Encyclopedia of British Horseracing

The *Encyclopedia of British Horseracing* offers an innovative approach to one of Britain's oldest sports. Whilst it considers the traditional themes of gambling and breeding, and contains biographies of both human personalities and equine stars, it also devotes significant space to previously neglected areas. Entries include:

- Social, economic and political forces that have influenced racing
- Controversial historical and contemporary issues
- Legal and illegal gambling, and racing finance
- The British impact on world horseracing
- History and heritage of horseracing
- Links between horseracing and the arts, media and technology
- Human and equine biographies
- Venues associated with racing
- Horseracing websites.

The *Encyclopedia of British Horseracing* provides a unique source of information and will be of great interest to sports historians as well as all those whose work or leisure brings them into the world of racing.

Wray Vamplew is Director of Research in Sports Studies at the University of Stirling, UK. He has written extensively on horseracing and is a consultant to the National Horseracing Museum at Newmarket.

Joyce Kay is a Research Fellow in Sports Studies at the University of Stirling, UK. She has published widely on horseracing for international encyclopedias and academic journals.

Encyclopedia of British Horseracing

Wray Vamplew and Joyce Kay

Routledge
Taylor & Francis Group

LONDON AND NEW YORK

First published 2005
by Routledge
2 Park Square, Milton Park, Abingdon Oxon OX14 4RN

Simultaneously published in the USA and Canada
by Routledge
270 Madison Ave, New York, NY 10016

Routledge is an imprint of the Taylor & Francis Group

© 2005 Wray Vamplew and Joyce Kay

Typeset in Goudy by
Newgen Imaging Systems (P) Ltd, Chennai, India
Printed and bound in Great Britain by
MPG Books Ltd, Bodmin

British Library Cataloguing in Publication Data
A catalogue record for this book is available from the British Library

Library of Congress Cataloging in Publication Data
A catalog record for this book has been requested

ISBN 0–714–65356–X (hbk)
ISBN 0–714–68292–6 (pbk)

Contents

Introduction

Horseracing, the first truly national sport in Britain, has a longer history than most, stretching back at least to the days of Henry VIII. It also has many unique features. First, there are two distinct codes, the traditional flat and the 'more recent' National Hunt which emerged in the nineteenth century. Second, it is highly professionalised with little room for the amateur. It has no grass roots, no junior level: while many spectators at cricket and football matches will have played the sport, few racegoers will have ridden a horse let alone raced one. Another unusual aspect of racing is that it has no fan base. Spectators seldom follow particular horses or jockeys as they would a local team and there is little shared, communal experience associated with winning...or losing. Racing is largely for individuals, both participants and spectators.

There are other major differences. Unlike most sports, there are few celebrities to empathise with or admire, although in Victorian times jockey Fred Archer was said to be the best known sportsman after W.G. Grace. Today Frankie Dettori is probably the only racing professional to be widely recognised and even his undoubted charisma does little to raise a positive profile. Nor is it a sport for the sedentary viewer as an afternoon at the races might only contain ten minutes of action. In other sports, you take your seat and the event unfolds before you. In racing, to get the most from the spectacle you have to follow proceedings from stand to paddock, from paddock to rails, from rails to winners' enclosure. Along the way you can place a bet, the original and still the main rationale for the sport. Racing and betting have always gone hand-in-hand, from the simple wager on match racing in the eighteenth century to the multi-million-pound industries of the twenty-first century. Other sports *have* betting but racing in Britain *needs* betting. It is because of this close connection that there is a widespread perception of the sport as corrupt.

Racing is so far removed from 'average' sport that it sometimes fails to recognise that it has a problem, particularly with its image. It sees nothing incongruous with trying to bring in a crowd on the basis of activities – funfairs, bouncy castles, shopping – which have no relevance to the contests taking place. Football fans take their children to see the main event, the match, not the sideshows. Given a free afternoon, most people would not choose to spend it at a racecourse. Horseracing now has to compete for the time and money of sports fans who have never had more choice, in an era of saturation coverage of football, at a time when investigative journalism and a sensationalist press are ever more adept at rooting out scandals and misdemeanours. It continues to function in an age when most of the population has no affinity with the land, with horses, with riding, hunting or country pursuits because the majority are from urban rather than rural backgrounds. It lacks fans to speak up for it as a sport partly because of the close-knit, navel-gazing world in which it operates and partly because its relationship with gambling still evokes disapproval. Against all this, what hope does racing have of maintaining itself as a viable, acceptable, wholesome product for future generations to enjoy?

Despite a few innovations such as artificial surfaces and computerised handicapping, the sport remains rooted in the past. Races are still measured in miles and furlongs, jockeys in stones and pounds and horse values in guineas. Nineteenth-century dress codes are still maintained in the exclusive enclosures at Royal Ascot and Epsom Downs on Derby day while the ordinary racegoer, in jeans and T-shirt, munches burgers beside the funfair. The two branches of racing are equally far apart. The flat has the wealth, the prestige and the international dimension while jumping retains its local links, lowly status and poorer prize money. Yet paradoxically the Grand National is the one race that captures the public attention on a worldwide basis.

This book, however, unlike most encyclopedias, will not list the winners of this and other big races or the champion jockeys of the past century. It will not describe each of the 59 British racecourses in detail, explain the intricacies of betting terminology or provide biographies, human or equine, of the hundreds of personalities who have contributed to the history of racing. Anyone interested in these minutiae of the turf will find ample reference books to satisfy his or her curiosity. Among the most useful are the range of recent publications by Channel Four racing and, in particular, the excellent but unfortunately out-of-print *Encyclopaedia of British Flat Racing* (Mortimer *et al.*, 1977). Other invaluable sources are the *Racing Calendar, Ruff's Guide to the Turf, the Daily Telegraph Chronicle* and of course, the press especially the *Racing Post*. This is now the only specialist racing paper following the demise of the *Sporting Life* and in addition to newsprint coverage provides an unparalleled website for racing enthusiasts.

Instead of recycling old material, this volume examines some previously neglected areas such as the link between racing and the arts, alcohol and the church, and looks at the social, economic and political forces that have shaped the development of the sport. The focus is on Britain (not just England!) and its influence on world racing as well as the impact of other racing nations on the domestic scene. A major theme is continuity and change in attitudes within the sport and outside racing circles. Issues such as animal welfare, levels of prize money and transparency of decision-making are ongoing. Those of state involvement, Jockey Club rule and the sanctity of the Sabbath have gone.

There will always be debate about aspects of horseracing, not least how to spell the word or words – is it horseracing, horse-racing or horse racing? There is no standard version but this book has opted for horseracing, as in the British Horseracing Board. Similarly, traditional racing measurements have been retained along with the simplest form of race names – sponsors have generally been omitted and commonly-accepted abbreviations have been adopted in the case of the King George (King George VI and Queen Elizabeth Diamond Stakes) and the Arc (Prix de l'Arc de Triomphe).

It is a daunting task to cover over three centuries of thoroughbred horseracing. It is equally daunting to keep up with the rapid changes that have affected the sport in the past decade. The last two years alone have seen the abolition of betting tax, the doubling of Sunday and evening fixtures, and the promise of both Tote privatisation and the relinquishing of the disciplinary power of the Jockey Club. The time-honoured fixture list is currently under threat and there are plans afoot for race meetings on Saturday mornings. As racing fights to secure its place in the twenty-first century leisure market, who knows what else will have changed by the time this book is published!

Wray Vamplew
Joyce Kay
June 2004

List of entries

A

Horsebox

Airborne was the last grey to win the Derby in 1946; he also won the St Leger, one of only four grey winners in the twentieth century, the most recent being Silver Patriarch (1997).

Aliysa won the Oaks in 1989 but was disqualified after failing a drugs test, handing the race to Snow Bride. The subsequent dispute with the Jockey Club led to her owner, the Aga Khan, removing his horses from Britain until 1995.

Alycidon, second to Black Tarquin in the 1948 St Leger, went on to win the stayers' triple crown (Ascot Gold Cup, Doncaster and Goodwood Cups) in 1949, the first horse to do so for 70 years.

Amrullah took part in 74 races between 1982 and 1992 without ever winning, although he earned over £26,000 in place money.

Androma is one of only two horses to have won the Scottish Grand National twice, in 1984 and 1985 – the other was Barona (1975 and 1976).

Aunt Edith was the first filly to win the King George, in 1966; there have only been four others (Park Top 1969, Dahlia 1973 and 1974, Pawneese 1976 and Time Charter 1983).

Abandonment

Racing can be abandoned at any time of year because of weather or ground conditions. Thunderstorms, fog, high wind, flooding and torrential rain may result in the loss or curtailment of a dozen flat race days each year while snow, frost and waterlogged courses have led to over 100 lost days during a winter jump season. In years of exceptionally bad weather, racing has been abandoned for weeks; in 1963 no meetings could be staged from January to early March because of heavy snow and frost while the summer drought of 1976, followed by an exceptionally wet autumn, saw nearly 90 days of jump racing alone lost to both hard ground and waterlogging. A total of 79 fixtures succumbed to the weather in 2002, a fairly average year, with a further 6 halted during the meeting.

Races may be abandoned for a variety of reasons. When Edward VII, a great supporter of racing for nearly 50 years, died in May 1910, all fixtures in Britain and Ireland were cancelled for two weeks – a total of 30 race days – although most took place at later dates. The funeral of Diana, Princess of Wales, in September 1997 also led to the cancellation of the racing programme as did the funeral in April 2002 of Queen Elizabeth, the Queen Mother, a great patron of National Hunt racing, and that of her late husband, George VI, 50 years earlier. Sixteen flat race fixtures were abandoned from April to June 1921 because of the industrial crisis (largely the repercussions for the railways of a miners' strike) and further meetings were lost in May 1926 as a result of the General Strike.

Another recent cause of abandonment was the outbreak of foot-and-mouth disease in 2001. Fears that transportation of horses and the gathering of spectators at racecourses might lead to accelerated spread of the virus resulted in a total shutdown of the sport for a week in early March. Although some courses in unaffected areas were able to resume promptly, others including the major National Hunt venue at Cheltenham found themselves in infected zones and therefore unable to hold meetings. The flagship Cheltenham National Hunt Festival in mid-March was abandoned for the first time in 57 years, causing dismay to thousands of British and Irish racegoers, trainers, owners and jockeys, none more so than the connections and fans of the Irish hurdling star, Istabraq. The three-time Champion Hurdle winner was to attempt a fourth consecutive victory, a feat never before achieved, but was robbed of his opportunity. Although he started the race in 2002, he was by then past his prime and was quickly pulled up and retired from racing.

As restrictions extended into the summer, flat racing in some areas was also affected. Over 120 days racing were eventually lost during the epidemic and with over 100 weather-related abandonments because of the unusually wet winter, 2001 proved to be the worst on record for lost racecards. A previous outbreak of foot-and-mouth, in the winter of 1967–68, also saw disruption to the racing programme. The sport was shut down completely for six weeks from the end of November to the beginning of January with a loss of 81 meetings and a further 29 days were added to the total thereafter because of regional restrictions. With little work in Britain, several top jockeys headed to France to race there. The impact of disease on horseracing fixtures, however, has a long history. In 1744 racing was prohibited by magistrates of many northern towns because of the 'direful distemper attending the horned cattle.'

The other major cause of abandonment, and by far the most serious in the first half of the twentieth century, was war. The curtailment of racing during the war years led to significant problems, not only for racecourses, trainers, jockeys and others employed in the industry but also for breeders. During both world wars the continuance of racing was viewed by many as unpatriotic and wasteful of fuel, but an exception was made for races at Newmarket where the local community was almost entirely dependent on the sport. Wartime Classics and other major races were transferred to the headquarters of racing and 1915 saw the Derby take place away from Epsom Downs for the first time in its history. A limited number of meetings were also held at Lingfield, Windsor and Gatwick, where substitute Grand Nationals were run during the period 1916–18, but northern racecourses remained closed, Newbury was turned into a POW camp and the Epsom grandstands were requisitioned by the army.

Between 1940 and 1945 flat racing was again subject to severe restrictions with fixtures sanctioned at only a handful of courses and horses banned from competing outside their own region. This time provision was made for northern racing at Pontefract and Stockton while further south Ascot, Windsor, Salisbury and Newmarket were allowed to hold meetings. The industry managed to survive without attracting criticism that it was impeding the war effort, aided by well-publicised support from the royal family – Sun Chariot and Big Game, running in the colours of George VI, won a wartime fillies' Triple Crown and the Two Thousand Guineas in 1942. The same year saw the Jockey Club take steps to reduce the size of the racehorse population to save on scarce fodder: horses of five years old and over were banned from handicaps, owners were encouraged to dispose of moderate animals especially geldings and the stock of broodmares was reduced by 25 per cent. Over 60 flat-race meetings were held in both 1943 and 1944 but National Hunt racing was less fortunate. There were no Grand Nationals from 1940 to 1945 – Aintree was taken over by American forces – and the entire jumps season was abandoned in 1942–43 and 1943–44. A limited number of race days was finally agreed from January 1945 and the Cheltenham Gold Cup was run for the first time since 1942.

In cases of cancellation resulting from weather, royal funerals or disease, replacement meetings are frequently organised by the British Horseracing Board, particularly if the original fixture included an important race. The King George VI Chase, the highlight of the Boxing Day racecard at Kempton Park, was lost to bad weather in 1995 and finally staged at nearby Sandown Park in early January. The two disasters affecting the Grand National in the 1990s, however, elicited different responses from the authorities. The 1993 race, declared void after two false starts, was never re-run but the 1997 race, abandoned on the Saturday because of an IRA bomb scare, took place instead on the following Monday in front of a small but defiant crowd. In general, re-scheduled fixtures, even for major meetings, seldom attract the anticipated numbers and revenues of the original race day and racecourse executives have cause to rue the intervention of any event that leads to abandonment.

Further reading

Mortimer, R., *The Flat* (London: Allen and Unwin, 1979).
Tyrrel, J., *Running Racing – the Jockey Club Years since 1750* (London: Quiller Press, 1997).

See also Weather.

Accidents

So much can go wrong at the track and on the gallops. Horses have minds of their own and surprising agility for their size. They can rear in the parade ring, charge the starting gate, bolt, cross their legs, break blood vessels, run out at bends, or strike the heels of another runner. Even ones that are well schooled in training sometimes react unpredictably when they come to fences on the racecourse itself while back in the stables and breeding sheds lads and handlers run risks from frightened or excited horses. Jockeys can be pulled off by the starting gate, fall off because of a saddle slipping, or have a rein snap so that they cannot control their mount. The condition of the course can lead to disaster if the ground is too hard or too soft or, as in September 1989 at Doncaster, if the drainage system subsides and produces deep holes in the running track. Even getting to the racecourse can be hazardous when you are driving tens of thousands of miles each year and, although no jockey has been killed flying to a meeting, Frankie Dettori and Ray Cochrane were lucky to escape with their lives in an accident at Newmarket in May 2002 in which their pilot died.

Jockey Club figures show that a fall can be expected every 14 rides over jumps and hurdles. Imagine the state of mind of a jockey who has not fallen for twenty rides knowing that one is almost inevitable in the very near future. But at least a jump jockey knows that most falls happen when his horse meets obstacles deliberately placed in its path and can be mentally prepared to take action. Flat racing has no such advance warning system and when a horse slips over at 30 mph or more, often in the midst of other 500-kilo creatures, the consequences can be severe. The 1962 Derby is a prime example when 26 runners set off but only 19 finished. A combination of poor horses falling back, good horses moving up, and badly placed horses switching position led to a crowded collision at Tattenham Corner. One horse had to be destroyed and six jockeys needed treatment, two of them suffering concussion.

One of the greatest dangers is a loose horse running out of control. The problem is worst at small tracks where the course is narrow and races take place over several laps. Sedgefield, for example, saw carnage in 1999 when three horses unseated their riders at the first fence in a novices chase and a well-intentioned, but unsuccessful, attempt to catch the leading loose horse merely headed them in the wrong direction. Had the next race not been over the flat, hurdles would still have been in place which might have halted the trio. As it was they met the rest of the field on a bend and in the collision another six horses were brought down. Three were killed instantly in what was a 60 mph crash.

Any serious accident is investigated thoroughly by the Jockey Club who will seek feedback from the jockeys on aspects of the race, from the course inspectors on the state of the ground, from the vets on the horses and from the doctors on the injured riders.

See also Safety.

Administration

See Weatherbys.

Africa

With racecourses named Newmarket and Gosforth Park and races called Queen's Plates, South African racing has obvious links with Britain. English settlers brought racing to Africa in the last decade of the eighteenth century and since then, in spite of its occasional isolation for political or medical reasons – fear of

African horse sickness led to strict quarantine conditions – there has continued to be a limited traffic in horses, jockeys and trainers between the continent and Britain. Although thoroughbred racing was also introduced to Zimbabwe, Kenya and other parts of East Africa, it has flourished most strongly in South Africa.

British punters have become more aware of the sport there since betting shops and satellite television began to feature meetings, initially when domestic racing was wiped out by bad weather. (Similar time zones allow South African races to be transmitted live in Britain during the afternoon.) But the only South African horse to have made a significant impact on the international scene has been Colorado King, who won in America in 1963, and Hawaii, a prolific winner in his homeland who became Champion Grass Horse of 1969 in the States. He went on to sire 1980 English Derby winner Henbit and 1978 runner-up Hawaiian Sound. A number of successful racehorses have gone in the opposite direction. Sunstone, son of 1911 Derby winner Sunstar, became champion sire in South Africa; Wilwyn, winner of 20 races in England and the first to capture the Washington DC International Stakes in 1952, also did well there as did Sybil's Nephew, a six-time winner and runner-up in the 1951 Derby. But in general horses exported to Africa have been moderate racers or unsuccessful sires. Royal Lancer, winner of the 1919 St Leger and Irish St Leger was shipped off to South Africa after failing as a sire in Britain; more recently Ribofilio, a son of Ribot, beaten favourite in the 1969 colt Classics and a great disappointment on the racecourse, was also sent there.

A few British riders have tried their luck in Africa. Ernie Johnson, 1969 Derby-winning jockey, also rode winners in Kenya, as well as India and Hong Kong, and Derek Stansfield, killed in a fall at Hamilton in the same year, rode regularly in East Africa. The Wootton family, trainer Richard and sons Stanley and Frank, worked in South Africa en route from their homeland, Australia, to a successful spell in Britain. Frank, aged 9 years 10 months, rode his first winner in South Africa and later became British champion jockey from 1909 to 1912. South African jockeys John Gorton and Michael Roberts also made an impact on British racing. Gorton was fortunate in his British contacts, having been apprenticed to Frederick Rickaby, son of a Newmarket trainer, and encouraged by veteran trainer Sir Jack Jarvis who maintained close links with South Africa. He rode regularly in Britain from 1969 to 1974, winning the Oaks with Sleeping Partner in 1969 and the Coronation Stakes at Royal Ascot with Jacinth in 1973. Roberts established himself in Britain in 1986, having won the champion jockey title 11 times in his native land. By 1994 he had ridden 1,000 winners on the British turf, won the King George on Mtoto in 1988 and Opera House in 1993, the Two Thousand Guineas on Mystiko in 1991 and the Oaks on Intrepidity in 1993. He was champion jockey in 1990 when he rode 206 winners.

South Africa has proved to be important for British racing in another context. The Joel brothers, Solomon and Jack, left London to make their fortunes in the diamond fields of Kimberley at the end of the nineteenth century and, with some of the proceeds, became important owners and breeders of racehorses back in Britain. Between them, they won 14 Classics and passed on their passion for racing to their children who won a further 8, as well as consecutive King Georges in 1967 with Busted and 1968 with Royal Palace. Jack's son, Jim, in particular continued to make a significant impact on both flat and jumps racing and was one of the last great English owner-breeders, reviving the fortunes of his father's Childwick Bury Stud. He was leading owner on the flat in 1967 and in National Hunt racing in 1979–80 and 1986–87, and is one of the few to have owned both a Derby and a Grand National winner – Royal Palace in 1967 and Maori Venture in 1987.

Further reading

Magee, S., *Channel Four Racing Complete A–Z of Horse Racing* (London: Channel 4 Books, 2001).
Roberts, M. and Tanner, M., *Champion's Story* (London: Headline, 1994).

Age

Descriptions of racehorses are often age-related. A foal is the term used for a horse from its birth until 1 January of the following year, while a yearling refers to any horse during the 12 months from then to 31 December. Thereafter, males aged two to four are colts, females are fillies, racing two-year-olds are sometimes referred to as juveniles, and animals still running at five, the age of thoroughbred maturity, or older, are horses or mares according to gender.

The age at which horses normally race has varied considerably over time and according to the distance run. During the seventeenth and eighteenth centuries, it was unusual for an animal to race until it was five or six years old and it often continued until it was ten or even twelve. Only mature horses were capable of competing in the gruelling 4-mile races, often run in heats, which were then in vogue. As shorter races became more fashionable, the racing age fell. The Derby, Oaks and St Leger, first run in the last quarter of the eighteenth century, were always restricted to three-year-olds, but at a time when control of racing was lax and rules often unenforceable, it was inevitable that frauds, involving the substitution of older for younger horses, would occur in these and other age-restricted races. The most notorious case was the 1844 Derby in which two of the runners were found to be four-year-olds after an examination of their teeth, the method by which age is normally determined. By the early nineteenth century, shorter races for two-year-olds, equally susceptible to fraud, had appeared and the fashion for sprints culminated in yearling races over as little as two furlongs. The Jockey Club banned yearlings from the racecourse in 1859 and gradually imposed tighter controls on the sport, reducing the possibility of age-related offences.

It has remained the norm for flatracers to start their careers at two and for most top-class horses to retire before they reach five. In human terms, this would be the equivalent of completing an athletic career while still at primary school. National Hunt racing, however, is different. Horses are not allowed to race over hurdles and fences until the age of three and four respectively but often continue until twelve or thirteen years old; steeplechasers are usually at their peak when aged eight or nine. Unlike flat racing, there are no jump races comparable to the Classics or other Pattern races which are restricted to a specific age group. The exceptions are the relatively minor National Hunt Flat Races or 'bumpers' in which horses must be aged between four and six, and riders must not be fully-fledged professional jockeys.

All racehorses celebrate their official birthday on 1 January, a rule first introduced at Newmarket in 1834 and followed elsewhere in 1858. This means that a foal born in February 2003 will have a three-month advantage over a foal born in May in terms of maturity and development, although both will be considered as yearlings in January 2004. A late-spring foal may benefit from better grass but it can lack the physical maturity to join its older peers on the racecourse at the beginning of the two-year-old racing season, a factor of some importance given the short competitive life of the average racer. There are carefully graded rules restricting the running of two-year-olds – none, for example may race over more than 5 furlongs before June, or 7 furlongs before August – and a complicated system of weights to be carried by horses at different levels of maturity, the weight-for-age scale, applies to all races which are not handicaps. This was originally devised in 1855 by Admiral Rous, senior steward of the Jockey Club and public handicapper, modified by him in 1873, and subsequently revised by the Jockey Club. It is intended as a guide to the weights which horses should carry over specific distances, the amount increasing month by month throughout the racing season. It aims to compensate for the immaturity of younger animals, allowing three-year-olds, in particular, to race alongside older horses.

Age is an important factor in deciding the campaign of any flat racehorse but particularly a top-class thoroughbred. In most cases it will be lightly raced as a two-year-old and, if it shows promise, it may be aimed at one of the recognised Classic trials before contesting the major age-restricted races, the English, French or Irish Classics, in its three-year-old season. If it is an exceptional horse, it may transfer from age-group races to those open to three-year-olds and upwards, such as the King George or the Arc, taking on older rivals. For colts, success in any of the principal European Group One races may result in either retirement to stud, where potential fees are likely to be higher than future racecourse winnings, or a four-year-old campaign in a few carefully selected Group races, the choice dependent on the preferred distance.

The increase in international races offering large prizes has sometimes tempted owners to keep successful horses in training as five or even six-year-olds. Swain won the King George in 1998 at six, Daylami was five when victorious in the 1999 Breeders' Cup Turf, but it is now unusual for a Derby winner to continue racing beyond the age of three. Some horses are trained on because they mature too late to be Classic winners and top-flight mares may have their retirement to stud postponed, while geldings can continue to race and earn because there is no lucrative competing career. The same is true of stayers, for whom stud demand is poor and opportunities abroad more extensive. Vintage Crop was seven when he won the Melbourne Cup for Ireland in 1993.

The more modest animals which form the majority of race fields are less constrained by the age factor and, in an effort to earn their keep, may be raced more frequently in mixed-age races, sometimes over a number of years.

Moderate flatracers are sometimes campaigned over hurdles during the winter or on one of the all-weather tracks, prolonging their season and the length of their racing life; it is not uncommon to find such horses running at the age of eight. National Hunt horses, starting over hurdles and graduating to steeple-chases, also tend to have long racing careers. In recent years, Grand National winners Little Polveir (1989) and Royal Athlete (1995) were twelve-year-olds while Mr Frisk (1990), Seagram (1991) and Miinnehoma (1994) were all eleven. But for versatility over a 10-year span, there is surely no better example than Sea Pigeon, winner of 16 flat and 21 hurdle races. Seventh in the 1973 Derby, he won the Ebor Handicap on the flat as a nine-year-old in 1979 and maintained a first class hurdling career throughout the winters of 1977–81, culminating in two successive Champion Hurdles (1980 and 1981).

Further reading

Magee, S., *The Channel Four Book of Racing* (London: Hamlyn, 1995).

Agents

There are two major groups of agents in racing, the bloodstock agents and the jockeys' agents, both willing to relieve, respectively, the owner or jockey of a percentage of his or her money. Bloodstock agents normally charge owners about 5 per cent of the purchase price for their advice in choosing a horse. Additionally they will sift through the sales and auction catalogues looking for a horse to suit their clients' requirements and budget, provide details of the animal's pedigree, arrange for veterinary examination and, if necessary, an independent valuation, as well as bidding for the animal in the sale ring or negotiating a private sale. The agents also help sell animals, again on a commission basis. Critics argue that many agents are no more than glib con artists, but the fact that the profession continues suggests that sufficient owners value the services provided.

One of the major pioneers was the British Bloodstock Agency, created in 1911 by journalists Edward Moorhouse, Ernest Coussell and Robert Bunsow. They published the *Bloodstock Breeders' Review* which provided information about racing and breeding throughout the world whilst simultaneously publicising their expertise and attracting clients. Over time virtually every racing country has had a champion sire imported through the Agency. These days the Agency utilises computer programming to assist its mating advisory service but whether this will ever have as far-reaching effects on the breeding industry as two deals in the mid-twentieth century is debatable. In 1938 the Agency secured Nearco for Martin Benson's Beech House Stud for the then record sum of £60,000. Fourteen years later it advised Canadian industrialist Eddie Taylor to purchase Lady Angela who was in foal to Nearco. The sale was conditional on obtaining a promise of a return nomination to the stallion. The subsequent mating produced Neartic, the sire of Northern Dancer whose progeny had an international impact on racing.

For jockeys, the commission of 10 per cent of riding fees and share of prize money paid to their agent is certainly worthwhile as it takes away the work and worry of seeking rides. Prior to this development a top jockey could spend as much time on the phone trying to secure rides as on the horses themselves. One can only wonder at how barely literate Fred Archer managed to arrange his 667 rides in 1885. Pioneered in Britain by Willie Carson who appointed Ted Eley to work for him in 1970, the employment of an agent has become widespread and today even some apprentices, no longer subject to the restrictions of the old indenture contract, also employ them. The use of agents who offer trainers their full client list obviously reduces the opportunities for spare mounts for the lesser riders and this has encouraged them also to seek a representative.

A good agent spends time studying the form and entry books, and watching races, usually via television to pinpoint likely future mounts for his clients and also to identify those dangerous or unreliable horses that they should avoid. They also spend time and money on the phone: leading agent Dave Roberts has a telephone bill of over £8,000 a year, unsurprising as he books over 4,000 mounts a season. Agents are in a fiduciary relationship with their clients and must always act in their best interest; they can, for example, only act for one party within a negotiation. Although there is some conflict when an agent handles several jockeys, all desirous of the same ride, this is not illegal. No agent will admit to betting as this would undermine the relationships of trust and respect that they have cultivated with trainers.

Within National Hunt racing the increased power wielded by the agents has created an elite group who obtain the bulk of the rides. With less opportunity of mounts there has been a dramatic slide in registered jockeys from 149 in 1991 to only 85 a decade later. The number of conditional riders has more than halved in the same period from 196 to 92.

Further reading

McCoy, T. and Duval, C., *The Real McCoy* (London: Hodder and Stoughton, 1998). www.bba.co.uk

Aintree

Aintree racecourse in the northern suburbs of Liverpool is known throughout the world as the home of the Grand National, its features and fences instantly recognised by the millions who watch the race annually on television. Yet for much of the year it is empty, desolate, one of the least used courses in Britain with only four days racing outside the famous spring festival meeting.

The chequered history of its development began in 1829 when William Lynn, a local hotelier, rented land from the Earl of Sefton for a flat race meeting. An elegant grandstand was erected and by 1835 Lynn was organising three meetings a year, including one for hurdle events. In 1836 he promoted the first steeplechase over two circuits of the 2-mile course and this race, renamed the Grand National in 1847, was held annually at the Liverpool Spring flat race meeting throughout the nineteenth and twentieth centuries. Liverpool racecourse, as it was usually known, continued to host two further flat meetings each year, in July and November, but their popularity declined and flat racing was abandoned in 1976.

Aintree remained the property of the Earls of Sefton until 1949 when it was sold to the Topham family, clerks of the course for over a century. Although a motor racing circuit was added in 1953 to boost revenues, it closed within ten years and in 1964 the entire venture was deemed to be uneconomic by Mirabel Topham, the course manager, who proposed to sell it for redevelopment. The original contract of sale drawn up by Lord Sefton's advisers had stipulated that the land should only be used for agricultural or racing purposes and a series of legal battles ensued, during which the course facilities became increasingly run down. Great uncertainty about its future continued for nearly 20 years. Although it was eventually sold to a property developer in 1973, it was rescued in 1975, first by Ladbrokes the bookmakers, who offered to run it for the next seven years, and then by the combined efforts of the Horserace Betting Levy Board, sponsor donations and public subscription. It is now owned by the Racecourse Holdings Trust, a non-profit making subsidiary of the Jockey Club; new grandstands and a visitor centre have been built, a golf course occupies the centre of the course and the future of a national institution appears to be secure.

There are two distinct circuits at Aintree which benefit from a free-draining, sandy soil, although there is a tendency to remember the instances of wet, gruelling conditions rather than the good going on bright spring days. The Grand National course of 2 miles 2 furlongs is the longest in Britain, flat, wide and roughly triangular in layout, a track so vast that it can be difficult to see the far side from the stands. The Mildmay course of 1 mile 4 furlongs is also level and left-handed, with the hurdles track outside it, but its sharp bends make it unsuitable for the relentlessly galloping 'National' horse. Until 1975, the fences on both steeplechase courses were of similar construction but the Mildmay fences are now built in the orthodox manner from birch while the 16 Grand National fences (all but two of which are jumped twice during the big race) are made of thorn dressed with specially imported Norway spruce. A staff of 150 is required on the big race day to dress and repair the obstacles. The course is unique in terms of distance, fence type and number, and although there are numerous plain fences, the names of the more spectacular obstacles have achieved notoriety – the Canal Turn, the Chair, Valentine's and, most famously, Becher's Brook. Fierce condemnation of the perpendicular fences, labelled dangerous by some critics, first led to modifications as long ago as 1961 which resulted in sloped take-off sides. Since then further safety measures have been undertaken to reduce unacceptable drops on the landing side and in 1989 the ditch at Becher's Brook was filled in.

The enormous public interest in the Grand National tends to overshadow other events at Aintree but the spring meeting hosts several Grade One races including the Aintree Hurdle and the Melling Chase, and a total of 11 Pattern races in all. The three days of the Grand National meeting in April are the biggest draw of the jump season after the National Hunt Festival at Cheltenham in March, with crowds of over 50,000 on Grand National Day. Twenty-four hours later, the curtains have closed again on Aintree racecourse, a poignant theatre of ghosts and memories in an urban wasteland.

Further reading

Magee, S. (ed.), *The Channel Four Racing Guide to Racecourses* (London: Channel 4 Books, 1998).
Seth-Smith, M. *et al.*, *The History of Steeplechasing* (London: Michael Joseph, 1966).
www.aintree.co.uk

See also Grand National.

Alcohol

All racecourses sell alcohol: it is seen as a significant contributor to revenue and part of the day out for many racegoers. Sometimes the bars are named after racing personalities as at Huntingdon which has the Steve Smith-Eccles Bar in tribute to the retired steeplechase jockey, the Giffords Bar named after the locally-born trainers, and the Hugo Bevan Bar honouring a long-serving clerk of the course. Or after horses as with the Lucius Bar at Carlisle, the Durham Edition Bar at Sedgefield and the Romany King Bar at Exeter.

In turn the alcohol industry has often assisted racing. Purveyors of alcohol have traditionally sponsored racing, usually at a local level as in the many Innkeepers Plates and Publicans Stakes found throughout the eighteenth- and nineteenth-century *Racing Calendars*. The alcohol trade was also to the fore in pioneering the modern era of racing sponsorship. Colonel W.H. 'Billy' Whitbread, chairman of the brewing company bearing his name, was a devotee of the turf and had completed the Grand National course twice as an amateur. He saw the commercial possibilities offered by racing and in 1957 his firm sponsored the Whitbread Gold Cup at Sandown Park to be followed in 1960 by the Mackeson Gold Cup at Cheltenham. During the 1990s Whitbread sponsored the November three-day Murphy's festival at the Cheltenham course for around £90,000, a significant sum by National Hunt standards. Seagrams were involved in the Grand National for eight years before an offshoot of the company, Martell, took over the sponsorship in 1992. Five years later they committed themselves to a package of £4.5 million to maintain the sponsorship till 2004. The Grand National, of course, is televised worldwide which provides Martell with international exposure. Hennessy Day at Newbury is another major jumping feature. On the flat, the John Smith's Cup at York, originally the Magnet Cup, is the oldest sponsored race still on the fixture list, celebrating its fortieth running as racing entered the new millennium. Further north the Northumberland Plate had the Fosters Lager imprint attached. Most but not all meetings have significant sponsorship from the alcohol trade and industry, ranging from champagne firms at Goodwood, Epsom and York to the Federation Brewery at Hexham. Overall about a fifth of racing sponsorship is alcohol related.

Champagne in particular has long featured in racing. In Champagne Stakes, common in the nineteenth century, winning owners had to give a crate of bubbly to the race committee. Jockeys too have received champagne from the early 1960s when Bollinger began to supply a dozen crates to the winner of both the Amateur and Professional National Hunt championships. For some years too the Möet and Chandon Silver Magnum for amateur riders was run over the

Derby course at Epsom. Jockeys drink champagne for both social and vocational reasons. Many believe that it is ideal for drinking in the sauna to assist the sweating process; others, like owners, trainers and racegoers, simply enjoy celebrating their victories.

Unfortunately some riders face alcohol problems because of the nature of their work. Every time jockeys race they are subject to public and employer appraisal; they are constantly watching their weight; and they anticipate injury each time they get on a horse. No wonder that so many appear to have used alcohol to escape reality or as a painkiller. Apocryphal stories abound for the nineteenth century. Charles Marlow is said to have lost a two-horse race for the 1850 Doncaster Cup on the odds-on favourite The Flying Dutchman because he was drunk; and, after a morning at the brandy bottle, Bill Scott is alleged to have been so intoxicated at the Derby of 1846 that he did not realise that the race had started. It is clear that Scott, winner of nine St Legers, and George Fordham, 14 times champion jockey, were alcoholics as was Tommy Loates, champion in three seasons towards the end of the century, Bernard Dillon, the Derby-winning rider in 1910, and perhaps American 'Skeets' Martin who tended to hit the bottle. In the modern era both Walter Swinburn and Steve Cauthen have acknowledged that they had drink problems. National Hunt riders, with notable exceptions such as teetotallers John Francome, Tony McCoy – despite being sponsored by Guinness – and Jonjo O'Neill, see drinking as part of the social life associated with their sport, and regard it as a means of winding down. Whether the stress or culture of their working lives contributes to jockeys resorting to alcohol more than other workers remains conjectural in the light of current research. The effects of alcohol are often aggravated by the lack of food; significantly both Cauthen and Swinburn were alleged to be bulimic. Although the idea of a drunken jockey aboard a horse is a frightening one, the Jockey Club took no action on this issue till October 1994 when, at the instigation of Michael Turner, their new chief medical adviser, a protocol was developed for the testing of riders for banned substances. These include alcohol, the threshold for this initially being set at the drink-driving limit but later reduced to half that level. Initially done by urine sample, breathalyser tests were introduced in 2003.

Further reading

Collins T. and Vamplew, W., *Mud, Sweat and Beers* (Oxford: Berg, 2002).
Smith Eccles, S. and Lee, A., *Turf Account* (London: Queen Anne Press, 1986).
Tanner, M. and Cranham, G., *Great Jockeys of the Flat* (Enfield: Guinness, 1992).

See also Inns.

All-weather racing

All-weather racing takes place on an artificial surface composed of sand and synthetic fibres instead of turf and, though popular overseas, was not introduced to Britain until 1989. It was originally intended to provide opportunities for both flat and jump racing and to ensure an income for the racing and betting industries during the winter months when frost, snow and waterlogging often caused the abandonment of race meetings. From modest beginnings, it now operates all year round at three tracks but is restricted to flat racing, accounting for nearly one-fifth of all flat-race days. This figure will rise if controversial proposals for new all-weather tracks in Essex and South Wales are finally approved or if existing venues such as Newmarket and Newbury are allowed to develop all-weather tracks.

All-weather racing was the Jockey Club's response to concerns in the 1980s about the number of meetings – and consequently income – lost during the months of January to March. With significant financial backing from the Horserace Betting Levy Board, the first tracks opened in the autumn of 1989 at two existing racecourses, Lingfield Park and Southwell, to be followed in December 1993 by Wolverhampton which pioneered Saturday evening races under floodlights. Although hurdling took place until 1994, it was suspended following a number of injuries and fatalities to horses. It was found that the artificial surfaces, Equitrack at Lingfield Park and Fibresand at Southwell and Wolverhampton, were less yielding than turf, resulting in more serious falls and breakages, and it has never been re-introduced. Instead the number of flat-race fixtures has steadily increased; in 2004 there were over 200, mainly concentrated from November to March but with 25 per cent taking place during the remaining months.

Fog, flood and high wind can occasionally lead to the abandonment of all race meetings and such weather conditions have beaten even artificial racetracks. Frost also causes the dirt surface to become crusty and lumpy, requiring constant harrowing to break down the clods and the early use of toxic antifreeze material had to be abandoned after it was alleged to have caused cases of poisoning. However, the winter of 2001, which was exceptionally wet with several spells of sub-zero temperatures, played havoc with the drainage at the artificial courses. Design defects together with age and lack of adequate maintenance, particularly at Lingfield, brought several abandonments of the all-weather, disparagingly referred to in the press henceforth as 'flat racing on sand – formerly known as all-weather racing'.

Although in reality the three all-weather courses lost fewer than 20 fixtures in their first 10 years of operation, the high-profile adverse publicity given to the spate of call-offs in 2001 resulted in the complete refurbishment of the Lingfield track at a cost of £3 million. The new surface, Polytrack, is a mishmash of recycled material, sand and polyester fibres woven together and coated with wax. A similar mixture had already been used for training gallops at Lambourn and Newmarket, and since its unveiling at Lingfield, there has been a very positive response from trainers and jockeys alike. A great advantage of Polytrack is the lack of kickback which used to leave horses and riders covered in lumps of wet sand (or occasionally clouds of dust!).

The amount of prize money available at all-weather meetings has always tended to be low, attracting horses of very moderate ability. Initially, this led to unflattering comparisons with dog racing and complaints from purists that the races, which can be extremely competitive and run at high speed, did little to improve the image of racing or the riding skills of jockeys. In recent years, however, a number of more valuable Listed races (Class A, just below Group level), together with some Class B and C contests have been added to the standard lower grade D to F races which make up most all-weather programmes. The Wulfrun Stakes at Wolverhampton, worth over £31,000 to the winner, was the first Listed race to be run on an artificial surface in 1997. The arrival of the new track at Lingfield brought with it increased prize money – the opening day in November 2001 saw two races for over £20,000 – and purses in general have increased at the three Arena Leisure-owned all-weather venues. Money has also been found for a trainers' and jockeys' championship, won in the inaugural season by Nick Littmoden and Jimmy Quinn, and although there are acknowledged all-weather specialists, many top-class handlers now send runners to these tracks. Even at the lower grades, there is sufficient money to be made in dirt racing to attract the type of horse that used to be destined for novice hurdling and there are fears that, in the long run, some poorly funded National Hunt fixtures will suffer.

While the more strident critics have yet to be won over, this branch of racing has also become increasingly popular with owners and spectators. Apart from providing opportunities for less successful or less experienced horses and jockeys, the all-weather racecourses offer modern facilities and aim to attract a wider public than many traditional venues. Although crowds were initially small, 2,000–3,000 spectators can now be found at Boxing Day and New Year's Day fixtures, at least the equal of an average jumps meeting, and all-round demand has been sufficiently high for the British Horseracing Board to sanction applications for new tracks. Several venues plan to offer evening racing under floodlights which has proved highly successful at Wolverhampton.

Although it takes place throughout the year, all-weather racing comes into its own during cold snaps or wet winters. When severe Christmas weather wiped out the Boxing Day programme at ten racecourses in 1996, emergency fixtures were brought in at the dirt tracks, admission prices were reduced and trainers were able to keep horses fit when their home gallops were frozen. This pattern of substitute meetings has been maintained in recent years and horses raced on the all-weather have often performed better at the start of the flat season in March than those denied the opportunity. It may be equine roulette in the eyes of its detractors but all-weather racing has had a significant impact on the racing year.

Further reading

Magee, S., *The Channel Four Racing Guide to Racecourses* (London: Channel 4 Books, 1998).
Wilson, J., in Armytage, G. and Seabrook, M. (eds), *Turf Accounts* (London: Gollancz/Witherby, 1994).

Amateur riders

The amateur participates in sport for fun. Certainly this must be the case in racing where the accident rate in point-to-point, the branch of horseracing solely for amateurs, is higher than in the professional branch of jump racing. Some amateurs, both in point-to-point but more often in National Hunt racing, are aiming for a career as a professional. Nevertheless most unpaid riders over the sticks are genuine amateurs in the accepted sense of the word, men and women who simply love their sport, its fellowship and traditions.

Historically there are rare examples of successful amateurs in flat racing such as 'Squire' Abington in the nineteenth century and Mr George Thursby, one of the few gentleman riders who could get down to less than 9 stone, which he did to finish second twice in the Derby, on John O'Gaunt in 1904 and on Picton two years later. However, few amateurs were prepared to sacrifice the good life sufficiently to ride at flat-race weights.

This was less often the case in National Hunt where jockeys can be heavier. Amateurs started steeplechasing and even when professionals came into the sport some could hold their own, among them Arthur Yates who won 460 races, double Grand National winners Maunsell Richardson and Ted Wilson, Arthur Coventry who became an official Jockey Club starter, and Roddy Owen who had 254 winners from 812 mounts in the decade from 1882 and then gave up racing after winning the 1892 Grand National on Father O'Flynn. Amateurs won 12 of the 15 Grand Nationals between 1871 and 1885 and five from 1885 to 1897. They were successful in three more before the First World War. In the interwar years unpaid riders – a few reputedly more expensive to hire than professionals – continued to take a leading part in the sport and in season 1926–27, for example, over 150 of them rode winners over hurdles and fences. In 1946 the first postwar Grand National was won by an amateur, Captain Bobby Petrie, recently demobilised from the Scots Guards, who brought home 25–1 outsider Lovely Cottage. Champion amateur rider in this year and the succeeding ones until his accidental drowning was Anthony (later Lord) Mildmay. At 6 ft 2 in he was no stereotype jockey but, having given up a career in the City to devote himself to steeplechasing, he could compete with the best as indicated by his fourth place in the overall National Hunt riders championship in 1946.

Earlier amateurs had won that title, though the last was Harry Brown in 1919. Today their target is the Amateur Championship, sponsored by Bollinger from 1963–64, the year it was won by Stephen Davenport. Among the other winners has been American George Sloan who for the 1977–78 season put aside a successful business to cross the Atlantic and become a full-time amateur rider in a determined campaign to lift the trophy. In 1999 the Amateur Jockeys Association decided not to follow the National Hunt precedent of ending the season in April but to continue with the traditional date in early June. Otherwise they feared that the hunter chase campaign, a core part of the amateur riders' season would be cut in half.

National Hunt racing remains one of the few sports in which the amateur can flourish even against professional opposition, though a permit system is in operation to ensure that only the fit and competent are allowed to compete. Since the 1960s the racing authorities have also adopted a policy of advising the most successful amateurs to turn professional on the grounds that they were depriving paid riders of their income. Among those so counselled have been

Terry Biddlecombe and Michael Scudamore, both of whom went on to win the professional championship. The Jockey Club now also requires owners to pay them the equivalent of a riding fee – which goes to charity – when they employ an amateur who has had 75 rides in races open to professionals. Such competition is not even allowed on the flat and, apart from novelty events, there are now no opportunities for amateurs to race against their paid counterparts in this branch of the sport. National Hunt amateurs can race against each other on the flat in bumper races, designed to give racecourse experience to potential hurdlers without the off-putting risk of falls, and there are occasional flat races solely for lighter-weight amateurs but it is in the point-to-point fields that the unpaid enthusiasts find their real home.

Further reading

Kidd, J. and Oaksey, J., *The Race for the Championship* (London: J.A. Allen, 1979).
Lee, A., *Jump Jockeys* (London: Ward Lock, 1980).

See also Baird, Point-to-Point.

American invasion

In 1895 a solitary American jockey, the Afro-American Willie Simms, rode in British racing and secured four wins, insufficient to rank him in the top 50 in the jockeys' championship, but the product of merely 19 mounts, a winning percentage amongst the highest in the land. Simms's visit was a precursor for an American invasion of the British turf in which a handful of men, small in stature but large in influence, revolutionised British racing.

Lester Reiff came over for a spell in 1896 and had 16 winners. Next to arrive was Tod Sloan. On his first short visit in autumn 1897 he had 53 mounts and won on 20 of them. He returned the following autumn, again as the punter's friend, with 43 winners out of 98 mounts. The shocked British experts argued that if Sloan came over for a full season it would be a different story. It was. His strike rate fell from 43.9 to 31.3 per cent but his 345 mounts yielded 108 victories placing him near the head of the jockeys' table. By 1900 four of the top ten riders in the championship were from the United States, including champion jockey, Lester Reiff. Nineteen-year-old Danny Maher arrived late that season and secured 27 wins from 128 rides, a sign of the talent which was to secure him the jockeys' championship in 1908 and again in 1913.

Most of the Americans were outstanding jockeys, but their ability was not the sole reason for their remarkable success in Britain. They brought with them a new style of racing and riding which could be distinguished at a glance. English jockeys rode in a similar style to the hunting field, sitting erect with a comparatively straight knee and a good length of rein; in contrast the Americans pushed the saddle forward, shortened both the stirrups and the reins, and rode with knees bent, crouching along the horse's neck. By cutting wind resistance and giving a better weight distribution on the horse, the monkey-on-a-stick style of riding was worth several pounds advantage. The Americans also brought a different style of racing. British jockeys had often raced almost half-paced in the earlier stages of a race and then swooped in the final furlong or so. Champions such as Sam Chifney, George Fordham and Fred Archer were all famous for their waiting game in which they came with a late rush to the winning post. In contrast the Americans often raced from the front if they felt their mount could cope with the pace. Indeed the fact that Sloan was frequently 'out on his own' led to 'on your tod' entering the English language. Most of the Americans were remarkable judges of pace because American trainers made more use of the stopwatch than their British counterparts who generally preferred to try their horses out against each other. The similarity of many American flat tracks made comparison of times more meaningful than in Britain where 'horses for courses' was a fair working rule.

The American jockeys also benefited from a concurrent invasion by American trainers. In the three years 1898–1900 John Huggins trained the winners of 162 races and was champion trainer in 1899; in 1900 Enoch Wishard headed the list of trainers with 54 winners; and his fellow-American, W. Duke put 31 into the winner's enclosure. Although American training methods contributed to their success with horses having better shoes fitted and being given more fresh air than was common in British establishments, the Americans also had skill in the use of drugs. American race meetings lasted for ten days or more and horses raced several times at one meet, leading to the use of dope to stimulate tired animals. Those who came to Britain were not averse to supplementing their training methods with the application of drugs to give their horses a further advantage. At the time doping was not a turf offence in Britain.

By 1902 the American invasion was virtually over. The success of Sloan and company and the growing employment of many lesser-ranked Americans persuaded British jockeys that they too had to take up the American style of riding and racing. Initially the pure American style was adopted but, although it was a decided improvement on the traditional British upright seat, it was not ideal for British courses that were more undulating than the American flat tracks. Difficulties in rebalancing horses led to a host of accidents and objections for foul riding. Soon, however, modified versions of the American seat appeared: the end result was that stirrups in general remained shorter than formerly, but the knees of most jockeys did not overlap the withers of their mounts, nor were reins grasped as tightly or held so close behind the ears as in the original American style.

The stay of the Americans was brief. Simms rode only that first season; Lester Reiff came back to ride from 1899 to 1901; his brother Johnny for the same three years; and Tod Sloan for only two full seasons. By 1902 only Danny Maher and 'Skeets' Martin were riding regularly in Britain but they were still successful: Maher third in the championship with 106 wins (and the highest winning percentage of 23.5) and Martin fourth with 80 wins. Significantly Maher had changed his style and taken up the Anglo-American seat. Equally significant Maher was regarded as respectable whereas many of the others had a blatant disregard for the rules of racing. Lester Reiff, champion jockey in 1900, was warned off by the Jockey Club in October 1901 for not trying to win at Manchester and Sloan, following an official reprimand for gambling which was against the rules of British racing, had it intimated to him that he need not bother to apply for a renewal of his licence the following season. Maher took up residence in Britain and continued to ride with success even when British riders adopted American techniques. In 1903 he was never out of the places in the Classics and won both the Derby and the St Leger on Rock Sand. In 1906 he was victorious in the Derby again, this time on Spearmint, and in the Oaks on Keystone II. Between 1900 and 1914 Maher rode 1,331 winners in Britain with a winning percentage of 25.3. Eventually he succumbed to tuberculosis, virtually the industrial disease of jockeys exacerbated by their constant efforts to lose weight. Martin also continued to ride in Britain with some success though he never challenged Maher as the leading American rider.

Further reading

Dizikes, J., *Yankee Doodle Dandy: The Life and Times of Tod Sloan* (New Haven: Yale University Press, 2000).
Vamplew, W., 'The American Invasion of the English Turf: A Study in Sporting Technological Transfer' in Toleneer, J. and Renson, R. (eds), *Old Borders, New Borders, No Borders* (Leuven: Meyer and Meyer, 2000).

See also Jockeys, Race riding.

Anti-racing lobby

Historically most of the objections to horseracing have centred on its association with gambling, both as a vehicle for betting in its own right and, in the nineteenth century, in the gaming booths rented out to thimblemen and card-sharps to bring in revenue for the prize fund. Such arguments had three thrusts. Morally, gambling was evil and the poor and gullible (often the same) needed protection; economically, gambling was an unproductive waste of resources; and socially it was linked with crime. Not only was it an illegal activity itself for many years but also it was associated with stealing by gamblers to finance their addiction and, more recently, with money laundering on the racecourse.

It was not just gambling that concerned the anti-racing lobby but also the other disreputable activities which race meetings generated. In the nineteenth century race weeks were a major event in the local social calendar and almost everywhere they resulted in an influx of prostitutes, an expansion of gaming houses in the locality, and a rise in uninhibited and inebriated behaviour, some of it criminal. Racing was held responsible for this and other frowned-on behaviour: for the pick pocketing that occurred in the large crowds, for the passing of counterfeit coinage in the hurried trading between races, and for the unholy trinity of betting, drinking and lack of sexual restraint associated with the sport. Employers also claimed that the local races led to staff absenteeism, to their mind an even worse crime!

As gambling has become more socially accepted – and government approved – and as racecourses have dampened the worst of the social misbehaviour, the opposition to racing has switched from a concern about the misdeeds of humans to one about the welfare of horses. Opposition to racing now comes mainly from animal rights activists. They believe racing is cruel, particularly National Hunt racing which asks a half-ton animal to leap a fence at 30 mph carrying a man on its back. Some argue that forcing horses to race is an act of cruelty in itself; others object more to the whipping and the injuries and deaths that occur. Campaigners consistently target horseracing for its exploitation of horses, a matter which intensifies after incidents at high-profile events such as the Grand National Meeting at Aintree in April 2000 where four horses were killed on the first day or the Cheltenham Festival the previous year where four horses also died. Groups such as Fight Against Animal Cruelty in Europe and the Animal Aid Society hold poster and leaflet campaigns outside betting shops, protest at race meetings (particularly at Aintree on Grand National day), and petition both racing and parliamentary authorities. In 1989 they persuaded Labour MP Tony Banks to table an unsuccessful House of Commons motion calling for the Grand National to be banned unless the Aintree course passed the safety standards demanded by animal welfare groups. They have no truck with racing apologists who argue that without the sport there would be no thoroughbreds to protect, nor with the view that the horse has died doing something that it instinctively wants to do and for which it is rewarded by being well looked after all its life. It has not helped racing's image with these groups that the British Horseracing Board gave financial support to the pro-hunting lobby.

Using its website as its public face, the Jockey Club has mustered arguments to defend its sport against the allegations of cruelty. Perhaps it is justified in pointing out that horses are herd animals and galloping alongside one another is a natural inclination. It is on less safe ground when it defends the use of the whip for safety, correction and encouragement but then argues that disciplinary action is taken against riders who apply it incorrectly. This implicitly accepts that abuse and cruelty does occur. The Club argues that the quality of life enjoyed by the racehorse is better than virtually any other animal in Britain and that most receive care and devotion far beyond that given to most domestic pets. The horses get individual attention from a loving lad or lass, all the food, drink, clothing and bedding they require, regular exercise on custom-made training grounds and expert veterinary care. They even get an annual rest or holiday! The Club even utilises the poor economic condition of the sport to argue that few people come into racing for the money; that it is the love of working with horses that attracts them not financial reward.

It is a sad fact that while high-profile, televised events can publicise racing's best qualities they can also bring the downside of the sport into living rooms across the country. When ten horses die at the 1996 Cheltenham Festival, three are killed in the 1998 Grand National and four lose their lives in a single day at Aintree in 2000, it can only strengthen the case of the animal activists. Following the death of the three horses in the 1998 Grand National the RSPCA stationed inspectors at each obstacle the following year to assess if the fences were 'jumpable'. Yet, despite a record of over one-third of the starters failing to finish and almost 30 equine fatalities since 1946, the Society has been reluctant to condemn the Grand National, perhaps because the event is part of Britain's sporting heritage. It has, however, criticised aspects of the race, particularly the structure of fences, the number of horses allowed to start, and the problem of rider-less animals. More generally regular discussions are now held with the Jockey Club and relevant course managements to improve safety standards and reduce risk to horses. Nevertheless many in the racing industry believe that a legal challenge to the existence of horseracing for inflicting cruelty on animals is inevitable.

Further reading

Huggins, M., *Flat Racing and British Society 1790–1914* (London: Cass, 2000). www.thejockeyclub.co.uk

See also Whipping.

Apprentices

Most licensed jockeys are either apprentices or conditional riders. An apprentice is a young flat-racing jockey who is tied by an annual renewable contract to a trainer from whom he will learn the skills of race riding. The National Hunt equivalent is a conditional rider. He or she can sign an agreement at 16 but cannot ride as an apprentice beyond the age of 24. Historically they were bound to their trainer by legal agreement for up to seven years, but by the 1970s an apprenticeship had been reduced to a minimum of three years. Until two decades ago apprentices were indentured to a trainer with whom they had to stay till they completed their articles. Today they have the freedom to switch stables, though, at the insistence of the Jockey Club, they are not allowed to race ride for the remainder of the season unless both trainers agree.

In the early twentieth century the Jockey Club introduced weight allowances for apprentices in recognition of their inexperience. Outstanding apprentices and conditional riders can thus do well. In 1923 Charlie Elliott was champion jockey whilst still an apprentice, as was Elijah Wheatly 18 years before him. During the Second World War the Jockey Club, fearing a shortage of jockeys in the post war years, brought in a sliding scale of apprentice weight allowances. Seven pounds could be claimed until six winners had been ridden, 5 lb till 20, and 3 lb till 40 winners or the apprentice had reached the age of 21. Many trainers responded to this cue and in 1951, 84 apprentices aggregated over 300 winners. Unfortunately in this period National Service proved a major bugbear to many trainers as their diminutive apprentices often returned muscled out and too heavy for a riding career. Under the scheme operating since 1991, the allowance is reduced progressively, disappearing completely after the total of winners reaches 85.

'Losing one's claim' to an allowance is a major rite of passage after which the young rider has to compete on ability alone. Even a leading apprentice has no guarantee of future success. Lester Piggott (1950), Pat Eddery (1971), Kevin Darley (1978) and Frankie Dettori (1989) were all champion apprentices who went on to become champion jockeys. Frankie Durr, joint champion apprentice in 1945, went on to ride over 2,000 winners. But who recalls David Coates or Richard Dicey, joint champion apprentices in 1968, or even the 1994 champion apprentice, Stephen Davies, winner of 45 races when attached to Henry Cecil's stables but who has since disappeared from the British racing scene?

It was in the training stables that the apprentices were supposed to be taught the skills of jockeyship: how to be smart out of the stalls, how to balance a horse, how to judge pace, and how to use the whip both left- and right-handed. Some stables, especially those with ex-jockeys on the staff, have taught apprentices how to race ride. Indeed where an apprenticeship promised the trainer half the boy's earnings it was in his interest to do so. Men such as Frenchie Nicholson, Ernie Davey, Sam Armstrong, and Major F.B. Sneyd, a first rate but hard teacher, from whose Sparsholt stables brothers Doug and Eph Smith and Joe Mercer graduated, earned a reputation as well as an income from their ability to produce good, young riders. Even those trainers who cared for their apprentices did not have an easy task in bringing on the boys, partly because they had no parental influence. Some got homesick and dispirited; others cocksure, unruly and unmanageable. Unfortunately, as is acknowledged in the industry, too many trainers simply regarded apprentices as cheap stable labour and would not give them the chance to ride in public. Not that this was always the trainer's fault; many owners were reluctant to put up a youngster, even with a weight allowance. Willie Carson, commenting on becoming champion jockey in 1972, noted that 'there may be a dozen others as good as me who will never be heard of because they did not get the chances I did' (Ayres and Newbon, p. 120). From the 1920s races solely for apprentices were developed to help budding jockeys to gain some race experience. These days any course that holds more than four days of racing is obliged to put on at least one such event. There are also 'bumper' races during the National Hunt season which are flat races for jumping horses ridden by apprentices, conditional riders or amateurs. Nevertheless the apprentices are riding alongside other novices not experienced jockeys from whom they might learn in the unforgiving environment of a race.

An alternative to in-house tuition was provided by training courses for apprentices which began in the early 1970s at Great Bookham near Leatherhead in Surrey. They were financed by the Horserace Betting Levy Board (HBLB) and by trainers of the 12 apprentices who attended each six-week course. In 1974 further courses financed by the HBLB commenced at the National Equestrian Centre at Stoneleigh in Warwickshire. They were for girls who wished to become apprentices and school-leavers who came from a non-racing background but were interested in a career in the industry. Neither significantly changed the face of apprenticeship and in the early 1980s an enquiry by John Marriage Q.C., onetime Home Office representative on the Levy Board, recommended the establishment of an apprentice training school. Yards were getting too big for traditional apprenticeship schemes to operate effectively as there was no time to offer proper tuition.

The British Racing School at Newmarket and, to a lesser extent, the Northern Racing College at Rossington Hall near Bawtry, took on this task. Purpose built at a cost of £1.5 million, the British Racing School came into being in 1983. Its first director, Major Barney Griffiths, a successful amateur rider himself, ran it like a boarding-school-cum-stables, attempting to replicate stable routine and stressing the importance of manners and smartness. In the late 1990s about a quarter of those trained have gone on to ride as apprentices. Four of the last six champion apprentices have come through the School. When the apprentices lose their 7-pound allowance they are given a three-day intermediate course dealing not so much with riding as with career management, money matters, interview techniques, fitness and diet.

The old apprentice system has now gone along with what many believed to be over harsh discipline, but, with nothing to tie an apprentice to the stable, the incentive to pass on advice and give young riders a chance has been weakened. Indeed, most apprentices are now virtually freelance riders and, though many trainers no longer take half their earnings, they no longer pay half their expenses. Most apprentices earn very little money for an outside chance of becoming a well-paid jockey. Money and fame tempt many to try, but throughout the history of racing the majority of apprentices have failed to become licensed jockeys. Of the 187 apprentices registered in 1900, only 75 became jockeys and a mere 23 (12 per cent) continued as such for more than three years. Little has changed. Current director of the British Racing School, Rory MacDonald, estimates that nine out of ten budding apprentices fail to become full professional jockeys.

Further reading

Ayres, M. and Newbon, G., *Under Starter's Orders* (Newton Abbot: David and Charles, 1975).
Magee, S., *The Channel Four Book of Racing* (London: Hamlyn, 1995).
www.brs.org.uk

See also Jockeys.

Arabian horses

When British breeders of racing horses in the seventeenth century decided that their stock needed improvement, it was to the Arab breed that they turned. Arabs, selectively bred by the Bedouin for centuries, were small, seldom more than 15.2 hands high, tough, and possessed both speed and stamina. No fewer than 150 stallions of Eastern blood were said to have been imported to Britain in the seventeenth and early eighteenth centuries although some of these were Turks or Barbs, related to the Arab breed. Poorly maintained records and name changes have led to difficulties in identifying and tracing the subsequent development of the thoroughbred but three horses in particular, the Byerley Turk, the Darley Arabian and the Godolphin Arabian, had a major impact on the evolution of the modern racehorse.

The Byerley Turk, foaled around 1680 of predominantly Arab blood, was captured from the Turkish army at Buda in 1687 and brought to England by Captain Robert Byerley. Said to have seen action at the Battle of the Boyne in 1689, the horse was sent to stud first in Durham and then in Yorkshire. His bloodline was established by his grandson, Partner, the best racehorse of his day at Newmarket, and his great-grandson, Herod, who sired the winners of over 1,000 races in the late eighteenth century. Two recent Derby winners, Blakeney (1969) and Dr Devious (1992) can trace their descent from the Byerley Turk.

The Darley Arabian was sent to England in 1704 as a four-year-old. A bay of 15 hands with a white blaze and three white feet, he had been bought in Syria by Thomas Darley for his father, James. He remained at stud on the Darley family estate in Yorkshire for around 25 years. He sired Flying Childers, said to be the first great English racehorse, and his brother Bartlet's Childers, the grandsire of Eclipse, and through them he is the ancestor in the direct male line of the vast majority of modern thoroughbreds. Northern Dancer, the most influential stallion of the late twentieth century, is descended from the Darley Arabian and, in naming their management company Darley, the Maktoums have acknowledged his early impact on British bloodstock.

The Godolphin, another name brought to the forefront of modern racing by Sheikh Mohammed's racing operation, may have been a Barb, similar to an Arab, and is thought to have come originally from the Yemen. A brown horse of less than 15 hands, he was a gift to Louis XV of France, and was bought in 1729 as a five-year-old by Edward Coke of Derbyshire. After Coke's death in 1733, he was acquired by Lord Godolphin and spent over 20 years at his stud near Newmarket where he produced Lath, one of the best racehorses of the 1730s. His grandson, Matchem, became one of the greatest sires of the eighteenth century and his bloodline, though less robust than that of the Darley Arabian, can be traced to Santa Claus, winner of the 1964 Derby.

Although these three stallions have traditionally been credited as the founding sires of the English thoroughbred, other Arabian horses may also have been influential. The Leedes Arabian features more commonly in the pedigree of most modern thoroughbreds, and the Curwen Bay Barb, bought from Louis XIV of France and noted for his impact on female lines, may have been undervalued in the past because nineteenth-century breeders discounted the female contribution to the development of the horse. Research undertaken in the late 1970s also noted that genealogical lines are not the same as genetic contributions to a breed. The findings confirmed that 80 per cent of modern thoroughbreds can trace their descent from the Darley Arabian in the male line but discovered that the total genetic contributions of the three founding stallions was little over 25 per cent.

The Arab horse has also featured on the racecourse in its own right. Although it was bred for racing in France for more than 100 years, it was developed largely for showing in Britain, where Arab racing had proved to be unsuccessful in the eighteenth century. It was not until the mid-1970s that the Arab Horse Society, with the approval of the Jockey Club, resurrected races for Arab horses. A split within that body in 1999 and the formation of a new group, the Arabian Racing Organisation, has recently led to a situation in which the Arab Horse Society continues to be the sole registration authority for Arabian horses in Britain and the new organisation is responsible for administering all Arab racing. Sometimes Arabian horseracing is tacked on to existing thoroughbred meetings but in many cases an entire race day is devoted to this branch of the sport. Sponsorship by the Maktoums and other Middle Eastern families has enabled it to expand from purely amateur beginnings to semi-professional status, with a mixture of amateur and professional trainers and jockeys, vastly increased prize money, and the kudos of racing at venues such as Epsom Downs, Newbury and Newmarket.

Further reading

Herbert, I. (ed.), *Horse Racing* (London: Collins, 1980).
Holland, A., *Stride by Stride* (London: Queen Anne Press, 1989).

See also Eighteenth-century horses.

Archer, Fred (1857–86)

No one seeing Frederick James Archer for the first time would have recognised him as a jockey. At 5 feet 10 inches he was tall for a flat-race rider and in winter he weighed nearly 11 st. Yet possibly he was the greatest jockey of all time in British racing. During his brief career, cut short by his suicide before he reached 30, he rode 2,748 winners (from 8,084 mounts), including 5 Derby victories and 16 other Classics. He also rode over 200 winners in a season seven times, a record no other rider has come near.

He was the second son of William Archer, a steeplechase rider who won the 1858 Grand National. Both his older brother William and younger brother Charles also became jockeys, the former dying of injuries received in a fall at Cheltenham. Fred attended school only intermittently and in later years relied on friends to write his correspondence. How he coped with organising the hundreds of mounts he took each season is a matter for conjecture. His racing education was provided first by his father but primarily by Mathew Dawson, the Newmarket trainer to whom he was apprenticed in 1868 and for whom he became stable jockey in 1873. At the age of 12 he won his first race, a steeplechase at Bangor, and the following year his first victory on the flat, on Athol Daisy at Chesterfield. Four years later he was champion jockey and remained so for 13 consecutive seasons.

He was a good judge of pace and of horses. Riding in the traditional upright English stance, he possessed marvellous hands and the ability to read a race. Competitive and determined, he rode hard, driving finishes in which he gave no quarter to rival jockeys – he once put his own brother through the rails. Especially in his early career, he was also severe on his mounts with whip and spurs. Yet he was suspended only once, in 1871 at Newmarket, for misconduct at the start.

His riding success made him wealthy and he left an estate valued at over £60,000. As an apprentice he obtained only 9 guineas in his first year, rising to 13 guineas in his fourth and fifth years, but, at his peak as a jockey, he earned around £8,000 per annum. Most of this came from retainers to secure his services and from presents from winning owners. It was alleged that he was involved in a jockeys' ring to fix races but there is no evidence of this. However, he did use his judgement of horses and riders to good effect in advising a betting syndicate. His love of money led to him being known in some quarters as 'The Tinman', tin being contemporary slang for currency. Yet he returned the balance of his retainer to the Duke of Portland when His Grace demanded that Archer end his association with George Baird, the brash son of a Scottish ironmaster, who was doing his best to outride and cuckold British racing society.

His death shocked racing. While riding in Ireland Archer had received a telegram from the Duchess of Montrose, owner of St Mirin, stating that 'my horse runs in the Cambridgeshire. I count on you to ride it'. Archer needed little persuasion. The Cambridgeshire was the one big race that had eluded him. He had been racing in Ireland at 9 st 4 lb but undertook to ride at 8 st 6 lb, a reduction of 12 lb in less than a week. He attempted to achieve this by not eating at all on three days, counteracting the intake at other times by doses of a purgative, especially devised for him by Dr Winter, a Newmarket physician, and, when not riding, making use of the Turkish bath attached to his Falmouth House residence. He still failed to make the weight by a pound and when he lost the race by only a head the overweight rider blamed himself. The effort to lose weight left him so weak that when riding on Wednesday 3 November at Brighton, eight days after the Cambridgeshire defeat, he contracted a chill, which he aggravated by insisting on fulfilling his engagement at Lewes the following day. He left that course in an extremely weakened state and was diagnosed on the morning of Monday 8 November as suffering from typhoid fever. The date was the second anniversary of his wife's death in childbirth. That afternoon his sister, who was taking care of him, heard a noise in his bedroom and found Archer with a revolver. She attempted to disarm him but he placed the muzzle in his mouth and fired. He died a victim of illness, depression, and wasting. Newmarket came to a halt for his funeral and the streets were lined with thousands paying their respects.

His record of 246 winners in the 1885 season was not broken until 1933, by Gordon Richards, by a macabre coincidence on the anniversary of Archer's death.

Further reading

Murray, A., *Race to the Finish, The Life and Times of Fred Archer* (London: Robson, 2003).
Welcome, J., *Fred Archer: A Complete Study* (London: Lambourn Press, 1990).

See also Nineteenth-century jockeys.

Architecture

Early thoroughbred racing took place without the formality of permanent racecourse structures. The aristocracy viewed the proceedings from horseback or from carriages while others, as can be seen in early eighteenth-century paintings, simply stood around. By the mid-1750s some supporters of elite racing were prepared to pay for the privilege of watching from more exclusive and weather-proof surroundings. The first grandstand at the Knavesmire racecourse in York was designed and built by John Carr in 1754 after 250 gentlemen had subscribed £5 each. A quarter of a century later the same architect was commissioned to design and oversee the construction of a grandstand at Doncaster which cost more than £2,500. Another early Georgian edifice at Richmond racecourse, where top-class racing ceased in 1891, was built in 1775 by public subscription. Even some small courses established permanent buildings with the help of wealthy benefactors. Kelso races in the Scottish borders benefited from the support of the Duke of Roxburghe who not only purchased land for a new course but funded a handsome stone grandstand with elegant arches and elaborate ironwork. Completed in 1822, it is still in use today and must be one of the few racecourse stands to contain a coal fire in the ladies' powder room! The original royal stand at Ascot, to a design by John Nash, the architect of London's Regent Street, was erected in the same year and the first at Epsom took shape in 1830.

During the Victorian era racecourse grandstands were amongst the largest structures in which crowds regularly gathered. Racing art of the period depicts numerous examples of large canopied buildings several stories high and viewing galleries crammed with spectators, many perched precariously on the top level, completely exposed to the elements. (The Edwardian stand at Ludlow and the 1974 creation at Cartmel are still roofless.) There was also an assortment of stewards' and judges' boxes, weighing rooms, clock towers, ornate entrance gates and little lodge houses, all built in local material of red brick, stone, timber or thatch embellished with wrought iron. Many of the structures became increasingly dilapidated or unsuitable for twentieth-century racegoing and have been replaced, as at Newbury and Leicester. Some stands, such as Warwick, are listed but have been sympathetically converted to present needs. Some survive with altered functions; the elegant columned and carved Georgian edifice at Doncaster is now a weighing room. Others, faded but recalling Victorian and Edwardian splendour, have been superseded by state-of-the-art facilities, and now incongruously play host to the least affluent patrons of the racecourse instead of the local gentry.

The last 25 years have seen a profusion of glass and concrete additions and replacements to racecourse architecture. The March Stand at Goodwood, opened in 1980, won the annual Concrete Society award. The Queen's Stand at Epsom, unveiled in 1992, won an architecture award from the *Financial Times*. Several Millennium grandstands have recently sprouted into life (Newmarket, Wetherby) and premier tracks such as York and Cheltenham seem to be in a permanent state of rebuilding. There has been substantial investment at many courses like these which come under the umbrella of the Racecourse Holdings Trust, an arm of the Jockey Club, while others have benefited from interest-free loans by the Horserace Betting Levy Board. Improvements are also ongoing at the tracks owned by the major commercial groups currently involved in racing (e.g. Arena Leisure, Northern Racing) and also at smaller independent venues such as Musselburgh, Stratford and Towcester.

Amongst the modern, functional architecture appearing on the racecourses of Britain, there are still isolated, unusual gems – a Victorian bandstand at Ripon, a pagoda and classical garden complete with Grecian urns at Fontwell Park, an old wooden judges' box at Sandown Park. Statues commemorating the stars of the track also adorn the scenes of their glory – Red Rum overlooks both Aintree and Ayr, Arkle, Golden Miller and Dawn Run form a triumvirate at Cheltenham and an unnamed bronze horse stands guard at Goodwood, permanent reminders of why racecourses and their buildings exist.

Further reading

Sampson, A., *Courses of Action: the Homes of Horse Racing* (London: Hale, 1984).

Arkle (1957–70) – by Archive out of Bright Cherry

Arkle was arguably the greatest steeplechaser of all time, winning 27 of his 35 races including the Cheltenham Gold Cup three times in succession. Bred in Ireland from a sire whose stud fee was less than 50 guineas, he was bought as a three-year-old for 1,150 guineas by Anne, Duchess of Westminster, and named after a mountain overlooking her Scottish estate. He was sent into training with Tom Dreaper and after several successes over hurdles in Ireland, he made a winning debut in a novice steeplechase at Cheltenham, finishing unbeaten in the 1962–63 season.

The next two years saw a series of meetings with the top English chaser, Mill House. Though Arkle lost their first encounter in the Hennessy Gold Cup at Newbury in November 1963, he was never to be beaten again by the English champion. In March 1964, he won the initial rematch at Cheltenham, recording the fastest ever time in the Gold Cup; he then beat him into fourth place in the 1964 Hennessy and followed this up with a second Cheltenham Gold Cup win of 20 lengths. He ended that season in Britain by winning the 1965 Whitbread Gold Cup at Sandown Park. In Ireland, where he had won the Grand National in 1964 and the Leopardstown Chase two years running, he not only became a folk hero, drawing huge crowds whenever he raced, but caused the rules of handicapping to be changed; his superiority was such that a different set of weights was applied when he ran.

The 1965–66 season saw his greatest triumphs. Carrying the maximum weight of 12 st 7 lb he beat the unfortunate Mill House again by 24 lengths in the Gallaher Gold Cup at Sandown, setting a new course record for 3 miles in the process, won the Hennessy again and the King George Vl Chase at Kempton Park as short-priced favourite (at odds of 1–6 and 1–7), and demolished the field in his third Cheltenham Gold Cup, winning by 30 lengths. These feats earned him the title of National Hunt Champion of 1966 and the highest National Hunt ranking to date in the *Timeform* ratings (212).

But his jumping days were nearly over. Beaten into second place in the Hennessy in November 1966 while conceding 35 pounds to the eventual winner, he won at Ascot before finishing second again, this time in the King George. Obviously lame at the end of the race, it was discovered that he had fractured the main bone in his off-fore hoof, and although there were hopes that he might race again, he was officially retired to his owner's Irish estate in October 1968. Throughout his brilliant career, in which he won 22 of his 26 steeplechases and amassed record prize money for a jumper of almost £75,000, he was usually partnered by Pat Taaffe, who regarded him as by far the best horse he had ever ridden.

Arkle did not spend long in retirement. Although he made a full recovery from his career-ending injury, he developed a progressive arthritic condition in his hind feet and was put down in May 1970 to spare him further suffering. He was only 13. By all accounts a calm and gentle horse, this bay gelding will be remembered for his pace, acceleration, and jumping ability – he never fell – and for his courageous running under severe handicap weights. He was mobbed at racecourses, particularly by the large Irish contingent who followed his exploits, and his star status produced sacks of fan mail and a song recorded in his honour. He is commemorated at Cheltenham by a statue facing the parade ring, the Arkle Bar, with its many souvenirs, and a major novice 2-mile race, the Arkle Chase. Although originally buried at the Duchess of Westminster's Irish home, his skeleton can now be found at the Irish Horse Museum, a tribute to his greatness but a touching and poignant end for such a great horse.

Further reading

Herbert, I., *Arkle, the Story of a Champion* (London: Pelham, 1966).
Randall, J. and Morris, T., *A Century of Champions* (Halifax: Portway Press, 1999).

Art

The horse has been painted, drawn and sculpted for thousands of year, from Egyptian wall paintings to the white chalk horses across English downs. Racing was first depicted in Roman chariot scenes but the earliest surviving picture of an English horserace is thought to be an etching entitled '*August 24 1684, The last horse race run before Charles II at Dorsett Ferry near Windsor Castle*' by Francis C. Barlow, dated 1687. Although it is more than 300 years old, there are many familiar appurtenances of racing on display: the jockeys wear peaked caps and breeches, the king views the race from a grandstand, the clerk of the scales is present and there is a cheering crowd urging the riders towards the winning post.

Barlow (*c*.1626–1704) is considered to be the father of British sporting art and his work, including views of hunting and illustrations of birds and fish, was strongly influenced by the Flemish artists of his time who were resident in England. After his death it was they who initially carried on the tradition. Jan Wyck concentrated on hunting and battle scenes but Peter Tillemans, who arrived from Holland in 1709, painted several panoramas of racing on the various courses at Newmarket Heath and '*The Watering Course on the Warren Hill, Newmarket*', a view of racehorses exercising on the same gallops which are used today. John Wootton, a pupil of Wyck, and James Seymour, both contemporaries of Tillemans, left behind similar canvases of races at Newmarket but they also specialised in portraits of notable horses such as the Byerley Turk and Flying Childers. One of the few early paintings of racing outside Newmarket purported to show the first York races, 'The Meeting at Clifton and Rawcliffe Ings, York, September 1709' by James Ross senior, now on display at the National Horseracing Museum.

The three branches of sporting art consisting of portraits, illustrations of actual events, and imagined subjects based on fact, were all represented by eighteenth-century painters and engravers. The greatest of these, George Stubbs (1724–1806), revolutionised the techniques of horse painting following a meticulous study of equine anatomy. His portraits of many great racehorses such as Eclipse and Gimcrack radiate authenticity – the bone and muscle, flesh and blood of the animal rendered more lifelike than the earlier works of Wootton and Seymour. He was also the first equine artist to integrate his subject with a natural landscape. Stubbs published his Anatomy of the Horse in 1766, painted a frieze of racehorses at Wentworth, experimented with enamel on porcelain and designed the horses for Josiah Wedgewood's china. His contemporaries included members of the Sartorius family, originally from Bavaria, and Sawrey Gilpin, elected President of the Society of Artists in 1773. Francis Sartorius and his son John Nost Sartorius made no attempt to refine their painting in the manner of Stubbs but continued the crude portrayals of an earlier era, depicting primitive racers in the 'rocking horse' gallop, with front and hind legs extended and necks stretched. However, they received many commissions from racehorse owners keen to capture the triumphs of their animals at moderate cost and have therefore left a considerable legacy of eighteenth-century race painting. Gilpin, though less skilled in anatomical detail than Stubbs, was a highly regarded equine artist, and was said to have been an early inspiration to the next great horse painter, Ben Marshall (1767–1835).

Originally known for his portraits, Marshall is credited with saying that many gentlemen were prepared to pay him 50 guineas for a picture of their horse but only 10 guineas for one of their wife! Whatever the truth of this statement, equine art was a sufficiently lucrative business to entice him to Newmarket where his commissions covered both hunting and racing, including 'The Match between Sir Joshua and Filho da Puta at Newmarket, 1816', a detailed study of the racegoers as much as the race. His fellow artist Clifton Tomson (1775–1828), however, was renowned for capturing the thrills of the sport itself with large fields of runners flashing past packed grandstands, as in his 'St Leger Stakes of 1812'.

Marshall had produced pieces for The Sporting Magazine and one of his pupils, Abraham Cooper (1787–1868) continued this work, together with a stream of racing and hunting scenes, over 300 of which were exhibited at the Royal Academy. Marshall's other famous pupil, and lifelong friend, was John Ferneley senior (1782–1860) who worked extensively in Ireland and made a good living from ten-guinea portraits of horses. He passed his skill in sporting art to his sons John junior and Claude Lorraine, and to his daughter Sarah who engraved several of his pictures in stone. Another family of artists were the Alkens who had arrived in Britain from Denmark during the eighteenth century but whose most famous member, Henry senior made an impression in the early Victorian period. He specialised in subjects which, along with portraits, had always been the most popular with racing painters, the starts and particularly the finishes of races. He and his son, Henry junior, made a special feature of the Epsom Derby but their wide-eyed, straining horses have more in common with the Sartorius style of racing than the more technically accurate work of Marshall, Tomson and Cooper.

With the Classics firmly established as high points of the racing year, the Derby and St Leger in particular became frequent subjects for many of the artists already mentioned. They were also prominent in the work of James Pollard and John Frederick Herring senior. Pollard, like Tomson, specialised in detailed crowd scenes while Herring was the better horse painter. The two collaborated on several canvases including *'Dead Heat for the Doncaster Great St Leger, 1839'* between Charles XII and Euclid, against a background of massed grandstands. Herring executed portraits of nearly 70 Classic winners during the period 1815–51 and also painted scenes of the relatively new sport of steeplechasing. The Alkens were also well known for their prints of jump races such as the moonlit *'Aylesbury Aristocratic Steeplechases'*.

The great period of hand-wrought racing prints lasted for around a hundred years until the 1870s, by which time they had been superseded by photography and cheaper reproduction processes. Etchings, line engravings, mezzotints, stipple-engravings and aquatints (some of the latter virtually indistinguishable from watercolours) were all used to popularise racing art. Some artists such as James Pollard and Henry Alken senior engraved their own designs, others handed their compositions to London publishing firms who employed tinters, engravers and colourists. With so many racing pictures commissioned and displayed privately, prints of original works were frequently the medium by which races and their participants came to the attention of a wider public.

Races and racehorses were not the only subjects to be immortalised in art. The caricaturist Thomas Rowlandson (1756–1827) produced many pen and ink sketches and cartoons poking fun at members of the Jockey Club and illustrating the levels of gambling and corruption in the sport. Personalities of the turf were painted, from Tregonwell Frampton, keeper of the royal running horses under four monarchs (William III, Anne and Georges I and II), portrayed by John Wootton, to Admiral Henry John Rous, Jockey Club steward for nearly 40 years of Queen Victoria's reign. The main street at Newmarket outside the Subscription Rooms was captured by Pollard in the 1820s and intricate crowd scenes or pictures of racing society, with or without the equine stars, were popularised in the second half of the nineteenth century by William Frith and Isaac Cullin. Frith's masterpiece, *'The Derby Day (all human life is here)'*, a copy of which hangs in the National Horseracing Museum, shows the seamier side of the racing crowd – the card sharps, gypsies, pickpockets, tipsters and swells who flocked to Epsom Downs each year. Cullin, originally a portrait painter, specialised in scenes of the winners' enclosure or the paddock at Newmarket, peopled with well-known figures of the turf such as Edward, Prince of Wales, the auctioneer Richard Tattersall and numerous members of the aristocracy. Others painted stylised groups of the smart set on the lawns at Goodwood and similar fashionable courses, with a fair sprinkling of elegantly costumed women. Fascinating insights into nineteenth-century social history, these scenes were almost like human versions of the composite equine paintings in which artists created imaginary races between famous horses. One, by Alfred de Prade, shows Derby winners Cotterstone (1843), The Flying Dutchman (1849), Voltigeur (1850) and West Australian (1853) racing against a field of equally illustrious animals.

Cullin also depicted areas of the racecourse which were off limits to the general public, including the weighing room, and prints, paintings and cartoons of its occupants, the jockeys, formed another branch of Victorian racing art. Many were painted on horseback, sometimes astride their greatest winning mounts, sometimes in the colours of a particular patron. Cartoonists Lib, Spy and Sem drew all the most successful jockeys as well as Jockey Club members and owners, often individually, but also in groups, as in the much-reproduced Lib cartoon containing an assortment of racing personalities from the famous jockey Fred Archer to the infamous Dowager Duchess of Montrose ('Newmarket 1885').

The arrival of photography largely killed off the sporting print and the satirical drawing but brought with it the opportunity to view the actual movement of a racehorse. The Eadward Muybridge consecutive series of photographs taken in 1887 demonstrated for the first time that animals did not gallop in the 'rocking horse' style and finally consigned this type of picture to the dustbin along with numerous inferior purveyors of racing art. With the demise of several families of British sporting painters (the Ferneleys, Herrings and Alkens had all died out by the 1890s), the late Victorian era saw wealthy owners turning to Europe for portraits of their horses. The German-born Emil Adam (1843–1924) became particularly sought after and received commissions from the Prince of Wales to paint his Derby winners Persimmon (1896) and Diamond Jubilee (1900) as well as his sole Grand National winner Ambush II (1900). James Lynwood Palmer (1868–1941) and Alfred Munnings (1878–1959, knighted in 1944) were two English artists to carry on the tradition of equine portraits. Others such as Joseph Crawhall and Sir John Lavery were influenced by the Impressionists and produced canvases that conveyed the speed and flashy colours of the racecourse. Gilbert Holiday and Lionel Edwards worked initially as illustrators, followed hounds and brought their knowledge of horses and horsemanship to their racing pictures. It was Munnings, however, who probably made the greatest impact on twentieth-century British sporting art. For 40 years from 1918 to 1958, he turned out a wealth of colourful race scenes based on his own observations at Newmarket and the racecourses around London. His greatest achievement, perhaps, was to raise the profile of the sporting artist to new heights with his election as President of the Royal Academy in 1944, an honour he held until 1949. In recent years, sales of his work have commanded particularly high prices in America.

The artists of the later twentieth century have continued the themes of their forebears. The start, the finish, the paddock, the portrait, and the exhilaration of the race have been the mainstay of racing art as they have been since the beginning. Owners still wish to see their champions commemorated in oils as they did 200 years ago. Portraits of Lester Piggott and Frankie Dettori are as prized now as those of Fred Archer and George Fordham were in Victorian times. However, there have also been changes. Women have increasingly featured in the list of sporting artists, spearheaded by Susan Crawford who has painted some 20 Derby winners, executed commissions for the royal family and the Maktoums, and exhibited widely at venues such as the Royal Academy. British racing sculpture, pioneered towards the end of the nineteenth century by John Willis Good and Austrian-born Joseph Edgar Boehm, was bolstered throughout the central decades of the twentieth by the work of John Skeaping (1901–80), Professor of Sculpture at the Royal College of Arts from the end of the Second World War until 1959. He was still sculpting in bronze in the late 1970s. More recently, ex-jockey Philip Blacker has been responsible for many of the racecourse sculptures on display in Britain including Red Rum at Aintree, Desert Orchid at Kempton Park and Generous at Epsom, while Marcia Astor has fashioned the large rearing stallion with his handler, erected near the National Stud as a millennium symbol of Newmarket.

The racing print is also enjoying a revival. Many race meetings feature retail outlets specialising in racing scenes and portraits of the favourite horses of recent years. The annual publication *Travelling the Turf* is copiously illustrated with examples of limited edition prints, together with work by many members of the Society of Equestrian Artists. Racecards sometimes advertise racing art and specialist catalogues offer books of sporting prints. The racehorse in art is over 300 years old and still going strong.

Further reading

Budd, G., *Racing Art and Memorabilia* (London: Wilson, 1997).
Paget, G., *Sporting Pictures of England* (London: Bracken, 1987).
West, J. (ed.), *Travelling the Turf* (Hexham: Kensington West, 1986).

Ascot

Ascot racecourse in Berkshire is synonymous with royalty and fashion. Established in 1711 by Queen Anne, it is still owned by the Crown and, until 1939, held only one meeting each year, the four days of Royal Ascot in June. It now hosts over 25 days racing, including National Hunt fixtures, and, with seven Group One contests and roughly 20 further Pattern races, can confidently claim to be the premier racecourse in the country.

Ascot is steeped in history. The first permanent grandstand was erected in 1793 while the oldest race on the card, the Ascot Gold Cup, once the most prestigious race in Britain after the Derby, has been staged since 1807. At $2\frac{1}{2}$ miles, it is now the longest Group One race of the flat season. The royal procession, which takes place during the Royal Ascot meeting, was started by George IV in the 1820s, and open carriages are still used to convey the Royal party from the gates of Windsor Park along the straight mile course to the Royal Enclosure, where morning suits remain obligatory. More recently, history was made at the Ascot Festival meeting in September 1996 when Frankie Dettori became the first jockey in Britain to win all seven races on a card.

The flat racing circuit, over 1 mile 6 furlongs, is triangular in shape with a short home straight which is largely uphill while the chase and hurdle courses, opened in 1965, are situated inside the main track. Drainage has often proved to be a problem with two days racing, including the Gold Cup, lost after torrential rain in 1964. Over 45 kilometres of piping were laid following this disaster but further waterlogging in 1974 put paid to another Group race, the Queen Elizabeth II Stakes. (It is highly unusual for important flat races to be abandoned because of the weather or the going.) Unlike Epsom Downs, Ascot has few awkward gradients, but the courses are still reckoned to be stiff, tending to suit horses with stamina. What Ascot does have in common with its equally famous neighbour is a traditional place in the sporting and social calendar. While Epsom Downs boasts the major Classic races and the carnival of Derby Day, Royal Ascot offers the highest quality meeting of the British flat racing season and the tradition of picnics on Ascot Heath.

Many races at Ascot have royal associations. The St James's Palace Stakes, first run in 1834, elevated to Group One status in 1988 and now the most valuable race at the Royal meeting, is for three-year-old colts over a mile and has been won recently by Giant's Causeway (2000) and Rock of Gibraltar (2002). The Group One Coronation Stakes is the fillies' equivalent at the same meeting. The Prince of Wales's Stakes, raised to Group One in 2000, the Queen Anne Stakes and the King Edward VII Stakes also take place at Royal Ascot but no 'royal' race is more famous than the King George VI and Queen Elizabeth Diamond Stakes. First run at the July meeting in 1951 as the King George VI and Queen Elizabeth Stakes, it is now one of the most important flat races in Britain, with prize money to match of over £750,000. Many of the top European middle-distance horses of the post war era have triumphed in this event, from Pinza, Ribot and Ballymoss in the 1950s, to Nijinsky, Mill Reef and Brigadier Gerard in the 1970s, and, in the last decade, the Maktoum-owned Lammtarra, Daylami and Swain, who won in two consecutive years, 1997 and 1998.

But there is more to Ascot than royal patronage and association. Charity race days have been held since the 1960s, Sunday racing takes place on several summer weekends and while the Royal meeting is the most prestigious, the Festival meeting in September offers the highest amount of prize money for a single day, as well as two further Group One races in the Queen Elizabeth II Stakes and the Fillies' Mile. Another novel day out has been provided recently by the Shergar Cup in August, an international team event for jockeys, pitting Great Britain and Ireland against the Rest of the World. Plans for a new grandstand, a re-alignment of the course and re-siting of the paddock aim to place Ascot amongst the very top racecourses in the world, but will put the venue out of action in 2005.

And then there is the fashion – hats galore, no bare shoulders or micro-minis in the Royal Enclosure, trouser suits permitted since 1970 (but jeans banned) and the whole carefully chosen ensemble liable to be wrecked by the British climate. The dilemma of what to wear at Royal Ascot in particular is not a creation of the last 50 years. The attire of the Victorian aristocracy was described at length in *The Times*, and fortunes were spent then, as now, on new and fashionable clothes. Even in the twenty-first century, to be seen beside the winning post or in the Royal Enclosure at Ascot, sporting mad hats and cleavages (and probably an umbrella) is a very British experience.

Further reading

Magee, S. and Aird, S. (eds), *Ascot: The History* (London: Methuen, 2002).
Onslow, R., *Royal Ascot* (Swindon: Crowood, 1990).
www.ascot.co.uk

Asia

Until recently, traffic between the worlds of British and Asian horseracing has been largely one way. Hong Kong, India, Japan and Singapore have all benefited from the impact of British racehorses, bloodstock, jockeys and trainers, with little corresponding Asian influence on the British turf. The success of Agnes World, the first Japanese-trained horse to win a race in England, during the summer of 2000, may have heralded the start of a new era.

Horseracing accompanied the army and administrators to the eastern outposts of the British Empire during the nineteenth century, and the Hong Kong Jockey Club and the Royal Western India Turf Club are survivors of British rule. Happy Valley racetrack in Hong Kong opened in 1846 and English trainers were employed by the 1860s to handle racehorses belonging to Messrs. Jardine, Matheson and other eminent merchants in the colony. The migration has continued. Ivan Allan, owner of 1984 St Leger winner Commanche Run, has been a successful trainer in Singapore and Malaysia since 1964 while Peter Chapple-Hyam of Newmarket spent several seasons in Hong Kong from 1999 as one of the 26 licensed trainers there.

Jockeys who earn their living on the flat in Britain have regularly wintered in Asia. Joe Mercer did so in the 1950s and Lester Piggott rode in Hong Kong, Singapore and India in the 1970s, returning to ride there during his comeback years in the 1990s. Philip Robinson was the first British jockey to become Hong Kong champion at the end of the 1980s. Frankie Dettori rode in Hong Kong in 1992, won the Young Jockeys' World Championship in Japan in 1993 for the second year running, and continues to ride at big meetings in the Far East. Kieren Fallon was contracted to ride in India in 1993 and still fulfils engagements in Asia in the close season. Many less successful jockeys also take the opportunity of earning a living in Asia during the winter months and a trickle of hopefuls now make the journey in reverse, with young Asian riders spending a short period on attachment to English stables. Yoshiba Okabe became the first Japanese rider to win a race at Epsom Downs in 1992.

Both Hong Kong and Singapore invested heavily in new facilities in the last decades of the twentieth century and the Hong Kong International races in December 2000 attracted 305 overseas entries from 16 countries. In 2002 this meeting staged four Group One events including the world's richest mile race and 5-furlong sprint. It is Japan, however, a relative newcomer to the racing business, which has made the most impact on the British and international scene, largely through its purchases of western bloodstock and yearlings. There was a time when stallions with unsound tendencies or little proven ability as sires would be despatched to Japan; unfashionable Derby horses Parthia and Larkspur, victorious in 1959 and 1962, were sent there, Grundy and Dancing Brave, winners of the King George in 1975 and 1986 suffered the same fate. During the 1990s, however, Japanese studs have paid enormous sums for winners of the Arc, Kentucky Derby and Breeders' Cup races, as well as five consecutive English Derby winners (1991–95), prompting fears that Japan is planning not merely to upgrade its bloodstock for domestic purposes but to launch a home-grown assault on international racing. Among the stallions standing in Japan in 2001 were Opera House, Pentire, and Pilsudski, all European Group One winners.

Until recently, Anglo-Asian racing had been confined to raiding parties from Britain, together with those from Europe, North America and Australasia, converging on Fuchu racecourse in Tokyo every November for the Japan Cup. An invitation race over $1\frac{1}{2}$ miles, it was launched in 1981 and offers one of the largest purses in world racing (over £2.6 million total prize money in 2002). Britain has claimed the event three times, with Jupiter Island (1986), Singspiel (1996) and Pilsudski (1997). In April 2000, however, another Japanese race, the Nakajama Jump, was opened to international competition for the first time, and with prize money of nearly £500,000, attracted seven overseas entrants – the British horse, The Outback Way, was third. By 2002, the prize fund had risen to £780,000.

Reverse raids on European racing have so far been limited, but Kooyonga, Irish-trained but Japanese-owned, won the Eclipse Stakes in 1992, the Group One Coronation Stakes and the Irish One Thousand Guineas in 1991, and also claimed the runner-up spot in the Queen Elizabeth II Stakes at Ascot. Her English triumphs placed Mitsuo Haga seventeenth in the list of winning owners for 1991, a long way behind the Maharajah of Baroda, the top Asian owner up till then. He was second in 1947 and 1948, thanks to the efforts of Sayajirao, winner of the 1947 St Leger and third in the Two Thousand Guineas and the Derby, and My Babu, winner of the 1948 Two Thousand Guineas.

Japanese racing made its most direct impact on Europe in 1999 when El Condor Pasa, partnered by leading Japanese jockey Yutaka Take, finished second in the Arc. So far, however, most Japanese success has been confined to sprints and to tilts at French prizes. In winning the top French 5-furlong race, the Prix de l'Abbaye, Agnes World became the first Japanese-trained horse to win a European Group One race. When he won the 6-furlong July Cup at Newmarket in 2000, he made British racing history. It remains to be seen whether Japanese horses continue to raid Britain, where prize money is relatively low in comparison with the rich pickings elsewhere.

Further reading

Magee, S., *Channel Four Racing Complete A–Z of Horse Racing* (London: Channel 4 Books, 2001).

Scott, B. and Cranham, G., *The World of Flat Racing* (London: Peerage, 1987).

Associations

Racing is a sport with myriad sectional groupings, all of which seem to have formed associations to promote their views and protect their interests, be it the Horseracing Sponsors Association, the Permit Trainers Association or the Amateur Riders Association. Perhaps unsurprisingly in an industry driven by breeding interests, the first collective organisation in racing was the Thoroughbred Breeders Association, established in 1917. That area of the sport has also produced the Federation of Bloodstock Agents. Within the stables there is the National Trainers Federation, based at Lambourn, which is the trade organisation responsible for all licensed thoroughbred racehorse trainers in the United Kingdom. Its governing body has a council of 18 members divided into two sub-committees representing each major branch of the sport. In 2002 the membership was around 90 per cent of all licence holders. At the other end of the stable hierarchy is the Stable Lads Association formed after the famous strike of 1975. At that time the lads involved had been members of the Transport and General Workers Union, but many, especially those at Lambourn, felt that this was too large and too political an organisation, as well as one which did not know the intricacies of the racing industry. Helped by Lord Oaksey, an amateur-rider-turned-journalist, and Jimmy Hill of the Professional Footballers' Association, the stable staff formed their own association with a former jockey and head lad Tommy Delaney as its first secretary.

Although jockeys are in competition with each other – both during the races themselves and also as rivals for mounts – there is a great deal of camaraderie, solidarity and good fellowship, resulting from the dangers of the sport that they all face. Risking life and limb and participating together in daily trials of courage can have a bonding effect. Nevertheless it was not until the 1960s that this solidarity manifested itself in organisational form, most particularly in the founding of the Jockeys Association in 1969, an amalgamation of the northern and southern sections of the Flat Race Jockeys Association and the Professional National Hunt Jockeys Association which had developed a few years earlier. The new association has concerned itself with matters of racecourse facilities and safety and also operates a pension fund, savings plans and insurance services. Although it negotiates with the Racehorse Owners Association on riding fees, in many respects it is more of a guild than a union with a prime aim of maintaining the highest standards of integrity among its members. It operates a system of having joint presidents, one from each code of racing.

The very fact that there are two branches of the sport, one far wealthier than the other, makes for difficulties in racing politics, but lobbying the Jockey Club and government has not been made any easier by the other schisms and divisions that have bedevilled racing. The associations have not always spoken with one voice. How easily can the Racehorse Owners Association represent both the views of syndicated owners who share the hind leg of a selling plater and of those who spend seven–figure sums on an equine superstar? There is tension within the Racecourse Association as two groups of tracks, those run by Arena Leisure and Northern Racing, are owned by shareholders whose aims statutorily have to be put first. This can lead to potential conflict with the Racecourse

Holdings Trust and individual courses, such as Ascot, Goodwood and York who are generally regarded to have the interests of racing at heart. Inevitably some organisations have fragmented. Bookmakers, for example, are now represented by the Bookmakers Protection Association, the National Association of Bookmakers, the Rails Bookmakers Association, the Betting Office Licensees Association and the British Betting Offices Association!

Racing is not generally regarded as a team sport except in the sense of the joint efforts of the trainer, jockey and horse so it is unsurprising that the associations within the sport have rarely come together. There was the notable exception of the Racing and Breeding Liaison Committee of 1958 which comprised members from the Racecourse Association, the Racehorse Owners Association and the Thoroughbred Breeders Association. It was melded into a Horseracing Advisory Council in 1980 which also contained representatives from the associations of trainers, jockeys, stable staff, racegoers, permit trainers, bloodstock agents, racehorse transporters, vets, point-to-point owners, amateur riders, lady jockeys and the Transport and General Workers Union. Until the early 1990s this continued solely as an advisory body with limited influence in the racing world and certainly no power. It has been superseded by the BHB, purportedly offering representation across the industry (except for bookmakers), but often in practise causing friction between the sectional associations who continue to put their own interests ahead of those of racing in general.

Further reading

Hill, C.R., *Horse Power: The Politics of the Turf* (Manchester: Manchester University Press, 1988).
Tyrrel, J., *Running Racing: The Jockey Club Years Since 1750* (London: Quiller, 1997).
www.racehorsetrainers.org
www.jagb.co.uk

See also British Horseracing Board.

Australasia

Horseracing in Australia and New Zealand owes much to British influence. With racecourses named Ascot, Epsom and Sandown Park, authorities called Jockey Clubs, and races entitled the Newmarket Handicap, the Queen Elizabeth Stakes, and the St Leger, many key elements in nineteenth-century racing were simply transplanted into the new colonies together with English thoroughbred stock. In the twentieth century, however, the tide has also run in the opposite direction, with horses, jockeys and trainers from Australasia making an impact on racing in Britain.

The 1900s saw the arrival on British shores of several jockeys from Australia, perhaps encouraged by the recent success of American riders. Frank Bullock and Bernard 'Brownie' Carslake raced in England for a short period before moving to Europe. Frank Wootton arrived in Britain via South Africa, accompanied by his trainer father, in 1906. He rode his first winner at 13 and became champion jockey four times, 1909–12, while still in his teens. Unable to ride flat-race weights after the war, he turned to hurdles and was runner-up in the National Hunt jockeys' championship in 1921. His younger brother, Stanley, took over the family stables at Epsom, headed the numerical list of winners five times and became a highly respected tutor of apprentices. Bullock and Carslake returned to Britain and developed successful careers in the 1920s; Bullock was runner-up in the jockeys' championship in 1921 and Carslake rode seven Classic winners in the period 1918–38.

In the 1930s, William 'Rae' Johnstone came to Europe, and though riding mostly in France, won 12 English Classics, eight in a brilliant spell from 1947 to 1951. Bill Williamson and Ron Hutchinson arrived in 1960, already in their thirties, and won themselves five Classics and reputations as highly competent jockeys. George Moore was based in France in 1959 when he won the Two Thousand Guineas on Taboun but on his second visit to Europe he rode for English trainer Noel Murless and won three Classics in 1967 with Royal Palace (Two Thousand Guineas and Derby) and Fleet (One Thousand Guineas). His strike rate that season was over 30 per cent. Neville Sellwood was less fortunate. Resident in France, he got a chance ride in the 1962 Epsom Derby on Larkspur, avoided the pile-up at Tattenham Corner and won the race, only to be killed in a fall at Maisons-Laffitte later that year. But the Australian who became a household name in the post war decades was Arthur 'Scobie' Breasley, four times champion jockey from 1957 to 1963, and winner of four English Classics as well as the King George and the Arc in 1958 on Ballymoss. He later trained the 1972 Irish Derby winner Steel Pulse but after six years at Epsom he moved to France, and later to the West Indies.

Horses from the antipodes have also made their mark on British racing. One of the earliest was Carbine, bred in New Zealand in 1885 from two ex-British horses. A winner of many top-class races in Australia, including the Melbourne Cup, he was bought by the Duke of Portland in 1895 to stand at his English stud, where he sired the 1906 Derby winner, Spearmint. In 1896, the actress Lillie Langtry purchased an Australian four-year-old named Merman who subsequently won both the Cesarewitch (1897) and the Ascot Gold Cup (1900). Although technically this makes him the first Australian horse to win at Royal Ascot, Choisir, victorious in the Group Two King's Stand Stakes, became the first Australian-trained winner at the meeting in 2003. Most immigrants, however, have been National Hunt rather than flatracers. Moifaa, the 1904 Grand National hero, was a nine-time winner in his native New Zealand. Crisp, runner-up to Red Rum in the 1973 Grand National and one of the unluckiest losers of the race, was a successful racehorse in Australia, while Seagram and Lord Gyllene, Grand National winners in 1991 and 1997, were both bred in New Zealand and bought by English owners. Consignments of New Zealand-bred horses had arrived previously in Britain: Royal Mail won the Whitbread Gold Cup in 1980, and Playschool won both the Hennessy Gold Cup and the Welsh National in 1987. On the flat, Balmerino, a Classic winner in his homeland, was prepared for his assault on the 1977 Arc from a base in England, coming second to Alleged.

There has always been traffic in the reverse direction. A number of good horses were exported for racing or stud duties in Australasia, from Fisherman, winner of two Ascot Gold Cups and 26 Royal Plates in the 1850s, to Niksar, Two Thousand Guineas winner of 1965, and Hopeful Venture, winner of seven European races, sent out in 1974. Fisherman is said to have been one of the great foundation sires in Australia; Foxbridge, a son of Foxlaw, a Gold Cup winner in the 1920s, was champion sire in New Zealand 11 times; Magpie, second in the 1917 Two Thousand Guineas, won the Melbourne Stakes and the Caulfield Stakes before a highly successful Australian stud career in which he was champion sire in 1929 and runner-up four times. Star Kingdom raced under the name of Star King in England and won the Gimcrack Stakes and several top-class sprints before his purchase by Stanley Wootton. Exported to Australia in 1951, he was leading sire of winners five times. More recently, it has become unnecessary to export top stallions permanently. Improvements in air travel allow European horses to visit the southern hemisphere during the covering season before resuming stud duties in Europe although some have failed to return. In bizarre circumstances, both Suave Dancer, the 1991 Arc winner on secondment from the National Stud, and Zafonic, 1993 Two Thousand Guineas winner, also sent out from Newmarket, were killed, the first in 1998 when he was struck by lightning in Melbourne, the second in 2002 when he broke his neck in a freak accident at a stud in New South Wales.

Long-haul flights have also permitted European horses and jockeys to compete in major Australasian races. Lester Piggott won the 1972 New Zealand International Invitation Stakes but the Irish horse, Vintage Crop, ridden by Michael Kinane and trained in Ireland by Dermot Weld, made history by winning the 1993 Melbourne Cup, the premier Australian handicap. It is true that European horses shipped out to Australia earlier in the twentieth century had subsequently won the race (Comedy King 1910, Backwood 1924) and the past 20 years have seen horses from the northern hemisphere sent to Australian trainers to be prepared for a tilt at the Cup. Both Robert Sangster (Beldale Ball, 1980) and Sheikh Hamdan al-Maktoum (At Talaq, 1986 and Jeune, 1994) have won the race but, as international owners, they have breeding and racing interests within Australia – At Talaq was one of a bunch of yearlings sent out from the Sheikh's Shadwell Stud base near Newmarket. The victory of Vintage Crop, however, was the first instance of a European-trained horse capturing Australia's richest and most famous prize. No longer confined to locally trained entrants, the Melbourne Cup now forms part of the international racing year and is contested regularly by overseas runners. After a lean spell in the 1990s, during which 22 British and Irish contestants managed only one second and two third places, the twenty-first century is proving to be more fruitful for European raiders. British-trained horses Give the Slip and Persian Punch filled the minor places in 2001 while Dermot Weld captured the trophy for a second time in 2002 with Media Puzzle. Another prestigious Australian race, the Caulfield Cup, was won by a British horse for the first time when Taufan's Melody, trained by Lady Herries and ridden by Ray Cochrane, triumphed in 1998.

Australia is an important racing nation, increasingly caught up in the global transfer of horses in spite of the costs and distances involved. Unlike Britain and

Ireland, it has gone over to metric measurements for its races. Even more surprisingly, Australians once displayed a sense of refinement totally lacking in the
northern hemisphere. When the modest British stayer called The Bastard – a
great grandson of Carbine – was sent out there over 80 years ago, an untypically
sensitive Australian renamed him The Buzzard. Perhaps the original was
deemed to be an inappropriate name for his new calling – he proved to be an
outstanding sire for the next 20 years!

Further reading

Freedman, H. and Lemon, A., *The History of Australian Thoroughbred Racing* (Melbourne:
    Classic Reproductions, 1987).
Scott, B. and Cranham, G., *The World of Flat Racing* (London: Peerage, 1987).

Awards

Racing, like football, film, theatre and other branches of the entertainment
industry, is not averse to annual self-congratulation, or monthly or daily self-
congratulation. Horses, or more accurately their trainers, are rewarded in the yearly
Cartier awards and in the racing journalists' 'Racehorse of the Year' award. Jockeys,
in addition to annual recognition, receive 'ride of the month' prizes and leading
rider trophies at major meetings such as Royal Ascot or the National Hunt Festival
at Cheltenham. Stable staff receive small awards on a daily basis, at fixtures up and
down the country or for being in charge of the best turned-out horse in a race. At
the other end of racing's social hierarchy Queen Elizabeth II was even acknowledged in a special Millennium presentation by Cartier in November 2000 for her
patronage of horseracing and her success as an owner/breeder.

The modern era of racing awards was probably ushered in by William Hill,
the bookmakers, whose 'Golden Spurs' were given to leading performers in the
sport from 1972, and the Racegoers' Club, founded in 1968, which nominates
an annual 'racecourse of the year' as well as regional winners. There is now a
plethora of equine-shaped prizes, some from the various sectional associations
within the industry but most from the racing media. They include the Channel
4 Racing Personality trophies and awards from the Horserace Writers' and
Photographers' Association – the Derbys. The latter take into consideration
not just achievements on the track but also helpfulness to the press (thus
excluding several well-known but rude or taciturn trainers and jockeys!).

The Cartier Racing Awards, run in conjunction with the Daily Telegraph,
were established in 1991 'to recognise excellence in the racehorse' in a number of categories including champion two- and three-year-old colts and fillies,
best sprinter, stayer and older horse, and 'Horse of the Year'. The decisions are
arrived at by aggregating points won in Pattern races, the votes of a group of
racing journalists and the 20-strong Cartier jury, and a poll of Daily Telegraph
readers. Amongst the recipients of awards of merit have been the Aga Khan
and Prince Khalid Abdulla for their contributions to racing and breeding, and
champion jump jockey Tony McCoy, winner of a special award in 2002 for his
outstanding riding achievements.

Jockeys have their big night out at the Lesters, named after the incomparable Piggott and inaugurated in 1990. They were the brainchild of Michael Caulfield, then in his second year as Secretary of the Jockeys' Association, who borrowed the idea after attending a Professional Footballers' Association dinner. Members of his organisation vote for the best flat and jump jockey, best flat and jump ride, best apprentice and conditional rider, and best woman rider. Additionally there are special recognition awards which have gone to both journeymen and champions. In 2000 one went to Gary Lyons, a National Hunt rider who had battled to win just over 100 races in a 13-year career. In the following year Ray Cochrane received one in his retiral season, during which he rescued Frankie Dettori from a crashed plane at Newmarket. Another was given to Scottish rider Peter Niven, who, despite amassing over 1,000 winners, remained an under-recognised jump jockey. In 2002 Michael Caulfield himself was a recipient in recognition of his services to the Association and to jockeys in general.

Racing, however, is a minority sport and receives little recognition from the wider public. The best that its champions have managed in the last 25 years of the BBC Sports Personality of the Year Awards are two third places – for Frankie Dettori in 1996, the year he rode seven winners in one day at Ascot, and for champion jump jockey Tony McCoy in 2002, the year in which he beat the British record for winning rides. The only other recognition for racing was the team award in 1981 when the fairytale duo of Bob Champion and Aldaniti triumphed over illness and injury to win the Grand National.

Moneybox

An **accumulator** is a bet combining several horses, usually more than three, in different races – if the first horse wins, the winnings and stake are placed on a second horse, and so on.

Added money is contributed by sponsors, the Levy Board and the racecourse, supplementing the entry fees of owners to form the prize fund for a race.

The Aga Khan has twice been a leading flat-horse owner: in 1981 his winnings of £441,654 were largely the result of Shergar's Derby, Irish Derby and King George victories, and in 2000 he won £1,694,280 thanks to Sinndar's performances in the same two Classics and the Arc.

Ante-Post betting occurs well before a race, usually weeks but sometimes several months. Higher odds than normal are obtained as the punter risks losing the bet if the horse does not run.

Arkle was the shortest-priced favourite ever to win the Cheltenham Gold Cup at odds of 1–10 in 1966.

The **Autumn Double** refers to the two big betting handicaps at Newmarket in October, the Cambridgeshire and the Cesarewitch.

B

Horsebox

Barathea, trained by Luca Cumani and ridden by Frankie Dettori, is the only British (should that be Italian?) winner to date of the Breeders' Cup Mile (1994).

Battleship, the American-bred Grand National winner of 1938, not only won the American Grand National in 1934 but went on to sire Shipboard who won it twice; he was the last entire horse to win the Aintree Grand National and the smallest of the twentieth century.

Bebe Grande is the only filly to be placed in the Two Thousand Guineas since 1946 (second to Nearula in 1953).

Bobbyjo won both the Irish and Aintree Grand Nationals, in 1998 and 1999 respectively; only two other horses have ever achieved this feat – Ascetic's Silver (1904 and 1906) and Rhyme 'n' Reason (1985 and 1988).

Brown Lad won the Irish Grand National three times (1975, 1976 and 1978), the only horse to do so in the post war period.

Bustino, winner of the 1974 St Leger, will always be remembered for his epic duel with Grundy in the 1975 King George, in which he lost by half a length. The pair, together with third-placed Dahlia, all broke the course record time.

Baird, George (1861–93)

At the age of eight George Alexander Baird inherited £2 million from his father and, six years later, a further £1 million from his uncle. He used the money to help him become the greatest amateur flat-race jockey of any era.

After quitting Eton, he spent two years at Cambridge University where he developed a passion for riding fast horses and adopted a Cambridge Blue cap as part of his first racing colours. He began his turf career in 1880 running a few hunter chasers. He raced as Mr Abington – taking the name from one of his Scottish estates – to hide the involvement from his trustees. By early 1882 he was riding regularly in hunters' flat races and also occasionally over hurdles. In one of the latter he won an important event at Kempton Park, narrowly beating Arthur Nightingall, one of the best jump jockeys of the time. However, in

April of that year he was warned off by the National Hunt Committee for threatening to put a fellow jockey over the rails. The Jockey Club extended the suspension to meetings under their jurisdiction, but the continental authorities did not follow suit so he was able to continue to race in France.

On his reinstatement in 1884 'The Squire' invested heavily in horse ownership, including Busybody which secured him Classic victories in the Oaks and One Thousand Guineas. These successes were not welcomed in racing society and when he won the Derby with Merry Hampton in 1887, he refused to lead in the horse, fearful of another snub from the turf establishment. That season he was also leading owner with 46 winners. Increasingly, however, he became more interested in riding and thus less concerned with attending the elite meetings frequented by those who put him down, as opportunities there for gentlemen riding at around 10 stone were sporadic. Elsewhere events for amateur jockeys, welter handicaps and plates, and selling races provided him with sufficient mounts, usually on one of the vast string of horses he had purchased. After his reinstatement he appears to have ridden and run his horses fairly. Nevertheless he continually flouted Jockey Club rules on running horses in other people's names, partly to give the impression that he was securing outside rides.

He resembled Fred Archer in being long and lanky, in fasting hard (a breakfast restricted to weak tea and cod liver oil), and, after tuition from the great man, also in riding style. He learned his lessons well and from 1885 to 1891 he was champion gentleman rider. In 1889 he won on five mounts in succession at Lichfield. That year he had his best season as a rider with 61 winners, 58 more than Willie Moore, his closest challenger in the amateur rider's list. More significantly 48 of these victories were against professional opposition.

He lived as hard as he rode. One contemporary newspaper felt he spent his life in 'horse racing, prize fighting and harlotry' (Onslow, 1980: 15). It omitted the regular drinking bouts, but was otherwise correct. He died aged only 31 in New Orleans where he had gone to sponsor a prizefight. His death was hastened by the tortuous wasting he underwent to make the weight. On his thirty-first birthday he had got down to only 9 st 5 lb to ride Alice in the Edinburgh Gold Cup at Musselburgh. That this, his last ride in public, was a winning one was a suitable epitaph.

Further reading

Onslow, R., *The Squire: A Life of George Alexander Baird Gentleman Rider 1861–1893* (London: Harrap, 1980).

See also Amateur riders.

Becher, Martin (1797–1864)

Steeplechase jockey 'Captain' Martin William Becher found lasting fame by taking refuge in a brook. Son of an army man turned Norfolk farmer and horse dealer, he secured a position in Brussels in the stores supplying Wellington's troops. His own rank of captain was an honorary one in the Buckinghamshire Yeomanry. On his return to Britain he worked initially as a horse dealer but later became first jockey for Thomas Coleman. Proprietor of the *Turf Hotel* at St Albans, Coleman is generally credited with pioneering the commercial development of steeplechasing when he promoted the St Albans Steeplechase in 1830. He encouraged Becher to take up riding over fences; not that the gallant captain required much persuasion for he had been taught to ride all manner of horses as a child and was a skilled horseman. Although qualified to ride in races restricted to gentlemen, Becher made a living from riding and from schooling horses over fences for their owners.

His name is indelibly associated with the Grand National Steeplechase. In 1836, riding The Duke, he won William Lynn's inaugural chase at Aintree and came third on the same horse two years later. However, it was in the 1839 race, usually recognised as the first Grand National even though the title was not formally adopted till 1847, that Becher gained racing immortality. When running second in a field of 17, his mount Conrad fell at a specially constructed jump in which a brook had been dammed to make it 8 ft wide and a $3\frac{1}{2}$ ft wooden fence set back about a yard in front of the water. The hazard was increased by the landing area being 3 ft or so lower than the take-off side. Becher landed in the water and sensibly crouched in safety in the deepest part of the brook till the rest of the horses had passed by. Less sensibly perhaps he remounted only to take another soaking at the next water jump. Although he never rode again in a Grand National, such was his fame that the fence at which he fell became known as Becher's Brook. His last public ride was at Doncaster's Cantley Common course on 19 March 1847. His horse fell. After giving up racing he was appointed Inspector of Sacks for the Great Northern Railway at Boston, Lincolnshire.

A boisterous character, he would drink and sing late into the night at post-race celebrations. His favourite party trick was to run around a room on the wainscoting without touching the floor. He died in 1864 and was buried at Willesden cemetery in North London. At an auction to dispose of his estate, his seven silk riding jerseys brought 5 shillings (25 pence). In 1990 Becher's Brook was filled in but it remains a challenging fence on the Aintree circuit, a fitting memorial to a tough and intrepid rider.

Further reading

Munting, R., *Hedges and Hurdles* (London: J.A. Allen, 1987).
Seth-Smith, M., *et al.*, *The History of Steeplechasing* (London: Michael Joseph, 1966).

See also Nineteenth-century jockeys.

Betting

Betting is the lifeblood of racing. The mission statement of the British Horseracing Board, the controlling body of the racing industry, acknowledges as much when it states that the Board 'will seek to maintain and promote horseracing as a competitive and attractive sport and betting medium'.

Without the contributions to racing via the levy on the clientele of the betting shops, the deductions from the customers of the Tote, and the gate-money from those who wish to bet at the racecourse, there would have been much less organised horseracing in Britain. It would not have disappeared as shown by the long tradition of point-to-pointing on Sundays, a day on which for many years bookmakers could not ply their trade.

Most bettors are recreational punters, persons looking for a modicum of excitement as they watch their fancies race either on the betting shop television or at the course itself. They choose their horses by various means, from examining the form to liking the name. Some of them develop elaborate staking systems depending on the size and success of the previous bet. Most of them bet on several races in a day, something the professional punter would not do. On rare occasions they can have a big win when an accumulator comes off; sometimes they can have a run when they more than break even; but generally they lose. They accept this as the price to be paid for the fun their hobby brings them. This is not to infer, as do many opponents of gambling, that betting is an unproductive activity. Such views ignore both the investment in the betting industry and the employment that it offers to some 40,000 people.

To the professionals betting is work that needs time and study. They regard a day at the races as a day in the office. They are not there for fun or excitement but to do business and try to make money. They cannot win all the time but a 10–1 shot every eight bets will suffice. They try to take advantage of the fact that bookmakers must offer odds on every horse in every race whereas they can be more selective. Such professionals do not simply try to select potential winners but also compare their evaluation of a horse's chances – often calculated via sophisticated computer programmes – with that of the bookmaker so as to assess which might be the better bets. Some professionals rely on their mathematical ability to take advantage of those bookmakers whose prices would allow almost every horse in a race to be backed and still yield a small profit. By using their knowledge of racing form they eliminate those with no chance, back the rest and count the money. Others are more sparing in their bets. Roger Darlington, known as the Plastic Bag Man from his habit of carrying his racecourse winnings around in supermarket bags, bets rarely and mainly on short-priced favourites often returning less than even money on his £30,000 outlays. All professionals bet on the course not only so that they can observe events as they unfold, but also to secure the best odds available on the day and, of most importance till recently, so that no betting duty is payable on their winnings.

One of the most famous punters to make racing pay was Phil Bull whose meticulously kept accounts show that when he gave up serious betting around 1974 he had taken the present day equivalent of over £5 million from the bookmakers. He was not a gambler but a rational bettor who gained intellectual stimulus from the challenge of the new set of horses that appeared each year. The basis of his betting was past racing performance, but not merely the relative finishing positions used by most students of form. He argued that a moderate horse could never become a great one but that any horse that ran a fast time was capable of replicating the feat when conditions were propitious.

From this idea came his development of *Timeform*, which he introduced to the racing public in 1948. In this detailed publication every racehorse in Britain was rated according to achieved speed. This major original contribution to racing became internationally recognised and was eventually mirrored by the Jockey Club in its handicapping system.

Publications such as *Timeform* helped open the stable doors to punters previously ignorant of what might be happening in the racing world. Yet bettors have always sought information and touts and tipsters have always been there to provide it. Some advertised in the Victorian press, guaranteeing a winner in the next big race for readers who sent in money. Their modern equivalents utilise the *Racing Post*, though some simply push literature (if home-produced pieces of card can be so classed) under windscreen wipers in racecourse car parks inviting punters to participate in 'genuine prepared plots'. Yet anonymity has not always been sought. Peter Carl McKay, better known as Prince Monolulu, was a flamboyant tipster on the inter war and post war racing scene. Two of his eye-catching jackets are on show in the National Horseracing Museum. Labelling himself 'The Black Prince' and using the catchphrase 'I Gotta Horse', his advice did not come cheap: he charged 10 shillings (50 pence) for an overnight letter and a pound for a telegram sent from the course. There is no record of how successful he was, unlike the professional tipsters employed by the press. Clearly they have no chance of successfully tipping winners in every race – though the editors demand that they try – and the annual tipping competitions for racing journalists are generally based on their 'nap' selection, their perceived best bet of the day. On a standard stake some of these do show a profit over a season but rarely from season to season and career records are in the red rather than the black.

Further reading

Ashforth, D., *Hitting the Turf, A Punting Life* (London: Headline, 1996).
Clapson, M., *A Bit of a Flutter* (Manchester: Manchester University Press, 1992).
Munting, R., *An Economic and Social History of Gambling in Britain and the USA* (Manchester: Manchester University Press, 1996).

See also Betting shops, Bookmaking and bookmakers.

Betting shops

The overwhelming amount of betting on horseracing takes place away from the course in betting shops, legalised in 1960 in a belated recognition by government of the public demand for off-course cash betting facilities. Although willing to tax the now legal activity, the government – aware of strong opposition from the anti-gambling stalwarts – did not wish to be seen as encouraging betting and hence insisted that the shops be unattractive and not allowed television, comfortable seating, the provision of refreshments, or even a toilet! Nevertheless the shops proved popular and by 1963 there were 14,388 across the country, a figure that peaked at 15,782 five years later. It should be emphasised that off-course cash betting was not new: all that had happened was that it was now legal and regulated. Prior to the betting shops a myriad of 'bookie's runners' – from milkmen to bar staff in pubs – would collect bets and pass them on to illegal bookmakers, often with a blind eye being turned by the local constabulary.

By the early 1990s the number of shops had fallen to 9,400 and a growing concentration of ownership was underway. Initially, the big bookmakers, such as Hills, Corals and Ladbrokes, were unenthusiastic about opening shops as they felt this was merely a continuation of the old unrespectable street book-making in a new legal guise. Eventually, however, economic logic prevailed and they elected to move in. Their problem was that most parts of the country were already well served and the law required the existence of an 'unstimulated demand' for any new shops to be licensed. This led to the beginnings of a takeover of the independent bookmakers and small chains by the larger operators which has reduced the numbers to around 8,500.

A radical change came in 1986, following legislation of 1985 that allowed shops to have televised coverage of racing and other sports, and to sell soft drinks in more comfortable, well-furnished surroundings. Bookmakers, especially the major ones, invested heavily to make their shops more attractive: indeed the provision of facilities and customer services have become the focus of competition between bookmaking firms in their running of betting shops. Most racecourses also open betting shops – outside the ring – during their meetings to give the gambling public another outlet for their money. Betting opportunities have also been broadened to include most sports and even political events.

Away from the sights, sounds and smells of the race meeting, the betting shop can be seen as a passive social environment with betting for many almost a routine afternoon diversion rather than an intellectual exercise or an exciting adjunct to a day out. Yet in aggregate the money placed in the shops dwarfs that bet at the track and it is this volume of betting that is important to the racing industry. Indeed racing has become dependent upon the betting shops, or, more precisely, upon their turnover. For most of the late twentieth century a substantial proportion of its revenue came via the betting levy by which some of the money raised from betting taxes was returned to the industry. This dependence influenced the racing fixture list which was organised to provide a regular betting medium for the betting shop punter. In turn the levy obtained helped make mid-week race meetings more viable. Even though a commercially negotiated agreement between bookmakers and the British Horseracing Board has now replaced the levy it is still the money spent in the betting shops that determines how much the bookies are prepared to pay.

Further reading

Munting, R., *An Economic and Social History of Gambling in Britain and the USA* (Manchester: Manchester University Press, 1996).

See also Betting, Bookmaking and bookmakers.

Betting tax

Towards the close of the 1926 flat racing season that greatest of Britons, Winston Churchill, at the time Chancellor of the Exchequer, introduced a betting tax of 2 per cent on racecourse transactions and 3.5 per cent on those taking place in bookmakers' offices. As might be anticipated, bookmakers objected vociferously to the tax and actually went on strike at Windsor in November 1926. Racecourse executives blamed the tax for a fall of 16 per cent in attendances between 1925 and 1927. In 1928 the tax was reduced to 1 per cent and 2 per cent respectively and eventually abandoned altogether. The badly drafted legislation was a charter for evasion and less than a third of the anticipated revenue had been raised. Churchill admitted that it had been a fiasco and substituted a turnover tax on tote betting and a fixed sum duty on bookmakers' telephones. Both these were dropped when Labour came to power in 1929.

More thought had been undertaken when a tax was successfully re-introduced in October 1966 at a level of 2.5 per cent on both on and off-course betting, the latter now legalised for cash betting. Bookmakers argued that the tax would simply drive betting underground: well, they would, wouldn't they! But they were wrong. The status of legal respectability had been a long time coming and was not going to be discarded lightly, even if it came at a price and an increasing one at that. The amount charged on bets away from the track steadily rose; though it was reduced to 6.75 per cent in April 1987 when, in the interests of racecourse attendances, the on-course tax was abandoned. Most of the money siphoned off from betting on horses did not return to racing. In 1975, for example, the government took 7.5 per cent of betting turnover and returned just 1 per cent to racing.

In the 1990s bets at the racecourse were free of tax but not those placed in the betting shop. Bookmakers charged the tax at 9 per cent with bettors having the option of paying this proportion out of their stake – hence they paid even if their selection lost – or from their winnings, in which case no tax was paid if the horse lost though the money disappeared just the same! That four-fifths of punters chose to pay the deduction from their stake may suggest something about the optimism of betting shop clients. Of every 9 pence paid over to the bookmakers as 'tax' 6.75 pence went to Customs and Excise, 1.25 pence to horseracing via the Levy, and the bookmaker retained the remainder as a contribution to administrative costs.

For years the various bookmakers' associations had argued for a reduction in the tax to stimulate betting, but their pleas had generally not been heeded. However, after Victor Chandler opted to move his bookmaking operations to Gibraltar in 1999 others followed to set up further offshore operations in gambling tax havens. Although Chandler charged punters 3 per cent as an administration fee, half of which he voluntarily returned to the sport, the Government was losing out. Most betting on British horseracing still came through the betting shops, but the relocation of some activity could be seen as the thin edge of the wedge. The Government was lobbied to cut the rate of tax to encourage home-based betting. In 2000, on the basis of what had happened in Ireland, bookmakers argued that a cut in the betting duty to 3 per cent would increase overall betting turnover by between £5 billion and £15 billion and government revenue by £230 million. The response was not what they expected. On 6 October 2001 the General Betting Duty – the betting tax to punters – no longer applied. Such was the subsequent increase in the volume of betting that the levy raised went up 21.4 per cent on the previous year.

Further reading

Hill, C.R., *Horse Power: The Politics of the Turf* (Manchester: Manchester University Press, 1988).
Vamplew, W., *The Turf* (London: Allen Lane, 1976).

See also Betting shops, Bookmaking and bookmakers, Horserace Betting Levy Board, Law and legislation.

Biddlecombe, Terry (1941–)

Terry Biddlecombe was champion National Hunt jockey three times and the first jumps rider to win over 100 races in two consecutive seasons. From a farming family, his early competitive riding experiences were at gymkhanas where both he and his brother Tony won the Ponies of Britain Championship. His brother went on to become champion Amateur National Hunt Jockey for the 1961–62 season. Terry too rode successfully as an amateur before being advised by the National Hunt Stewards to take out a professional licence. His first winner under Rules was Burnella in a novice hurdle at Wincanton in March 1958.

At the close of his first season as a professional, in which he rode 18 winners, he secured a retainer as second jockey for Fred Rimell, one of the most successful National Hunt trainers in Britain. After 41 winners from 287 mounts in 1962–63, he became first jockey when Bobby Beasley moved on and he stayed with Rimell until turning freelance in 1972. He retired in 1974 with a career total of 908 winners, the best of which he regards as Woodland Venture in the 1967 Cheltenham Gold Cup when he lost his nearside rein jumping the last fence. He was champion jockey in 1964–65, 1965–66 and shared the title with Bob Davies, his brother-in-law, in 1968–69. His last ride fittingly was at Cheltenham, the home of National Hunt racing, in March 1974.

Surprisingly for a tall man brought up in the hunting field, he rode with short leathers and rein; his unique style was complemented by tactical awareness. The 'blond bomber' had a voracious appetite for life and played as hard as he rode. A day's racing would often be followed by a night on the town and in turn a visit to one of London's fashionable Turkish baths. Biddlecombe was not a natural lightweight and the baths became almost a second home.

His list of injuries exemplifies the dangers facing jump jockeys. During his career he broke a shoulder-blade six times, his wrists five times, bones in his left hand five times, his left collar-bone, elbow, forearm and ankle once each, as well as cracking two vertebrae, dislocating his right ankle, breaking a rib, and chipping a bone in his shin; not to mention over 100 cases of concussion. Injury cost him a winning ride on Gay Trip in the 1970 Grand National, a race he never won, though he came a close second on the same horse in 1972.

A man of courage and humour, he could not cope with retirement and hit the bottle. His alcoholism cost him two marriages and almost his life, though he has not had a drink since 1993. He now works with his current wife, the successful Wantage trainer, Henrietta Knight. They met when she was interviewed on 'Terry's Tips', a racing slot that Biddlecombe hosted on Central TV. Labelled as one of the 'three musketeers' of National Hunt racing along with Josh Gifford and David Nicholson, he had a cavalier approach to his profession, one that he acknowledges he would not tolerate today in any rider of his wife's horses.

Further reading

Biddlecombe, T. and Lucas, P., *Winner's Disclosure* (London: Stanley Paul, 1982).

Bookmaking and bookmakers

Around 1,000 bookmakers turned up at Sandown Park on Sunday 14 December 1998, not for the racing – there wasn't any that day – but to participate in the first public auction of racecourse pitches, one of the last bastions of inherited jobs in British industry. Until then a newcomer was only allowed in when a bookmaker did not have family to whom to pass on the betting site; some men had been on the waiting list for 20 years. The new system not only brought in fresh blood; it also gave existing bookmakers the chance to buy an improved position and it provided a retirement pot for those leaving the trade. At that first sale 333 pitches brought in almost £3 million, including £105,000 for the prime site at Cheltenham. There is money in bookmaking.

Initially betting on horses was wagering between individuals, usually race-horse owners or their friends, who held different views of the likely outcome of a match between two thoroughbreds. Bookmaking emerged when one man was willing to accept bets from many people on any animal in a race. The first to do this on any scale was allegedly Harry Ogden, a Lancastrian who established a business in Newmarket in the 1790s. Making a 'book' on a race involves the bookmaker offering odds that, in his opinion, reflect the likelihood of a par-ticular horse winning. Once bets start to be placed turf accountancy takes over and the odds are shortened or lengthened depending on how much is being bet on each horse. Successful bookmakers tend not to take a personal view on the chances of a horse – except perhaps in the opening price offered – but are happy to make a small percentage on a large turnover. To achieve this they must be able to think quickly on their feet and react calmly under pressure, trying to balance their books while tic tac signals send money round the ring and runners dash down the line laying bets from off-course offices.

The clients of Ogden and his ilk came from the higher social groups who mostly bet on credit and settled their accounts once a week generally at Tattersalls in London or Newmarket. However, the propensity to gamble is not restricted by class and by the 1840s list bookmaking had developed in which the odds on named horses in specified races were posted in places frequented by working-class backers: public houses, barbers' shops, billiard saloons and tobacconists. Here bookmakers and their agents would accept small cash bets from their clients. Organised betting had come down the social scale but worries over the social evil of gambling by the working class led to the suppression of such betting houses by Parliament in 1853. The main effect was to drive betting into the streets. Aided by rising real incomes and the development of the racing press, mass gambling emerged in the last two decades of the nineteenth century. Such was the volume of betting taking place that Parliament was persuaded to follow the line of many local councils that had passed byelaws against street betting and prohibit the activity. From 1906 off-course cash betting became illegal and remained so until betting shops were allowed in 1960. Although credit betting was legal, this was not a realistic option for most working-class bettors and, despite being a criminal offence, off-course cash betting flourished as part of the local underground economy. Barbers, tobacconists, confectioners, milkmen and newspaper sellers acted either on their own behalf or as agents for bookmakers to accept bets from their clientele. When betting offices were licensed such petty bookmaking began to disappear, though illegal betting at the beginning of the twenty-first century has been estimated at about £1 million, though not all of it on horseracing.

Although there is still room for the smaller, independent operators, most off-course bookmaking today is dominated by the 'Big Three', the firms of Ladbrokes, Corals and William Hill (who took over fourth-ranked Mecca Bookmakers in 1989). Ladbrokes had an offer to take over Corals accepted in 1998 but the Monopolies and Mergers Commission prohibited the deal on the grounds that it would dilute competition too much. Instead Corals joined forces with Eurobet, the first company to take bets online. By this time all the major firms were offering web-based betting, often in a multi-lingual format and covering sport worldwide. British bookmaking had gone global.

1996 was a key date in bookmaking history. Not only did the Internet start to be used for betting activities, it was also the year that Victor Chandler began his telephone betting service in Gibraltar to take bets on the European Football Championships. Three years later he shook his competitors (and the British government) by transferring almost all his telephone betting operations from Britain, where betting tax of 9 per cent was paid, to Gibraltar where a government, grateful for the employment boost as the Ministry of Defence was pulling out, charged nothing. His move started a stampede of bookmakers into betting tax havens, a development that eventually forced the British government to change the way in which racing was financed.

The bulk of British betting on horseracing takes place in the betting shops but it is at the track that the starting prices are determined which fix the odds at which winning shop punters are paid. In all about 800 bookmakers are licensed to operate on British racecourses. The vast majority work in the betting ring where they stand on coloured stands and boxes loudly shouting the odds on animals for which they want to attract bets whilst their boards (now electronic rather than chalk) display all prices available. Personality can attract punters and in order to stand out from the crowd such bookies can be as outrageous in word as a few of them are in clothing. In contrast the rails bookmakers, well-dressed corporate men, stand at ground level between the Members and Tattersalls Enclosure, shouting the odds almost sotto voce in voices that match their outfits. Generally they deal only in large stakes, a point of honour being to accommodate any bet no matter how large. Rails' betting thus is often on credit whereas cash rules in the ring. In Britain the Tote has never become the dominant form of racecourse betting unlike many other countries where the surplus revenue contributes much more to racing's finances. The bookmaking interests argue that they bring colour and excitement that can attract people to racing. Betting with the bookie is a personal encounter and a challenge to find and secure the best odds available. However bookmakers often know more than their clients. They will be aware whether a jockey will or will not be trying or whether a horse is on or off form. From the earliest days bookmakers employed touts to spy on horses in training and in trials to assess their form. Today bookmakers still pay for information, often in the form of a free bet. They want to know if a horse is coughing, how it has gone on the gallops, if extra weight was secretly being carried in a trial. Such intelligence obtained from stable lads, work riders and horsebox drivers can give the layer of odds an advantage over the punter in the betting market.

Bookmakers have an image problem. Not just because of the loud clothes and louder voices used to attract the racecourse punter, but also in the way they are regarded both by the public at large and within racing circles. The study of modern racing by ethnographer Kate Fox argues that bookmakers are used as convenient and universal villains within the sport's culture. She argues that, although both bettors and bookmakers are aiming to make a profit out of each other, it is the latter that are caricatured as necessary evils. This demonology has a long tradition. The very fact that for over a century they were undertaking an illegal activity was enough for them to be labelled criminals. Anti-gamblers went much further describing them as sinful, social parasites, greedy men out to cheat and fleece, their pursuit of profit leading to numerous social and economic evils. Recent revisionist historians have painted a different picture. Instead of the grasping exploiter of the masses, they see a respectable, local businessman offering a needed service. As always in historical debates the truth lies somewhere in between these polarised views. Many of the early illegal bookmakers came from working-class areas where street fighting was common and violence was often used to settle both territorial and betting disputes. However, the vast majority were honest men and many cultivated a reputation for local charitable works. No doubt as they grew more wealthy they grew more respectable!

In aggregate bookmakers are castigated by many in racing for not contributing enough to the sport on which they owe their livelihood. They were also criticised for collectively rounding up the betting tax deduction from punters' stakes or winnings and pocketing the difference. Yet the British Betting Offices Association points out that in 2001 less than 1,000 complaints out of some 1.2 billion bets made in Britain reached the Independent Betting Arbitration System, a level of dissatisfaction they argued was far less than in the financial, real estate and legal sectors. In fairness to the bookmakers it should be noted that gambling debts are not enforceable at law and bad debts undermine bookmakers' profits more than in most other industries.

The most famous bookmaker of the nineteenth century was William Edmund Davies, who earned the sobriquet 'Leviathan' for the size of the bets he accepted both individually and in total. He began taking bets while continuing to work as a carpenter but then became a pioneer of the betting lists. By the time these had been banned in 1853 Davies had become a wealthy man. He had also moved up the betting market, abandoning his 'silver book' and setting a minimum bet of a pound. At the other end of the scale he appears to have set no limit. The Derby victories of Daniel O'Rourke in 1852 and West Australian the following year saw him paying out £100,000 and £48,000. He still died a rich man. In an era of turf corruption he had a reputation for honesty and winning betting tickets from Davies became as negotiable as banknotes.

Although women are widely employed in the gambling industry via betting shops and the tote, female bookmakers are still a rarity. Helen Vernet is often cited as the first female to take bets on course. While at the races she became aware that many women wished to bet in small amounts which bookmakers on the rails were reluctant to accept. During the 1918 racing season she let it be known among her friends that she would accept such bets handed to her in writing. This was illegal and as her clientele increased the professional bookmakers objected and had her warned off by racecourse officials. However, Arthur Bendir, who had established the bookmaking firm of Ladbrokes in 1902, saw the economic potential and publicity value of employing her as the first female licensed bookmaker on British racecourses. In 1928 she purchased a partnership in Ladbrokes.

William Hill is a name synonymous with bookmaking. He began collecting bets aged 18 using an old motorcycle to get round the streets to pick up the six pences and shillings of working-class bettors. Before his retirement in the 1950s he would take his position on the rails and take bets in tens of thousands of pounds. He also entered the racing industry in a different way and bred the winners of the 1949 Derby (Nimbus) and the 1959 St Leger (Cantelo).

A more recent high-profile figure is Victor Chandler, whose grandfather set up the firm that bears his name in 1946. The family built Walthamstow Greyhound Stadium while Victor's father expanded the bookmaking business into a chain of some 40 betting shops. Educated at Millfield School, Victor took over the firm aged only 21 following the sudden death of his father. He eventually sold off the shops, but retains his position on the rails at major courses. However, he has been in the vanguard of a move into world sports betting. Beginning offshore in 1996 with a landline, two mobiles and three employees, within four years his turnover was almost £1 billion (though bets in several currencies were accepted). Whilst not ignoring domestic racing – indeed he continues to sponsor many events – he has seen that more money is to be made by facilitating gamblers to bet from home on live sports events around the world. He has paid out a winning individual bet on the horses of £1 million but also collected a losing one of £1.5 million on a football match.

Further reading

Clapson, M., *A Bit of a Flutter* (Manchester: Manchester University Press, 1992).
Munting, R., *An Economic and Social History of Gambling in Britain and the USA* (Manchester: Manchester University Press, 1996).
www.bboa.co.uk

See also Betting, Betting shops, Betting tax, Economics.

Boyd-Rochfort, Captain Sir Cecil (1887–1983)

The career of Captain Cecil Boyd-Rochfort spanned seven decades and, as flat-race trainer to the royal family from 1943 to 1968, he was responsible for a period of considerable royal success. Born in 1887 in Co. Meath and educated at Eton, he graduated from pupil trainer with H.S. Persse in 1906, to assistant trainer to Captain R. Dewhurst in 1908. In 1912, he became racing manager to multi-millionaire Sir Ernest Cassel and, after wartime service in the Scots Guards, he resumed this post before setting up on his own account at Freemason Lodge, Newmarket.

His first major success was in 1929 when Royal Minstrel, second in the previous year's Two Thousand Guineas, won the Eclipse Stakes, and in 1933 he won his first Classic, the One Thousand Guineas, with Brown Betty, owned by one of his rich American patrons, William Woodward, chairman of the New York Jockey Club. His links with American owners led him to visit and study the methods used in the United States, some of which he incorporated at his own yard. His growing reputation in the 1930s as a trainer of stayers was enhanced by the victory of Boswell, another Woodward horse, in the 1936 St Leger, and two consecutive Ascot Gold Cups, with Precipitation in 1937 and Flares in 1938. He was leading trainer in both these years, an achievement which was repeated in 1954, 1955 and 1959, and he won a third Gold Cup in 1957 with Zarathustra.

His association with the royal family began in 1943 and his winners for King George VI included Hypericum in the One Thousand Guineas of 1946, the first royal Classic triumph for 18 years, and Above Board in the 1950 Cesarewitch. As trainer for Queen Elizabeth II, he was responsible for the horses bred at the Royal Stud and one of his greatest successes from that establishment was Aureole. A temperamental colt who was difficult to train, he won seven races including the King George in 1954, the first of two years in which the Queen was leading owner (the other was 1957). He also trained a royal Classic winner in Pall Mall (1958 Two Thousand Guineas).

Among his other owners were Sir Humphrey de Trafford, whose colt Alcide won the St Leger in 1958 and the King George in 1959, and Lady Zia Wernher for whom Meld won the fillies' Triple Crown in 1955. Boyd-Rochfort trained 13 Classic winners in total, maintaining his early reputation with stayers by winning six St Legers. His sole success in the Derby was with de Trafford's Parthia in 1959, ridden by W.H. Carr, whose 18-year partnership with the trainer as stable jockey helped to deliver three trainers' championships and two runner-up spots in the years 1954–58. During this period, he became the first trainer to amass over £1 million in prize money for his owners.

He was a patient man, who refused to hurry his horses and it was said that his stable seldom struck top form before the Royal Ascot meeting in June. He maintained a consistent record of success in the 30 years from 1929 to 1959 but, although he continued to train during the 1960s, winning the Eclipse Stakes for the Queen with Canisbay in 1965 and the Goodwood Cup four times out of five from 1962 to 1966, the golden years were over and he retired in 1968, leaving his stable in the hands of his assistant trainer and stepson,

Henry Cecil. His large presence – he was 6 ft 4 in tall – had been a significant feature of British racing for 40 years. He was knighted in 1968 and spent his retirement in Ireland, where he died in 1983, aged 95.

Further reading

Curling, B., *The Captain – A Biography of Captain Sir Cecil Boyd-Rochfort*, (London: Barrie and Jenkins, 1970).

Breeding

All the major racing nations of the world have imported the English thoroughbred and based their own breeding on the English model. Yet this itself was dependent upon foreign horses since all thoroughbreds in modern racing stem from three stallions imported into the country centuries ago: the Byerley Turk, the Darley Arabian and the Godolphin Arabian. Paradoxically, given their supposed influence on modern racing, none of these Arab horses was recorded as having ever raced. The value of eastern blood lay in the toughness and stamina of desert horses which, combined in selective breeding with the best of British stock, produced the thoroughbred, a term first used in the *General Stud Book* in 1822. Subsequent controlled inbreeding (where the same horse or family appears on both sides of the pedigree) and outcrossing (where the parents do not share ancestors in their recent pedigree) has resulted in the modern racehorse, that compound of power and elegance, strength and beauty, stamina and speed. Today around 80 per cent of genes in the modern thoroughbred derive from only 31 original ancestors, 11 of which were British, all of them mares. En route fresh overseas blood has been introduced, particularly in the twentieth century when British breeders discarded some of their insularity and realised that foreign-bred horses such as Sea Bird II, Nijinsky and Mill Reef had much to offer to domestic bloodstock. Breeders have also responded to the market. As races became shorter and younger horses participated, so there came an emphasis on early development. Thus by the mid-nineteenth century the average thoroughbred was about 6 in taller than the foundation Arabian stallions. More recently, middle-distance horses have been bred to run best at $1\frac{1}{4}$ miles, the Kentucky Derby distance, rather than the $1\frac{1}{2}$ miles of the English Derby, perhaps a reflection of the relative prize money offered.

Some stallions have exerted a major influence on racing's bloodlines, beginning with Matchem, Herod and Eclipse in the eighteenth century through to Sadler's Wells in the twenty-first. Herod was champion sire for eight consecutive years from 1774. In 1781 his progeny won 121 races, a record not broken till 1866 by the offspring of Stockwell. St Simon (foaled 1881) never even ran in a Classic yet is still regarded as one of Britain's greatest racehorses. Despite having sent out six Derby winners, trainer Mat Dawson believed St Simon to be the best horse from his stables, maintaining that the colt was unbeatable over any distance from 1 furlong to 3 miles. His reputation came as much from his stud as his racetrack performance. An absolutely sound animal, he passed on no flaws of constitution or conformation to his stock. He was champion sire nine times, seven of them in succession, and second or third a further five times. Ten of his offspring won a total of 17 Classics, including Triple-Crown winner Diamond Jubilee, the brilliant filly La Flèche, Persimmon and Sceptre (see separate entry). Other leading sires in the first half of the twentieth century have included Persimmon (four times champion between 1902 and 1912), Polymelus (five times between 1914 and 1921), Fairway (four times between 1936 and 1944) and Hyperion (six times between 1940 and 1954). Canadian-born Northern Dancer was retired from stud duties in 1987 after becoming the dominant influence in world breeding for two decades. His progeny included Derby winners Nijinsky, The Minstrel and Secreto. The current leading sire – measured in terms of his progeny's earnings – is Sadler's Wells who has held the title every year since 1990 with the exception of 1991. To the end of the 2002 flat-racing season he has produced 54 Group One and Grade One winners.

In the past three decades breeding at the top level has changed from being an expensive hobby for rich individuals to an equally expensive multi-national business. Yet not all of the thoroughbred foals born in Britain are the produce of Sheikh Mohammed's impressive Dalham Hall Stud near Newmarket or others like it. Although as regards flat racing it is true that a small number of large breeding operations dominate the market, many of the 7,000 thoroughbred breeders in the United Kingdom are working farmers with only one or two brood mares looking to sell their produce eventually into National Hunt racing. Few of the breeding businesses make significant profits unless they have a star stallion. The owners of such stud stallions can really make money and for them potential profits in the breeding sector of the racing industry dwarf earnings from prize money. Many stallions are syndicated into 36 or 40 shares whose owners can elect to have their own mare covered or sell the nomination in any year to another breeder. Stud fees vary according to the racing reputation of the stallion and also his offspring. Sadler's Wells covers between 150 and 200 mares each season at a fee of £180,000 a time. Most contracts have a no foal – no fee clause. To ensure that the foals are of an appropriate age to compete in racing, the covering season is usually mid-February to mid-July. The number of coverings are limited to prevent the over supply of one stallion's offspring in the market but increasingly, thanks to improved air travel, some horses labelled shuttle stallions are now having a second covering season in the southern hemisphere.

For many years, however, breeders attempted to produce outstanding horses without any theoretical backing to their efforts; they merely appreciated that in some way qualities could be passed on from generation to generation. Whilst they showed an appreciation of racecourse performance and immediate family record, they were unaware that the female line was just as important as the male. Considering the respective biological limitations to the reproductive capabilities of stallions and mares this is hardly surprising as a stallion has many more chances of producing good racehorses than a mare. Not till Mendel's work on heredity became better known in the late nineteenth century did racehorse breeders begin to act on any explicit theoretical basis. Since then more scientifically-based research has assisted breeders, but there is no magic formula. The breeder is looking for the right combinations of temperament, speed, stamina, soundness and toughness, all, except for the richest of owners, within a budget constraint. In selecting which horses to breed from, emphasis is placed on conformation and pedigree. The former is subjective as personal preferences as to how a horse should look can influence the decision. Pedigree is more objective as it allows an assessment of the racing qualities of an animal's forebears to be considered. Were they stayers or sprinters? What grade of racing did they win at? Did they win at all? Much care often goes into planning the mating, but biological chronology and racing restrictions mean that it is two or three years before the results can be assessed on the track. Owners can insure against a stallion being infertile but not against his offspring being mediocre racing performers. Theories have proved incapable of identifying any more than a loose pattern for successful mating. A judicious union of selected blood strains is more likely to produce good horses than random coupling but still many great horses have inflicted some wretched offspring on the racing world. John Hislop, breeder of Brigadier Gerard, summed up the position well when he stated that all that a breeder can do is attempt to arrange matters so that there is a reasonable chance of a good genetic make-up emerging…and then hope for the best. That said, recent advances in genetics offer the possibility of identifying those genes responsible for particular performance traits such as speed, stamina, fertility and perhaps predisposition to bleeding or wind problems.

There are several irrationalities in the breeding industry. First the covering season is limited to five months from mid-February. This is forced on the breeding sector by the imposition on racing of a universal 'birthdate' of 1 January no matter when the animal is born in the year. Hence any horse foaled in say October or November would be classed as one year old only a few months later and thus at a major disadvantage in races restricted to particular age groups. Second the use of artificial insemination is prohibited, although this is widely used elsewhere in agriculture and even in some sectors of horse breeding where the technology is considered to lessen the risk of disease, cut costs and ease the international transfer of semen. Nevertheless all recognised stud books will register only the offspring of natural cover and the act of equine intercourse is generally photographed both to substantiate this and to provide evidence in any later disputes between the owners of the mare and the stallion. The money involved in breeding raises suspicion and insecurity. Witnessing and photographing the mating is still not regarded as a sufficient guarantee of paternity and British stud managers now have to provide a DNA sample (which replaced blood sampling from 2001) from each foal which is then tested by Weatherbys so as to establish parentage. The argument against artificial insemination focuses on the dangers of too much cross-breeding, but this is weakened by the fact that only 6 per cent of colts ever go to stud and a few dozen stallions dominate the breeding scene. More feasible is the generally hidden agenda that an oversupply of stock fathered by the same sire might undermine the value of that line of bloodstock.

Some commentators might also see a third irrationality in the high prices that were paid in the 1980s when hyperinflation, fuelled by the money and ego of oil-rich Arabs, pools millionaire Robert Sangster, and a few competitive and prosperous Americans, entered the international bloodstock market. Unraced horses went for astronomical amounts, most spectacularly in the case of Snaafi

Dancer which was bought by the Maktoums for $10.2 million and proved so inept that it never saw a racecourse. Average prices at the Newmarket Highflyer auctions for yearlings jumped from 14,167 guineas in 1977 to 96,710 guineas only a decade later. Eventually the bubble burst and stallion prices and stud fees reverted to levels more appropriate to the potential racetrack earnings of their offspring. For a time Northern Dancer could command a fee of a million dollars for a single nomination; by the late 1990s top stallions were available for only a fifth of that amount.

Further reading

Cassidy, R., *The Sport of Kings* (Cambridge: Cambridge University Press, 2002).
De Moubray, J., *The Thoroughbred Business* (London: Hamish Hamilton, 1987).
Robinson, P. and Robinson, N., *Horsetrader* (London: HarperCollins, 1994).
www.bba.co.uk

See also Arabian horses, General Stud book, National Stud, Weatherbys.

Brigadier Gerard (1968–89) – by Queen's Hussar out of La Paiva

Brigadier Gerard, a bay colt of 16.2 hands, was probably the finest European miler of the twentieth century. He was bred by his owners John and Jean Hislop at a small stud near Newbury and was descended on his dam's side from the great Edwardian mare, Pretty Polly. Named after a brave but boastful French cavalry officer in an Arthur Conan Doyle novel, he was sent to trainer Dick Hern and was unbeaten in his four two-year-old races, including the prestigious Middle Park Stakes at Newmarket. But 1970 was a vintage year for two-year-olds and he was rated only third behind Mill Reef and My Swallow.

His first outing in the following season was the Two Thousand Guineas in which he was pitted against these highly-rated colts but 'The Brigadier' stormed home to win by three lengths. He won four further mile races at Ascot and Goodwood in the summer of 1971, including the St James's Palace Stakes and the Sussex Stakes which his sire, Queen's Hussar had won in 1963. He then stepped up to $1\frac{1}{4}$ miles for the Champion Stakes at Newmarket, beating a field of ten runners in soft conditions, which he hated.

1972 saw further triumphs at this distance, including the Eclipse Stakes at Sandown, in which he was partnered as always by jockey Joe Mercer. Perhaps his greatest victory was in the lengthier King George at Ascot, one of the most important flat races in the calendar. He was now unbeaten in 15 starts, over distances ranging from six furlongs to $1\frac{1}{2}$ miles, thought at one time to be beyond the limits of his stamina. A rematch with Mill Reef had been eagerly anticipated all year but illness and injury prevented a further meeting of the rival four-year-old champions. Instead Brigadier Gerard came up against recent Derby winner Roberto in the inaugural Benson and Hedges Cup at York in August. Sent out as odds-on favourite, he was beaten into second place for the first and only time.

His career ended on a winning note, however, with a second successive victory in the Queen Elizabeth II Stakes over a mile at Ascot in September and a final win at Newmarket, again in the Champion Stakes. Hard-nosed racing correspondents, listening to the cheers as he approached the winning post for the last time declared that his reception was one of the most moving ever witnessed at a flat race meeting in recent times. He retired with winnings of nearly £250,000, the second-top stake winner in Europe after Mill Reef. He had raced 18 times and earned 17 victories and a runner-up spot, breaking the course record even when finishing second!

Although he sired the 1980 St Leger winner, Light Cavalry, ridden by his old partner, Joe Mercer, and the 1981 Champion Stakes winner Vayrann, his days at stud in Newmarket were somewhat disappointing and far less successful than his great rival, Mill Reef. He died at the age of 21, one of the great British racehorses of the century, unbeaten over one mile in three seasons, leading money winner and Racehorse of the Year in 1972. His statue overlooks the parade ring at Newmarket's Rowley Mile, where he triumphed on four occasions, and he is also commemorated in the Brigadier Gerard Stakes at Sandown Park.

Further reading

Hislop, J., *The Brigadier* (London: Book Club Associates, 1974).
Randall, J. and Morris, T., *A Century of Champions* (Halifax: Portway, 1999).

British Horseracing Board

To ask the question 'who runs racing?' would have been relatively easy to answer till very recently. For most of the past 200 years British racing was controlled by the Jockey Club, a self-elected body. As public money – via a levy on bookmakers and on Tote turnover – became increasingly important in the finance of racing, concern was expressed that control of the sport still lay in the hands of a private, self-perpetuating body.

In 1991 a Home Affairs Select Committee inquiry into the financial structure of racing argued that it was in the sport's interest for the fragmented sectors to cooperate in a modernised power structure. The government had rarely responded to the entreaties of the industry because it did not provide a united front. Consequently in June 1993 the British Horseracing Board (BHB) was set up under the chairmanship of Lord Hartington, an ex-Senior Steward of the Jockey Club, to give owners, trainers and others in the industry more say. Its remit included the important functions of strategic planning, finance, fixtures, training and education, public relations, negotiating racing's share of the betting levy and marketing the sport. The BHB had predecessors – the Racing and Breeding Liaison Committee (1958), the Joint Associations' Liaison Committee (1964), the Bloodstock and Racecourse Industries Confederation (1974), the Racehorse Industries Liaison Committee (1976) and the Horserace Advisory Council (1980) – but none of these had any power and they remained talking shops of various interest groups, technically consulted but rarely listened to by the Jockey Club. The new body was in a different position as it took on the responsibility for the direction of racing. Of its 11 members 4 came from the Jockey Club, 2 each from the Racecourse Association and the Racehorse Owners Association and 3 from the Horserace Advisory Council (subsequently known as the Industry Committee) in recognition of the numerous interests it supposedly represented, including trainers, breeders, jockeys, stable staff and racegoers.

The Jockey Club retained its mandate as the regulatory body for the industry, including disciplinary matters, licensing and security, and the operation of the training facilities at Newmarket and the racecourses owned by the Racecourse Holdings Trust. It still formulates, enforces and administers the rules of racing, investigates possible breaches of those rules and punishes offenders, appoints stewards to control individual meetings, supplies and licences officials and authorises programmes. However, after more than two centuries, the real power has shifted towards a more representative body within the racing industry, though jockeys and racegoers do not yet have direct representation on the board and bookmakers are ignored altogether.

Further reading

Hill, C.R., *Horse Power: The Politics of the Turf* (Manchester: Manchester University Press, 1988).
Tyrrel, J., *Running Racing: The Jockey Club Years Since 1750* (London: Quiller, 1997).
www.bhb.co.uk

See also Horserace Betting Levy Board, Jockey Club.

Broadcast media

History was made in 1927 when BBC Radio first broadcast the Grand National. The following year the house publication, *The Radio Times*, featured the story of Aintree on its front page and a detailed map of the course and fences within the covers. For the 1927 transmission of the Derby, there was a light-hearted sketch of Epsom racecourse, complete with a policeman directing the horses round Tattenham Corner, with the suggestion to 'use this drawing when you listen to the Derby broadcast.' Although there were 23 runners, the finish was not difficult to call as it became a two-horse race between Call Boy and Hot Night with the third horse eight lengths behind. Nor was the commentator troubled by the issue of starting prices: the BBC Board of Governors refused to allow any mention of betting or tips in case there were accusations of encouraging the public to gamble.

The first attempt to televise the Derby took place in 1931 courtesy of John Logie Baird, and the following year it was broadcast to an audience in a London cinema; a similar transmission took place in 1938. It was not until the post war period, however, that televised racing began on a regular basis. The BBC featured races from Sandown in 1948, Ascot in 1951 and its first Grand National broadcast in 1960. With the advent of commercial television in 1955, regular news and features programmes on horseracing were also shown, something which the BBC had never tried and, with no restrictions on the announcement of odds, ITV was on to a winner. (The advent of betting shops in 1961 finally forced the BBC to acknowledge the existence of gambling.) Amongst those involved in the early transmission of radio and television races were Raymond Glendenning, Clive Graham and Peter Dimmock for the BBC and Tony Cooke and John Rickman for ITV. Two names who were to dominate the airwaves for the next 40 years started their racecourse careers at this time – commentator Peter O'Sullevan, who was to become the voice of racing, and Peter Bromley, later BBC Radio's chief racing correspondent.

As with football, the great debate in the 1950s was whether television was good for the sport because it brought racing into the living rooms of potential racegoers or whether it kept people away from the course. Racecourse executives were divided. There was evidence that attendance at a variety of meetings from Brighton to Redcar had increased after they were first televised and with the arrival of ITV, there was the added incentive of rising television fees paid to courses. A few took exception to live broadcasts. The management of Bogside (a course which closed in 1965) decided not to continue its arrangement with the BBC to show the Scottish Grand National in the mid-1950s as it was feared that punters were staying at home to watch instead of paying at the turnstiles. Other racing professionals had reason to be wary of the new eye on proceedings. A poor start by the official was now clear for all to see while excess use of the whip by a jockey was more easily spotted. Television was about to have a considerable impact on the conduct of racing.

In the meantime, radio commentary continued to grow with about 50 races, mostly big handicaps, covered in 1960. A few years later, early morning bulletins on the state of the going at the day's meetings were introduced and are still given just before 7 am on Radio Five Live. The daily reading of race results, however, has been consigned to history as an anachronism in an age of multi-media access to information. Unlike television, the BBC has had little competition over the years in radio coverage of horseracing. At the beginning of the twenty-first century, it delivers commentaries on the big races, no longer mainly the handicaps but the major Pattern races of the season, and produces programmes from the most prestigious meetings at Aintree, Ascot, Cheltenham, Goodwood, Newmarket and York, to name a few.

Television coverage by the BBC soon lagged behind the ITV network. The peak output of racing on both channels was reached in 1974 when a total of 826 races were broadcast, over 500 on the commercial channel. Amongst the consequences of virtually saturation output on Saturday afternoons during the 1960s and 1970s was an increased following for jump racing – the drama and danger of which was well suited to television – and a rise in both off-course betting and the amount of race sponsorship, attracted by guaranteed television coverage. (The amount of publicity available to racing apparently led to horses called Rugby Special – owned by a syndicate from the BBC television programme, and Today, raced by members of the long-running BBC Radio show, taking to the tracks in the early 1970s. The 'Today' horse even won at Epsom!) Disappointing viewing figures, however, led to cutbacks in the early 1980s. Midweek racing on ITV moved to

Channel Four in 1984; by the end of 1985, all independent racing production was covered on the more specialist channel and with it went most of the big fixtures.

The BBC has retained transmission of Aintree, Royal Ascot, Goodwood and four other British courses and in 2001 it resumed broadcasting the Derby meeting lost in 1979. It has also covered the Dubai World Cup meeting at Nad al Sheba at the end of March and the Arc meeting at Longchamp in October. Although it features midweek dedicated racing, its weekend mixing of live races with other sport on 'Grandstand' has given it higher viewing figures and a wider audience than Channel Four. For many years it also benefited from the presence of the highly respected Peter O'Sullevan, the lynchpin of BBC television racing. He finally retired in 1997, having called his first race for the BBC 50 years earlier, and his knowledge and delivery of horseracing made him a household name. His autobiography, *Calling the Horses*, became a bestseller, something virtually unknown in the world of racing. Since then, the appointment of Clare Balding, daughter of trainer Ian, to the role of main presenter has done much to modernise recent output; she has often been twinned with ex-champion flat jockey Willie Carson as the 'expert summariser.'

Channel Four Racing built its early reputation on a collection of extremely knowledgeable racing professionals. Using a team of ex-jockeys – from National Hunt champion John Francome to amateur steeplechase riders John (Lord) Oaksey and Derek Thompson – together with racing journalists Brough Scott, Alastair Down, Timeforms's Jim McGrath and commentator Simon Holt, it delivered an easygoing brand of informative output to the diehard racing fan. With a greater emphasis on personality, the ace in the pack was John McCririck, an irreverent, irrepressible betting expert who is one of the best known faces in racing. Channel Four devoted entire afternoons to racing coverage and since 1989 has shown 'The Morning Line' on Saturdays, an hour-long features programme which previews the day's cards and topical issues.

The battle for coverage of racing in Britain over the past 15 years has become increasingly complicated. Perhaps the most influential player has been SIS (Satellite Information Services) which struck a ten-year deal with racecourses in 1992 to provide televised racing in betting shops. Starting up in May 1987 with live transmission of horse and greyhound racing to a limited number of betting outlets, it expanded rapidly, led to increased betting turnover and left racecourses wondering whether the big bookmakers, as major shareholders in the service, had been the main beneficiaries rather than racing itself. Next on the scene was Sky Sport which began to offer evening racing in 1993, to be followed two years later by the Racing Channel, the world's first television station dedicated to a single sport. With broadcasting on this scale, earlier doubts about whether the medium was good for racing were overturned although some smaller courses continued to feel that they were being discriminated against. To make matters worse, the Racing Channel ceased transmission in 2003. Into the breach stepped Attheraces, a consortium formed by Channel Four, Arena Leisure and Sky broadcasting on terrestrial television but although it negotiated a lucrative ten-year deal with the majority of racecourses, it terminated the contract abruptly in early 2004, leaving terrestrial television rights once more open to offers.

Another spin-off from the demands of broadcasting has been the media training offered to jockeys to help them cope with the ubiquitous post-race interview. Improvements in technology including overhead camera shots from airships, head-on views of the finish and the use of mini-cameras mounted on jockey helmets to give viewers a taste of what it is like to jump a fence like Becher's Brook have brought much greater immediacy, clarity and excitement to television racing. But now some racegoers never have to leave the bar – they have a better view of proceedings out on the track from the close-circuit television set in the corner!

Further reading

Cope's Racegoers Encyclopaedia, 1958–1960 (London: Cope's Publications).
Huggins, M., *Horseracing and the British 1919–39* (Manchester: Manchester University Press, 2003).

Buckle, Frank (1766–1832)

Sixteen-year-old Frank Buckle, weighing only 3 st 13 lb, made his racecourse debut on Wolf at Newmarket in May 1783 and aged 65 rode his last race on Conservator also at Newmarket in November 1831, just three months before his death. Neither of the horses won but in between times Buckle notched up 27 Classic victories, including the Epsom double twice and the Guineas double six times. This record number of Classic wins stood until 1984 when Lester Piggott won the St Leger on Commanche Run. Piggott, however, had five opportunities a year but Buckle only three till the Two Thousand and One Thousand Guineas were established in 1809 and 1814 respectively.

Son of a Newmarket saddler Buckle was orphaned at 12 and apprenticed to trainer the Hon. Richard Vernon who had been impressed by the boy's riding in private trials. He then began to ride for the first Earl Grosvenor for whom he won two Derbys and two Oaks. After Grosvenor's death he rode for Newmarket trainer Robert Robson, whose principal patron was the third Duke of Grafton. Dubbed the 'Pocket Hercules' on account of the power he could exert for his size, Buckle's forte was the waiting race where he held up his horse prior to a late rush to the winning post. Such a tactic paid off well in the many match races in which he was involved, most notably when he piloted Hambletonian to victory against Diamond, ridden by Dennis Fitzpatrick, for a purse of 3,000 guineas. Over the 4 miles, 1 furlong, and 138 yards of Newmarket's Beacon Course, Buckle judged things to perfection to win by half a neck. One match that he did not win was a 2-mile race against Alicia Thornton at York in 1805. Riding side-saddle she beat Buckle who was, it should be said, giving her a considerable weight advantage.

Generally he disliked making the running, preferring to hang back and then to make a late challenge as he did successfully on Scotia and Tyrant to win the Derby and Oaks of 1802. In those days jockeys were allowed to bet and it is said that Buckle won a tidy sum on that Epsom Classic double. Unlike many jockeys he chose not to live in a major training area, settling as a farmer near Peterborough where he pursued breeding of cattle, greyhounds, bulldogs and fighting cocks. This often necessitated a 90-mile round trip to ride trials at Newmarket which he undertook on one of his immaculately turned-out hacks (a matter of personal pride) with his riding saddle strapped across his back. Allegedly he banned discussion of racing at home to deter his sons from following him into a riding career. The idea was successful as they became a solicitor, a chemist and a brewer. One of his whips, silver coated and emblazoned with details of his Classic triumphs, became a racing trophy in Germany.

Further reading

Mortimer, R., Onslow, R. and Willett, P., *Biographical Encyclopaedia of British Flat Racing* (London: Macdonald and Jane's, 1978).
Tanner, M., *Great Jockeys of the Flat* (London: Guinness, 1992).

Moneybox

Ballymoss held the record in 1958 for most money earned in a career by a horse trained in Britain – £114,150 (over £1.5 million in current values) from eight wins, five seconds and a third.

Barnes Park and **Bellefella** share the dubious distinction of being the longest-odds placed colts in the Two Thousand Guineas since 1912, both at 100–1; Barnes Park in 1949, Bellefella in 1988. Barnes Park was also a 33–1 shot in 1951 when he won the Lincoln Handicap.

Baron Blakeney, son of the 1969 Derby winner, Blakeney, was Martin Pipe's first big race winner, a 66–1 shot in the Triumph Hurdle of 1981.

Marcia, **Lady Beaverbrook**, is said to have spent over £1.5 million between 1966 and 1976 at the sale rings (some £12 million in present terms) including a British record of £202,000 guineas for a Mill Reef colt (which won two minor races).

When Commander-in-Chief won the 1993 Derby, he was followed home by two 150–1 outsiders, **Blue Judge** (2nd) and **Blues Traveller** (3rd).

French industrialist **Marcel Boussac** was leading owner in Britain in 1950 when three Classics (Derby, Oaks and St Leger) and eight other wins brought him £57,044 (over £1 million today); he was also leading owner the following year when 17 wins netted him £39,339 (nearly £700,000 in current values).

C

Horsebox

Cadeaux Genereux won three of the top sprints in Europe – the July Cup at Newmarket and the Nunthorpe Stakes at York in 1989, and the Prix de l'Abbaye at Longchamp in 1988 but was disqualified from the latter for interference.

Caller Ou won 51 of her 101 races in the 1860s including the 1861 St Leger and the Northumberland Plate twice (1863, 1864).

The **Champion Stakes** was won by French horses in 3 out of 4 years in the 1990s – Tel Quel in 1991 and Dernier Empereur in 1994, both trained by Andre Fabre, and Hatoof in 1993, trained by Criquette Head.

Commissar won the Lincoln Handicap, the first big betting event of the flat race season, in 1948 from a field of 58 runners, the largest ever field in a British flat race.

Corbiere is well known for winning the Grand National in 1983, the first horse to be trained by a woman, Jenny Pitman, but he was also third in 1984 and 1985.

The **Coronation Cup** has only been won twice on three occasions, and the winners were all fillies – Pretty Polly (1905 and 1906), Petite Etoile (1960 and 1961) and Triptych (1987 and 1988).

Cannon family

Tom Cannon (1846–1917) provides a link between two famous horseracing dynasties. He married Catherine, the daughter of John Day, the Danebury trainer, and his own daughter, Margaret, married the steeplechase jockey Ernest Piggott, the grandfather of Lester.

At the age of 13 he was apprenticed to a Mr Sextie who ran a small training stable in Wiltshire. His first win came the following year when, weighing only 3 st 12 lb he piloted Lord Portsmouth's My Uncle to victory in a 6-furlong heats race at Plymouth. In 1872 he became champion jockey with 87 winners. He had only one Derby triumph – Shotover in 1882 – but his 32 years in the saddle brought him 12 other English Classics, several major French races, and a career total of 1,544 winners.

He was physically slight, riding as a lightweight for most of his career, but a graceful jockey to whom the epithet 'polished' was often applied by contemporaries. Cannon had a gentle touch. He rarely used the whip and was renowned for his ability to coax the best even from a highly-strung two-year-old: indeed many contemporaries regarded him as unequalled in his handling of young horses. His major fault, shared with many other jockeys, was to try and win by the narrowest of margins in an attempt to deceive the handicapper, though his judgement was such that it cost him fewer races than most. What he did not share with many other jockeys of the time was a reputation for dishonesty: no trace of scandal tinged his career.

Unusually, whilst still riding he turned to training, taking over the lease of the Danebury stables from his father-in-law, John Day, in 1879, though not actual possession until after Day's death three years later. Most of the horses which he trained, he also owned; his most successful were Curzon, second in the 1895 Derby and Playfair, winner of the 1888 Grand National.

Cannon was even better at training riders. Leading jockeys, John Watts, Sam Loates and 'Jack' Robinson all served their apprenticeships at Danebury. He also passed on his knowledge to Arthur Coventry, an outstanding gentleman rider, as well as to his three sons who all became jockeys. Tom Cannon junior (1872–1945) rode 33 winners before weight problems forced him into training in 1889. Kempton (1879–1951) won three Classics. The most successful was Mornington (1873–1962), named after a horse on which his father won at Bath on the day of his birth. Mornington's first winner was the day before his fourteenth birthday on Flint at Salisbury. Four years later he was champion jockey with 137 winners. A beautiful horseman who excelled at waiting tactics, he gained the title a further five times between 1892 and 1897. His most productive season was 1895 with 184 winners, though 1899 may have been more memorable as he won the Triple Crown of Derby, Two Thousand Guineas and St Leger on the Duke of Westminster's Flying Fox. His last Classic win was in 1903 on Our Lassie in the Oaks. He retired in 1907.

Tom Cannon's younger brother Joseph (1849–1933) won the Grand National on Regal in 1876 and then began training at Newmarket for Captain Machell. In 1882 he became private trainer to Lord Rosebery. Although he won the Two Thousand Guineas twice and the One Thousand Guineas once, his forte was important handicaps such as the Manchester November one which he secured four times. His son Noel also became a trainer and won three Classics, but is generally more noted for bringing over the Australian jockey, 'Scobie' Breasley, to ride in England.

Further reading

Mortimer, R., Onslow, R. and Willett, P., *Biographical Encyclopaedia of British Flat Racing* (London: Macdonald and Jane's, 1978).
Tanner, M., *Great Jockeys of the Flat* (Enfield: Guinness, 1992).

See also Nineteenth-century jockeys.

Carson, Willie (1942–)

Unlike other champion jockeys such as Lester Piggott, Pat Eddery or Frankie Dettori, Willie Carson had no racing pedigree. Their fathers were jockeys or trainers; his was a warehouse foreman. However Carson did inherit his mother's small stature which led to suggestions that he should become a jockey. He used money earned on a paper round to pay for lessons at a Stirling riding school and in 1958 became apprenticed to Gerard Armstrong at Middleham. At first he hated it: he did not see his parents for nearly a year and he got only 2/6d a week in contrast to the 10/6d plus tips delivering newspapers. His first ride was on Marija at Redcar on 18 May 1959 when he finished last. He had to wait over three years, till 19 July 1962, for his first win when he piloted home Pinkers Pond at Catterick. Gerald Armstrong trained both these horses but he retired that year and Carson moved to his brother Sam's Newmarket stables.

In 1972 Carson won the jockeys' championship, the first Scot to carry it off. In all he won the title five times, but ironically not in 1990 (the year he rode his 3,000th winner) when he found himself second to Pat Eddery despite 187 victories, his highest seasonal aggregate. In 1977 he replaced Joe Mercer as first jockey to Major Dick Hern, the latter job leading to the majority of his 17 Classic victories.

Like most leading jockeys Carson has had his share of accidents. In 1968 he broke his jaw, wrist and leg and had to have 27 stitches in his face, not from a fall but a car crash. He was unable to walk without callipers for several months and this delayed his breakthrough into the big time. Falls did occur and three of them were serious. At York in 1981 he fractured his skull when Silken Knot fatally snapped her leg. Three years later a fall in Milan put him out for five weeks and meant that for the first time since 1970 he did not ride a century of winners. Then in 1996 he was kicked across the paddock at Newbury by two-year-old filly Muhred, receiving severe injuries which eventually forced his retirement. Unlike many jockeys he was not content to win narrowly but drove his mounts out whether challenged or not. His Oaks victory on Sun Princess was by a record 12 lengths and his Derby on Troy by 7, the widest winning margin for half a century.

In 1976 he won 5 races from his 5 mounts at Redcar, scene of his first ride in public, and 14 years later he went one better at Newcastle, though this time he had 7 rides. In India, perhaps in a less competitive environment, he once rode 8 winners in 9 mounts and was only narrowly beaten on the losing ride.

He moved into breeding and in 1988 he became the first jockey to ride a Classic winner that he had bred himself when he piloted Minster Son to victory in the St Leger. After retirement he extended his breeding interests and has stables in Gloucestershire with a dozen mares. He is also British racing manager for the Thoroughbred Corporation. Additionally Carson has become a television racing pundit, his diminutive figure often boosted by a box on which to stand to hold conversations with other commentators.

Further reading

Carson, W. and Scott, B., *Willie Carson Up Front* (London: Stanley Paul, 1993).
Duval, C., *Willie Carson* (London: Stanley Paul, 1980).

See also Twentieth-century jockeys.

Cecil, Henry (1943–)

Henry Cecil is probably the most successful British trainer of the past 30 years and one of the most enigmatic. The stepson of Captain Cecil Boyd-Rochfort, he began his racing career in 1964 as assistant to his stepfather, taking over the Freemason Lodge stables in 1968 when the Captain retired.

His reputation as a winner of big races began in 1969 with Wolver Hollow in the Eclipse Stakes and Approval in the Observer Gold Cup, a Group One race now retitled the Racing Post Trophy, which he won four times in five years between 1989 and 1993. His first Classic success came in Ireland when Cloonagh won the 1973 Irish One Thousand Guineas, and Bolkonski, ridden by Gianfranco Dettori (father of Frankie) picked up not only a first English Classic in the 1975 Two Thousand Guineas but also the St James's Palace Stakes and the Sussex Stakes that year. When the same Anglo-Italian combination of trainer, jockey and owner (Carlo d'Alessio) won the Two Thousand Guineas in 1976 with Wollow, a son of Wolver Hollow, Cecil was on his way to becoming champion trainer for the first time.

His subsequent career has combined glittering triumph with consistent success. A twentieth-century Classic winning record (23) sits side by side with ten trainers' championships and records for the most consecutive seasons (9) with over 100 wins and the fastest 100 winners in a flat season (1987). After taking over Newmarket's Warren Place stables in 1977 from his father-in-law Noel Murless – Julie Murless and Henry Cecil were divorced in 1990 – he sent out the first of six One Thousand Guineas winners in 1979 (One in a Million). The 1980s saw 11 Classic successes including a first Derby in 1985 with Slip Anchor and a fillies' Triple Crown in the same year with Oh So Sharp, owned by Sheikh Mohammed al Maktoum. For the next ten years the two shared a formidable partnership – Cecil was leading trainer five times from 1985 to 1993 while Sheikh Mohammed was leading owner in eight out of nine seasons during the same period. Their big race successes included victories in the Oaks with Diminuendo (1988), the Prix de Diane (1987) with Indian Skimmer and the King George with King's Theatre (1994) and Belmez (1990, the year in which they were also responsible for the second horse, Old Vic, winner of the 1989 Irish Derby). During this spell Cecil won the Derby twice, with Reference Point, champion racehorse of the year in 1987, and Commander-in-Chief in 1993, and two further Classics in 1989, the Oaks with Snow Bride and the St Leger with Michelozzo.

His much-publicised split with Sheikh Mohammed in 1995 appeared to have little impact on his Classic wins. Eight more were to follow, mostly with good fillies such as Bosra Sham, winner of the One Thousand Guineas and

Champion Stakes in 1996, and Ramruna, who won the Epsom, Irish and Yorkshire Oaks in 1999. Oath brought him his fourth Derby that same year and Love Divine a seventh Oaks in 2000 but it is ten years since he has won a train-ers' title and recent major success has been limited. Unlike other top trainers, Cecil has been unwilling to send his charges on globe trotting exploits to America, Dubai or Japan. Closer to home he has never won the Arc although Ardross, winner of consecutive Ascot Gold Cups (1981 and 1982) was runner-up in 1982. In Britain, his turbulent private life and interest in clothes and gar-dening have resulted in almost as much media coverage as his training feats. His overall record of success, however, is unparalleled by a British flat race trainer in the later twentieth century.

Further reading

Cecil, H., *On the Level* (London: Harrap, 1983).
Magee, S., *Channel Four Racing Complete A–Z of Horse Racing* (London: Channel 4 Books, 2001).

Charities

Some charities begin at home. Jockeys hurt at work are now aided by the Injured Jockeys' Fund which stemmed from serious accidents to Tim Brookshaw and Paddy Farrell in the 1963–64 jumping season. Brookshaw broke his back when the mare Lucky Dora belied her name and crashed through the wing of a hurdle at Aintree and a few months later, in the 1964 Grand National, Farrell also broke his back there when Border Flight fell at the Chair fence. A public appeal raised nearly £48,000 for them, but another £6,000 came in after the appeal had been closed and this was used as the basis for the Injured National Hunt Jockeys' Fund. In 1971 this was renamed the Injured Jockeys' Fund to incorporate flat-race jockeys, though, as might be anticipated, the demands on its resources have tended to be dominated by those who ride over hedges and hurdles. As a registered charity the Fund is dependent on public goodwill and, using the slogan 'one fall can ruin a jockey's career', money is raised through the sale of Christmas cards, calendars, key rings, computer mats and the like as well as donations from individual and company benefactors. Events such as charity cricket matches involving a jockeys XI in the 1960s and donkey derbies in more recent times also contribute to the funds.

   Three registered racing charities designed to help those in the industry and their families are supported by the Jockey Club who recognise that many who work in racing – the lads, grooms, horsebox drivers, loaders, gatemen and stud staff – are poorly paid and often have few resources to draw upon in adversity. Each year over 3,000 requests for assistance are dealt with, some just for help in filling out forms but others from people in real financial distress. Of the three the oldest is the Stable Lads Welfare Trust which was founded in the 1970s for the benefit of stud and stable staff. It provides help and welfare counselling from re-housing to aiding benefit claims as well as supporting sports and social centres used by stable personnel. Retirement housing is also made available in and around the training centres of Newmarket, Lambourn, Arundel, West Ilsley and Kingsclere. The Racing Welfare Charities, established in 1988, provides flats and sheltered accommodation in both Newmarket and Lambourn. Finally the Jockey Club Charitable Trust administers a number of trusts and benevolent funds that provide support to those in need because of age, sickness, accident or misfortune.

The racing industry was much slower to respond to the needs of its equine participants. In 1995 a controversial television programme 'They Shoot Horses Don't They', portrayed it as uncaring towards racehorses once they had finished running for prize money. Some hardhearted owners are simply not prepared to look after their horses when their racing career is over and many animals are subsequently passed from hand to hand, often ending up being ill-treated, destroyed or exported – sometimes in horrific conditions – for meat. Others are owned by syndicates or businesspeople who are willing to help but who do not have the knowledge to care for them. Trainers, of course, cannot afford to fill their stables with non-runners.

There were in fact several charities for retired racehorses: Greatwood Caring for Retired Racehorses, run by the Yeadon family since 1990 at Rainscombe in the Wiltshire Downs; the Moorcroft Centre in Surrey (named after the steeple-chaser Moorcroft Boy) under the direction of Graham Oldfield, a dressage trainer; and Carrie Humble's Thoroughbred Rehabilitation Centre in Lancashire. All three, however, had to raise their own funds. Additionally some owners contributed to an Emergency Relief for Thoroughbreds Fund. The industry responded to the television allegations by setting up the Retired Racehorses Welfare Charity to establish a fund to produce £200,000 annually which would be shared between the three approved centres for racehorse rehabilitation. Chaired by Brigadier Andrew Parker Bowles, it has obtained a commitment of £10,000 from the British Horseracing Board and £12,500 from two equine trusts. The remainder will come via a voluntary agreement for racecourses to give £50 a meeting, trainers and jockeys to pay an additional £10 on their licence fee, owners to contribute five pence on every entry; and other sums to come from racehorse transporters, breeders and auctioneers. Although the racing industry now contributes far more than it did, donations from caring individuals and organisations are still indispensable and all three charities could expand their activities as there is a long waiting list of horses needing rehabilitation.

Individual racing personalities have often been generous to charities outside the sport. In November 2000 owner Robert Hitchins, while quietly celebrating a win of £4,682 in the opening race at Ascot, decided to pledge £1 million to the BBC's 'Children in Need' Appeal. The racing industry also often assists by holding race days from which a proportion of the profits of turnover as well as the proceeds of dedicated collections go to charity. Leicester holds a regular charity day for Menphys and Doncaster for the Fund for Epilepsy. Ascot's Charity 2000 Appeal benefited four charities supporting people with impaired sight and hearing. One patron was leading jockey, Richard Quinn, who himself is deaf in his right ear following a teenage accident. In over 30 years the *Timeform* Charity Saturday at York has raised over £2 million for good causes. The Lambourn stables have had an Open Day since the early 1980s that has contributed over £400,000 to local charities. Jockeys such as Walter Swinburn have undertaken sponsored walks to aid favoured charities or, in the case of Sharron Murgatroyd – herself paralysed from a fall in 1991 – a sponsored wheelchair push to assist the Midlands Spinal Unit.

Some organisations have combined involvement in racing with their charitable activities. From 1996 the Race For Life charity has held a raffle in which the holder of the winning ticket became an 'owner' of a Grand National runner for the day of the event. Various charities including the Bob Champion Cancer Trust have benefited to the tune of over £500,000. The Betting Office Licensees Association has gone further with its raffle and has three winners sharing a horse for a whole season, though any racing winnings over £25,000 are split with the beneficiary charities including the Racing Welfare group.

Further reading

www.racing-network.co.uk/racingwelfare
www.mrwc.org
www.racehorsesgreatwood.org

Cheltenham

Cheltenham racecourse, situated at the foot of Cleeve Hill in Gloucestershire, is the Mecca of National Hunt racing for participants and spectators alike. The entire jumps season for top-class hurdlers and steeplechasers is geared towards the three-day National Hunt Festival held there in mid-March and the postponement and eventual cancellation of the fixture in 2001 as a result of the foot-and-mouth epidemic was a disaster not only for the local economy but also for the world of racing.

Although races had been held nearby since the 1830s, including flat racing up to 1855, the present course at Prestbury Park dates from 1902 and is now owned by the Racecourse Holdings Trust, an arm of the Jockey Club. The most prestigious events, the Cheltenham Gold Cup and the Champion Hurdle, were inaugurated in the 1920s, but at that time Cheltenham was just an average National Hunt track and neither race boasted the status or value which it was to achieve in later years. Even when Golden Miller won the Gold Cup in five consecutive years from 1932 to 1936, the race was only worth one-tenth of the amount offered in prize money for the Grand National and was still used as a trial for Aintree. The Champion Hurdle was of even less consequence because of the lowly standing of this branch of the sport but the Irish invasion of the post war years helped to lift the profile and prize money of racing at Cheltenham. There were four Irish victories in the Champion Hurdle from 1946 to 1951, three courtesy of Hatton's Grace and trainer Vincent O'Brien, and from 1951 to 1954 the winning hurdler received higher earnings than the Gold Cup winner. This race was also dominated by the Irish from 1946 to 1953, with Vincent O'Brien's Cottage Rake taking the honours in three successive seasons (1948–50). The Irish champion trainer sent runners to Cheltenham over a 12-year period (1948–59) and never went home empty-handed. Since then Irish challengers and their exuberant supporters have continued to descend on Gloucestershire in March and frequently walked off with the major trophies – Arkle, L'Escargot and Monksfield in the 1960s and 1970s and more recently, Istabraq, to name a few.

The racecourse has four distinct racing circuits, the Old Course, the New Course, the Park Course and the cross country course, constructed in 1995 from natural hedges, banks and timber. The first two in particular, with their significant undulations and punishing uphill finish, provide a stern test for jump racers, and the fences are reckoned to be stiff but fair. Facilities at the course are excellent, helping to ensure that Cheltenham was voted Racecourse of the Year by the Racegoers' Club seven times in eight years during the 1990s. A new grandstand, containing a glass-fronted restaurant with panoramic views of the course, was opened in 1997 and the Hall of Fame, established in 1994, celebrates the history of steeplechasing and the famous names associated with National Hunt racing.

Cheltenham has had many heroes – Cottage Rake and Arkle, both three-time winners of the Gold Cup, and Sir Ken, Persian War, Hatton's Grace, See You Then and Istabraq, all three-time winners of the Champion Hurdle, as well as equine and human celebrities such as Desert Orchid and Dawn Run, trainers Vincent O'Brien, Michael Dickinson and Fulke Walwyn, and jockeys Pat Taaffe and Jonjo O'Neill. The Irish influence is still strong; it was once suggested that a sudden run on the Irish punt during early March 1986 could have been attributed to the annual Cheltenham pilgrimage while 20 per cent of entrants to the major races in 2000 were trained in Ireland. Major sponsorship by Irish brewers has further cemented the relationship between England's top National Hunt course and the Republic, and the atmosphere at Cheltenham during the Festival is unique in British racing.

The popularity of the Festival meeting led to significant overcrowding in the 1990s, culminating in 58,500 spectators on Gold Cup day in 1997, but since then, attendance has been restricted to 50,000 each day. Those who join the throng are treated to top-class racing, including not only the Gold Cup and Champion Hurdle but also the Supreme Novices' Hurdle, the Arkle Chase and the Queen Mother Champion Chase. This fixture alone contains nearly half of the annual Grade One National Hunt races in Britain and with all the hype surrounding the climax of jump racing it is easy to forget that Cheltenham stages another 12 race days each year from October to May. The Paddy Power Gold Cup, at one time the Mackeson, takes place in November and heralds the start of the serious winter jumps campaign. The evening meeting generally in May closes Cheltenham's contribution to the season, leaving Britain's most prestigious National Hunt course to be presided over for the summer by the statues of three of its great champions, Arkle, Golden Miller and Dawn Run.

Further reading

Lee, A., *Cheltenham Racecourse* (London: Pelham, 1985).
Magee, S. (ed.), *Channel Four Racing Complete A–Z of Horse Racing* (London: Channel 4 Books, 2001).
www.cheltenham.co.uk

See also Hurdling and hurdlers, Steeplechasing and steeplechasers.

Chifney family

Samuel Chifney (1753–1807) was both the greatest trainer and greatest jockey of his era: at least that is what he proclaimed in his memoirs, conceitedly entitled *Genius Genuine*. His vanity was reflected in his dress with its ruffs and frills and bundles of ribbons adorning his boots. He combined inherent horse sense with acquired tactical cunning to become an outstanding jockey. He began to ride in races in 1770 when attached to the stables of the Newmarket trainer Foxe. He had light hands and did not believe in hard pulling a horse. Only 5 ft 5 in in height, he could go to the scales at 7 st 12 lb up to the end of his career. He won the Oaks four times and in 1789 completed the Epsom double when he was also victorious in the Derby on Skyscraper. Only two years later he was banned from Newmarket over the inconsistent running of the Prince of Wales's horse Escape. Although the Prince stood by his jockey and promised to continue to pay his retainer, Sam sold the annuity for £1,260 and ended his days in Fleet prison as a debtor.

Encouraged by their father, his sons William (1784–1862) and Samuel (1786–1854) also achieved fame on the turf, as trainer and jockey respectively. William, the more intelligent, was taught training and stable management, while young Sam, an even tempered individual of few words who virtually lived in the saddle, was educated in all aspects of race riding, including the famous 'Chifney Rush' in which a waiting race was climaxed by a surge to the front in the last few strides. For several years the brothers prospered, especially after William trained and Sam rode the winners of the Derby in 1818 (Sam, named after the jockey by owner Thomas Thornhill) and 1820 (Sailor, also owned by Thornhill). Powerful rather than elegant in the saddle, Sam, like his father, also did well in the Oaks, winning that Classic five times. The brothers engineered several betting coups, the most rewarding of which occurred when William trained his own horse Priam to win the 1830 Derby. Unfortunately the brothers tried to repeat the feat in 1834 when they plunged on Shilelagh, another animal from William's stables, which was narrowly beaten by Plenipotentiary. This loss forced them to sell their properties to meet the debts. William's old age was spent in poverty but Sam was left a house and stables by a grateful Thomas Thornhill. Sam continued to ride till 1843 and in that year, aged 57, he won his last Classic, the One Thousand Guineas on Extempore. However, for the later part of his career he increasingly picked his rides and wasted only if he really fancied a mount. His last visit to a racecourse was in 1853 to see his nephew, Frank Butler, win the Derby on West Australian.

Further reading

Mortimer, R., Onslow, R. and Willett, P., *Biographical Encyclopaedia of British Flat Racing* (London: Macdonald and Jane's, 1978).
Onslow, R., *Great Racing Gambles and Frauds* (Swindon: Marlborough, 1991).

Children

Racing is easy for a child to understand. There is no complicated offside rule or leg before wicket to be explained; simply the basic fact that the horses race from here to there and the first to finish is the winner. The race itself is even more child-friendly because it is of brief duration, suitable for the attention span of a five-year-old. Children are now part of racecourse marketing in that executives try to attract families by offering cheap, often free, entry to children, providing entertainment and also crèches with qualified supervisory staff. One social anthropological study suggests that children enjoy a day at the races whether it is part of an initiation into the sport by knowledgeable parents or simply a family day out with chips and bouncy castles to supplement the horses. Families now form a significant proportion of Saturday racegoers and dominate the Sunday scene.

Children themselves are the targets of a recent British Horseracing Board initiative to get racing into the classroom. National Curriculum packs have been developed for primary schools and visits to studs, training yards and racecourses arranged for older children. The teaching involves the use of betting odds in mathematics, breeding within biology, and colours and fabrics within textile technology.

Then there were those children who rode rather than watched. In the early nineteenth century, prior to minimum weight legislation, owners sometimes resorted to child riders. The official weight of little Kitchener when he won the Chester Cup in 1844 was a feather (nominally 4 stone), but his actual body weight has been alleged as 2 st 12 lb. Such low weights imply very little strength and if a horse proved troublesome there was little that the diminutive rider could do. Fifteen-year-old George Fordham weighed only 3 st 12 lb when he won the 1852 Cambridgeshire, and his horse allegedly ran on into Newmarket before he could pull it up. Five years later, in the Goodwood Stakes, Chevy Chase could not be controlled by his jockey, a little boy named Hearden, and brought down seven other horses and put two jockeys in hospital for several weeks. Although the days of the 'infant phenomenon' were legislated away, child riders continued well into the twentieth century. Eddie Hide was 13 when he had his first official ride in 1950; Lester Piggott rode his first winner at Haydock Park in 1948 aged only 12; and Josh Gifford broke his maiden at 10 in 1951. Significantly for those critics who feared for the safety of jockeys and horses with such young riders, Hide, weighing just over 4 stone, found it difficult to control his mount which collided with the rails. In the 1960s the minimum age for riding in public was set at 15 and is now 16.

Further reading

Fox, K., *The Racing Tribe* (London: Metro, 1999).

See also Apprentices, Marketing.

Church, The

Racing and the church have had an uneasy relationship for nearly 200 years. While religious festivals and holy days throughout the eighteenth century led to fairs and entertainment which often included horseraces, and racegoing clergymen were not uncommon, religious opposition to racing and its twin arm, gambling, increased during the Victorian era. The twentieth century saw the continuance of disapproval, if not outright condemnation, but with the advent of charity race days and recent marketing of the sport as family-friendly, some churchmen have adopted a more benign attitude to horseracing. This change was exemplified in 1991 when the Dean of St Paul's opened a new betting shop in London by placing a £100 bet for charity, and in 2000 when the chaplain at Newmarket, interviewed for the BBC religious programme *Songs of Praise*, suggested that the church had perhaps been too critical in the past of the ways in which people earned their living.

The Reverend Henry Goodricke was the rector of Aldborough in North Yorkshire and the owner of St Leger winners Imperatrix (1782) and Quiz (1801). As the son of a local nobleman and a keen huntsman, his interest in horseracing was not unusual at a time when the upper classes were enthusiastic supporters of race meetings and hunts, the dates of which were often announced from the pulpit. Many younger sons found employment in the Church of England, at least ten clergymen were said to have attended York races in 1813 and in 1860 a parson named Drake allegedly took part in the Grand National under an assumed name. Not all, however, were prepared to tolerate a sport at which drink, sex and gambling were all part of the fun. The local vicar at Cheltenham is said to have orchestrated a campaign against racing which resulted in the grandstand being burnt down in 1830. When the Reverend John King, the vicar of Ashby-de-la-Launde in Lincolnshire, won the fillies' Triple Crown (the One Thousand Guineas, the Oaks and the St Leger) in 1874 with Apology, press coverage led to his resignation. King came from a racing family, had inherited his father's stud and had never, apparently, been present at a race meeting or gambled during his lifetime. His misfortune was to be successful on the racecourse in an age when a sporting clergyman was seen as 'a great evil in a parish' (Huggins, 2000: p. 207). Attitudes in Ireland may have been different – the 1905 Grand National winner, Kirkland, was bred in Co. Limerick by the Reverend Clifford.

As racehorse owners, both Goodricke and King raced under assumed names, a common nineteenth-century practice. The difference in their treatment may have reflected not only a change in opinions about racing clergy but a matter of geography. Yorkshire has always been a centre of racehorse breeding and training and it would appear that the church was unwilling to denounce racing in areas where there was strong regional support. In Newmarket, a town heavily dependent on the fortunes of the turf, the relationship between church and community seemed equally tolerant. A local vicar is said to have ordered the ringing of the church bells in 1863 when a Newmarket horse won the Derby; trainer Martin Gurry presented his church with a gift of communion plate after the success of his Derby winner in 1890; and winning owner Ambrose Gorham, whose horse Shannon Lass won the 1902 Grand National, donated prize money to church restoration funds. Where local interest waned, however, races became more vulnerable to attack from church hierarchies; the death in 1850 of a wealthy supporter of Stirling races opened the way for heavy criticism from a Free Kirk elder and the meetings were abandoned in 1854.

The last decades of the nineteenth century saw efforts by Sunday Schools and religious organisations to provide alternative entertainment for children during holiday weeks when racing traditionally took place, in an attempt to keep them away from a sinful environment. At the end of the twentieth century, a racecourse is perceived to be a far less threatening or wicked place. The introduction of Sunday racing in Britain, albeit after a strenuous campaign of opposition by church groups, has led to an increase in family-centred leisure activity at racecourses. This change in attitude, resulting from a more secular and tolerant society, may have been assisted by the willingness of racing to become involved with charitable organisations; many racecourses now hold charity race days, benefiting a wide range of national, as well as racing charities. The industry itself even helps to fund its own chaplain, based at the Racing Welfare offices at Newmarket.

If it is now considered acceptable for a race to be named after a racegoing cleric (at Chepstow in the early 1990s), and a man of religion can be found on Newmarket Heath every morning amongst the trainers and staff, it would suggest that, as in the eighteenth century, racing and the Church are not incompatible.

Further reading

Huggins, M., *Flat Racing and British Society, 1790–1914* (London: Frank Cass, 2000).
Mortimer, R., Onslow, R. and Willett, P., *Biographical Encyclopaedia of British Flat Racing* (London: Macdonald and Jane's, 1978).

Classics

When Colonel Anthony St Leger first suggested a race for three-year-olds over 2 miles at Doncaster in September 1776, he was not to know that 100 years later his brainchild would form the last leg of a series know as 'The Classics'. Over Georgian dinner tables, numerous gentlemen dreamed up competitions for their racehorses, with hefty sums of money wagered on the outcome. The Oaks and the Derby are both believed to have started in the same way, the first as a race for three-year-old fillies over $1\frac{1}{2}$ miles at Epsom in 1779, the second at the same venue a year later but for colts and fillies over 1 mile. The Earl of Derby and Sir Charles Bunbury were instrumental in the founding of the two Epsom races and each won an inaugural event, Derby taking the Oaks with Bridget, and Bunbury the Derby with his colt, Diomed.

All three races continued to evolve over the next 50 years. The oldest, originally nameless, was run as St Leger's Stakes between 1778 and 1785 and oscillated between the St Leger Stakes and the Great St Leger Stakes until 1845. It was eventually reduced from 2 miles to 1 mile 6 furlongs and roughly 132 yards, the distance over which it takes place today. Initially staged at Cantley Common, Doncaster, it was moved to the Town Moor in 1778 and, with the exception of the twentieth-century world wars (when it was run at Newmarket, Thirsk, Manchester and York) and track subsidence in 1989, which caused the race to be shifted to Ayr, it has been there ever since. The Oakes Stakes, re-spelt as The Oaks from 1787, remained a 12-furlong contest for fillies while The Derby Stakes was lengthened to the same distance in 1784. They have both been held at Epsom throughout their history, apart from wartime spells at Newmarket (1915–18, 1940–44).

During the last quarter of the eighteenth century, three-year-old races which did not involve heats were still a novel idea and seemed to capture the imagination of owners. By 1800, the Derby, Oaks and St Leger were already regarded as the three great races of the year. Fields averaged between eight and ten but were sometimes smaller – only four took part in the 1794 Derby, 1799 Oaks and both the 1783 and 1785 St Leger. However, this was not unusual at a time when horses were walked to race meetings and, until 1815, Britain was almost constantly at war. (Military officers were amongst the greatest enthusiasts of the turf.) A glance at the winning names of this era illustrates the dominance of the aristocracy; in the first 35 years, 28 of the Derby and 26 of the Oaks-winning owners held titles, though only 17 aristocrats won the St Leger.

In 1809 the headquarters of racing decided to muscle in on the success of these three races by instituting the Two Thousand Guineas Stakes for three-year-old colts and fillies over the Rowley Mile at Newmarket in May. This was followed in 1814 by the One Thousand Guineas Stakes for fillies at the same course but over a distance slightly below 1 mile. (The lengths of both contests were finally standardised at 1 mile 11 yards in 1889 and 1 mile in 1902.) Like the original three, the early winners were largely owned by the aristocracy but the Guineas were initially regarded as little more than stepping stones to the big summer races, a fact reflected in prize money which was seldom more than half that for the Derby and Oaks. From the outset they were less popular – the field for the Two Thousand Guineas only reached double figures six times before 1850 while the number of Derby contestants between 1809 and 1850 was never lower than 10 and peaked at 32. There was even a walkover for the 1825 One Thousand Guineas at a time when the Oaks regularly attracted 10–15 fillies.

When the colt West Australian won the Two Thousand Guineas, Derby and St Leger in 1853, he became the first of only 15 to achieve this milestone. By the time his success was repeated in 1865 (by Gladiateur) and 1866 (by Lord Lyon), it had been generally acknowledged that the five three-year-old contests formed a set in which horses extended their stamina – and reputations – over a four-month period. From then on, they came to be known as 'The Classics' while victories in the Two Thousand Guineas, Derby and St Leger received the title 'Triple Crown'. Fillies were – and still are – technically allowed to enter all five races, colts were always restricted to three. The first winner of the fillies' Triple Crown (One Thousand Guineas, Derby and St Leger) was Formosa in 1868 (as it happened she also won the Two Thousand Guineas), followed by Hannah in 1871 and Apology in 1874. The concept of Classics, either as the most important individual races of the year or a pattern to test the top three-year-olds has since been adopted throughout the racing world.

For the next 100 years, the Triple Crown was the most coveted achievement for any three-year-old, although the Derby remained the single most prestigious race. In attempting to win all three legs, a colt or filly had to demonstrate sufficient speed over a relatively short distance on the flat expanse of Newmarket's Rowley Mile in early May, follow this by coping with 4 additional furlongs over the tricky switchback course at Epsom Downs – where balance and agility at speed were crucial – at the beginning of June, and end the season in September by covering 14 stamina-sapping furlongs at Doncaster, a track more similar to Newmarket. Any animal which could beat the cream of its generation in three such different contests passed the supreme test of the three-year-old thoroughbred and very few were successful. Although 15 colts and 9 fillies attained the treble, 4 of these were won in wartime when the races were run at Newmarket, a somewhat easier prospect than Epsom. Only 20 horses won bona fide Triple Crowns from the first in 1853 to the most recent, the filly Oh So Sharp, in 1985. In the intervening 132 years, the majority of triple champions (11) were foaled in the last half of the nineteenth-century, and only two, the filly Meld (1955) and the colt Nijinsky (1970) have won the accolade since 1945. Most of the Triple Crown wins occurred in years when competition was limited – Common (1891) beat only 9, 11 and 9 respectively in the Two Thousand Guineas, Derby and St Leger; Flying Fox 8,12 and 6, and the filly La Flèche only 7, 7 and 11 in the fillies' equivalent.

The early twentieth century saw further standardisation. Within the first five years, geldings were banned from the Classics (no gelding had ever won a Classic but Courlan was third in the 1900 St Leger). Weights to be carried were fixed at 9 stone throughout for colts and for fillies in their own races, 8 st 9 lb for fillies in the colt Classics and 8 st 11 lb for fillies in the St Leger. Although few have successfully taken advantage of this allowance in the Two Thousand Guineas and the Derby – only Sceptre (1902) and Garden Path (1944) have won the former and Signorinetta (1908), Tagalie (1912) and Fifinella (1916) the latter – there have been 13 female winners of the St Leger since 1900, the most recent being User Friendly in 1992, and 9 runners-up. A further change from late Victorian times was the increase in entries to the races. The 1920s and 1930s regularly saw over 20 colts tackle the first two Classics of their season. Craig an Eran beat 26 rivals to win the 1921 Guineas while Blue Peter led a field of 25 to victory in 1939. Captain Cuttle was the first of 30 horses in the 1922 Derby. The winning owners were all peers of the realm, a situation which had changed very little for over 100 years. Roughly 50 per cent of Classic-winning owners in the period 1900–39 were commoners – but equally, half still boasted titles!

The post war period saw enormous change in the breeding of thoroughbreds, resulting in increased specialisation among the three-year-old cohort. All-rounders were no longer prized as they had been in the nineteenth century and the concept of the Triple Crown all but disappeared. Competition from alternative Classic races such as the French and Irish Derbys and an ever-growing number of valuable Pattern races throughout Europe have diluted competition for the English Classics, all of which resorted to sponsorship in 1984. Before Ever Ready stepped in, at least a dozen races throughout the world were said to be more valuable than the Epsom Derby and only continued injections of money since then have helped to stem the flow away from Britain's most important flat race. (The first prize more than doubled between 1992 and 2002 to over £800,000.) Derby fields which frequently topped 20 and occasionally reached 30 from the 1950s to the 1970s have fallen more recently to an average of 16. Other attempts to rejuvenate this early summer fixture have angered traditionalists, particularly the move from its Wednesday slot to Saturday. Even this appears to have failed to halt the decline not only in attendance but in general interest in the race. Compared with the Melbourne Cup or the Kentucky Derby, it is a non-event.

Although the Guineas have to some extent benefited from the emphasis on speed brought about by American bloodlines – milers have never been more esteemed – the 1990s produced some poorly rated winners. Even Rock of Gibraltar, triumphant in the 2002 colt Classic and six subsequent Group One races, failed to please the international handicappers, with an end of year rating of only 128. The St Leger has probably suffered most of all, with staying power no longer valued and the Triple Crown dead – it is 15 years since any colt was in a position to attempt it (Nashwan) and 33 years since the last winner. Top-class horses are diverted to the English and Irish Champion Stakes, the Arc, the Breeders' Cup, anywhere it seems except Doncaster. Numbers recently have sometimes remained in single figures and the quality of entries has fallen dramatically in the last 25 years. (The same might be said of Classic owners! The last British peer to win the Derby was Lord Howard de Walden in 1985 while Lady Beaverbrook was the last titled person to win the St Leger in 1988. They have, of course, been replaced by overseas aristocrats in the shape of the Dubai and Saudi royal families.)

The five Classics seem to have come full circle, reverting to their pre-1850 position in which each had a separate identity, with fewer horses taking part in any two, let alone three, of the contests. Many Guineas participants fail to stay the distance at Epsom, fewer even try, given the highly prestigious and well-funded mile races now available. The last Epsom winner to triumph in the St Leger was the Oaks success User Friendly in 1992. What would the Colonel think if he could see his race now!

Further reading

Randall, J. and Morris, T., *A Century of Champions* (Halifax: Portway, 1999).

Clubs

The Jockey Club emerged in the mid-eighteenth century when an associational world was developing in Britain to cover a host of activities including sport. The club at the time was a distinctly British social phenomenon, recognised as such by contemporary and continental observers. Joining with others who share similar interests has remained a feature of British recreational life, a facet from which racing has not escaped.

The initial aim of the Jockey Club was to organise races at Newmarket for its members. Elsewhere clubs from another branch of equestrian sport, hunting, organised several early race meetings. In Scotland, for example, the Royal Caledonian Hunt Club hosted an annual meeting using various geographical locations from the late eighteenth century while more permanent venues were used by the Perth Hunt Club (from around 1785) and the United Border Hunt which ran National Hunt Racing from its inception at Kelso (only changing the name to Kelso Races in 1951). Point-to-point races, still mainly run by individual hunt clubs, were also organised well into the twentieth century for members of clubs of London lawyers or city brokers.

Some racing clubs are essentially owners' syndicates that have brought ownership if not to the masses at least well down the socio-economic scale. Of these the most well known is the Elite Racing Club which was founded in 1992 and ten years later was ranked 28th in the list of winning owners with prize money of £187,000. Another is the Winning Line Club established by professional punter and tipster Stanley Winstanley, large enough with about 50 active members to have its own hospitality tent at the Cheltenham Festival. More regional in their coverage are The Epsom Downs Racing Club and the North West Racing Club. The former, sponsored by United Racecourses, combines ownership of horses trained at Epsom and a diary of social events including organised gallop visits, stable tours, an Oaks Day party and reduced admission at Epsom, Kempton and Sandown. The latter, in business for nearly quarter of a century, is a non-profit organisation accommodating around 400 racing enthusiasts in the North West of England and North Wales. The Group One Racing Club specialises in National Hunt horse ownership, a much cheaper option than being involved on the flat. Any winnings are a bonus for the members of these clubs, the majority of whom join for the excitement of participation as an owner and the consequent tickets to the paddock, visits to trainers' yards, and an opportunity to meet leading jockeys.

More economically motivated than the owners' clubs but still socially attractive organisations are the breeders' clubs set up by the National Stud. For a one-off payment of £750 (or alternatively £150 a year for the five years of the club's existence) a share is obtained in a group that collectively purchase a few broodmares to be covered by National Stud stallions. However, unlike the owner's clubs, these are wound up after five years.

Racegoers too have not been immune from the desire to be part of a club. In the early nineteenth century several racing clubs were formed with their own rooms, though these were more often used for betting than convivial sociability. In the mid-nineteenth century some urban clubs primarily formed for non-racing purposes rented hospitality booths at the courses for major race days. Slightly later the new enclosed courses specifically established separate club enclosures for those willing to pay a fee (and at that time also have the necessary social cachet) to keep them away from those of lower social standing. Most courses today still have a members' stand, although now anyone can gain admittance as segregation is by price not status. Away from the individual course the Racegoers Club was established in 1969 with the objective of encouraging people to go racing by using its buying power to secure cheaper admission to meetings. It has been recognised for consultation purposes by the British Horseracing Board as the voice of the racing consumer.

Further reading

Huggins, M., *Flat Racing and British Society 1790–1914* (London: Cass, 2000).
www.eliteracingclub.co.uk

Colours

Racehorses have six official colours – bay, black, brown, chestnut, grey and roan – but their jockeys seem to be attired in infinite shades and combinations of colour. At one time this was probably true but racehorse ownership has become so popular during the twentieth century that restrictions have had to be placed on new registrations both in terms of colour and pattern of racing silks. Owners must register their choice annually with Weatherbys instead of adopting a colour scheme for life but once registered the colours belong to the owner and cannot be used by anyone else.

The first attempt to control a rider's dress came in 1762 when a Jockey Club resolution suggested that owners provide a specific set of clothes for their jockeys to aid recognition and prevent disputes. This proposal appears to have been largely disregarded; nearly half a century later, only 70 gentlemen had bothered to nominate colours and so many of these were identical that it can scarcely have assisted either judge or spectators. (In 1808, there were six sets of plain black and four of plain white.) Others were elaborately designed with scarlet trim or gold buttonholes and the caps tied with different coloured ribbon, details which could not possibly be identified at speed or distance. More obvious were contrasting sleeves, said to have originated from hunting attire, where jackets would be removed to reveal coloured waistcoats over differently coloured shirt sleeves.

Compulsory registration arrived in 1890 at which time roughly 1,000 individual racing colours were identified. A century later, the number had increased tenfold but new registrations had to be in combinations of 18 basic colours, 27 jacket designs, 12 sleeve types and 10 cap patterns. Blues, for example, are now restricted to light, royal and dark but, as colours can be bought or inherited, it is still possible to see aquamarine, peacock, sky, Oxford and Eton blues at the racecourse! Patterns can be hoops or stripes, spots or checks, stars or diamonds, and numerous variations, but they are all designed to be bold, symmetrical and easily distinguishable.

In the nineteenth century, a jockey's 'silks' were just that, but this beautiful material has been replaced by lightweight, man-made fibres for flat jockeys and wool for National Hunt riders. The most prolific and wealthy owners sometimes registered two sets of colours in their name and the garments were handmade by a specialist firm. In recent times, personal association has given way in many instances to multiple or corporate ownership, with horses running in the colours of studs and racing syndicates as well as individuals. Second sets today may identify the overseas branch of a racing empire rather than a wealthy owner and the colours of a 'Lord' are more likely to refer to captains of industry or show business than members of the British aristocracy.

With so many new owners and combinations of colour and design, it is increasingly difficult for spectators to recognise racehorse ownership, even with the aid of colour diagrams now printed in many racecards or racing publications. Some, however, are seen too regularly to be forgotten. Sheikh Mohammed's maroon with white sleeves, J.P. McManus's emerald green and orange hoops and Khalid Abdulla's green, white sleeves and pink sash are frequently spotted at the head of the field. The British royal colours of purple, gold braid and scarlet sleeves are less prominent now, eclipsed by the royal blue of Godolphin and the royal blue and white designs of Sheikhs Hamdan and Maktoum al Maktoum. But the brilliance of the multi-coloured runners as they flash past is still one of the great spectacles of racing.

Further reading

Magee, S., *The Channel Four Book of Racing* (London: Hamlyn, 1995).

Corruption

Corruption and racing are intertwined: not merely in the rip-offs of the touts and tipsters, or the activities of the cardsharps and their nineteenth-century equivalent, the thimble men, or the use of the racetrack and betting office by criminals to launder money, but in the actual racing itself. No sport which daily redistributes large amounts of tax-free money will ever be immune from crooked behaviour. In early 1998 a survey organised by the *Sporting Life* suggested that almost half of regular patrons of betting shops believed that racing was dishonest. Although some of this belief might be attributed to punters talking through their pockets, no one with any knowledge of the turf would deny that malpractice occurs.

A subculture of corruption has long existed in racing because of its connection with gambling. Knowing that a particular horse will not win gives a gambler an advantage in the betting markets. Additionally racing has almost institutionalised corruption by the existence of handicap racing which tempts owners and trainers to deceive those setting the weights as to the true ability of their horses. Although doping has played its part, it is the jockey who is central to most means of stopping a horse from winning. Jockeys would be fools to risk riding doped horses – the game is dangerous enough – but making sure that a horse does not feature in a finish is still relatively easy even with the race patrol cameras and Jockey Club regulations on riding out. A tactically injudicious race might be ridden or an animal might not be helped at obstacles. Most jockeys understand that in an overcrowded labour market riding to orders is crucial to their future employment prospects and those orders are not always to win. Sometimes this is to deceive the handicapper and improve the horse's chances next time out; on other occasions it might be part of a betting conspiracy. In 1998 the media were replete with rumours of jockeys fixing races; at one stage it was alleged that up to 50 jockeys were involved. Although eventually several jockeys were arrested, none were ever brought to court. In October 2000 a 'Panorama' television exposé made public the open secret within racing that some jockeys have close associations with big punters and bookmakers. Although such associations might merely lead to the passing on of information rather than any deliberate dishonesty, it is against the rules of racing.

In the late nineteenth century many jockeys argued that they had to gamble because owners often refused to pay their riding fees. In 1880 the Jockey Club ruled that all such fees had to be deposited with the clerk of the course before the race took place. However, betting by jockeys did not cease and, annoyed by this and by rumours of race fixing, in 1884 the turf authorities made gambling by jockeys an offence punishable by loss of licence. Three years later they added a ban on jockeys owning or having an interest in a horse. These issues have been treated seriously as vital to the integrity of racing and some big-name riders such as Charley Wood, Tod Sloan and Charlie Smirke were warned off. Yet such punishments for this and other turf offences failed to act as a complete deterrent as sentences were indeterminate and those warned off or with a suspended licence were at liberty to apply for reinstatement. Pressure by owners, anxious not to lose the services of good quality jockeys, was often exerted on the stewards.

One way to beat the bookmaker is the use of the 'ring in' in which one horse is substituted for another of similar experience. The most famous incident here is the 1844 Derby won by Running Rein which was in reality Maccabeus, a horse actually a year older, which no doubt gave him an advantage in a race supposedly restricted to three-year-olds. Just over a century later, in July 1953, a coup almost succeeded at Bath when Santa Amaro was substituted for Francasal. The conspirators arranged for the telephone lines to the course to be cut so that the bookmakers would not know of the heavy off-course betting and thus the starting price was not lowered but remained at a lucrative 10–1. Those involved stood to win £60,000, but all bets on Francasal were eventually declared void. Four men received prison sentences. Although identification procedures were tightened in the 1970s, substitutions are still attempted. Gay Future ran in its own name in 1976 at Cartmel but had another inferior animal impersonate him on the gallops. In 1978 In The Money ran as Cobbler's March at Newton Abbot and in 1982 Good Hand masqueraded as Flockton Gray at Leicester.

Impersonation of a different kind featured in 1998 when a professional jockey, warned off in the United States, was discovered to have assumed a false identity to become a leading amateur rider in Britain. After riding five winners from 21 mounts and becoming favourite for the Bollinger-sponsored, amateur rider's flat-racing championship, Angel Jacobs attracted attention because his polished style was certainly not that of a 7 lb claiming rider. He turned out to be Puerto-Rican, Angel Monserrate, who had been warned off in the United States for drug offences in 1995 and riding under an assumed name the following year. The Angel's wings were clipped by a Jockey Club ban of ten years.

In early 2004 corruption within the bloodstock industry was highlighted following a court case in which it was claimed that a trainer had received a kickback from a bloodstock agent to ensure the sale of a horse. This money was deducted from the price without the knowledge of the owner. Subsequent press investigations revealed endemic malpractice of collective bidding to force up prices, agents covertly acting for both buyer and seller, and a host of secret commissions and payments. In response the Jockey Club called a summit of racing and bloodstock organisations together with auctioneers to discuss how to introduce more transparency into sales transactions.

Racing may have its difficulties, but other sports also face drugs problems, bribery allegations and gambling scams, some of them far worse than on the turf. Nor are the racing stables as dirty as those in some areas of public life, notably in the financial services industry whose mis-selling disgraces in the past two decades have far outstripped any sporting corruption.

Further reading

Onslow, R., *Great Racing Gambles and Frauds* 3 vols (Swindon: Marlborough, 1991–93).

See also Security.

Moneybox

Henry Cecil became the first British trainer to amass over £1 million in win and place money in one season, 1985 (£1,148,189 from 132 races).

The **Champion Hurdle** was worth only £365 to the first winner, Blaris, in 1927, the equivalent of roughly £13,000 now; the winner in 2002, Hors La Loi III received over £156,000, indicating the greatly increased prestige of the race.

Charlottown, winner of the Epsom Derby and runner-up in the Irish Derby in 1966, became the leading British money earner of the century (£78,000 – over £850,000 now) overtaking the record highest winnings in a season set by Tulyar in 1953.

The **Cheltenham Gold Cup** was won by 15 favourites from 1946 to 1999. When Prince Regent came home at 4–7 in 1946, his winnings were £1,130. In 1995 Master Oats (at 100–30) received £122,540, the equivalent of a six-fold increase in the value of the race.

A **claiming race** is one where a horse can be entered with a price stated at which it can be bought. An additional 15 per cent must be paid to the race-course.

Countess Crossett was backed at 5,000–1 at Kelso in 1992, the longest odds ever offered on a British racecourse. The mare finished ninth.

A day at the races 1750

I know horses. My workers plough with them. I use them to drag my carts, to manure my land, and to carry my produce to market. Without horses on my farm I'd be like my great grandfather back in the last century, struggling to eke out a subsistence living. I've done well for myself. Took up the new crops and rotations. Got enough money to buy a few quality horses. Two pull my carriage; the other I canter with across the country. Can't afford a thoroughbred though. Wish I could. I'd be on him next week at Exham races up the road. They're on the Wednesday this year so as to avoid market day. Us farmers can't miss that.

Not too many around here own thoroughbreds so we usually only have a single prize, but they race in heats until one horse wins twice. Last year it was all over in two races so I mounted my old grey and had a match against the brown half-breed from across the valley. Won easily I did, but I'd rather race on a thoroughbred. At 10 st I could manage that. This year there are four horses entered. By the articles they have to be stabled at the *Crown* for three days before the race. I've been around to have a look at them. As I said, I know horses and a couple of them are real beauties. Conformation like Regulus and *he* won nine King's Plates.

As long as I can recall we've had a meeting at Exham most years. Though not four years ago as we couldn't raise the prize money. Parliament decided that we had to offer at least £50 and with the Earl's widow not willing to contribute there was no chance. Landlord of the *Crown* always gives a few sovereigns. He gets to run the refreshment booth and have the horses and their grooms at his place. But without the Earl's donation £50 was beyond us. The Countess didn't like the races. I don't think it was the actual racing that put her off but the crowd who came. She's a stickler for manners and people knowing their place. Our race meeting used to be on the feast of Saint Bartholomew, not that there was all that much holy about what went on. Out in the countryside, we don't have much organised entertainment so with the races some folks go daft. By late August the harvest is in and the hard work is over for the year. So what happens is too much drinking, fighting and – how shall I put it on – carrying on. The new Earl, however, he started the races again once he was 21. Anyway, Parliament has just given up the idea of a minimum prize so we'll be all right from now on.

D

Horsebox

Dahlia, the only dual winner of the King George (1973, 1974) won top-class races in five countries, including the Irish Oaks (1973), the Washington DC International (1973), the Grand Prix de Saint-Cloud (1974) and the Canadian International at Woodbine.

Dayjur will always be remembered as the British horse that lost the 1990 Breeders' Cup Sprint in the last 100 yards by jumping a shadow; he had previously won five consecutive Group One sprints in Europe.

Docklands Express, trained by Kim Bailey, was a two-time winner of the Racing Post Chase (1991 and 1992), as well as the Whitbread Gold Cup in 1991 following the disqualification of Cahervillahow.

Double Trigger, trained by Mark Johnston, won the stayers' triple crown (Ascot Gold Cup, Doncaster and Goodwood Cups) in 1995, winning the last two twice more, as well as five other Pattern races.

Dream Well won both the French and Irish Derby in 1998 (as did Montjeu in 1999).

Drum Taps won the Ascot Gold Cup in two successive years (1992 and 1993), thereby becoming the oldest winner, a seven-year-old, since 1929.

Dancing Brave (1983–99) – by Lyphard out of Navajo Princess

No-one who has seen the video footage of Dancing Brave powering his way past 15 rivals in the 1986 Epsom Derby could deny his astonishing burst of speed and few would disagree that he was unfortunate not to beat the sixteenth, Shahrastani. He was one of the most exciting horses to race in Britain in the last 25 years, won eight of his ten starts and is reckoned to be one of the greatest and most unlucky colts not to win the Derby.

His owner Khalid Abdulla had bought the bay horse, bred in the United States from a son of Northern Dancer, as a yearling and sent him to trainer Guy Harwood in Sussex. He ran in only two minor races as a two-year-old, winning on both occasions. His three-year-old season, however, produced sensational highs and lows. He won the Craven Stakes and the Two Thousand Guineas at Newmarket and was 2–1 favourite for the Derby, despite concerns about his stamina. But his jockey, Greville Starkey, rode a tactically controversial race, holding him up at the back of the field and only sending him on within the final two furlongs. Although he produced a stunning finish, he was unable to make up all the ground and was beaten by half a length. Starkey later partnered Dancing Brave to win the Eclipse Stakes but was replaced by Pat Eddery in the King George, in which the horse gained revenge over Shahrastani. He was then aimed at the Arc and was such a certainty to win his warm-up race at Goodwood that no starting price was returned. He followed this by trouncing a high-class Arc field in spectacular fashion, breaking the course record at Longchamp with a burst of speed similar to that of the Derby. This time he won by a length and a half. His exploits in one outstanding season ranked him as the greatest English champion since Mill Reef and Brigadier Gerard, and his official rating (141) was the highest since the introduction of international classifications in 1977.

It had already been decided that he would retire to stud as a three-year-old but, as Champion Racehorse of Europe, he was sent to the United States to take part in his final race, the third running of the Breeders' Cup Turf. Whether he failed to acclimatise or was simply feeling the effects of a long summer campaign, he could only finish fourth and never raced again, having won over £400,000.

Syndicated for £14 million, he stood at Sheikh Mohammed's Dalham Hall stud at Newmarket for five years, siring the 1993 Derby and Irish Derby winner, Commander-in-Chief, but his fertility was affected by illness and in 1991 he was exported for stud duties in Japan. He died there of a suspected heart attack in 1999, aged 16. Noted for his tremendous acceleration, he may be best remembered for the race he failed to win.

Further reading

Wilson, J., *The Great Racehorses* (London: Little, Brown and Co., 1998).

Darling, Frederick (1884–1953)

Fred Darling was reckoned to be the greatest trainer of his generation, winning six trainers' championships during a 21-year period and saddling seven Derby winners, a twentieth-century record. He came from a racing family; his father, Samuel, and elder brother were both trainers, his great-grandfather had been a jockey, and he began his own career as an apprentice to his father.

He started training near Newmarket in 1907, moving to Germany for a successful spell from 1909 to 1913, before returning to Britain to take over his father's stables at Beckhampton on the Wiltshire Downs. His first Classic winner was Hurry On, in the substitute St Leger of 1916, and during the 1920s he produced three Derby winners for his major patrons, Lord Woolavington and Mr H.E. Morriss, two of which, Captain Cuttle and Coronach, were sons of Hurry On. He was leading trainer for the first time in 1926, and in 1931 trained

Cameronian to win both the Two Thousand Guineas and the Derby for his other principal owner, Mr J.A. Dewar.

With Gordon Richards as principal stable jockey from 1931 to 1947, the Beckhampton establishment saw considerable success. Richards won the Two Thousand Guineas three times on Darling-trained colts – in 1938, 1942 and 1947 – as well as the fillies' Triple Crown in 1942 on Sun Chariot. But although the stable won the Derby three times in four years with Bois Roussel (1938), Pont l'Eveque (1940), owned by Darling himself, and Owen Tudor (1941), Richards was unable to take any of the rides because of injury and previous retainers. However, the trainer/jockey partnership was responsible for winning many important races over 16 years, including the Goodwood Cup in 1932 with Bruletta, the Stewards' Cup in 1937 with Firozepora, the Eclipse Stakes in 1938 with the Two Thousand Guineas winner, Pasch, and the Ascot Gold Cup in 1942 with Derby winner, Owen Tudor.

The 1940s turned out to be Darling's most successful decade; he was leading trainer on four occasions (1940–42 and 1947) and won eight Classics, including four in one year for King George VI, with Big Game and Sun Chariot. But he had been dogged with ill-health for several years and retired from training at the end of the 1947 season, achieving a final Classic victory in the Two Thousand Guineas with Tudor Minstrel, and a total of 19 Classic winners in all.

Reputed to be a strict disciplinarian and meticulous organiser, he regarded frequent training gallops and trials as unnecessary but almost invariably produced his horses at the racecourse in peak condition. In retirement, he concentrated on breeding and lived just long enough to know that one of his home-bred colts, Pinza, had given Richards his first Derby winner in 1953. An outstandingly successful trainer, his name is commemorated in the Fred Darling Stakes at Newbury, an important One Thousand Guineas trial.

Further reading

Mortimer, R., *The Flat* (London: Allen and Unwin, 1979).
Mortimer, R., Onslow, R. and Willett, P., *Biographical Encyclopaedia of British Flat Racing* (London: Macdonald and Jane's, 1978).

Dawn Run (1978–86) – by Deep Run out of Twilight Slave

Dawn Run was a unique champion. Not only was she the first horse to win both the Champion Hurdle and the Cheltenham Gold Cup, a feat still unequalled, but she also achieved an outstanding treble, winning the British, Irish and French Champion Hurdles in one season. In her tragically short life she became the most popular Irish jumper since Arkle, sharing with him the accolade of a commemorative statue at Cheltenham, the scene of her greatest triumphs.

A big bay mare, nearly 17 hands high, she was foaled in 1978 in Co. Cork and sold at auction as a three-year-old to Mrs Charmian Hill, an indomitable horsewoman who was still riding under Rules at the age of 62. She sent Dawn

Run to trainer Paddy Mullins but rode the mare herself in three flat races for National Hunt horses during 1982, winning at the third attempt. Switching to hurdles the following year, the horse was partnered regularly by Tony Mullins, son of the trainer, and the pair developed a flamboyant, front-running style. They won seven races in 1983, both in Ireland, where they triumphed by ten lengths in the Champion Novices' Hurdle at Punchestown, and in England, where they won a valuable handicap under top weight at Aintree and came out again the next day to finish second to the British champion hurdler, Gaye Brief.

Tony Mullins was often replaced by a more experienced jockey in the most prestigious races – Ron Barry had steered the horse to second place in the Sun Alliance Novices' Hurdle at Cheltenham in 1983 – and it was with Jonjo O'Neill that Dawn Run produced her major British victories, taking the Christmas Hurdle at Kempton Park from Gaye Brief, followed by the 1984 Champion Hurdle at Cheltenham as odds-on favourite. She was the first mare to win the race since 1939, undoubtedly benefiting from the recent increase in weight allowance for mares, from 3 pounds to 5 pounds. Some would even argue that Dawn Run was not an outstanding horse but merely the lucky beneficiary of a timely rule change. Nevertheless she continued her winning ways in the Irish and French Champion Hurdles with front-running displays under Tony Mullins. The French race, the Grande Course de Haies at over 3 miles, was half a mile longer than she had ever previously run but she still won by six lengths as 6–5 favourite. Her earnings for the season, from eight out of ten starts, amounted to almost £150,000, a record for a hurdler, and it was not surprising that she was National Hunt Racehorse of the Year.

The following season was an anticlimax as her winning debut over fences was halted by an injury which sidelined her for the remainder of the year but a three-month spell in 1986 brought glory and despair. She returned to Cheltenham to win the Gold Cup with Jonjo O'Neill in a course record time, having only raced in four previous steeplechases. There were scenes of Irish jubilation at this unique Cheltenham double, with her owner and jockey lifted shoulder high by the crowd, but popular and charismatic as she was, she was not, according to O'Neill, a natural jumper and sadly her downfall was swift.

She unseated him at the first fence in her next outing at Aintree and he was never to ride her again, retiring before her next race. It was with Tony Mullins on board that she took part in a match at Punchestown with Buck House, an old rival and winner of the Queen Mother Champion Chase at Cheltenham. In front of a large, adoring Irish crowd, she won by $2\frac{1}{2}$ lengths before heading to Auteuil in preparation for a second tilt at the Grande Course de Haies. Beaten in her warm-up race, it was decided to engage an experienced French jockey, Michel Chirol. On a hot June day, while contesting the lead with two others at a cracking pace, she fell heavily and fatally, breaking her neck. She was only eight.

Further reading

Herbert, I. and Smyly, P., *The Winter Kings* (London: Penguin, 1989).
Holland, A., *Dawn Run* (London: Arthur Barker, 1986).

Dawson family

The Dawson brothers, Thomas (1809–80), Mathew (1820–98), Joseph (1825–80) and John (1827–1903) were the most successful training family in British racing. Between them they won 42 Classics, including 9 Derby victories. According to one contemporary journal, their judgement of a yearling was held in as high repute as their irreproachable taste for whisky. The brothers were four of the 17 children of racehorse trainer George Dawson and his wife Jean. All were brought up around their father's training stable at Stamford Hall, Gullane, in East Lothian where he had moved from Bogside in Ayrshire.

Thomas, the eldest, left Gullane in 1830 and settled at Middleham in north Yorkshire, first at Brecongill and later at the Tupgill stables where he trained for Lord Eglinton. In 1838 he was joined by his brother Mat as head lad, and later both Joseph and John served apprenticeships there. He pioneered the training of horses without sweating them under heavy rugs to get rid of supposed surplus flesh. His training methods produced five Classic winners.

In 1840 Mat returned to Scotland to train on his own account. Shortly after the death of his father in November 1846 he went south again to train for Lord John Scott and his racing partner Sir John Don-Wauchope. When Sir John gave up racing in 1857 Mat arranged the sale of his stud to the wealthy Scottish ironmaster, James Merry, and became Merry's private trainer at Russley on the Berkshire Downs near Lambourn. In 1860 he won the Derby for Merry with Thormanby. Six years later he left Russley, following differences with Merry, never an easy man to serve, and started as a public trainer at Newmarket, where he took Heath House. There his principal owners were the heavy-betting Dukes of Hamilton and Newcastle, both of whom were ultimately forced to leave the turf because of their gambling losses. In 1869, however, he secured the non-betting Lord Falmouth as a patron. Falmouth was concerned only with winning important races and together with Dawson and Fred Archer, the trio were victorious in the Derby twice and each of the other Classics three times. In 1885, the year after Falmouth retired from the turf, Mat handed over Heath House to his nephew, George Dawson, and moved to Exning Manor with just a few horses. Nevertheless, at the age of 75 he trained Sir Visto to win both the Derby and St Leger of 1895 for fellow-Scot Lord Rosebery. Small in stature, immaculate in dress, and justifiably autocratic in his training methods, he secured 28 Classic victories including six in the Derby. Such was his reputation that in his declining years, when gout hampered his walking, he received special Jockey Club dispensation to take a carriage onto Newmarket Heath to supervise his horses.

Joseph left Middleham to run a yard at East Ilsley in Berkshire. From there he went to Newmarket to be private trainer to the Earl of Stamford at Heath House, premises later taken over by his brother Mat after Joseph and the Earl fell out, forcing Dawson to sue his patron for money owed him. He then moved to Bedford Lodge, also at Newmarket. Joseph never won a Derby but he gained five other Classic victories. He was most famous, however, for revolutionising stud management. He decided that his two-year-olds should have their strength developed from birth and fed them as foals and yearlings on the best of fodder.

This policy of forcing his young stock paid off as he won the Middle Park Plate, a major race for two-year-olds, in its inaugural year of 1866 and on three subsequent occasions. He was also reckoned to be the first Newmarket trainer totally to abandon the heavy sweating of horses. In this he followed the pioneering ideas of his brother Thomas at Middleham.

In 1857 John left Middleham and took Roden House at Compton in Berkshire, a village adjoining Ilsley. There he trained Bel Esperanza, the first of the four winners which he saddled in the Lincolnshire Handicap. In 1861 he moved to Warren House, Newmarket where he lived for the remainder of his life. Shortly after settling there he was appointed private trainer to the Hungarian nobleman, Prince Batthyany and also General Peel. When the Prince died in 1883 his executors sold all his stock and thus John missed the opportunity to train the outstanding St Simon, that opportunity going instead to his brother Mat who trained for the Duke of Portland, the purchaser of the horse. John gave up training in 1900, handing over Warren House to his son George. His career encompassed four Classic wins including the 1875 Derby with Galopin, a horse in which he had such confidence that he gave it only one prior race, and that in an easy match with moderate filly, Stray Shot.

Although Mat himself was childless, the Dawson racing dynasty continued with John's sons, George (c.1853–1913) and John junior (?–1942) and Thomas's son also called Thomas (1840–86), who all enjoyed a reputation as trainers, especially George. He had been a brewer at Burton-on-Trent before being selected to succeed his uncle at Heath House. After serving for six months as Mat's assistant he took over, but, unlike his uncle, he opted to be a private trainer employed by a consortium of owners and in seven seasons won ten Classics, all for the Duke of Portland. In 1888 his horses won £77,914, a training record that stood for 43 years. In 1900 he moved to Warren House when his father retired. Both he and John, who trained at St Albans House, Newmarket till his retirement in 1929, gained their initial tuition in their uncle's yard, John being head lad there for a while. Their sister Helen Rose married champion jockey, Fred Archer. Thomas won the Chester Cup with Tim Whiffler in 1862 and subsequently became clerk of the course at Lanark, Haydock Park, Redcar, Thirsk and York.

Further reading

Humphris, E.M., *The Life of Mathew Dawson* (London: 1928).
McConnell, T., *The Tartan Turf* (Edinburgh: Mainstream, 1988).
Mortimer, R., Onslow, R. and Willett, P., *Biographical Encyclopaedia of British Flat Racing* (London: Macdonald and Jane's, 1978).

See also Training and trainers.

Day family

The record of the Day family as jockeys and trainers in Classic races is unsurpassed. Over two generations they rode 30 winners and trained 22.

John Barham Day was that rare racing figure, a successful jockey who became a successful trainer. As a lightweight rider (in contrast to his 20 st father), he won 16 Classics in the early nineteenth century, though never a Derby. From 1835 he trained at Danebury in Hampshire, using the uphill gallop there for hard preparation to make his charges absolutely fit providing that their constitution was robust enough. Seven Classic winners emerged from this regimen, though again not including a Derby. Four of his brothers Charles, William, James and Sam became jockeys, the latter winning five Classics including three Derbys, the first and last 25 years apart. After his second Derby win in 1830 he retired to become a farmer but was unsuccessful and shed over 3 st to resume riding, later winning the Epsom Classic double in 1846.

John handed over his Danebury stables to his son John Day junior and set up another son, William in a stable at Woodyates in Wiltshire. From here William won the autumn double of Cambridgeshire and Cesarewitch in 1860 and sent out three Classic winners. He wrote two practical treatises on breeding and training racehorses as well as the autobiographical *William Day's Reminiscences of the Turf* (1886) and *Turf Celebrities I Have Known* (1891). John junior won the Two Thousand Guineas in 1844 as a jockey on Ugly Buck, owned and trained by his father. Shortly afterwards he commenced training and won a dozen Classics. Another son Alfred rode his first winner aged 14 and weighing only 6 st on Flea in the Goodwood Stakes. In addition to two other Classic victories he won the Derby, Oaks and two Two Thousand Guineas for his brother John and another Two Thousand Guineas for William. Second son Samuel became the youngest jockey to win the St Leger when, aged 18, he brought home Mango in 1837. A year later he died from a fall when out hunting.

There was a third, less successful generation. Alfred, the younger son of Woodyates trainer William, began training in 1887 and brought off several coups but never trained any high calibre horses. After his retirement in 1924 he laid out a National Hunt course on his old gallops at Fontwell Park.

A huge bettor, John Barham Day was sarcastically referred to in turf circles as 'Honest John' and racing historians have often labelled him and other members of the Day clan cheats and castigated their devious behaviour to secure favourable odds for their horses. Yet only William was ever warned off, temporarily as it turned out, for his part in an attempt to stop Old England winning the 1845 Derby. This may say more about the state of racing administration than the honesty of the Days. Nevertheless, when Admiral Rous later accused John Day junior of turf malfeasance, he sued for libel and won an apology from Rous, albeit a qualified one.

Further reading

Day, W., *William Day's Reminiscences of the Turf* (London: 1886).
Mortimer, R., Onslow, R. and Willett, P., *Biographical Encyclopaedia of British Flat Racing* (London: Macdonald and Jane's, 1978).

Deaths

Racing is dangerous, especially for National Hunt horses. There is one death roughly every 500 runs in jump and hurdle racing, usually as a result of a broken neck, back or leg. Horses are bred to run and jump and trained for the purpose, but they are brittle animals. Deaths of flatracers are less common simply because they are not trying to clear obstacles but broken legs or heart attacks still take their toll. Not all horses are killed outright but are humanely put down to save them pain and their owners money. They are rarely saved for stud purposes as the cost far outweighs the potential return; and of course most National Hunt horses are gelded. However, exceptions have been made. Mill Reef, the 1971 Derby winner, fractured a leg while exercising in 1972 but was successfully saved for stud duties. More recently Sheikh Mohammed's favourite horse, Dubai Millennium broke a leg on the gallops in 2000 but was saved for breeding only to succumb to a fatal attack of grass sickness the following year. Overall the sport loses around 220 horses a year as a result of accidents at the racetrack and on the training gallops.

The racing community is not hard-hearted. Although riders become resigned to equine fatalities, most of them are affected by the death of their mount, particularly if they have ridden it several times. Jonjo O'Neill contemplated quitting the sport when Alverton, the horse on which he captured the Cheltenham Gold Cup in 1979, died during the Grand National two weeks later. Tony McCoy was convulsed with grief when budding star Gloria Victis was put down after fracturing a leg in the 2000 Gold Cup and even more so two years later when potential wonder horse Valiramix suffered a fatal fall in the Champion Hurdle. Those who had daily contact with the animals, the lads and lasses who looked after them in the stables, however, feel the greatest loss. Rebecca Cassidy's ethnographic study of racing suggests that, for a stablehand, the death of a horse on the track is comparable to losing a family member. According to eight-times National Hunt champion rider Peter Scudamore, some handlers never forgive a jockey if a horse dies while he has been riding it.

Some jockeys too have died at work. Emmanuel 'Manny' Mercer, one of the best of the post-war generation of flat-race jockeys was killed instantly when, cantering to the starting gate in the fifth race at Ascot in September 1959, his fractious mount Paddy Fair, whipped round, unseated him and then kicked him in the face as he lay on the ground. Generally, however, it is the lesser riders that have to ride the lower quality, more dangerous horses. Since 1980 there have been 14 deaths on the British turf, three on the flat, five in National Hunt racing and the rest in point-to-point. Apprentice Joe Blanks died at Brighton in 1981 when his mount Sleigh Queen clipped the heels of a horse in front and fell. Blanks was galloped over by several horses and received head and chest injuries from which he died eight days later, never having recovered consciousness. Thirteen years later northern lightweight jockey Steve Wood was fatally injured in a three-horse pile up at Lingfield Park after his horse Kalar caught the heels of the horse immediately in front of him, stumbled and catapulted Wood to the ground where he was trampled by following horses, one of which crushed his chest. The other victim on the flat was 64-year-old, Trevor Radford who died in hospital in October 2000, two months after sustaining a head injury when he fell from his own horse Landican Lane in a race for amateur riders at Goodwood.

Jayne Thompson was Britain's leading professional female rider over jumps in 1984. Two years later she died from head injuries received in a fall at

Catterick when Hot Betty fell at the first flight in a selling hurdle. In the same year amateur rider Michael Blackmore died on his way to hospital after a fall at Market Rasen. Vivian Kennedy, son of the same-named Irish trainer, broke his neck and suffered severe head injuries when Wessex Milord, having his first outing over hurdles, fell two flights from home at Huntingdon in August 1988. Conditional jockey Philip Barnard was killed at Wincanton on Boxing Day 1991 when Sayyure fell heavily at the second-last flight of hurdles. Richard Davis suffered fatal internal injuries at Southwell in July 1996 when he was crushed under an inexperienced horse which simply failed to rise at the first fence. Point-to-point racing has claimed six riders since 1980, most recently Rachel Atkinson, a rider with the Belvoir Hunt, who broke her back, neck and sternum when It's On The Cards, the horse she owned and rode, fell in a point-to-point at Wolverhampton in May 2002. Although released from hospital after being fitted with a body brace, she died in Leicester Royal Infirmary from internal bleeding three weeks after the accident.

Nor are the gallops safe. Three stable hands have been killed in the past five years. Indeed with about 4,500 lads and lasses riding out some 13,500 horses on a daily basis even more deaths might have been anticipated. The most recent was in September 2002 when Rebecca Davies was unseated while riding out for Lincolnshire trainer James Given, but, instead of being thrown clear, her foot stuck in the iron and she was dragged for over 400 metres. Five years earlier two young women died within a couple of months of each other after training accidents on the Newmarket gallops. Natasha Glynn, only 17, collapsed and drowned in her bath shortly after being released from Addenbrookes Hospital following a fall on a colt Young Sheba. Less than ten weeks later South African Shana Golden sustained severe head injuries while riding work for Derby-winning trainer William Haggas. Her mount, a three-year-old filly, All In Leather, bolted and collided with a tree. Golden had secured the job at Newmarket only three days before.

Other jockeys died away from the course or gallops but with their deaths influenced by their profession. Wasting certainly contributed to the early deaths of Victorian riders Tom French, John Charlton and Tom Chalenor, all of them Classic winners, John Wells, twice champion jockey, and Fred Archer, 13 times champion, and in the early twentieth century both three-times champion, Danny Maher, and Australian Brownie Carslake.

British racing has never had the major crowd disasters that have disfigured some other sports. Nevertheless spectators have been killed at race meetings, some, like a carpenter at Northampton in 1901 and suffragette Emily Davison at Epsom Downs in 1913, because they got in the way of the horses, others unexpectedly such as the 15-year-old youth who was shot dead at Liverpool when standing behind the boards at the back of a shooting gallery, erected as part of the festivities for Liverpool races in July 1854. Others have fallen victim to freak weather conditions. Twice Royal Ascot race meetings have suffered fatalities from lightning. In June 1930 a bookmaker sheltering in the Tattersalls enclosure from a severe thunderstorm was struck by lighting and killed instantly. A quarter of a century later lightning struck again on Gold Cup day and killed two spectators.

See also Accidents, Hurdling and hurdlers, Injuries, Safety.

Derby

See Classics.

Desert Orchid (1979–) – by Grey Mirage out of Flower Child

Desert Orchid is one of those rare equine stars who capture the imagination of the general public as well as the racing world. Bred by James Burridge, and owned by himself, his son Richard and Simon Bullimore, 'The Grey Horse' or 'Dessie', as he was affectionately known to his many fans, began life in Leicestershire, the first foal of the Burridges' moderate hunter-chaser, Flower Child, by a winning flat-race stallion, Grey Mirage. Partnered by jockey Colin Brown, his racing career began inauspiciously in a novice hurdle at Kempton Park in 1983 where he fell at the last flight and was so badly winded that there were fears for his life. He recovered but, although he managed a second place later that year, it was the following season before he recorded his first win in a novice hurdle at Ascot, one of six victories in 1983–84.

Switching to steeplechasing in 1985, he won novice races at Devon, Ascot and Sandown Park, before coming third in the Arkle Chase at Cheltenham in March 1986. His first major success occurred on Boxing Day of that year in the King George VI Chase at Kempton, a race with which he became closely associated. Considered to be a 2-mile specialist, he won the 3-mile King George comfortably before recording victories at Sandown and Wincanton over similar distances.

Desert Orchid's popularity was based not only on his distinctive grey colour but on his courageous front-running style and his obvious enjoyment of jumping. A born showman, he conquered distances from 2 miles to 3 miles 5 furlongs and a variety of ground conditions but seemed to have a distinct preference for good going and right-handed tracks. His Cheltenham Gold Cup win of 1989, in heavy going on a left-handed circuit, was therefore hailed as an outstanding triumph for his trainer, David Elsworth and jockey Simon Sherwood, who had taken over the reins following the retirement of Colin Brown in 1988.

'Dessie' ran 70 times, notching up 34 wins and 19 places, and amassed prize money of over £540,000. Among his major successes were the Whitbread Gold Cup at Sandown in 1988, the Irish Grand National in 1990 with Richard Dunwoody, his final partner, and the King George VI Chase on three further occasions from 1988 to 1990. He was also third in the Cheltenham Gold Cup in 1990 and 1991 and was voted the National Hunt Horse of the Year by the Racegoers' Club in four consecutive seasons (1987–90). In his final race, at Kempton in 1991, watched by a record crowd, he fell attempting to win the King George for the fifth time, and was immediately retired, aged nearly 13.

But the bare facts of his career fail to conjure up the impact of the grey gelding on National Hunt racing and the wider public. His racecourse appearances attracted huge crowds and he was the most popular racehorse of recent times, with his own fan club, together with books and videos of his racing days. He had an orchid named after him, a race dedicated to him at Wincanton and a statue erected in his memory at Kempton, scene of so many triumphs. In retirement, he has opened supermarkets and betting shops, and when he suffered a life-threatening illness in 1992, regular bulletins on his condition were broadcast on national radio. 'Dessie' was no ordinary champion.

Further reading

Burridge, R., *The Grey Horse* (London: Penguin, 1992).

Dettori, Frankie (1970–)

At school in Italy the ambitions of Lanfranco 'Frankie' Dettori were limited to wanting to become a petrol pump attendant, but fortunately for racing, genes won out. His father Gianfranco was leading Italian rider 13 times and had travelled to Newmarket to win the Two Thousand Guineas in 1975 and 1976. He arranged for his son to spend some time gaining experience in the Newmarket stables of another Italian based in England, Luca Cumani. What was to be a six-month stay turned into an offer of an apprenticeship. Frankie was still too young to race here but not in Italy where he had his first winner on Rif at Turin in November 1986. His first victory in Britain came at Goodwood in June the following year on Lizzy Hare, a horse named after Cumani's secretary. In 1989 Frankie became champion apprentice with 75 winners (equalling Eddie Hide's post war record) and Cumani appointed him stable jockey. Next year he became the first teenager since Lester Piggott to ride a century of winners, actually totalling 141 to finish fourth in the jockeys' championship. He also won his first Group One race on Markofdistinction in the Queen Elizabeth II Stakes at Ascot.

He has always been willing to learn. His trademark flying dismount was copied from the American rider, Angel Cordero. In 1992 he also changed his riding style along American lines. He had always ridden in a low crouched position but with his feet well in the irons. Now he began to ride with only the toe in the iron and with an even lower flat-back profile and shorter rein. In 1993 he ended an eight-year association with Cumani after agreeing a two-year contract to ride in Hong Kong, but he was refused a licence to ride there after a police caution for possession of recreational drugs. He then signed up to ride for Sheikh Mohammed. In 1994 he set his sights on becoming champion jockey and made an early start to his season riding on the all-weather tracks. By the start of the turf season he had already notched up 51 winners. Ultimately after 1,318 rides he took the title with 233 winners, beating by six the post war European record held by his father. He won the championship again in 1995, this time with 217 wins, but then left that battle to others and concentrated on the big races as stable jockey for Godolphin. He has now won over 100 Group One races, including nine Classics.

On 28 September 1996 Frankie rode into racing history at Ascot when he became the first jockey to win all seven races on a card. Even before his memorable Ascot feat, the Anglicised Italian jockey had already established himself as a firm favourite with the racing public. With his accented English, trademark leap from his winning mounts in the unsaddling enclosure, and enthusiasm for the sport, he had taken some of the stuffy insularity out of English racing. He is one of the turf personalities to become a celebrity outside the sport, making appearances on *Top of the Pops* and becoming a team captain on *A Question of Sport*. Both the Tote and the British Horseracing Board have used him to promote the sport and in 2000 he received an MBE for services to racing. This was the year that Dettori narrowly escaped death when his plane crashed on take-off from Newmarket. The pilot was killed but Dettori was dragged clear of the burning wreckage by fellow passenger, jockey Ray Cochrane who, on retirement from riding, became Dettori's agent.

Further reading

Dettori, F., *A Year in the Life of Frankie Dettori* (London: Heinemann, 1996).

'Dictators of the Turf'

Commonly referred to by racing historians as the 'Dictators of the Turf', Sir Charles Bunbury (1740–1821), Lord George Bentinck (1802–48) and Admiral Henry Rous (1795–1877) did much to cleanse the racing stables by suppressing corruption and punishing malefactors. Nevertheless they were no holy trinity, especially Bentinck and Rous.

Sir Charles Bunbury, MP for Mildenhall and one-time Chief Secretary for Ireland, became a Jockey Club steward in 1768 and remained a powerful influence in turf affairs into the early years of the nineteenth century. In 1791 he led the inquiry into the running of Escape which resulted in the Prince of Wales being told not to employ Sam Chifney whom it was felt had pulled the horse in one race to secure more favourable odds in a later one. In 1803 he authorised the publication of the Jockey Club's rules of racing and in his later years campaigned against the presence of defaulters at race meetings. Even if he had not been virtual perpetual president of the Jockey Club he would have a place in turf history as the owner of Diomed, the winner of the first Derby. He also won further Derbys with Eleanor in 1801 and Smolensko in 1813.

MP for King's Lynn, Lord George Bentinck, the son of the fifth Earl of Portland, was a respected but not popular figure of the British turf. His racing stable, at one time the largest in Britain, helped make Goodwood 'glorious', but he was also a devious character who engineered a major betting coup by pretending that his horse Elis would not run in the St Leger and then, when the odds had widened, vanning the horse to Doncaster where it won the Yorkshire Classic. In his early turf career he raced his horses in the names of others to hide his involvement from his family who had been forced to settle his debts after a disastrous betting plunge on the losing favourite in the 1826 St Leger. He fought two duels, one against Squire George Osbaldeston when he was palpably in the wrong. Although a member of the organisation, Bentinck did not hold the Jockey Club in high regard, feeling that it was too reluctant to pursue turf malefactors and occasionally made decisions in favour of vested interests, not usually ones he agreed with. He became obsessed with ridding racing of defaulters and those who practise skulduggery and took it upon himself to investigate the Running Rein scandal when the winner of the 1844 Derby, a race for three-year-olds, was found to be a year older than it should have been. For this he received public acclaim, election as a Jockey Club steward, and a testimonial from fellow members of the Jockey Club which he used to form a charitable fund to aid impoverished jockeys, trainers and their families. Bentinck also prompted more effective weighing of jockeys and better starting arrangements. He also deserves praise for innovations that helped the spectator, such as the use of telegraph frames at Goodwood to display the names of jockeys and numbers of horses, the establishment of betting enclosures around the stands at Goodwood, Epsom and Liverpool, and saddling areas near the grandstand at the same courses. At the Goodwood meeting of July 1846 he shocked racing society by announcing his retirement from the turf and selling his bloodstock of three stallions, 50 horses in training, 70 brood mares, 50 yearlings and 45 foals for £10,000, well below their market value. To his chagrin, one yearling Surplice went on to win the Derby. On his death, only two years after he left racing, Bentinck was described by Disraeli as 'Lord Paramount of the British Turf'.

Henry John Rous, the younger son of Lord Stradbroke, retired from the Navy in 1836. Two years later he became senior steward of the Jockey Club, to which he had been elected in 1821. His life then became devoted to the turf and its administration. A man of strong opinions, contemporaries judged him to be completely honest with an abiding hatred of tobacco, heavy betting and turf corruption, and a nostalgic preference for the social order that labelled jockeys as 'riding grooms'. His classic advice to owners was 'to keep yourself in the best company and your horses in the worst' (Mortimer, 276). He became an expert handicapper, particularly for matches (challenge races between two horses), and developed the first weight-for-age scale that allowed for differences over the year. Between 1840 and 1861 he acted as racing manager for the Duke of Bedford, arranging matches and negotiating the stakes, weights and distances. In 1850 he published *The Laws and Practices of Horse-Racing* which, among other things, set out for purposes of precedence the judgements of the Jockey Club stewards in a variety of cases, gave an analytical explanation of the rules of racing, and defined the duties of all racing officials. It was, however, as senior steward, a position that he retained till death, that he achieved both fame and notoriety. He had the vision to produce workable legislation and the thoroughness to pursue and suppress malpractice, ridding racing of many unscrupulous characters. In 1866 Jockey Club members presented him with an inscribed centre piece for a dining table (now in the National Horseracing Museum) to mark 25 years of 'valuable zealour and disinterested services'. However, power led to arrogance and old age was accompanied by intemperate prejudice and irascibility. He persecuted as well as prosecuted, often being unwilling to cease hostilities even when in the wrong. Increasingly he was forced by threats of legal action to write letters of apology to those whom he had criticised unfairly.

Further reading

Mortimer, R., *The Encyclopaedia of Flat Racing* (London: Robert Hale, 1971).
Onslow, R., *Great Racing Gambles And Frauds* (Swindon: Marlborough, 1991).
Seth-Smith, M., *Lord Paramount of the Turf* (London: Faber, 1971).

See also Corruption.

Distances

There are three official meanings for the word 'distance' in horseracing terminology, which can be somewhat confusing for the uninitiated. To make matters
worse, the average person would probably add a fourth as the most obvious use
of 'distance' refers to the length of a horserace. This varies according to the
type of racing – flat or jumps – and has changed considerably over time. Flat
races in the eighteenth century were usually much longer than they are today,
often 4 miles in length, while the nineteenth century saw a fashion for increasingly short sprints, some of no more than 4 furlongs. These were eventually
banned by the Jockey Club and the minimum distance set at 5 furlongs; today
most flat races are for 12 furlongs or less, with a few over 2 miles. They are
advertised as '1 mile' or '1 mile 2 furlongs' but there is a good deal of approxi-
mation in race distances; race cards frequently state 'about 1 mile' or '1 mile
about 2 furlongs', sometimes with more exact figures in brackets ('1 mile about
100 yards' or '10 furlongs about 36 yards'). Jump racing, both hurdling and
steeplechasing, still takes place over longer distances, normally 2 to 3 miles.
The Cheltenham Gold Cup, at 3 miles $2\frac{1}{2}$ furlongs, is unusual. The Grand
National, at $4\frac{1}{2}$ miles, is unique. In all British racing, however, the traditional
furlong (220 yards) is still the standard measurement while metrication is
notable by its absence.

Every race result includes 'the distances', that is, the official margin separat-
ing the winning horses. Automatically recorded by the photo-finish camera,
the shortest distances are short head, head and neck. Thereafter they are
declared in lengths and parts of a length, based on the accepted measurement
of a horse from nose to tail, approximately 8 feet equalling one length. The distances ascend by quarter lengths from half a length to one and three-quarter
lengths and are subsequently given in half and whole lengths. On the rare
occasions, almost exclusive to jump racing, when the first and second are separated by over 30 lengths, the official term 'a distance' is used. Even Arkle,
reckoned to be the greatest chaser of the twentieth century, seldom trounced
the opposition by a distance. He won the Cheltenham Gold Cup by 20 lengths
in 1965 and 30 lengths in 1966, and his superiority in the King George VI
Chase at Kempton in 1965 resulted in him recording a distance victory. More
recently Red Marauder won the 2001 Grand National by a distance from
Smarty in very gruelling conditions.

A distance of over 30 lengths (80 yards) should not be confused with the
archaic 'distance' used in describing the length of a racecourse. Nineteenth-
century courses, particularly the variously named stretches on Newmarket
Heath, were listed in the *Racing Calendar* as a number of miles 'and a
distance'; for example, the Cambridgeshire Course was 'the last mile and a distance, straight', that is 1 mile 240 yards of the Beacon Course. '*The distance*' is
a term given to an unmarked point 240 yards (just over a furlong) from the
winning post. In the days when races were run in heats, any horse which finished more than 240 yards behind the one in front was said to have been 'dis-
tanced' and was not permitted to compete in further heats. Although the site
of the distance judge's chair resulted in the naming of 'the Chair' fence at

Aintree, the highest on the Grand National circuit, there is no rationale for the continued use of the phrase in modern racing.

Donoghue, Steve (1884–1945)

Steve Donoghue was champion jockey from 1914 to 1923. Unusually for a jockey he had neither a rural nor a racing background. His father Patrick was a steelworker in Warrington and family poverty forced him to take employment in his father's works, but at the age of 14 he walked from Warrington to Chester races to secure employment in the Kingsclere stables of famous trainer, John Porter. Within four months homesickness brought him back to a job at a Warrington wireworks. Then, fearing he had killed a bully in a fight, he fled with his younger brother to the Middleham stables of Dobson Peacock, a leading northern trainer. However, they had given assumed names and left with the arrival of census officials, this time to Newmarket where Steve joined the stables of Alfred Sadler junior. Next came France where he gained experience of race riding and won for the first time, on Hanoi at Hyères in April 1905. Two years later he went to ride for Philip Behan's stable in Ireland where he became leading Irish jockey. In 1910 he was retained by Henry Persse at Stockbridge, Hampshire to replace American Danny Maher, who was suffering from tuberculosis, and by 1914 had won the first of ten consecutive champion jockey titles. Rejected as unfit for military service, he rode two wartime Derby winners in 1915 and 1917, both of them at Newmarket to which the race had been transferred from Epsom.

He developed a reputation for having other riders 'jocked off' mounts in major races and was no respecter of his own contracts if he fancied the chances of another owner's horses. Although this enabled him to win four out of five Derbys between 1921 and 1925, ultimately it cost him the chance of retainers later in his career as no owner or trainer would trust him to honour his obligations. After 1925 he rode no more classic winners till he piloted Exhibitionnist to victory in the 1937 Oaks and One Thousand Guineas. At the end of that season he retired to become a trainer at Blewbury, though only with modest success. He also did some broadcasting. He was a fearless jockey with great tactical skill, soft hands and perfect balance, though never as strong in a finish after an accident in the 1925 Grand Prix de Paris in which he dislocated and fractured his left shoulder. Donoghue was not continually successful. During the 1928 racing season he rode 108 consecutive losers. Worse was to follow. In September of that year a bankruptcy petition showed that he had debts estimated at £15,000 and assets of less than £600. His generosity to friends accounted for some of the problem but primarily it was due to illegal (for a jockey) and unsuccessful betting. Rescue came in the form of a retainer from Sir Victor Sassoon and a decision by his creditors to accept 5 shillings in the pound.

Two horses are indelibly associated with Donoghue. At the start of his career he rode 'the spotted wonder', the unbeaten The Tetrarch, and later he piloted Brown Jack to six consecutive wins in the Queen Alexandra Stakes from 1929 to 1934. In 1957 a pair of gates dedicated to his memory was erected at the entrance to the Epsom grandstand.

Further reading

Seth-Smith, M., *Steve: The Life and Times of Steve Donoghue* (London: Faber and Faber, 1974).

Doping

With its links to betting, horseracing has always been a potential target for performance-enhancing and performance-inhibiting substances. In the non-scientific days of the early nineteenth century sophisticated drugs were not available but there was one sure way to stop a horse: poison it. The first recorded case occurred in 1809 when 13 horses trained by J. Stevens were poisoned at Newmarket, two of which subsequently died. Two years later, again at Newmarket, three horses of Sir Frank Standish also died from drinking poisoned water. The dead horses had been fancied to win at the Newmarket Spring Meeting, so much so that some bookmakers stood to lose heavily if they were successful. They had accepted ante-post bets months earlier which offered higher odds because of unknown form and the risk that the stake would be lost if the horses did not run. Two bookmakers in particular, the Bland brothers, Jim and Joe, saw salvation in the non-runner clause and recruited Daniel Dawson, a training groom turned tout, to stop the animals from racing. He arranged to have arsenic added to the water trough used by their trainer, Richard Prince. A 500-guinea reward offered by the Jockey Club led to Dawson's arrest and, although he was acquitted on a technicality, he was found guilty of the earlier poisoning of Stevens' horses and hung.

The last major proven incidence of the doping of an ante-post favourite was Pinturischio in 1961. After winning his debut race in spring, he finished a close fourth in the Two Thousand Guineas and was installed as favourite for the Derby. A victory at Epsom would have cost the bookmakers a fortune and someone was determined that this would not happen. He was doped to prevent him running in the Classic.

Doping a horse was not against the rules of racing in Britain until 1904. The decision to render it illegal followed the American invasion of the British turf at the turn of the century. Horses at American race meetings could race several times in just a few days and this led to the use of drugs to stimulate jaded animals. The practice of doping accompanied the American jockeys and trainers on their trans-Atlantic migration. Initially the Jockey Club felt the issue was a minor one, but the Hon. George Lambton, trainer brother of Lord Durham, forced them to take action by doping five of his own horses, animals that had shown no form but which under the influence of drugs gained four first places and a second. He did this to demonstrate that unregulated doping could ruin the British turf by allowing animals to win that could not do so otherwise. Such tolerance would make it difficult to assess which horses would make the best breeding stock. Additionally it would not allow gamblers to make a true assessment of racing form. Yet improving the breed was the official rationale of racing and betting its actual reason for existence.

Doping legislation in American racing remains different from that of Britain which can cause problems for British owners and trainers who wish to race their animals in the United States. The racing authorities there allow the use of both bute (phenylbutazone), an effective painkiller and anti-inflammatory drug that relieves the aches and pains of wear and tear, and Lasix, a diuretic that also stops bleeding in a horse's lungs during exertion. The dilemma facing the Britons is that the use of such drugs may give American horses an advantage, but, if they follow suit, potential breeders might worry that the animal actually needed assistance to overcome genetic unsoundness. Some proponents claim that the use of Lasix is actually humanitarian as most bleeding is caused by infection in the lungs and is rife among racehorses; thus to reduce the horse's distress from bleeding is good veterinary practice. On the other hand, as a diuretic, it could also be used to hide the use of performance-enhancing drugs.

No scientific means of detecting the use of dope existed until the development of the saliva test in 1910. Detection processes have improved since then, but generally the equine pharmacists are one step ahead in the doping race. In the early 1950s nobblers used curare which caused horses to lose full use of their back legs. This gave way to hyoscine and atrophine, both of which allowed for a delayed reaction, and then pheno-barbitone. In the late 1970s anabolic steroids made their presence felt via the building up of the physique of young horses. More recently, there has been use of the fast-acting sedative acetylpromazine (ACP), often used in stables to calm down excitable horses but prohibited on the racetrack. Allegations are also being made that the use of erythropoietin (EPO) has spread from athletics and cycling into horseracing.

Norman Pegg, who wrote as Gimcrack in the *Daily Sketch*, estimated that from 1945 to 1961 there were at least 200 known cases of horses being doped, but there were no arrests or charges, let alone convictions. In the 1960s bookmaker-inspired gangs raided trainers' yards and doped horses to lose, but this lessened after some severe sentences were meted out at the Lewes and Reading Crown Courts. However, doping still occurs. In September 1990 three horses, Bravefoot, Norwich and Flying Diva, were all doped within a week and in 1997, Avanti Express, second favourite in what was – despite the size of the field – virtually a two-horse race at Exeter, and Lively Knight, hot favourite in a three-horse race at Plumpton, were both found to have been given ACP. It is still not a criminal offence to dope a racehorse and cases have to be brought under the charge of conspiracy to defraud which are notoriously difficult to prove. The recent collapse of a case whose investigation lasted three-and-a half years and cost the taxpayer £3 million has demonstrated the current inadequacies of the law.

The responsibility for doped horses was always laid at the feet of the trainer who stood to have his licence suspended if any of his horses was found to have been drugged. In 1952 Lord Rosebery, a powerful figure on the turf, began a campaign to have this changed. He argued that only in cases of stimulants could the stable be blamed for they would know if the horse was ready for a particular race whereas they could slow it down by methods other than drugs. Eventually, following the Norfolk Committee Report in 1961 trainers had to be shown to have been negligent in making anti-doping safeguards before they lost their licences.

Today tests are carried out on each winner, virtually every beaten favourite and any other horse that runs markedly above or below form as well as some selected randomly and others on the basis of intelligence reports. In total over 7,000 tests are carried out each year of which only a handful are positive, far fewer than in most other racing countries. Of these many are attributable to mistakes relating to the administration of legitimate medicines, veterinary treatments being given too close to a race, confusion over feed buckets, or something eaten in the fields. From the 1980s there has been international agreement on admissible threshold levels of those substances that some horses carry naturally or can be ingested in fodder made from natural ingredients. These post-race tests are based on urine samples, but occasionally, as part of a programme to ensure that the sport is clean, horses are blood-tested before racing.

Jockeys are rarely accused of doping horses, certainly not the ones that they ride themselves as this would be foolhardy. That said, some riders have failed to pass the drugs tests introduced by the Jockey Club in 1994 when, at the instigation of Michael Turner, their new chief medical adviser, a protocol was developed for the testing of riders for banned substances. These included marijuana, cocaine, amphetamines and alcohol. To 2001 only one jockey, one apprentice and two conditional riders were suspended for recreational drug use, though it should be noted that amphetamines, the banned substance in two of the cases, speed up metabolism and can be used for weight loss. However, in a six-month period in 2002 five drug tests on jockeys proved positive, a worrying trend for the racing authorities, though three of these were for substances not on the Jockey Club prohibited list. One involved an anabolic agent that formed part of a medical prescription; another was a cold and flu remedy; while the third was for a dietary product. The other two jockeys were found to have cocaine in their system, one of them, Dean Gallagher, having already been banned for six months in 2000 after testing positive three times for the same drug in France. To the end of 2003 a further two British-based jockeys have tested positive for cocaine and have received suspensions.

Further reading

Lambton, G., *Men and Horses I Have Known* (London: 1924).
Onslow, R., *Great Racing Gambles and Frauds* 3 vols (Swindon: Marlborough, 1991–94).

See also Corruption.

Dunwoody, Richard (1964–)

Richard Dunwoody rode 1,699 winners, at the time the most by any jump jockey, and had a career strike rate of 18 per cent. He is one of only four jockeys to have won the big three of Grand National, Cheltenham Gold Cup and Champion Hurdle. He rode two Grand National winners, West Tip in 1986, when at 22 he was the youngest rider in the field, and Miinnehoma eight years later. His two major Cheltenham victories were on Charter Party in the 1988 Gold Cup and Kribensis in the Champion Hurdle of 1990. He also won four King George VI Chases. Indeed of the major races only the Hennessy Gold Cup and the Queen Mother Champion Chase have eluded him. He won races on every jumps track in Britain and Ireland except Catterick, Bellewstown and Wexford.

He was born in Belfast in 1964 into a racing family. His father George trained in Antrim and then at Newmarket; his mother Gillian was daughter of trainer Dick Thrale. So determined was he to become a jockey that he became anorexic when at school. The severity of the illness convinced him to eat sparingly but sensibly during a riding career where he was always watching his weight. He started as a pupil to Paul Kelleway and later John Bosley and Tim Forster. His first public ride came in August 1982 and his first winner under National Hunt Rules was at Cheltenham on 4 May 1983, on Game Trust, a horse that he had previously ridden to his first victory in a point-to-point. From 1986 to 1993 he was stable jockey for David Nicholson and, on the retirement of Peter Scudamore, took his position with Martin Pipe. He notched up the first of his ten centuries of winners in 1989–90, had his best year in 1993–94 with 197 wins, and was champion jockey in that and the adjacent seasons.

His obsession with riding, and more so winning, cost him his marriage in 1996 and almost his sanity in 1994 during a titanic struggle with Adrian Maguire for the jockey's championship which went to the last day of the season. After leaving his wife he released himself from his contract with Martin Pipe, began to accept less rides, and opted out of the chase for the title.

His final ride, though he did not know it at the time, resulted in victory on Twin Falls at Perth on 25 August 1999. He retired (reluctantly) four months later at the age of 35 on medical advice that further damage to a neck injury could result in him losing the use of his right arm. For 18 months he had ridden with a significant lack of strength in that arm and had been forced to whip left-handed in any driving finish. In a career spanning over 10,000 rides he had already had 699 falls though he had only spent one night in hospital – in intensive care after breaking his sternum in a fall from See More Business in 1997 at Kempton. Remarkably he was riding again only 13 days later. Similarly when his employer, David Nicholson, advised him to take three weeks rest to heal after six falls in one three-day meeting at Ascot, he was back at work within three days. Ultimately it was not the fear of paralysis that caused him to step down, but the realisation that he could not be as effective a rider as he had been.

Further reading

Dunwoody, R., *Obsessed: The Autobiography* (London: Headline, 2000).

Moneybox

Dancing Brave, racehorse of the year, winner of the Two Thousand Guineas, the King George, the Eclipse Stakes and the Arc, lifted over £423,000 in prize money in 1986, a British record (nearly £750,000 now).

The **Derby** was won by 35 favourites during the twentieth century and, unlike the other Classics, its value has more than kept pace with inflation; it was worth a third as much again in 1999 (£611,450) as the equivalent amount in 1900 (£5,450).

When **Frankie Dettori** completed his famous seven wins at Ascot in September 1996, any punter who had backed him to go through the card would have received accumulated odds of 25,095–1.

Lady James Douglas was the first woman to top the leading owner table (in 1918), thanks to the exploits of her colt Gainsborough, who won a wartime Triple Crown. He later became champion sire (in 1932 and 1933 his progeny won races valued at nearly £73,000), as did his most famous son Hyperion, the Derby and St Leger winner of 1933.

When **Drumcree** won the 1903 Grand National as 13–2 favourite, he picked up only £2,000, the equivalent of £138,000 today, less than half the current prize money.

The **Dubai World Cup**, first run in 1996, is now the richest race in the world, with total prize money of over £4.25 million. Street Cry, the 2002 winner, picked up £2,465,753.

E

> **Horsebox**
>
> **Earth Summit**, trained by Nigel Twiston-Davies, won the Scottish Grand National in 1994, the Welsh National in 1997 and the Aintree Grand National in 1998.
>
> **El Gran Senor**, a son of Northern Dancer, was rated the top horse in Europe in 1984, with wins in the Two Thousand Guineas, (the last English Classic win for trainer Vincent O'Brien), Irish Derby and a close second in the Epsom Derby.
>
> **Erhaab** won the 1994 Derby, the last of Willie Carson's four Derby winners and 17 Classic successes, from the largest field (25) since 1978.
>
> **E.S.B.** with jockey Dave Dick on board was the unsung winner of the Grand National in 1956, the year in which the Queen Mother's Devon Loch collapsed inexplicably on the run-in – his name would no longer be allowed under rules of naming that exclude initials or punctuation.
>
> **Eyecatcher** is the only mare to have been placed twice in the Grand National, third behind Rag Trade and Red Rum in 1976 and behind Red Rum and Churchtown Boy in 1977.
>
> **Ezzoud**, winner of the 1994 Eclipse Stakes, unseated his jockey Walter Swinburn at the start of that year's King George and continued riderless to the finish, impeding several major contenders including Erhaab, the Derby winner. The race was won by King's Theatre, second in the Derby, but Ezzoud redeemed himself somewhat by winning the International Stakes at York for the second year running.

Eclipse (1764–89) – by Marske out of Spiletta

Eclipse was the racing superstar of the eighteenth century, unbeaten in 18 races. He was bred and owned by William, Duke of Cumberland, and is said to have been named after the eclipse of the sun in 1764, the year of his birth. He was a big horse by the standards of the time, over 15.2 hands high, and his portraits by George Stubbs show him to be a chestnut with an Arab profile, a white blaze and one white sock.

His owner died when he was a yearling and he was sold for 75 guineas to William Wildman who had a stud in Surrey. He developed into a fiery, excitable horse and was apparently fortunate not to be gelded. In keeping with the custom of the eighteenth century, Eclipse was not raced until he was five years old, and his first racecourse outing was at Epsom Downs against four other horses. The race was run in three 4-mile heats, the standard format of the times, and Eclipse won the first two so emphatically that the remaining horses were not officially placed. This is the occasion at which the Irish gambler Dennis O'Kelly is alleged to have forecast the outcome of the race with the statement, 'Eclipse first, the rest nowhere' although, as with much in horseracing folklore, its historical accuracy is highly doubtful. Following this triumph, however, he purchased a half share in the horse for 650 guineas; the next year he paid a further 1,100 guineas for sole ownership.

Eclipse was entered for 17 races during 1769 and 1770 but his reputation was such that many owners refused to start their horses against him. Frequently carrying weights of 12 stone and invariably an odds-on favourite, he is said to have beaten no more than 20 horses, often by distances of over a furlong. He is known to have run in the most prestigious races of his day, including 11 King's Plates and the Great Subscription race at York but seven of his victories were walkovers. He was retired to stud aged six, never having been stretched on a racecourse.

He stood near Epsom, initially for a fee of 50 guineas, although this was later dropped to between 20 and 30 guineas, and his presence in the neighbourhood is said to have contributed to the heightened profile of racing on the Downs. His progeny won over 850 races, including three of the first five Derby Stakes, and had a considerable impact on the development of the nineteenth-century thoroughbred. Even modern racehorses, such as Nashwan, winner of the 1989 Two Thousand Guineas and Derby, can trace their descent directly from Eclipse.

When he died at the age of 24, his skeleton was preserved for examination by veterinary experts in an effort to find reasons for his extraordinary speed, and it can still be seen at the National Horseracing Museum at Newmarket. Other memorabilia include a statue of the horse at Newmarket racecourse and a hoof mounted on a gold plate and presented to the Jockey Club by William IV as a racing trophy. His fame is also commemorated in the Eclipse Stakes, run at Sandown Park since 1886, the oldest Group One race in the flat-race calendar and the Eclipse Awards, the most prestigious accolades in American racing.

Further reading

Mortimer, R., Onslow, R. and Willett, P., *Biographical Encyclopaedia of British Flat Racing* (London: Macdonald and Jane's, 1978).
Wilson, J., *The Great Racehorses* (London: Little, Brown and Co., 1998).

Economics

Although individuals and even groups within the industry can do very well financially, owners compete for sums that cover only a quarter of the cost of keeping horses in training; the vast majority of jockeys fail to make a decent living out of the sport; many trainers run at a loss; racecourses are often under-utilised; and even the perceived saviours, the bookmakers, claim that they cannot afford to give much more to the sport. Many find the economic struggle too much. Each year about 10 per cent of trainers and an even larger proportion of owners quit racing though at the moment replacements continue to come forward. This is less the case with jockeys, especially in National Hunt where the numbers have almost halved in a decade. Yet there are some indications that racing is better off than it has ever been. Attendances are the highest for several decades, prize money is at a record level, and the recent commercial deal on media rights has significantly increased the contribution to racing from the bookmaking sector.

All this, however, is dependent on two groups, the owners and the punters. Throughout its history horseracing has relied on owners to partly finance the sport. Even after the coming of the enclosed course – beginning at Sandown Park in 1875 – when spectators had to pay to see the racing, owners still contributed much of the prize money themselves. They still do and it is also on their money that breeders, trainers, jockeys and stable staff rely. The bettor is now the other vital cog in the financial wheels of racing. Without his or her belief that they can outguess the bookmakers the latter would not be in business; nor would the jockeys and trainers. However, it was not until the 1930s that the surplus from Tote operations began to drop into racing's coffers and bookmakers and their clients did not contribute directly to the funding of racing until the introduction of the levy in 1961. Some saw this as a state subsidy but in reality it was a price paid for the racing product which brought betting tax revenue to the national exchequer. For the next 40 years or so disbursements from the Levy Board provided a substantial proportion of racecourse finance and an annual set of arguments and negotiations as both racing and bookmaking pleaded their respective cases of poverty! An era ended in 2002 when, fed up with the squabbling and concerned about the relocation of bookmaking activity to overseas tax havens, the government abandoned racing to its own devices, forcing the parties involved to undertake commercial negotiations rather than rely on others to set the rate of redistribution from gambling to racing. The whole industry had become dependent on the money raised from betting duty and Tote profits. Although this is set to change with the abolition of the betting tax and a greater reliance on the sale of media rights to the betting sector, it is still the volume of bets by individual punters that will underpin any deal.

What the sport has to sell is pre-race information on runners and riders and actual races for telecast. It is generally acknowledged that these were sold far too cheaply in the past, perhaps because of the financial safety net provided by the levy money. Pre-race information is one of the few items of value owned by the British Horseracing Board (BHB). For many years it was virtually gifted to the betting industry. In the 1990s the BHB received only £350,000 for data covering 1,200 fixtures, 7,000 races and around 150,000 entries, information which it is estimated cost about £4 million to produce! The racecourses also failed to grasp the potentiality of the sale of live pictures when the first deal was made with Satellite Information Systems in the 1980s for transmission to the betting shops. Now, although there has been a split among the ranks of the Racecourse Association with separate deals being negotiated with different broadcasters, collectively the fees earned more than doubled. The contract signed on behalf of 49 courses (of the 59 in Britain) with Attheraces, a joint endeavour of Arena Leisure, BSkyB and Channel Four, was for £307 million over 10 years. In October 2003 the Office of Fair Trading declared that the deal breached competition law and that it should be renegotiated. The broadcasting consortium has announced that it intends to drastically reduce its offer and indeed has formally terminated the original agreement.

It had been a long-standing grievance in many sectors of racing that bookmakers did not make a larger contribution to the sport. Yet no one in power, either in racing or politics, was prepared either to charge the bookmakers a more realistic fee or, even more unthinkable (in Britain) give the Tote a monopoly. In many countries bookmaking is less significant than in Britain and most betting is through a totalisator system. This allowed racing there to take a larger slice of betting turnover than was forthcoming through a betting levy. In turn this led to greater levels of prize money, cheaper attendance costs and better racecourse facilities than in the United Kingdom.

In 2002, after much acrimony, legal threats and personality clashes, the BHB secured an agreement with the bookmakers' organisations for around £160 million, more than twice what it had obtained through the levy, to cover the copyright material and the signal sent into the betting shops. The hope of the bookmakers was that the abolition of the betting duty would encourage punters to bet more and thus raise their profits.

The racing industry is viable only because owners are prepared to regard their participation more as a hobby than a business; aspirant trainers are willing to replace those who withdraw from a sport that cannot provide them with a satisfactory living; and stable staff love working with horses more than they want a decent wage. Its continuation has been dependent on implicit subsidies from those within the industry as well as a government-imposed redistribution of income. The latter has now gone as the betting levy and duty have been replaced by a commercially negotiated contract for media rights.

Racing is a minority sport striving to keep its economic balance on an inclined plane leading to sporting obscurity. Two major problems have to be faced if it is to survive: the increasing age profile of those who support racing by either attending meetings or placing bets, and the growing competition for the gambling pound. Walk into any betting shop or stand by the turnstiles at most racecourses and it is clear that racing's 'audience' is an ageing one. Even televised racing gears its adverts towards viewers interested in retirement benefits and funeral arrangements! The image that the sport presents to the younger generation does not appeal. Apart from possibly Frankie Dettori, no jockey exudes charismatic qualities that might rival footballers in the poster-on-the-bedroom-wall stakes. Not that this will matter if racing loses the support of the punter. To continue to be important in the betting market, horseracing must preserve its integrity so as to keep the trust of the bettor. Currently this is under review as television documentaries and media follow-up have revealed some rotten apples in the racing barrel. There have been corruption scandals in the past but the punters always came back. Now there are more alternatives available, be it simple numbers as in the National Lottery or the vast range of sports betting available through the internet or in the betting shop itself.

See also Industry, Marketing.

Eddery, Pat (1952–)

In 1999 the sight of Pat Eddery riding on the all-weather surfaces enlivened winter racing in Britain. He was in pursuit of a milestone in his career, a twenty-sixth century of winners to break Lester Piggott's British record. He finally achieved this on Sirine at Southwell on 22 November. This meant that he had scored a century every year since 1973 except in 1982 when he rode mainly in his native Ireland and won the championship there.

Born in 1952, Patrick James Eddery was one of the 12 children of Irish champion jockey, Jimmy Eddery, who won the Irish Derby on Panaslipper in 1955 and was second on the same horse in the Derby. His maternal grandfather was Jack Moylan who had also been Irish champion. At the age of eight he began riding out at the Leopardstown stables of Seamus McGrath, where his father had become assistant trainer and six years later was apprenticed there. In 1967 he moved to England to complete his apprenticeship with Frenchie Nicholson, that great educator of jockeys.

His first ride in England was on a lively filly that ran through the starting tapes and deposited him on the ground. After over a year and a further 69 rides he landed his first winner, Alvaro in the Spring Apprentices Handicap at Epsom. In 1970 he rode a five-timer at Haydock, the year in which two seven-day suspensions probably cost him the title of champion apprentice: he was earning himself the soubriquet 'Polyfilla' for his tendency to go for any gaps! Next year he did win it with 71 victories, though he did have 655 rides, the third most of any jockey. Six years after breaking his duck he became champion jockey, at 22 the youngest holder of the title since Gordon Richards in 1925. Ten more titles came his way, along with three Derbys, four Arcs, a Japan Cup and two Breeders' Cup races.

Motivation has never been a problem. Even when his brother Michael had to have a leg amputated following a fall at Newcastle in 1972, this did not deter him from wanting to be not just a jockey but the best that there was. He has a deserved reputation for being conscientious and turning up on time – a lesson learned thanks to the occasional heavy hand of Frenchie Nicholson – which, apart from his superb riding record, appeals to owners and trainers.

In 1977 he had been champion for four consecutive seasons when the virus hit Peter Walwyn's stables, from whom he held a retainer, and drastically cut his winning opportunities. He remained loyal to Walwyn for three years but then had an offer from Irish trainer Vincent O'Brien that was too good to turn down. His retainer was increased fivefold, he was to be paid all expenses, and he had a nomination at stud for one horse of his choosing every year. Yet this meant that he could not really challenge for the British jockeys championship and after six years he returned to a mainland stable to ride for Prince Khalid Abdulla.

In 1990 he determined to break the two-century mark and took rides where he could get them. After a five-timer at York on 10 October bookmakers stopped taking bets on whether he would achieve the target, which he did at Chepstow on 23 October, 14 racing days before the end of the season. His final total was 209. During that phenomenal season he passed the career winning totals of both Fred Archer and Joe Mercer. In 1991 he achieved the fastest ever 3,000 winners in British turf history, taking 22 years and 3 months. In 1997 he rode his 4,000th winner and in June 2002 he moved into second place in the all-time list of winning jockeys in British racing. He retired in November 2003 with a career total of 4,632 winners.

Further reading

Eddery, P. and Lee, A., *To Be A Champion* (London: Hodder and Stoughton, 1992).

Eighteenth-century horses

Eighteenth-century racehorses were markedly different from their counterparts today. To begin with, they were much smaller; two of the founding fathers of the modern thoroughbred, the Darley and Godolphin Arabians, were probably no more than 15 hands high. They never raced but Gimcrack certainly did – he is said to have won 26 races between 1764 and 1771, yet measured little more than 14 hands. His contemporary, Eclipse, was 15.3 hands and reckoned to be a big horse in his day; even the famous duo Voltigeur and The Flying Dutchman who raced 80 years later were no taller. A similar thoroughbred in the twenty-first century would be thought undersized.

Their careers were also very different. Few saw a racecourse before they were five or even six years old and in the early part of the century, they may only have raced two or three times. Flying Childers, son of the Darley Arabian and said to be the first great English racehorse, only ran twice while his grandson, Snap, foaled in 1750, ran four times over two seasons. Neither was raced till they were six years old. On the other hand, Matchem, a grandson of the Godolphin Arabian, had at least ten starts over six years and won on eight occasions, while by the end of the century, Hambletonian, a descendant of Eclipse and the greatest racehorse in the north of England, won over 20 races including the St Leger.

The races in which they competed also bore little resemblance to horseracing as we know it today. For much of the century racing at the elite level either took the form of matches between two horses or sweepstakes run in heats, often over a distance of 4 miles. The winner was the first to triumph in two heats. The horses, carrying weights of up to 12 stone, were often ridden by their owners and sometimes raced for pitifully small prizes and trophies, especially at the smaller race meetings. It was only in the last decades that shorter races for younger horses became widespread, requiring lower weights and the employment of professional jockeys.

It was against this background that the most famous racehorses emerged. Flying Childers, bred in Yorkshire but sold to the Duke of Devonshire, took part in two matches, for 500 guineas and 1,000 guineas against solitary opposition in 1721 and 1722. His power and speed impressed contemporary observers and his reputation was such that none could be found to challenge him. In the following decade, Lath, a son of the Godolphin Arabian was said to be the best horse of his time, and in the 1740s Regulus, his half-brother, won nine King's Plates and was never beaten.

However, there is a general lack of knowledge about the racing exploits of many eighteenth-century horses. Those whose names survive in written accounts appear to have made their reputations by their prowess as stallions rather than as racehorses. Matchem won eight races over a six-year period (1753–58), including two each at York and Newmarket but was twice beaten in the recently-founded Jockey Club Plate. He is better remembered as a leading sire. His contemporary, Marske, the sire of Eclipse, won the Jockey Club Plate but was beaten on two occasions by Snap and was not reckoned to be a top-class racer. His appearance in the records is largely as a result of his famous son and his numerous other progeny. Even Herod, who was to become leading sire eight times, only won six of his ten starts from 1763 to 1767 and at least three of those were matches. His son, Highflyer, appears to have been the consummate thoroughbred of the period. Unbeaten in 12 races, he went on to be champion sire 12 times with three Derby winners to his credit. However, the reputations of two great racehorses in the last third of the century were based as much on the fear factor as on their racecourse performances. Eclipse (see separate entry) won 18 races but at least seven were walkovers. His son Pot-8-Os won 28 races in eight years but ten were similarly uncontested.

The advent of the St Leger (1776), Oaks (1779) and Derby (1780) for three-year-olds and the beginning of two-year-old contests around the same time brought a different dimension to eighteenth-century horseracing and would lead to profound changes in the development of the racehorse. Quick-maturing, speedy, lightweight horses came to be prized more than those which displayed stamina over long distances and strength under heavy weights. The two continued to co-exist but a small number of sires exerted a disproportionate influence on the early Classic races. Six of the first ten renewals of the Derby were won by the offspring of Eclipse or Highflyer, who had also sired four St Leger winners by 1788. One of his sons, the 1787 Derby winner Sir Peter Teazle, was in turn reckoned to be the outstanding horse of his era. He won 16 races and was responsible for five Classic victories before 1800 and a further five in the new century.

No-one knows how good these horses were. At a time when the improvement of the breed was alleged to be the main justification for racing, Admiral Rous, senior steward of the Jockey Club, was highly disparaging of these early thoroughbred racers. He doubted whether Flying Childers could even win a £30 plate in the 1850s, acknowledged that Eclipse and Highflyer might scrape home in a seller for a purse of £50 but reckoned that £200 was the best they could manage at sale. His comments reflected a personal view of the constant progress achieved by breeders over the century since these animals had raced. Perhaps he was correct but there is no means of judging.

Horseracing in general did not change overnight. Alongside shorter races and the first handicaps, the traditional matches between the horses of the aristocracy and 4-mile races, run in heats, continued to be run. Fields were often small, prizes seldom large. Away from Newmarket and a handful of high-class courses, racing and racehorses exhibited as much continuity as change at the end of the century.

Further reading

Dawes, R. (ed.), *The Illustrated Encyclopedia of World Horse Racing* (London: Marshall Cavendish, 1989).

Mortimer, R., Onslow, R. and Willett, P., *Biographical Encyclopaedia of British Flat Racing* (London: Macdonald and Jane's, 1978).

See also Arabian horses.

Epsom Downs

The racecourse at Epsom Downs is best known for its hosting of the Derby and the Oaks, the traditional high spots of the flat racing year. A hundred years ago, it was also associated with a great unofficial public holiday, Derby Day, the Victorian essence of which was captured by William Frith in his famous painting of 1858, subtitled 'all human life is here'. Parliament may no longer adjourn for the day as it did in the nineteenth century but Epsom in early June still attracts worldwide interest.

Horseracing has taken place in this part of Surrey since the seventeenth century and during the reign of Charles II (1660–85) fashionable society came both to race and to sample the recently discovered waters known as Epsom salts. By 1730, an annual race meeting was held every spring and the 1770s saw increased interest in Epsom, with the retirement to stud nearby of the great racehorse Eclipse, and the founding of the Oaks and the Derby in 1779 and 1780. Its proximity to the capital led to ever-increasing crowds and 80,000 were said to have attended Derby meetings in the 1820s. The visit of Queen Victoria in 1840 and the advent of a direct rail link in 1847 further contributed to its popularity and by the end of the century, Derby Day crowds were estimated at anything from 250,000 to 500,000. Although a large grandstand was completed in 1830 and replaced in 1927, access to the Downs remained free and unenclosed as it did for most of the twentieth century, and the scenes at Epsom on Derby Day in the 1950s retained much that would have been familiar to the Victorians. The lines of open-topped buses, pearly kings and queens, sideshows and rides together with the carnival atmosphere, picnics and frivolity on the Downs continued to contrast sharply with the top hats and tails in the grandstand. However, the course was finally enclosed in 1985, an additional grandstand opened in 1992 and efforts made to rejuvenate and modernise a venue which had become increasingly tawdry.

The present course, left-handed and horseshoe-shaped over 1 mile 4 furlongs, has been in use since 1872 and is noted for its steep gradients, sharp bends and awkward camber. It is intended to be the supreme test of the three-year-old thoroughbred racehorse, requiring speed, stamina and balance but its eccentricities have led to accusations that it is not a fair, accurate or even safe trial. Few favourites win here, and numerous Derby winners have subsequently failed to win another race, including a recent sequence from 1996 to 1999. The steep left-handed bend of Tattenham Corner has seen both equine and human accidents, from the seven-faller pile-up during the 1962 Derby to the death of suffragette Emily Davison, knocked down by a horse during the 1913 race. The 5-furlong track, said to be one of the quickest in the world, saw Indigenous record the fastest time for this distance in 1960, at 53.6 seconds, although this was timed by hand from a starting gate. In 1970 Raffingora set up a world record for the same distance at the same track, electrically timed at 53.89 from starting stalls.

Epsom is not simply the home of the Derby and the Oaks. Its third Group One race, the Coronation Cup run on Oaks day over the Classic course, is for older horses and tends to attract small but high-class fields. First staged in 1902, it has been won by many previous Classic winners later in their careers, notably Mill Reef (1972) and Roberto (1973), both victorious in the Derby, Silver Patriarch and Mutafaweq, St Leger winners of 1998 and 2001, and the Oaks-winning Petite Etoile who notched up consecutive successes in 1960 and 1961. Frankie Dettori has won the race four times in six recent attempts on Swain (1996), Singspiel (1997), Daylami (1999) and Mutafaweq (2001). The Group Three Diomed Stakes on Derby Day commemorates the first winner of the colts Classic and the Great Metropolitan Handicap, founded in 1846 and funded by local publicans (hence its alternative name 'The Publicans' Derby'), is still staged here although it is no longer a race of any consequence. There are also popular summer evening fixtures amongst the 11 annual race days at the course.

Epsom Downs is now owned by the Racecourse Holdings Trust, a non-profit making subsidiary of the Jockey Club. It was an army camp during the First World War, the site of the first attempted television transmission of an outdoor event (the Derby meeting of 1931), and the location for a James Bond movie in 1995. But it is still largely synonymous in the eyes of the world with its two famous Classic races and the folk festival which took place on Derby Day.

Further reading

Hunn, D., *Epsom Racecourse* (London: Davis–Poynter, 1973).

Magee, S. (ed.), *The Channel Four Racing Guide to Racecourses* (London: Channel 4 Books, 1998).

www.epsomderby.co.uk

Equipment

The equipment required by participants in horseracing is somewhat more complicated than the footballer's boots and ball and the cricketer's bat, pad and box! Jockeys need armour in the shape of crash helmets and body protectors, tights to keep out the cold, aerodynamic silks to cut wind resistance at 30 mph and several lightweight racing saddles for their day's work. Horses need all manner of straps, cloths, buckles, bandages and special racing plates. Owners may need the morning suit and binoculars and preferably a large chequebook – and this is just at the racecourse!

The range of tack assembled for a racehorse is nothing like the saddle, bit and bridle to be found at the local riding stables. Some is for protection, some for control. A horse may wear bandages or leather boots on its legs to guard against damage when jumping fences; a tongue strap to prevent tongue-swallowing during a race; a variety of breast girths and additional straps to stop the saddle from slipping and ear plugs if it is likely to be upset by racecourse noise. (What a pity these weren't available to Devon Loch in the 1956 Grand National, as jockey Dick Francis always maintained that it was the deafening cheers from the grandstands that caused the Queen Mother's horse to collapse on the run-in.) The basic snaffle bit and bridle can be supplemented by sheepskin or crossover nosebands to encourage the horse to keep its head in an optimum position and a brush-pricker attached to the bit, the pricking sensation from which theoretically keeps a horse straight instead of tending to hang in one direction. Various blinkers (eye shields to limit the vision and encourage concentration), visors (blinkers with eye slits to allow some lateral sight) and hoods (which cover the ears and therefore perform the same function as ear plugs but make the poor animal look much more scary) are also fastened to the horse's head in the hope of improving racecourse behaviour.

Training equipment at modern stables might include horse walkers – power-driven frames which look like giant rotary clothes-driers, to which several horses can be tied and exercised at the same time – and swimming pools for muscle toning and cardiovascular workout (for the horses, that is!) Flat racehorses have to be schooled in the use of starting stalls, hurdlers and steeplechasers in how to jump fences. All animals have to become accustomed to the motorised horseboxes that ferry them around the country and, in the case of the elite few, the boxes in which they will be loaded for flights around the world.

Technology at the racecourse includes a range of camera equipment and electronic timing apparatus. The photo finish was first introduced at Epsom in 1947, the patrol camera at Newmarket in 1960 (where the first colour photo finish was displayed in public in 1989) and the first finish to be determined by an electronic camera took place at Goodwood in 1995. The responsibility for provision and operation of all technical photographic support at racecourses, from coverage of the race for the benefit of officials and supplementary material for television broadcasters to close-circuit and big screen facilities for the general public, lies with Racetech (Racecourse Technical Services Ltd). They also supply the starting stalls and their teams, are responsible for racecourse cable installations, and operate the first sectional-timing equipment in Britain, at the Rowley Mile course, Newmarket. Commonly used in America, this facility for analysing the speed of a horse at different points in a race is also available at the all-weather tracks. It works by means of the computerised connection of wiring points under the course to electronic chips in a horse's number cloth.

Europe

Britain had established racing connections within Europe by the early nineteenth century. Bloodstock was exported widely – the Derby winner Gustavus (1821) was sold to Prussia, Middleton (1825) to Russia, and the victors of two consecutive Epsom Classics ended up in Hungary (Teddington, 1851 and Daniel O'Rourke, 1852). Although the closest links were forged with Ireland and France (see separate entries) British racehorses, jockeys and trainers have travelled throughout the continent for over 100 years while more recently Italians and Germans in particular have tried their luck in Britain. The last decades of the twentieth century have also seen close co-operation between European racing authorities, leading to systems of European pattern racing, handicapping and sponsorship.

The French were the first European raiders on British soil in the second half of the nineteenth century and successful invaders from other states only began to appear 100 years later. Bella Paola, winner of the One Thousand Guineas and Oaks in 1958 was trained in France but was a predominantly German horse. Before 1914, the Hoppegarten district of East Berlin was the Chantilly of Germany with British trainers, jockeys and stable staff working there. German attempts to upgrade bloodstock had been of limited success and early in the twentieth century British Derby winners were still being bought for German studs. Ard Patrick (1902) was exported there and Galtee More (1897), originally sent out to Russia where he had proved to be very successful, was sold on to Germany where he became the maternal grandsire of the greatest German inter war horse, Oleander. After the wars, German racing began to recover in the early 1960s but it was British raiders together with those from other European countries who often picked up the newly funded prizes such as the Grosser Preis von Baden and the Preis von Europa (a race won in 2000 by John Dunlop trained Golden Snake). An isolated German success abroad was Star Appeal in 1975, winner of the Eclipse and the Arc. In 2002, however, Boreal (Coronation Cup) and Kazzia (One Thousand Guineas and Oaks) broke a 27-year drought by winning British Group One races.

Italians have fared better, particularly jockeys, owners and trainers. The Dettoris, Gianfranco and his more famous son, Lanfranco (Frankie) have both ridden successfully in Britain, the father capturing the Two Thousand Guineas in consecutive years for Italian owner Carlo d'Alessio (with Bolkonski in 1975 and Wollow in 1976), the son becoming champion jockey in 1994 and 1995. Frankie Dettori, with seven Classic wins and four King Georges to his credit, has been one of the most popular personalities in the flat racing world in recent years. Both father and son have ridden for Luca Cumani, the Newmarket-based Italian trainer who won the Derby twice with Kahyasi (1988) and High-Rise (1998) and the St Leger with Commanche Run (1984). Another well-known Italian was millionaire Carlo Vittadini, owner of Grundy, whose horses were regularly seen on British tracks in the 1960s and 1970s. The best Italian horse of recent times was Ribot, foaled at the English National Stud and one of the last products of the great Italian breeder, Federico Tesio. Reckoned to be one of the most brilliant European colts of the twentieth century, he was unbeaten in 16 starts and won the King George on his only racecourse appearance in Britain in 1956. He stood in England for a year after his retirement and sired five Classic winners. The Italian-trained horse Ruysdael was placed in the 1967 St Leger and 1988 Arc winner Tony Bin, trained by Luigi Camici was third in the King George that year. But in general raiding parties move in the opposite direction. Trainer Ian Balding sent out Glint of Gold to win the Derby Italiano in 1981, the first year it was re-opened to foreign horses and no Italian horse has won the race since 1988. Of the 25 Pattern races held in Italy in 2000, British-trained horses won seven.

The British have probably made more impact on Europe than Europeans have here. British flat and jump jockeys ride regularly on the continent and have done so for 150 years. Some travelled over for occasional races on Sundays, others rode regularly abroad, sometimes capturing overseas championships – Colin Astbury was champion jump jockey in Norway in 1977 and Paul Hamblett was champion flat jockey there in 1979. Others have made a living abroad when progress proved to be too difficult at home – David Richardson and Steve Eccles became top jockeys in Germany in the 1980s. When the Norwegian Grand National was launched in 1970 British jockey David Nicholson won the inaugural race on a Swedish horse; English rider John Williams has won it twice since then. Reverse raids have not been so successful. When Norwegian Grand National winner Trinitro contested the Aintree equivalent in 2000, he fell at the first fence. Although the Scandinavian countries began to import British bloodstock in a big way during the 1960s – English-bred stallions were responsible for the winners of 17 out of 21 Scandinavian Classics from 1962 to 1968 – their horses are not yet of a sufficiently high standard to compete throughout Europe.

British horses have walked off with numerous top prizes since The Ranger won the first Grand Prix de Paris in 1863, notably the 11 English-trained winners of the Prix de l'Arc de Triomphe. The opening of European Classic races to foreign-bred horses in the last decades of the twentieth century has frequently seen national prizes scooped up by English raiders, particularly in Scandinavia. In jump racing, British horses won the Grand Steeplechase de Flandres in Belgium and the Grand Steeplechase de Paris as long ago as 1910 (Jerry M). Troytown won the French event in 1919 and, perhaps most famously, Mandarin in 1962, the year in which jockey Fred Winter had to negotiate the course without the advantage of a bit in the horse's mouth! A British jockey won the very first Velka Pardubice, the Czech equivalent of the Grand National, in 1874 and there have been two more recent successes, in 1973 when amateur rider Chris Collins won and in 1995 when Charlie Mann partnered It's A Snip.

The development of the European pattern system for top grade races, introduced in 1971, has helped to smooth out disparities between the top five racing nations – Britain, Ireland, France, Germany and Italy – and has been followed by another important European initiative, the establishment of the European Breeders' Fund (EBF), the largest individual sponsor of British racing. Founded in 1984, it distributes sums raised by stallion owners in the form of racecourse prize money, breeders' prizes and veterinary research funds, and operates a reciprocal arrangement with its American counterpart, the Breeders' Cup Limited.

Further reading

Hedges, D., *Horses and Courses* (London: Secker and Warburg, 1972).
Herbert, I. (ed.), *Horse Racing* (London: Collins, 1980).

See also Pattern races.

Evening racing

Evening racing was first introduced in Britain at Hamilton Park racecourse near Glasgow in July 1947. The meeting, arranged on the Friday preceding a planned Saturday visit to the races by the royal family, attracted a crowd of 18,000, but was viewed with a mixture of scepticism and amusement. Although a few courses in the North and Midlands continued the experiment, it was 1955 before a London course, Alexandra Park, staged its first evening event. The main significance of this meeting was probably the arrival by plane of several riders who had already taken part in the afternoon races at Leicester, heralding a new era in jockey travel.

These early attempts to entice the working population to mid-week racing were not without difficulty. The traffic jam created by the first evening meeting at Leicester in 1955 caused many spectators to miss the opening races, and at most courses a 6 pm start, coinciding with the evening rush hour has proved to be a perennial problem. The programming of meetings in the 1950s, often on two consecutive nights, was ill-thought-out, usually resulting in a large turnout on the first evening and a poor one the next. Jockeys and trainers, though accepting the need to offer novel alternatives to the racegoing public, complained of the long hours, increased travel and disruption to stable routines.

1962 saw the first Saturday evening meeting, at Wolverhampton, but 25 years later less than half of the racecourses in Britain staged an evening fixture, few of these were in the South, and prestigious courses were notable by their absence. There was certainly nothing to compare with the few gala evenings organised at Longchamp, near Paris, in the 1930s when dance floors with orchestras, floodlit boxing matches and fireworks vied with the horseracing.

The picture has changed considerably since the 1970s. At the beginning of the twenty-first century, most racecourses hold at least one evening meeting each year; the remainder are mostly small winter jump courses. The fixtures take place from mid April to late August; many of the winter jump tracks such as Aintree, Cheltenham, Towcester and Wetherby sign off their season with an evening fixture. While there were roughly 60 meetings in 1971, there were over 220 in 2004 with southern racecourses now well represented and even major venues such as Epsom Downs, Goodwood, and Newmarket offering evening racing. The relaxation of betting laws in 1993 has enabled betting shops to stay open until 10 pm during the summer months and television coverage was extended in the same year to include these fixtures.

Mid-week racing is popular around London with Kempton Park offering around eight cards and Windsor, an early pioneer, holding a weekly series of Monday meetings throughout the summer but the trend has been towards Friday and Saturday fixtures with family entertainment and live music during and after the races. There is now an evening race meeting somewhere in Britain on 20 consecutive Saturdays to the end of August. The summer National Hunt programme allows spectators to view both flat and jump racing on long light evenings and the all-weather track at Wolverhampton has extended the season by featuring floodlit racing on Saturday nights during the winter months. As for the pioneering course, nearly half of Hamilton's races are now held in the evening. The novelty is here to stay.

Moneybox

Each way bets are effectively two bets with the stake split evenly between one for a win and one for a place (which includes finishing in first place).

The **Eclipse Stakes** was worth more than twice as much as the Derby (£10,000) when it was first run in 1886 – nearly £750,000 in current value.

American **Charles Engelhard** was leading owner in 1970 (winning £182,059), largely thanks to Nijinsky's Triple Crown success.

Enstone Spark won the One Thousand Guineas in 1978 at odds of 35–1 and never won another race.

Entrepreneur (4–6 in 1997) and **El Gran Senor** (8–11 in 1984) were the shortest-priced losing Derby favourites since Tudor Minstrel (4–7 in 1947). El Gran Senor was beaten a short head by Secreto, the other two finished fourth.

An **Exacta** is a Tote bet requiring punters to pick the first and second in a race.

F

Horsebox

Fair Salinia gave Michael Stoute his first Classic win in the 1978 Oaks, having finished second in the One Thousand Guineas; she was the first filly to win the Epsom, Irish and Yorkshire Oaks.

Siblings **Fairway** and **Fair Isle** (by Phalaris out of Scapa Flow) both won Classics. Fairway won the St Leger in 1928 while **Fair Isle** won the One Thousand Guineas in 1930.

Flakey Dove is one of only three mares to win the Champion Hurdle (in 1994) – the others were African Sister (1939) and Dawn Run (1984).

Fortina was the last entire horse to win the Cheltenham Gold Cup, in 1947, and his jockey Dick Black was one of only three amateurs to win the race.

Freddie is one of four post-war horses to be second in the Grand National in consecutive years (1965, 1966) – the others were Tudor Line (1954, 1955), Greasepaint (1983, 1984) and Suny Bay (1997, 1998) while Durham Edition was second in 1988 and 1990.

Further Flight is the only horse to have won the same Pattern race five times in consecutive years, scooping the Group Three Jockey Club Cup at Newmarket every year from 1991 to 1995; he was also twice winner of the Doncaster Cup (1991, 1992).

Facilities

Gone are the days when racecourses could offer little more than a draughty concrete edifice or a wooden shack for a grandstand, a muddy field for a car park and a few burger stalls for sustenance and expect to get away with it. As opportunities for leisure have burgeoned in the past 50 years, racecourse managements have been faced with a stark choice – modernise and diversify or die. (15 courses have closed down for a variety of reasons in that period.) Not only must they provide more comfortable facilities for the diehard punter, the bread-and-butter of their survival, but they must also attract both new racegoers and commercial activities to supplement the racing fixtures.

The realisation that seedy, down-at-heel venues which were barely adequate in the 1950s were unlikely to appeal to a late twentieth-century audience, has seen massive rebuilding and rethinking at the most progressive racecourses. Glass-fronted restaurants, on-site hotels, smart conference suites and reception areas capable of hosting weddings and exhibitions have appeared at the top British tracks, together with hospitality boxes and function rooms for corporate entertaining. Infield areas boast golf courses and caravan parks and even smaller racecourses open up for car boot sales on non-race days in an effort to improve revenues during the weeks of the year – the vast majority – when no racing takes place.

Horseracing itself is now marketed along with a host of different attractions. Family days, Sundays and charity meetings in particular put on Punch and Judy shows, face painting, fun fairs, clowns, bungee jumping, barbecues, live music, falconry displays and bouncy castles. Sports personalities pay visits and parades of veteran racehorses are regular race day features. For the dedicated racegoer rather than the family group, improvements in facilities occasionally extend to close circuit television with race previews and interviews, and large screen viewing of the races. Many punters, however, are still thankful if there is an adequate supply of betting outlets, clean toilets and bars serving fresh coffee and chilled lager.

With different clienteles, budgets and standards of racing, it would be unrealistic to expect small rural tracks in the north and west of Britain to provide the same amenities as the prestigious courses concentrated mostly in the south. Nevertheless, racegoers ought to receive certain basic facilities when they part with the not-inconsiderable sums required to enter a racecourse. Car parking that does not involve a squelch through ankle-deep mud is the first prerequisite. A racecard which offers more than a list of runners and riders, including information for the novice punter and the sort of news and views regularly presented in football programmes, would be helpful and perhaps entertaining. Adequate shelter for those race days when the weather turns sour is not too much to ask, together with access and viewing areas for wheelchair users. The opportunity to purchase a range of food and drink, from a decent lunch with wine to a fresh sandwich and a cup of tea, is not unreasonable given the hours spent at the course. The chance to bet or brush up without joining long queues should be mandatory (although racecourses appear to be one of the few leisure outlets where female toilets are under-utilised!). The possibility of viewing the entire race cycle, from paddock to winners' enclosure, which is surely the raison d'etre of the whole experience, should also be available with the minimum of discomfort and hassle. To do so in an aesthetically pleasant setting, with flower beds and hanging baskets or warm, carpeted vantage points, according to the season, is the only way in which racecourses will entice the elusive floating punter rather than the hardened veteran back through the turnstiles.

Further reading

Lee, A., *The Course Inspector* (London: CollinsWillow, 2001).

Fallon, Kieren (1965–)

In his early days of riding, six times champion jockey, Kieren Fallon, caused as much consternation among racing scribes regarding the correct spelling of his forename as he has in later years to owners and trainers with his behaviour on and off the course. His talent for riding has been matched by an ability to rub people up the wrong way.

Born in Co. Clare, Fallon grew up on a small farm in a family with no racing connections. He first joined Irish trainer Kevin Prendergast and after riding 38 winners in six years transferred in 1988 to Jimmy Fitzgerald at Malton. His first winner for that stable was on Evichstar at Thirsk. From 1993 to 1995 he rode as stable jockey for Lynda Ramsden. For the 1997 season he came south and joined Henry Cecil, a partnership that brought him his first Classic winner on Sleepytime in the One Thousand Guineas, four other Classics, and three successive double centuries of winners – a feat matched only by Fred Archer and Sir Gordon Richards – along with the jockeys' title in each of those seasons. The run was brought to an end by an accident at Royal Ascot in 2000 when he was hit just below the shoulder by a hoof. This severed the main nerve in his left arm as well as rupturing the axillary artery. Had a leading nerve surgeon not operated on him within 24 hours he might never have ridden again. As it was he did not return until the 2001 season.

His style is to be one of the slowest away from the starting stalls and build up the momentum from about halfway through a race, though he does his homework and knows which horses and jockeys he should track. Nor does he ride flat out from the start of the season, preferring to avoid Sundays and evenings for a while, but when the title is on the line later in the year he will go to Wolverhampton to ride on the dirt on a Saturday night.

Controversy has dogged his career. He has a short fuse and in 1994 pulled rival jockey, Stuart Webster, from his horse after a race at Beverley. Fisticuffs allegedly followed leaving Webster with a broken nose and Fallon with a six-month ban from riding. It was not his first ban nor would it be his last: his list of turf misdemeanours is a long one. During his enforced absence he spent some time in the United States where he developed a better feeling for pace. In 1995 his ride in the Swaffham Handicap at Newmarket became the centre of a libel action when trainer Lynda Ramsden was falsely accused by the *Sporting Life* of not letting her horse Top Cees run on its merits. Fallon was the jockey involved and he pocketed £70,000 when the court found against the paper. In 1996 he was beaten in controversial circumstances in the Eclipse when he got himself boxed in on Bosra Sham and was publicly castigated by Cecil. Three years later Cecil terminated his contract after rumours of a sexual relationship with Cecil's wife, a charge that Fallon has consistently denied. He moved to Sir Michael Stoute's yard in Newmarket and picked up consecutive Two Thousand Guineas on King's Best and Golan. Then in 2002 he lost his job as retained jockey for Stoute because several of the owners, most notably the Aga Khan, no longer wanted him to ride their horses. However, the trainer himself continued to employ Fallon in his freelance capacity. The season ended with him being named in an investigatory television programme as a man who mixed with gangsters in Hong Kong and him suing a tabloid newspaper for repeating the allegation. He still won the champion jockey title, though with a reduced total of 144 winners as he rode much more abroad, and piloted Golan to a win in the King George. In early 2003 it was announced that Fallon was seeking treatment for alcohol problems, but he still rode the winners of the Derby and One Thousand Guineas in that year. In 2004 he won both the Derby and Oaks.

Families

The family trees of many of those involved in racing can rival the pedigrees of the horses that they ride, train and own. Consider Francis Pratt, an undistinguished Cheltenham trainer of the Victorian era. He married a sister of the great champion jockey Fred Archer. Her father William Archer rode the Grand National winner in 1858 and two of her remaining brothers also became jockeys. Fred Archer himself married into the Dawson family (see separate entry) with its three generations of successful trainers. Francis had three sons, Charles, Fred and William, all of whom entered racing. Charles became travelling head lad to Harry Cottrill (remember the name) before setting up as a trainer himself; Fred rode the winner of the One Thousand Guineas in 1895 and later became a private trainer to James de Rothschild winning another One Thousand Guineas in 1911; William became a successful jockey and trainer in France. William married his cousin Ethel Archer, daughter of Charles who was Francis Pratt's brother-in-law. They had three daughters. One married Claude Halsey who rode and trained in France; his father William Halsey was also a trainer but had earlier ridden both on the flat and under National Hunt Rules, coming second in the 1900 Grand National and winning the Two Thousand Guineas the year after. Another daughter married trainer John Frederick Watts, grandson of famous jockey John Watts, and son of John Evelyn Watts who trained the Derby winner in 1927; their son, also John, became the fourth generation of the Watts' family to train at Newmarket. The third daughter also married a trainer, Humphrey Cottrill, who was the son of Harry Cottrill , the employer of her Uncle Charles a generation before.

Little has changed since then. The twenty-first century world of racing is still peopled with a relatively small number of families, many of whom are connected by blood and marriage. The Scudamores are into their fourth generation as racing professionals – Tom, champion amateur jump jockey in 2000–01 is now riding for a living, like his illustrious father Peter and grandfather Michael, winner of the 1959 Grand National on Oxo. Tom's great-grandfather, Geoffrey was a trainer. There have been numerous sets of racing brothers: the Wraggs, Harry, Sam and Arthur during the inter war period (Harry and his son Geoff became trainers); the Edderys, Pat, Paul and Michael throughout the last decades of the twentieth century (their father Jimmy was Irish champion jockey); and at the present time the Hills, jockey twins Michael and Richard whose father Barry and elder brother John are both trainers. The Dunlops, father John and son Ed, both train. The Dickinson family played musical chairs in their stable for 20 years as the training licence was held first by father Tony (1968–80), then son Michael (1980–85) and finally mother Monica (1985–89). All three had been successful jump riders. Cecil Boyd-Rochfort passed his Newmarket stable on to his stepson Henry Cecil, Peter Easterby handed the reins of his Yorkshire yard to his son Tim and in these enlightened times Sussex trainer Guy Harwood has been followed at Pulborough by his daughter Amanda Perrett. Training is simply another form of business in which the family firm continues through the generations.

Even those who leave the firm often stay in the racing business. Some work for racecourses, others become officials or, as in the case of Clare Balding, daughter of trainer Ian and niece of Toby, racing journalists. Others marry into it. Racing may have changed significantly since Fred Archer married into the Dawson dynasty but many jockeys and apprentice trainers still cement relationships by marrying a trainer's daughter. Tommy Carberry who piloted L'Escargot to successive Cheltenham Gold Cups, married Pamela Moore, daughter of trainer Dan Moore. Lester Piggott married Susan Armstrong, daughter of Newmarket trainer Sam. (One of their daughters married local handler William Haggas.) Susan took over the Piggott yard in 1988 when Lester was imprisoned while Mercy Rimell, married to jump jockey-turned-trainer Fred, carried on the business on his death, turning out 1983 Champion Hurdle winner Gaye Brief.

And so the merry-go-round spins on. There is one famous racing name, however, that continues without the ties of kinship. Vincent O'Brien, one of the outstanding trainers of the twentieth century, operated from Ballydoyle, Co. Tipperary for over 40 years. There is still an O'Brien at the Ballydoyle yard – but twice champion British flat trainer Aidan O'Brien is not a relation! Instead he was assistant to his wife, champion Irish jumps trainer Anne-Marie Crowley in 1992–93 before striking out on his own. The Crowleys are another family business: Anne-Marie took over the yard from her father Joe, her sister has been running it since Anne-Marie retired...yet another example of the racing family.

Film and drama

When photographer Eadward Muybridge first recorded a galloping thoroughbred on film in 1878, he was able to demonstrate conclusively the four-beat stride of the racehorse. His famous sequence of shots, taken by a series of still cameras, proved that the animal did not gallop in the way artists had portrayed it for centuries with front and hind legs extended. With the invention of the telephoto lens in 1891, it was technically possible to film the action of a horserace and the two were linked when the Epsom Derby became one of the earliest sporting events captured on camera. Both Birt Acres and Cecil Hepworth, pioneers of the British film industry, chose it as a subject for their cinematography: Acres in 1895 when the winner was Lord Rosebery's Sir Visto, Hepworth, filming from the top of a horse-drawn bus, in 1899 when the Duke of Westminster's Flying Fox was victorious. Unfortunately at least one camera ran out of film as the leading horses approached the finishing line.

For the next 50 years, many of the films featuring horseracing emanated from Hollywood although the best known, *National Velvet*, had a British connection. Adapted from a novel by Enid Bagnol, and starring Mickey Rooney and the young Elizabeth Taylor, it told how two youngsters trained their horse to win the Grand National, a highly dubious but heart-warming yarn for the wartime audiences of 1944. The race scenes, purporting to show Aintree, were apparently filmed on a Pasadena golf course. An earlier Hollywood feature, *Knight Without Armour* (1936) starring Marlene Dietrich was actually filmed in Britain and contained a re-enactment of the 1913 Ascot race meeting as part of a portrayal of traditional British cultural values, American-style.

Homegrown racing films tended to be escapist rags-to-riches stories of punters winning against all odds and stable lads training Derby winners. Many were comedies: *Educated Evans* (1936) and its sequel *Thank Evans* (1938) starred comedian Max Miller as a tipster-turned-trainer. Singer-comedian George Formby, a former professional jockey, made several racing films in the inter-war years, culminating in *Come On George* (1939) in which our hero outwits a gang of crooks and rides an unmanageable horse to victory in the big race. The popular jockey Steve Donohue also starred in a number of short films made at Islington Studios between 1925 and 1937, and was apparently praised for his acting ability.

The postwar years saw more of the same with racing films tending to feature tales of petty crime or absurd comedy – sometimes combining the two. An adaptation of Graham Greene's novel about racecourse gangs, *Brighton Rock*, starring Richard Attenborough and directed by John Boulting, hit the screens in 1947. *Derby Day*, directed by Herbert Wilcox (1952), showed the unlikely adventures of four racegoers at Epsom; *The Rainbow Jacket*, from Ealing Studios (1954), followed the fortunes of a middle-aged jockey, banned for accepting a bribe, and his young and increasingly successful protégé; and *Dry Rot* (1956), based on the stage farce which opened at London's West End in 1954, starred Brian Rix and Sid James and involved the switching of horses by unscrupulous bookies. One of the few exceptions to this genre was the 1949 adaptation of a D.H. Lawrence tale, *The Rocking Horse Winner*, in which a boy discovers that he has the ability to predict winners while pretending to be a jockey on his own rocking horse. The sexual undertones and other subject matter of this film place it in a different category from the usual racing fare.

The increasing sophistication of audiences in the postwar era has virtually ended the film industry's interest in this area of sport. The 'crime and horseracing' theme was trotted out once more in Tony Richardson's 1974 direction of *Dead Cert*, based on the first novel, of the same name, by ex-jockey Dick Francis. The screenplay was co-authored by John Oaksey, amateur jockey, racing correspondent and Channel 4 racing presenter, and once again centred around Britain's most well-known steeplechase, the Grand National. Although this was the only film adaptation of a Dick Francis novel, a television series based on his characters, entitled 'The Racing Game' was shown in 1979. In the 1980s, big screen interest was rekindled with the tear-jerker *Champions* (1983) starring John Hurt as Bob Champion, the National Hunt jockey who battled through cancer to partner Aldaniti to Grand National success in 1981. The same year saw an Australian film industry production, *Phar Lap*, based on the story of Australia's most famous racehorse.

If films about horseracing have either emphasised the seedier or more poignant aspects of the business, snapshots about the world of racing have usually focused on the glamorous side. One of the most famous film scenes to feature a horse race – although it fails to show any racehorses! – is that featured in the 1964 musical, *My Fair Lady*. There is no comparable sequence in the original George Bernard Shaw play, *Pygmalion*, on which the film is based, but the 1960s version for stage and screen included a day at Royal Ascot, complete with hats and high fashion. The excitement of the race unfortunately causes the heroine, erstwhile flowergirl Eliza Doolittle, to lose her cool, forget that she is supposed to be a lady and shout the highly unladylike words, 'Move your bloomin' arse!' at her chosen horse as the runners storm towards the finish. The upmarket was even merged with the criminal image of racing in the 1985 James Bond feature, *A View to a Kill*, in which a rich and successful racehorse owner and breeder is found to be implanting his animals with a chemical substance that can be activated by use of the jockey's whip. Jockey Kelly Marks, who had ridden in both Europe and America, won a role in this film and also in *Champions*. Another Bond movie, *Goldeneye*, used the Queen's Stand at Epsom as a film set.

As well as fictional entertainment there have been many factual recordings of horseracing. The original film of the Derby was a forerunner of the black and white newsreels for cinema audiences popularised by Pathe and British Movietone News which showed the big betting races such as the Derby, St Leger and Grand National and occasional interviews with jockeys such as Donohue. When the British horse Papyrus took on the American champion Zev at Belmont Park, New York in 1923, footage of his journey, training and the race itself was recorded by Pathe News. More recently the arrival of the home video player has seen documentaries about well-loved horses like Desert Orchid, collections of great races and celebrations of particular courses and events such as Cheltenham and the National Hunt Festival.

While several of the above films were adapted from novels, others started life on the stage. There has been a connection between racing and the theatre since the eighteenth century when the annual races in cities such as York and Edinburgh proceeded to the accompaniment of dances, assemblies and plays patronised by the great and the good. The Victorian theatre, both London and provincial, moved a stage further, performing plays about racing such as *The Derby Horse* or *A Run of Luck* in which scenes were set at the racing stables or on the course. A musical comedy entitled *The Sporting Duchess* parodied Caroline, Duchess of Montrose, a well-known figure of the Victorian turf but in general the themes of betting and horse nobbling predominated as they did in twentieth-century film. The confined space and relatively static nature of theatre productions meant that horse races had to be imagined by the audience whereas the advent of moving film at least enabled directors to convey the action and excitement of racing. Occasionally, however, animals have been required to perform on stage. It is alleged that after Voluptuary won the 1884 Grand National, he was sold to an actor and appeared nightly at London's Drury Lane Theatre in a version of *The Prodigal's Daughter*, during which he had to negotiate a water jump! It was much easier to accommodate jockeys than horses. When Jem Snowden, the Derby winning jockey of 1864 was discovered in the audience at Weston's Music Hall in London after the race, he was brought on stage by the proprietor and applauded by the patrons.

Twentieth-century stage plays tended to cover the same themes as their film counterparts. *The Sport of Kings*, a comedy about betting, and *The Calendar*, an

Edgar Wallace crime script, were both filmed in 1931 while another play based on bookies and crime, *The Naughty Age* was turned into the film *Strictly Illegal* (1934). One of the most popular theatre comedies of the inter war years, *Me and My Girl* featured bookie Bill Snibson, played by Lupino Lane, as its hero – it was filmed as *The Lambeth Walk* in 1939. All of these productions painted amusing, light-hearted and generally positive images of stereotypical racing folk – monocled toffs and aristocrats, dishonest or cheerful bookies, lucky or unfortunate punters and seedy small-time crooks. It is not hard to see why their adventures on stage and screen had virtually disappeared by the last decades of the century. In the 1990s revival of *Me and My Girl*, the racing theme has been jettisoned completely and the leading man turned into a Cockney barrow boy.

However, the twenty-first century has seen an unexpected revival of the 'rags-to-riches' racing saga. The 2003 film, *Seabiscuit*, based on a true story and the award-winning book of the same name, follows the adventures of three men in 1930s America as they turn a no-hoper animal into Racehorse of the Year 1938. Who says cinema audiences are more sophisticated than they were 50 year ago?

Further reading

Huggins, M., *Horseracing and the British 1919–39* (Manchester: Manchester University Press, 2003).
Pym, J. (ed.), *Time Out Film Guide* (London: Penguin 2000).
Walker, J. (ed.), *Halliwell's Film & Video Guide 2003* (London: Harper Collins, 2002).

Finishing

A few minutes work on the day was all a judge needed to do to earn his money, a mere matter of watching the finish of a few races and declaring the result. It may sound easy and it could be when horses trailed each other home, but a close finish in bad weather was a different story. In the blur of arms as the jockeys pressed their mounts to victory, especially in the days when many owners registered similar colours, decisions were more difficult. How could anyone hope to distinguish between sky blue, light blue, Mexican blue, mazarine blue, Eton blue, Oxford blue, peacock blue, blue-gown blue, blue bird's eye and plain ordinary blue, all registered colours in 1870. Before 1838 too there was no rule to prevent spectators riding in with the jockeys, which on one famous occasion led to a judge, frustrated by the charge of the mounted gentry, declaring that the first horse home was ridden by 'a tall gentleman in a white coat', none other than Lord George Bentinck, later to become a major force for turf reform.

Judges were the earliest professional Jockey Club officials. Following a dispute in 1776 between stewards who were acting as judges, the Club decided to appoint John Hilton to officiate at Newmarket. As the Jockey Club gained disciplinary control over British racing the numbers expanded and by 1900 there were ten officials licensed to judge at authorised meetings. To reduce the risk of corruption winning owners were banned from giving presents to judges who themselves were prohibited from owning horses or having any financial interest in any race in which they adjudicated.

Judges do make mistakes. In May 1864 (on Friday the 13th!) the Stonehenge Plate at Salisbury had to be rerun because the judge was not in his box. Fortunately for everyone the result of the second race was the same as the first. Insight II was placed third in the 1927 Cambridgeshire, a race that he clearly won. At Kempton Park in May 1984 the judge gave two disputed decisions when the camera operators were on strike. More recently a judge at Newmarket was suspended and ordered to undergo retraining for first giving the closely-fought 1999 Weatherbys Superlative Stakes to one horse, then 30 seconds later changing her mind and awarding it to another. Only three weeks before at Lingfield she had made a similar error but did not spot it until after the weigh-in.

In the days before the camera was there to assist the judges and they had to rely on their eyes alone there were more dead heats than are called today. The photo-finish camera was introduced to British racing in 1947 and called on for the first time at Epsom on 22 April to place Parhelion in second place ahead of Salubrious in the Great Metropolitan Handicap. Initially only Newmarket, Epsom, Goodwood, Birmingham and Doncaster, where the first photographed dead-heat was recorded in 1947, had cameras but by 1952, 24 courses were so equipped. Yet there were still problems and, following an erroneous decision by an official at Goodwood who judged that the Bentinck Stakes had been won by High Stakes rather than Hornet III, two major changes were made, one technical, the other administrative. First, reflected images were introduced so that the judge could see the finish from both sides of the course and, second, the rules of racing were amended so that judges could alter their decisions regardless of whether or not 'weighed in' had been signalled.

Until very recently judges have agonised with their magnifying glasses on the photo-finish image for up to ten minutes before declaring a result. Waiting for the negative and print would already have taken another ten. This had knock-on effects as the delay prevented sponsors making their presentations and perhaps missing a prime-time television slot. It also affected betting turnover as punters often will not bet again until they know a result. Fortunately computer technology has come to the rescue. The modern procedure for photographing horses as they cross the line is fully computerised and uses two digital cameras placed high in the stand. One covers the whole width of the track and the other focuses on that part of the course furthest away from the cameras in order to make best use of the strip of mirror attached to the winning post. The pictures these cameras take are made up of millions of tiny dots and a vertical line of these photographs the activity at the winning line up to 2,000 times a second to build up an image of the horses going through. This is presented to the judge instantly on a monitor with the aim of normally announcing the result within 20 seconds and within three minutes for even the hardest decision. The computer can judge to one thousandth of a second: anything less deserves to be called a dead-heat. There has been debate as to whether the determination of races by such narrow margins is against the spirit of the sport. Some people have suggested that in really close calls dead-heats should be announced but the Jockey Club has been reluctant to go down this track, fearful that irate owners might have a photograph independently analysed and resort to the courts.

The judge's initial decision is not always final. Riders can object and stewards can initiate enquiries if they feel the rules of racing have been broken. Usually, however, the result is still declared on the day of the race...but not always, especially where doping is involved. On 3 March 1987 Torymore Green won a novices' chase at Nottingham but then failed the dope test as it had ingested a prohibited substance contained in a chocolate biscuit. So three months later, during the close season, jockey Peter Scudamore, rider of the second-placed horse, found he had an extra winner.

Further reading

www.racetech.co.uk

Fixtures

Racecourses are not allowed to organise meetings whenever they want. The British Horseracing Board (BHB) effectively determines both when and where meetings will take place, though approval can be given to fixture exchange or sale. Although the social calendar, local holidays and especially tradition all have a role in influencing the allocation of meetings, an over-riding issue is the creation of a daily betting market. Generally at least two meetings are scheduled for a Monday and Tuesday, two to three on Wednesdays and Thursdays and more on Fridays, Saturdays and at holiday times. New fixtures can be brought in to meet the demand of course executives and to offer more races to owners and trainers. In 1995, for example, the BHB added £500,000 in prize money for 21 new National Hunt fixtures scheduled for June and July at six courses. These included 13 evening meetings for summer race-goers. The BHB also has the responsibility for rescheduling postponed or abandoned meetings if they can be fitted in to the overall schedule without causing problems for competing courses. In 1993 this led to the unusual situation of Southwell running two meetings on the same day; a turf meeting in the afternoon followed by an all-weather in the evening!

The Office of Fair Trading has looked at the question of racecourse fixtures and indicated that a more competitive system should be introduced. Certainly it sees no future for the archaic ruling that forbids a meeting within 50 miles of another on the same day. The BHB is keen to introduce competition between racecourses, possibly by 'auctioning' some fixtures which would go to those courses that guaranteed the most prize money for the meeting. Auctions would also allow entrepreneurs to build new courses knowing that they could compete effectively for fixtures. The Racecourse Association is opposed to such a move. Its position is to try to maintain a status quo so that a course can hang on to its fixtures no matter how poorly it performs, unless it opts to sell them as Newton Abbot did. For five years to 1999 Newton Abbot's Boxing Day fixture has been abandoned because of frost or waterlogging. This led the course executive to offer to sell the meeting for £400,000 plus a summer fixture. They had already sold two January meetings to Newcastle for £200,000. There are, however, some racecourses that would favour total deregulation of the fixture list. The two limited companies, Arena Leisure and Northern Racing, have a duty to their shareholders not to racing in general and would stand to gain by putting on more low-grade racing simply for the punters in the betting shops and striking their own media rights deal with the bookmakers. Now that the levy is being replaced by a commercial agreement between the betting industry and racing, the fixture list could prove to be a bargaining tool in future dealings between the BHB and the bookmakers. The former has already 'threatened' that it might encourage more evening and Sunday fixtures for the benefit of racegoers and racecourses rather than the weekday and Saturday afternoon meetings preferred by the betting shop proprietors. A lot depends on how much and what type of competition the Office of Fair Trading insists upon.

Further reading

Clark, N., *Neoliberals Frighten the Horses*, New Statesman, 8 September 2003.

Flatman, Nat (1810–60)

In 1846 Elnathan 'Nat' Flatman headed the first officially recognised jockeys' championship with 81 winners. He remained champion till 1853, his most successful season numerically being 1848 when he had 104 victories including the St Leger on Surplice. Born in Suffolk in 1810, the son of a small farmer, he became an apprentice in the Newmarket stables of William Cooper. At the time he weighed but 4 st. Although soon promoted to riding training trials, he did not have a mount in public till he was 19, a relatively late age for a first race ride.

Flatman was an honest professional in an age when racing's stables needed to be cleansed. He was a natural lightweight, which, coupled with his skill at riding two-year-olds and his reputation for honesty, secured him sufficient rides to become one of the first jockeys to earn £5,000 in a season. Such was his integrity that he would not give even a hint of the outcome of trials to anyone but the relevant owner and trainer. Unusually for a southern-based jockey of his time, he obtained many rides (and winners) at northern meetings, in particular after 1844 for John Scott's Malton stables. However, his favourite course was Ascot, where, although there was only one meeting a year, he rode over 100 winners including a dozen in 1845 and only one short of that in 1847.

Nat was regarded as a good jockey who used his head during a race rather than an intuitive horseman and he was certainly never considered an elegant rider. He won 10 Classics, the first in 1835 on Preserve in the One Thousand Guineas. No more came till the controversial Derby of 1844 when, although his mount Orlando was beaten into second place, the original winner Running Rein was subsequently disqualified for being over age. Another of his more famous races was in the 1850 Doncaster Cup when his ride, Lord Zetland's Voltigeur, lowered the colours of The Flying Dutchman for the first and only time.

He died, aged 50, at Newmarket in August 1860. His demise was accelerated by two accidents the previous year. First, his mount Sudbury fell at Bath and a splintered rib pierced Flatman's lung. Then, in September at Newmarket, he was kicked viciously by Golden Pippen as he dismounted the filly.

Further reading

Mortimer, R., Onslow, R. and Willett, P., *Biographical Encyclopaedia of British Flat Racing* (London: Macdonald and Jane's, 1978).
Tanner, M., *Great Jockeys of the Flat* (Enfield: Guinness, 1992).

Fordham, George (1837–87)

George Fordham became champion jockey in 1855 at the age of 18 and won the title a further 13 times, once sharing with Charles Maidment. He was apprenticed to Middleham trainer, Dick Drewitt, for whom his uncle was travelling head lad, and moved to Lewes when that trainer went south. His first race ride was in 1850 at nearby Brighton when, with heavy clothing and a large saddle making up his 3 st 8 lb to the required 5 st, he trailed in last. Next year aged 14 he gained his first victory in the Trial Stakes for two-year-olds on the same course.

In 1852 he won his first big race, the Cambridgeshire, but had to wait six more years for his initial Classic win, which came on Mayonnaise in the One Thousand Guineas, the first of seven successes in that Newmarket event, still a record for any jockey. He had a knack of riding fillies and also won five Oaks. Surprisingly for a jockey of his talent, he had only two victories in the Two Thousand Guineas, a solitary Derby (from 22 attempts), and not one St Leger (again from 22 appearances). His most productive season was 1862 when he won 166 races, but perhaps his greatest riding feat was at Stockbridge on 18 June 1867 when he won six races and deadheated in the seventh before losing the run-off. He also often rode in France and won the Grand Prix de Paris three times, the Prix du Jockey Club twice, and the Prix de Diane once.

He was known as 'The Demon', famous for his 'kidding' where he would feign that his horse was distressed but then come with a rush. His seat was ungainly with, for the time, very short leathers, but he had sound judgement of pace and a light touch which made him an ideal rider for young horses. He frequently rode without whip or spurs and was reluctant to strike a horse, except in the last few strides of a tight finish.

A rough and ready character, he eschewed the high life that his earnings could have brought. He enjoyed hunting, shooting, cricket, a hand of whist, and the odd practical joke. His weakness was alcohol. In 1875 he retired from the turf, lost heavily in continental stocks when duped by a French financier, and took refuge in the gin bottle. Sir George Chetwynd persuaded him to dry out and ride again: which he did to the tune of a further 482 winners, including five Classics. His final win, like his first, was at Brighton where he secured the 1883 Brighton Cup on Brag. He rode only twice the next season. His last race was at Windsor in August 1884 when he finished fourth on Aladdin in the Park Stakes.

After he won the 1853 Cambridgeshire, Mr W. Smith, the owner of the successful Little David, presented him with a whip inscribed 'honesty is the best policy'. He followed this maxim throughout his career and indeed refused to ride again for both William Day and Captain Machell when they accused him of not trying. He even reported Day to the Jockey Club Stewards for his comments.

Several contemporary jockeys and trainers, including Henry Custance, John Osborne, Richard Marsh, John Porter, and even Mat Dawson rated him a better all-round rider than Fred Archer. In a deathbed letter (now held in York Racing Museum) to fellow jockey, Charlie Wood, he expressed appreciation for the few 'fair friends, considering all others gave me up and at any moment I may go'. A silver plate on his coffin proclaimed 'Tis the pace that kills'.

Further reading

Mortimer, R., Onslow, R. and Willett, P., *Biographical Encyclopaedia of British Flat Racing* (London: Macdonald and Jane's, 1978).
Tanner, M. and Cranham, G., *Great Jockeys of the Past* (Enfield: Guinness, 1992).

France

France and Britain have been rivals in horseracing as in many fields. Even before Gladiateur, 'The Avenger of Waterloo', strode away with the Triple Crown in 1865 and first called into question the supremacy of the English thoroughbred, owners and trainers had eyed prizes across the water, and horses and jockeys had criss-crossed the Channel in pursuit of them. These raiding parties have taken place for more than 150 years, and the implementation in 1971 of the Pattern system for grading top European races was intended to encourage Anglo-French and other trans-European competition at the highest level.

To begin with, honours were evenly distributed. Top-class racing at Epsom Downs, Ascot, York, Doncaster and several other venues, had been established in Britain for over 30 years before the opening of the racecourse at Chantilly near Paris in 1834; when the inaugural running of the Prix du Jockey-Club, the French equivalent of the Derby, took place there in 1836, more than half a century had elapsed since the first Epsom Classic. Although the complacency of British racing men may have been shaken slightly when Beggarman, owned by the Duc d'Orleans, won the Goodwood Cup in 1840, they consoled themselves that he was English-bred. When the same race was won in 1853 by the French filly, Jouvence, she became the first French-bred animal to win a trophy in England, but at least she had been trained at Epsom by Ralph Sherwood. Revenge came 10 years later in the form of The Ranger, an English horse which triumphed in the first staging of the Grand Prix de Paris, the showpiece race at the recently opened Longchamp racecourse. Downright hostility, however, greeted the victory of Fille de l'Air, the first French-owned winner of an English Classic, the 1864 Oaks. Some said that the horse had to be escorted to the winners' enclosure by a group of hired prizefighters, others that the jockey had to be protected by mounted police with drawn sabres as he attempted to weigh in. The following year, however, dismay and despondency surrounded the victory of Gladiateur in the Derby. The horse was French-owned and bred, and trained by an Englishman who had learned his trade in France; it had already won the Two Thousand Guineas and was about to claim the St Leger, and, in 1866, the Ascot Gold Cup. So significant was Gladiateur to French racing that a life-size statue was erected in his memory at the main gates to Longchamp racecourse. His exploits heralded a new era in English–French flat-racing history.

The next 15 years saw a succession of French winners of major British races with little scope for retaliation as the French Classics were restricted to home-bred talent. Regular British participation in the Grand Prix resulted in only two victories, scant recompense for defeats in four Ascot Gold Cups, two Oaks, a St Leger, a Two Thousand Guineas and a further Derby. Fortunes were reversed in jump-racing, however. After the opening of the racecourse at Auteuil, Paris, in 1874, a succession of English horses raided France to pick up the major prizes, the Grand Steeple-Chase de Paris, by 1910 the richest jump race in the world, and the Grande Course de Haies, the top hurdle race. The only notable French victory on British soil was in the 1909 Grand National when Lutteur III, French-bred and ridden but trained in England, became the last five-year-old to win the race.

The presence at Chantilly, now the Newmarket of France, of a significant number of English trainers and jockeys, working for French owners, led to heavy criticism in Britain, particularly when their French charges walked off with English prizes. Tom Jennings, who had served his apprenticeship at Chantilly in the 1830s, became trainer for Count Frederic de Lagrange, the owner of Gladiateur, firstly in France but, after 1857, at Newmarket where he later trained for a number of French owners. An entire community of Englishmen and their families settled at Chantilly during the second half of the nineteenth century. English Classic winner The Flying Dutchman took up stud duties in France in 1858 and jockey Thomas Lane won the Prix du Jockey-Club and Prix de Diane (French Oaks) before scooping the Grand Prix six times in 12 years, including a four-season spell from 1890 to 1893. The British are still there. John Hammond moved to France after working as an assistant trainer in England and Ireland; he won the King George in 2000 with Montjeu, a year after his successes in the Irish Derby, Prix du Jockey-Club and the Arc. He also trained the top-class Suave Dancer to win the two major French races in 1991. From 1999 to 2001, David Loder ran a training establishment for two-year-olds at Evry, a former racecourse south of Paris, on behalf of the Maktoums.

French domination of English flat racing was at its peak after the Second World War. Although there had been severe disruption on both sides of the Channel, the immediate postwar years saw the sport flourish, largely to the detriment of British owners and trainers. The statistics speak for themselves. French horses filled the first three places in the 1946 Ascot Gold Cup, the

1954 Oaks and the 1957 King George while four French-bred horses finished in the first six in the 1948 Derby. Marcel Boussac, leading French owner 19 times in his own country, won the Derby, Oaks and St Leger in 1950 and was the top owner in Britain in 1950 and 1951, while his trainer, Charles Semblat, topped the British trainers' championship without setting foot in the country. Between 1948 and 1966 French-trained horses won nine Ascot Gold Cups and five King Georges in addition to 27 Classics. Included among these were Derby victories for the Francois Mathet-trained Phil Drake (1955) and Relko (1963), and in 1965 the horse generally reckoned to have been the finest Derby winner of the century, Sea Bird II, from the yard of Etienne Pollet. It seemed that higher levels of prize money in Britain attracted French entrants, and that the British emphasis on sprints and races for fast-maturing horses played into the hands of the French, who bred a far higher proportion of stayers and animals capable of racing over 10 furlongs.

The British were not without their triumphs. English victories in the Grand Prix of 1920 and 1921, the inaugural Arc in 1920 and the same race in 1948 turned into regular raids on major French prizes in the 1960s and 1970s. Mill Reef and Rheingold won the Arc in 1971 and 1973 while British sprinters walked off with the premier 5-furlong race, the Prix de l'Abbaye, five times between 1968 and 1973. With the French Classics now open to overseas competitors, Highclere won the Prix de Diane in 1974. The 1980s and 1990s also saw considerable British success with victories in the Prix du Jockey-Club for Old Vic, Sanglamore and Celtic Swing in 1989, 1990 and 1995, the Prix de Diane for Indian Skimmer and Sil Sila in 1987 and 1996, and the Arc for Dancing Brave, Carroll House and Lammtarra in 1986, 1989 and 1995. British horses continued to dominate the top French sprints, from the triumvirate of Marwell, Sharpo and Habibti in consecutive years (1981–83), through Lochsong in 1993 and 1994, to the 2002 winner Continent.

With the exception of 1976, when jockey Yves Saint-Martin won three English Classics on French-trained horses, the recent French impact on elite British flat racing has been more limited. Trainer Francois Boutin was responsible for four Classic wins including the One Thousand Guineas with Miesque (1987); Andre Fabre trained Toulon (1991 St Leger), Zafonic and Intrepidity (1993 Two Thousand Guineas and Oaks), and Pennekamp (1995 Two Thousand Guineas) while Criquette Head won the One Thousand Guineas three times with Ma Biche (1983), ridden by brother Freddie, Ravinella (1988) and Hatoof (1992). Jockey Olivier Peslier, four-time champion in France from 1996 to 2000 has had several Group One successes in Britain, most notably with the Luca Cumani trained High-Rise in the 1998 Derby. However, only one French colt won a British Group race in 1998, the year in which British-trained equivalents occupied the first four places in the Poule d'Essai des Poulains (French Two Thousand Guineas). Increased levels of prize money in France in the final decades of the twentieth century and richer pickings elsewhere have largely contributed to French disregard of British racing. British trainers, in contrast, are increasingly sending their strings to France, to contest the opening races of the flat season at Cagnes-sur-Mer in January and February or one of the valuable Group races at Saint-Cloud or Deauville. The annual

British pilgrimage to Longchamp for the Arc meeting in early October has become a highlight of the racing calendar although there was little to cheer for some years until the Godolphin-owned Sakhee and Marienbard landed the prize in consecutive years, 2001 and 2002.

In National Hunt racing, English trainers have increasingly looked to France for prospective young steeplechasers while French handler Francois Doumen has been waging a one-man campaign on British soil for almost two decades. When Nupsala won the King George VI Chase in 1987 he was the first French jumper to win in Britain for 25 years. Since then Doumen has won the race four times with The Fellow (1991 and 1992), Algan (1994) and First Gold (2000). His greatest success has been with The Fellow, Cheltenham Gold Cup winner of 1994, and runner-up in 1991 and 1992. The latest top-class French raider, Jair du Cochet, even had the temerity to beat Britain's current favourite steeplechaser, Best Mate, in November 2003. Rivalry and inter-connections between French and British racing still abound at the beginning of the twenty-first century.

Further reading

Magee, S., *The Channel Four Book of Racing* (London: Hamlyn, 1995).
Mortimer, R., *The Flat* (London: Allen and Unwin, 1979).

Francome, John (1952–)

National Hunt rider, John Francome was the first jump jockey to ride four consecutive centuries of winners and one of the few to have ridden over 1,000 winners. He was champion seven times, the first in 1975–76. Six years later, in a memorable demonstration of sportsmanship, he shared the championship with Peter Scudamore. After reaching the same total of winners as his rival, who had been well in the lead for the title till he was sidelined with a broken leg, Francome refused any more rides so as not to deprive his fellow rider of the title.

Son of a railway fireman at Swindon who later turned to building, he left school in 1969 aged 16, spent a month working in a car repair shop and then became an apprentice with Fred Winter in Lambourn. He claimed that the trainer liked his sense of humour: when asked what his lightest weight was he had replied '7 lb 3 oz'! Francome had had some riding experience.

His parents bought his first pony from the local milkman but initially they could not also afford a saddle. Riding bareback taught Francome how to grip properly with his legs. He graduated to junior international honours in show-jumping and hunted on a regular basis. His first racing mount, Multi Grey was a winner. His second resulted in a fall and a broken wrist, demonstrating the dangers of a novice rider on a novice chaser!

Francome did not hold back on his opinions and hence his career was not without incident. He had no time for pompous officials and insisted that the race stewards call him Mr Francome rather than the unprefixed Francome many of them had used to demean riders. The racing establishment had its revenge when in 1978 he was suspended for his relationship with bookmaker

John Banks. The racing authorities charged him with supplying confidential information to Banks. Francome openly admitted that he had talked to Banks about horses but said that he did not know that this was against the *Rules of Racing*, an anthology that he had never read! He also maintained that the information was not confidential and that he had never stopped a horse as racetrack rumour was implying. All this was to no avail. Francome was fined £750 and suspended for six weeks; Banks had to pay £2,500 and was banned from all racecourses for three years.

Despite the impression that he gave of being laid-back, he actually worked very hard for his success. He rode his last winner in 1985, reaching a grand total of 1,138, a record not broken till 1989, ironically by Peter Scudamore. Despite his winning totals he gained success in only one Cheltenham Gold Cup (in 1978 on Midnight Court) and one Champion Hurdle (in 1981 on Sea Pigeon) and never won a Grand National.

On quitting the saddle he had a brief and unsuccessful flirtation with training – perhaps it was a portent that his first runner fell and died – before becoming a newspaper columnist, best-selling novelist, and a television racing pundit where his no-frills directness have made him popular. Advertised as being 'out of the same stable as Dick Francis' he has produced a book a year since his retirement, all of them, of course, based on horseracing.

Further reading

Francome, J., *Born Lucky: An Autobiography* (London: Pelham, 1985).

Moneybox

When **Falbrav** and Frankie Dettori won the Japan Cup in 2002, they picked up a first prize of £1,328,000.

Favourites, or joint favourites, the shortest-priced horses in the betting, win roughly 40 per cent of all races.

Fet won the Cesarewitch in October 1936 having been bought for 200 guineas after a selling race only two months earlier.

Flying Water, winner of the 1976 One Thousand Guineas, was one of a hat trick of English Classic successes for French owner Daniel Wildenstein, enabling him to top the leading owner table that year with £244,501; the others were Oaks winner Pawneese and St Leger winner Crow.

Foinavon (1967) was not the only 100–1 winner of the Grand National in the twentieth century; there were three others, Tipperary Tim (1928), Gregalach (1929) and Caughoo (1947).

A forfeit is paid by a horse's connections if it is withdrawn from a race.

A day at the races 1800

I'm off to the St Leger. A Yorkshire squire has to support his big race meeting. Local man, Colonel Anthony St Leger, began it in 1776, first of the great races for three-year-olds. They've tried to copy it down south, but the Derby and Oaks, they don't test the best. They run 14 furlongs up here at Doncaster, not the 12 or so they do at Epsom. Any horse can sprint but how many of them can keep up a good pace? That's what we look for at Donny.

Some of my labourers will walk the 15 miles to the Town Moor. And back for the next day's work. Not me. I'll stay the full three days. There's plenty to do in the town. The City Theatre has a new play on and the Mayor is hosting a civic dinner. Then, of course, there's the gambling clubs. 'Hells' some people call them but if you've got the money what's wrong with cards? Sithee, I don't hold with those thimblemen at the course. The public are too gullible. Why don't they realise the pea is never under the thimble at all but hidden in his long fingernail?

I don't know too much about the runners this year. I've subscribed to Weatherbys' *Calendar* since '93 – you get your name mentioned inside – but none of these St Leger horses raced as two-year-olds so you've got to rely on their pedigrees. Young Weatherby's *Stud Book* can be handy for that, but I bet none of them have the class of Hambletonian. Great Yorkshire horse, he was. He were odds on when he won St Leger in '95. Mind you I got better than that with Ogden as I put my money on a couple of months before the race. Probably I'll back Champion this time. Good name for a good Yorkshire horse. Some folks reckon his owner Mr Wilson is from Doncaster but he's from Tadcaster. That's Yorkshire enough for me.

You know, Yorkshire really is the place for horseracing. We've the Kiplingcotes race that's been run since sixteen hundred and odd, more Royal Plates than anywhere else, and the St Leger itself. And we've got plenty of horses. Never understood why the Jockey Club insisted on basing itself at Newmarket. Dreadful place. Too many different courses. You never know where you are supposed to be. Saw Buckle ride Hambletonian there last year against that southern horse. Plenty of us Tykes went down to support him. Won by a neck but I knew me money were safe. We breed tough horses up here.

Yon Buckle's not a bad rider for a southerner, but the best jockeys come from up north. Chifney had to cheat to beat them, you know. I remember seeing John Singleton win that first St Leger. Saw John Jackson win it in '91 and Bill Pierse in '93. And Ben Smith, there was a man. I was at York four years ago when a horse kicked him at the start but he won the race. Four miles, it was. Turned out he had a broken leg. Tell you what. I'm reet certain that if that Napoleon fellow invaded up here, half a dozen Yorkshire jockeys would see him off.

G

Horsebox

Game Spirit, numerically the most successful horse owned by the Queen Mother, won 21 races and ran third in the 1974 Cheltenham Gold Cup but dropped dead after a race at Newbury, his favourite track, in 1977.

Glass Slipper was the dam of a Classic winner in two consecutive seasons; Light Cavalry by Brigadier Gerard, St Leger winner of 1980 and Fairy Footsteps by Mill Reef, One Thousand Guineas winner in 1981.

Gingembre won the Scottish Grand National in 2001, beating the largest post-war field for the event (30 runners).

Gloria Victis, the young Martin Pipe-trained winner of the Racing Post Chase in 2000, was killed only weeks later attempting to win the Cheltenham Gold Cup as a 6-year-old, a feat only achieved three times since the war (Fortina 1947, Mont Tremblant 1952 and Mill House 1963).

Golan won the Two Thousand Guineas in 2001, the seventh Classic winner for jockey Kieren Fallon and the tenth for trainer Michael Stoute.

Golden Fleece, a son of Nijinsky, trained in Ireland by Vincent O'Brien and unbeaten in three races, won the Epsom Derby in 1982 and never won again – he died in 1984.

Gambling

See Betting.

General Stud Book

The thoroughbred racehorse has the best-documented genealogy of any species. Whereas humans often have trouble tracing their family trees back before 1837 when birth registration became compulsory in Britain, virtually the entire thoroughbred population can be tracked back 40 or so generations. Or so we used to think. James Weatherby, nephew of the man who had become the Jockey Club's racing administrator, began this historical record with his publication of the *General Stud Book* in 1791, though it is now recognised that William Sydney Towers undertook the actual research. Weatherbys has maintained the records for

Britain and Ireland ever since and the model has been emulated throughout the world.

One reason for the appearance of the *Stud Book* was to offset two problems that were bedevilling racing: the passing off of horses of supposedly fashionable pedigrees when selling and the pretence that horses were badly bred when negotiating the terms of match races. Once owners accepted the value of the work it became an authoritative source. These days to be eligible for the *General Stud Book*, a horse must trace all lines of its pedigree to other animals already registered there (or in one of the other 50 or so approved studbooks elsewhere in the world) for at least eight or nine crosses of pure blood. It must also be shown that the turf performance of the immediate family is such as to warrant a belief in purity of the blood.

The latter clause suggests that the *Stud Book* by itself is not sufficient proof that a horse is a thoroughbred, interestingly a term that does not appear in the *Stud Book* until the 1822 edition. Clearly some early pedigrees could not be completely verified. Reliant as he was on private studbooks and early racing results, Towers could not guarantee the absolute accuracy of his first volume. There were few written inventories of studs for him to consult; names of horses often changed with their ownership; some horses, especially female, were not named at all; and authenticating dates was difficult. Later document-based research, however, revealed only a few errors and it has been assumed to be reasonably reliable.

Since the late 1980s the *Stud Book* has been maintained under a strict registration process that requires the verification of parentage by blood-typing and DNA analysis. Any of the very few mistakes detected have been quickly corrected. However more recent advances in genetic technology have exposed long-standing errors in the *Stud Book* entries. Horses inherit most of their DNA from both parents, but mitochondrial DNA is passed on only through the female line and is passed on in its entirety. Hence all members of a family back to the foundation mare should have possessed the same mitochondrial DNA. However, in 2002 a study by geneticists, Dr Emmeline Hill and Professor Patrick Cunningham, of 100 thoroughbreds from supposedly 19 distinct families revealed that nearly half had at least one animal whose DNA sequence did not match the rest of the family members. The early history of the thoroughbred will have to be rewritten. Fortunately DNA analysis, as well as discovering the anomalies, can be used to correct them. Whether it matters to modern breeders that the historical record is wrong is a moot point. Most, if not all, would argue that the influence of distant ancestors is now negligible and that the recent ancestry of the horses with which they are immediately concerned is not in question.

Further reading

Hill, E.W. *et al.*, 'History and Integrity of Throughbred Dam Lines Revealed in Equine mtDNA Variation', *Animal Genetics* 33.4, 2002, 287–294.

Prior, C.W., *The History of the Racing Calendar and Stud Book* (Sporting Life: London, 1926).

See also Breeding.

Geography

The geography of horseracing is largely about the location of racecourses. To some extent it is also concerned with the sites of training yards across Britain but these tend to congregate near courses. The major training centres are situated in areas where there are significant opportunities for horses to work out and race: Middleham, with its adjacent moor, and Malton in Yorkshire, and Lambourn on the Berkshire Downs, all with numerous racetracks nearby, and Newmarket, the centre of thoroughbred racing and the wide expanses of Newmarket Heath.

Racecourses, together with golf courses, form the largest sites on the sporting landscape. In the days before enclosure, the main requirement for racing was an area of relatively flat, well-drained land that was sufficiently accessible to attract a crowd, although some meetings were deliberately held on the estates of the nobility to render them private affairs. Common land, such as the Town Moor at Doncaster, provided a popular venue. River meadows and even beaches were appropriated for racing but problems with floods, tides and heavy going restricted their use. York races had to be relocated early in the eighteenth century because the River Ouse regularly burst its banks (it still does!) while racing on the sands at Leith near Edinburgh was abandoned in 1816 in favour of a permanent site on the sandy soils of Musselburgh Links, where the course still shares its home with a golf club. Those tracks which have continued to occupy river banks – Windsor, Worcester and Nottingham, to name a few – run the risk of soft ground at best and regular abandonment at worst. Perth on the banks of the River Tay lost its flagship April meeting in two consecutive years (1999 and 2000) through waterlogging.

History has left its mark on the landscape of British racing in numerous ways. The availability of vast open spaces has taken precedence over the suitability of the land, saddling racecourses with variable soils, awkward microclimates and unusual shapes. Many meetings take place on sites and at times of the year mapped out in the first half of the nineteenth century or even earlier, which is why Chester racecourse finds itself sandwiched between the city walls and the River Dee, with a tight circuit on which horses are almost constantly turning, and with its major fixture in May, as it has been since 1758. Bath, Brighton and Goodwood are situated on hill tops with the consequent risk of low cloud and sea mist; Exeter borders Dartmoor and is susceptible to fog; Pontefract with its main meetings in high summer used to suffer from hard going before the introduction of a watering system; and many courses in the Midlands have to put up with heavy clay soils. Following the contours of the land or avoiding areas of poor drainage have resulted in strange layouts – Brighton, Goodwood and Epsom Downs are constrained by their hilly positions, York by the need to skirt the boggier sections of the flat Knavesmire (the word 'mire' is significant).

Racing on fair days and holidays, on town land or parkland, took place widely throughout Britain during the nineteenth century. At the peak of its popularity, authorised flat-race meetings were held at 140 different venues, not counting the local events too small-scale to feature in the official records. By 1904, the number was reduced to 50 and their location was far more concentrated. By 2000, only 17 purely flat racecourses were left, together with 18 dual flat and jumps courses, including three all-weather, and 24 National Hunt tracks. The most northerly course is Perth, the most southerly Newton Abbot, both small jump courses. There is no flat racing in the West Country beyond Bath or in Wales beyond the border town of Chepstow. Racing in Scotland, never popular in the north, had virtually retrenched to the Central Lowlands by the middle of the nineteenth century. Eight of the strictly flat race courses occupy positions south of, and including, Newmarket, while six of the remaining nine are in Yorkshire. Lancashire, north of Haydock Park, is a completely racing-free zone; so are Hampshire and Dorset; and there are no courses north of the Thames from the coast of Essex to Towcester, north-west of Milton Keynes.

How and why the racecourse map of Britain has evolved in this way is debatable and is largely a legacy of nineteenth-century change. Only a few additional courses – Newbury 1905, Fontwell Park 1924, Chepstow 1926 and Taunton 1927 – have opened their gates during the past hundred years although all-weather circuits have developed at existing venues, and 15 tracks have closed since 1948. It seems likely that changes to Jockey Club rules in the 1870s put paid to numerous small race meetings which were unable to afford the additional prize money required. The advent of enclosed courses led to a shift from rural to urban population centres – Sandown and Kempton Parks, for example, in suburban London, and Leicester, Nottingham and Hamilton Park near Glasgow were all opened in the last decades of the century. Inadequate transport may have sounded the death knell for race meetings in some of the more remote parts of the south-west, Wales and East Anglia, further concentrating racing into central and southern areas. The exception to this trend has been Yorkshire, always a heartland of British racing which still boasts of the 59 existing courses. Of the 15 closures in the post-1945 period, Bogside and Lanark in Scotland were denied further Levy Board finance, a fate which also befell Alexandra Palace, Lewes, Lincoln and Rothbury. Others such as Birmingham, Hurst Park and Manchester were sold to property developers, a far more lucrative option for their racecourse executives than staging race meetings. A few including Musselburgh and Aintree are only around today because of strenuous campaigns to save them.

The location of several courses make them heavily dependent on holiday meetings. Newton Abbot in south Devon concentrates most of its fixtures in the summer to take advantage of tourists; Brighton, Redcar and Yarmouth are also seaside, holidaymaker tracks featuring flat racing; Cartmel in the Lake District only races on the late spring and summer bank holidays while several small jump tracks from Perth to Worcester are officially summer National Hunt courses. Regular summer evening meetings are staged near large population centres, especially near London with Kempton Park and Windsor offering at least half-a-dozen each from May to August to attract commuters after a day's work. Numerous courses benefit from close proximity to railways, some – Epsom, Kempton, Newbury, Sandown and Southwell – have adjacent stations. For most, however, good access by road and adequate car parking have become essential as they try to overcome their Georgian and Victorian heritage in the battle to entice twenty-first century spectators with money and leisure to spare.

Further reading

Magee, S. (ed.), *The Channel Four Racing Guide to Racecourses* (London: Channel 4 Books, 1998).
Pitt, Chris, *A Long Time Gone* (Halifax: Portway, 1996).

See also Racecourses.

Going

Phil Bull, professional punter and inventor of the *Timeform* system of rating racehorses, said 50 years ago that the state of the ground was the most critical element in assessing a race. It was 'a variable that greatly affects performance'. Listen to almost any interview with a trainer or jockey today and you will hear a similar story: 'the horse didn't act on the going,' (from a losing rider), 'he 'll love the ground, he's a real mudlark,' (from a trainer sending out a horse on a heavy track). The condition of the racetrack can have far-reaching consequences, not only affecting the outcome of a race but sometimes increasing the risk of injury to racehorses and jeopardising their future careers. No wonder trainers become angry with any clerk of the course who misjudges the state of the going, allowing racing to go ahead when it should have been called off, or watering injudiciously. Conversely, given the British climate, who would be a clerk of the course attempting to follow the Jockey Club instruction to aim for good going at jump meetings and good to firm on the flat?

Traditionally the clerk of the course assessed the going by prodding a stick into the earth as he walked the track or by gut feeling aided by a judicious boot heel. Although the penetrometer, a more scientific device using a metal rod and weights, is widely employed abroad, it was pronounced unsuitable for British racecourses after trials in the 1990s, resulting in a continued tension between racecourses eager to attract sizeable fields and competitive racing, and trainers anxious to run horses in optimum conditions. It is hoped that the latest electro-mechanical device – the Goingstick – will finally solve the problem of assessing racecourse turf but until this latest invention is given the green light by Jockey Club officials, racecourses will continue to rely on unscientific measures.

Turf racing vocabulary includes seven categories to describe the ground conditions at a racecourse and horses will run or sometimes be withdrawn on the strength of the present situation, the predicted weather and any potential change in the going. All-weather tracks have only three categories of going: fast, standard and slow. The official turf descriptions – heavy, soft, good to soft (it used to be called 'yielding'), good, good to firm, firm, hard – are available well in advance of a race meeting and updated as necessary to take account of rain, frost, drought or other meteorological circumstances. Conditions can change rapidly, and not always evenly, on a racecourse. A sustained period of heavy rain, for example, can result in good going turning uniformly soft or irregular deterioration of the track, leading to hybrid surfaces such as 'good to soft, soft in places.' Prolonged rain on already heavy ground may produce waterlogging and the abandonment of a fixture, particularly on courses with poor-draining clay sub-soils. The unusually wet winters of 2000 and 2001 caused significant problems for a number of courses, especially those at risk of flooding from nearby rivers. Maintenance and upgrading of drainage is therefore a matter of great importance.

A lack of rain causes other difficulties. Strong spring sun and the rapid drying out of ground on which large fields have already run can cause uneven and dangerous surfaces. In summer, trainers are often unwilling to run their charges on ground labelled firm or, in a really dry season, hard, although these conditions frequently produce course record times. The notorious drought of 1976 saw the temporary closure of several courses when watering was banned, while others continued to operate with small fields on bone dry surfaces. Since then, major racetracks have installed permanent irrigation systems but others, particularly small, rural jump courses often have to rely on portable sprays. For some, costs are prohibitive while the practical difficulties of watering a racecourse that extends over 2 miles can result in damaging delays. And the problems don't stop there. Pop-up sprinklers are unable to water evenly, resulting in patchy, false ground. Specialist turf consultants have suggested that watering encourages grass with a shallow root structure which is unable to withstand frost, leading to substandard and worn surfaces the following spring. This is even more of a problem for those courses whose flat-race surface doubles up as a hurdle track during the winter months. Detailed surveys have also shown that few racecourses can boast uniform soil depth and type, making the job of ground maintenance particularly difficult. Varying soils and exposures can lead to surface inconsistencies, and jockeys will often be seen heading their mounts towards particular strips of ground to take advantage of better conditions.

Winter jump racing has its own special problems. The take-off and landing sides of fences begin to resemble the bare, muddy goal mouths of 1960s' football grounds after fields of thundering horses have battered their way round a course, and there is no chance of recovery in winter when the grass has stopped growing. On wider tracks, it is sometimes possible to move the running rails in an effort to minimise the wear and tear on a concentrated area, and palletised turf technology, with trays of new grass to replace worn areas, has been suggested as a solution to the damage around fences. All of this, however, costs money which only the largest and most prestigious National Hunt courses could afford. Aintree also has to deal with the Melling Road which crosses the racecourse and has to be adequately covered during race meetings. A similar problem affects Epsom Downs and Ascot where grass pallets have been tried out.

Even the all-weather courses are not immune to track difficulties. Problems of drainage and inconsistency of surface led to the replacement of the original Fibresand material at Lingfield with the more reliable Polytrack, a solution which may also have to be implemented at Wolverhampton after rain forced the abandonment of a meeting in December 2003. Adverse weather can produce patchy surfaces at artificial as well as turf courses, resulting in racing that is not only unfair but sometimes dangerous. The state of the going continues to be a thorny problem for racecourse officials, trainers, jockeys and punters, just as it was in Phil Bull's day.

Further reading

Kay, J. and Vamplew, W., *Weatherbeaten: Sport in the British Climate* (Edinburgh: Mainstream, 2002).

See also All-weather racing, Weather.

Golden Miller (1927–57) – by Goldcourt out of Miller's Pride

Golden Miller's achievements were unique and unlikely to be repeated. He won the Cheltenham Gold Cup on five consecutive occasions between 1932 and 1936, and the Grand National in 1934, the only horse ever to have achieved the double in one season. His exploits made him the first National Hunt racing superstar, the Arkle or Desert Orchid of his era and the most popular steeplechaser of the 1930s.

Golden Miller was foaled in 1927 near Dublin and his early years saw some modest success. Trained at Newmarket by Basil Briscoe, he was unplaced in his first hurdle race in 1930 but won at Leicester and Nottingham the following year, before his debut over fences, in which he was second. He continued to contest hurdle races in the autumn of 1931 before being sold for 6,000 guineas to Miss Dorothy Paget and embarking on a steeplechase career which lasted seven years. His four races in early 1932 included a win and a second, culminating in the Cheltenham Gold Cup which he won comfortably under Ted Leader. The 1932–33 season saw four more victories and a second Gold Cup although his first attempt at the Grand National, a far more lucrative and prestigious race at that time, ended in failure.

The following season saw his greatest triumphs. Partnered by champion jockey Gerry Wilson, he won his third Gold Cup, as 6–5 favourite, before returning to Aintree, a course which apparently did not suit his style of jumping. This time, however, he won the Grand National by five lengths and his record-breaking victory was not surpassed until 1973, when the duel between Crisp and Red Rum resulted in a faster race. Although he took part in three further Nationals, once, in 1935, as the hottest ante-post favourite ever for the race, he never again completed the course, refusing to jump the eleventh fence on two occasions. The controversy surrounding his 1935 failure resulted in a change of trainer and he finished his racing days with Owen Anthony.

But he made the Cheltenham Gold Cup his own. He won in record time in 1935, and, with Evan Williams up, triumphed for the fifth year in succession in 1936, at odds of 21–20. A sixth consecutive win was ruled out in 1937 when bad weather forced the abandonment of the National Hunt Festival and by 1938, Golden Miller, now 11 years old, was past his peak. He could only finish second, his sole defeat at Cheltenham, and was retired after one more race, having won 29 of his 55 starts without ever falling.

In retirement, the bay gelding remained a popular hero, making guest appearances at horse shows. He was finally put down in 1957, at the age of 30, and his statue now overlooks the paddock at Cheltenham.

Further reading

Blaxford, G., *Golden Miller* (London: Constable, 1972).
Herbert, I. and Smyly, P., *The Winter Kings* (London: Penguin, 1989).

Goodwood

Goodwood racecourse, high on the Sussex Downs above Chichester, is best known for its flagship summer meeting to which the word 'glorious' is often applied. Following Royal Ascot in June, its four days of racing in late July signalled the end of the London social season and remained the sole fixture at the course until the 1960s. It now hosts 20 flat racing days each year with quality events in May and August as well as 'Glorious Goodwood', one of the few British flat-race meetings to extend over five consecutive days.

The first public race meeting took place here in 1802 on the Duke of Richmond's estate and the family have continued to be involved with racing ever since. Lord George Bentinck, an influential supporter of the Turf, was closely associated with the development of the course during the 1830s. The Goodwood Cup was inaugurated in 1812, the Nassau Stakes and the Stewards' Cup, still a great betting handicap over 6 furlongs, in 1840 and the Sussex Stakes, run over a mile, in 1841. The July meeting, however, was invariably an occasion for wealthy and fashionable society to gather, with the racing sometimes little more than a sideshow; Edward VII was a regular visitor at the house parties organised at Goodwood House in the early twentieth century. However, like its elite southern rivals, Epsom Downs and Ascot, Goodwood also offered viewing for the masses, from a picnic vantage point on Trundle Hill. Today the members' lawns, seafood restaurants and champagne bars are still prominent but with the advent of summer Sunday and evening meetings, jazz and steel bands and family days complete with creche and children's playground, Goodwood appears to have finally shaken off its aristocratic and exclusive reputation.

The course itself, on a crest of the Downs, is unique, even bizarre, both in shape and setting, with a chalky subsoil which ensures that it rarely suffers from heavy going. Commanding spectacular views of the English Channel on a clear day, it has a 6-furlong straight, a looping triangular circuit for longer races and two alternative bends, the Top and Lower. With its confusing layout and steepish, undulating gradients – the 5-furlong track is mostly downhill and fast – it is a course for agile horses and alert jockeys. Navigational errors have been made, not just on those days when visibility is reduced by sea mist!

Two Group One races are staged at Goodwood, the Sussex Stakes over a mile and the Nassau Stakes over 10 furlongs. The Sussex Stakes, originally for three-year-olds, is now open to four-year-olds and over, and provides the first Group One opportunity for younger milers to take on more mature rivals. With only ten older horses scooping the prize in the last 43 renewals, the Sussex Stakes continues to be won by the top three-year-olds, from Petite Etoile (1959) and Brigadier Gerard (1971) to recent champions Giant's Causeway (2000) and Rock of Gibraltar (2002). The Nassau Stakes, elevated to Group One status in 1999, is for fillies and mares of three years old and over. Amongst the illustrious winners have been La Flèche (1892), Sceptre (1902) and Pretty Polly (1904) while recent successes include Crimplene (2000), one of the top three-year-old fillies of the year. The July fixture also includes major races such as the Group Two Richmond Stakes for two-year-olds, the Group Three Gordon Stakes and the Goodwood Cup over 2 miles, won three times by the much-loved Double Trigger (1995, 1997, 1998). The Stewards' Cup has become so popular in recent years that there is now a consolation Stewards' Sprint Handicap for horses balloted out of the main event. Earlier meetings feature Classic trials and August sees the Celebration Mile.

Among its other claims to fame, Goodwood was the first British course to install a public address system in 1952 and, allegedly, the first to embrace that type of corporate hospitality in which grandstand boxes face away from the racetrack! It also saw the first British Pattern race win for Sheikh Mohammed Al Maktoum in 1977 when Hatta won the Group Three Molecomb Stakes, while in 1987 it was the venue for Frankie Dettori's first winning ride in Britain on Lizzy Hare.

Further reading

Ennor, G., Onslow, R. and Cecil, C., *Glorious Goodwood* (London: Kenneth Mason, 2002).
Lee, A., *The Course Inspector* (London: CollinsWillow, 2001).
Tyrrel, J., *Racecourses on the Flat* (Marlborough: Crowood Press, 1989).
www.goodwood.co.uk

Grand National

The Grand National is the most famous steeplechase in the world. More reams of paper have probably been devoted to its history than any other race and for over 150 years it has attracted international competitors and global interest. It has been subjected to false starts, bomb scares, animal rights protests, blizzards and threats of extinction. It has turned horses such as Devon Loch and Red Rum into household names and immortalised Captain Martin Becher. It has been broadcast annually to a worldwide audience of 500 million and shamelessly overhyped. Its uniqueness – the length of the race ($4\frac{1}{2}$ miles), the challenge of the 30 fences, and the drama and controversy which always seem to surround the event – have ensured that it is not only a focus for the jump racing fraternity but for the public at large.

The long history of the race (159 renewals) and the large number of runners and riders (now restricted to 40 but peaking at 66 in 1929) make it a paradise for statisticians and anoraks. Apart from the obvious records – starters, fallers, finishers, highest–lowest winning odds, fastest times, winning margins, oldest–youngest horses and jockeys – there are a seemingly endless number of 'firsts'. The first Royal victory was in 1900 when Ambush II won for Edward, Prince of Wales and then became the first horse to represent a reigning monarch three years later (though he failed to complete the course on that occasion). The first radio broadcast took place in 1927, the first Saturday race was in 1947 (it had previously been run on Fridays), and it was televised for the first time in 1960. Charity was the first mare to win (1841), Lady Nelson was the first female winning owner (of Ally Sloper in 1915), Charlotte Brew was the first woman rider to compete (1977), Geraldine Rees was the first to complete the course (1982), and Jenny Pitman was the first and so far the only female trainer to send out a National winner (with Corbiere in 1983, and Royal Athlete in 1995).

Controversy has surrounded the race since the very beginning. Although most historians accepted that the first Liverpool Great Steeple Chase, won by Jem Mason on Lottery, took place at Aintree in 1839, recent research has suggested that the 'Liverpool Grand Steeple-Chase' of 29 February 1836 was in fact the inaugural 'Grand National', a name finally bestowed on the race in 1847. Late twentieth-century protests about cruelty to horses, and criticisms of the stiff fences and unreasonable dangers of the race are just the latest in a century-old debate about Aintree's most famous spectacle. A close finish between The Colonel and The Doctor in 1870 allegedly resulted in a summons against the losing jockey, brought by the Society for the Prevention of Cruelty to Animals for excessive whipping. When only 3 out of 32 finished without a fall in 1922, the RSPCA protested again.

The unique Aintree fences have often been condemned, sometimes unreasonably. As long ago as 1863, modifications were made to reduce their size and further alterations took place in 1870. Much publicity attended the unveiling of the 'new' Becher's Brook in autumn 1989 after the deaths of two horses there six months previously. Sixty years earlier, a similar incident had occurred at the Canal Turn resulting in such a shambles that half the field was halted. Only one horse, 100–1 shot Tipperary Tim completed the course without falling and press reports were scathing, dubbing the race 'burlesque steeplechasing.' The ditch was removed before the 1929 race. The new-look Becher's also saw the filling-in of the notorious brook, together with the removal of the landing-side 'lip' to prevent animals slipping backwards and becoming fatally wedged. One of the most significant changes took place in 1960 after a series of equine deaths. The fences, virtually perpendicular, were henceforth sloped on the take-off side to allow horses to stand off and gain the necessary height for clearing the obstacles.

Supporters of the Grand National have argued for decades that many of the mishaps occur not because the fences are dangerous but as a result of the mediocrity and inexperience of the horses and riders. The charge to the first obstacle has frequently resulted in the decimation of the field – 12 fell there in 1951, 10 in 1952, 10 in 1982 and 5 in 1998. This had nothing to do with the difficulty of the fence but resulted from the speed at which the horses thundered towards it and simply misjudged their first jump. After the record-breaking 66 had tackled the course in 1929 (47 were already out by the halfway point) and over 40 in the two subsequent years, restrictions were introduced in 1932 in an attempt to keep out the worst contenders. In future any horse entered for the race had to have been previously placed in a steeplechase at Liverpool or in one worth at least £200 to the winner, and of at least 3 miles, elsewhere. Consistency, however, was not the strong point of the race organisers. In 1937 minimum weights which had been raised to 10 st 7 lb were lowered again to 10 st, once more encouraging indifferent entrants.

The popularity and excitement of the Grand National have tended to over-shadow the fact that it has not been a contest for great champion steeple-chasers throughout its history but a handicap for sometimes very moderate jumpers. For the first few renewals, all entrants carried 12 st but since 1843, weight and chance have played a significant part in the outcome of the race. During the nineteenth and early twentieth centuries it offered generous prize money and, with few competing chases, attracted a higher quality of field than in the 1920s and, particularly, in the post-1945 period. When Golden Miller won five Cheltenham Gold Cups in the 1930s, it was still necessary for him to demonstrate his class by taking part in the Grand National as well; he remains the only horse to have won both races in one season (1934).

The status of the two contests was reversed after the war. The much publi-cised and oft-recounted stories surrounding the sale of Aintree racecourse and uncertainty about the future of the National itself throughout the 1960s and 1970s did nothing to enhance its reputation or the quality of the horses taking part. Popular 1970s' hero Red Rum, the only three-time winner of the race, was nevertheless a resolute galloper and would have struggled to compete success-fully in the now more prestigious Gold Cup while it was no longer thought nec-essary for steeplechase champions such as Arkle and Desert Orchid to prove their superiority (or take unnecessary risks) in the Grand National. The pres-tige of the race hit an all-time low in the aftermath of the 1993 starting gate fiasco – the only instance in its history when it was declared void – but sub-stantial sponsorship and racecourse improvements in recent years have helped to maintain public interest and equine numbers. The kudos of being a National winner and the rapid escalation of prize money have continued to tempt the owners of some superior horses to Aintree.

The worldwide fame of the Grand National has also led to many overseas entries in the shape of owners, horses and jockeys. The French Viscomte de Namurs owned the 1862 winner Huntsman, the Hungarian Count Charles Kinsky both owned and rode Zoedone to victory in 1883 and the American actor and film star Gregory Peck visited Aintree in 1968 to see his horse Different Class gain third place. Two Soviet horses, Grifel and Reljef and their jockeys took part in 1961; Czech rider Vaclav Chaloupka twice competed, in 1986 on Essex and in 1991 with Fraze; and 18-year-old Thierry Doumen, son of trainer Francois, had his first National ride in 1998. Few can compare, however, with the Spanish Duque d'Alburquerque whose fixation with the National apparently began when he saw a film of the race at the age of eight. Between 1952 and 1976 he competed regularly, unsuccessfully and often painfully, suffering numerous injuries along the way. In 1974 at the age of 55 he finally completed the course in eighth place. He tried again in 1976 but was badly injured although he would have persisted with his attempts to win if the Jockey Club had not introduced a medical examination for prospective riders.

Now the third-richest race in Britain, the Grand National is viewed even in the twenty-first century as a national institution. Ordinary people who have little interest in horseracing and who seldom venture inside a betting shop will read about, tune in to and bet on the National. It has regularly attracted a domestic television audience of 10–15 million and the volume of bets on the race is four times higher than on the next most popular event, the Epsom Derby: one-third of the adult population is said to gamble an average of £6 each. Even those who normally ignore racing are at least aware, from the amount of media coverage, that something exceptional is taking place in a suburb of Liverpool at around 4 pm on a Saturday in early April.

Further reading

Green, R., *National Heroes. The Aintree Legend* (Edinburgh: Mainstream, 1997).
Pinfold, J., Where the Champion Horses Run: The Origins of Aintree Racecourse and the Grand National, *The International Journal of the History of Sport*, 15.2 (1998), 137–51.

See also Aintree.

Moneybox

Gay Crusader (2–11) was the shortest-priced twentieth-century winner of the St Leger in 1917.

Generous, winner of the Derby, Irish Derby and King George in 1991, was the leading money winner in Britain that year, and third in the all time list behind Pebbles and Ibn Bey, with career earnings of £1,119,944.

Giant's Causeway, winner of five consecutive Group One races in the summer of 2000, is currently rated one of the most valuable stallions in the world with a covering fee of 100,000 Irish guineas.

The **Grand National** has been won by only six favourites since 1946, at odds ranging from 13–2 (Merryman II in 1960) to 10–1 (Freebooter in 1950).

Grundy held the record in 1975 for most money earned in a career by a horse trained in Britain – £326,421 (over £1.5 million today) from eight wins and two seconds.

A **guinea** (£1.05) is still the currency used for bloodstock sales in Britain and Ireland.

H

Horsebox

Habibti was one of the best sprint fillies of recent years; unbeaten in nine sprints over two years from July 1982, she won the July Cup, the Nunthorpe Stakes, the Haydock Sprint Cup and the Prix de l'Abbaye in 1983, partnered by Willie Carson.

Halloween holds the record for most placed horse in the Cheltenham Gold Cup, second in 1953 and 1955, third in 1954 and 1956.

Harayir was the last of trainer Dick Hern's 16 Classic winners when taking the 1995 One Thousand Guineas; Hethersett (1962 St Leger) was the first.

Hidden Meaning beat 45 horses to win the Cambridgeshire Handicap in 1962, the largest post-war field.

High Line won the 2-mile Jockey Club Cup at Newmarket in three consecutive years 1969–71.

High Top won the Two Thousand Guineas in 1972, the first English Classic winner for Willie Carson, and the first of four horses whose names contained the word 'high' to have won an English Classic in the last 30 years – the others were Highclere (1974 One Thousand Guineas), High-Rise (1998 Derby) and High Chaparral (2002 Derby).

Heritage

Racing is one of the oldest sports and its history can be seen all around: in streets and roads carrying the names of defunct courses and dead administrators, in weed-covered buildings no longer hosting hundreds of racegoers, and in the contours of tracks only visible to the discerning eye. Some courses that have modernised have deliberately retained historical features; elsewhere much has disappeared... but not all. At Lincoln, closed in 1964, the grandstand surveys the road now running past it into the city and Alexandra Park, shut down in 1970, still has its running rail. Such large items are non-collectable racing artefacts, unlike silks and equipment associated with famous horses and their riders, or entry badges, metal and card, reflecting the hierarchical structure of race viewing and racing officialdom.

High-class commemorative wares with a racing theme are relatively rare, perhaps because of the popularity and affordability of racing art and prints. Transfer-printing on to ceramic became possible by the 1820s and nineteenth-century plates, vases and porcelain trophies were sometimes decorated with famous racehorses. Glassware, much of it made at Newcastle, also featured northern champions. Fans and particularly silk scarves commemorating Derby winners were produced from Victorian times to the Second World War. At the lower end of the market, jockeys found their way onto mugs and other functional items. The great Fred Archer spawned an entire craft industry of memorabilia, from earthenware jugs and plates to silver matchboxes; he was also the first sportsman to be featured as a waxwork at Madame Tussaud's in London.

At the cheaper end of the memorabilia market are cigarette cards and racecards, both of which are a source of not just racing but also social history. Cigarette cards featuring horses or jockeys, sometimes both, demonstrate that the cult of the personality existed in racing in the 1930s. Some cards of the previous decade also covered owners, trainers and famous racing colours, scarcely subjects to grasp the imagination of today's younger generation, but valuable to the racing historian. A glance at racecards over the past 150 years reveals even more about societal changes and how racing has accommodated them, sometimes with a considerable time lag. Information about the best position for viewing from a private carriage gave way to extracts from railway timetables (including, for Goodwood, details of the first-class Pullman service from London to Chichester) and later to maps showing where racegoers could park their cars. Advertisements for hotels – for overnight stays during meetings – and theatres in which to spend the evening before the next day's racing now rarely feature. Instead the cards are more likely to advertise the products of the meetings' sponsors. Another identifiable change is the reduction in the number of titles among the stewards, although officials are still listed before any of the runners and riders.

Several features stand out in a more specific comparison of racecards for meetings at York in 1909 and 1999. Both give full details of the race conditions (entry fees, penalty weights, age and quality restrictions and so on), information really only useful to the aficionado and professional punter. Other things, however, are different. At the end of the twentieth century it is the name of the horse that gets prominence but in the earlier card first mention goes to the owner. The key difference though is that the 1909 meeting has no sponsors. Races were named after local dignitaries, places and the champion nineteenth-century Yorkshire racehorse The Flying Dutchman. In 1999 the whole programme had commercial sponsors.

Among the more unusual racing artefacts are parts of the racehorses themselves. The National Horseracing Museum at Newmarket has a collection ranging from framed tail hairs and racing plates belonging to famous horses to hooves mounted in silver. The skeleton of the famous eighteenth-century champion, Eclipse and the stuffed head of the 1896 Derby winner, Persimmon, are also on display.

Further reading

Bracegirdle, H., *A Concise History of British Horseracing* (Derby: English Life Publications, 1999).
Budd, G., *Racing Art and Memorabilia* (London: Wilson, 1997).

See also Architecture, Museums.

Horserace Betting Levy Board

In a ground-breaking move for the financing of British racing, the Horseracing Betting Levy Board (more generally referred to as the Levy Board) was established in 1961 to assess and collect monetary contributions from bookmakers and the Tote. It originated as a compensation scheme for racing when off-course cash betting was legalised in 1960 and punters no longer had to attend a race meeting to bet legally in cash. Initially based on the number of betting shops owned by a bookmaker, in 1969 the levy changed to one based on turnover and later it became a function of gross profits, though every year there was a political struggle as to the precise amount to be raised. By 2001, 10 per cent was charged on annual profits exceeding £150,000 with a proportionate reduction for those betting shops that fell short of this figure. In the first year of operations a substantial minority of bookmakers refused to co-operate with the scheme but were brought into line by making a certificate of compliance an essential requirement of an application for a licence renewal.

Under the leadership of Field Marshall Lord Hardy of Petherton, the Board took over many of the revenue distribution functions of the Horseracing Totalisator Board which was left to run the Tote and make a contribution to the levy. Among the early decisions made by the Levy Board were the establishment of a veterinary research laboratory, improved travelling allowances for horses, the provision of photo-finish and patrol cameras, the financing of starting stalls, and the development of anti-doping measures.

The Levy Board is a statutory body with the prescribed function of applying the funds raised to the improvement of horseracing, the improvement of breeds of horses, and the advancement of veterinary science and education. Some 90 per cent of expenditure goes on interest-free loans and grants to racecourses to improve their facilities and infrastructure, and on supplementing the prize money coming from owners, sponsors and racecourses themselves. As well as owning the Horseracing Forensic Laboratory at Newmarket where dope testing takes place, it is also responsible for the National Stud and authorises the National Joint Pitch Council that allocates on-course betting sites for bookmakers.

One recent major initiative was an interest-free loan to Lingfield Park to finance its new all-weather Polytrack as this was considered vital in helping racing, and the betting market, keep going when turf racing was abandoned. Such a move has increased in significance as the recent commercial deal between the British Horseracing Board (BHB) and the bookmakers now excludes a levy on bets taken on overseas racing, a source of income that had been worth about £5 million a year and provided a useful cash flow during spells of lengthy abandonments at home.

The Board has eight members. The Secretary of State for the Department of Culture, Media and Sport appoints the Chairman, Deputy Chairman and one other member. The Chairman of the Tote and the Chairman of the Bookmakers' Committee each have a seat. The other three positions are for the nominees of the Jockey Club but in practice this power has been delegated to the BHB.

Critics have argued that the Board too readily accepted less from the bookmakers than it could have obtained. Others believe that the financial crutch provided to racing by the levy to some extent deterred enterprise within the industry. In the light of the restructuring of racing's institutional financial arrangements, the future of the Board is uncertain and it is currently scheduled for closure in September 2005.

Further reading

Hill, C.R., *Horse Power: The Politics of the Turf* (Manchester: Manchester University Press, 1988).
www.hblb.org.uk

Hurdling and hurdlers

Hurdling is not only the junior branch of the racing family but also the poor relation. It has been so overlooked and unfashionable that most books about horseracing fail to mention it, except perhaps in relation to its major contest, the Champion Hurdle at Cheltenham. Yet every National Hunt course has to have a designated area, partially or wholly separate from the steeplechase track, on which to stage hurdling, and 50 per cent of the Grade One jump races are for hurdlers. It also took place on the all-weather tracks for a number of years but after 12 equine deaths in a period of six weeks in early 1994, all-weather hurdling was suspended and has never resumed.

Hurdles are wooden frames standing no less than 3 ft 6 in high into which gorse and birch are woven. Flimsier than steeplechase fences, they are designed to give on contact with a field of galloping horses, the less experienced of whom often seem to plough through them. As in human hurdle races, hitting the obstacle may cause a fall but is more likely to upset the speed, rhythm and stride pattern of the jumper. In recent years artificial flights of birch have been tried out and more substantial hurdles used to encourage horses to jump rather than flatten the fence, thereby providing potential chasers with a smaller but more realistic version of steeplechase jumps.

Hurdling, however, is an intermediate type of racing. Although it may be a training ground for horses that will step up to bigger fences, it also provides mature flatracers with an opportunity to continue their careers by utilising their natural speed. There has been a tendency in recent years for the smaller, lighter flat-type horse to compete in top-level hurdling and for fewer hurdlers to graduate to larger obstacles. Three-time Champion Hurdle winner, Istabraq (1998–2000), is a son of champion flat sire Sadler's Wells, a close relative of Derby winner Secreto and raced on the flat for three years. See You Then, another three-time winner of the race (1985–87), was sired by 1967 Derby and Two Thousand Guineas winner Royal Palace. The top National Hunt sire of the 1980s, Deep Run, was second in the Irish St Leger and, as a four-year-old, was runner-up to Nijinsky in the initial outing of his Triple-Crown-winning season (1970). That said, hurdling is sometimes still used as preparation for experienced steeplechasers at the start of their winter campaign to sharpen them up and remind them of the racecourse environment.

The position of a hurdle circuit varies – some as at Fontwell Park are on the outside of the chase course but many, such as Bangor, Haydock Park and Kelso, form the inside track and therefore have fairly tight bends. The number of hurdles on any circuit is usually about half the number of fences; there must be a minimum of eight flights in the first 2 miles of a race and a further obstacle every $\frac{1}{4}$ mile thereafter. Like steeplechasing, the hurdling programme is divided into races for juveniles (a three-year-old in autumn, a four-year-old in spring), novices (horses who have not won a hurdle before 1 May of the previous season) over 2 to $2\frac{1}{2}$ miles, and regular hurdlers over distances of 2 to $3\frac{1}{4}$ miles. Amongst the Grade One hurdle races are the 2-mile Christmas Hurdle at Kempton Park, the $2\frac{1}{2}$-mile Challow Hurdle for novices at Newbury, the Supreme Novices' (2-mile), Champion (2-mile), Stayers' (3-mile) and Triumph (2-mile juvenile) Hurdles at Cheltenham and the $3\frac{1}{4}$-mile Long Walk Hurdle at Ascot. Important Grade Two hurdles are also run at Wetherby, Newcastle, Sandown Park, Doncaster, Chepstow, Haydock Park and Aintree.

The first hurdle race was said to have taken place at Durdham Down, near Bristol in 1821 and by the mid-nineteenth century hurdles appeared regularly in the *Racing Calendar* in a variety of flat-race fixtures from Brighton to Thirsk though mostly throughout the Shires. In the early twentieth century, the most important race was the Imperial Cup at Sandown Park, first held in March 1907 and reckoned to be the most prestigious hurdle of the season until 1939. It was worth over £1,000 in 1927 – although the major handicap hurdle at Liverpool at this time was awarding prize money of over £2,000 – significantly more than the princely sum of £365 offered to the winner of the inaugural Champion Hurdle at Cheltenham that year. With rewards of this magnitude, it is not surprising that the pre war winners of the race were rated amongst the poorest in its history, or that Brown Jack, the four-year-old that won the second renewal in 1928, was aimed at more lucrative flat races for the remainder of his career, retiring with earnings of over £21,000. (To put hurdling into perspective, the Classics were each worth between £9,000 and £13,000 at the end of the 1920s, as were the Eclipse Stakes and the Grand National.)

The Champion Hurdle, however, was a weight-for-age contest at a time when handicaps dominated the hurdling calendar. The post war years saw its profile heighten with consecutive three-time winners, the Irish-trained Hatton's Grace (1949–51) and the French-bred Sir Ken (1952–54). The Triumph Hurdle for four-year-olds, though first run in 1939 at Hurst Park, was transferred to Cheltenham in 1965 and the inaugural Christmas Hurdle at Kempton Park, destined to be the hurdling equivalent of the King George VI Chase, was held in 1969. Cliché though it may be, the next 15 years were undoubtedly the 'golden age' of the sport. Only seven horses won the

Champion Hurdle from 1968 to 1981 and each was an outstanding hurdler. Persian War won it three times (1968–70) and was runner-up in 1971, having also lifted the Triumph Hurdle in 1967. He won or was placed in 36 of his 51 races over the sticks. Five horses were double winners of the race – Bula (1971, 1972), Comedy of Errors (1973, 1975), Night Nurse (1976, 1977), reckoned by many to be the greatest hurdler of modern times, Monksfield (1978, 1979) and Sea Pigeon (1980, 1981). The 1974 winner Lanzarote would have been a great champion in any other era, with 20 victories in 33 races including two Christmas Hurdles and a Welsh Champion Hurdle but he was overshadowed by Comedy of Errors for many years.

Bula was the top novice hurdler of 1969–70 and won 21 of 26 hurdle races during his career. Comedy of Errors became the first jumper in Britain or Ireland to win £100,000 in prize money. Night Nurse was unplaced only three times in 32 starts, with 19 victories which included the Champion Hurdle and the Irish, Scottish and Welsh equivalents in 1975–76. In his second championship year, he beat the most high-quality field ever seen in the race, coming home ahead of Monksfield (2nd) and Sea Pigeon (4th), and two other highly-rated horses in Dramatist (3rd) and Birds Nest (5th), respective winners of the 1976 and 1979 Christmas Hurdle. Monksfield not only won the Champion Hurdle twice, he was also twice runner-up (1977, 1980) as was Sea Pigeon (to Monksfield in 1978 and 1979). As the trainer of both Night Nurse and Sea Pigeon, Peter Easterby who also won in 1967 with Saucy Kit, has the best record in the race.

One of the interesting features of all these champions was their versatility. Some, like Bula and Night Nurse, made successful transitions to steeplechasing and were each placed in the Cheltenham Gold Cup. (Dawn Run, of course, became the only horse to win both races in 1984 and 1986 – see separate entry – while Morley Street, 1991 champion, won the Breeders' Steeplechase Cup in America twice, in 1991 and 1992.) Others graduated to hurdles from flat racing. Royal Gait, having broken the course record time in winning the 1988 Ascot Gold Cup only to be subsequently disqualified, capped a lengthy period on the flat by taking the 1992 Champion Hurdle as a novice nine-year-old, the least experienced winner since 1956.

Sea Pigeon, a son of 1965 Derby winner Sea Bird II, even sustained a dual career in both codes, winning the Ebor Handicap under 10 st in 1979, the year in which he was again runner-up in the Champion Hurdle. He also won the Chester Cup twice and a further 13 flat races together with 21 hurdle victories (and eight seconds) over a period of 11 seasons in training, a modern-day equivalent of Brown Jack. Sea Pigeon had Classic potential – he ran seventh in the 1973 Derby – but Aurelius actually won the 1961 St Leger as well as two Group races at Royal Ascot before, in quick succession, being (1) retired to stud (2) gelded (3) sent hurdling (4) ridden into second place in the 1967 Champion Hurdle (5) disqualified from the race (6) sent over fences, winning at Ascot and Sandown in 1968. Thereafter he refused in all his subsequent chases and was dishonourably retired. Beat that!

In the past 15 years there have been changes in the sport. The advent of all-weather racing has led to fewer flat-race horses being campaigned over hurdles during the winter. The impact of ex-flatracers has increased – the 1990s saw not only Royal Gait and Istabraq take the Champion Hurdle but also flat winner Alderbrook (successful in 1995 and second in 1996). Six weeks after his victory he was second in the Group One flat race, the Prix Ganay at Longchamp! Both Sir Michael Stoute (trainer of 1990 winner Kribensis, another flat winner) and Aidan O'Brien (trainer of Istabraq) run overwhelmingly flat-race stables. French-bred and trained horses have also made their presence felt – Francois Doumen and his jockey son Thierry won the Triumph Hurdle in 2000 with Snow Drop while the 2002 Champion Hurdle winner Hors La Loi III was bred in France where horses are introduced to obstacles at an earlier age than in Britain.

At the elite level, hurdling can be exhilarating. There are few sights in racing to equal a field of top-class horses streaming over the obstacles at speed, brushing them aside as they charge down the course. At many of Britain's smaller racetracks, however, hurdle races are little more than fillers in a programme, an opportunity for mediocre flat racers or apprentice chasers to earn their keep – or not, given the relatively low prize money in this branch of racing.

Further reading

Randall, J. and Morris, T., *A Century of Champions* (Halifax: Portway, 1999).
Tanner, M., *Champion Hurdle 1927–2002* (Edinburgh: Mainstream, 2002).

Moneybox

A **handicap** is a race in which weights are allocated on the basis of a horse's past performance in order to give them all an equal chance of winning if they run to form.

Hedging occurs when bookmakers themselves bet on horses on which they have liabilities so as to reduce the potential loss.

The late **Dick Hern** was the only other man to win more than one flat-racing trainers' championship in the period 1980–2000, breaking the virtual stranglehold of Henry Cecil (seven wins), Sir Michael Stoute (six wins) and Saeed bin Suroor (three wins).

A **Heinz** is a multiple bet involving six horses which are backed in 15 doubles, 20 trebles, 15 four-horse accumulators, 6 five-horse accumulators and a six-horse accumulator. In all these are 57 varieties of bet.

When **High Chaparral** won the 2002 Derby, his winnings amounted to £800,400.

Hyperion was leading sire six times between 1940 and 1954; his offspring were winners of around 750 races in Britain worth £557,009 (about £9 million now).

I

Horsebox

The French-bred and trained **Imprudence**, ridden by Australian jockey Rae Johnstone, not only won the 1947 Oaks but also the One Thousand Guineas and the French equivalent, the Poule d'Essai des Pouliches.

Imagine, trained by Aidan O'Brien, won the English Oaks and the Irish One Thousand Guineas in the same year (2001).

Indian Skimmer, trained by Henry Cecil and rated the best three-year-old filly in Europe in 1987, was one of four English fillies to win the French Prix de Diane from 1980 to 1990 – Mrs Penny and Madam Gay were successful with Lester Piggott in 1980 and 1981, and Rafha with Willie Carson in 1990.

Insurance, the first double winner of the Champion Hurdle, beat his rivals by 12 lengths in 1932, the longest winning margin in the history of the race, but the opposition consisted of only two inferior horses; he won by only $\frac{3}{4}$ length in 1933.

Intermezzo won the St Leger in 1969, the lowest rated winner according to the Timeform system of ratings. He never won again and was exported to Japan.

Intrepidity holds the fastest time for the Oaks (1993 – 2.34.19).

Industry

Racing is a sizeable leisure industry whether measured by employment or by income. Racecourses need managers, officials, administrative and catering staff, gatemen, security stewards and many others. Training yards require stable staff – at least one for every three or four horses – and give ancillary employment to vets, farriers, blacksmiths and saddlers among others. Stud farms replicate the needs of the training stables. Between them racing and breeding directly employ around 35,500 persons of whom over 12,000 are full-time employees. Many of those employed work in the rural economy. When indirect employment is also considered – and with due allowance for part-time work – the racing and breeding sector is responsible for about one-eighth of the agricultural labour force. It is a highly important employer in the local economies of Epsom, Lambourn, Malton, Middleham and especially Newmarket.

The racing industry generates over £830 million of income including over £230 million from the five million or so visitors to race meetings each year (who also spend £70 million offsite). The tax yield from the industry was estimated in 1999 to be £150 million from the income tax and national insurance payments of those employed directly and indirectly as well as VAT, local taxes and fuel duty.

Any consideration of the racing industry cannot avoid its links with the betting sector of the economy for which horseracing is the staple source of income. In fact about 28,000 jobs in the betting industry can be attributed to racing. In 1999 legal off-course bookmaking had a turnover of almost £5 billion, approximately 70 per cent of betting in the United Kingdom. From this about £58 million was returned to racing through the Levy Board and over £300 million paid in general betting duty to the government. It is estimated that the bookmakers' net receipts generate expenditure of approximately £650 million in the economy as well as significant government revenue through income tax, business rates and corporation tax. Clearly in abandoning the direct tax on betting the government itself is taking a gamble that the cheaper cost of betting will increase bookmaking revenue sufficiently for the consequent income and corporation tax yield to more than offset the loss of the betting tax revenue.

Within the combined racing and betting industries different sectors look to varying revenue sources. Racecourses search for sponsorship, charge gate money, sell media rights and negotiate with the British Horseracing Board (BHB) for part of the money raised from bookmakers and the Tote. Breeders sell their produce to owners at home and abroad. Owners seek sponsorship, anticipate that prize money will contribute towards covering their costs, and hope that their horses will peak when the money is on. Trainers rely on owners, a share of prize money won, and inside knowledge to assist their gambling. Stable staff dream of 'doing' a winning horse and supplementing their meagre incomes with a share of the prize money, a well-placed bet, and perhaps a present from a grateful owner or trainer. The bookmakers, at least those who are turf accountants rather than gamblers, count the cash.

All of them are affected by the state of the economy which determines the level of disposable consumer income either for betting or horse ownership. Between 1990 and 1993, for example, economic recession led to a fall of 11 per cent in the number of horses in training. Downturns in the economy pose a particular problem to the BHB who will be faced with the dilemma of either cutting prize money – which annoys the owners and has a cascade effect on to trainers and their employees – or reducing the number of fixtures which saves them £35,000–£40,000 for each one but can lead to a reduction in betting turnover. Moreover under the new commercial agreement the bookmakers only pay a broadcasting rights fee when racing takes place so curtailing the fixture list may not prove to be as economic as intended.

See also Economics.

Injuries

Such is the danger of racing that an ambulance always follows the riders around. And it gets used. By 2000, 39-year-old Brendan Powell, the senior National Hunt rider, had ridden in nearly 7,000 races. En route he had broken his femur (twice), tibia and fibula – there is an 8 inch metal rod in his left leg – wrist, arm, fingers, hand, collarbone (three times), and all his ribs as well as puncturing his lung and rupturing his stomach. His experience is not untypical of the jump jockey. John Francome, seven times National Hunt champion jockey, calculated that in 15 seasons he lost 460 days through injury and many jump jockeys have metal wires, plates or screws holding damaged joints and bones together. Flat-race riders can also expect serious injuries in their career, for, although they have no fences to get over, their horses can come down unexpectedly and at high speed.

All workers run the risk of industrial injury though for most the risk is minimal. For jockeys, however, serious injury at work is not a possibility or even a probability: it is inevitable. Leading jockeys, whether flat or National Hunt, have all suffered serious injury during their careers. One survey of 700 jockeys found that they aggregated over 1,000 fractures, mainly limbs. Although comparative calculations are difficult because of inadequate measures of participation, it has been suggested that jump racing ranks below only mountaineering and aerial sports in risk of fatality and injury. In professional sports, a jump jockey faces no more risk of being hurt than a footballer and less than a rugby player. However the nature of their injuries is different, simply because they are thrown to the ground at 25–30 mph, even more in sprint races. Indeed half of racing injuries consist of broken collarbones caused by landing on the shoulder after being thrown. Broken wrists, elbows, arms and dislocated shoulders account for another 30 per cent. The most serious injuries occur when a horse, an animal weighing around 500 kilos, lands on the rider. Statistically the most dangerous equestrian event is point-to-point racing as it involves amateurs who often lack both the experience and skills to cope with dangerous situations. Yet even top riders in this branch of the sport can run into trouble. In 2002 three leading point-to-point jockeys were sidelined for the season: Adrian Whintle broke his back, Richard Burton dislocated his shoulder and Stuart Morris received severe facial injuries.

Not till the mid-twentieth century was an insurance scheme established to look after the interests of professional jockeys. Up to that point injured riders had to appeal to the trustees of various funds for assistance. The nineteenth century had seen the Bentinck Benevolent and Rous Memorial Funds both set up to honour distinguished turf administrators. In 1923 the Jockey Club inaugurated the Jockeys' Accident Fund, but it was stressed that this was not an insurance scheme and that, despite its nomenclature, no jockey had a right to draw upon it. Jump jockeys had recourse to nothing but individual charity till the Rendlesham Benevolent Fund of 1902 made some provision for those killed or injured while riding in National Hunt races. It was open only to licensed professionals and payment was entirely at the discretion of the management committee. After the First World War this was reinforced by the National Hunt Accident Fund which paid £1,000 in instances of death and £3 a week for 26 weeks for temporary disablement. The fund was initially financed by half of the jockeys' licence fees with supplementation after the 1920s from the Racecourse Betting Control Board (later the Horserace Betting Levy Board). In 1964 the Injured National Hunt Jockeys Fund (renamed the Injured Jockeys Fund in 1971) was established as a registered charity.

The Fund is not designed to cope with short-term injuries. For this there is the Professional Riders Insurance Scheme which has emerged out of the Racehorse Owners Compensation Fund. It is financed by a mandatory levy on all riding fees paid by owners. This raises about £500,000 per annum of which about half is spent on weekly compensation for temporary injuries and most of the rest on premiums to insure all professional jockeys against death or career-ending injuries. The temporary weekly benefits are paid on a sliding scale dependent upon the number of rides the jockey had the previous season. However, what is being compensated for is the loss of riding fees not the share of prize money lost and thus some jockeys also subscribe to private insurance schemes, though premiums are not cheap and cover is limited.

Racing is hazardous. Among the holidaymakers who went to Tenerife in 2002 on the tenth annual trip organised by the Injured Jockeys' Fund was Rebecca Hewitt recently confined to a wheelchair by a fall in a hunter chase at Hereford. Five years earlier Shane Broderick was paralysed from the neck down in a fall at Fairyhouse, only days after finishing third on Dorans Pride in the Cheltenham Gold Cup: a career ended at 22. Other attendees included Sharron Murgatroyd, crippled by a fall at the last at Bangor-on-Dee in 1990; Sam Berry just 20 when he was disabled at Sedgefield in 1985; Dennis Wicketts severely disabled in a point-to-point at Crimp in Cornwall 18 years ago; and Jenny Litson who rode over 70 winners before a horse fell on her at Larkhill and deprived her of both speech and mobility.

Also present in the Canaries were brain-damaged flat-race jockeys, Des Cullen and Ronnie Singer. To them movement was not a problem, but memory and coherence were. It is now acknowledged that many jockeys exhibit a 'punch drunk' syndrome similar to that of boxers, the result of repeated concussion from hitting the ground at speed. Terry Biddlecombe, champion jockey in the late 1950s, had more than a hundred instances of concussion. In his day, however, a jockey could have a terrible fall but, if showing no signs of distress, be allowed to ride in the next race. In 1988 the Jockey Club introduced mandatory bans of 2, 6 or 21 days depending on how long a rider had been unconscious. A decade later a more flexible method – based on experience in Australian Rules football – was adopted which requires jockeys to sit a seven-minute written test to demonstrate that their co-ordination is back to normal. Serious head injuries involving brain bruising or convulsions, however, can lead to a year out of the saddle.

National Hunt riders, in particular, are always just one fall away from paralysis. Although the domination of rides by the leading jockeys increases their chances of injury, it is the journeymen who have to ride the bad horses, of which, to quote Guy Lewis, one such rider, there are 'bad useless and bad horrible', the latter a dangerous mount. Yet, as Sharron Murgatroyd argues, although unlucky to be severely injured, many of the crippled riders were lucky to have felt the euphoria of bringing home a winner; lucky, compared to many lads and lasses in the stables, to have ever got the chance to ride in public.

Further reading

Magee, S. and Lewis, G., *To Win Just Once* (London: Headline, 1998).
Murgatroyd, S., *Life on the Other Side of the Fence* (London: Romney, 2001).

See also Accidents, Charities, Deaths.

Inns

Inns, hotels and public houses have a long association with the turf. The Jockey Club first met in the *Star and Garter* in London's Pall Mall in the early 1750s and also gathered at the *Thatched House* in St James's Street, the *Clarendon* in Bond Street, both of these in London, and the *Old Red Lion* at Newmarket. The idea for the St Leger, the first of the English Classics, stemmed from a meeting of local landowners and sportsmen in the upper room of the *Salutation Inn* at Doncaster. It was here that the stallion Catton stood at stud for a 15 sovereign fee (plus one for the groom) in 1827. In that same year similar breeding opportunities were offered at the *Rose and Crown*, Beverley, the *Grantham Arms*, Boroughbridge and the *King's Arms Yard*, Pimlico and such advertisements continued in the *Racing Calendar* until the early 1860s. Sometimes mares and their offspring were also offered stable facilities.

Traditionally it was in the stables of inns and hotels that horses were accommodated prior to race meetings. Many advertisements for races in the eighteenth century specified that the horses had to be stabled in the town for between two and nine days before race day. This widespread condition of entry to the races was formulated to allow the local innkeepers to recoup their investment in the race prizes. It is certain that the groom who accompanied the horse, and perhaps other servants, and even the owner might also be accommodated there, thus increasing the inns' profit. Spectators might visit the inns to examine the horses, and spend money there too. The requirement to stable horses at certain inns died away in the railway age as racecourses increasingly provided their own yards.

It was at the appropriately named Doncaster inn, the *Turf Tavern*, that Elis arrived in his van to be stabled prior to his St Leger win in 1836. Many other inn names are associated with horseracing, either in a general sense via the ubiquitous *Horse and Jockey* or more specifically commemorating famous races or their winners. Derby victors a century apart were celebrated in the Epsom pubs *Amato* (1838) and *Blenheim* (1930). St Leger winner *Rockingham* (1833) is appropriately recorded in a Doncaster hostelry. Seventeen other Classic winners are listed in Larwood and Hotten's study of English inn signs as having public houses or hotels named after them in the nineteenth century alone. Other drinking establishments such as the *Chester Cup* in Plymouth, and the *St Leger* at Warrington were named after the race itself rather than the horse which won it, to celebrate, it is alleged, gambling wins which enabled the publican to set up shop.

Even though fewer jockeys than in the past stay away overnight, racing inns are still popular with owners and the travelling public. Indeed an annual review, *Travelling The Turf*, first published in 1986, provides recommendations for local hotels, restaurants and pubs for every course in Britain. Generally it features the better class of accommodation. Among these is the *Queen's Hotel* on the Promenade at Cheltenham, closely associated with the National Hunt Festival and catering to the wealthier Irish gamblers in its own Gold Cup room.

Further reading

Larwood, J. and Hotten, J.C., *English Inn Signs* (Exeter: Blaketon Hall, 1986).
Wentworth Day, J., *Inns of Sport* (London: Naldrett, 1949).
West, J., *Travelling the Turf* (Hexham: Kensington West, 1998).

See also Alcohol.

International

When his mount Lammtarra won the Prix de l'Arc de Triomphe at Longchamp in 1995, Frankie Dettori noted that the British national anthem was played to salute the success of a horse bred in the United States, trained and owned by Dubaians and ridden by an Italian, an indication of how globalised racing had become. In 1990 the top ten jockeys in the British championship presented literally a league of nations, featuring three Irishmen, two Scots, two Welshmen, an American, a South African and, of course, one Italian. Yet the regular international movement of jockeys is no modern phenomenon. It dates back well into the nineteenth century, coinciding with the development of railway networks in Britain and Europe. British jockeys took advantage of the absence of Sunday racing in Britain to ride in France and Belgium. It is equally clear from the *Racing Calendar* that European riders, French jockeys in particular, came to England to participate in Classic and other elite races, usually on mounts from European stables. The ease of air travel now means that many British jockeys build riding in Europe and even other continents into their timetables.

The racehorse has become an international commodity. In breeding what was formerly a series of small national markets with some interlopers from foreign parts has been transformed into a vast international market. The top yearling sales are now organised on a global basis, beginning in July with the Keeneland Sales in Kentucky, moving on to Deauville, then to Goff's Sales in Ireland and ending with Tattersalls' October Sales at Newmarket.

Horses themselves have become globetrotters. Take the case of the American-bred Fantastic Light. As a three-year-old he had ten races, only venturing outside Britain for one of them, and that only across the Channel to Longchamp. His real travels began the following year, beginning with a trip to the Emirates where he won the Dubai Sheema Classic. Races back in Britain followed at Epsom, Sandown and Ascot. Then came two at Belmont and one at Churchill Downs in the United States, an unsuccessful tilt at the Japan Cup in Tokyo and a win to end his four-year-old season in the Hong Kong Cup at Sha Tin. Next year began with a second place in the Dubai Sheema Classic before wins at The Curragh, Ascot and Leopardstown and a triumphant finale in the Breeders' Cup Turf at Belmont. His riders included Irish, English, American and Italian jockeys.

Where in the past national Classics and other elite events were targeted by a few overseas raiders, some meetings and individual races have now been specifically organised with the international horse in mind. The World Turf Championships at Sha Tin, Hong Kong, the Japan Cup in Tokyo and the World Cup meeting in Dubai are all examples of fixtures which have offered substantial prize money to attract top horses from a variety of countries. Individual races at these meetings also form part of the Emirates World Series, an unofficial world championship instigated in 1999 by Sheikh Mohammed al Maktoum. Points are awarded for the jockeys, trainers and owners of placed horses in a collection of 12 international races spanning the globe from North America via Europe and Asia to Australia. Cynics might suggest that the Sheikh has been intent on self-aggrandisement since his trainer Saeed bin Suroor and jockey Frankie Dettori have been the human recipients of the first four awards, thanks to the success of Maktoum horses Daylami, Fantastic Light (twice) and Grandera.

Internet

Racing is an inherently conservative sport in which tradition is important. It still deals in guineas and sovereigns and has not yet adopted metrication for its distances and weights. Nevertheless it has embraced computer technology, particularly in respect of the Internet. All racecourses, most organisations and a few trainers and riders possess dedicated websites to provide information to a computer-literate audience. Basically the Internet allows documents stored on one computer to be distributed on request and viewed on any other computer connected to the web. These documents – termed pages – can contain text, multimedia elements such as graphics, photographs, sound and video (ideal for trainers and bloodstock agents), and even interactive computer programs (particularly used for betting).

Unlike football, and this might say something about the fan base of racing, there are few websites organised by devotees of the sport or devoted to stars of the turf. Even Frankie Dettori, possibly the celebrity figure in racing, can only be found on an American website. What the Internet does do for racing is provide masses of statistical data, give access to breaking news and archived press material, allow communication between people in the industry, offer live racing and enable interactive betting to take place.

The provision of live pictures of racing on the net began with experimental webcasts of meetings at Ascot and Aintree in 2001 but during 2002 attheraces.com – a consortium of track owners and television channels – opted to show some 4,000 hours, making horseracing the most webcasted sport in

Britain. Initially the quality of pictures resembled a Degas racing painting with a running commentary, but it has improved rapidly, though it still lags behind normal television viewing.

Live racing on the net has allowed bookmakers to show more races from abroad and lengthened their betting day. All the major bookmakers have set up sites, but the pioneers were the smaller bookmakers such as Sportingbet, begun in 1988 by Mark Blanford. He sold his four betting shops and two race-course pitches to set up the first British company to offer tax-free betting from Alderney via the Internet. The site is now available in several languages and claims to be the world's largest Internet betting site. Although the move abroad to establish web-based betting sites led to the abolition of the betting duty, it has not been the saviour that many firms hoped for. Slow downloading and poor web design have affected some but the greatest problem, for the book-ies, has been the competitive market that the web facilitates. Online customers tend to be shrewd operators who search for the best odds and have little loy-alty to one bookmaker, unlike the habitué of the local betting shop. Margins consequently are lower than in their traditional lines of business. Many Internet punters are also patronising the betting exchange sites where they can bet with each other at mutually agreed odds. The proprietors of these sites such as the Dublin-based Betdaq and the mainland pioneer Betfair take 5 per cent from the successful punter's winnings, significantly less than the deductions of the bookies. Punters appreciate this and within two years of introducing the new system in 2000 Betfair had a turnover of £50 million.

Further reading

www.racingpost.com

See also Virtual racing.

Ireland

Ireland is a small country which exerts an enormous influence on British, and world, horseracing. When both sides of the border are included, as they are for Irish racing purposes, it has a population scarcely bigger than Scotland or Denmark, minnows of the Turf, and only one-tenth the size of France, a lead-ing player. Yet the Irish Classics are hotly contested by international fields, Irish horses have swept up valuable and prestigious prizes around the globe and the top Irish stables and studs are synonymous with wealth, power and success.

It was not always so; the development of racing in Ireland fluctuated with the political, social and economic history of this troubled state. The begin-ning of formal organisation and control occurred as it had in Britain with the establishment of an Irish Turf Club, similar to the Jockey Club, and the publication of an Irish Racing Calendar from 1790. Before that, British gar-risons stationed at The Curragh had indulged in hunting, shooting and country sports on that vast tract of land in Co. Kildare which forms the Irish equivalent of Newmarket. The first recorded race was held there in 1741. Since the early eighteenth century the local aristocracy and ultimately, the British monarchy, had encouraged both horseracing and breeding by offering prizes, the chief of which were the Royal Plates, valued at 100 guineas. By the 1820s, 16 of these took place mostly at The Curragh but also at Down Royal and Bellewstown.

The impact of Irish bloodstock even began to be felt not only in Britain but throughout the racing world during the mid-nineteenth century. Harkaway, bred in Co. Down won all his races as a three-year-old at The Curragh before taking on English opposition. He won the Goodwood Cup twice, in 1838 and 1839, together with six other races on English soil. Retired to stud in Berwickshire, he eventually became the maternal great-grandsire of the prolific St Simon. Birdcatcher, often referred to as Irish Birdcatcher, never raced outside Ireland but his reputation for speed led him to be much sought after as a stallion. He was twice champion sire in Britain (1852 and 1856) and his son The Baron, 1845 St Leger winner, later sired Stockwell, one of the most influential British stallions of the century. Birdcatcher's full brother, Faugh-a-Ballagh, also bred in Ireland, won the 1844 St Leger and later sired Fille de l'Air, the first French-owned filly to win the Oaks in 1864 (and dam of Reine who won the same race and the One Thousand Guineas in 1869). His son Leamington was exported to the United States where he sired Iroquois, the first American-bred winner of the Epsom Derby in 1881.

But a century of trauma and turbulence, from the potato famine of the 1840s to the Second World War, ensured that the progress of Irish racing stuttered and faltered. Although the Irish Derby was first staged in 1866, it failed to attract entries and, together with other more valuable Irish races such as the Royal Plates, was initially won by English raiders. The first two Irish Derby winners, Selim and Golden Plover, were English-owned and trained; the Turf Club subsequently banned the entry of horses that had not been trained for the previous six months in Ireland. A continued lack of interest in the Irish Derby resulted in the race becoming a handicap, and although the other Irish Classics were all founded between 1895 and 1922, they remained of national rather than international interest. Prize money for Irish racing was no better in 1939, in real terms, than it had been 100 years earlier. Ireland, however, had a limestone soil and mild climate which suited horse breeding and a rural population for whom horses were part of daily life. While some were content to breed and run a few animals in a small way at country meetings, others sought fame and fortune across the Irish Sea. In the nineteenth century most who did so were involved in jump racing.

The Irish are said to have invented steeplechasing in the 1750s. Less than a century later, they began an assault on British jump racing that has seldom flagged. Alan McDonough and Brunette took on England's foremost rider Jem Mason and the 1840 Grand National winner Jerry in a match and won. The first Irish victory in the Aintree steeplechase was in 1847 when Matthew and jockey Dennis Wynne triumphed. The first dual winner of the race, Abd-el-Kadar was Irish-bred and ridden in 1851 by little-known amateur T. Abbott (or Abbot). From then on, Ireland became the nursery of British jumpers. The great steeplechaser Manifesto was bred there; so were The Lamb, Cloister, Wild Man from Borneo, Why Not, Empress, The Soarer, Woodbrook – all winners of the Grand National between 1868 and 1899. The names of Drogheda (1898 winner) and Drumcree (1903) also give them away. Throughout the twentieth century, National Hunt statistics listing trainers of major winners are full of Irish residents. The columns 'bred in …' mention France, occasionally America, but there is no longer any point in compiling data on Irish-breds. Winning steeplechasers are nearly all Irish-bred!

The history of Irish horseracing and its relationship with Britain have become increasingly significant in the last 50 years. There had been a minor upsurge of Irish success on the English flat at the beginning of the twentieth century with the first Irish-trained Epsom Derby winner, Orby (1907), who also won the Irish Derby, and Rhodora, 1908 English One Thousand Guineas winner, both owned by Irish-American Richard Croker. Ireland was also recognised as highly suitable horse breeding territory by owners such as the Aga Khan, one of the most influential and successful in Britain during the inter war period; he bought five studs in Co. Kildare. In general, however, Irish flat racing was held in low esteem. The Irish Classics, restored to level weights in 1945, were poorly funded but still fair game for English horses unable to win an equivalent race at home. Three men, Vincent O'Brien (see separate entry), Paddy Prendergast and Joe McGrath changed all that.

O'Brien, initially a trainer of jump horses, won the major British National Hunt contests, the Champion Hurdle and Gold Cup at Cheltenham and the Grand National three times each between 1948 and 1955. He then turned his attention to flat racing, producing Ballymoss, the greatest Irish horse of the 1950s, winner of several top English races and the first Irish horse to win the prestigious Prix de l'Arc de Triomphe at Longchamp. Prendergast made a habit of winning the major two-year-old races in England, took the leading trainers' title in three consecutive seasons (1963–65), and won four English Classics. McGrath put Irish racing on the international map by masterminding the sponsorship of the Irish Derby. In 1962 the race leapt from being an £8,000 domestic event to a £50,000 international extravaganza, the Irish Hospitals Sweepstakes Derby 30 per cent more valuable than its English counterpart. The re-launched Irish Classic attracted horses and media attention from around the globe and was won by a top French colt, Tambourine II, trained at Chantilly but bred and owned in America. Elite Irish racing has never looked back. The winners of the Irish Derby in the past 40 years have been the cream of European three-year-olds and the race is scheduled at a time, around the end of June, which allows contestants from both the English Derby and the Prix du Jockey-Club to participate. Thirteen Epsom Derby and four Prix du Jockey-Club winners have won at The Curragh since 1962.

The importance of horse breeding in Ireland has also grown significantly over the same period. During the Second World War the English National

Stud, located at Co. Kildare since 1916, was finally handed over to Ireland, becoming the Irish National Stud. This was followed by government incentives aimed at the expansion of bloodstock breeding and, during the 1960s, the cementing of strong links between trainer Vincent O'Brien and American owners. O'Brien began to visit the yearling sales in North America, bought the yearling colt Nijinsky and in so doing started a process which culminated in Coolmore, Co. Tipperary, now the leading stud farm in Europe. His partnership with Robert Sangster and John Magnier, dating from 1975, saw millions of dollars change hands at the Keeneland Sales in Kentucky where O'Brien regularly chose yearlings sired by the Canadian stallion Northern Dancer. The import of North American bloodstock on a large scale changed the course of thoroughbred breeding in Ireland while the offspring of Northern Dancer dominated European racing throughout the 1980s. One of his sons, Sadler's Wells, has since taken over the mantle; standing at Coolmore, he is currently the champion sire in Europe and has been for most of the 1990s. Following O'Brien's retirement, John Magnier has masterminded the racing and breeding operation based there, and many of the top European horses in recent years are products of the stud, owned and raced by Magnier and his partners (including his wife Susan, O'Brien's daughter) and trained by the other O'Brien, Aidan. Other rich international owners and breeders, such as the Maktoums, also maintain studs in Ireland.

Not content with bringing equine talent to its shores, Ireland has sent out many world champions of its own. Vincent O'Brien, in the twilight of his outstanding career, picked up the 1990 Breeders' Cup Mile with Royal Academy and John Oxx, trainer of 2000 Epsom Derby winner, Sinndar, took the same American race with Ridgewood Pearl in 1995. Dermot Weld has twice won the Melbourne Cup with horses from his Curragh yard (Vintage Crop in 1993 and Media Puzzle in 2002) as well as US Triple Crown race, the Belmont Stakes, in 1990 with Go And Go. He has been champion trainer in Ireland by prize money on eight occasions and by number of winners 18 times since 1972. Irish-trained horses have won 34 English Classics from 1957 to 2002. In jump racing they have picked up 9 Champion Hurdles and 11 Cheltenham Gold Cups since 1960, though only four Grand Nationals (three in the past six years: Bobbyjo in 1999, Papillon in 2000 and Mouty's Pass in 2003). The 'Master of Ballydoyle', the incomparable Vincent, has now been replaced at the famous yard by Aidan O'Brien (no relation), leading trainer in Britain in 2001 and 2002.

Then there are the jockeys, from current jump champion Tony McCoy (see separate entry) and fellow riders Mick Fitzgerald and Norman Williamson to great names now retired such as Jonjo O'Neill and Richard Dunwoody (see separate entries). Pat Taaffe, Willie Robinson and Tommy Stack partnered three of Britain's favourite steeplechasers – Arkle, Mill House and Red Rum. During the winter jumps season, it sometimes seems that every winning jockey interviewed boasts an Irish accent. On the flat, Michael Kinane, John Reid and Johnny Murtagh have all won big races in England during the 1990s while Pat Eddery and Kieren Fallon (see separate entries) have won 16 British jockey championships between them. It is impossible to contemplate horseracing in England without the input of Ireland and the Irish.

Further reading

Scally, J., *Them and Us: the Irish at Cheltenham* (Edinburgh: Mainstream, 1999).
Smith, R., *Vincent O'Brien. The Master of Ballydoyle* (London: Stanley Paul, 1992).
www.hri.ic

See also O'Brien, Vincent.

Moneybox

Indian Queen, one of the few fillies to win the Ascot Gold Cup (1991) was also the longest priced winner of the race in the post war period, at 25–1.

Information is a key currency in betting circles and in racing usually refers to inside intelligence, often from a stable, which reveals whether a horse is fancied to win (or lose).

In the Groove was bought for only 20,000 guineas as a yearling in 1988 but won races worth £700,000.

The Injured Jockeys Fund has paid out over £4 million in assistance since it was founded in 1964.

The **Irish Champion Stakes**, run at Leopardstown in September, is the only Irish race to be included in the prestigious Emirates World Series programme of races. It was worth £384,475 to the 2001 winner, Giant's Causeway.

Istabraq was favourite for each of his three Champion Hurdle successes, at odds of 3–1 (1998), 4–9 (1999) and 8–15 (2000).

A day at the races 1850

Dearest Mama,

I am in a state of agitation. Charles has been invited to Ascot on Gold Cup day, which is, as you know, the most fashionable of the week, and I am to accompany him. We are to join the Fitzwilliams for luncheon and view the races from the grandstand. Charles says that over 2,000 people can be accommodated in the stand and that the ladies are all exceedingly well-dressed. Oh dear, what am I to wear? It cannot be my pink silk nor the amber satin for I fear my condition will be too advanced. Does my sister Louisa still have the cream muslin? It would be very suitable as the weather in June is often oppressive – my cousin Charlotte had to endure a thunderstorm when she attended the Derby at Epsom and her parasol offered little protection from the elements, or the riff-raff who surrounded the carriage. Her husband Henry had to chase away scores of little gypsy children! Charles says I must not worry as we will be safe in the grandstand.

I hope we shall arrive in time to see the Royal carriage procession drive down the course. When Charles was at Ascot last year with Colonel Foster, he told me that he had walked past the Royal Enclosure which extends from the stand to the rails and had seen several members of the Royal Household. I should very much like to see the Queen – I have read in *The Times* that she frequently appears at the window of the Royal Box.

Do you remember the year we attended with the Brownings? It was such a delightful day and the children so enjoyed the picnic. I am sure we saw very few of the races even from the carriage – it was a pity James could not find a stance nearer to the course – but Jenkins had prepared such a delicious repast that our disappointment was soon forgotten. Charles assures me that we shall have an excellent luncheon from the caterers – a London firm, I believe – and that I may retire to the ladies' rooms if I become fatigued.

Oh, by the way, Charles says to tell Papa that The Flying Dutchman is much fancied for the Gold Cup – no, I must remember it is called the Emperor's Plate now in honour of Tsar Nicholas – after it won the Derby and St Leger last year. He intends to wager 20 guineas and recommends Papa to do the same, though he fears the horse will be the favourite.

Do ask Louisa to send that dress.

Your loving daughter,
Emma

J

Horsebox

Jay Trump, bred and raced in the United States, became trainer Fred Winter's first of two successive Grand National winners in 1965, ridden by amateur jockey C. Smith – the 50–1 Anglo was the second. Winter had also won the race twice as a jockey with Sundew 1957 and Kilmore 1962.

Jerry M. was second in the 1910 Grand National but is remembered as one of only two winning horses to carry 12 st 7 lb to victory, in 1912; the other was Poethlyn (1919).

Jet Ski Lady won the 1991 Oaks for Sheikh Maktoum, the longest priced winner (50–1) and the second longest winning margin (10 lengths) of the twentieth century.

Jodami won the 1993 Cheltenham Gold Cup, becoming National Hunt Champion of the year; he was second in 1994 and completed a unique hat trick of Hennessy Irish Gold Cups in 1995.

Johannesburg was two-year-old colt of the year in 2001, after his victory in the Breeders' Cup Juvenile but failed in his only three starts in 2002.

Juliette Marny won the Epsom and Irish Oaks in 1975; her full brother Julio Mariner (by Blakeney out of Set Free) won the St Leger in 1978, the first Classic winner for Clive Brittain.

Jargon

Every sport has its own set of rules, code of behaviour and language. Football has its offside and sweeper, rugby its garryowen and lineout, figure skating its triple salchow. None, however, has the amount of jargon and complexity of language found in horseracing, a situation which is the complete reverse of the sport. Racing could hardly be simpler: the horses run from A to B and the first one to get there wins. Unfortunately, the jargon employed to describe this act and the operations surrounding it would fill a book.

Almost everything about the language of racing is designed to exclude, baffle and demean. In spite of the marketing, the emphasis on family days and friendliness and the exhortations to 'come racing', a racecourse can be an intimidating venue for the fledgling racegoer. Turn up at most courses and you can't even gain admission without deciphering a code. Can you pay to be a 'member'? (you know you aren't one but it looks as if you can join by paying at the gate). Are 'club' and 'members' the same? What is the difference between Tattersalls and the Silver Ring? The three-tier entry system employed by some racecourses is reminiscent of the days when railways had first, second and third-class carriages (toffs, white collar, plebs).

Everyone connected with racing uses jargon. There is the language of the horse itself, its conformation, the 'points of a horse' from the blaze on its face (a patch of white) to all the parts of its legs which are vitally important if it is to race properly – pasterns, fetlocks, cannon bones. (In racing parlance, if a horse has 'got a leg', this is shorthand for suffering from tendon strain, in which case it is likely to 'break down'.) Then there is jockey-speak. Giving the horse a 'backhander' indicates a stroke of the whip, a 'reminder' is something the same, intended to keep the horse focused on the job of racing. In his post-race report, usually explaining why he didn't win, the jockey might suggest that the horse 'put in a short one' (an extra stride before a fence, possibly resulting in a sharp exit from the race!). Or the horse 'didn't stay' (the race was too long). Then there is the statement frequently trotted out for the media, 'I asked him the question and ...'. (What question? The horse can't talk! The question, basically, is 'Horse, have you got any more petrol in the tank/could you run a bit faster please because if you can't, we won't win this race.')

There is racecourse terminology. 'Weighed in', intoned across the tannoy some time after the horses have returned to the unsaddling area means that the jockey and his saddle have come back from the race at the correct weight, having been weighed out and the figure noted at the start. (The 'winner all right' phrase used in Ireland seems to make more sense.) There is also the language of the race, trotted out glibly by the racing broadcasters – 'tailed off' (the horse, probably the one you have backed, is miles behind the rest), 'on/off the bridle/bit' (either going well ... or not).

The Plain English Campaign has already had a go at explaining betting terminology with its 'double carpet', and 'Burlington Bertie'. Why has it bothered? Any group of people who have invented a language as complex as this and persist in using it in the twenty-first century have only one object – to keep out those who are not part of their gang, their secret society. Social anthropologists agree that the complexity of language is an inverse correlation of what is being described. The more complicated something sounds, the more outsiders will be in awe of those using the terminology. Where betting is concerned, however, it is really quite unnecessary. A visit to the Tote window with £5 each way on number 4 in the 3.30 is all that is required. The sooner everyone accepts that betting language is not quaint and colourful but either plain daft or just intimidating twaddle, the more chance of making a racecourse an inviting place. As an example, how about 'the jolly'? This is apparently slang for the favourite and is short for 'the jolly old favourite'. When did you last hear anyone talk about 'the jolly old...'? 1914? 1954? Who in their right mind is going to use this sort of terminology in 2004, apart from those who already do? How can the marketing arm of the racing business propel it forward when there is language like this around to cast it back at least 50 years?

There are signs of change. New and younger managers and marketing personnel are attempting to jettison some of the more antiquated terms particularly those surrounding payment and entry to the course. Help desks, information points and racecards at the most forward-looking venues are all trying to demystify the racing experience. But in many areas racing still has a problem. It can keep on preaching to the converted few, the insiders who know the jargon, or it can strip away the mystique and open up the sport to ordinary sports fans by simplifying its terminology. Foreign languages are no longer compulsory in the British education system. Why should anyone in the twenty-first century bother to learn this one?

Further reading

Cassidy, R., *The Sport of Kings* (Cambridge: Cambridge University Press, 2002).
Fox, K., *The Racing Tribe* (London: Metro, 1999).

Jockey Club

The Jockey Club is the regulatory authority for horseracing in Britain. It is responsible for the licensing of trainers, riders, valets and racecourses; security, anti-doping measures and disciplinary matters; the employment and direction of racing officials and racecourse medical and veterinary arrangements for horses and riders. Additionally through the Racecourse Holdings Trust, the Club owns and operates 13 racecourses, re-investing the profits into racing, and through the Jockey Club Estates it manages the 2,800 acres of training grounds around Newmarket.

Initially formed around 1752 to arrange match races at Newmarket and settle gambling debts between members, generally from the aristocracy or great landed families, it gradually took more responsibility for organising racing at Newmarket. It gained authority because of the status of its members and by the early nineteenth century those who raced elsewhere were asking the Club to adjudicate on racing issues, particularly gambling. The Club opted out of betting disputes but chose to determine actual racing matters, though only if the events had been held under the Club's rules of racing. By the late nineteenth century to hold a meeting not recognised by the Jockey Club was tantamount to being cast into the racing wilderness. Although by 1900 the Club controlled flat racing, jump racing remained outside its authority. Indeed the Club had not wished to involve itself in that side of the sport, although Admiral Rous, senior Jockey Club steward at the time, had assisted the National Hunt Club in formulating its rules when it was established in 1866. In 1968 the two bodies were merged to provide racing with a unified controlling body, a precursor to incorporation by Royal Charter in 1970. Although this had the disadvantage that any change to its constitution, however trivial, required Privy Council permission, it did offer significant protection from political interference.

Elections are held each December and usually about five new members are selected. They are elected (for life) for their knowledge and experience of racing and the contribution that it is felt they could make to the regulation of the sport. Of the 84 'active' members in 2002 – defined by the Club as those of the 123 members under 70 years of age – 96 per cent were past or current registered owners, 54 per cent were breeders, 51 per cent acted as racecourse stewards, 42 per cent were racecourse directors, 30 per cent have sat on the licensing committee, 29 per cent on the disciplinary committee, 26 per cent were ex-jockeys (mainly amateur) and 17 per cent were past or present holders of a licence or permit to train. Seven stewards are elected from the members and, together with the Jockey Club executive, are responsible for strategy and policy. Members are expected to sit on Jockey Club and other racing committees.

Despite opposition from those in the industry who felt that it was morally wrong for racing to be run by a private club, one so exclusive that most of the talent in the sport was denied any opportunity to influence or implement policy, the Jockey Club survived unscathed for almost two and a half centuries. Perhaps those who complained feared interference from government even more than they disliked being dictated to by an organisation in which bloodlines seemed to be as important as in horse breeding. Hence the Jockey Club continued to have the dominant voice in determining the direction of British racing, but it tended to be reactive rather than pro-active, acting as a policeman rather than as a facilitator. Decisions were arrived at and implemented slowly; partly because of the thoroughness with which all points were discussed but also because of the innate conservatism of a traditional leisure industry. Progressive leadership was not prominent.

Eventually, in 1993, the British Horseracing Board (BHB) was established to take over responsibility for strategic planning, political negotiation and marketing though the Club retained its responsibility for regulation of the sport. It is not responsible for the regulation of betting which falls within the province of the law, but which, of course, lies behind many of racing's security problems.

In 2001 the Club underwent a corporate restructure to recognise its four major roles of regulating racing, supporting the work of the BHB, owning and running racecourses, and operating training facilities. The vital regulatory role was ring-fenced from the Club's other activities and became the specific responsibility of Regulatory Stewards who as well as overseeing such matters appointed the members of the Disciplinary and Licensing Committees. The individuals holding the key appointments in the four areas – the Chairman of the Racecourse Holdings Trust, the Chairman of the Jockey Club Estates, the nominated Directors on the BHB and the Regulatory Stewards – are all on the main board of the Jockey Club to help provide a forum for effective discussion of overall strategy.

Recent legal discussion has focussed on the independence of the Jockey Club and the suggestion that members who own and race horses cannot be truly unbiased in making judgements about the sport and on those who work in the industry. In February 2003 the Club announced that it would be relinquishing its position as regulator and disciplinary authority of the British turf. An independent body is set to take over these roles at the end of 2004.

Further reading

Hill, C.R., *Horse Power: The Politics of the Turf* (Manchester: Manchester University Press, 1988).
Tyrrel, J., *Running Racing: The Jockey Club Years Since 1750* (London: Quiller, 1997).
www.thejockeyclub.co.uk

See also British Horseracing Board.

Jockeys

Jockeys are extraordinary sportspersons. They contrast with others uniquely in terms of their physique, age, gender and the danger of their occupation. In what other job are participants expected to peak mentally and physically five or six times a day – even more if there are evening meetings – for six and increasingly seven days a week; risk serious injury every time they go to work; and all the time restrict themselves to a diet designed to keep their weight well below the norm?

Other things being equal, and often when they are not, it is the skill of the jockey that determines the result of a race. Leading jockeys earn six-figure incomes because they have the ability to make that split-second decision during a race which can mean the difference between winning and losing, between success and failure, between a horse being worth a few million pounds or a few hundred thousand. Even without the presents from grateful owners and backers, and retainers to secure the services of the best performers, it is clear that there is an earnings pyramid with rewards reflecting the skewed distribution of mounts and even more so that of winning rides. Perhaps five or six riders make an exceptional living from propelling 500 kilos of horseflesh faster than most others. Next come the four dozen or so who can ride perhaps 20 winners a season. They are followed by a large band of men (and women) who struggle to make ends meet, earning relatively little and obtaining most of that from riding work rather than races. The money to be earned from jump and hurdle racing bears little comparison with that available on the flat. The basic riding fee is higher but the level of prize money is substantially lower and always has been. As on the flat a few outstanding individuals dominate the earnings pyramid. One estimate is that 250 rides and 20 winners are now required to show a profit at the end of the season, a figure attained by around 30 jockeys.

Then there is the matter of psychic income from the applause of the crowd and the plaudits of the media. Not till the 1820s were the names of jockeys generally featured in the newspapers or even the *Racing Calendar*. Even then, most of them would be regarded by their employers as liveried servants, wearing the colours of their masters. The development of the sporting press stimulated jockey worship among the masses by quoting their opinions, reporting their activities and creating identities for them both on and off the racecourse. The first jockey to achieve 'superstar' status was Fred Archer (see separate entry), the long-legged 'Tinman', who won over a third of the 8,004 races in which he rode, including 21 Classics. Town criers announced his arrival, reproductions of his image had record sales, special trains brought adoring crowds to his wedding, and on the day of his funeral Newmarket closed. Today's equivalent is Frankie Dettori (see separate entry). He inhabits a much more media-aware world in which he is used by racing to promote the sport, not only to existing racegoers but also to the uninitiated. Until Dettori's era riders rarely exhibited excitement, emotion, or even enthusiasm for their job. However, his flying leap from winning mounts, accented English, and charismatic flamboyance has endeared him to the racing public.

Two skills are essential to jockeys. 'Hands', the ability to control and encourage a horse independently of physical strength, is almost always a natural gift; whereas 'head', the capacity to note circumstances within a race and without hesitation know what is the correct thing to so, is partly instinctive but doubtless can be picked up by practice, observation and experience. Jockeys who make it to the top possess distinctive attributes of their own. In the eighteenth century Sam Chifney had his late rush; in the nineteenth George Fordham was renowned for his 'kid' by which he persuaded other riders that his own mount was faring less well than it was and in the twentieth Lester Piggott was as ruthless on the track as in his business dealings off it.

Once apprentices become fully-fledged jockeys they are on their own; all further skills acquisition is very much a matter of 'independent learning'. To some extent this involves picking up tips from admired senior riders: Edgar Britt taught Eddie Hide to hold the reins shorter on a tight track and Frankie Durr showed him how to catch hold of the mane in the starting stalls so as to give the horse full freedom when it jumped out. Otherwise it is down to experience. Racing itself is the best way to appreciate that different tracks require different skills: that Brighton's long, uphill finish is a different proposition to the sharp, ill-cambered final bend and short run-in at Catterick; that Chester's sharp left-hand bends do not suit big horses; and that the steep and perilous descent to Tattenham Corner at Epsom can cause tired horses to drop back and impede other runners.

As this suggests, many skills are acquired or refined simply via 'learning by doing'. At times, however, new skills have to be developed as a matter of urgency. In 1965 the introduction of starting stalls in flat racing meant that the experience of jockeys who knew how different starters operated the gate and had the ability to manoeuvre horses ready for the off was rendered redundant virtually overnight. Now what had to be learned was the art of keeping horses ready for the opening of the stalls and being prepared to go instantly from a standing start. In the late 1980s the introduction of all-weather tracks on which a smooth run was all-important necessitated the development of new tactics. Some riders grasped the essentials more quickly than others and it was on such tracks at Wolverhampton, and particularly Southwell, that Alex Greaves established herself as 'Queen of the Sands'. More recently furore has erupted over new restrictions placed on the use of whips. Jockeys propel their mounts mainly by physical effort and skill, using legs, hands and heels, and sometimes their voices, but the only material aid permitted is the whip.

Recently the Jockey Club, under the pressure of public opinion, has taken exception to 'excessive' use of this implement and it has taken many riders some time to come to terms with what is now required.

Leading jockeys may be millionaires, but they still tip their caps to the owners of their mounts and call them 'Sir' when they enter the saddling enclosure. Anthropologist Kate Fox has argued that the body language indicates that this is a vestigial gesture rather than an expression of genuine deference, particularly since syndicalisation has to a degree democratised ownership. Yet it is the owner who ultimately decides whether or not he wants a particular jockey to ride his horse and many trainers and owners still believe in a master and servant relationship. Tact and diplomacy remain vital components for success. Owners do not like to acknowledge that they have purchased a dud and would rather blame the jockey than his mount. Loyalty by owners to riders is not a feature of racing. All jockeys get sacked in what Michael Caulfield, Executive Manager of the Jockeys Association, labels a working life of confidence-sapping mental abuse.

Further reading

Dettori, F., *A Year in the Life of Frankie Dettori* (London: Mandarin, 1997).

Magee, S. and Lewis, G., *To Win Just Once: The Life of the Journeyman Jump Jockey* (London: Headline, 1997).

Vamplew, W., 'Still Crazy After All Those Years: Continuity in a Changing Labour Market for Professional Jockeys', *Journal of Contemporary British History* (2000), 115–45.

See also Nineteenth-century jockeys, Twentieth-century jockeys, Weight, Whipping.

Moneybox

A **Jackpot** is a Tote bet in which punters have to select the winners of the first six races at a given meeting.

Japan hosts the most valuable jump race in the world, the Nakayama Grand Jump – the winner of the inaugural running (2000), the French-trained Boca Boca, won nearly £500,000 in prize money.

Jeddah was the first 100–1 winner of the Derby in 1898; the only others have been Signorinetta (1908) and Aboyeur (1913).

The **Jockeys Association** negotiates the basic riding fees for flat-race jockeys and National Hunt riders.

Jockey Treble, at 100–1, was the longest priced post-war winner of the Lincoln Handicap in the third largest field (46 runners in 1947).

H.J. (Jim) Joel was leading National Hunt owner twice, in 1979–80 and 1986–87, at the ages of 85 and 92.

K

Horsebox

Lanzarote, the Champion Hurdle winner of 1974, also won the Christmas Hurdle at Kempton twice (1973, 1975) and a total of 20 of his 33 hurdle races; he was killed in the 1977 Cheltenham Gold Cup.

Legal Steps gave champion jump jockey Tony McCoy his first win in March 1991 – on the flat at Thurles in Ireland.

Le Moss became the first horse to complete the stayers' triple crown (Ascot Gold Cup, Goodwood Cup and Doncaster Cup) twice in 1979 and 1980; he was also second in the 1978 St Leger. His full brother was Levmoss, winner of the Ascot Gold Cup and Prix de l'Arc de Triomphe in 1969.

Little Polveir won both the Scottish Grand National (1987) and the Aintree Grand National (1989).

Lomond, a son of Northern Dancer, won the Two Thousand Guineas in 1983, one of Vincent O'Brien's last English Classic winners, but failed to win again, unplaced in two races and second in the Irish Two Thousand Guineas.

Love Divine gave Henry Cecil his most recent English Classic winner in the 2000 Oaks, having also won the race in 1996 with Lady Carla.

Lambourn

Berkshire is the home of Ascot and Windsor racecourses, and a number of famous training stables at Kingsclere, Wantage, and East and West Ilsley are congregated not far from the third course, Newbury. Across the boundary in Wiltshire, the Marlborough Downs have also attracted racing establishments but the greatest concentration of racing yards outside Newmarket is to be found some 10 miles north-west of Newbury, at Lambourn. Here around 30 trainers, mostly over jumps, have based themselves in an area dubbed the 'valley of the racehorse'.

Lambourn first claimed attention when the 1855 Derby was won by the Berkshire-trained Wild Dayrell, and by the end of the nineteenth century the Lambourn Downs had developed into a popular training centre. Centuries of sheep farming had helped to nourish natural grassland which the great Victorian trainer John Porter reckoned to be vastly superior to the flat, artificially managed gallops of Newmarket Heath. A century later, the Downs region boasts six all-weather tracks as well as over 600 acres of traditional turf. The men who finally put the name of Lambourn on the racing map, however, were the two post war National Hunt trainers, Fulke Walwyn and Fred Winter. A string of successes in the Cheltenham Gold Cup and Champion Hurdle between 1962 and 1978 together with three consecutive Grand National winners (the Walwyn-trained Team Spirit in 1964 and Winter's Jay Trump and Anglo in 1965 and 1966) were testament to the quality of the Downs. Between them, the two champion trainers sent out over 3,500 winners from their Saxon House and Uplands yards and many of the current generation of local trainers worked as their assistants at one time, including Nicky Henderson, Oliver Sherwood and Nick Gaselee. There have also been incomers. With over half the work force in the village said to be Irish, it is not surprising that Irish trainer Noel Chance is also at home there, picking up two Cheltenham Gold Cups in five years with Mr Mulligan (1997) and Looks Like Trouble (2000).

Although Lambourn is better known for its jumping associations, the area has also played host to some prominent flat trainers. Peter Walwyn, cousin of Fulke, set up there in 1960 and was twice champion trainer in 1974 and 1975, while Barry Hills moved from Newmarket to his own yard at Lambourn in 1969 and still operates there. Quickly established by training the 1973 Arc winner Rheingold, his most recent big race success was Hula Angel in the 1999 Irish One Thousand Guineas; in between he has been one of the few to train a Pattern race winner every season and pass the milestone of 2,000 flat winners in a career. He favours the downland over the Newmarket gallops because it offers stiffer exercise and horses attain fitness more readily. (The fashion for interval training – using steeply inclined all-weather tracks for repeated shorter gallops instead of the traditional lengthier workouts – is well suited to the local hilly terrain.) Jamie Osborne and Brian Meehan, both successful at the all-weather courses recently are two more Lambourn trainers who ply their trade on the flat. Marcus Tregoning, trainer for Sheikh Hamdan al Maktoum and Henry Candy, veteran of over 30 seasons, also train nearby.

Other famous names have had connections with the village. The Pitmans, Richard and Jenny, worked here and son Mark maintains the family connection. John Francome, champion jockey seven times and now a broadcaster and writer, spent his entire career with Fred Winter; he continues to live locally. Merrick Francis, son of novelist Dick and a former trainer himself, runs the local racehorse transport business. Apart from these, there are probably 700 or 800 people directly employed in racing in the immediate vicinity and a similar number providing services to the industry, from feed merchants to horse dentists. With almost half of the population connected in some way to racing, it is little wonder that Lambourn, which stages a charity Open Day every spring for the general public, has been called 'the village of racing'.

Further reading

Lee, A., *Lambourn: Village of Racing* (London: Barker, 1982).
Oakley, R., *Valley of the Racehorse* (London: Headline, 2000).

Language

See Jargon.

Law and legislation

Those involved in sport often think (falsely) that aspects of their activity are beyond the law. This attitude has developed because for most instances of mis-conduct within a sport the legal authorities – *and* those involved in the misbe-haviour – were content to leave matters to the jurisdiction of the sporting bodies. Racing has been no exception and generally disciplinary measures were left to the Jockey Club.

Until the end of the twentieth century the Jockey Club used this power without much regard to the niceties of the law. Indeed as late as 2000 it brought in a rule that anyone who refused to supply information on request would be deemed to have committed an offence, in effect denying persons the right to silence. Yet this is one of the basic tenets of the European Convention on Human Rights. The Club is now struggling to come to grips with the Human Rights Act to which it is bound as a public authority. In particular licensed persons coming under Jockey Club jurisdiction now have the right to a fair and public hearing by an independent and impartial tribunal. Most of the current closed-door enquiries will have to be open to the public and reasons will have to be given publicly for all decisions made.

Racing participants are subject to the normal laws of the land and racing itself, as an industry, is liable to all the intricacies of contract, employment and discrimination legislation. In the third quarter of the twentieth century, for example, Equal Opportunity laws forced the Jockey Club to issue riding and training licences to women. Within racing the past decade has seen an increas-ing tendency to resort to law. As the turf wars between the British Horseracing Board and the various sectional interests have become personal and bitter, writs have been threatened on such matters as the fixture list, the negotiation of media rights, and even statements on the future of the industry. Additionally those at the receiving end of the Jockey Club's disciplinary actions are no longer willing to accept what it does, even if it is trying to protect the integrity of the sport. In the late 1990s the senior stewards temporarily suspended the riding licences of five jockeys arrested in connection with race-fixing but not at the time convicted of any offence. Three of them – Jamie Osborne, Dean Gallagher and Leighton Aspell – with the support of the Jockeys Association, threatened to go to law on the grounds that this was an illegal restraint of trade. In other occupations suspension on full pay is often used but these individuals, like most jockeys, were self-employed. On the advice of its own legal team, the Jockey Club was forced to lift the suspensions. The men never actually faced trial.

One area where the law has not yet intervened is on the issue of injuries to riders sustained during a race. The High Court has accepted the view that when small men ride large animals at high speed in close proximity they do not have much chance to avoid or reduce the risk of collision. Hence recklessness and intentional dangerous riding are difficult to establish legally and no claim for negligence against a jockey has yet been successful in the courts.

It is not often that private organisations plead for more regulation, but the Jockey Club is concerned about the vulnerability of racing to corrupt activity. It believes that, in comparison to other forms of gaming and betting, the business of bookmaking is under-regulated and lacks the necessary measures to deter corruption and thus renders racing open to malpractice. The Club acknowledges that betting and racing are being used for money laundering purposes, that there is some corruption in racing by criminals, and that there is large-scale illegal betting which is to the detriment of both government and racing revenues. Hence the Club would like more substantive criminal offences to be introduced directly related to corrupt behaviour in racing such as the doping of a horse and the bribery of participants or officials.

Most government-imposed regulation on racing has come about because of its association with gambling but historically there has been some more direct legislation. In 1740 an Act of Parliament declared that prizes at all race meetings must be at least £50. The government felt that there was too much racing which was leading to idleness and poverty in the population. The Act was repealed within a decade and the next time minimum prize money was set it was by the Jockey Club in the 1870s. However, Parliamentary legislation was used in 1879 to end unauthorised metropolitan race meetings that were leading to spectator disorder.

Most parliamentary intervention has lain in the betting side of the industry. In the late 1920s the government approved the establishment of the Tote and legalised the apparatus for it to transfer money into the racing industry. For most of the last four decades of the twentieth century, betting on horses was regulated by the Betting Gaming and Lotteries Act of 1963, again with a mechanism to dip a bucket on behalf of racing into the financial stream from betting on its activities. In 2002, however, a shock wave went through the racing industry when the government announced the end of the betting tax and betting levy, forcing the various sectors of the industry to negotiate a new financial structure. It has also decided that the Tote will be privatised. There has never been a single government department with direct responsibility for horseracing. The Department of Culture, Media and Sport has rarely viewed the turf as coming within its ambit; the Home Office's remit has covered the Horseracing Betting Levy Board, the Tote and regulated betting and both the Treasury and Customs and Excise have had an interest in the betting tax. Now the sport is to be completely cut adrift from both government subsidy and direct regulation.

Literature and writing

Horseracing and literature seldom inhabit the same breath, let alone the same sentence. Most members of the public are only concerned with the sport because of their interest in gambling, which is why numerous books on form and betting systems make their way on to the high street bookshelves. Those who earn their living in racing have little time or inclination to read about its past triumphs and disasters, its detailed histories and memoirs. When Jack Fairfax-Blakeborough, one of the foremost twentieth-century authorities on the sport, wrote his series on *Northern Turf History*, this prolific writer was obliged to publish his fourth and final volume privately in 1973: there was no commercial market any longer for his brand of anecdote and folklore. The racing world to which he and 'turfists' such as the Hon. George Lambton, author of an acknowledged racing classic *Men and Horses I Have Known* (1924), belonged had virtually disappeared by the 1960s.

Some racegoers, however, are happy to have pictorial reminders of racing's recent past, and the last 30 years have seen a proliferation of glossy coffee table books crammed with photographs of 'greatest' horses, 'royal' horses or 'Grand National-winning' horses. These, together with biographies of the top jockeys, histories of individual stars like Desert Orchid and Istabraq, a selection of informative but mostly uncritical volumes on British racecourses, a handful of anthologies, and a few yearbooks detailing the exploits of the season past, make up the current stock of books about racing. There have been no Nick-Hornby-type revelations of a misspent youth around the racecourses of Britain. Or maybe there have been and they have gone unnoticed. (The closest would probably be David Ashforth's *Hitting the Turf: A Punting Life* which obviously falls into the gambling rather than horsey category.) Horseracing, after all, is a minority sport, with a twenty-first-century following whose reading habits are most likely to begin and end with the *Racing Post*. Is that unfair? Perhaps. A Dick Francis novel, then.

Francis, ex-champion jockey, forever associated with Devon Loch's extraordinary collapse at the end of the 1956 Grand National, used his knowledge of racing to produce a novel a year for 40 years. Hardly literature, these thrillers have nevertheless sold over 60 million copies, have been translated into 35 languages and earned Francis a more than comfortable living. He won the Edgar Allan Poe award for best novel, given by the Mystery Writers of America, on three occasions (1970, 1981 and 1996) and received further accolades from the Crime Writers Association (1965 and 1980). The biggest 'whodunit' in recent years revolved around speculation that the author was actually Francis' wife, Mary, who was known to have helped him with research and editing but who was suspected of contributing rather more to the writing partnership. The truth is immaterial. The books have been phenomenally successful and have paved the way for other racing personalities such as ex-jockey Richard Pitman, his former wife, trainer Jenny Pitman, and seven-time champion jockey John Francome to continue this type of fare.

Not that Francis was the first to write racing fiction. Nat Gould was a prolific exponent of the genre but, with titles such as *The Rajah's Racer* and *Racecourse and Battlefield*, his work belongs to another age. More serious non-fiction about racing, however, has also had its day and reflects the ever-diminishing profile of the sport from the heady days of the early-to-mid twentieth century. At one time, it was possible to ask a fellow drinker or traveller for the winner of the 3.30 at Kempton as well as the top-of-the-table clash between Arsenal and Chelsea and be greeted with more than a blank stare. Now only the football query is likely to elicit an answer. Outside the close-knit world of 'connections' and habitual punters, the general population has no knowledge of and little interest in horseracing, and the shelf space allocated to the sport in major bookshops mirrors this situation. Without the series of books published by Channel 4 Racing throughout the 1990s, the numerous books about the Grand National by race expert Reg Green and a trickle of biographies about turf personalities, the range would be thinner still. Even the success of the American prizewinning sports book, Seabiscuit, based on a true story about a racehorse in the 1930s, is unlikely to produce any British imitations.

Yet there would appear to be sufficient interest in the subject to support several second-hand bookshops and catalogues specialising in racing and the horse, largely operating around Newmarket. A glance through these highlights a number of specific fields not normally found in high street booksellers – books on breeding and veterinary practice, sporting art, Arabian horses, hunting and copies of standard reference volumes such as *Horses in Training, Ruff's Guide to the Turf* and the *Bloodstock Breeders' Review*. Collections of Weatherbys' *Racing Calendar* are much prized and scarcely available. It is a salutary observation that second-hand copies of many works appearing on the market have inscribed flyleaves which identify their original owners as members of the military, landed gentry or minor aristocracy: families who bred, owned, raced and hunted horses at one time but whose estates and possessions have increasingly been broken up and dispersed.

Horseracing, however, has occasionally found itself a bit part in literature. Emile Zola in his novel, *Nana*, builds an entire chapter around the scene at Longchamp in 1870 before and during the running of the premier French race of the time, the Grand Prix de Paris. A highlight of the Parisian social calendar, comparable to Royal Ascot, the race description is particularly interesting to British eyes because of the presence of English horses and jockeys, a matter of some historical accuracy. The best known British novel to feature racing is Graham Greene's *Brighton Rock*, set amongst the razor gangs of the 1930s and their rival protection rackets at the south-coast racecourse. (Brighton has had some difficulty in living that one down!) More recently, Graham Swift's 1996 Booker prize winner, *Last Orders*, contains a character, Ray 'Lucky' Johnson whose expertise as a punter sometimes realises large sums of money at crucial times. We sweat with him as he sits nursing his drink in the pub, waiting to see whether 33-1shot Miracle Worker will oblige in the 3.05 at Doncaster to help out a dying mate. Neither of these English-language books actually involve themselves greatly with the races; both focus on the seedy, money-grabbing aspects of the sport; neither is likely to be cited in a British Horseracing Board (BHB) marketing campaign!

Racing used to figure more regularly in British literature. Adam Lindsay-Gordon, a mid-nineteenth-century hunting man, wrote poetry about chasing and point-to-point, as did Siegfried Sassoon and Will Ogilvie. Anthony Trollope dealt with equine sport in his *Hunting Scenes* (1865) and several other works, from the early *The Kellys and the O'Kellys* (1848) to *The Duke's*

Children (1880). Twentieth-century poets have considered other aspects of racing. Philip Larkin reflected on the lives of former racehorses and their brief days of fame in *At Grass*, and John Betjeman visited the Berkshire training centre in his poem *Upper Lambourne* (although the real village is spelt without that final letter!) W.B. Yeats described the scene *At Galway Races*, Robert Hughes wrote simply about *The Races*.

Prime ministers, past and present, have also included horseracing in their writings. Benjamin Disraeli discussed it in his novel, *Sybil*; the fifth Earl of Rosebery, the only serving prime minister to own a Derby winner (Ladas II, 1894) wrote verses about his triumph; and Sir Winston Churchill, another racehorse owner, referred to it in his letters. Amongst the present generation of politicians both Robin Cook, sometime cabinet minister in the Blair governments, and Alex Salmond, for many years leader of the Scottish National Party at Westminster, have combined their love of the sport with newspaper columns on the subject. Robin Oakley, former political editor of the BBC, has gone beyond this by writing a book on the 1999/2000 season from the perspective of Lambourn's racing population.

Occasionally the names of racehorses crop up in literature – the winner of the 1904 Ascot Gold Cup, Throwaway, makes an appearance in James Joyce's *Ulysses* – but more frequently characters from literature appear on the racecard. The most famous of these was probably 1970s champion Brigadier Gerard, named after a French Napoleonic cavalry officer in Arthur Conan Doyle's *The Adventures of Brigadier Gerard*. It is unlikely, however, that many racegoers in Britain, watching the 2001 Irish Two Thousand Guineas winner Black Minnaloushe walk off with the St James's Palace Stakes that summer, would have associated him with the feline star of W.B. Yeats' poem *The Cat and the Moon*. And it will probably be some time before anyone in Britain publishes a children's book about a famous horserace, as happened in Australia with *The World's Greatest Handicap (After Dad)*, a story about the Melbourne Cup. No doubt the BHB in its endless quest for the next generation of racegoers would welcome this idea!

Further reading

Bedford, J., *The Racing Man's Bedside Book* (Cambridge: Colt, 1997).
Huggins, M., *Horseracing and the British 1919–1939* (Manchester: Manchester University Press, 2003).

Moneybox

Lanark racecourse was closed in 1977 when the Levy Board withdrew its support as part of a rationalisation plan for British racing.

Laying off is similar to hedging in that bookmakers pass on some of their received bets to other bookmakers so as to reduce their liabilities.

The betting **levy** was introduced in 1962 and raised £1.8 million in its first year of operation.

Nick Littmoden was leading all-weather trainer in 2002 with total prize money of over £260,000.

Perhaps the unluckiest **loser** of 1994 was the owner of Mister Chippendale who won a point-to-point but whose rider failed to weigh in: this was in a walk over!

Luck money is a tradition at bloodstock auctions worldwide by which a seller voluntarily gives a financial thank you to a buyer after the sale.

M

Horsebox

Meadow Court, winner of the 1965 Irish Derby and the King George, was owned by Bing Crosby.

Miesque, trained by Francois Boutin, won consecutive Breeders' Cup Miles for France in 1987 and 1988.

Moonax, the 40–1 winner of the St Leger in 1994, is the last horse to have won a French/English Classic double, scooping the Prix Royal-Oak in the same year, though he was rated 122, one of the poorest St Leger winners of the century.

Morley Street beat 23 others to win the Champion Hurdle in 1991 as 4–1 favourite, a field only equalled in the post-war period in 1964 when Magic Court won.

Muhtarram, ridden by Willie Carson, won the Group One Prince of Wales's Stakes at Ascot twice in 1994 and 1995.

Mystiko is the only grey to have won the Two Thousand Guineas in the last 50 years.

McCoy, Tony (1974–)

Aided by Martin Pipe's horses, a twelve-month riding season and an almost injury free career, Tony 'A P' McCoy has broken almost every National Hunt riding record. In 1997–98 he rode 200 winners almost two months earlier than Peter Scudamore's record. Two years later he reached 100 winners on 21 November, beating Scudamore's existing record by 30 days, and the following season he achieved the century mark 16 days sooner. That year he rode 253 winners, a record for a jump jockey. In 1999–2000 he reached 1,000 career winners in five years and 95 days, beating Scudamore's record by the incredible margin of five years and 72 days. Stan Mellor had taken 17 years, John Francombe 14, and Peter Scudamore and Richard Dunwoody each 11 years. In 2001–02 he broke Gordon Richards' long-standing record aggregate for flat or jumps by bringing home 289 winners. On Boxing Day 2002 he reached 200 winners in a season 16 days earlier than the previous record, held, of course, by himself. In January 2004 he became the first National Hunt jockey to ride 2,000 winners in Britain.

Tony McCoy was one of six children. He did little schoolwork. By the age of 12 he was a regular truant, cycling away from school to the stables of Billy Rock. Identified by Rock as a future champion, he was recommended to Irish Classic-winning trainer Jim Bolger and apprenticed with him for four years. 'Wee Aunthnay', as he was labelled by trainer Rock, had hoped to be a flat-race jockey but his weight ballooned from 7 st 10 lb to 9 st 7 lb when he was out injured in 1993 with a broken leg sustained on the training gallops. He joined English trainer Toby Balding and within a month of arriving on the mainland rode his first winner, Chickabiddy at Exeter. When he arrived in England in August 1994 he had never ridden in a steeplechase, yet in his first full season he won the conditional jockeys' title (with a record total of 74) and finished seventh in the full jockeys' championship. Next season he was champion National Hunt rider and has been ever since, each year with an increased number of winners.

He undertakes an incredible workload on the daily treadmill. In 2001–02 he rode in a record (again) 1,006 races. At almost six feet tall he continually has to watch his weight. A non-drinker, non-smoker and at times virtually a non-eater, he undergoes an agonising diet regime. His rock-bottom riding weight is 10 st which is about 20 lbs below his natural weight. No matter how small the prize money, how poor the quality of the horse, he always gives everything. It is generally acknowledged, even by his competitors, that he has won more races on horses on which his rivals would not have succeeded. However, his determination to be successful, to be first at the line, has led to several suspensions for overuse of the whip. He makes £200,000 a year – substantially less than his flat-race counterparts – but mainly from riding as he has little celebrity status outside racing, though in 2002 he did make third place in the BBC Sports Personality of the Year. In 2003 he was awarded an MBE.

Further reading

McCoy, T. and Taylor, S., *McCoy: The Autobiography* (London: Michael Joseph, 2002).

Machell, James (1837–1902)

Captain James Octavius Machell, referred to as 'Captain MacHell' by the bookmaking fraternity, was a ruthless gambler, a successful racehorse owner, and an astute racing manager.

In 1857 he was commissioned into the 14th Regiment of Foot and, after being posted to The Curragh, exploited the opportunities to race there. By 1862, at the age of only 24, he was the leading owner in Ireland, five of his horses having won 18 races valued at £1,035. He resigned from the army in 1863 – when a new commanding officer refused him leave to attend the St Leger – and established a small training stable at Kennett, 4 miles north of Newmarket.

His first major plunge on the English turf came the following spring when, taking advantage of the low weight of 6 stone allotted to his Irish horse, Bacchus, in the Prince of Wales's Handicap, he laid out £400 and won £10,000.

Another coup came in the Grand National of 1873 when the bookmakers offered 50–1 against Disturbance, a small horse that they thought unsuited to the stiff Aintree fences. Machell knew the animal much better and put on £200 at these odds. To the bookmakers' chagrin and Machell's delight, the horse came home 6 lengths in front. Two of his other horses also won the Grand National, Reugny in 1874 and Regal two years later. Over his racing career his horses won 540 races worth over £110,000, the last one being Lady Help ridden by American jockey Danny Maher at Lincoln on 18 March 1902.

Despite this success as an owner, it was as a racing manager that Machell excelled. He took horses into his stables but relied on others to perform the training, whilst he concentrated on making race entries and advising the owners what horses to purchase and when to bet. His first employer was the young Lincolnshire squire, Henry Chaplin, for whom, with Machell's assistance, 66–1 shot Hermit won the 1867 Derby, even though the horse had burst a blood vessel only a week before the race. Other young men with large inheritances and a desire to enter racing circles followed, including the Yorkshire baronet, Sir Charles Legard, the seventh Earl of Aylesford, the second Lord Gerard, and the banking heir, Harry McCalmont. For the latter Machell obtained the mare that foaled Isinglass, the 1893 Derby, Two Thousand Guineas, and St Leger winner. Several of 'Machell's Young Men', as they were referred to in racing circles, dissipated their fortunes but usually because they ignored Machell's advice to back only fancied runners from his Bedford Cottage stables.

An astute gambler, he won enough on the turf to buy back the family's Westmoreland estate. He was a better judge of horses than of people. His acerbic tongue cost him the services of leading jockeys George Fordham and Fred Archer when he accused them of not trying on horses that he had backed. He was respected rather than liked and in his latter years was severely depressed, aware that his suspicious nature had cost him several racing friendships.

Further reading

Onslow, R., *Captain Machell* (Swindon: Marlborough, 1994).

Maktoum family

The Maktoum brothers, Sheikhs Maktoum, Hamdan, Mohammed and Ahmed, and other members of their family have made an increasingly significant contribution to British racing since the late 1970s, although in recent years their influence has acquired a more global dimension. Sons of the late Sheikh Rashid bin Saeed Al Maktoum, they form the ruling dynasty in Dubai, an important and wealthy state within the United Arab Emirates, and their wealth has enabled them to buy, breed and race some of the best horses in the world.

When Sheikh Mohammed had his first British winner in 1977, few could have anticipated the extent to which the family would dominate the turf in Britain over the next 25 years. Their influence has been felt in a variety of areas, from sponsorship of races such as the Dubai Champion Stakes to the launch of the *Racing Post* newspaper, from the funding of the Al Bahathri all-weather gallops at Newmarket to the ownership of the Gainsborough, Shadwell and Dalham Hall studs. Their entry into the global bloodstock market in the early 1980s drove up yearling prices, particularly at the Kentucky sales, to unprecedented heights; the naming of these horses introduced reams of unpronounceable Arabic words to British racegoers.

The impact of the Maktoums has been immense. The family members won 35 English Classics between them from 1982 to 2002, including the Derby four times, and carried off the King George nine times from 1988 to 1999. For ten years they completely dominated the fillies' Classics, winning the One Thousand Guineas in four consecutive years from 1989 to 1992 and the Oaks at every renewal bar one between 1987 and 1995. Their most famous horses include the colts Nashwan, the only horse to complete the quartet of Two Thousand Guineas, Epsom Derby, Eclipse and King George in one season (1989), Fantastic Light, a globe-trotting double Emirates World Series winner in 2000 and 2001, and Daylami. Originally bred by the Aga Khan and raced by him until the age of three, Daylami was kept in training for two more years and matured from a miler to an outstanding middle distance horse, winning the Eclipse, King George, Irish Champion Stakes and Breeders' Cup Turf. Oh So Sharp was the most recent winner of the fillies' Triple Crown in 1985 while Dayjur was one of the top sprinters of recent times, with five consecutive Pattern wins in 1990.

The Maktoum roll of honour over 20 years is extensive and impossible to list – Pebbles and Barathea, Breeders' Cup champions, Opera House and Swain, King George winners, Singspiel and Dubai Millenium, victors in the Dubai World Cup, Mtoto and Halling, both two-time winners of the Eclipse Stakes, Winged Love and Balanchine, triumphant in the Irish Derby, Erhaab and Lammtarra in the English Derby, Old Vic and Indian Skimmer in the Prix du Jockey-Club and Prix de Diane, Classic Cliché and Mutafaweq, winners of the St Leger, and Kayf Tara, twice holder of the Ascot Gold Cup are but a few of their successes. They have been utterly dominant in British racing since 1985. Sheikh Mohammed topped the leading owners' table in nine consecutive years to 1993, and has won four more times under the banner of Godolphin, most recently in 2002. Sheikh Hamdan was leading owner in 1990, 1994, 1995 and 2001 and runner-up on several occasions. The Aga Khan (2000) and Khalid Abdulla (2003) are the only non-Maktoum recipients of the title in the past 19 years.

The influence of the Maktoums is increasingly a worldwide phenomenon. They have breeding and racing interests in Australia, where Sheikh Hamdan won the Melbourne Cup in 1986 and 1994, and in the United States, where an academy was launched in 2000 with a view to capturing the Kentucky Derby and other major American races. During the 1990s, their ongoing criticism of British racing, with its low levels of prize money, high betting taxes, and large number of mediocre racecourses, has led to threats of scaling down their operations in Britain, particularly since the foundation of Godolphin Racing, based in Dubai, in 1993. The brainchild of Sheikh Mohammed, the most influential of the brothers, the Godolphin enterprise overwinters horses in Dubai before returning them to its own training establishments worldwide and a selected number of European stables in Britain, Ireland and France. By so doing, it has removed many promising two-year-olds from their original trainers and reduced their yards to little more than nurseries. The policy has undoubtedly been successful, though not universally popular; within five seasons, the Godolphin colours had registered a full set of English Classic wins. With little left to prove in Britain, however, many horses are now aimed at races abroad.

It is hard to over-estimate the impact of the Maktoums on horseracing in Britain. The family has been hailed by many as the saviour of the sport in the past two decades, and Sheikh Mohammed as one of the key figures in twentieth-century British racing. Although Godolphin now has its own stables, trainer (Saeed bin Suroor) and retained jockey (Frankie Dettori), the brothers have had lucrative partnerships with many top British racing personnel over the years including trainers Dick Hern, Michael Stoute, Henry Cecil, John Dunlop and Barry Hills, and jockeys Willie Carson, Pat Eddery, Steve Cauthen and Walter Swinburn. The money they have poured into the industry would be difficult to replace.

Further reading

Magee, S., *Channel Four Racing Complete A–Z of Horse Racing* (London: Channel 4 Books, 2001).
Thompson, L., *Quest for Greatness* (London: Penguin, 1996).

Marketing

When the great Newmarket jockey Fred Archer was scheduled to ride at distant meetings, local town criers would announce his plans. Today leading riders and champion horses can feature at a meeting without anyone but the readers of the racing pages being aware of their presence. Indeed, so poorly is modern racing marketed that sometimes one would not know that racing was taking place except for the odd horsebox on the local roads.

Marketing involves matching a company's capabilities with the wants of consumers so as to satisfy the objectives of both parties. It is not just advertising – though that has a key role – but can involve the creation of a brand, the promotion of an image, and the development of stratified pricing for selling to segmented markets. A good marketing strategy necessitates becoming aware of consumer expectations. Following a consultancy report in 2000 between them the British Horseracing Board and the Levy Board allocated some £10 million to be spent over the next three years in developing such a national strategy for the racing industry. The report had revealed that only 2 per cent of Britain's adult population went to the races even once a year and only 6 per cent regularly bet on the horses (in stark contrast to over 70 per cent that played the lottery). Launched as Discover Racing, the new strategy was designed to boost racecourse attendances from 5 million to 6 million and increase betting on horseracing by 1 per cent above the rate of inflation. This was to be achieved by targeting the under 30s, the middle class and the family racegoer. Surprisingly both targets were met.

Those undertaking the marketing task faced a major problem in that the image of the sport, often a major marketing tool, was sadly tarnished by media revelations of corruption within racing. On the other hand so poor was the existing state of marketing that improvements would not be hard to implement. For example the start of the flat season had no 'wow' factor to grab the attention of the media. Perhaps it is the time of year, when rain and grey skies often disguise the spring, or maybe it is the Doncaster track which many find unappealing, but why should the first day contain both an apprentices' race and a ladies race, hardly events to attract racegoers or publicity? Those running the marketing strategy have declared that they wish to get more clarity into the racing season by giving it a rhythm and a distinct climax but so far the traditional mainly continues. A racing 'Grand Slam' with £5 million up for grabs for the 'super horse' that won four nominated races was introduced in 2003 but it did not influence owners and trainers and hence had little impact on attracting racegoers. Nor has the campaign team taken the opportunity to market horses or jockeys – why are the head-to-head contests between Frankie Dettori and Kieren Fallon not advertised?

Possibly such marketing lies in the province of the individual racecourse rather than as part of a national strategy. At this level a few tracks have failed to drag themselves into the twentieth century, let alone the twenty-first. They rarely view what they offer through the eyes of potential consumers. Others are more progressive and have developed relationships with the local community to encourage loyalty and a future generation of racegoers. Some have also attempted to cater to a wide range of customers, appreciating that many niche markets can be satisfied simultaneously. There are those who want more than just racing, hence the Irish band at Wetherby and the Sinatra-style crooner at Catterick. There are those not interested in the sport at all which explains the ubiquitous bouncy castle and the often politically-incorrect Punch and Judy show. Others, however, do appreciate racing and can be attracted by a parade of champions or even the guest appearance of an old favourite such as retired National Hunt star Desert Orchid. No other course has yet followed Towcester where racegoers are admitted free in an attempt (so far successful) to swell betting revenue and income from food and drink.

Perhaps getting newcomers to racing in the first place is the most difficult task. Many of the general public express a profound ignorance of racing: many have never ridden a horse so whereas the excitement of scoring a goal, taking a wicket or serving an ace can be readily understood, the techniques and tactics of racing may not be fully appreciated. Clearly the racing pages are no place to attract their attention. Ascot tried to reach them by leaflet drops, posters on sites around London, television commercials and the local press all selling the message that it offered an 'unforgettable' day of fun and entertainment for all the family. More generally the local newspaper, often of the free variety, is sometimes used to feature a nearby meeting, accompanied on most occasions by discount vouchers or a competition for free tickets. One success of the Discover Racing campaign has been the 'racing village', a road show bringing together a dozen or so racing organisations to take the sport to people by visiting agricultural shows and displaying aspects of racing from breeding and owning to riding and betting. The road show also encourages the computer literate to use a website where they can receive offers of cheap tickets, free drinks and gifts. This knits into a basic objective of developing a single gateway with centralised information and ticketing, accessible by telephone and internet. Regional marketing by groups representing Scottish racing and the nine Yorkshire tracks reinforce the national approach offering discount railway travel and a free bet on the tote.

But it is not enough simply to persuade new spectators to turn up. Repeat custom is the name of the game. The archaic language and insider terminology may appeal to the traditionalist and be understood by the initiated, but they can be baffling to the newcomer. What is a furlong? Or the Silver Ring? And how can you back a horse each way when they only run in one direction? The mysteries of the sport have to be explained. To their credit several courses attempt to do this in their race cards, though more often than not these have to be paid for in addition to the entry fee.

Of course not all marketing is aimed at the racegoer. Racecourses are unused for their primary purpose most of the time and other revenue streams are sought. So the corporate sector is prevailed upon to use the conference facilities available in the stands; other advertising concentrates on the wedding and banqueting market. When Douglas Erskine-Crum took over as chief executive at Ascot in 1994 the course was open only 24 days annually; within three years he had driven this up to over 300 days without any additional racing fixtures. The competition for the exhibition, concert and wedding market is fierce but racecourses have one prime advantage: they can usually offer free parking.

See also Jargon.

Mellor, Stan (1937–)

In 1959, only seven years after his first public ride, Stan Mellor became champion National Hunt jockey at the age of 22. He retained the title for the next two years and was heading for a fourth when a horrific accident in the Schweppes Gold Trophy at Aintree smashed his jaw and cheekbones in 14 places. This failed to deter him and when Ouzo won at Nottingham on 18 December 1971, Stan Mellor became the first jump jockey to ride 1,000 winners. Eventually, after a career lasting two decades, he totalled 1,035 career victories, a record haul that stood for 12 years until passed by John Francombe. Surprisingly he never won any of the big three National Hunt races.

Born in 1937, he left school at 13 and joined George Owen's Cheshire stables. Although he had no background in racing, his father, a successful Manchester timber merchant, had encouraged him to become a successful juvenile showjumper. He had his first public ride at 15 and, after riding as an amateur for just one season, he turned professional, winning on his first mount, Straight Border at Wolverhampton. He stayed in the north until after his first title, but, even when he moved south, it was not to one of the large jumping stables, but to the yard of Derek Ancil, a trainer with only 21 horses. One of his great strengths was his masterly timing of the take-off into a fence, a lesson learned from showjumping, hunting and constant practice.

After retiring from the saddle he took up training at the Linkslade Stables in Lambourn, later moving to Foxhill where he named his yard Pollardstown after the 1979 Triumph Hurdle winner, his first big race success as a trainer. To this he added a Whitbread Gold Cup and another Triumph Hurdle, but generally his accomplishments were limited. Mellor acknowledged that he loved horses too much to run them on hard ground and was not commercial enough in seeking out new clients. Towards the end of his training career he switched from National Hunt horses to dual purpose ones that would run on good to firm going. After a couple of seasons with only single figure totals of winners and less than 20 horses under his wing, he retired from training in 2001 and sold his stables to Sir Richard and Lady Colthurst for use in training eventers. Until the new owners moved in he continued as caretaker with just two horses, one of them, Shepherds Rest, bringing him his last victory when it won a handicap chase at Folkestone.

He was held in high regard by his colleagues; and not just for his racing ability. When the National Hunt Jockeys' Association was formed in 1964 Mellor was elected chairman and he remained as a vice-chairman on its merger with its flat racing counterpart. He also gave his time freely to advising the trustees of the Injured Jockeys Fund. In 1970 he was awarded an MBE for his services to racing.

Further reading

Fitzgeorge-Parker, T., *Steeplechase Jockeys: The Great Ones* (London: Pelham, 1971).

Middle East

In the 1980s no book about the world's great racecourses, owners or horseracing nations included Middle Eastern states. All that has changed with the rise to power and influence of the Maktoum family of Dubai. Their impact on British and subsequently world racing has ensured that the Middle East can no longer be overlooked as a major horseracing region.

It could be argued that it has taken nearly 300 years to complete the circle from Godolphin to Godolphin, from the arrival in England of one of the founding Arabian stallions in the early eighteenth century to the international racing operation masterminded by Sheikh Mohammed bin Rashid al Maktoum whose royal blue Godolphin colours first appeared on a British racecourse in 1994. The Byerley Turk, the Darley Arabian, the Godolphin Arabian and several others were brought over from the Middle East between the 1680s and the 1730s and played a vital role in the development of the English thoroughbred. Three centuries later, the ruling family of the tiny oil-rich state of Dubai, second largest of the United Arab Emirates, began their assault on the English turf in 1977, having earlier acquired a British education and a passion for racehorses. The intervening period saw few obvious racing links between the two areas.

Several Saudi Arabian princes such as Khalid Abdulla and the brothers Fahd and Ahmed Salman became involved in British racing at about the same time as the Maktoums. Khalid Abdulla has had eight English Classic winners, the most famous of which was probably Dancing Brave, Two Thousand Guineas and Prix de l'Arc de Triomphe winner in 1986. He also owns the worldwide Juddmonte Studs operation. Fahd Salman, his son-in-law, owned Generous, winner of the 1991 Derby, Irish Derby and King George, and 1999 Oaks winner Ramruma. Ahmed Salman, younger brother of Fahd, won the Epsom Derby in 1999 with Oath and the Kentucky Derby in 2002 with War Emblem, the first Arab owner to win the American Classic. His international racing operation, under the banner of the Thoroughbred Corporation, was managed in Europe by former champion jockey Willie Carson. Wafic Said, another Arabian owner, won the 1996 Oaks with Lady Carla. In National Hunt racing, Saudi businessman Sheikh Ali Abu Khamsin was leading jumps owner four times in the 1980s before retiring from the sport. His Gaye Brief won the Champion Hurdle in 1983 and the partnership of trainer Fred Winter and Richard Linley lifted the Mackeson Gold Cup (now the Paddy Power) at Cheltenham for him three times, once with Fifty Dollars More (1983), and twice with Half Free (1984, 1985).

However, the main connection between Britain and the Middle East in racing terms remains the exploits of the Dubai royal family, their stables, studs and phenomenally successful horses. Their dominance of British racing in the 1980s was followed by the development and expansion of thoroughbred racing in their homeland. The opening of the top class Nad al Sheba racecourse in 1992, the founding of the UAE Racing Association in 1993, the inaugural Dubai World Cup, the world's richest horse race, in 1996 and the setting up of the Emirates World Series in 1999 as an unofficial world championship of racing have stemmed largely from the drive of Sheikh Mohammed. They have also fostered worldwide interest in the little desert state where on Dubai World Cup day the fashionable attire (and hats) are reminiscent of Royal Ascot, the racecourse commentary (in English!) is provided by Derek Thompson of Channel Four racing fame and the pre-race procession includes Bedouin horsemen and camels. However, betting is not allowed, either on or off the course.

The lynchpin of the current Godolphin training operation in Britain is the wintering of the Maktoum horses, particularly promising youngsters, in the warmth of Dubai before their return to Newmarket the following spring. Balanchine became the first horse trained in the Middle East to win an English Classic (the 1994 Oaks) and since then the system appears to have worked well – the Dubai string is often well ahead of its rivals who train within the confines of the British climate. Successes have included four leading owner and three trainer titles for the Godolphin team under Saeed bin Suroor between 1996 and 2001 together with 11 Classic wins and four King Georges since 1994. Victories in big international races such as the Irish Champion Stakes, the Breeders' Cup Turf, the Hong Kong Cup and the Singapore Cup have also enabled three of their horses, Daylami, Fantastic Light and Grandera to be consecutive Emirates World Series' winners.

Between them, the Middle Eastern royal families have exerted enormous influence on British racing and have also been generous benefactors of the sport, sponsoring events such as the Shergar Cup day at Ascot. But one of their most obvious legacies has been to saddle British punters, bookies and media personnel with a wealth of virtually unpronounceable equine names – try cheering for Almutawakel or Mutafaweq in a close finish! On the other hand, be thankful that Hal Hoo Yaroom and Haya Ya Kefaah never made the big time!

Further reading

Magee, S., *Channel Four Racing Complete A–Z of Horse Racing* (London: Channel 4 Books, 2001).

See also Arabian horses, Maktoum family.

Mill Reef (1968–86) – by Never Bend out of Milan Mill

Mill Reef was one of the most brilliant horses of his generation, both on the racecourse and at stud. A compact bay colt, standing only 15.2 hands high, he was bred in the United States by his owner, Paul Mellon, and named after a stretch of coast near his Antiguan home. Trained in England by Ian Balding and ridden throughout his career by Geoff Lewis, he made his winning debut at Salisbury in 1970 and, as a two-year-old, won five of his six races. Convincing performances in the Gimcrack Stakes at York and the Dewhurst Stakes at Newmarket saw him enter his three-year-old season as favourite for the colt Classics.

In the Two Thousand Guineas, however, he encountered the sharp, unbeaten Brigadier Gerard and suffered the second, and last, defeat of his career, finishing runner-up. But he more than atoned for this disappointment during the year. He followed a two-length win in the Derby with a record-breaking time in the Eclipse Stakes, beating the French four-year-old champion, Caro. He then won the King George at Ascot by a record six lengths before completing an outstanding season with victory in the Arc. Starting as odds-on favourite, he set a new record time for $1\frac{1}{2}$ miles at Longchamp. This treble – the Derby, King George and Arc in one year – has only been achieved once since 1971 and he ended the season as Racehorse of the Year and leading European prize money winner with over £300,000.

1972 opened promisingly with wins in the Prix Ganay at Longchamp and the Coronation Cup at Epsom Downs and a rematch with Brigadier Gerard was eagerly awaited. But he never ran again. Struck down by the virus which swept through British racing stables that year, he was unable to race all summer and at the end of August, as he was being prepared for a second Arc, he broke a foreleg on the training gallops. He was saved for stud duties by outstanding veterinary skill and his own placid temperament, and embarked on a second, equally successful career. Retired to the National Stud, he produced winners of numerous top-class international races, including Shirley Heights in the English Derby, Acamus in the Prix du Jockey-Club, Lashkari in the Breeders' Cup Turf and Fairy Footsteps in the One Thousand Guineas. He was Champion Sire in 1978 and grandsire of another Derby winner, Slip Anchor, in 1985.

A heart operation that year was only partially successful and when his condition deteriorated, he was put down in 1986 at the age of 18. His importance as a stallion was underlined when his colt Reference Point won the Derby, King George and St Leger in 1987, resulting in a second, posthumous, title of Champion Sire. It is fitting that his statue can be found at the National Stud and that his name is commemorated in the Mill Reef Stakes at Newbury.

Further reading

Oaksey, J., *The Story of Mill Reef* (London: J.A. Allen, 1974).

Museums

Although some racing artefacts are on public display at racing museums – the Natural History Museum houses the skeleton of St Simon, and that of Arkle is on view at the Irish Horse Museum, Kildare – it is the museums devoted to the turf that are the public face of racing history. British racing has several such institutions to record and interpret the sport's heritage. They include the National Horseracing Museum at Newmarket, the National Hunt Hall of Fame at Cheltenham, the Derby Hall of Fame at Epsom, and, till recently, York Racing Museum. It is in their collections of photographs, archives and memorabilia that the history of the turf can be documented and illustrated and the drama and emotion of the sport replicated.

York had the oldest racing museum in Britain which was housed on the fourth floor of the five-storey Tattersall's grandstand, at the Knavesmire course. When the stand was being constructed in 1965 the racecourse executive decided to incorporate a museum as 'a celebration of racing history'. Advice was sought from turf antiquarian, Major Jack Fairfax-Blakeborough, and a public appeal for racing memorabilia produced many donations and loans, many from Fairfax-Blakeborough himself. Of particular interest are a set of racing silks worn by Fred Archer, champion jockey from 1874 to 1886, and the tail of Voltigeur, the losing horse in the famous match race against The Flying Dutchman at York in 1851. Recent exhibits have commemorated Phil Bull, founder of the betting guide *Timeform*, and Frankie Dettori's seven-in-a-row at Ascot with racing plates from the winners and a photocopied cheque from a lucky punter on the day. A major feature of the museum is the associated racing library which contains not only several hundred volumes of modern material but also *Racing Calendars* dating back to the earliest issues and almost complete runs of *Ruffs Guides to the Turf*, the *General Stud Book* and other bloodstock literature. Unhappily rebuilding in 2003 led to a decision to close the museum (hopefully temporarily) though access to the library can be arranged by appointment.

The Hall of Fame is an American sports concept that has developed in Britain in the past decade. When organised with annual inductions there can be renewed publicity each year though neither of the British racecourses with Halls of Fame have yet done this. Cheltenham's National Hunt Hall of Fame was opened in 1993 and celebrates steeplechasing and its history. Honoured there are jumping legends such as Golden Miller, Cottage Rake, Arkle, and Desert Orchid, but also featured are racegoers, riders, and trainers as well as the influence of the Irish. Permanently playing videos depict classic Champion Hurdle and Gold Cup winners as well as winners of other major races. On display also are the colours Pat Taaffe wore when Arkle won the Gold Cup, Dawn Run's Gold Cup winning bridle and Simon Sherwood's saddle when victorious on Desert Orchid. Epsom's Hall of Fame, opened in 1994, deals with the Derby, though it remains closed on most race days including Derby Day itself!

Opened by the Queen in 1983, the major repository for racing memorabilia accessible to the public in Britain is the National Horseracing Museum at Newmarket, located in the former Subscription Rooms on the High Street next to the Jockey Club. At one end of the display spectrum it houses the British Sporting Art Trust collection of paintings; at the other it offers hands-on education through entertainment. In the Practical Gallery, one that is staffed by retired trainers and jockeys, visitors can tack up a model horse, find out about the daily routine in a training stable, dress up in silks, weigh out and ride a horse simulator. Like most leading museums these days it has developed a teacher's pack and offers activities for children related to the key stages of the National Curriculum. Special exhibitions are held regularly and have included ones on racing scandals, royalty and racing, the history of betting and the work of jockey-turned-writer, Dick Francis.

In these days of soaring prices for all forms of sporting memorabilia, racing museums have a difficult task in developing their collections. The racing industry itself, whilst appreciative of history in the guise of the formbook and studbook, is generally focused on the here-and-now and the production of winners for tomorrow. Fortunately there are generous individuals and fund-raising 'friends of the museum' without whom the curators would find it difficult to convey the excitement of thoroughbred racing to the general public and make their displays more than merely glorified trophy rooms.

Further reading

Bracegirdle, H., *A Concise History of British Horseracing* (Derby: English Life, 1999).
www.cheltenham.co.uk
www.nhrm.co.uk

Music

Horseracing takes place against a backdrop of sound – the drumming of hooves, the crack of whips, the ringing of bells, the shouts, gasps, cheers and groans of the crowd. Music, however, does not play an integral part in the sport. Racegoers, unlike football fans, are not bound together in the singing of anthems, either national or popular. There are no team songs, no communal chants. The world of racing – its theatres, participants and spectators – revolves around the individual.

The early connections between racing and music largely evolved outside the racecourse. Race meetings in the Georgian era were associated with assemblies, balls and concerts to which the local gentry flocked during race weeks. Horseracing was the excuse for having a good time and musical activities took place because of the races but without reference to them. In Scotland, for example, the Caledonian Hunt Club sponsored racing from its inception in 1777 and employed a regular group of musicians at its balls. The leader of 'Gow's Band', the fiddler Neil Gow, even composed a piece entitled '*The Caledonian Hunt's Delight*' to play on these occasions.

At the opposite end of the social spectrum, music and racing were linked in working-class song and ballad. Recent studies of Tyneside have shown that the well-known '*Blaydon Races*' is only one of many songs written in the nineteenth century for performance at taverns, concerts and music halls, while others were also printed as collections of sheet music for home entertainment. Although a few celebrated the triumphs of popular local horses – '*The Ballad of Bonny Bee'swing*', in eight verses and chorus, extolled the virtues of a north-country mare who won over 50 races – the majority appear to have centred either on betting (and losing!) at the races or the general mayhem surrounding race days. They often contained colourful descriptions of the fighting, drinking, card playing and chatting up which were all part of the day out but seldom referred to the actual sport. Even '*The Blaydon Races*' is more concerned with the adventures encountered in getting to the racetrack and the antics of the crowd gathered there than racing. In fact the only horses to feature in the song are those on the roundabout! '*Swaggering at the Races*' and '*Ye've Lost a Whole Half-Crown*' sum up the subject matter of most Geordie racing songs! But if hunt clubs and local race meetings throughout Britain replicated the musical associations found in Scotland and north-east England, horseracing may have inspired a wealth of local song and dance, now largely forgotten.

The modern racecourse, however, has developed its own relationship with music. Trad jazz and brass bands are regular entertainments before, between and sometimes after the races at many venues. Royal Ascot has always featured a military band, Goodwood has recently followed the football ground in adopting a theme tune (although somewhat bizarrely it dumbed down and chose a recent chart hit while many soccer clubs went upmarket by raiding the popular classics for their leitmotif). Newmarket, along with many courses that stage summer evening meetings, goes in for live pop groups, Cheltenham in Festival week has everything from ceilidh bands to karaoke. Though featured more widely today, none of this is entirely new. When Wolverhampton staged Britain's first Saturday evening meeting back in 1962, 30 years before its all-weather floodlit weekend nights, there was both a skiffle group and a regimental band to play for the crowd!

Further reading

Gregson, K. and Huggins, M., Sport, Music-hall Culture and Popular Song in Nineteenth-century England, *Culture, Sport, Society*, 2.2 (1999), pp. 82–102.

Moneybox

J.P. McManus, owner of the legendary Istabraq, has spent a lifetime dealing in money – as a bookmaker in Ireland, as a player on the international money markets and as one of the biggest punters of recent times.

Sheikh Hamdan al Maktoum, the second of the four Maktoum brothers, is the Minister of Finance in his native Dubai.

Mandarin became the first British or Irish National Hunt horse to win over £50,000 – his 19 wins, 13 seconds and 5 thirds gave him a career earnings total of £51,496 in 1962 (nearly £650,000 in 2002 prices).

A **match** race is a head-to-head challenge contest between two horses.

The **Melbourne Cup**, staged at Flemington racecourse in November, is worth nearly 2 million Australian dollars to the winner.

Noel Murless became the first British trainer to amass six-figure winnings in one season; 32 winners of 48 races brought him over £116,000 in 1957 (over £1.5 million in current value). Ten years later, he became the first trainer to win over £200,000.

A day at the races 1900

'Say, Buddy', asked the American visitor, 'Why don't your English jockeys get their heads down?' He had a point. Half-a-dozen diminutive Yankees riding like monkeys-on-a-stick were causing gloom and despondency among their domestic counterparts whose more upright style cost them several lengths in wind resistance. A day at the races was almost becoming a matter of betting on the jockey rather than the horse!

'Yes, but your fellows don't play the game. The horses they ride are doped. That's not the done thing.'
'It's not against the Rules of Racing.'
'But it's not in the spirit of the sport. Anyway your fellows don't know how to really ride. In a close finish Otto and Morny can control their horses. Your fellows are all over the track.'
'We don't ride close finishes. We get out in front and we stay there.'
He had another point.

Time to go on the offensive. 'Sloan might have won the One Thousand last year but that's all you got. And this year who rode the Prince's Diamond Jubilee for the Triple Crown? Not Sloan, one of the Reiffs or Danny Maher that's for sure. The Prince recognises a good jockey when he sees one and he chose young Herbert Jones. And look at the other Classics. Morny won the Oaks and Sammy Loates the One Thousand. Not a solitary Classic did you get.'
'Yes, but Lester Reiff will be champion jockey this year.'
And another.

'Well, there's the Grand National. The Prince won that as well you know. There wasn't an American even riding in the race. Too much horsemanship required over those fences for you Yanks.'
'Yes, but it wasn't an English jockey was it? I'm sure that Algy Anthony is an Irishman.'
One more.
'Tell me, how many courses do you have in England?'
'Over 100. We used to have a lot more but the Jockey Club insisted on a minimum level of prize money and that put paid to quite a few.'
'Still over 100. That doesn't seem very efficient. Back home we centralise our racing and have meetings that last for weeks. The track at East St Louis once had 354 days of consecutive racing. We also like our courses to be similar so that form can be compared easily.'
'Sounds very boring, old chap. Going round and round the same circuit. Here we have a saying that it's "horses for courses" because our tracks vary so much.'

'That's why your jockeys can't judge pace.'
Is anyone keeping the score?

'My dear fellow, you seem to have an answer to everything, but do you know when Good Friday last fell on Boxing Day?'
'Is this something to do with your English religious festivals?'
'Try Wolverhampton on 26 December last year. In the Thorneycroft Steeplechase.'
Game, set and match!

N

Horsebox

Nearco, winner of all his 14 races, became one of the most influential twentieth-century stallions to stand in Britain. He sired two Derby winners, Dante (1945) and Nimbus (1949) and was grandsire of world champion stallion Northern Dancer.

Nicolaus Silver won the Grand National in 1961, the first grey to do so for 90 years (since The Lamb).

Nickel Coin was the last mare to win the Grand National (1951), three years after Sheila's Cottage in 1948. The previous female winner was in 1902 (Shannon Lass).

Night Nurse, winner of the Champion Hurdle in 1976 and 1977 and third in 1978, was the top rated hurdler since classification began 40 years ago.

Nobiliary is the only filly to be placed in the Derby – second to Grundy in 1975 – since Fifinella won in 1916.

Nupsala, trained in France by Francois Doumen, was the horse that prevented Desert Orchid from winning five consecutive King George VI Chases from 1986 to 1990, beating him into second place in 1987.

Names

Naming a racehorse today is a matter of some importance to owners with sentimental, witty or blatantly commercial motives, to Weatherbys (the administrative body charged with the vetting and registration of names) and to the punters, bookmakers and broadcasters who have to pronounce them. Three hundred years ago the Arabian stallions responsible for the development of the English thoroughbred were merely called after their owner, for example, the Byerley Turk named after Robert Byerley. At the end of the eighteenth century, horses often ran without a name and the records simply refer to Lord X's bay colt or Mr Y's chestnut filly. Even Classic winning horses could be nameless – the 1797 Derby winner was the Duke of Bedford's brown colt by Fidget, and Lord Foley's brown filly by Selim won the One Thousand

Guineas in 1815. Owners who could be bothered often chose simple names such as Star, Bess, or Raven while others – Pudenda, Little Yid, Sweetest When Naked – would be barred in an age of political correctness on the grounds of taste and decency.

A racehorse cannot be registered at Weatherbys until it is a yearling and it cannot be given a name which is already registered; there are nearly 250,000 at present. But with the increasing international traffic in racehorses it is possible that a horse born outside Britain could be racing alongside a home-bred animal of the same name. Overseas horses are distinguished by the use of initials (USA, IRE, FRA) to denote the country of origin. Current British rules stipulate a maximum of 18 letters and spaces, together with a ban on initials and punctuation marks, and any name which could cause offence or confusion is vetoed. There is also a list of protected names including those of Classic and other big race winners and well known horses, to prevent the appearance of a second Mill Reef or Desert Orchid.

Having eliminated the unacceptable, there are several established methods of choosing a name. A combination of the sire and dam (Golden Corn by Golden Sun out of Corn Cockle, Step on Eyre by Step Together out of Jane Eyre) is a common tradition. Humour in all its forms has always been popular, from the nineteenth-century Sour Grapes by Claret, and Nun Nicer (the 1898 One Thousand Guineas winner, not to be confused with None Nicer, a staying filly of the 1950s) to the recent Don't Tell the Wife, Loop the Loup (by Petit Loup), Jim and Tonic and Blue Suede Hoofs. Place names (Calcutta, Fort Knox), literary names (Hamlet, Dr Zhivago), musical names (Bach, Stravinsky) and sporting names (Bryan Robson, Lennox Lewis) vie with the loving (You're Special, Love Divine) and the poignant (Roses Have Thorns). The inclusion of lad/lass, girl/boy, lord/lady/knight continue to find favour and more recently Bint, 'daughter of' in Arabic. Certain colours have also been popular – red (Red Rum, Red Alligator, Red Marauder), blue (Blue Peter, Blue Gown, Blue Cashmere), silver (Silver Patriarch, Silver Buck, Silver Charm) and green (Green Dancer, Green Desert, Green Ruby) but there are very few yellows or oranges.

Commercial naming, which has now extended to Classic winners (Mister Baileys, 1994 Two Thousand Guineas winner was named to promote his owner's firm) has also been around for a long time. Horses named Celledema Blister and Celladema Ointment advertised products as far back as 1898; more recent commercial sponsors have included Pontin-Go, fifth in the 1964 Grand National and owned by the Pontins holiday camp boss, and Schweppeshire Lad who advertised his sponsors' name in the 1970s from the winners' enclosure at Royal Ascot to New Zealand where he became a champion sprinter. A company called Equiname was even set up to name racehorses for advertisers without requiring them to purchase a horse. The unfortunate animal that acted as a mobile advertisement for the parent company (Call Equiname) even won some major races, including the Queen Mother Champion Chase at Cheltenham in 1999. The proliferation of Arabic names, a reflection of the importance of Middle-Eastern owners to British racing, is another feature of recent times.

It is said to be unlucky to change the name of a racehorse although Saffron Waldon, winner of the 1999 Irish Two Thousand Guineas was re-registered as

Saffron Walden, the East Anglian town from which he originally took his misspelt name. Obviously there are no similar qualms about racecourses – both Edinburgh and Liverpool changed their names during the 1990s to the more geographically appropriate Musselburgh and Aintree.

Further reading

Bateman, R., *The Business of Racing* (Cambridge: Hobsons, 1989).
Magee, S. (ed.), *The Channel Four Racing Guide to Racehorses* (London: Channel 4 Books, 1999).

National Stud

In November 1915 Colonel William Hall Walker (later Lord Wavertree) offered his bloodstock – 2 stallions, 30 mares, 10 yearling fillies, 20 foals and 8 horses in training – to form the basis of a national stud provided that the government would purchase his own breeding property at Tully, Co. Kildare and his training stables at Russley near Lambourn. Initially his offer was refused but, when he then elected to break up the stud and put up its constituent parts for auction at the Newmarket December sales, the government relented. This came after pressure from the Army Council who wanted the thoroughbreds to form the foundation of the military's light horse stock. Britain was at war and the horse was still regarded as important for military purposes. Concern was expressed in some quarters that the stud would be mismanaged if run by the state or that it would offer unfair subsidised competition to the private sector. In practice neither occurred and the stud paid its way as a commercial concern. The initial director was Captain Henry Greer, an experienced owner and breeder, who was knighted for his services in 1925.

By the late 1920s Russley, originally intended as a depot from which stallions would travel the country servicing farmers' mares, had been sold and the emphasis of the stud had switched to producing racing stock with little attention being paid to military needs, which, of course, were declining as the Army mechanised. The rationale had shifted to the important contribution that the export of bloodstock could make to Britain's balance of payments. Most of the produce was sold as yearlings at public auction though some fillies were retained for future breeding purposes and were leased out during their racing careers.

When Ireland secured independence in 1921 it meant that the British National Stud was now in a foreign country, but both the Irish and British governments tolerated this until the Second World War emphasised the illogicality and inconvenience of the situation. In 1944 Tully was vested in the Irish Government and became Ireland's national stud and the British government purchased the Sandley Stud in Dorset, close to the Somerset and Wiltshire borders, from the executors of Lord Furness. Facilities were expanded after the Second World War by the further acquisition of a stud at West Grinstead in Sussex.

In 1963, when responsibility for the Stud was transferred from the Ministry of Agriculture to the Levy Board, two policy changes were instituted. First it was decided that the stud should sell its mares and become a stallion station.

Second, both existing facilities were sold and a new stud was built at Newmarket on 500 acres of land leased from the Jockey Club near the July Course. This opened in 1967. Possibly the best stallion at the National Stud has been Mill Reef who sired winners of the Derby (Shirley Heights 1978 and Reference Point 1987), One Thousand Guineas (Fairy Footsteps 1984) and the St Leger (Reference Point 1987) while the best horse foaled there was Ribot, unbeaten in 16 races including the Arc twice and the King George.

With the growing domination of Arab, American and Japanese breeders, the Stud has been unable to maintain its previous considerable influence in world breeding. It still has reputable horses standing, though from the late 1980s emphasis has been given to stallions with fees affordable to owners of most British mares. In the past few years international collaboration has come on the agenda. The Stud has sent Celtic Swing, Puissance and Suave Dancer on lease to Australia, Be My Chief to the Brazilian National Stud, and Derby winner Shammit as the first stallion to undertake shuttle duties between Europe and South Africa. In turn the French Classic winner Hector Protector has come to the Stud on lease from Japan.

The Stud offers a range of services to breeders including not only stallions at stud but also seasonal and permanent boarding, sales preparation and quarantine facilities. For many years too it has trained young people for work in the thoroughbred industry and now offers both Diploma and NVQ courses. However, the government has recently announced that the Stud will be gifted to racing or sold off by mid-2005. Their preference is to hand over the venture to a charitable trust, but the decision hinges on the stud broadening its appeal to a variety of horse breeds ranging from the Shetland Pony to the Suffolk Punch, rather than concentrating solely on thoroughbreds.

Further reading

Rasmussen, L. and Napier, M., *Treasures of the Bloodstock Breeders Review* (London: J.A. Allen, 1990).
www.race-horses.co./studs/national

See also Breeding.

Newmarket

Newmarket is the home of British racing, with a history dating back to the seventeenth century. A small town of around 17,000 people and 4,000 racehorses, it is situated on the flat windswept Newmarket Heath, about 12 miles from Cambridge. It plays host to the Jockey Club, the National Stud and National Horseracing Museum, Tattersalls Sale Ring, over 60 training stables and 57 miles of horsewalks (an equine version of cycle paths). Racing takes place on two separate courses, each with its own facilities, the July Course for summer meetings and the Rowley Mile for the remainder of the flat season.

Although James I (reigned 1603–25) is credited with introducing blood sports to the Heath, it was his grandson, Charles II (1660–85) who established horseracing there. His twice-yearly visits began the Newmarket tradition of spring and autumn meetings which is still maintained today, and the Rowley Mile course is said to be named after his favourite hack, Old Rowley. Charles kept his race-horses at the Palace House Stables, which survived as a training yard until the 1980s, and in 1665 he inaugurated the Newmarket Town Plate, until 1972 the only race under Jockey Club or National Hunt rules to allow female competitors.

The fortunes of Newmarket ebbed and flowed over the next 200 years. The establishment of the Jockey Club there during the 1750s was the first step in the development of the town as the headquarters of British racing. Its acquisition of large parts of the Heath by 1820 aimed to consolidate that position, and the introduction of two further Classic races, the Two Thousand Guineas for three-year-old colts in 1809 and the One Thousand Guineas for three-year-old fillies in 1814, run over the Rowley Mile course, sought to emulate the success of the Epsom Derby and Oaks. But the middle decades of the nineteenth century saw Newmarket fall from favour as a training centre, largely because its gallops were said to be too firm in the summer for fragile thoroughbreds. Statistics of Derby winners illustrate its demise. From 1788 to 1832, all but three champion colts were based at Newmarket, but from 1833 to 1862, no more than three were trained there. Relief arrived in the 1860s in the shape of Scottish trainers such as the Dawson brothers, Joseph and Mathew, French horses which were increasingly prepared at Newmarket by Tom Jennings for challenges in British races, and the success of Macaroni in the 1863 Derby.

Thereafter, Newmarket regained its position as the centre of British racing, attracting top trainers and jockeys but distancing itself from the efforts to woo spectators which were taking place at the newly-developed enclosed race-courses of the late nineteenth and early twentieth centuries. Newmarket had always held more race meetings than any other course, six or seven annually throughout its history, but it was both socially exclusive and physically remote. Its two courses are separated by an ancient earthwork which bisects the Heath, the Devil's Dyke, and with a variety of different starting and finishing posts, it was far from convenient for the general public. Until the economic pressures of post war British racing finally persuaded Newmarket and its owners to change their approach, they maintained a somewhat disdainful attitude to racegoers. The courses are now owned by the Racecourse Holdings Trust, a subsidiary of the Jockey Club which remains the major landowner in the town, with 4,500 acres of training grounds, stud farms and other property.

Newmarket stages over 20 Pattern races throughout the year, including seven Group One races. The Craven Meeting in April is the first high-class flat meeting of the season, with two important Guineas trials, the Nell Gwyn Stakes for fillies and the Craven Stakes for colts. Future champions that began their Classic campaigns here include Shadeed (1985) and Dancing Brave (1986) in the Craven, and Pebbles (1984) and Oh So Sharp (1985) in the Nell Gwyn. May sees the Guineas meeting before racing switches to the July Course where the sole Group race is the 6-furlong July Cup. Back at the Rowley Mile, the major October meetings include three end-of-season two-year-old contests, the Cheveley, Middle Park and Dewhurst Stakes. The Dewhurst in particular, run over 7 furlongs, counts future stars Pinza, Crepello, Nijinsky, Grundy, The

Minstrel, Generous and Rock of Gibraltar among its previous winners. The Champion Stakes, the last Group One of the year at Newmarket, was twice won by the fillies Triptych in 1986 and 1987 and Alborada in 1998 and 1999, as well as Classic winners Petite Etoile (1959), Sir Ivor (1968) and Bosra Sham (1996). The course also plays host to two major late-season handicaps, the Cambridgeshire and the Cesarewitch.

In recent years, both racecourse facilities and the management approach to racing have been extensively updated. With 37 race days in 2004, including eight summer evening meetings featuring post-race musical entertainment, the installation of electronic sectional timing and a new Millenium grandstand on the Rowley Mile, and its first female clerk of the course, Newmarket has entered the twenty-first century with a more modern public image. Privately, however, the town maintains its own rhythms and a certain distance from the world out there. It has been built almost entirely around the thoroughbred; during the two world wars, governments were prevailed on to keep the racing and breeding industries ticking over to maintain the local economy. It does not readily accept newcomers to its way of life and many of the families who train in Newmarket have done so for generations.

In training terms it has been highly successful. In 1996, Newmarket horses won all five Classics and 72 per cent of English Group One races. The National Stud, once home to Mill Reef, the most important British sire of his generation, has recently hosted stallions such as Silver Patriarch. Within a 10-mile radius of the town are another 40 private studs while in the town centre Tattersalls auctioneers presided over £34.5 million guineas worth of yearlings in just three days during October 1999. It is hardly surprising that a statue of a rearing stallion was chosen to guard the entrance to the town, a symbol of Newmarket's lifeblood. There are other areas of Britain with substantial racehorse populations, numerous training yards and a considerable dependence on racing but none on the scale of Newmarket.

Further reading

Cassidy, R., *The Sport of Kings* (Cambridge: Cambridge University Press, 2002).
Onslow, R., *Headquarters* (Cambridge: Great Ouse Press, 1983).
www.newmarketracecourses.co.uk

Nijinsky (1967–92) – by Northern Dancer out of Flaming Page

Nijinsky is the only horse to have won the Triple Crown (the Two Thousand Guineas, the Derby and the St Leger) since 1935. His granddam was named after a ballerina and his own name continued the dance themes of his fore-bears. A big, handsome bay colt, almost 17 hands high, he was bred in Canada in 1967, bought as a yearling on behalf of his owner Charles Engelhard and sent to be trained with Vincent O'Brien in Ireland. He was unbeaten in 1969, winning his first outing at The Curragh, followed by successes in three of the most important two-year-old races in the Republic. He finished the season with an easy victory in the Dewhurst Stakes at Newmarket and the accolade of top-ranked juvenile.

1970 was Nijinsky's year. Another success at The Curragh was a prelude to the Two Thousand Guineas which he won comfortably, partnered by Lester Piggott. He went on to record the fastest Derby win since 1936 and, as 4–11 favourite, continued his winning ways in the Irish Derby under Liam Ward, his regular jockey in Ireland. Piggott then rode him to victory in the King George. His owner had already expressed the intention of retiring the horse to stud at the end of the season and so, unbeaten to date, he was aimed at both the St Leger and the Arc.

Although he suffered a setback in August, developing a bad case of ringworm, he still managed to beat an undistinguished St Leger field with ease, and arrived at Longchamp three weeks later with a string of 11 victories behind him. Some reports suggest that Piggott rode a poor tactical race, keeping Nijinsky near the back of the field for too long and enabling the French Derby winner, Sassifras, to defeat him by a head, though others reckon that he was given every opportunity to prove himself. Whatever the opinion, it was a bitter disappointment for his connections. He was given a final outing only two weeks later in the Champion Stakes at Newmarket and a huge crowd turned up to see him but he failed again, beaten into second place. It may be that his lengthy season and frequent travelling contributed to his loss of form or that his recent illness had crucially undermined his abilities. In spite of his defeats he was the leading prize money winner and Champion Racehorse of 1970 and only the fifteenth Triple Crown winner of all time. He was said by Lester Piggott to be one of the three greatest horses he ever rode.

Syndicated for over £2.25 million to stand in Kentucky, his career at stud was equally impressive. He sired three English Derby winners – Golden Fleece (1982), Shahrastani (1986) and Lammtarra (1995) – and his offspring won numerous top-class international races including Green Dancer (1975 Poule d'Essai des Poulains), Ile de Bourbon (1978 King George), Caerleon (1983 Prix du Jockey-Club), Ferdinand (1987 Breeders' Cup Classic) and Royal Academy (1990 Breeders' Cup Mile). He was also the grandsire of two further Derby winners in Kahyasi (1988) and Generous (1991).

He died in 1992 at the age of 25, and his former trainer Vincent O'Brien unveiled a statue of the great horse at The Curragh in 1998.

Further reading

Baerlein, R., *Nijinsky: Triple Crown Winner* (London: Pelham, 1971).
Sampson, L., *Nijinsky: Blue Riband Sire* (London: J.A. Allen, 1985).

Nineteenth-century horses

The career of a top nineteenth-century racehorse was often markedly different from that of a similar animal today. When Eleanor became the first filly to win the Derby in 1801, she completed the double the following day by winning the Oaks and, astonishingly, continued to race, often at minor meetings, until she was seven. A current racehorse of this quality would be unlikely to take part in two championships in 24 hours or subsequently contest low-class races, and would frequently be retired to stud by the age of four. The expectations of a Classic winner of that period are inconceivable to modern racegoers. Priam, reckoned to be one of the best Derby winners in the first half of the nineteenth century, never ran as a two-year-old, won two preliminary races in 1830 prior to his Epsom victory and, in the same season, won the Goodwood Cup over $2\frac{1}{2}$ miles. The following year, he won this race again as well as a 4-mile Royal Plate, and was then retired. Nowadays no horse who had won a Derby would be entered for a contest of nearly twice that length only two months later and would never be asked to race 4 miles – there have been no flat races of that length for over 100 years. Even in 1860, versatility was still the name of the game. The three-year-old filly Sweetsauce won the 6-furlong Stewards' Cup sprint at Goodwood before returning two days later to take the Goodwood Cup. Such a combination of speed with endurance is no longer expected and flatracers are bred to be middle-distance performers, specialist sprinters or stayers, not all three at once! The career of a steeplechaser, in contrast, has changed far less, sometimes spanning eight or nine years and still requiring heavy weights to be carried over long distances.

The horses that left their mark on the history of nineteenth-century British flat racing were inevitably winners of the Classics and the Ascot Gold Cup, the most important race after the Derby, or those with record-breaking careers in racing or breeding. Many are now little more than names in lists. Champion was the first colt to secure both the Derby and the St Leger in 1800 while in 1822 Pastille was the only filly to triumph in the Two Thousand Guineas and the Oaks. Cadland and The Colonel are remembered for fighting out one of only two dead-heats in the Derby, in 1828 (the second was in 1884); Cadland, the Two Thousand Guineas winner, won the run-off that same afternoon, following the custom of the time, and The Colonel went on to win the St Leger. In 1838 Amato became the only nineteenth-century Derby winner to be trained at Epsom. It was his first race – and also his last! His career was very different from that of Alice Hawthorn, foaled in the same year but remarkably the winner of 52 of her 71 starts in a seven-year span. British records were set by Catherina who won 79 out of 174 (or in some versions, 176) races between 1833 and 1841, and Fisherman, first past the post in 23 races in 1856, still the greatest number of victories in a single season.

Other horses left behind more than statistics. Bee'swing, sired in 1833 by Dr Syntax, a popular and prolific stallion on northern racecourses, became the pride of Northumberland and one of the best-loved horses of her generation. She won over 50 races, mostly of 2 miles and upwards, including the Ascot, Chester, Doncaster, and Newcastle Cups (the latter on six occasions), and her achievements are commemorated in an old north-country ballad, *Bonny Bee'swing*. At a time when northern trainers were particularly successful, the two outstanding Yorkshire-based stallions, The Flying Dutchman and Voltigeur, each having won the Derby and St Leger, in 1849 and 1850, met in the Doncaster Cup, which Voltigeur won. The re-match, arranged in May 1851 over 2 miles at York, attracted enormous interest and a large crowd gathered to witness The Flying Dutchman gain his revenge in what became one of the most well-documented races of the century.

1853 saw the first winner of the Triple Crown – the Two Thousand Guineas, Derby and St Leger – and for the remainder of the century, this became the goal of all Classic colts. West Australian was the first horse to achieve the feat, adding the Ascot Gold Cup the following year, and a further 10, 7 colts and 3 fillies, won three Classic races, the fillies' Triple Crown consisting of the One Thousand Guineas, Oaks and St Leger. Formosa capped these performances by taking four Classics – she won the fillies' Triple Crown in 1868 and forced a dead-heat in the Two Thousand Guineas – but this achievement seemed to count for little, as, like Eleanor 70 years earlier, she was still racing for paltry sums as a five-year-old. The lower stud value of fillies has often kept them in training, and potentially earning, longer than colts able to command high serving fees.

The most noteworthy winners of the Triple Crown were probably Gladiateur (1865), the first overseas poacher of the top English races, Ormonde (1886), unbeaten in 16 races, La Flèche (1892), the filly who nearly won the Derby as well, and Isinglass (1893) who secured more prize money than any subsequent racehorse for nearly 60 years. Gladiateur was the scourge of Britain and the hero of France. Bred and owned by Count de Lagrange but trained at Newmarket by Englishman Tom Jennings, he beat a field of 28 in the Derby, becoming the first overseas winner of the English Classic. Only three weeks later, he turned out for the Grand Prix de Paris, the premier race in France, and duly won that contest. His Triple Crown success was greeted with dismay and despondency by followers of British racing, particularly as he followed it up with victory in the Ascot Gold Cup of 1866. He had destroyed the belief in the superiority of the English thoroughbred.

Although La Flèche sounded French, she was English-bred, a daughter of the famous St Simon (see below), and trained by John Porter. Unbeaten in four races as a two-year-old, she won the fillies' Triple Crown and was second in the Derby in 1892, a race she could have won but for the incompetence of her jockey, George Barrett. The following year, when Isinglass captured the colt Classics, she seemed to lose form, but returned to the racecourse to win the Ascot Gold Cup in 1894, the year in which Isinglass, now four, won the Princess of Wales's Stakes, the Eclipse Stakes, then worth twice as much as the Derby, and the Jockey Club Cup. He too won the Gold Cup as a five-year-old and retired with record winnings of over £57,000, an enormous sum in 1895, and only surpassed once before 1960.

In the eyes of many contemporaries, however, the outstanding horse of the nineteenth century was Ormonde, winner of all his 16 races at a time of high-class competition. Bred and owned by the Duke of Westminster and trained by John Porter, he won the 1886 Triple Crown and five other races as a three-year-old, including the St James's Palace, Hardwicke and Champion Stakes, and although found to be unsound in wind, he gained three further successes in his four-year-old season. He won over distances ranging from 6 furlongs to 1 mile 6 furlongs and the scenes at Ascot after his final victory there were said to be unmatched until the heyday of Brown Jack nearly 40 years later.

Fame on the racetrack was sometimes followed by a successful career at stud. Whalebone won the Derby in 1810 but is better remembered for his profound influence on nineteenth-century bloodstock. His grandson, Touchstone, winner of the St Leger in 1834 and the Ascot Gold Cup in 1836 and 1837, sired the winners of 11 Classics and a total of 738 races. In mid-century, the outstanding sire was Stockwell, winner of the Two Thousand Guineas and St Leger in 1852 and champion sire on seven occasions, with three Derby winners to his credit. One hundred years later, he still held the record for siring the greatest number of winners in one season (1866 – 132 races won). In the 1890s, Persimmon won the 1896 Derby and St Leger, followed by the Ascot Gold Cup and Eclipse Stakes in 1897. He went on to become champion sire on four occasions and his offspring included the famous filly, Sceptre, and four other Classic winners. However, it was his sire, St Simon, who became synonymous with stud brilliance. A winner of the Ascot and Goodwood Cups, he produced ten foals that became Classic winners, including La Flèche, Persimmon and Diamond Jubilee, the Triple Crown winner in 1900, the year in which all five races fell to his stock. He was champion sire in eight consecutive seasons, 1887–94, and ten years in total.

In National Hunt racing, the racing year was much less structured, with no equivalent to the Classics. The sport only became established in the 1830s and, with no Cheltenham Festival or major handicaps at this time, the Grand National at Aintree dominated the nineteenth-century jumping season. The best horses took part in it because there were few alternatives, and winners of this marathon race are predominant in any selection of steeplechase champions.

Before the inaugural 'Liverpool Grand Steeple-Chase' of 1836, the race which would later become the Grand National, the most important contest in the early 1830s was the St Albans or Hertfordshire Steeplechase. The winner of this race on two occasions was Moonraker, a bay horse who won eight times in his career, and was said to be a good galloper and jumper. Immortalised in a painting of 1831, he is reckoned to be one of the greatest horses of his time. The first two steeplechases at Liverpool over the Grand National course were held in 1836 and 1837 and both were won by The Duke, who also came third in 1838. Although he was ridden in two of these three races by the famous Captain Becher, his achievement has been largely overlooked and the name of Lottery has entered history as the first winner of the Grand National in 1839 and the champion steeplechaser of his day. Lottery ran in his first jump race in 1836 as a six-year-old, and was finally retired in 1844, having carried weights of up to 13 st 3 lb to victory.

Apart from The Duke, only five horses won the Grand National twice during the century. Peter Simple, victorious in 1849, won again in 1853 at the age of 15, carrying 10 st 10 lb; he entered the contest six times. 1850 and 1851 saw Abd-el-Kader, a small bay animal, bred in Ireland, take the honours, setting a new course record time of 9 minutes 57.5 seconds for his first win. (The fastest times in the twentieth century are almost one minute less.) The Lamb and The Colonel divided the spoils between them from 1868 to 1871. Both were only six-year-olds when they won for the first time, The Lamb in 1868, The Colonel in 1869. The Lamb, bred in Ireland and no bigger than 15.2 hands, was said to be a powerful and agile jumper, the last grey to win the race for 90 years. The Colonel was still, unusually, an entire (a stallion) throughout his steeplechasing years and when his racing days were over, he embarked on a new career in one of the German Imperial studs. Cloister, second in two consecutive years (1891 and 1892), only won the race once but became the first horse to carry 12 st 7 lb to victory in 1893 while setting a course record time that stood for 40 years.

The steeplechaser who probably enjoyed the greatest reputation in the later nineteenth century, however, was Manifesto. He was entered for the race on eight occasions between 1895 and 1904, emerging with a fourth place, three thirds and two victories, in 1897 and 1899. He carried 12 st 7 lb in 1899 and 12 st 13 lb the following year, when he was third, conceding 3 st to the second horse. He won the Irish Champion Chase and several other big races but his exploits in the Grand National earned him a reputation comparable to twentieth-century hero, Red Rum, at a time when the Aintree fences were probably more daunting and dangerous than they are today.

In general, the elite nineteenth-century flat racehorse ran more often, over longer distances and for less money than his twentieth-century counterpart but lengthier careers may have helped to establish a place in history. The level of corruption in the sport ensured that the best animals occasionally failed to win but the reputation and popularity of the star turns drew increasingly large crowds to the racecourses.

Further reading

Mortimer, R., Onslow, R. and Willett, P., *Biographical Encyclopaedia of British Flat Racing* (London: Macdonald and Jane's, 1978).

Seth-Smith, Michael *et al.*, *The History of Steeplechasing* (London: Michael Joseph, 1966).

Wilson, J., *The Great Racehorses* (London: Little, Brown and Co., 1998).

Nineteenth-century jockeys

Frank Buckle and the younger Sam Chifney (see separate entries) were the most well-known riders of the late Georgian period, but Jem Robinson ran them close. Son of a Newmarket farm labourer, Robinson enjoyed the good life: at least in winter when his weight would balloon to over $9\frac{1}{2}$ st. Yet in the racing season he was a dedicated rider, reportedly using laxatives and long walks in heavy clothing to shed the pounds. This willingness to suffer for his trade paid off. He was second only to Frank Buckle in riding Classic winners and his 24 victories included nine Two Thousand Guineas and six Derbys, a total not bettered till 1972 (by Lester Piggott). His first win in the Epsom event came in 1817 on Azor, at 50–1 the longest outsider to win the blue riband of the turf. Although a stylish rider, he could be harsh on his mounts leading to the comment by contemporary John Day, of the famous riding and training family (see separate entry) that he could 'punish a horse most in the least time'.

His career was effectively ended after being thrown at Newmarket before a two-year-old match race in 1852. The incident smashed his thigh and left him with one leg four inches shorter than the other. Like many jockeys he failed to look after his money and in his retirement relied on the generosity of two former patrons, the Dukes of Rutland and Bedford.

Frank Butler, the first rider to win the Triple Crown, was a nephew of the younger Sam Chifney and won 14 Classics, ten of them for John Scott after the latter fell out with his brother Bill (see separate entry). His Triple Crown came on West Australian in 1853. He won the Oaks four times in a row from 1849, a feat never replicated. He died in 1856, a victim of attempting to control his weight too much. John 'Brusher' Wells was twice champion jockey in the 1850s, taking the title from its first holder Nat Flatman (see separate entry) and won eight Classics before he too died of excessive wasting in 1873 aged 39. His initial nickname was 'Tiny' and he could still do 6 st in 1853, the year of his first championship, but later he found difficulty in getting down to even $8\frac{1}{2}$ st. When he won Sir Joseph Hawley a third Derby, on Blue Gown in 1868, allegedly the owner presented him with the entire stakes of £6,800. Although he had one extravagance – wearing flamboyant clothes – unlike many of his contemporaries in the saddle he invested rather than consumed his earnings, thus providing for his family after his death.

The mid to late Victorian years starred George Fordham and Fred Archer (see separate entries) who between them won 27 championships. Those that followed were never able to exert similar dominance. Despite Jack Watts's ability, his weight problems restricted the number of mounts that he could take and thus he never became champion jockey, though he was runner-up in 1891 with 114 winners. In the winter of 1895 he contemplated retirement because of the difficulty in controlling his weight, but was persuaded not to by trainer, Richard Marsh, which led to him riding the Prince of Wales's Persimmon to victory in the 1896 Derby, his third success in that race. In all he rode 19 classic winners. Taught by Tom Cannon (see separate entry), he was a quiet and unspectacular rider who relied on timing and 'hands', and getting the best out of a horse when apparently doing very little. He was undemonstrative and, according to trainer, the Hon. George Lambton, would enter the winner's circle 'looking as solemn as a judge who had just passed the death sentence'. His health undermined by excessive wasting, Watts retired from the saddle in 1900 to become a trainer but he died only two years later. Two of his sons were jockeys, one of them, also known as Jack, later becoming a trainer at Newmarket, as did Watts' grandson and great grandson. Charles Wood did become champion jockey, in 1887, but he was also accused of organising a jockeys' ring, an allegation that was never sustained, and of being the cause of the irregular running of Sir George Chetwynd's horses, a charge that was. He lost his licence for several years but when it was returned in 1897 he rode Galtee More to a Triple Crown.

Tommy Loates rode his first winner in 1883 when he was 15. Six years later he was champion jockey. He again occupied first place in 1890 and, after a two-year retirement possibly associated with his alcoholism, he was champion again in 1893, his most successful season with 222 winning mounts, only the second jockey ever to top the double century mark. Short-legged he sometimes had difficulty in coaxing the best out of bigger horses, but he was a resourceful rider who was quick to take advantage of openings that presented themselves during a race. In 1896 he had three nasty riding accidents including one in which he broke his thigh, though he continued to ride till 1900 when, after having trouble with his eyes, he relinquished his licence. Unlike many working-class professional sportsmen of the time, he hung on to the money he had made and left almost £75,000.

Although almost all early steeplechases were supposedly restricted to gentlemen riders, men such as Martin Becher (see separate entry), Jem Mason and Tom Oliver certainly were paid to compete over jumps. Leicestershire-born Mason learned to ride as a child in assisting his father who was a horse breeder. As a rider he was perfectly balanced and rarely fell. He won the first Grand National on Lottery, a horse on which he had considerable success. A dandy, he always rode in white kid gloves and had his boots and coats made in London. He died of throat cancer in 1866 and such was his popularity that Tattersalls got up a public subscription to take care of his family. Oliver, known as 'Black Tom' because of his swarthy appearance, was a more rough and ready rider but could triumph in a hard finish. Born in Sussex, one of 16 children, he worked in his uncle's training stables at Epsom. Often in trouble with the law, usually for debt problems, he won three Grand Nationals, the first and last eleven years apart, and was placed a further four times. While a publican at Prestbury, Oliver taught the Cheltenham schoolboy, Adam Lindsay Gordon, to ride and was later rewarded by a stanza from the poet:

> He cares not for the bubbles of fortune's fickle tide
> Who like Bendigo can battle and like Oliver can ride

Two others coached by Oliver were Tommy Pickernell and George Stevens. Pickernell won three Grand Nationals but was forced to retire after a fall in 1877 in which he broke his jaw and lost an eye. He then became the first National Hunt Inspector of Courses. Stevens won his first major race, the Grand Annual Steeplechase at Wolverhampton in 1851, when he was 18 and went on to triumph in an unequalled five Grand Nationals. His tactics were to keep back initially so as to avoid the early scrimmages and falls and then to use his judgement of pace to offer a late challenge that often swept him past his tiring opponents. He was killed when he fractured his skull following a fall when riding at exercise.

By the mid-nineteenth century the fiction of the gentleman rider had gone as more races open to all comers emerged. In 1854 there were at least 110 professional jump jockeys, a figure that had almost doubled at the turn of the century. Of these the outstanding rider was Arthur Nightingall, son of a trainer, who in 15 Grand Nationals had three wins, a second and four thirds.

Further reading

Seth-Smith, M. *et al.*, *The History of Steeplechasing* (London: Michael Joseph, 1971).
Tanner, M. and Cranham, G., *Great Jockeys of the Flat* (London: Guinness, 1992).

North America

America, like all British colonies imported horseracing along with its early governors and settlers. The first racecourse was allegedly laid out on Long Island in 1665, around the time when the English monarchy was popularising racing back home at Newmarket. During the eighteenth century several sons of the founding Arabian stallions were said to have arrived in Virginia and Maryland including Bulle Rocke, a son of the Darley Arabian, Childers, a son of Flying Childers, and Janus, a grandson of the Godolphin. The most famous and well-documented import, however, was Diomed, the first winner of the Derby. A relative failure at stud in England, he was exported to Virginia at the age of 21 and through his son, Sir Archy, founded the dominant American male line of the nineteenth century.

Before the War of Independence, the results of American races were occasionally listed in the *Racing Calendar* and not long after the cessation of hostilities the volumes also contained the names of North American subscribers. By the middle of the nineteenth century these included the American Jockey Club, the editor of the *Spirit of the Times*, New York, a lieutenant in Nova Scotia and Richard Ten Broeck. In 1857, Ten Broeck became the first American owner to try out his horses in Britain, bringing over Prioress to win the Cesarewitch that year and Starke to capture the Goodwood Stakes and Goodwood Cup in 1859. Where he paved the way, others followed. The assault on the British turf, begun in earnest by the French in the 1860s, gathered pace in 1879 when an American tobacco merchant of French descent, Pierre Lorillard, sent a number of horses across the Atlantic. Parole won both the City and Suburban Handicap and the Great Metropolitan Handicap at Epsom on consecutive days in 1879. Two years later, partnered by Fred Archer, Iroquois became the first American-bred horse to win the Derby and later the St Leger. At the end of the century, Lorillard tasted success again when the US-bred Sibola, running in the name of his racing partner Sir William Beresford and ridden by Tod Sloan, won the 1899 One Thousand Guineas.

Sloan was one of several top American jockeys who briefly rode in Britain with considerable success in what came to be known as 'The American Invasion' (see separate entry). From roughly 1896 to 1902, some half dozen dominated British racing, lifting champion jockey titles and Classics, and causing home-grown jockeys to change their riding style. American trainers arrived too, but although some of their methods were later adopted, others including the doping of horses were unacceptable in Britain and they moved on to continental Europe. The culmination of this period in Anglo-American relations was the so-called Jersey Act of 1913 in which the Jockey Club banned horses with American bloodlines from the *General Stud Book*. Traffic in the opposite direction, meanwhile, had been limited to the occasional Derby winner exported for stud purposes, although two of these, Blue Gown (1868) and Kingcraft (1870) died on the Atlantic passage.

There was little Anglo-American competition on the track before the Second World War. Although Rubio became the first American-bred winner of the Grand National in 1908, he had been imported to Britain as a yearling. In 1923, however, Papyrus, the Derby winner of that year, became the first long distance British raider when he was sent to race in a match against the Kentucky Derby winner, Zev. The result was no different from most modern forays to contest the Breeders' Cup. Papyrus had never run on dirt, was not fitted with American racing plates and had to contend with a sopping wet Belmont track. He lost. American runners seemed to fare better in Europe. Battleship was a son of the American champion Man' O War and after a successful jumping career at home, including victory in the 1934 Grand National at Belmont, he was sent by his owner, Marion du Pont, wife of the film star, Randolph Scott, to attempt the British equivalent. Although only 15.2 hands high, an entire (a stallion) – the last to win the race – and ridden by a 17-year-old jockey, Bruce Hobbs, he beat 35 runners to triumph by a head, the shortest winning margin in the Grand National during the twentieth century. He won six further races in Britain before returning to America where he became leading sire on five occasions.

If the Americans still had little to fear from British racehorses, they had much to gain from British bloodstock. Two Derby winners of the 1930s, Blenheim II (1930) and Mahmoud (1936) were exported to the States and had a major impact on bloodlines, both becoming champion sires. A son of British champion Hyperion, Heliopolis, was champion US sire in 1950. The drain continued after the war with British Classic winners Tudor Minstrel and Tulyar also departing for America. One of the most influential exports was Nasrullah, bred like Mahmoud and Tulyar by the Aga Khan. He was champion sire in Britain in 1951 and after his sale to America became champion sire there five times. The Trans-Atlantic thoroughbred was born.

With the advent of long-distance commercial flights after the war, traffic in racehorses also began to grow. When the first Washington DC International Stakes was held at Laurel Park, Maryland in 1952, the English horse Wilwyn won in a course record time with his travelling companion Zucchero third. The journey to America with two re-fuelling stops had taken 28 hours. The same race was won twice by Lester Piggott, on the American-bred but Irish-trained Sir Ivor in 1968 and on Karabas in 1969. The 1960s, however, had seen the start of the second 'American Invasion' but this time it was in bloodstock not jockeys. With the modification of the Jersey Act in 1949, the way was clear for American-breds to compete again in Britain. The involvement of Americans such as Raymond Guest (owner of Sir Ivor), Charles Engelhard (owner of Nijinsky), and Paul Mellon (owner of Mill Reef) in British racing increasingly led to the import of yearlings bought at the Kentucky sales. In the 30 years from 1968 when Sir Ivor won the Epsom Derby there were 14 North-American bred winners of this race, 13 in the Two Thousand Guineas, 10 in the fillies' equivalent and 11 in the King George. The Canadian contribution to bloodstock has, of course, been world champion Northern Dancer whose impact on international racing has been unprecedented.

The Atlantic continues to be criss-crossed by horses, jockeys and trainers. American Steve Cauthen became British champion jockey in 1984 having been US champion in 1977. He was the first to complete the double since Danny Maher in 1908 but the only winning rider so far of both the Kentucky and Epsom Derbys (in 1978 with US Triple Crown winner Affirmed and 1985 with Slip

Anchor, the year in which he also won a British fillies' Triple Crown with Oh So Sharp). British trainer Michael Dickinson went in the opposite direction, launching a new career on the flat in America after three National Hunt championships at home. Newmarket handler John Gosden trained for eight years in California, winning the inaugural Breeders' Cup Mile in 1984 with Royal Heroine before returning to Britain. Further royal success on an America racecourse went to owner Queen Elizabeth II when, in her first attempt for 35 years, she had her initial US winner in 1989 with Unknown Quantity in the Grade 1 Arlington Handicap in Chicago.

European success on North American dirt tracks remains spasmodic. Although the Breeders' Cup series was framed to attract horses from this side of the Atlantic, including a turf race, there was little to show in the first 15 years. Surfaces, riding styles, tactics and track layout are all different in America where drugs are still part of the racehorse diet, and British horses struggled to overcome the differences. Up to 1999 there had only been 5 winners, 3 – Pebbles (1985), Pilsudski (1996) and Daylami (1999) – in the Breeders' Cup Turf. The Alex Scott trained Sheikh Albadou took the 1991 Sprint, and Barathea won the Mile in 1994, a race also captured by two Irish-trained horses, Royal Academy in 1990 and Ridgewood Pearl in 1995. There were also some spectacular downfalls – Dancing Brave, champion racehorse of Europe in 1986, could only finish fourth in the Turf – and unlucky failures – Dayjur was beaten a neck in the 1990 Sprint after jumping a shadow only yards from the winning post. However, a new century has brought increased success. British horses have won the Turf in four years out of four – Kalanisi (2000), Fantastic Light (2001) and High Chaparral twice, outright in 2002 and equal first in 2003. Islington also became the first British winner of the Filly and Mare in 2003. But assaults on the American Triple Crown (Kentucky Derby, Preakness Stakes and Belmont Stakes) have continued to be unrewarding: the best English effort to date has been Bold Arrangement, runner-up in the Derby of 1986. British horses have fared rather better in the Canadian International run at Woodbine, Toronto on turf, with several winners in recent years, (Singspiel 1996, Royal Anthem 1998, Mutafaweq 2000 and Mutaman 2001).

Further reading

Randall, J. and Morris, T., *A Century of Champions* (Halifax: Portway, 1999).
www.racingpost.co.uk

Moneybox

A **nap** is a racing tipster's best bet of the day.

Nashwan was the shortest priced winner of the King George in its history, at 2–9 in 1989; his four major wins (Two Thousand Guineas, Epsom Derby, Eclipse Stakes and King George) made him leading prize money winner of the year (£770,000).

David Nicolson is the only National Hunt trainer to break Martin Pipe's total dominance of jump racing since 1988/89, holding the record for top prize money earnings in 1993/94 and 1994/95.

Nijinsky, first winner of the Triple Crown since Bahram in 1935, victorious in the Irish Derby and runner-up in the Arc, smashed the record for leading British money winner, amassing nearly £160,000 in one season (1970) – almost £1.5 million today.

Northern Dancer was four times champion sire in Great Britain – 1970, 1977, 1983, 1984 – and in the last of these years his progeny won races valued at over £1 million (or £2 million now), an all-time record.

Norton's Coin (1990) was the longest priced winner of the Cheltenham Gold Cup (100–1).

O

Horsebox

Oath gave Henry Cecil the most recent of his four Derby winners in 1999 but was the lowest-rated winner (123) of the post-war era.

When **Oh So Sharp** won the St Leger (and the fillies Triple Crown) for Henry Cecil in 1985, he became the first post-war trainer to win four English Classics in a season (the Cecil-trained Slip Anchor had already won the Derby).

One in a Million, evens favourite for the 1979 One Thousand Guineas, became the first Classic winner to be owned by a business company, Helena Springfield Ltd, for advertising purposes.

One Man, a popular grey horse reminiscent of the great Desert Orchid, won the King George VI Chase twice in 1995 and 1996, as well as the Hennessy Cognac Gold Cup at Newbury and the Queen Mother Champion Chase at Cheltenham before suffering a fatal fall at Aintree in April 1998.

On the House, a 33–1 chance in the 1982 One Thousand Guineas, gave jockey John Reid his first Classic win.

Oscar Schindler is one of three horses in the last decade to have won the Irish St Leger twice, in 1996 and 1997 – the race is open to three- and four-year-olds and has also been won twice by Vintage Crop, 1993 and 1994, and Kayf Tara, 1998 and 1999.

Oaks

See Classics.

O'Brien, Vincent (1917–)

Vincent O'Brien, who was based at Ballydoyle House, Co. Tipperary, was the most successful overseas trainer to grace the British racing scene during the twentieth century. In an extraordinary career, he switched from National Hunt to flat racing, notching up four seasons as leading trainer in Britain, twice under each code of rules, and became a national hero in Ireland.

His father was a small-scale breeder and trainer and Vincent rode as an amateur jockey before the war, taking out a training licence in 1943. By the end of the decade, he had won the Cheltenham Gold Cup in three consecutive years with Cottage Rake (1948–50) and was soon to emulate this feat by winning the Champion Hurdle three times with Hatton's Grace (1949–51). He then trained the Irish Grand National winner of 1952 (Alberoni), followed by three winners of the Aintree Grand National – Early Mist (1953), Royal Tan (1954) and Quare Times (1955), as well as a fourth Gold Cup winner in Knock Hard (1953). In addition to his string of champion National Hunt horses, he ran some flatracers, saddling the 1953 Irish Derby winner, Chamier, and it was to this branch of the sport that he turned in the later 1950s.

His first major success was the brilliant Ballymoss, winner of the Irish Derby in 1957, second in the English Derby and the first Irish winner of the English St Leger, whose four-year-old season included consecutive victories in the Coronation Cup, Eclipse Stakes, King George and the Arc. Around this time he began a long association with wealthy American patrons, the most well-known of whom were Charles Engelhard and Raymond Guest, owners of Nijinsky and Sir Ivor, and formed a lasting partnership with Lester Piggott who was to ride most of his English runners and many of his big winners over the next two decades.

The years 1968–78 were particularly fruitful for O'Brien. Sir Ivor won the Two Thousand Guineas, Derby and Washington DC International in 1968, while Nijinsky became the fifteenth and last horse to date to win the Triple Crown, in 1970. There were two further Derby winners, Roberto in 1972 and The Minstrel, who also won the King George, in 1977. He saddled nine Irish Classic winners during this period and capped his success with Alleged, one of the few horses to complete a double in the Arc, in 1977 and 1978. He was leading British trainer in 1977.

During the 1970s, Vincent O'Brien began to frequent the Kentucky yearling sales and became closely associated with breeder/owner Robert Sangster in the purchase and training of American-bred horses, particularly the offspring of top sire, Northern Dancer. The partnership, together with John Magnier, built up the Coolmore Stud in Ireland to become one of the most important in Europe and the inmates of the Ballydoyle training stable were largely descended from American thoroughbred lines.

There were more successes over the next 16 years including Golden Fleece in the Epsom Derby (1982), Caerleon in the Prix du Jockey-Club (1983), Sadler's Wells (later to become leading sire at Coolmore) in the Eclipse and the Irish Two Thousand Guineas, and El Gran Senor in the Two Thousand Guineas and the Irish Derby (all in 1984), and Royal Academy in the Breeders' Cup Mile (1990). O'Brien won a total of 44 European Classics, including 6 English Derby wins, a record which will be hard to match, and his successes in France and the United States underline his importance. He retired in 1994, aged 77, undoubtedly one of the top international trainers of the twentieth century, and received the Cartier/Sir Peter O'Sullevan award in 2001 for his lifetime achievements in racing.

Further reading

Randall, J. and Morris, T., *A Century of Champions* (Halifax: Portway, 1999).
Smith, R., *Vincent O'Brien. The Master of Ballydoyle* (London: Stanley Paul, 1992).

See also Ireland.

Officials

Impartial officials are vital to the long-term success both of individual meetings and racing in general. Unless it is believed that handicappers will allocate fair weights, starters not give some horses an advantage, judges keep their eyes focused on the finishing line, and stewards not turn a blind one to foul riding then ultimately few will wish to participate in or support racing. To ensure that this does not occur the Jockey Club employs around 200 officials who work to keep racing safe and fair. Access to the racecourse stables is protected by security guards; the clerk of the scales weighs out the jockeys prior to every race and ensures that the correct weight (set by the handicapper), colours and numbers are carried; the stewards' secretary and the veterinary officer view the horses in the parade ring; the starter assumes control of the field when they arrive at the start and oversees any problems such as tack adjustments or withdrawals; the judge calls the result of the race and announces the winning margins and times; the stewards' secretaries and stipendiary steward review the race to see if any rules might have been broken; the clerk of the scales weighs in jockeys after the race to ensure that the correct weight was carried; and the veterinary officers organise the dope testing of nominated horses and send the samples to the forensic laboratory in Newmarket.

A key member of racing officialdom is the handicapper who performs most of his work before the racing takes place. Whereas the judge's role is to separate the horses at the finish the handicapper blissfully dreams of multiple dead-heats, the ultimate accolade of his capacity to allocate weights so as to produce a fair race. To a degree handicapping is a contest between owners, anxious to disguise the true ability of their horses, and the handicapper, hoping to set weights which will attract sufficient horses and produce a good race. The main problem with handicappers in the nineteenth century was inexperience and incompetence with too many meetings being handicapped on a one-off basis by men out of touch with racing form. A good handicapper must regularly attend meetings in order to assess what racing conditions were like and how well horses had run. Recorded distances are no substitute for personal observation; a short head victory by a tired horse means something very different from a similar win by an animal with plenty in hand. However, few handicappers were prepared to incur the costs of travelling to meetings unless they could be guaranteed employment so the Jockey Club took the lead by appointing public handicappers and certifying others as competent officials. They still had to find their own work, not too difficult a task once they had a track record but not easy when a beginner. From 1935 the Jockey Club appointed handicappers to meetings. In 1973 handicapping became computerised and centralised so that the same handicap figure was applied to all races, thus removing the differences that could occur between meetings when individual handicappers provided the assessments.

Others who expend most of their efforts before the meeting takes place are the clerks of the course and the inspector of racecourses. Although licensed by the Jockey Club, clerks of the course are employed by racecourse executives and several of them work at more than one track. Their basic function is to plan the race programme, including the types of races that will be run and the conditions that will apply to entries. This is done in conjunction with the British Horseracing Board's Race Planning Department. They also supervise the preparation and maintenance of the courses and oversee the operation of racing on the day of the meeting. The first inspector of racecourses was appointed in 1907 with the right to suggest alterations in track width, gradients, drainage, contours and fencing. Northallerton was one of the first to hear that starting in rows, because the course was too narrow, was not an acceptable practice. Other racecourse executives were told that the run-in should be fully fenced off to prevent people straying on to the track and possibly interfering with the finish.

Whereas most racing officials became professionalised in the nineteenth century, there was one place where amateurism still reigned: the stewards' room. Throughout the century – and beyond – stewards tended to be selected from the aristocracy and gentry, a legacy from the days when local patronage was vital to the success of a meeting. Unfortunately many accepted the honour but not the responsibility to be aware of the rules of racing and to watch the races closely to identify when those rules were being broken. Their ineffectiveness was not always their own fault. Not till the early twentieth century did the Jockey Club suggest that the stewards could act on their own initiative rather than wait for an objection to be lodged by an owner, trainer or jockey. Despite decades of complaint, not till 1936 did the Jockey Club appoint the first stewards' secretaries to advise and assist the local men (there were no female stewards till after the Second World War) and regardless of regular calls for stipendiary stewards to assist the local honorary officials, nothing happened till the 1980s.

It is generally acknowledged that the standard of stewardship has now risen, thanks to an age limit of 75 and all appointments by the local executive having to be approved by the Jockey Club. Additionally assistance is given by the secretaries on racing matters and by the camera patrol on riding ones so that the officials no longer have to rely on memory recall and fleeting impressions. Nonetheless there is still no qualification required other than social esteem and no evaluation is made of their performance, though those local stewards who preside at inquiries now have to attend seminars, discussions and dress rehearsals. Every race is now watched live and on video (from four camera angles) by at least six officials – four local stewards, one stipendiary steward and one or two stewards' secretaries. The latter meet regularly for training days to aid the consistency of decision-making. The appointment of stipendary stewards has made a big difference, especially now that more are coming directly from the industry. Of the 13 'stipes' employed in 2000, four were ex-jockeys and two were ex-trainers. Their role is to assist the local stewards by also observing the races and acting as 'clerk of the court' and advisors at inquiries. They are also used to re-educate erring young jockeys sent for compulsory courses at the British Racing School.

Further reading

Vamplew, W., *The Turf* (London: Allen Lane, 1976).

See also Finishing, Starting.

On-course communication

With their white gloves on the end of whirling arms the tic tac men are a unique feature of British racing. Their code of signals provides an instant visual message of changing odds and other betting information from one part of the racecourse to another. Even if allowed – which they are not – trying to listen to a mobile phone message in the noisy atmosphere of the betting ring would not be easy so the men with racing's version of semaphore have survived the technological revolution. Their transmission of betting market information is easy to comprehend by anyone prepared to learn the basic code, but many of them also operate a second system, decipherable only by those bookmakers' agents who lay off money from the betting shops to reduce the starting price and their employers' off-course commitments. A major communication link between the racecourse and the betting world outside came with the development of 'the blower', initially a telegraphic connection but later a phone-based one which enabled up-to-the-minute racing and betting information to be transmitted directly from the course to subscribing bookmakers and laying off facilities in the reverse direction.

Some traditional means of visual communications still remain important at the racecourse. A letter 'P' on the number board fairly obviously indicates that the judge has called a photo finish. Signal flags of various colours hoisted at the weighing room and on the number board indicate objections, the results of stewards' enquiries, and, of importance for those waiting to collect from their winning bets, that the jockeys have weighed in. Strangely on most courses the attention of the public is drawn to these signals by means of the tannoy! Shades of Sandown Park in the 1930s where a siren hooter was sounded in the event of an objection and to inform racegoers that a special notice had been put up on the number boards; or of Goodwood where alarm bells were rung if a horse was withdrawn. Flags are also used to indicate the need for an ambulance (white), a doctor (red with a white cross) or a vet (orange).

The race card is an important form of communication for spectators, especially if they fancy a bet. Perhaps most readers can conceive that 1, 2 and 3 in the form guide show that a horse has finished in the first three but most race cards supply an explanation of the apparent scrabble hands held by some horses with BF (beaten favourite), B (brought down), F (fell), P (pulled up), R (refused), S (slipped up), U (unseated), d (disqualified) and r (ran out). Lots more information is usually provided ranging from what happens if racing is abandoned or what to do if the course has to be evacuated to lists of the officials acting at the meeting and warnings on not making undue noise, playing radios, using mobile phones and baring one's chest! Material on betting covers points for punters, how to bet on the Tote, and how many runners there must be for bookmakers to accept each-way bets. Directions are given where to obtain food and drink, place bets, and see prints of a photo finish. Most cards are now supplied by Weatherbys but racecourses often individualise them, usually with advertisements from sponsors of the meeting and details of future fixtures.

At the track racegoers generally rely on the commentary to tell them what is going on, be it the official one or that on the ubiquitous television set in the bars, eating and indoor betting areas. Very occasionally the commentators can have an off day. At Sandown Park in 1987 the wrong result was announced and the error was not corrected before the betting shops and bookmakers had paid out. Subsequently the Jockey Club determined that the judge should confirm what was going to be announced and also listen to the announcement.

Large outside television screens supplied by Racetech Services are now a common feature at tracks, enabling spectators to follow a race visually without having to leave their place in the stands or rely on the use of binoculars. They can also be used to pass on messages to the public, most notably in 1997 at Aintree when they flashed up the message 'Will all persons please leave all areas immediately' thus assisting in the evacuation following the bomb threat to the Grand National that year.

O'Neill, Jonjo (1952–)

When Supreme Quest won at Uttoxeter on 1 April 2002, John Joseph (Jonjo) O'Neill became the first person to win 100 races in a British season as both a jockey and a trainer.

Born in Co. Cork in 1952, O'Neill was apprenticed to Michael Connolly at The Curragh and rode his first winner, Lana, on the flat at his home course on 9 September 1970. He left after the trainer blamed him for the death of Irish Painter by riding the horse too hard. He migrated to England in 1973 to ride for jump trainer Gordon W. Richards. In 1977/78 he was champion jockey with 149 winners, a total that easily beat the previous best of 125 by Ron Barry. Another championship followed and two further seasons of over 100 winners as well as dual victories at the Cheltenham Festival in both the Gold Cup and Champion Hurdle. Despite riding in the Grand National eight times he was never placed: how could he be when he failed to complete the course on each occasion! Although he won Cheltenham Gold Cups on Alverton and Dawn Run, and also the Champion Hurdle on the latter horse, he is always associated with Sea Pigeon which he rode in 24 jump races, winning 11 times including the Champion Hurdle in 1980. What is less well known is that he also partnered the horse seven times on the flat, winning on four occasions including the Ebor Handicap at York in 1979 (at 18–1!).

In 1979 he bought Ivy House, a neglected farmhouse and smallholding of 43 acres in Cumbria, with the intention of having a few horses. The following year he shattered his right leg in a fall at Bangor, the second time it had been broken. He aggravated the injury by trying to ride again too soon and at one time it was feared that he might have to have the leg amputated. He did not return to the racecourse for 14 months but, on his first day back, won on Realt Na Nona at Wetherby. The plate and nine screws that held his leg together after the fall are exhibited in the National Hunt Hall of Fame as a gruesome reminder of the inherent dangers of being a jump jockey.

In 1986 he retired from the saddle with a total of 901 winners and took up training full time, only to face a year-long battle against cancer of the lymph glands and spinal column. He had had 18 horses and many owners reneged on their promise to let him have them back when he regained his health. He was left with only two so he had little income and no insurance. But, as demonstrated by his fightback against injury, Jonjo was no quitter. By 1999 he had developed Ivy House into modern racing stables set in 100 acres and had a thriving business with 50 horses. Nevertheless he cut a moderate rather than a significant figure in training circles and not till 2000/01 did he achieve his first half-century of winners. This was the first indication of the success that would follow from a move south to Jackdaws Castle, a purpose-built training stables less than 10 miles from Cheltenham, at the behest of its new owner, J.P. McManus, one of his leading patrons. In three seasons there he has saddled over 300 winners.

Further reading

O'Neill, J. and Richards, T., *Jonjo* (London: Stanley Paul, 1985).

One Thousand Guineas

See Classics.

Ownership and owners

The odds are stacked against the racehorse owner in Britain. Not only does merely one horse in ten ever win a race, but, in aggregate, prize money covers less than a quarter of ownership costs (not including the purchase price of the horse which generally devalues about 70 per cent between purchase and later sale!). Although some owners can make money, in general they pay for their pleasure. Hence, though they might hanker after triumphs, the majority of owners regard the sport as a hobby not as a business activity and are prepared to subsidise it. What they hope, as Sheikh Mohammed graphically put it in his Gimcrack Dinner speech of 1997, is that having emptied their pockets they are allowed to keep the lining.

While profitability was never the main motive for the majority of people who became racehorse owners, the poor balance between prize money and costs was a commonly cited reason given by those owners who exited the industry. Owners have received increased assistance towards covering part of their costs since 1993 via sponsorship, appearance money and a VAT refund scheme. Sponsorship, now worth over £4 million per annum, has come in several forms including an owner gaining it for either one specific horse or all of his horses, a trainer negotiating a yard deal, or participation in a sponsored number cloth scheme. Appearance money, funded principally by the Levy Board, was brought in to increase the size of fields by paying owners a sum that helped cover the cost of bringing their animal to the fixture. It was seen as being possibly self-funding as larger fields would make for a larger betting market. These sources of income have enabled owners to take advantage of a scheme which allows them to offset VAT charged on their costs against that on sponsorship, appearance money and other business sources. This was introduced in 1993 as a response to the differential tax rates that applied to racehorse ownership and purchase costs in Britain compared to the European Union. Currently the VAT scheme covers about 75 per cent of horses in training and refunds owners around £15 million a year. Some owners have remained outside the scheme as they do not feel their level of involvement in the sport warrants the administrative burden, others cannot attract sufficient income through sponsorship, and some regard their racing as a hobby pure and simple.

Unfortunately at the same time as prize money and other forms of potential income have increased, so have the costs of training and racing a horse. In the last five years of the twentieth century, training costs rose faster than inflation and were expected to rise even faster as the effects of the minimum wage, the working time directive and more Sunday fixtures fed through to owners. Each year about 30 per cent of owners drop out but they are usually replaced. The British Horseracing Board now makes efforts to bring new owners into the sport by organising two-day seminars, eight times a year. Potential owners visit a stud farm, breakfast with a trainer, watch the horses on the gallops, listen to talks from experts and spend an afternoon at the races. The cost of £265 is refunded if a horse is purchased and registered within a year.

Winning races or making money is not the ultimate goal of most owners, but the icing on the cake of social cachet. Three other major motives appear to operate. There are those who own horses so that they can socialise by inviting friends to the track to see the racing or to Sunday brunch at the training stables. Others are horse lovers for whom the animal is a 'super pet'. Third, there are the corporate owners who use racing as an impressive venue at which to entertain their clients. Additionally many trainers own horses – usually more than they would like – so that they have something to sell when a prospective owner comes to their yard. They also often take shares in horses that they train to give confidence to their clients. What must not be forgotten is that for most owners racing is fun. Conjuring up an appropriate name for a newly purchased yearling, deciding what colours to have, and feeding your horse an apple at the training stables are all part of the enjoyment. Added to this is the excitement of watching your animal perform on the track and, for some, the celebrity status however fleeting, of having all eyes focused on you in the winner's enclosure.

As there are around 9,000 active racehorse owners and only about 14,000 horses in training, it follows that most owners operate on a small scale. But it is those who can afford to participate on a grand scale that reap most glory. The turf has never been a democratic institution, especially where ownership is concerned: outstanding horses have generally had wealthy owners. Between

1880 and 1900, three such men, the Dukes of Westminster and Portland and the Earl of Rosebery bred and owned the winners of 29 Classics. A century later it was pools millionaire Robert Sangster and the Maktoums who bought and bred their way to the top of the owners' prize list. Sangster was leading owner five times between 1977 and 1984, and since then (apart from 2000 when it was the Aga Khan) the title has gone to the Maktoums in the guise of Sheikh Mohammed, Sheikh Hamdan or Godolphin. National Hunt ownership has always cost less money than the flat, at least for the initial purchase of the animal. Yet wealth is still a major determinant of being a leading owner, though surprisingly not for the man who won most races since 1945, trainer Arthur Stephenson with 465, who beat the Queen Mother by 20. Stephenson was an outstanding trainer with a career total of 2,644 wins, but for the first 14 post war seasons he was a permit holder, training only for himself. Even when he became a public trainer, he continued to buy young horses, train them to win novice events, and then sell them on to patrons of his yard. Although millionaire heiress Dorothy Paget ranks third in post war wins with 359 between 1945 and her death in 1960, it is likely that she holds the all-time record as an owner over jumps but official statistics were not collated until 1939–40. She set the post war seasonal record with 50 wins in 1951–52 and won more races than any other owner for eight consecutive seasons from 1946–47. She also owned flat horses and won the 1943 Derby with Straight Deal. Like Paget, Jim Joel, whose father made millions in the South African diamond industry, also won a Grand National (Maori Venture in 1987) and a Derby (Royal Palace in 1967). He was primarily a flat-race owner but still won 353 races over jumps between 1949 and 1992, though he headed the numerical list only once in 1972–73.

Ownership is spreading down the socio-economic scale. The Jockey Club sanctioned syndicates in 1969 and they have become a way of spreading the costs – and joys – of ownership. In 1985 around one-fifth of horses were owned by syndicates; today it is approaching one-third. Kate Fox, a social anthropologist, estimates that over 30 per cent of owners might now be from working-class backgrounds thanks to the development of large syndicates. Some of them can still be relatively expensive; to join the Boudoir group costs £12,000 up front and the Royal Ascot Racing Club charges £4,000 to join and a further £3,500 each year. This is still cheaper than attempting to compete as an individual as the estimated cost of keeping a horse in training is around £1,300 a month which will cover jockey and trainer fees, veterinary expenses, transportation and entry fees. More populist is the Manchester United Racing Club in which a two-year membership can be bought for only £235, a sum significantly less than a season ticket to Old Trafford! Another possibility is to become a short-term owner for a season, month or meeting by hiring a horse from another owner or a trainer. There will always be wealthy, large-scale owners willing to pay for their pleasure, but it is likely that the trend towards part-ownership will continue, thus allowing racing enthusiasts to have a sporting interest while lowering their financial outlay by a significant proportion.

Further reading

Hey, S., *An Arm and Four Legs* (London: Yellow Jersey Press, 2000).
KPMG Consulting, *The Economic Impact of the VAT Scheme for Racehorse Owners* (London: British Horseracing Board, 2001).

Moneybox

Any owner, trainer, rider, official or steward may raise an **objection** to a horse if it is thought to have infringed the rules of racing.

Aidan O'Brien, champion trainer in 2001, won over £3 million in total prize money that year.

Sir Robert Ogden has been leading jumps owner three times, in seasons 1996/97, 1999/2000 and 2000/01.

The **One Thousand Guineas** was worth £5,450 (£376,000 in current value) to the winner, Sceptre, in 1902, but only around £174,000 to Kazzia, in 2002.

Opera House was the leading money winner of 1993, with over £500,000 in prize money, having won the King George, Coronation Cup and Eclipse Stakes.

Sir Peter O'Sullevan, the well-known racing commentator, owned the high-class sprinter Be Friendly in the 1960s, winner of 12 races worth nearly £44,000 (over £450,000 in current value) including the first and second runnings of the November Sprint Cup at Haydock (1966, 1967), the Ayr Gold Cup (1967) and the top French sprint, the Prix de l'Abbaye (1968).

P

Horsebox

Parthia, winner of the 1959 Derby, proved to be the last of trainer Cecil Boyd-Rochfort's 13 Classic winners; he also gave jockey Harry Carr his only Derby success, beating his son-in-law Joe Mercer on Fidalgo into second place.

Peggy's Pet took part in 94 races on the flat and over hurdles and fences between 1962 and 1969 without ever winning.

Peintre Celebre holds the fastest winning time for the Prix de l'Arc de Triomphe (2.24.6 in 1997); he won the Prix du Jockey-Club and the Grand Prix de Paris in the same year and retired as one of the top-rated French horses of recent years (139).

Pendil won the King George VI Chase twice (1972, 1973) and the Racing Post Chase twice (1973, 1974) but failed when twice favourite for the Cheltenham Gold Cup.

Polygamy gave Pat Eddery the first of his 14 Classic wins in the 1974 Oaks.

Popham Down was the loose horse that caused mayhem at the 23rd fence in the 1967 Grand National. By halting most of the field he allowed rank outsider Foinavon to become the first 100–1 winner for 20 years.

Pattern races

The Pattern is a system of structuring the most important contests in the racing calendar to ensure that a series of races is available to all elite racehorses throughout the season. First established for flat racing in 1971 to include the major races of Britain, France and Ireland, it has imposed a framework on what had been a haphazard assortment of national events.

In Britain, the racing year had been built around the five three-year-old Classics – the One Thousand and Two Thousand Guineas over 1 mile in late spring, the Derby and Oaks over $1\frac{1}{2}$ miles in early June, and the St Leger over 1 mile 6 furlongs in September. The idea of a planned programme of races for all ages, over a variety of distances, was first mooted by Lord Ilchester's Racing Reorganisation Committee in 1943. Noting that the emphasis on two-year-old racing was likely to prove detrimental to the soundness and constitution of the British thoroughbred, it recommended restrictions on two-year-old races before June and additional prize money for four-year-old contests. These points, ignored at the time, were picked up over 20 years later by the Duke of Norfolk's Pattern of Racing Committee, which had been charged with the task of recommending a programme of racing with particular emphasis on high class, non-handicap races. Once the general principles were laid down, a further committee met in 1967 under Lord Porchester to identify specific races both in Britain and abroad which could provide adequate tests for outstanding horses and, from these deliberations, the Pattern was born. The final discussions were held in 1970 when the racing authorities in Britain, France and Ireland worked out a system of races which would allow carefully staged and balanced competition between the racehorses of the participating countries, taking different levels of prize money and penalties into consideration. The international Group System was launched in 1971 and soon expanded to include Italy and Germany; in 1973, there were 275 internationally agreed Group races with roughly 100 apiece in France and Britain. By 2002, the number had risen to 331.

There are four categories of Pattern races. Group One consists of the domestic Classics and major international weight-for-age races, such as the King George and the Arc; Group Two comprises races just below championship standard; Group Three contains preparatory races such as Classic trials; and the fourth division are designated as Listed races for good horses below Group standard. In 2000, there were 27 Group One races in Britain, 29 Group Two, 54 Group Three and over 80 Listed races. Of those in the top category, 18 were for three-year-olds and upwards, over 1 mile to 1 mile 6 furlongs, indicating the current emphasis on the middle-distance performer.

The Pattern is not fixed, and periodic reviews allow racing authorities to adjust key elements within the overall shape of the season. In 1973, the St James's Palace Stakes and the Coronation Stakes, run over 1 mile at the Royal Ascot meeting, were ranked as Group Two but both were elevated to Group One in 1988 and have become logical follow-up races for horses which featured prominently in the Guineas. Conversely, the Norfolk, Coventry and Queen Mary Stakes for two-year-olds at the same meeting have been downgraded to Group Three, reducing the importance of juvenile races at this June fixture.

In National Hunt racing, the rationale of the Pattern is not muddied by the issue of improving the breed, as most male jump horses are geldings, but it is similar to flat racing in attempting to provide a balanced structure to the racing year. There are over 100 top races, designated Grades One, Two and Three, in which Grade One consists of the top two contests in each of 12 categories ranging from 2-mile novice hurdles to 3-mile chases. The races are spaced to encourage competition between the top performers and include such valuable events as the King George VI Chase at Kempton Park, the Cheltenham Gold Cup and the Champion Hurdle. Grade Two comprises over 60 further high-class races in the same 12 categories while Grade Three contains the major handicaps such as the Grand National, the Scottish and Welsh Nationals, and the Gold Cups run at Newbury and Sandown Park.

With the diminishing status of the English St Leger and even, some would say, the Derby, there is an increasing tendency to aim the top horses at prestigious end-of-season fixtures abroad. This used to mean the Arc meeting at Longchamp in October and the American Breeders' Cup series in November but, with valuable races now available in the Far East and Australia towards the end of the year, many top European horses are being sent further afield. It is sometimes argued that the European Pattern is being devalued by the absence of the greatest horses and there certainly appear to have been fewer multiple Group race winners since the mid-1990s. The obvious exceptions are Giant's Causeway (2000) and Rock of Gibraltar (2002) who each won five Group Ones as three-year-olds, although both horses were milers or 10-furlong specialists. Some would point to this as evidence of the increasing competitiveness of top-class European racing but it could equally suggest that, with the top horses jetting around the globe, the stay-at-homes are uniformly average. No doubt the shape of the European Pattern will continue to evolve during the twenty-first century.

Further reading

Cranham, G. and Poole, C., *The Guinness Book of Flat Racing* (London: Guinness Publishing, 1990).

Magee, S., *Channel Four Racing Complete A–Z of Horse Racing* (London: Channel 4 Books, 2001).

Mortimer, R., *The Flat* (London: Allen and Unwin, 1979).

Piggott, Lester (1935–)

Lester Piggott won 7 French, 16 Irish and 30 English Classics, including the Derby 7 times, and was champion jockey on 11 occasions. Yet, like Fred Archer a century before, the Cambridgeshire eluded him.

It could be claimed that he was bred for his career! His father Keith rode around 500 winners as both a flat and jump jockey, before becoming a trainer. His paternal grandfather Ernest was a successful trainer who had won three Grand Nationals as a jockey and the same number of National Hunt jockey titles. His maternal grandmother, Margaret, was sister of leading flat-race jockeys Mornington and Kempton Cannon, themselves the offspring of the great Tom Cannon. His mother Iris came from the Rickaby family which included great-grandfather Fred who trained a Derby winner, father Fred who rode three Classic winners, and a brother Fred who rode five. Of Piggott's Rickaby cousins, Bill was a top jockey for many years and Fred became champion trainer in South Africa.

An only child, he began his apprenticeship in his father's stables and had his first public ride at the age of 12 when he weighed less than 5 st. His first win was on 18 August 1948 on The Chase at Haydock. Just over two years later he had ridden out his claim and had been champion apprentice twice, the second time despite breaking his leg in August and missing the rest of the season. Almost from the beginning, his career was dogged by controversy. In October

1950 he was suspended by the Jockey Club for the remainder of the season following several instances of crossing and boring. By 1954 he had received seven suspensions, almost all for rough riding, and then, shortly after winning his first Derby on Never Say Die, he was given a six-month ban and told to work for a trainer other than his father. Typically the first ride on his return was a winning one and he remained a brave and thrusting rider. He also rode some races over hurdles till 1959 and had 20 winners, including one at the Cheltenham Festival.

He spent 12 years as stable jockey to Noel Murless but in 1966 they split when Piggott insisted on riding Vincent O'Brien's Valoris in the Oaks rather than one of Murless's fillies. Needless to say Valoris and Piggott won the race. He then went freelance and, though initially rides were less easy to come by, he still won the jockeys' championship with just 117 winners. He gained a reputation in pre-agent days of having other riders 'jocked off' if he fancied a particular mount in a big race. Piggott exploited the fact that owners pay the bills and are entitled to put up whom they wish. This was not always well received by the racing public, most notably in 1972 when Piggott's machinations lost Bill Williamson a Derby-winning ride on Roberto. Piggott's view was that racing is a hard game and it is part of a self-employed jockey's job to get on the best horses. His fellow professionals respected him and he was elected Vice-President of the Jockeys Association on its foundation in 1969.

He retired for the first time in October 1985 and began training, gaining 30 winners in his first season but generally having far less success than when he rode. In 1987 he was jailed for three years for tax evasion and forced to hand back his OBE, awarded in 1975 for services to racing. He returned to the saddle in 1990 and within a week had won the Breeders' Cup Mile in New York on Royal Academy, in money terms the most valuable race of his career. In May 1992 Rodrigo de Triano brought him his thirtieth Classic win, an individual riding record that still stands. He finally retired in April 1995, six months short of his sixtieth birthday. His last win was at Haydock, scene of his first victory 26 years previously. His career wins on the flat in Britain totalled 4,493, but he had also ridden winners in 35 other countries on 4 continents. He is commemorated in the Lesters, the annual jockey awards, and in the Piggott Gates at Epsom that bear the phrase 'an iconoclast who became an icon', words penned by the racing commentator, Sir Peter O'Sullevan.

Further reading

Piggott, L., *Lester* (London: Partridge, 1995).
Pryor, S., *Lester* (London: Sidgwick and Jackson, 1985).

Pipe, Martin (1945–)

On 30 August 1999, Martin Pipe became the most successful jumps trainer in Britain when Bamapour won at Newton Abbot to enable him to pass Arthur Stephenson's total of 2,644. Then on 4 February 2000, victory by Through the

Rye at Folkestone saw him pass Stephenson's aggregate of 2,988 winners for flat and jump racing. Stephenson took 46 years, Pipe only 26, though there was no summer jumping in Stephenson's day.

In 1972, his father David Pipe, a highly successful West Country bookmaker, sold all but one of his 35 betting shops and bought Pond Farm in Somerset, some 73 acres with a few derelict buildings. It is now a fully equipped 300-acre training establishment. When Martin began training he had little knowledge of the racing industry apart from a few point-to-point rides, one of which resulted in a broken thigh – the reason why he bikes around the yard instead of walking. What he did have was an enquiring mind, a willingness to learn and a highly competitive nature.

He has done more than any other trainer to modernise the art of producing racehorses peaked to run at their best by taking the guesswork out of his profession. He took a 'racing industry' course at Worcester Agricultural College – winning the best student award – and also attended courses at the Animal Health Trust. Pipe went away bearing in mind the relative importance of blood, weight, temperature, avoidance of viruses, nourishment and exercise. He abandoned the idea of long-distance cantering as he found no practical reason for it and so his horses do most of their work up and down a short but steep hill. They also swim a lot, bask in a solarium, have their temperatures taken twice a day, are regularly weighed especially before and after races, and have their blood analysed by a resident expert. Pipe acknowledges that this will not tell you whether a horse will win but it will identify those who have little chance.

His first winner, as a permit holder in May 1975, was Hit Parade in the Last Chance Selling Hurdle at Taunton. He took out a full training licence in 1977. Nine seasons later he had his first century of winners and virtually each season since has done it earlier and earlier. He became the first trainer to send out 100 winners before Christmas in 1989, the year that he also became the first trainer to achieve 150 winners in a National Hunt season. He has broken the 200 barrier seven times; no other National Hunt trainer has done it even once.

A workaholic, Pipe is insistent that the details are done correctly. Some do not take kindly to his demand of getting things exactly as he likes them to be. Hence, displaying his humorous side, Pipe named one of the six races he sponsored at Taunton in 1997 the 'Martin Pipe Am I Being Too Difficult Handicap Hurdle'. He insists on written reports from all his jockeys but they are happy to do so because he supplies them with potential winning material. 'Ridden by Peter Scudamore, trained by Martin Pipe' featured in the winner's enclosure 792 times. More recently his relationship has been with Tony McCoy: of Pipe's first 200 winners in 1999, the Irishman had ridden 143. Their joint efforts in the 2001–02 season enabled Pipe to complete the fastest century of wins by a jumps trainer when Turkestan headed the field at Ascot on 3 November.

There has been much criticism in racing of his success. This is partly snobbery inflamed by the fact that a bookmaker's son with no experience of the industry has sent out so many winners. Others argue he goes for quantity rather than quality. There is some evidence for this. If you measure the achievement of a trainer by his total of winners Pipe has been the leading exponent of his trade since1985–86, but if you look to the volume of prize money won, he has been less successful only being champion from 1988–89 except in 1993–94 and 1994–95! He has been leading trainer twice at the National Hunt Festival at Cheltenham and, along with Jenny Pitman, he holds the distinction of having won the Aintree Grand National as well as the Scottish, Welsh and Irish equivalents.

As befits his modern approach to the sport, his website is one of the most advanced and commercial of those developed by racing interests. It combines video action, audio interviews, and a gamut of adverts ranging from stable memorabilia to the products of his sponsors.

Further reading

Pipe, M. and Pitman, R., *Martin Pipe* (London: Headline, 1993).
www.martinpipe.co.uk

Pitman, Jenny (1946–)

Jenny Pitman was the most successful female trainer of the late twentieth century at a time when women in National Hunt racing were still sometimes viewed with suspicion. She was born Jennifer Harvey on a small farm in Leicestershire, the middle of seven children, and developed an interest in horses from an early age. She graduated from riding ponies in local shows and hunting with the Quorn to a weekend job at nearby racing stables, and by the age of 18 she was working full time with racehorses at a yard in Lambourn, Berkshire, one of the main centres of training. Marriage to the National Hunt jockey, Richard Pitman, and two sons quickly followed but her love of horses soon led to the purchase of a small yard of her own. To begin with, she specialised in rehabilitating injured horses and in 1974 started to race point-to-pointers. The following year she successfully applied for a licence to train under Jockey Club rules and embarked on a career as a trainer which was to span nearly 25 years.

Although she trained her first winner in 1975, her earliest big success came in 1982 when Corbiere won the Welsh National at Chepstow, a race which another of her talented horses, Burrough Hill Lad, won the following year. She first captured the attention of the racing public at Aintree in 1983 when Corbiere won the Grand National, making her the first woman to train a National winner. It was the success of Burrough Hill Lad in the 1984 Cheltenham Gold Cup, however, which finally marked her acceptance by the racing press and professionals. The horse went on to win both the Hennessy Gold Cup at Newbury under a top weight of 12 st and the King George VI Chase at Kempton Park, earning him the accolade of National Hunt Champion of 1984.

Other major successes followed. She captured the Welsh National for the third time in 1986 with Stearsby, won the Cheltenham Gold Cup again in 1991 with

Garrison Savannah, ridden by her elder son, Mark, and nearly pulled off a historic double when the horse was narrowly beaten in the Grand National three weeks later. She suffered the agony of 'winning' the void National of 1993 with Esha Ness but triumphed in the 1995 race with Royal Athlete. She also trained the winners of the Scottish Grand National in 1995 (Willsford) and the Irish Grand National in 1997 (Mudahim).

There were also setbacks. Her first marriage broke up, ill-health dogged much of her career and she was sometimes portrayed as a controversial character by sections of the press, with whom she had, at times, a stormy relationship. But her pioneering achievements as a woman trainer were recognised with the award of an OBE in 1998 for services to horseracing and with a special award by the BBC in 1999 when she finally retired from training.

Further reading

Pitman, J., *Jenny Pitman – The Autobiography* (London: Bantam Books, 1999).

Point-to-point

Point-to-point racing is steeplechasing for amateurs. It is run under Jockey Club regulations but organised at the local level by a hunt or a recognised point-to-point club. Most races are run over 3 miles with a minimum of 18 fences to be jumped, though there are a few longer races of up to 4 miles and a small number of 2-mile races for horses that have never won a race. Unlike National Hunt racing there is a limited season of six months starting in January. At the beginning of the twenty-first century there are just over 200 fixtures, the majority of them held at the weekends. It is one of the last truly amateur sports at the elite level, and not just for those riding: all course staff from parking attendant to doctor, from farrier to commentator are volunteers. The sport is generally promoted as a family day out complete with picnic and wellington boots. Except when current or old racecourses are used, there are no permanent buildings or facilities available to the racegoers.

Although steeplechasing was begun by huntsmen keen to compete in races against their sporting colleagues, by the later nineteenth century that branch of racing was becoming increasingly professionalised with paid jockeys riding thoroughbred horses that had often been specially trained for jump races, which themselves were now often at enclosed racecourses rather than over natural terrain. In an attempt to restore the original aim of the sport, hunts, individually and collectively, moved to stage cross-country races from which thoroughbreds and professional jockeys were excluded. The spirit of amateurism prevailed and in the 1890s both the Stock Exchange and the legal fraternity in the Pegasus Club promoted participation by their specific occupational groups. Initially each meeting set its own rules but in 1913 the Master of Hounds Point-to-Point Association established a nationally applicable set of regulations. One interesting spin-off was that these rules, unlike those for both National Hunt and flat racing, did not prohibit women from participating as riders against men, a situation that prevailed till 1929. From 1967 female riders could compete against men in hunt members' races and seven years later in such races run by adjacent hunts. In 1976 came equality: men and women could race against each other in all events save for those open races specifically confined to one gender. At the same time a rule was imposed banning anyone from racing under the age of 16; previously this had been 18 for women.

By the 1930s the issue of professionalisation had again come to the fore. A common complaint was that the sport was becoming too much like steeple-chasing with too many ex-racehorses competing. New rules were brought in which banned professional riders including apprentices, hunt servants, stable hands, grooms and anyone who had 'ridden for hire'. At the same time other regulations prohibited participation by horses that were trained by a licensed trainer unless they were his own property. The administration of the sport remained with the Masters of Foxhounds till the 1935 season when point-to-pointing came directly under the jurisdiction of the National Hunt Committee (and in 1969 the Jockey Club itself). For the most part the existing rules were maintained though several important changes were made including a clear definition of what constituted a [non-eligible] professional rider, the appointment of accredited course inspectors, and restrictions on horses that had won too often in open nomination races.

To ensure that the racing retains its amateur characteristics – and also its traditional relationship with hunting – riders, owners and horses are subject to rules of eligibility. Owners must be member, subscriber or farmer of a recognised pack and their horses must have been 'regularly and fairly' hunted with a recognised pack of foxhounds, bloodhounds, draghounds or harriers. All jockeys must hold a Rider's Qualification Certificate, an item that is generally issued only to masters, members, farmers and subscribers of a hunt or their sons, daughters or partners. In the past there was some rule bending and lip service paid to the hunting regulation, today most of the horses running have been out after foxes and other hunted species. Perhaps the greatest force for amateurism is the limit set to prize money. Although there is no handicapping and only limited penalties on previous winners, the money to be made does not encourage profit seekers. The 1977 season saw the first rise since 1961 when the winner of an open event was entitled to £50 – previously £40 – but the ceiling on first prize in all other races remained at a lowly £30. Two further rises occurred in 1979 and 1990 when it reached its current level of a maximum of £250 in aggregate for winning and placed horses in open events and £175 for other races. There is a downside to the amateurism. The inclusive nature of point-to-pointing allows many inexperienced riders to participate, along with inexperienced horses. This makes the sport very dangerous and falls and injury rates are much higher than in the professional sectors of racing.

Whilst essentially remaining a fun day out for participants and spectators, point-to-pointing has provided an avenue into National Hunt racing for both jockeys and horses. Joe Tizzard, for one, moved from being leading novice rider to becoming stable jockey to Paul Nicholls. Some horses have gone on to make a successful transition to racing under Rules, including in the 1960s What A Myth and in the 1970s The Dikler which both won the Cheltenham Gold

Cup. More recent successful equine graduates from the amateur side include See More Business and Cool Dawn, both Cheltenham Gold Cup winners, Teeton Mill, Harwell Lad and Coome Hill, respectively winners of the King George VI Chase, the Whitbread Gold Cup and the Hennessy Cognac Gold Cup. Ideas have also moved into the professional branch of jump racing. Sunday racing with betting was pioneered at point-to-point tracks as was the dolling off of fences to protect stricken riders and horses without causing a race to be abandoned.

Point-to-point meetings and Hunt races were virtually out of the same stable, both being promoted by the local hunt. The main difference between bona fide hunt meetings and point-to-pointing was that the former were allowed to hold their meetings over an enclosed course and charge a modest entry fee to spectators whereas point-to-point meetings did not charge admission. Generally the horses and riders competing tended to be the same at both type of event and over time the hunt meetings were submerged within the point-to-point calendar. By 1949 the bona fida hunt meetings had completely disappeared from the scene. Half a century later point-to-pointing itself is under threat by proposed anti-hunting legislation. In 1998 a survey of point-to-point secretaries suggested that more than half the sponsoring hunts would no longer hold race meetings if hunting was banned. What other groups, if any, would step in to keep the sport alive is now on racing's agenda.

Further reading

Williams, M., *Point to Pointing in Our Time* (London: Quiller, 1998).
www.thejockeyclub.co.uk

Porter, John (1838–1922)

During a career of nearly 50 years straddling the Victorian and Edwardian period, John Porter trained the winners of 1,063 races worth £720,021, including 23 Classics. He began his racing career as an apprentice jockey in the stables of John Barham Day, but received few rides as another of the apprentices there was John Wells who went on to become champion jockey twice and win eight Classics. But Porter was learning his trade within the stables and out on the training gallops. In 1855, at the age of 17, he became head lad for William Goater and in 1863, on the recommendation of Lord Westmorland, one of Goater's patrons, he was appointed as private trainer at Sir Joseph Hawley's Cannons Heath yard to replace the recently deceased George Manning. Stable jockey there was one John Wells! He rode both of Porter's first winners as a trainer, Washington and Columbia, in successive races at Doncaster on St Leger day 1863.

By the end of 1867 the Cannons Heath stable had become successful enough to convince Sir Joseph to expand his operations and Porter moved into newly built premises at Kingsclere where he trained Blue Gown to win the Derby of 1868 and Pero Gomez the St Leger of 1869. On the death of Sir Joseph in 1875

Porter exercised his option to buy Kingsclere for £4,000 and subsequently expended five times as much on its enlargement.

In his early years as a public trainer he was very reliant on the horses of Frederick Gratton with which he captured several major handicaps. Eventually, however, trainer and owner split because of the manner of Gratton's gambling coups, involving a deviousness that led to a victory in the 1880 Liverpool Autumn Handicap being booed by the public. Other owners soon replaced Gratton, including the Duke of Westminster for whom Porter landed the 1882 Derby with Shotover and Lord Stamford whose Geheimniss won the Oaks the same year. The great days of John Porter at Kingsclere had begun. The next four years saw six Classic wins including the Triple Crown by Ormonde in 1886. Three more Triple Crowns followed: Common in 1891, Flying Fox in 1899 and La Flèche with the fillies' version in 1892.

He did not push his horses hard and rarely ran them in trials, fearing that it could be a race too many for the fragile creatures that thoroughbreds often are. He looked after his staff as well as his horses. The expansion of Kingsclere included the construction of bathrooms and lavatories for his lads and apprentices, and although the indentures of the time commonly entitled trainers to all riding fees of their apprentices, Porter took only half. He also advocated low minimum weights so as to give younger riders more chance of securing mounts.

On his retirement at the end of the 1905 season he handed on the Kingsclere stable to William Waugh. He continued in racing by acting as managing director of Newbury racecourse, which he helped found in 1906. That course commemorates his contribution to racing in the John Porter Stakes, a $1\frac{1}{2}$ mile Group Three race, run in April.

Further reading

Mortimer, R., Onslow, R. and Willett, P., *Biographical Encyclopaedia of British Flat Racing* (London: Macdonald and Jane's, 1978).

Porter, J. and Moorhouse, E., *John Porter of Kingsclere* (London: 1919).

Pretty Polly (1901–31) – by Gallinule out of Admiration

Pretty Polly was the greatest filly ever to race in Britain and the idol of the Edwardian racing crowds; a century later her achievements have yet to be surpassed. At the end of her outstanding racing career, she went on to found a highly significant bloodline through her four fillies.

She was bred in Ireland by her owner Major Eustace Loder and was sent to trainer Peter Gilpin at Newmarket. A large chestnut with a white star, she made her debut as a two-year-old at Sandown Park, winning by 10 lengths in impressive style. In her next race she led from start to finish, and followed this with seven successive victories, including the Cheveley Park Stakes, the Criterion Stakes and the Middle Park Plate at Newmarket, sent off on each occasion as odds-on favourite.

In 1904 she made all the running in the One Thousand Guineas and comfortably beat three opponents in the Oaks, for which she started at 8–100, the shortest-ever price for an English Classic. She won the Coronation Stakes at Ascot and the Nassau Stakes at Goodwood before an autumn trip to Doncaster, accompanied as always by her faithful travelling companion, a horse whose presence apparently kept her calm in the paddock. She not only won the St Leger in record time, trouncing the Two Thousand Guineas and Derby winner, St Amant, but came out again two days later to win the Park Hill Stakes over the same distance. It was not the victories themselves but the manner in which she achieved them that marked her out as an exceptional filly and a popular one with the racing public.

Having demolished the best three-year-olds in England, it was decided to send her across the Channel to deal likewise with the French. But a bad sea crossing, delays, heavy going at Longchamp and a change of jockey all conspired against her. Her regular partner, William Lane, had been badly injured after the St Leger meeting and his replacement, the American Danny Maher, could only bring her in second in the Prix du Conseil Municipal over $1\frac{1}{2}$ miles. Maher reckoned that she was not a true stayer but English racegoers, a contingent of whom had travelled to Paris for the race, were dismayed.

She redeemed her reputation somewhat by winning the Free Handicap at Newmarket in October, carrying top weight, and she was unbeaten as a four-year-old, winning four major races including the Coronation Cup at Epsom Downs in a time 6 seconds faster than the previous day's Derby winner. But a strain caused her to miss the summer fixtures and she was kept in training for a fourth year. She won at Newmarket and repeated her success in the Coronation Cup before turning out at Ascot for the Gold Cup, a true stayers' race at $2\frac{1}{2}$ miles. She was beaten by a length and although there were mitigating factors – the lancing of a wart a few days earlier, a torrid day with huge crowds, a jockey who may have disobeyed orders and the apparent absence of her travelling companion – she never raced again. She had won 22 of her 24 races.

It used to be said that she was not a first-rate brood mare but she produced four winning fillies who in turn began a highly successful line. Amongst the champions descended from Pretty Polly are Brigadier Gerard, Derby winners Psidium and St Paddy, Arc winner Carroll House, Neartic, sire of Northern Dancer and recent international globetrotters Vintage Crop and Swain. She finally retired to Ireland where she died, aged 30, one of the most brilliant mares of the twentieth century.

Further reading

Randall, J. and Morris, T., *A Century of Champions* (Halifax: Portway Press, 1999).
Wilson, J., *The Great Racehorses* (London: Little, Brown & Co., 1998).

Prize money

Prize money offered in British flat and National Hunt racing in 1999 was a British record at £72 million and it has continued to rise to its current level of just above £80 million. Yet the Racehorse Owners Association complains vociferously that it is still insufficiently low compared to costs. In the late 1990s

Britain was ranked 36th of racing nations in the prize money recovered by owners as a percentage of keep and training costs: on average it was just under a quarter here compared to 47 per cent in the United States, 49 per cent in France, 83 per cent in Japan and 100 per cent in the United Arab Emirates. For every £1,000 outlaid by owners racing in Britain they got back about £250. And this does not include the cost of buying the horse in the first place.

Moreover much of the prize money actually comes from the owners themselves. In 1913, the first year for which comprehensive data are available, owners supplied 63 per cent of prize money by way of entry fees and forfeits. In 2002, thanks to the Tote, the betting levy and sponsorship, the proportion was down to 14 per cent, still well above the 6 per cent in both France and Australia. Most of the rest came from the British Horseracing Board (BHB) (47 per cent), sponsors (20 per cent) and the racecourses (17 per cent).

Bookmakers have always had a bad [racing] press for their failure to contribute more money to racing, but with the new commercial deal for media rights the racecourses are also being criticised for not passing on more of their income in prize money. The BHB point out that in 2002 an additional £46 million was provided to racecourses but aggregate prize money went up only by £5 million. A survey of winning prize money offered for jump racing in 2002 revealed that whereas Aintree averaged £33,086 per race and Cheltenham £25,058, 18 of the other 40 courses paid out less than £4,000 and Hexham delivered only £2,772, scarcely enough to warrant the costs of participating. But owners and trainers have the option of not entering races at particular courses: that they continue to do so will do little to persuade track owners to offer more money.

To some extent the blame for the paucity of prize money can also be laid at the door of the BHB and the Levy Board who could have required higher minimum levels to be provided by the courses. In the 1870s the Jockey Club helped revolutionise racing when it set a minimum level of prize money which drove out those courses attempting to race on the cheap. The policy of minimum prize money has continued and now applies to each grade of race. Hence the racing authorities could demand that racecourses attempt to provide more cash stimulus to owners.

Another bone of contention between owners and racecourse executives is that many courses deduct the cost of any trophies from the winner's prize money. It was estimated that in 1999 such deductions cost owners about £500,000. However, most of these were in fact optional with owners preferring the prize to the prize money. The real issue is where there is no choice, a major problem where partnerships, and especially syndicates, are involved.

Prize money is important to more than owners as trainers, jockeys and stable staff all receive a proportion to supplement their income. It is likely to increase substantially as a result of the new financial arrangements for racing when commercial negotiation with the bookmakers replaces the betting levy. However, the unanswered questions are how the growth will compare with the rise in costs and how the aggregate level will compare with that offered by foreign rivals.

See also Ownership and owners, Sponsorship, Trophies and Prizes.

Moneybox

Pari-mutuel is the equivalent of Tote betting in France.

Penalty value is the amount of prize money won by a victorious horse before deductions and is used in the calculation of penalties for future races.

Pilsudski's globetrotting exploits, winner and runner-up in Group races in England, Ireland, Germany, France, Canada and Japan, earned nearly £3 million in prize money in the 1990s.

Martin Pipe became the first jumps trainer to net a seven-figure sum in prize money, which he achieved in season 1990/91 (£1,203,014).

A **Placepot** is a Tote bet in which horses are selected for the first six races at any meeting, normally for a place but, in a race with fewer than five runners, for a win.

Psidium was the longest odds post-war Derby winner in 1961, the same year in which Rockavon was the longest odds Two Thousand Guineas winner, both at 66–1.

A day at the races 1950

Rode myself before the War. Point-to-point and hunt races. Easy enough to get leave from the regiment for that. Made Brigadier during the War. Demobbed in '46 and have adjusted to peacetime a damn sight better than most racecourses. One just needs to look across the Channel. Compared to Longchamp, Auteuil and Deauville, most of our courses look like they've had an air raid. And the French only pay a fifth of what we do. Racegoers won't return if facilities don't improve, you know. The *Telegraph* says that over 10,000 attended every day in 1948 but that's down to 8,500 now. The French do it with their pari-mutuel, that's the Gallic version of the totalisator. Puts a massive surplus into their tracks. A good officer admits his mistakes and I was wrong about the Tote. When it came in I was against it. More bureaucracy, I thought. But it does generate money for racing. But then, what would British racing be without the bookies?

Mind you, have to sympathise with the course executives. Damn government is hamstringing them with all its regulations and restrictions. Difficult to get a licence to make repairs when materials are needed for houses. However, one can't object to 'homes fit for heroes', can one? At least petrol rationing has ended so might drive down to the races. But food is still rationed so there won't be much of a spread. That's not all that is in short supply. Wonder if HMG knows that one has to pay a shilling deposit on a cup and saucer at the London tracks! Then there's the entertainment tax: costs enough to get into the races even without that. And don't get one started on nationalisation. Mind you, one doesn't object to the National Stud. Run by military men and at least it's now in England. Damn silly having our National Stud in a foreign country.

The French have also got their act together on the track. When one was there in '45 who would have guessed that only two years later they would win the Oaks, Derby and Coronation Cup. And this year just look at the Oaks: Ashmena owned by Monsieur Boussac and trained by Charles Semblat. And the Derby: Galcador owned by Monsieur Boussac and trained by Charles Semblat. One felt almost unpatriotic backing their Scratch II for the St Leger but 9–2 was too good to miss!

One notes that Gordon rode his 4,000th winner last May. You know, when war broke out he turned down the offer to ride in Ireland and took up ARP duties. Even applied to join the fly boys but was turned down as unfit because of his brush with tuberculosis in '26. One doubts if young Piggott will do as well. He's just lost his claiming allowance but he'll be lucky not to lose his licence as well. No discipline. Needs some time in the army.

One doesn't like the way racing is going. There's no need for photo finishes. If the judge can't separate 'em, then call it a dead-heat. And who wants to go racing in the evening? Scottish idea, wasn't it? Damn good soldiers those Jocks, but they know nothing about racing. One struggles to name a Scottish trainer or jockey. All that racing needs is a return to what we had before the War.

Q

Horsebox

Quashed is one of only six fillies to have won the Ascot Gold Cup, in 1936; only two others have done so in the twentieth century, Gladness (1958) and Indian Queen (1991). Her name is a clever reference to those of her sire (Obliterate) and dam (Verdict).

Queenpot won the 1948 One Thousand Guineas by a head. She never won again.

Queen's Taste won the Scottish Grand National three times (1953, 1954 and 1956).

Quest for Fame won the 1990 Derby. When he won a race at Santa Anita, California in 1992, he became the first Derby winner since Isinglass in 1895 to win as a five-year-old.

Quick as Lightning, first of three One Thousand Guineas winners for John Dunlop, won the 1980 race but never won again; his other winners were Salsabil 1990 and Shadayid 1991.

Quinlan Terry won the Cambridgeshire in 1988.

Quantification

Racing is an anorak's dream. There are statistics on everything from the conventional lists of winning jockeys, trainers and owners, through the youngest and oldest jockeys, numbers of starters and finishers in major steeple-chase races, fastest times, winning margins, and a host of 'the first...' to the outright bizarre correlations of colour of horse with success on particular tracks.

Some might consider the way that the various titles are calculated borders, if not on the bizarre, then towards the irrational. Certainly it is applied inconsistently between the various categories of championship. When that for flat-race jockeys was instituted in 1848, it went to the rider of most winners during the defined racing season whether the mounts were in selling plates or the Classics. Even now no cognisance is taken of either prize money or the quality of the races won; nor is there any place for strike rates which some would see as a more meaningful figure. Computer whiz, John Whitley, has devised a system of measuring the 'added value' that different jockeys contribute to a horse's performance and by his analysis Ray Cochrane was the outstanding jockey of the past decade, but Cochrane never won a title. In the case of owners, trainers and stallions – for which technically there is no official championship, merely a generally acknowledged 'leading' label – it used to be the value of the races won by their horses or offspring that counted. However, pressure from those who felt that second or third place in a Group One race should not be discounted brought all winnings into consideration from 1999. This immediately cost Paul Nicholls the National Hunt trainers' title. He was more than £100,000 in front of Martin Pipe thanks to trebles at Cheltenham and the Scottish Grand National meeting, but Pipe had twice as many horses and the numerical superiority eventually told. In 1969 Peter Walwyn would have been champion trainer under the current system of counting total prize money, but in those days only winning prize money was considered so the title went to Arthur Budgett. Perhaps even more unfortunate was Arthur Stephenson who, in terms of numbers of winners, led other trainers ten times and other owners three times but was never prize-money champion in either capacity. One other problem in ranking owners is that caused by partnerships and syndicates. In 2002, for example, the list of the top 50 owners included Mrs John Magnier in fourth place in partnership with Michael Tabor, in sixth place individually, in tenth with Sir Alex Ferguson, and in fourteenth again with Michael Tabor but with their names reversed!

Then there is the matter of the length of the racing season to be used in the calculations. Traditionally the flat season ran from late March to mid-November, but then the coming of the all-weather course raised the possibility of year-round racing. In 1993 William Hill, the bookmakers, approached the Jockeys Association to seek guidance on the parameters of the championship. Hill then agreed to sponsor the title chase and it was agreed that from 1994 the flat season would run from New Year's Day right through to the end of the year, thus incorporating early and late year racing on the all-weather tracks into the championship, but also effectively removing from championship contention those jockeys who chose to stick to the conventional season. Following further consultation with the Jockeys Association, this has now been modified to allow both all-weather and turf winners to count, but only from late March to early November. In other words, despite the existence of racing throughout the year, the actual defined season is now shorter than it ever was, though all-weather racing now also has its own championship. The Gold Cup meeting at Sandown in April, now denotes the end of the National Hunt season which runs all year to that date and then starts again the following Monday.

The racehorse is bred for a specific purpose: to win races. Some aren't very good at this. Quixall Crossett retired in 2001 after racing 103 times and never making the winner's enclosure, though he finished second on two occasions. The previous worst losing streak was Amrullah with a mere 74 defeats. On the other hand in 1861 the filly Nancy won 12 races in one season. This was out of only 13 starts and included victories in the Chester Cup, Goodwood Cup and Ebor Handicap. One hundred and fifty years later Madame Jones repeated the feat of 12 victories but at a lower level of racing: she would have been rated about 4 st below Nancy. Both must yield the palm to Nagwa who won 13 races in 1975. This trio of fillies, however, ran in handicaps. Those who raced in weight-for-age or non-handicap races could garner more victories, as there was no official to penalise them for success by imposing more weight on their backs. In 1856, three-year-old Fisherman won 23 races: he also won 21 in each of the next two flat-racing seasons. The post war record is 16 held by Provideo (1984) and Timeless Times (1990), both two-year-olds trained by Bill O'Gorman. The record for a filly or mare is 21 by Alice Hawthorn in 1874 and Lilian 30 years later, both of them outstanding stayers. Over the jumps Bybrook won 11 handicaps in 1975–76.

In career terms Catherina, daughter of the 1816 Derby winner Whisker, is credited with more wins than any other British horse. The *Racing Calendar* shows that she ran in 176 races and won 79 of them but when allowance is made for the heats system she actually had 134 wins in 304 starts. However, apart from an unplaced attempt at the Oaks, she rarely raced at the top level and won only about £5,000 in her racing career. She was retired at the age of 11 and as a brood mare gave birth to nine foals. The post war record is 34 set by Le Garcon d'Or between 1960 and 1972, but Palacegate Touch was only one behind at the end of 2001 ... and was still one behind at the end of the 2002 season, this despite some 200 races.

As for jockeys, it is top riders who have both most winners and most losers because of the number of mounts they take. Frankie Dettori holds the record for the greatest number of losing rides in a flat season with 1,085 in 1994 and Richard Johnson has the most over jumps with 728 in 2000–01. Clearly the expansion of racing to include Sundays, evenings, all-year jumping, and all-weather tracks combined with easier travel for riders has greatly increased the opportunities for not finishing first. Johnson is also the National Hunt jockey with the second highest number of winners as a runner-up in the championship, 161 to Tony McCoy's 191 in 2000–01. Pride of place here, if that is not too much of an accolade for someone finishing second, goes to Adrian Maguire who lost out to Richard Dunwoody in 1993–94 by 194–197. On the flat Jason Weaver had 200 winners in 1994 but was beaten by Frankie Dettori who rode 233 horses to victory in spite of his massive losing aggregate that year. Not counting the dead-heat in 1923 between Steve Donoghue and Charlie Elliott the narrowest championship margins on the flat were the one winner that separated Gordon Richards and Freddy Fox in 1930 and the two between Steve Cauthen and Pat Eddery in 1987. Over the sticks, discounting the contrived dead-heat between John Francome and Peter Scudamore in 1981–82 the narrowest margin was the three between Dunwoody and Maguire in 1993–94. At the other end of the scale Gordon Richards beat runner-up Billy Nevett by a margin of 187 in 1933 and over jumps Tony McCoy led second-placed Richard Johnson by 157 in 2001–02.

Moneybox

A **Quadpot** is a Tote bet requiring a selection of four horses to be placed in the last four races of a Placepot.

Quashed, winner of the Ascot Gold Cup in 1936, won the Oaks in 1935 at odds of 33–1, one of the longest priced winners of the race in the twentieth century.

The Queen has twice been leading owner, winning nearly £41,000 in 1954 and £62,211 in 1957 (£656,000 and £871,000 in present values).

Queen's Hussar was leading sire in 1972 (£185,337), thanks to the winning ways of his son Brigadier Gerard.

Queen of Trumps, winner of the 1835 St Leger, was made 10–1 on favourite for the Scarborough Stakes three days later, but was brought down by a dog that ran on to the Doncaster track.

A **Quinella** is an American (and Australian) bet requiring punters to pick the first two finishers in either order, the equivalent of the now discontinued Tote Dual Forecast.

R

Horsebox

Rambo's Hall won the 1992 Cambridgeshire Handicap as a seven-year-old, having previously won the race in 1989.

Rockfel is probably the only failure in a selling race to become a dual Classic winner. After finishing eighth of 11 on her racecourse debut, she won the One Thousand Guineas and Oaks in 1938 as well as the Champion Stakes.

Rock Roi has the doubtful distinction of twice winning the Ascot Gold Cup (1971 and 1972) and being disqualified, once for testing positive for 'bute', the second time for interference.

Rodrigo de Triano gave Lester Piggott the last of his 30 English Classic winners in the Two Thousand Guineas of 1992 – the horse won the Irish Two Thousand Guineas of that year as well, only the fourth twentieth-century colt to achieve the double (the others were Right Tack 1969, Don't Forget Me 1987 and Tirol 1990).

Rose Bowl is the only filly to have won the Queen Elizabeth II Stakes twice (1975 and 1976), the only other dual winner of the race being Brigadier Gerard (1971 and 1972).

Royal Gait was disqualified from the Ascot Gold Cup in 1988 – the winner Sadeem went on to win it again in 1989.

Racecourse layout

Racecourses occupy far larger areas of land than most sporting venues and are often situated on the outskirts of towns or several miles from centres of population. The majority of British courses are complete circuits – the exceptions are Brighton, Epsom Downs, Newmarket and York – so that a significant part of any racecourse is located inside the racetrack and largely under-utilised, although some feature golf courses. There are circular tracks (Chester), square tracks (Fakenham), roughly triangular tracks (Newcastle) and two figures-of-eight (Fontwell and Windsor), but most are laid out in a more or less irregular oval shape. Many have chutes or spurs attached to accommodate sprints which are run over a straight 5 or 6 furlongs. A few have two separate courses as at Aintree where the much shorter Mildmay course operates alongside the famous Grand National circuit. Dual-purpose courses often have three separate tracks laid out for flat races, hurdles and steeplechases.

All racecourses have certain key features in common. There are areas where racing takes place; areas where spectators gather in grandstands, bars or betting halls; areas where horses make appearances in parade and pre-parade rings, unsaddling or winners' enclosures; and areas reserved for racing personnel such as weighing rooms, stables and judges' boxes. Beyond these are the ubiquitous car and coach parks, some on hard surfaces, many still occupying adjacent muddy fields. Another common feature is the prominent situation of betting outlets either in the form of bookmakers' stands or Tote booths. These are located throughout the public areas although the main betting ring is normally found in the grandstand or Tattersalls' enclosure. Some courses have light air-craft or helicopter landing areas and big screen television coverage opposite the stands while others, operating with limited resources, have little more than basic facilities for punters and participants alike.

Racecourse buildings, often congregated at one corner of the raceground close to the winning post, usually consist of a hotch-potch of grandstands and enclosures, reflecting different architectural styles and periods of course devel-opment, together with catering, betting and retail outlets. At the most presti-gious courses, grandstands can extend for several furlongs along the finishing straight, with the cheapest at a considerable distance from the winning line. Even the most expensive stands are not guaranteed to provide good views of the entire race. Low or poorly sited buildings combined with obstacles such as trees or running rails, and undulating terrain or sheer distance to the far side of the course can result in horses disappearing from sight. On racedays, the per-manent stands are sometimes augmented by tented villages, temporary stalls and mobile fast-food units. Even racecourses, it seems, are not immune from the early twenty-first century disease of shopping and it is often possible to buy sporting prints, photographs and books, crafts and bric-a-brac, hats, umbrellas and outdoor clothing on site. Some of the larger courses have their own sou-venir shops offering everything from ties to cuddly toys.

The size and straggling layout of public areas at racecourses invariably means more footslogging than at those sports events where all the action takes place on a limited playing arena. Opportunities for pre-viewing runners and riders can depend on the proximity of the parade ring to spectator enclosures. Some rings and their environs are aesthetically pleasing, with flowers or trees, notably the Rhododendron Walk at Sandown Park, but many have no such pretensions and winter jump tracks are at an obvious disadvantage. A few, as at Doncaster or Market Rasen, are situated in front of the stands but the major-ity are to be found behind or to the side of the main buildings, requiring a fair amount of walking and considerable discomfort in bad weather. However, when it comes to the actual races, many on-course bars and restaurants have close-circuit television of the action ensuring that it is possible to go racing without ever venturing outside!

Further reading

Lee, A., *The Course Inspector* (London: CollinsWillow, 2001).
Somerville, D. (ed.), *Aerofilms Guide to Race Courses* (Surrey: Dial House, 1995).

Racecourses

The phrase 'horses for courses' would make little sense in America where most tracks look alike – oval, flat, dirt, 10 furlongs and left-handed. It is an expression designed for racing in Britain where no two racecourses seem the same, either to spectators or participants. Circuits are left- or right-handed (in a ratio of 3 : 2), flat or undulating, triangular, square, oval or figure-of-eight shaped. Some are not circuits at all but straights, like the Rowley Mile at Newmarket or switchbacks with left- and right-hand bends like the notorious Derby course at Epsom. Some, like Aintree and Pontefract, are longer than 2 miles, others like Chester are barely 1 mile round. Some have smart new grandstands of concrete and glass (Leicester, Newbury), others have bleak and cheerless sheds reminiscent of non-league football grounds, one (Bangor-on-Dee) has no stand at all. Some are places to be or be seen, others are little more than outdoor betting shops with muddy fields attached. The standard of product on display, that is the actual racing, varies not only from course to course but from meeting to meeting. A day at Cheltenham in October is not the same as at the National Hunt Festival in March, a visit to Doncaster in February is not like St Leger day in September, any more than Ascot resembles Market Rasen or Wolverhampton seems like Newmarket. Each course, because of its unique history, location, layout and facilities, can offer members of the racing world a different experience at various times of year.

There are 59 racecourses in Britain, 60 if you count the two completely separate tracks at Newmarket. They can be divided into 24 jump courses, 17 flat courses and 18 offering a mixture of both codes, including all-weather races. Of these, 19 are situated north of Doncaster, 18 south of Bath and the remaining 22 occupy the central areas of the country. Generally speaking, the more you travel towards the south-east of Britain, the more prestigious the course. Although York, Cheltenham and Newmarket all offer top quality racing outside this area, and Folkestone, Plumpton and Fontwell dispense modest fare within it, the relative proximity to London of premier courses Ascot, Epsom, Goodwood, Newbury and Sandown tends to support this view. Beyond the south-east, the heartland of flat racing is Yorkshire while a majority of jump courses are located in west and central England. National Hunt racing is spread more widely across the country than flat racing, reflecting the more localised, small-scale nature of the races and their links with hunting, point-to-point and the rural and farming communities in general.

A journey from north to south starts in Scotland, never a stronghold of thoroughbred racing, with only five courses. Perth and Kelso are small National Hunt tracks with good local support and long histories of racing, both staging around a dozen race days each year. The present course at Kelso was founded by the Duke of Roxburghe in 1822 and has always had a following on both sides of the border. Perth, the most northerly racetrack in Britain, was laid out in the grounds of Scone Palace in 1908 although races had been held intermittently around the town since the eighteenth century. It was recently voted Small Racecourse of the Year by the Racegoers' Club. The survival of both courses is probably helped by their sensible division of the racing year with Kelso operating from October to May and Perth opting for a summer jumps programme from April to September. Between these two lie three racecourses serving the major population centres: Ayr, the largest but most dismal of the Scottish tracks, Musselburgh on the Firth of Forth, formerly called Edinburgh to the disgust of the local inhabitants, and Hamilton Park near Glasgow which offers solely flat racing. Ayr has much in common with Doncaster, whose 1989 St Leger it staged after subsidence ruled out the Yorkshire venue. They both have wide, galloping tracks, long associations with racing – the St Leger dates back to 1776, the Ayr Gold Cup to 1804 – some 25 days racing each year and an air of seediness and despondency. The Group Three Scottish Classic is the only flat race of any quality here, although there is always a good turnout for the Gold Cup, one of the major sprint handicaps of the year. The Scottish Grand National has been held at Ayr since 1966 following the demise of nearby Bogside and the marathon race, which takes place over a distance of 4 miles and 1 furlong about two weeks after the Aintree fixture, is another which attracts a high-class field. Musselburgh, a small, unpretentious course with energetic management and much improved facilities, introduced jump racing in 1987, and has a reputation for staging meetings when wintry weather has wiped out racecards the length and breadth of Britain. Hamilton Park, a pretty and go-ahead track which is not a circuit but a 6-furlong straight with a loop attached, pioneered evening racing in 1947. It now devotes nearly half of its annual quota of 17 days to these fixtures.

Just across the border are Hexham, Carlisle and Newcastle. Hexham, high, bleak and windswept, is one of Britain's more remote racecourses with a tendency to heavy going and a small National Hunt following. Carlisle, managed on behalf of the Jockey Club by the Racecourse Holdings Trust, offers all-year racing of a moderate sort. An undulating course susceptible to waterlogging, it stages its major flat-race meeting, including the race for the sixteenth-century Carlisle Bell, in June. Newcastle racecourse at Gosforth Park north of the city, which also races year-round, has recently come under the umbrella of the Northern Racing group. It shows due deference to history – the band is always keen to strike up 'The Blaydon Races', the famous northern mare Bee'swing is commemorated in a Group Three race in July and the Northumberland Plate, first run in 1833, is still a major summer handicap in the north. With the inclusion of several Pattern races over the sticks, Newcastle remains a course of some significance. Sedgefield and Cartmel, the final two venues of the north, are both representatives of the rural jump scene. Tiny Cartmel in the southern Lake District is a unique and idiosyncratic racetrack offering carnival-style racing and picnic opportunities on only five days a year. Sedgefield, to the east of the Pennines, provides frequent, modest, virtually year-round racing for a local clientele.

Yorkshire supplies the other nine northern racecourses. Most of them – York, Thirsk, Ripon, Beverley, Pontefract and Redcar – operate strictly on the flat,

Wetherby is a jumps course, and Catterick and Doncaster are dual purpose. York is in a class of its own – the best racecourse in the north, some would argue the best in Britain, with first-class facilities and no fewer than ten Group races (see separate entry). The other five flat courses offer unspectacular but adequate racing, each for up to 18 days a year, the first three in pleasant rural surroundings. This is not Pattern racing but local racing territory, although Ripon stages a well-known 6-furlong handicap, the Great St Wilfred, and Redcar has two valuable races in the Zetland Gold Cup and the Two-Year-Old Trophy. There were race meetings at Beverley and Pontefract in the seventeenth century and racing at Redcar originally took place along the beach. Wetherby, which stages its major meeting at Christmas and a further 14 days throughout the winter, offers good quality sport and a state-of-the-art grandstand. Catterick races modestly all year and advertises itself as 'the course with character'.

Which leaves Doncaster. A victim of its dreary surroundings, this, like Ayr, is a grade one course which has fallen on hard times. The perceived decline in the importance of the St Leger meeting and the lack of investment in modern facilities have had an adverse effect on this historic course, despite its first-class track and its staging of numerous graded races under both rules. There are several top two-year-old events here in September – the Group Two Champagne Stakes and Flying Childers Stakes and the Group Three May Hill Stakes – while the final Group One of the year, the Racing Post Trophy in October is also for juveniles. The Doncaster Cup, another Group Three race, forms the final leg of the so-called stayers' Triple Crown following the Ascot and Goodwood Cups but although Doncaster features nearly as many Pattern races as York, including a Classic, it is hard not to make unfavourable comparisons.

The Midlands is the heartland of jump racing with 13 National Hunt out of 14 regional courses. They range from Southwell, a minor venue now better known for its all-weather track, to Cheltenham, the premier British jumps course which has no rival (see separate entry). Modest racing has taken place at Hereford, Ludlow, Stratford and Worcester since the eighteenth century; the first two in winter, the remaining duo now opting for summer fixtures. Rather better fare is available at Towcester, near Northampton, a squarish course in a country estate setting which has made a considerable effort to improve facilities in recent years. The same might be said of Market Rasen, the only course in Lincolnshire, and another of those managed by the Racecourse Holdings Trust along with Huntingdon, Warwick and Nottingham. The latter, with around 20 days racing a year, used to operate under both sets of rules but became a purely flat racing course in 1996. Warwick and Leicester are dual-purpose courses, with over 50 annual race days between them and a history of racing on their present sites for over a century. Uttoxeter, under the banner of the Northern Racing Group, hosts the Midlands Grand National in March and continues to stage National Hunt fixtures throughout the summer. Finally, Wolverhampton holds a few jump days but is now best known for its all-weather surface, opened in 1993 as part of an Arena Leisure complex that boasts five restaurants and floodlit Saturday evening meetings. Few of the Midlands racetracks provide quality racing but they and others like them form the backbone of the sport in Britain and the bread-and-butter for many trainers and jockeys. Those with progressive management have at least made efforts to upgrade facilities even if the performers are seldom top-flight.

The remaining courses in the centre of the country are to be found in Wales, East Anglia and around Merseyside. Aintree (see separate entry) has a unique place in British jump racing. So, on the flat, does Chester, the oldest and smallest racecourse of them all, dating from the sixteenth century. Its May meeting features two Group Three races in the Chester Vase and the Ormonde Stakes while the Chester Cup, first run in 1824, is one of the most historic handicaps in the calendar. Haydock Park in central Lancashire offers good quality racing all year round and is one of the few courses to compete successfully with the southern 'premier league'. A member of the big seven operating under the banner of the Racecourse Holdings Trust (along with Aintree, Cheltenham, Newmarket, Epsom, Sandown and Kempton) it has 30 race days per year, the Group One Sprint Cup in September and a strong programme of races under both codes. Racing in Wales is restricted to two courses, Bangor-on-Dee, a small National Hunt track which saw the great Fred Archer ride his first winner and Chepstow, home of the Welsh National, a dual-purpose 'modern' course (dating from 1926) with over 20 annual race days. On the opposite side of the country, East Anglia has three venues: Yarmouth, catering for summer holiday flat racing, Fakenham, a square-shaped track providing only 8 days of local jumps racing, and Newmarket, headquarters of British racing and the only course to stage above 35 race days a year (see separate entry). It is the home of the first two Classics of the year, the One Thousand and Two Thousand Guineas, and roughly 20 further Pattern races on the flat.

The 18 racecourses in the south are divided between 6 in the south-west and 12, including the most prestigious, in the south-east. Taunton, established in 1927, and Wincanton in Somerset, and Exeter in Devon have traditional winter jump programmes while nearby Newton Abbot concentrates on summer meetings. Wincanton offers the highest quality racing in this area and has strong associations with Desert Orchid who won six times here. Bath and Salisbury are both situated on hills above their respective towns (Bath is the highest racetrack in Britain) and offer moderate flat racing. The same applies to Windsor which specialises in Monday evening fixtures throughout the summer. Fontwell and Plumpton are near neighbours in Sussex, each providing around 16 days of winter jump racing although Fontwell, with an unusual figure-of-eight layout (like Windsor), is reckoned to be the best small racecourse in the south. Folkestone, the only course in Kent, is another small but more dilapidated venue featuring both codes of racing whereas Brighton, the other south coast track high on the Downs is for flat racers only. Lingfield in Surrey opened the first British all-weather surface in 1989. With roughly 60 fixtures each year, it provides turf racing in summer and dirt racing throughout the winter with a few jump days thrown in.

The other six racecourses between them account for the majority of top-class race days in Britain. Kempton Park is the setting for one of the most famous Grade One steeplechases in the calendar, the King George VI Chase on Boxing Day, a race won by Arkle, Mill House and, on four occasions, by Desert Orchid. It also stages the Christmas Hurdle at the same meeting, the Racing Post Chase in February and a number of other high-class races. Flat racing is less important here but rumours that the course has considered switching to an all-weather track have been greeted with dismay by the racing press and public. Newbury in Berkshire, opened in 1905, has unveiled two new grandstands in the last decade. A wide, relatively flat and eminently fair racetrack offering both flat and jump racing, it stages the Group One Lockinge Stakes for milers, the Greenham Stakes, a Classic trial for colts and the equiv-alent Fred Darling Stakes for fillies, and a further half-a-dozen Pattern races. November sees the Hennessy Cognac Gold Cup and February the Tote Gold Trophy, two important handicaps in the jumping season. The remaining four courses, Goodwood and Epsom Downs on the flat and Ascot and Sandown Park with flat and jumps are sufficiently important to warrant separate entries. Between them they account for 8 top-class chases and hurdles, half of the annual Group One flat races and a further 40 of the remaining Pattern.

British racecourses all have distinctive characteristics in the same way as British football grounds and clubs. To the outsider they may have more simi-larities than differences but there are Premiership players and bottom-of-the-league triers, theatres of dreams and relics of better days in racing as well as football. Racecourses also have their championship days and mid-season doldrums, their local supporters and fans who travel far to experience the best. There are just fewer of them.

Further reading

Lee, A., *The Course Inspector* (London: CollinsWillow, 2001).
Magee, S. (ed.), *The Channel Four Racing Guide to Racecourses* (London: Channel 4 Books, 1998).
Tyrrel, J., *Racecourses on the Flat* (Marlborough: Crowood Press, 1989).
Tyrrel, J., *Chasing Around Britain* (Swindon: Crowood Press, 1990).
www.bhb.co.uk

See also Fixtures.

Race names

Race names are constantly changing, particularly in an age of widespread spon-sorship. Although they sometimes commemorate local personalities and places, as they have done for decades, the trend is towards cumbersome titles that reflect the substantial input of businesses seeking a novel form of advertisement.

At the beginning of the nineteenth century only a handful of races were given names, often indicating the donor of the prize such as the Corporation Plate at Doncaster, the Duke of Marlborough's Plate at Oxford and the Jockey Club Plate at Newmarket. Some reflected the locality – the Newmarket Stakes, the Pavilion Stakes at Brighton, the Belvoir Stakes at Leicester – or the calendar, as in the July Stakes at Newmarket but for the most part they were listed only as 'the gold cup' or 'sweepstakes' or 'a handicap plate.'

A century later, there were more named races but the naming pattern was similar. The Liverpool spring flat meeting, during which the Grand National was run, boasted the Liverpool Spring Cup, the Sefton Park Plate and the Earl of Sefton's Plate (the Earls of Sefton owned the land on which Aintree was built), and the March Two-Year-Old Selling Plate. A summer meeting at Alexandra Park, London, featured the Islington Welter Plate, the Middlesex Selling Plate and the July Handicap. Even at Newmarket, where significant races such as the Cesarewitch and the Cheveley Park Stakes had entered the calendar, there were still featureless contests under general headings – a 'Mile Selling Plate', the 'Autumn Handicap', the 'Second October Nursery Stakes'.

A major change took place from the 1950s as racing entered the modern era of sponsorship. Following the inaugural Whitbread Gold Cup in 1957, a variety of top races at the most prestigious courses began to sprout sponsored titles. The Magnet Cup, first run at York in 1960 (from 1998 the John Smith's Cup) is the oldest continuously sponsored flat race of the season, but most of the important sponsored contests were over the sticks – the Hennessy Cognac Gold Cup (1957) and the Tote Gold Trophy (1963) at Newbury, and the Mackeson Gold Cup at Cheltenham (1960). Flat racing began to introduce more commemorative race names such as the Nell Gwyn Stakes at Newmarket (1962) after the mistress of Charles II who popularised horseracing there in the 1660s, and the Dante Stakes at York (1958) after the only Yorkshire-trained Derby winner. Royal names, always popular, continued to flourish; the Prince of Wales's Stakes (1862), named after the future Edward VII, the Queen Anne Stakes (1930) and the King George VI Chase (1937) were joined by the King George VI and Queen Elizabeth Stakes (1951) and the Queen Elizabeth II Stakes at Ascot (1955) and the Queen Mother Champion Chase at Cheltenham (1959).

By the 1970s, there were races named after former champion horses Arkle, Ormonde, Diomed, Hyperion, Voltigeur, Mill Reef, St Simon and Mandarin, top trainers Fred Darling and John Porter, past owners Sir Winston Churchill and the Earls of Rosebery, administrator Geoffrey Freer and cartoon character Andy Capp. The Cheveley Park Stakes was now the William Hill Cheveley Park Stakes and the Welsh National had become the Coral's Welsh National. The process has continued to the present day with race names becoming ever longer and more bizarrre; the Hoechst Roussel Panacur European Breeders Fund Mares Only 'National Hunt' Novices' Hurdle Race at Exeter, the Nag's Head, Pickhill, 'Here's to the Next 25 Years' Handicap Stakes at Catterick Bridge, the Tote Ten to Follow Handicap Stakes at Doncaster, the Try Sponsorship at Musselburgh Claiming Stakes and the Hire a Private Box at Southwell Maiden Stakes are prime examples. The trend for commemoration has included the Happy Birthday Eddie Moll Rated Stakes at Beverley and the Richard Merton Happy Retirement Handicap Steeplechase at Exeter. Themed racecards are another recent ploy. One at Wolverhampton included races with 'star' names – Orion, Andromeda, Perseus and Ursa Major while Leicester's wildlife theme featured hares, shelducks, badgers and red deer.

The beginning of the twenty-first century has seen a proliferation of inter-net titles and a tendency for traditional names to be dropped or downplayed in favour of blatant advertising. However, this may be little different from the acknowledgement of prize donorship implicit in the City Purse at Edinburgh or the County Members Plate at Winchester in 1810.

See also Sponsorship.

Race riding

Riding a race is not a question of getting on board and letting the horse run. Judgements have to be made. Jockeys have to be aware of the state of the ground: will it be soft and tire out the early leaders or will it be firm so that con-tact ought to be maintained with the front runners? The varying nature of British racetracks means that 'horses for courses' is a valid cliché and the jockey needs to assess how a particular animal will run downhill, round a tight bend or in an anticlockwise direction. What are the idiosyncrasies of his mount? Is it a natural frontrunner or should it be covered up in the pack? Here he can be aided – or hindered! – by instructions from the trainer or an insistent owner. Unless strategy has been totally predetermined, the jockey earns his money by his ability to adapt to changing circumstances during a race.

Historically British jockeys rode waiting races, an art perfected by the two Sam Chifneys, father and son. Their practice was to keep a slack rein early on and then come with a rush at the finish to nick the race by the shortest possible mar-gin. Such tactics were born of an age when many races were run in long-distance heats in which it was no use riding a horse flat out to win as half an hour later it would be running again. Energy had to be conserved for the next heat or even heats until one horse had won twice. Yet riding at a moderate rate for the first part of a race before quickening for the business end persisted well past the age of heats. One reason was the development of the handicap system where it did not pay to reveal the horse's true merits. Another perhaps was simply tradition in a conservative industry where new ideas are often treated with suspicion.

It took foreigners to demonstrate that things could be done differently and better. An invasion of jockeys from across the Atlantic in the late nineteenth century showed that races could be won from the front and certainly that the actual racing should start earlier. The Americans also revolutionised riding style by pushing the saddle forward, shortening the stirrups and reins, and vir-tually crouching along the horse's neck. By cutting wind resistance and giving a better weight distribution on the horse they gained a significant advantage. In order to compete, British jockeys had to follow suit and adopt the American methods. In the 1980s came another American-led innovation, the flat-back style, an even more aerodynamic crouch with the knees below the pommel of the saddle, just the toes in the irons, and the chest down between the knees.

In National Hunt racing taking the inside rail is important as not only does it provide the shortest route, it also means that a rider need only worry about horses on his outside. However, etiquette has developed among jockeys regard-ing when and when not to give way on the inner so, for example, a rider allows someone to come through on the inside when his own chance has gone, but no quarter is given towards the end of the race from any rider in contention. A jump jockey also needs to know the formbook so that he can avoid trailing bad jumpers that might bring other horses down. Experienced riders on such animals will tend to take the outside to lessen the risk to fellow jockeys. Racing over hurdles is different from steeplechasing and requires different tactics. Many riders prefer to come with a run at the second last, or just before it in hurdling, whereas over fences they feel that they have to be up near the front to keep out of trouble.

Racing on the all-weather tracks calls for yet another type of strategy, usually of getting to the front and staying there so as to avoid the kickback of dirt and the difficulties of changing pace on the soft surface. Many traditionalists do not like the 'hell for leather' style on equine motorbikes which they feel does not contribute to the skills of race riding.

Whatever the surface and whatever the type of race the jockey has to make decisions as to his or her riding tactics. Sometimes they pay off and plaudits are received, but on other occasions there are serious errors of judgement that cost the race and bring the sting of public criticism. Greville Starkey was blamed by many for the defeat of hot favourite Dancing Brave in the 1986 Derby. He kept the horse at the back until the closing stages of the race and then accelerated past the field to finish just half-a-length behind the winner. British jockeys riding in the Breeders Cup races in America often fail to adjust their riding to American conditions: both Frankie Dettori on Swain in 1998 and Mick Kinane on Rock of Gibralter in 2002 were criticised for not giving their mounts a better chance of winning because of the tactics they adopted.

Further reading

Tanner, M., *Great Jockeys of the Flat* (London: Guinness, 1992).

Race types

Horse races are divided not only into different distances but into several categories, each with a set of criteria largely reflecting the weight to be carried and the experience of the horses. Currently all meetings are arranged to include a variety of these race types and restrictions are imposed by the British Horseracing Board (BHB) to ensure a balanced programme of racing.

The principal distinction is between handicaps and weight-for-age races. A handicap is a race in which every horse carries a weight based on its past performance, with the objective of giving each entrant a theoretically equal chance of winning. The rating of every racehorse, from 0 to 140 for flatracers, from 0 to 175 for jumpers, is adjusted weekly by the official BHB handicappers to reflect changes in performance. If a horse has won too recently for its official rating to be altered, it will be subject to a penalty on its next outing. A typical handicap on the flat may see variations of over 2 st between contestants, from roughly 10 st to 7 st 7 lb, but a 'limited handicap' restricts the weight range while a 'rated stakes' narrows it even further. In each case, the horse reckoned by the handicapper to have the best chance carries top weight and the least fancied runner carries the lowest. In National Hunt handicaps, weights may vary from approximately 12 to 10 st. The major handicaps of the flat season include the Lincoln and November Handicaps at Doncaster during the first and last meetings of the year, the Cambridgeshire and Cesarewitch at Newmarket in October, and summer handicaps such as the Royal Hunt Cup at Royal Ascot and the Ebor Handicap at York. Important National Hunt handicaps range from the Gold Cups run at Newbury and Sandown Park to the Grand National.

Any race that is not a handicap is a weight-for-age contest in which the amount carried is determined by the age and gender of the horse; fillies and mares are allotted lower weights than colts and geldings of the same age. The weight-for-age scale, originally devised over a century ago by Admiral Rous, the famous Jockey Club steward and handicapper, seeks to compensate younger horses for their immaturity in relation to older animals, and varies according to the month of the year. Three-year-olds competing against four-year-olds over 1 mile in June, for example, would benefit by roughly 1 st in weight but by October, the rapid development of the younger animals would have reduced the differential to less than 7 lb.

There are numerous other distinctions between races. Maiden races are for horses that have yet to win while novice events, either hurdles or steeplechases, are for horses which have not won either type of race before 1 May of the previous season. In selling and claiming races, horses can be bought immediately after the contest. National Hunt racing offers hunter-chases, for horses which have been regularly hunted during the season, and 'bumpers' or flat races for young National Hunt horses, aged four to six, that have yet to run under the Rules of Racing. Others specify particular conditions relating to age, sex or experience of horses or jockeys – ladies' races, apprentice races, races restricted to fillies or amateur riders – and this gives added opportunities for riding and more variety to any racecard.

Further reading

Magee, S., *The Channel Four Book of Racing* (London: Hamlyn, 1995).

Racing Calendar

The first *Racing Calendar* was published in 1727 and it has continued ever since, forming an unbroken sequence of turf records. It was produced by John Cheny of Arundel and was intended to be an account of all the horseraces run in England for which the prize money exceeded £10. It included the names of owners, the colours of horses, the conditions of the races and the results. It was, in essence, the first form book and Cheny, noting that the book would be published in the winter, recommended it as an 'agreeable amusement' for whiling away dark nights.

In 1732, he began to issue sheet calendars, which subscribers received fortnightly by post for an extra half-a-guinea a year. From mid-April to the end of October, they gave details of the previous two weeks' racing as well as information about future races. By 1741, meetings in Wales, Scotland and Ireland had been added; in 1743 a further 56 pages were devoted to pedigrees of principal runners. When Cheny died in 1751, two rival works appeared, *Heber's Calendar* and the *Sporting Kalendar* compiled by John Pond, an auctioneer. The format for these was virtually identical to that used by Cheny but Pond's venture ceased after 1757 while Reginald Heber continued to publish his calendar until his death in 1768.

Once more, two separate volumes competed for subscribers. *Walker's Calendar* disappeared after the second issue leaving the field clear for the *Sporting Calendar* jointly produced by William Tuting and Thomas Fawconer. Tuting was the Keeper of the Match Book at Newmarket and Fawconer was referred to as the Secretary of the Jockey Club. The partnership broke up in 1772, Tuting died in 1773 and in stepped James Weatherby who had been appointed Keeper of the Match Book in succession to Tuting in 1771. His first *Racing Calendar* was published in 1773 alongside that of Fawconer. The rivalry was maintained until 1776 but Fawconer died the following year and thereafter Weatherby became the sole name associated with the calendar of turf affairs. The family retained ownership for the next 123 years.

The main purpose of the publication was to provide an accurate list of race results together with advertisements of future meetings; from 1846 these were listed in a separate book, *Races to Come*. With the formation of the Grand National Steeplechase Committee in 1866, a further *Steeplechase Calendar* was issued and the results of hurdle races, formerly listed in the *Racing Calendar*, were transferred to the new volume. Throughout the nineteenth century the three contained a vast amount of additional detail about horseracing in Britain – where and when it took place, the register of owners' racing colours, the lengths of racecourses, particularly those at Newmarket, and the regular subscribers, from His Majesty through members of the aristocracy (in ranking order) to ordinary gentlemen of the realm. Further information included a list of members of the Jockey Club, major cockfights (until 1840 when they were banned), stallions and studs for the season and the Rules of Racing. These, together with cases decided by the Jockey Club, increased steadily over the years as the *Racing Calendar* became the unofficial mouthpiece of the sport's governing body. It was finally taken over by the Jockey Club in 1901 although Weatherbys continued as printers and publishers.

The *Racing Calendar* still fulfils the same major functions in the twenty-first century as it did in the eighteenth. Issued weekly, it contains details of all race meetings, prints the particulars, conditions and entries of every race, and reports objections and disqualifications. It also publishes alterations to rules and information on matters of concern (such as a list of the substances prohibited in horseracing).

Further reading

Kay, J., 'The Actress, the Politician and the Brigadier – British Horseracing through the pages of Weatherby's Racing Calendar' in T. Gonzalez Aja *et al.* (eds), *Proceedings of the 5th International CESH Congress* (Madrid, 2002), 367–75.

Prior, C.W., *The History of the Racing Calendar and Stud Book* (London: Sporting Life, 1926).

Radio

See Broadcast media.

Red Rum (1965–95) – by Quorum out of Mared

Red Rum was one of the racing superstars of the twentieth century and became a household name in the 1970s. A bay gelding, bred in Ireland, he first raced on the flat as a two-year-old at Aintree, dead-heating for first place in a selling race at the Grand National meeting. Little did the racing world realise the extent to which the fortunes of Red Rum and Aintree would be linked during the following decade.

He ran in ten flat races, winning three times, before switching to hurdles, and was second on his National Hunt debut at Cheltenham in 1968. He went on to win 3 hurdle races out of 24, and then turned to steeplechasing, in which he started well, winning 3 of his first 4 novice chases. His progress was inconsistent, however, and when it was discovered that he had a foot disease, he was packed off to the Doncaster Sales. By this point in his career, he had passed through the hands of two owners and four trainers, but his prospects improved when he was purchased by small-time Southport trainer, Donald 'Ginger' McCain, on behalf of a local retired businessman, Noel le Mare. The fairy tale was about to begin.

Working on the sands and in the sea at Southport seemed to cure his foot problems and he began to make a name for himself in the north as a stayer. In 1973, Red Rum was entered for what many thought would be the final Grand National at Aintree, as the course was to be sold for redevelopment. He started as 9–1 joint favourite with Crisp, and no one who saw the race will ever forget the manner in which it was won and lost. Crisp, having built up what appeared to be an unassailable lead, was headed by Red Rum and jockey Brian Fletcher inside the final 100 yards. They had broken the course record, held by Golden Miller for nearly 40 years, by over 18 seconds, fought out probably the most memorable finish of recent times, and helped to restore the tarnished prestige of the race. The sympathy was with Crisp, conceding 23 lb to his rival, but the eight-year-old Red Rum had displayed great jumping ability and indomitable courage, particularly as he had sustained a slight injury in the race, causing him to be sidelined for the remainder of the season.

With the fate of Aintree still in the balance, he re-appeared the following year, carrying 12 st and won again, giving Brian Fletcher his third National success (he had won on Red Alligator in 1968). Red Rum then made history by winning the Scottish Grand National at Ayr three weeks later, the only horse to have won both races in the same season, and became National Hunt Champion of 1974. Giving nearly a stone to his vanquishers, he was beaten into second place by L'Escargot in 1975 and Rag Trade in 1976, but in 1977, with the future of Aintree temporarily secured, in front of a crowd of over 50,000, he entered the record books by winning a third Grand National. Ridden on this occasion by Tommy Stack, the twelve-year-old had won by 25 lengths and was given a rapturous reception.

He was kept in training for a further year but injury prevented another Aintree appearance and he was retired from racing in 1978, the winner of 21 steeplechases. His enormous popularity with the general public, however, immediately opened a new career and 'Rummy' became an equine superstar, making television appearances, switching on the Blackpool illuminations, opening betting shops and supermarkets and heading the parade of champions at subsequent Grand National meetings. He earned more as a personality (with his own company, Red Rum Limited) than he ever did on the racecourse, and responded patiently to the crowds and cameras, and the adulation which greeted him wherever he went.

He remained with 'Ginger' McCain in Lancashire throughout his long life and statues in his honour were erected at both Aintree and Ayr. He died in 1995, aged 30, a commercial success and a racing legend, and it is both poignant and appropriate that this local hero, whose feats helped to restore the fortunes of his favourite racecourse, should be buried beside the winning post at Aintree.

Further reading

Herbert, I., *Red Rum 1965–1995* (London: Century, 1995).
McCain, G., *Red Rum. A Racing Legend* (London: Weidenfeld and Nicholson, 1995).

Retirement

All jockeys retire earlier than the average citizen. This is reflected in the successful lobbying by the Jockeys Association for a lowering of the age at which jockeys could claim their pension: at 35 in National Hunt racing and 45 on the flat. The pension fund is financed by a 0.06 per cent levy on prize money with jockeys being allocated a proportion according to the number of rides they have had. Weight problems, loss of nerve and accidents end the careers of some, but for the majority it is a matter of too few rides and too many losers. However, although the typical jockey's career is short, it is possible to have a lengthy professional riding life. In his autobiography Frankie Dettori noted that he rode alongside the incomparable Lester Piggott when the latter was approaching his sixtieth birthday and almost 50 years in the saddle. Willie Carson was in his mid-fifties when he had his last ride as, in earlier decades, were Scobie Breasley, Frankie Durr, Charlie Smirke and Gordon Richards. Clearly experience counts in Britain's 'horses for courses' situation. Retirement comes earlier over the sticks. By the age of 30 the elder statesman stage has been reached. John Francome called it a day at 32 after a fall too many at Chepstow in 1985 and

8-times champion Peter Scudamore did likewise at 34. When Simon McNeil retired in 1998, aged 42, he was the oldest jump jockey around.

Most retired jockeys try to remain connected with the sport as most of the skills that they possess are specific to the racing industry and not easily transferable to other occupations. For the articulate and successful there are media opportunities. Others have secured positions as clerks of courses, racecourse inspectors, agents and valets. Some, especially in National Hunt racing, move on to become trainers though they find business sense as vital as horse sense if they are to be successful. Yet others, particularly the failed apprentices, return to the stables where, unlike the market for jockeys, there is always a labour shortage. For the younger ones today there is the Jockeys Employment and Training Scheme initiated by the Jockeys Association to provide some of the basic skills required to secure employment when they finally opt out. Talk of retirement used to be taboo in the changing room but times have changed and career advice and training are now more accepted.

Each year about 4,000 horses come out of training. Many mares but far fewer stallions go to stud in Britain or are sent to overseas breeding markets. The smaller horses often move into polo; the ex-chaser becomes a hunter, races in point-to-points, or takes up eventing, show-jumping or just hacking. Devon Loch, so unlucky in the 1956 Grand National, became the hack of trainer Noel Murless and Champion Hurdle winner, Comedy of Errors, performed the same task for Mercy Rimell. A few others become police horses. However, about 200 animals annually find themselves on the scrap heap, literally. Some are rescued by charities devoted to the purpose; those that cannot be rehabilitated are put down.

Further reading

www.jagb.co.uk

See also Charities.

Richards, Sir Gordon (1904–86)

One of eight surviving children of a Shropshire miner, Gordon Richards was champion jockey on all but three occasions from 1925 to 1953. In 1926 tuberculosis kept him out of the saddle to the benefit of Tommy Weston; 1930 saw Freddy Fox beat him on the last day of the season; and in 1941 he lost part of the wartime season through injury and gave way to Harry Wragg. Otherwise for almost three decades it was Gordon at the front.

At the age of 15 he became a stable lad and later an apprentice for Martin Hartigan who trained at Foxhill in Wiltshire. His second year with Hartigan brought him his first winner, Gay Lord, in an apprentice race at Leicester in April 1921. From 1925 to 1931 he was stable jockey for Tommy Hogg, who trained for Lord Glanely, and then he began a 16-year partnership with Fred Darling. On Darling's retirement Richards signed up with his successor Noel Murless. Working for these trainers helped Richards accumulate 4,870 winners from 21,815 rides, which remains a British record total of career victories.

Perhaps his most remarkable riding feat began on 3 October 1933, when he rode the last winner at Nottingham, before going through the six-race card at Chepstow the following day. He then rode the first five winners at that course the next day, but came third on a 3–1 on shot in the unlucky thirteenth race. These victories contributed to a seasonal total of 259, a record broken by Richards himself in 1947 with 269 successes. Overall he rode 14 Classic winners but for 28 years the Derby eluded him until in 1953, the year he was knighted for services to racing, he piloted Pinza home. It is not reported how the Queen felt when she bestowed the honour as it was her horse that finished second!

A small – half an inch under 5 feet – short-legged man to whom wasting was not a problem, he was easily able to make 8 st and hence often secured rides at most races of a meeting. Seven times he had over 900 mounts in a season and in 1933 he topped the 1,000 mark. Yet, unlike several jockeys of his era, he rarely rode abroad: he won only three races in France and never participated in American racing. He had perfect balance aided by his powerful legs and knees, was a quick thinker with the patience to wait for an opportunity, and was sharp at the gate because he kept his eye on the starter's hand or, if hidden, on his shoulder for a clue as to when the lever might be pressed. Despite his success he was a worrier; falls, injuries or a long losing run could damage his surprisingly fragile confidence. He twice suffered severe bouts of depression that stopped him from riding.

He was forced to retire in 1954 after having his pelvis smashed when Abergeldie reared and fell on him in the paddock at Sandown Park. He then became a trainer for a while with only moderate success though he was responsible for Pipe of Peace, the champion two-year-old colt of 1956 and Reform, the leading miler of 1967. When he abandoned training in 1969 he became racing manager for Lady Beaverbrook and Sir Michael Sobell. The following year he was elected an honorary member of the Jockey Club, a unique distinction for a former professional jockey. He died in 1986 aged 82.

Further reading

Seth-Smith, M., *Knight of the Turf* (London: Hodder and Stoughton, 1980).
Tanner, M., *Great Jockeys of the Flat* (London: Guinness, 1992).

Royal Plates

The races known as Royal Plates are an early example of patronage in sport and it is generally accepted that they were founded by Charles II, an enthusiastic rider and supporter of racing. Beginning with the King's Plate at Newmarket, valued at 100 guineas, their number reached a peak of 50 in the 1830s, including 2 in Scotland and 16 in Ireland, and remained at this level for much of the nineteenth century. Their prestige was such that a separate list of winners was printed annually in the *Racing Calendar*, but their importance declined in the 1870s and they were finally abandoned in 1887.

Initially, Royal Plates followed the race pattern of the times, run in heats over distances of 3.5–4 miles. Although most were for all ages and types, some laid down conditions – for mares and fillies only, for three- and four-year-olds, or in the case of Ascot, for horses hunted with His Majesty's staghounds. By the 1820s, however, the majority of races were for four-year-olds carrying approximately 10 st 7 lb or five-year-olds at a stone heavier. They tended to attract small fields of 2–4 runners but this was not unusual at a time when horses were walked between race meetings.

In the following 50 years, the races became less, rather than more, standardised. Winners became younger, distances got shorter and some fields grew larger, particularly in Ireland where ten horses sometimes raced for the Royal Plates at The Curragh. By 1860, half of Her Majesty's Plates were won by three-year-olds carrying less than 8 st over 2-mile courses, with only five meetings maintaining the traditional distance. The weights and race lengths became so varied and complex that a schedule of rules and conditions had to be issued by the Master of the Royal Horse for annual publication in the *Racing Calendar*. What did not alter was the prize money, still restricted to 100 guineas at a time when many meetings could boast a handicap valued at twice that amount and the Derby was 50 times more lucrative.

Eventually the use of government money to support horseracing was raised in the House of Commons. (The Royal Plates were funded from the Royal Household expenditure, approved annually by Parliament.) It had always been assumed that the prizes were paid from the public purse as an incentive to breeding strong stayers suitable for army use but the reduction in trials of stamina during the nineteenth century, together with the appearance of geldings at numerous meetings, including prestigious courses such as Newmarket and Ascot, suggests that breeding for military purposes was not the sole rationale. Few winning stallions appeared to become successful racehorse sires either and it is little wonder that the system was called into question.

The races were reprieved in the 1860s because of their alleged importance to the smaller race meetings, and lingered on for a further 20 years. However, with dwindling fields and lack of interest, a Royal Commission on Horse Breeding in 1888 recommended that the 3,300 guineas of public money would be better spent on premiums designed to produce half-bred general purpose mounts and they were finally discontinued.

Further reading

Kay, J., 'Closing the Stable Door and the Public Purse: The Rise and Fall of the Royal Plates', *The Sports Historian*, 20(1) (2000), 18–32.

Royalty

The British royal family has been involved with horseracing for over 300 years as owners, breeders, riders and supporters. Although there are references to Elizabeth I attending races in the 1580s, and James I is credited with discovering the suitability of Newmarket Heath for riding and hunting, it was Charles II (reigned from 1660 to 1685) who initially promoted horseracing there. He is said to have been a good horseman and the only reigning monarch to have ridden a winner; he twice won the Newmarket Town Plate, the race founded by him in 1665 and still contested today. During the regular spring and autumn race meetings established in his reign, the business of the court was conducted from his palace at Newmarket, and the town became the acknowledged headquarters of English racing. The Rowley Mile course is allegedly named after Old Rowley, his favourite hack.

Both William III (1689–1702) and his successor Anne (1702–14) extended royal support of horseracing. William founded the Royal Stud at Hampton Court and employed a Keeper of the Royal Running Horses, Tregonwell Frampton, as the first royal trainer-manager, to arrange matches between royal horses and those of other sportsmen. Anne founded the racecourse at Ascot, still owned by the Crown, and donated prizes in the form of gold plate and cups at several venues throughout the country, including Newmarket and York. Royal patronage was continued throughout the eighteenth century in the form of Royal Plates, races worth 100 guineas funded by the monarch, and the keen personal interest of several royal princes including the Duke of Cumberland, second son of George II, and the two elder sons of George III. Cumberland was the breeder of Eclipse, the most successful racehorse and influential stallion of the century, and the two princes became the first royal winners of the Derby in 1788 and 1816, with Sir Thomas and Prince Leopold.

William IV (1830–37), like many of his successors, appeared to think that horseracing, a nationally popular sport, deserved royal support. During his short reign, he concentrated his equine interests on the development of the Royal Stud but within months of his death, it was closed and the bloodstock sold off. The new sovereign, Victoria, was apparently bored by horseracing but her husband, Albert, persuaded her to revive the Hampton Court Stud in 1851 and it bred seven Classic winners during her reign, including the Triple Crown filly, La Flèche. Although they attended Royal Ascot as a social occasion for many years, Victoria ceased to visit after the death of Albert in 1861. Her growing disapproval of racing and particularly gambling did not prevent her eldest son, the future Edward VII, becoming one of the leading patrons of the turf. As Prince of Wales, he embarked on racehorse ownership in the 1870s, initially with steeplechasers, established his own stud at Sandringham in 1886, and eventually won the Derby and St Leger with Persimmon, and the One Thousand Guineas with Thais in 1896. He bettered this in 1900 when not only did Ambush II win him the Grand National but the Triple Crown success of Diamond Jubilee also enabled him to become leading owner of the year.

The twentieth century witnessed considerable royal interest and success on the racecourse (although in an era before the photo-finish camera it was said to be traditional for the judge to award a race against the royal family in a close finish to avoid accusations of favouritism). When his horse, Minoru, won the Derby in 1909 having earlier won the Two Thousand Guineas, Edward VII became the only reigning monarch to achieve this feat. His son, George V, and grandson, George VI, saw the royal colours of purple and scarlet, with gold braid and black cap, carried to victory in several Classics, notably when Sun Chariot won the wartime fillies' Triple Crown in 1942. The current royal family, however, can boast of more than the thrill of winning ownership, with Charles, the Prince of Wales taking part in National Hunt races during the 1980/81 season, and Anne, the Princess Royal, an accomplished horsewoman, riding winners under both codes, including the top ladies' race of 1987 at Ascot.

When the present Queen, then Princess Elizabeth, was given a young racehorse as a wedding present, it heralded a lifelong enthusiasm for racing and breeding. The filly, Astrakhan, was her first flat-race winner in 1950, but she had already become a winning owner the previous year when Monaveen, a steeplechaser jointly owned with her mother, had triumphed in a handicap chase at Fontwell. After the death of her father in 1952, the new Queen Elizabeth focused her interest on flat racing while the Queen Mother, who had registered the colours of her ancestors, the Earls of Strathmore – pale blue with buff stripes and black cap – in 1950, concentrated on National Hunt racing.

The Queen's horses were very successful during the 1950s and the victories of Aureole in the King George and Carrozza in the Oaks enabled her to top the list of leading owners in 1954 and 1957. Aureole went on to become the leading sire in 1960 and 1961, responsible for the 1960 Derby and St Leger winner, St Paddy, and two further Classic winners. The Queen also won the Two Thousand Guineas in 1958 with Pall Mall, and although the following decade brought fewer rewards, her fortunes revived during the 1970s when the fillies Highclere and Dunfermline won two Classics apiece. Highclere, having won the One Thousand Guineas in 1974, went on to capture the Prix de Diane (the French Oaks) while Dunfermline took the Oaks and St Leger in 1977. Her horses have been less successful in recent years but she has continued to take a keen interest in breeding and racing.

When the Queen Mother won the Sir Peter O'Sullevan award in 1999 for lifelong support of racing, it was a further public acknowledgement of her role in raising the profile and status of National Hunt racing, always the poor relation of the Flat. In half a century, she amassed over 400 winners and although she owned several top steeplechasers, such as Special Cargo, winner of the Whitbread Gold Cup in 1984, she will forever be associated with Devon Loch, one of the unluckiest losers of the Grand National.

Numerous race names, particularly at Ascot, continue to demonstrate the link between royalty and racing. There are races named after Queen Anne, Queen Mary, King Edward VII and Queen Alexandra; others bear the titles of the Prince of Wales, the Duke of York, the Princess Royal and the Queen Mother. The British Royal Family, however, are not the only dynasty to be represented on the English Turf. Saudi Arabian princes (Khalid Abdulla) and Islamic leaders (the Aga Khans) have more recently been joined by the Dubai royal family, the Maktoums, as owners, breeders and supporters of horseracing in Britain.

Further reading

Pitman, R., *Fit for a Queen* (Chorley: Pride of Place, 1995).
Seth-Smith, M., *Bred for the Purple* (London: Frewin, 1969).
Smith, S., *Royal Racing* (London: BBC Worldwide, 2001).

Rules

Punters groan when they hear that Rule 4 applies as it means that a horse has been withdrawn before coming under starter's orders and that all winning bets have a percentage deducted to compensate the bookmakers for having to repay bets on the errant animal. The rule, like all those involving gambling transactions, has no legal force but is accepted – sometimes grudgingly – by bettors and bookmakers alike, along with all the other *Rules on Betting* authorised by Tattersall's Committee. These rules govern all betting transactions and no bookmaker can enforce any of his own rules that are contrary to those of the Committee. The Committee also has the authority to adjudicate in betting disputes associated with horseracing and, at their discretion, report defaulters to the Jockey Club who could then warn them off, thus banning them from race meetings.

The origins of the Committee lay in the development of Subscription Rooms at Richard Tattersall's bloodstock sales venue in London. Here gentlemen were allowed to bet on credit providing that they were members of the Rooms. In the mid-Victorian era an annual subscription would cost them 2 guineas. A similar institution was established at Newmarket. At both these places committees emerged to control what were in effect gentlemen's' clubs and also to arbitrate on betting disputes between members. In 1843 the Jockey Club renounced all intention of intervening in gambling disputes and increasingly such disagreements were handled by the two committees. In 1899 they amalgamated for this purpose under the name of Tattersall's Committee, though they continued to exist separately and up to 1929 each nominated members to a joint tribunal. The Committee then became a collection of 12 experienced racing men plus two members nominated by the Jockey Club with any vacancies filled by co-option, subject to Jockey Club approval.

Horseracing itself also requires a set of rules so that the event can be seen to be fair to all of the competitors. As there was no central governing body in the sport in the early eighteenth century, the organisers of each race meeting at that time devised a set of articles – a legally binding code of conduct between the owners of the horses and the people who provided the prize – to suit themselves and local conditions. Generally they followed a similar pattern and covered the basic arrangements of place, date and time; the distance, number of heats and route to be run; the type of horse and weight to be carried; the appointment of an official to act as clerk of the course; the financial arrangements; and the means by which disputes would be resolved. The articles were not usually available in printed form but were always shown to competitors when they formally entered for the race. In contrast the Jockey Club published its rules of racing in the *Racing Calendar* from an early date. In 1807 there were seven pages devoted to such rules; by 1904, when the Jockey Club was firmly in control of racing throughout

Britain, this had risen to 56 pages including a 12-page index. No wonder that trainers and jockeys do not have to demonstrate any knowledge of the rules of racing to obtain their licence, merely agree to obey them!

The most important rule in racing today is that which states that 'every horse which runs in a race shall be run on its merits'. Of course this does not always happen: trainers and jockeys riding to instructions still try to deceive the handicapper. However, those who flout the rules can be called to account with suspensions and fines. The penalties for not trying were substantially increased in 1998 and at the same time racecourse stewards were empowered to ask trainers to account for the running of their horses in cases of both improved and worsened performances.

Trying too hard by overuse of the whip or barging through gaps can also incur the wrath of the racecourse stewards who have the responsibility for monitoring the conduct of each day's racing. They watch each race both live and on video and where they consider that there may have been a breach of the rules of racing they hold an enquiry. In 2001, almost 4,700 such investigations were held. If they perceive that the rules have been broken they can apply the appropriate disciplinary measures, usually a suspension or fine. More serious offences are referred to the Jockey Club for further examination by its stewards. These days the work of the stewards is supplemented by an off-course monitoring system in which staff in London review a random selection of races but also target certain types such as maiden races and handicaps with large fields.

One problem with enforcing the rules is that many turf offences, including doping, are not necessarily regarded as illegal by the law. This often limits the action of the Jockey Club when dealing with individuals who are not part of the sport. All that can be done is to ban them from all premises owned, licensed or controlled by the Club. Within racing it is easier to deal with malefactors as their licences to be trainers or jockeys can be withdrawn, fines imposed, suspensions meted out, and a disqualification given from involvement in any aspect of racing.

Further reading

Racing Calendar (London: Jockey Club, 2002).

See also Officials, Whipping.

Moneybox

The **Maharaja of Rajpipla** bought Windsor Lad as a yearling as he was sired by Blandford whose offspring were winning big races. The horse went on to win the 1934 Derby, the third by a Blandford colt.

Reams of Verse is one of only two odds-on favourites to win the Oaks since 1946, at 5–6 in 1997; the other was Noblesse, 4–11 in 1963, who justified her price in winning by 10 lengths.

Red Rum had amassed career earnings of £145,234 by 1977 (over £500,000 now), a British record for a National Hunt horse, with 24 wins, 14 seconds and 21 thirds.

Reference Point, winner of the Epsom Derby, King George and St Leger in 1987, set a new record for prize money earned by one horse in a single season (£774,275) – currently more than £1.25 million.

A **retainer** is the sum of money paid to a jockey to ensure a first claim on his services by either a trainer or an owner; the amount is registered at Weatherbys.

Royal Athlete, Jenny Pitman's second Grand National winner in 1995, was the longest priced victor (40–1) since Last Suspect (50–1 in 1985).

S

Safety

Aintree, a fast, galloping circuit, often with a high number of runners in major events, has a reputation as a severe test of horses. Sixty horses have died there in the past two decades. The Duchess of Westminster, owner of the incomparable Arkle, refused to let her equine star race there as she considered the course unacceptably dangerous. Until 1989 any horse that had run three times over fences could enter the Grand National but, following the deaths of two horses within seconds of each other at Becher's Brook that year, a minimum handicap rating was required. This quality threshold was raised again in 2000, a year in which the management had the Grand National course watered in a bid to slow down the field and jockeys were advised to rein back their mounts to avoid a cavalry charge at the early fences. These days, jockeys with less than 15 wins over jumps are no longer allowed to compete and a safety limit of

40 runners has been imposed. Formal veterinary checks are carried out before the race and more staff are employed to repair the ground on the day.

These moves at Aintree reflect the growing importance attached to safety generally by the Jockey Club which, over the past 25 years in consultation with the Jockeys Association, has taken huge steps to make racing less dangerous for participants, both equine and human. If jockeys are concerned about the safety of a course the Jockey Club actually authorises a deputation of three senior jockeys to explain their case to the stewards. Numbers of runners are now limited according to the size of the course. The Derby run on Epsom's tough undulating track with a tight bend at Tattenham Corner is limited to 20 runners. If the number of declarations in any race exceeds the safety limit then the lowest weighted in handicaps or the lowest rated in Pattern races are eliminated; sometimes this necessitates a ballot when horses are equally ranked. When there are substantial numbers involved another strategy adopted is to divide the race into two. Much has also been done to lessen the chances of injury from course layout and construction: posts and rails are now mainly plastic, turns have been made less stiff, heights of fences and hurdles have been regulated, and the jumps themselves redesigned to encourage horses to take off correctly. In 1994 four horses were killed in a single week racing over hurdles on the all-weather tracks at Lingfield and Southwell. Subsequently the Jockey Club decided that the risk of injury to horses (and by implication also riders) was too great on surfaces that were less yielding than turf and jumping at all-weather courses was banned. Two years later the Club also outlawed chase or hurdle racing on any going officially described as 'hard', a possibility in summer National Hunt fixtures.

Today's jockeys must wear helmets and body protectors but well into the twentieth century little safety equipment was available to protect the rider. In 1923 crash helmets for jump jockeys became compulsory following the death of amateur rider Captain Bennet at Wolverhampton, but this was only for racing and was not enforced for training gallops till the 1970s. Initially the helmets were made of cork but today polystyrene offers lightweight safety. Body protectors, made of panels of polystyrene that cover the chest and both the upper and lower back, became mandatory in 1988 and design improvements now allow jockeys to curl up in a tight ball when they fall. Sometimes riders have to be protected from themselves as those desperate to make the weight opt to disregard the safety instructions: therefore the clerk of scales is instructed to check that jockeys are wearing the correct equipment.

Only recently has the protection of jockeys from the actions of their colleagues become a priority on the safety agenda. Although child riders were banned in the nineteenth century because of their inability to control their mounts, riding under the influence of drink or drugs was not made a turf offence until 1994. As part of the new safety regime, when jockey Jonathan Lower was diagnosed as an insulin diabetic his licence was immediately withdrawn because of the possibility, however remote, that it might affect his co-ordination and control in a race. Eventually he was reinstated but with limits on his lowest riding weight and the number of daily rides he could accept as well as a rigid programme developed by the Jockey Club medical adviser to control and monitor his blood sugar levels. In most sports diuretics are banned because they are regarded as masking agents, flushing out an athlete's system to hide the fact that he or she may have taken drugs. In racing in 1999 they were prohibited on safety grounds. Jockeys take them for immediate and drastic weight loss – a pint of fluid can weigh almost a kilo – but Jockey Club medical experts became concerned that the possible side effects of severe stomach cramps, nausea, weakness and disorientation could lessen a rider's concentration and lead to hazardous situations on the track. Similarly in 1999 the Club warned riders not to celebrate too soon or too enthusiastically. In big races the custom had developed for winning jockeys to punch the air or flourish their whip. Inevitably lesser riders in lesser events began to imitate their betters, leading to fears that they might lose control of their mounts. Jockeys have also developed their own risk-minimisation procedures. Particularly in National Hunt racing they will use the dressing room and 'the mill' at the start to discuss their plans through the first obstacles so as to avoid calamity in early traffic. During the race, information on positions and gaps is readily exchanged.

One aspect of rider safety remains untouched: overwork. With Sunday and evening meetings now a norm in summer months, jockeys can be racing on over 100 consecutive days in addition to riding work in the early morning and travelling to and from their engagements. The suggestion of restricting jockeys to only one meeting a day has been debated but rejected as unworkable and probably illegal.

Horses too are now subject to increased safety standards. Thoroughbred racehorses are highly strung animals, inclined at the best of times to be fractious, especially when young. Inexperienced horses can also be dangerous but the 'schooling' of horses, particularly over hurdles and jumps, has never been a major priority in Britain. However, following the death of Richard Davis at Southwell in July 1996, when his inexperienced mount – it had never actually completed a race – simply ran into the first fence, horses with appalling jumping records, defined as falling in three consecutive races or failing to finish in four on the trot, are banned until they have been re-schooled and assessed.

Further reading

www.thejockeyclub.co.uk

See also Accidents.

St Leger

See Classics.

Sales

'Selling plater' is a disparaging term used in racing about poor quality horses whose owners enter them in selling races in the hope that they might attract a purchaser in the auction following the race. Such sales, from which the racecourse executive takes a percentage, were more common in the nineteenth century when a card at a Victorian meeting might include two or even three selling races. Today higher quality horses are generally sold privately or via the major bloodstock sales at Doncaster and Newmarket.

To most people in racing the term bloodstock sales is synonymous with the firm of Tattersalls which for over two centuries has been the dominant bloodstock auction house in Britain. In its early days the firm sold all manner of horses including ponies, hacks and hunters and even ventured in the selling of hounds and carriages, but now it deals solely with thoroughbred bloodstock. The firm also used to conduct sales all over Britain at stud farms and at specialist sales at Doncaster, but from the 1960s concentrated its English activities at Newmarket. It continued operations in Ireland, opening a purpose-built complex at Fairyhouse where the emphasis is on National Hunt animals. [In 1962 Ken Oliver and Willie Stephenson resurrected the Doncaster Bloodstock Sales which has gone on to become another leading sales firm.]

Tattersalls hold eight sales at Newmarket which they claim include market leaders in every category. The flagship is the Houghton Yearling Sale, restricted to only 300 lots and unrivalled as a source of Classic winners; the October Yearling Sale produces more two-year-old winners than any other European yearling sale; the unique Autumn Horses in Training Sale is the largest of its kind in the world; the Autumn Yearling sale is a prolific source of two-year-old winners; and the December Sale of 2,500 broodmares, foals and yearlings, is widely regarded as the most international thoroughbred sale in the world. Their portfolio is completed by the Breeze-Up Sale, Europe's premier sale of two-year-olds in training, the July Sale of horses in training and breeding stock, and the February Sale also for horses in training, breeding stock and yearlings. Half of the firm's turnover is generated in Ireland, but Tattersalls' staff still travel the world to inspect all horses offered for sale, visiting studs and stables several months in advance of the sales. Nevertheless, apart from having all yearlings tested for their wind, the firm still applies the rule of 'caveat emptor' and refuses to guarantee the soundness of any horse that it sells.

Other things have changed. Sales days are less mixed than they used to be and specialist weeks will concentrate on foals and yearlings and on fillies and broodmares. Similarly the sales are delineated by their perceived quality of horses offered, primacy being given to the September event, named after Highflyer, the famous stallion owned by Richard Tattersall. All their auctioneers attend voice-training classes. Electronic sales boards show bids in all leading currencies, though the traditional use of guineas for actual bidding still holds sway. And, following an incident in 1983 when a final purchaser reneged on his offer, video cameras are now used to identify bidders.

In the United States x-rays and endoscopic images are made available by the vendors but in Britain the vetting of horses prior to sale is usually confined to non-invasive techniques such as checking eyes, heart and lungs, feeling the legs, and watching the horse walk. It is akin to buying a car by looking at the bodywork and upholstery but not starting the engine and driving it. Once the purchase has been made the horse, especially if a yearling, is often exercised to test its wind and the sale can be voided if the animal shows a breathing problem unless the possibility had been mentioned in the auctioneer's catalogue. Buyers may now request a blood test of an animal after purchase to check for non-steroidal antiinflammatory drugs; if positive the horse can be returned to the seller.

Given the poor financial returns from racehorse ownership, the auction sales figures are surprising. Tattersalls' turnover in 1999 was 121.9 million 'guineas' and in 2000 the annual three-day Houghton Sale produced an average of over £250,000: this for yearlings that had never seen a racecourse and could be judged solely on their conformation and breeding! Some of this spending has to be attributed to the fear of letting a rival owner or breeder secure the next wonder horse, though, of course, no one can predict which of the unraced animals will gain that accolade.

Further reading

www.tattersalls.com
www.thoroughbredauction.com

See also Agents, Tattersall family.

Sandown Park

Sandown Park has always been a pioneer amongst racecourses. The first in Britain to be fully enclosed (1875), it was also the first to be covered by network television (1947) and the first to stage a commercially sponsored race, the Whitbread Gold Cup in 1957. Its suburban situation to the south-west of London, adjacent to Esher railway station, has always ensured its popularity and it has regularly been voted Racecourse of the Year by the Racegoers Club.

Sandown came to prominence as the original enclosed course for which everyone paid an admission charge; until then only patrons of grandstands were required to pay, with the remainder of a course open to all. By charging half-a-crown (12.5 pence) the racecourse management hoped to keep out the seedier elements of society and to tempt middle-class female racegoers to what had been predominantly a male and working-class preserve. The 'park' course model with its more refined atmosphere was replicated throughout Britain at venues such as Kempton, Lingfield, Haydock and Hamilton over the following two decades. To further enhance its growing reputation Sandown staged the inaugural Eclipse Stakes, over 10 furlongs, in 1886, the first British race worth £10,000 (more than twice as valuable as the Derby at that time). From the outset, however, it also hosted jump racing. Since 1887 it has been the home of the annual Grand Military fixture and its mixed meeting at the end of April still heralds the official finish of the National Hunt season.

The flat-racing circuit at Sandown is an oval of 1 mile 5 furlongs with a separate 5-furlong straight. The jumps course with 11 fences weaves its way in and out of the flat but both use the same finishing straight which climbs steadily uphill. The elevated position of the grandstand ensures good views of the entire course with even the 'Railway Fences' visible on the far side. (Sandown must be one of the few courses in Britain offering punters a background panorama of suburban trains whistling past and planes simultaneously taking off from the nearby airport.) The back of the stand overlooks the paddock and the famous Rhododendron Walk down which the horses parade to the start.

Sandown hosts a single Group One flat race, the Eclipse in July, and three Grade One National Hunt races including the 2-mile Tingle Creek Chase and the Tolworth Hurdle. The Eclipse, sandwiched between the Derby and the King George, is the first opportunity for the current three-year-old crop to take on their middle-distance elders. It has been won by Derby winners such as Mill Reef (1971) and Nashwan (1989) and by other star performers who preferred a shorter distance – Brigadier Gerard (1972), Pebbles (1985), the first filly to win the race, and more recently Giant's Causeway (2000). Mtoto won in consecutive years (1987 and 1988) as did Halling (1995 and 1996). Other flat meetings, mostly held on summer evenings and weekends, include Classic trials in April and a charity race day in August.

The Tingle Creek Chase, named after the horse who twice set the course record over 2 miles in the 1970s, is held in December and the Imperial Cup, founded in 1907 and originally the most valuable hurdle race in the calendar, still forms part of the Grand Military Meeting in early March. The most famous steeplechase at Sandown used to be the Whitbread Gold Cup, the finale of the jump season in April, and a race won by many of the legends of the National Hunt scene – Arkle (1965), Mill House (1967), Desert Orchid (1988) and Mr Frisk in 1990, the year of his Grand National triumph. But after 45 years of sponsorship, Whitbread has now withdrawn its support and the race, which had recently been failing to attract many of the top names, will find it difficult to recapture its former prestige.

Sandown Park is the headquarters of the United Racecourses Group which, along with Kempton Park and Epsom Downs, forms part of the Racecourse Holdings Trust, a non-profit making management arm of the Jockey Club. It stages around 25 race days each year, many as prime Saturday fixtures, as befits one of the premier courses in Britain.

Further reading

Magee, S. (ed.), *The Channel Four Racing Guide to Racecourses* (London: Channel 4 Books, 1998).
Tyrrel, J., *Chasing Around Britain* (Swindon: Crowood, 1990).
www.sandown.co.uk

Sceptre (1899–1926) – by Persimmon out of Ornament

Sceptre is the only horse to have been entered in all five English Classics and to have won four of them; reports suggest that with more skilful handling she could have swept the board. A well-bred bay filly, related to both St Simon and Ormonde, she had the misfortune to be sold as a yearling for the record price of 10,000 guineas to the gambler, Robert Sievier, who was not only determined to make as much money as possible from her racing exploitsbut decided to train her himself throughout her crucial three-year-old season.

She won the Woodcote Stakes at Epsom Downs and the July Stakes at Newmarket as a two-year-old when trained by Charles Morton but Sievier took over her preparation in 1902 and entered her in the Lincolnshire Handicap, a strange choice for a Classic filly but not for an inveterate gambler. She was second. However, her condition improved so rapidly that she won the Two Thousand Guineas in record time and followed this achievement two days later with victory in the One Thousand Guineas, partnered on both occasions by Herbert Randall.

Although her training schedule was interrupted by a bruised foot, she was entered in both Epsom Classics. Her fourth place in the Derby was attributed to poor race tactics by Randall, riding in his first professional season, particularly as she turned out for the Oaks two days later and won in a canter. She was then sent to Paris for the Grand Prix, in which she was beaten and Randall again got the blame. When she failed once more, in the Coronation Stakes at Ascot three days after her French trip, Randall was sacked, and with a new jockey on board, she won the St James's Palace Stakes the following day. She had competed in what would now be five Group One races within two weeks.

Her punishing schedule was maintained throughout the season, with two races at Goodwood and two more at Doncaster. She won the Nassau Stakes and the St Leger but was beaten in the Sussex Stakes and the Park Hill Stakes. Although she had raced 12 times, winning over £23,000, her owner's financial difficulties still dictated her progress. Sent to the Newmarket sales at a reserve price of 24,000 guineas, she failed to attract a bid but when she was unplaced in the 1903 Lincolnshire, Sievier, having gambled heavily on her success, was finally forced to sell her for what he could get.

Her new owner, William Bass, sent her to the future champion trainer, Alec Taylor, and at last she received treatment worthy of an outstanding racehorse. She was beaten a neck by Ard Patrick, the 1902 Derby winner, in the Eclipse Stakes, thought to be one of the greatest races of the twentieth century, but went on to win all her remaining starts that year, the Hardwicke Stakes at Ascot, the Duke of York Stakes at Kempton Park, and the Jockey Club Stakes, Champion Stakes and Limekiln Stakes at Newmarket. Kept in training as a five-year-old, she failed to win in three attempts and was promptly retired.

Her success at stud was limited. She produced only eight moderate foals, although her filly Maid of Corinth was second in the One Thousand Guineas, but her later descendants included two Derby winners, April the Fifth (1932) and Relko (1963). Her achievement of four Classic wins is unlikely to be repeated.

Further reading

Wilson, J., *The Great Racehorses* (London: Little, Brown and Co., 1998).

Scotland

Horseracing is said to be the most widely followed sport in Scotland after football and Scots have made an impact on the turf in Britain as jockeys, trainers, owners and administrators. Within Scotland, however, the profile of the sport is low key. There are few top-class races or competitors at Scottish racecourses and those with ambition in the racing industry have tended to ply their trade in England, from the Dawsons, highly successful nineteenth-century trainers, to Willie Carson, champion jockey of more recent times (see separate entry). Even the contribution to racing of King James VI of Scotland occurred south of the border; as James I of England, he is credited with discovering the potential of Newmarket, later to be the headquarters of British racing, in 1605.

Horseracing in Scotland undoubtedly took place as early as the sixteenth century, when races were part of the festivities at local fairs or on annual holidays. Trophies were sometimes awarded by town councils or wealthy landowners but the race entrants were more likely to be farmers' horses than thoroughbreds. By the eighteenth century, however, quality meetings were taking place at venues which still exist today – Kelso, Ayr and Edinburgh – as well as at sites which have long disappeared from the racing calendar such as Dumfries and Haddington. During the 1820s, 16 racecourses held events, from Aberdeen and Inverness in the north to Hawick and Coldstream in the Borders, but thereafter the number declined. Eight courses remained in 1900 but with the closure of Paisley, Bogside and Lanark – the latter as recently as 1977 – Scotland now boasts only five, with flat racing at Hamilton Park and National Hunt at Kelso and Perth, while facilities for both exist at Ayr and Musselburgh (the more accurate name for Edinburgh racecourse). Point-to-point races, the amateur version of jump racing, are also held at a number of Scottish venues.

Geography and economics have both played a part in limiting the amount and the quality of racing in Scotland. The Scottish aristocracy, many of whom spent lengthy periods in England, had moved their stables south by the early nineteenth century and racing enthusiasts, such as James Merry, a wealthy Glasgow ironmaster, soon followed. Before the advent of good roads and railways, the movement of racehorses was restricted and race meetings tended to feature only local runners. By mid-century, an improved infrastructure had led to greater mobility and an influx of English horses but significant transport costs were incurred in any foray north of the border. Yorkshire stables in particular sent considerable numbers to Scottish race meetings but low prize money and sheer distance have often restricted entries from southern England, where most of the top-class trainers are based. Investment in modern course facilities, higher levels of sponsorship and joint-marketing initiatives by the five courses, together with Sunday racing and evening meetings, pioneered at Hamilton as early as 1947, have spearheaded attempts to encourage the sport in Scotland. But even at Ayr, the premier Scottish track, top-quality horses and jockeys are a rarity and Scotland continues to suffer from its northern location. Racing at most Scottish courses was, and still is, reckoned to be 'moderate'.

There have been some successes south of the border. Apart from five-time champion Willie Carson, both Duncan Keith and Sandy Barclay carved out careers as flat-race jockeys in England during the 1960s and 1970s. Keith won the Two Thousand Guineas on Niksar in 1965 and had the misfortune to be twice disqualified when first past the post with Rock Roi in the Ascot Gold Cup (1971 and 1972). Barclay was champion apprentice in 1966 and won the 1968 One Thousand Guineas with Caergwrle and the 1970 Oaks with Lupe before spending some years riding in France for Francois Boutin. More recently, Richard Quinn (born, like Carson, in Stirling) was champion apprentice in 1984, won the St Leger on Snurge in 1990 and both the Oaks and the St Leger in 2000 with Love Divine and Millenary. He also has the distinction of being the first winning jockey on the all-weather in Britain, at Lingfield in 1989, and has twice been runner-up in the jockeys' championship (1999, 2000). Human Scots have been far more successful than their equine counterparts. The only Scottish-trained flat racehorse to make any impact on the English turf was Rockavon, trained by George Boyd at Dunbar. He won the 1961 Two Thousand Guineas at a starting price of 66–1, but his only subsequent victory was in a two-horse race and he was reckoned to be one of the poorest Classic winners of the century.

Scotland has also made a significant contribution to National Hunt racing. Scottish jump jockey Peter Niven retired in May 2001 having joined the elite group who have ridden more than 1,000 winners over the sticks. The 1960 Aintree Grand National was won by Merryman II, already successful in the Scottish equivalent the previous year. Bred by the Marquess of Linlithgow and owned by Miss Winifred Wallace, a formidable amateur rider in Scottish point-to-points, he was second at Aintree in 1961, just failing to concede 25 lb to the eventual winner, Nicolaus Silver. Freddie, owned and trained by Border farmer Reg Tweedie, was twice runner-up in the Aintree marathon in 1965 and 1966 but won the Foxhunters' Chase at Cheltenham, the Mildmay/Cazalet Chase at Sandown and was second to Arkle in the Hennessy, no mean achievement. The popular Peaty Sandy, trained in the Borders by permit-holder Helen Hamilton, won the Welsh National in 1981 and ten races at Newcastle, the last as a thirteen-year-old in 1987.

The most successful Scottish trainer of the post-war period, however, was Ken Oliver who sent out nearly 1,000 winners from his Border yard. His best known horse was Wyndburgh who ran in six consecutive Grand Nationals from 1957 and was runner-up three times (to Sundew in 1957, Oxo in 1959 and Kilmore in 1962). Oliver won the Scottish Grand National five times from 1963 (Pappageno's Cottage) to 1982 (Cockle Strand), including 1979 when Fighting Fit also won the Hennessy Gold Cup. The year 1979 was a good year for the Scots as Rubstic became the only Scottish-trained winner of the Grand National. Handled by John Leadbetter of Roxburghshire, he was twice second in the Scottish National and competed at Aintree again in 1980 and 1981. Unfortunately, the closest Scotland has come to another success in the race has been in the name of the 1980 winner – Ben Nevis.

Further reading

Burnett, J., *Riot, Revelry and Rout* (East Lothian: Tuckwell, 2000).
McConnell, T., *The Tartan Turf: Scottish Racing, its History and Heroes* (Edinburgh: Mainstream, 1988).
www.scottishracing.co.uk

Scott brothers

William (1797–1848) and John Scott (1794–1871) were a formidable nineteenth-century racing partnership. Sons of a jockey-turned trainer, Bill went on to become an outstanding rider, but John, despite winning his first race aged only 13, fought a losing battle against increasing weight and eventually opted to become a flat-race trainer, the most successful ever from the North. Based in Yorkshire, they made a speciality of winning their local Classic, the St Leger. Bill rode nine winners of the Doncaster event and John trained 16, 6 of them being joint triumphs with his brother.

Both were first employed in their father's stables, at Chippenham near Newmarket, before moving on to the Middleham establishment of James Croft in 1814. Here John was put in charge of Filho da Puta who won the St Leger the following year. He then became private trainer to Mr Houldsworth of Rockhill in Sherwood Forest, a position that he retained for eight years before training for the Hon. Edward Petre at Mansfield. While in this later position he won his first St Leger with Theodore in 1822. Three years after this victory, Scott purchased Whitewall House at Malton which had training stables capable of accommodating over a hundred horses. Here Scott became renowned as 'the Wizard of the North' as from his stables came a further 41 Classic winners, including 15 more of the St Leger, 9 of the Oaks, and 6 of the Derby. In 1853 one of his horses, West Australian, became the first to win the Triple Crown of the Two Thousand Guineas, the Derby and the St Leger. He rented gallops at Pigburn, near Doncaster and at Leatherhead, a few miles from Epsom, at which his horses were often given their final preparation for the St Leger and Derby challenges. A dignified figure, with long white hair in his old age, he often entertained local villagers in his dining room, carving the beef with a knife whose handle was made from the shank bone of Rowton, his third St Leger winner.

Bill Scott became stable jockey and a partner in his brother's Whitewall enterprise from the outset. Together the trainer and jockey siblings enjoyed success after success. Bill's triumphs as a rider included three Two Thousand Guineas, an equal number of Oaks, the Derby four times, as well as nine St Legers, still a record for a jockey. Coarse in both character and riding style, he verbally intimidated other jockeys and rode so aggressively that his career was interrupted by a number of injuries resulting from falls. He was hard on his mounts and Jack Spignot, his first St Leger winner in 1821, apparently hated him so much that it had to be blindfolded to allow Scott to mount. However, that hardness enabled him to force Mündig home by a head in the 1835 Derby, which allegedly brought the brothers some £20,000 in winning bets. Like many other jockeys he had a drinking problem and too much brandy on the morning of the race is said to have cost him a Derby – and the first Triple

Crown – on Sir Tatton Sykes in 1846. Reputedly he was so busy arguing with the starter that he missed the 'off' and then was beaten by only a neck. After quarrelling with his brother, he set up a training establishment of his own in 1844 at Highfield House, near Malton with William Oates as trainer and himself as stable jockey. However, with Scott by then verging on alcoholism, the venture was not a success except for two Classic wins in 1846 on Sir Tatton Sykes, his own horse. Following the split between the brothers, Frank Butler rode 10 Classic winners for John Scott.

Further reading

Mortimer, R., Onslow, R. and Willett, P., *Biographical Encyclopaedia of British Flat Racing* (London: Macdonald and Jane's, 1978).
Tanner, M., *Great Jockeys of the Flat* (Enfield: Guinness, 1992).

Scudamore, Peter (1959–)

In 1989, Peter Scudamore became the first National Hunt jockey to ride 200 (221 in total) winners in a season, and, even more remarkably, the first jockey from either code to do so since Gordon Richards in 1933. Of these 158 wins emanated from a fruitful partnership with Martin Pipe at a phenomenal strike rate of 44 per cent.

In November 1966 a pile-up in a hurdle race at Wolverhampton ended the illustrious riding career of his father Michael. He moved successfully into training and Peter began riding out for him at the age of 13. In 1975, when he was 16, he had his first public ride on one of his father's horses on the flat at Leicester. Next year he had his first ride – and fall – in a point-to-point at Belmont before having his first mount under Rules at Chepstow ten days later, on which he finished fourth. His first winner under National Hunt Rules was Rolyat in a hurdle race at Devon and Exeter on 31 August 1978.

After learning to ride races as an amateur – and combining racing with work as an estate agent – he accepted an offer to work as an assistant trainer to David Nicolson, a device that would have allowed him to continue to ride as an amateur. However, he soon decided to turn professional and actually won on his debut, unlike his father who took 70 rides to break his duck. He became stable jockey first to David Nicholson and then succeeded John Francome as number one rider for Fred Winter.

He shared the National Hunt Rider's Championship in 1981–82 with Francome, after an act of generosity from the latter who refused any more rides after drawing level with Scudamore who was out injured. He was champion in his own right from 1985–86 to 1991–92, many of his winners coming from the stables of Martin Pipe for whom he became stable jockey in 1986. In 1990 he was awarded an MBE for services to National Hunt racing.

Towards the end of the 1992–93 season he realised that, although he still enjoyed the big meetings, he did not relish chasing round the minor tracks on moderate horses. On his retirement aged 34, appropriately after a winning ride, he had totalled 1,678 victories – 792 of them for Martin Pipe – at the time a record aggregate for a jumps jockey. That final season saw him complete his eighth consecutive century of winners. Yet he never won the Grand National or the Cheltenham Gold Cup. He moved on to become a television racing presenter and assistant to trainer Nigel Twiston-Davies, a contemporary from his point-to-point days.

In his retirement year he replicated Squire George Osbaldestone's famous 1831 challenge of riding 200 miles in less than 10 hours. Using 50 horses Scudamore achieved the target in 8 hours 37 minutes and 51 seconds, beating Osbaldestone's time by 4 minutes 9 seconds. However, whereas the Squire did it for a wager Scudamore was raising funds for the Animal Health Trust.

Further reading

Scudamore, P., *Scu* (London: Headline, 1993).

Security

In the week preceding the 1958 Derby, the ante-post favourite Alcide was savagely beaten in its training stables by an intruder and put out of the race, thus costing punters all the money they had bet on Cecil Boyd-Rochfort's horse. Imagine how much more difficult it would have been to ensure the safety of horses in the nineteenth century when many of them walked to meetings, guarded only by a stable lad or a young apprentice. Yet protecting horses from being 'nobbled' by dope or assault is important for the integrity of racing. For many years the racing authorities simply put the responsibility for the security of their charges on to the trainers. Moreover they applied the concept of 'strict liability' – which reverses the onus of proof normally required in a court of law – and often penalised the trainer concerned by fines, suspensions or even the loss of licence if anything untoward happened. This was seen as essential summary justice since the Jockey Club firmly believed that if racing was not kept clean it would not survive. In Alcide's case Boyd-Rochfort was not charged as he withdrew the horse from the Derby as any trainer is fully entitled to do. A different tack was taken when the Peter Walwyn-trained Rock Roi won the Ascot Gold Cup in 1971 only to be subsequently disqualified when traces of a painkiller were found after a routine dope test. Although the Jockey Club exonerated Walwyn from any suggestion of corrupt practice, they still fined him £100.

One of the reasons for placing the blame at the stable door of trainers was that the Jockey Club lacked the resources to fund an extensive security organisation and infrastructure. Until 1972, when money became available from the Levy Board to establish Racecourse Security Services, security was simply one of the many functions of the Jockey Club Racecourse Personnel Organisation. Fourteen years later security came under the direct control of the Jockey Club and was renamed the Jockey Club Security Department (JCSD).

The JCSD is at the core of the Club's efforts to protect the integrity of racing. Its activities include gathering intelligence, undertaking investigations, inspecting training establishments, monitoring moves in the betting market and the provision of security staff at racecourse stables. In recent years the Club has expanded the number of employees in the department, often recruiting experienced investigators from the police special branch and military intelligence. They see their prime task as the prevention of corruption by their presence rather than the detection of malefactors after the event. Accordingly they have the authority to visit stables unannounced. The department has introduced a secure hot line for informants, built up working relationships with the customs and police, and installed CCTV coverage of racecourse stables. No jockeys are allowed access to the racecourse stables: indeed the only persons allowed in are lads sent to look after their stable's mount. Mobile phones are now banned from the weighing room to prevent any information being communicated in or out. However, the Jockey Club has no powers of arrest, search or seizure and can only enforce the rules of racing not the law relating to criminal activity. In its licensing role the Club exercises a function in the public interest analogous to that of the Gaming Board. It regards it as essential that anyone it approves of being a 'fit and proper' person to hold a licence or be granted registration should be of a high standard of probity. Unfortunately this is hampered by a lack of access to criminal records in respect of those it licences, registers or employs.

Despite its efforts the Jockey Club has struggled to establish public confidence in the JCSD. The choice of Roger Buffham as Head of Security proved a public relations disaster for the Jockey Club. He lifted the profile of security and deterrents but mishandled the much-publicised race-fixing affair when five jockeys were arrested but released before the case went to court. He was sacked following allegations of serious misconduct and then went on to advise the makers of a 'Panorama' television documentary that lampooned the Jockey Club for its inaction in the face of information on jockeys mixing with criminals. The 'Panorama' exposé led to the resignation of his successor, Jeremy Phipps, the SAS officer who planned the ending to the siege of the Iranian Embassy in 1980, but failed to spot hidden cameras when he was interviewed by Buffham.

Even keen-eyed racegoers have sometimes not noticed when one horse has been substituted for a lookalike animal of vastly different ability. In such cases the betting market will not reflect the true odds of that horse's chances in the race. Technology is now being utilised to prevent such ring-ins (and also to identify horses discovered in a neglected condition after retirement) by having all foals microchipped so as to provide a quick, permanent and effective way of recognising horses. This system, still an adjunct to the passport that identifies horses by means of their markings, was introduced in 1999. By mid-2001 almost 41,000 of the 12 mm chips had been implanted; only 47 foals had had an adverse reaction and a mere 156 chips had proved unreadable when scanned electronically.

Spectators also have to be protected. On Derby Day 1867, 600 police were deployed around the Epsom course to keep order. In 1911 the number was up to 800. Fully enclosed courses perhaps found it easier by simply excluding undesirables. It might be thought that the emergence of human rights legislation would now make it more difficult for racecourse executives to announce, as did Sandown Park in its race cards of the 1930s, that 'known bad characters, persons infringing the provisions of the betting Act or creating any noise, disturbance or obstruction or otherwise misconducting themselves, will be removed by the Police. The management reserve the right to refuse admission, or to eject anyone from the Park, without assigning a reason for doing so'. But Doncaster was still issuing similar edicts in 2000, though Sandown had added a rider that this was only applied in 'extreme circumstances'. A general provision to exclude potential troublemakers was utilised against racecourse gangs in the inter-war years. The 1920s saw so much gang warfare on many courses as a direct result of criminal protection schemes being operated against bookmakers, that in 1924 the Home Secretary ordered the police to make racecourses safe. This had some success, as did a Jockey Club decision in 1929 to have bookmakers' pitches allocated under their auspices in conjunction with the local Bookmakers Protection Association. Recent decades have seen racing establish a reputation for reasonably orderly crowds who can enjoy themselves, the racing, gambling and alcohol without causing mayhem. Disturbances caused by friction between bettors and bookmakers have been curtailed by the employment of betting inspectors to settle disputes between bookmakers and their clients. Punters have now been given more protection from cheating bookmakers (or from misunderstandings over the nature of the bet) by the compulsory introduction of computerised betting tickets which give full details of the agreed transaction. More generally from the late 1980s the handling of rowdiness and hooliganism has been left to the police, the JCSD concentrating on other tasks.

Terrorism has perhaps replaced crowd disorder as the major threat to spectator security. The Grand National bomb warning in 1997 was taken seriously and Aintree was cleared of spectators and participants. However, since the events of 11 September 2001 anti-terrorist insurance premiums have soared and some courses have had to reduce the amount of cover. Others, it is reported, have decided to call the bluff of the phone-callers and carry on. One problem is that standard police procedure is to offer safety advice rather than specific instructions, leaving it to the racecourse authorities to make the decision whether or not to cancel. In turn this can lead to potential hassles with the insurance companies. Appeals to the government to act as insurer of last resort have not been heeded on the grounds that sport cannot be treated as a special case.

Further reading

Payne, N. and Hart, D., *Everyone Must Leave* (Mainstream: Edinburgh, 1998).
www.thejockeyclub.co.uk

See also Corruption, Doping.

Smith brothers

Sons of a Berkshire farmer, Doug and Eph Smith were the most successful pair of jockey siblings in the twentieth century. Eric Ephraim (1915–72) and his younger brother Douglas (1917–89) were both apprenticed to Major Frederick Sneyd. Eph rode his first winner in 1930, Red Queen at Windsor. Doug broke his maiden two years later on Denia at Salisbury. The horse carried 6 st but 17 lb of that was lead in the diminutive Smith's saddle bag. Neither of them suffered real weight problems and were able to ride comparatively light throughout their careers. In terms of winners both had their best season in 1947, Doug securing 173 victories and Eph 144. Unfortunately for them this was the year that Gordon Richards won 269.

Doug suffered the frustration of riding at the same time as Richards, finishing second in the jockeys' championship to him every year between 1946 and 1953 except 1948 when illness kept him out of action till July. When Richards retired, Doug, who had modelled his riding style on Harry Wragg, took the title in 1954, retained it for two years and then secured it again in 1958 and 1959. Unusually he won less Classics than championship titles, gaining victory in only four, all of them at Newmarket. One of these was the One Thousand Guineas on Hypericum while he was royal jockey for George VI. He excelled in staying races winning the Doncaster Cup seven times, the Goodwood Cup three times and the Ascot Gold Cup twice. He was always wanted for the Cesarewitch by trainers because of his ability to ride light in this major handicap in which he was successful six times. On four occasions the horse carried 7 st 8 lb and once only 7 st 5 lb. Few experienced jockeys could do these weights and few apprentices had Smith's knowledge of the track or the strength to ride a tough finish after $2\frac{1}{4}$ miles of a cavalry charge. After a career in which he rode 3,112 winners from some 20,000 mounts, Doug took up training in 1968 and won with his first runner, Owen Anthony at Doncaster. He also finally won an Epsom Classic, the 1969 Oaks with Lord Rosebery's Sleeping Partner. Two years later he won 74 races, more than any other trainer that season. In 1979 he became a bloodstock agent. Ten years later he was found dead in his Newmarket swimming pool.

Eph was never champion jockey, though, unlike his brother, he did ride an Epsom Classic winner, Blue Peter in the 1939 Derby. He won two other Classics. Eph was partially deaf and eventually had to wear a hearing aid. Many observers thought he had more talent than his brother, but he also had less tact and his forthrightness cost him rides from those owners who did not like to hear the truth about their horses. Neither brother liked the idea of aggressive freelancing, preferring trainers to approach them with rides: indeed Eph had only two first claims on his services for most of his career, Jack Jarvis from 1933 to 1948 and then H.J. Joel to 1963. Ill-health forced Eph to retire in 1965 after riding 2,313 winners though he continued to ride work for Noel Murless. He was found dead in a brook near Newmarket in 1972; a verdict of misadventure was recorded.

Further reading

Smith, D. and Willett, P., *Five Times Champion* (London: Pelham, 1968).

Social anthropology

The average race meeting has always attracted a diverse social crowd. In the nineteenth century, royalty and pickpockets represented the opposite ends of the spectrum, with many sectors of society, both respectable and criminal, in between. 'Connections' – owners, trainers and jockeys – cut across social boundaries in similar fashion while officials and administrators were increasingly members of the middle classes. Twentieth-century racegoers and professionals, though less aristocratic, were equally varied, a fact borne out by recent anthropological work conducted on racing.

Contrary to popular myth, racegoers are not compulsive gamblers according to these studies. Although the majority are well-informed enthusiasts, a substantial minority attend race meetings for purely social reasons and have little understanding of the sport. Racing is viewed as a good day out by a number of social groups – families, attracted particularly at weekends by picnic and child-friendly facilities, office workers enticed to summer evening meetings, 'hen parties' celebrating birthdays or imminent weddings, or businessmen dispensing corporate hospitality. The spectacle of horseracing is almost incidental, a sideshow amidst the eating, drinking and socialising aspects of the day out and in this respect, it has changed little over the centuries.

The same anthropological studies found that rules and rituals were highly prevalent amongst the 'racing tribe', as those most closely associated with racehorses were described. Superstitions, dress codes and their own language were further attributes of tribe members whose behaviour at a variety of racecourses was noted and compared. A race day pattern was identified, not only for spectators but also for the main participants in racing such as trainers, jockeys and officials. Celebrations or post mortems were conducted in similar fashion throughout the country, with champagne and eternal optimism forming major ingredients. Patterns of etiquette were observed, such as the manner in which jockeys and trainers treated owners or the unfailing courtesy of the Tote ladies when dealing with novice punters.

Different groups within racing were allotted titles according to the function which they performed for the tribe. Jockeys went out to do battle and were therefore the tribal warriors; trainers often accomplished miracles and were likened to witch doctors; racecourse officials were deemed to be tribal elders; and journalists from the racing press were both scribes and oracles, interpreting the past and predicting the future. The role of bookmakers was that of universal scapegoats, a marginalised subgroup of racing society.

Horseracing, a sport which has traditionally been linked with gambling and some of the seedier elements in society, seems to have been transformed into a safe and sanitised entertainment for twenty-first-century crowds, far removed from the unsavoury 'carnivals of drunkenness' which could be found in mid-Victorian Britain. The presence of women in large numbers at contemporary race meetings, up to one-third of total racegoers, contrasts with their more limited attendance at other major spectator sports and their position a century ago, when ladies were segregated from the masses and prostitution was as common at race meetings as gambling and drinking. The modern 'racing tribe' is neither disorderly nor unsavoury.

Further reading

Cassidy, R., *The Sport of Kings* (Cambridge: Cambridge University Press, 2002).
Fox, K., *The Racing Tribe* (London: Metro Books, 1999).
Huggins, M., *Flat Racing and British Society 1790–1914* (London: Frank Cass, 2000).

South America

Racing in South America has closer connections with the United States than with Europe. Jockeys such as Laffit Pincay junior, Jorge Velasquez and Jacinto Vasquez left their native Panama to become winners of the Kentucky Derby and top prize money earners in America while Chilean-bred Cougar II became Champion Grass Horse in America in 1972.

However, Britain has also had racing links with South America. The champion horse from Argentina, Forli, was a grandson of Hyperion, top English sire on six occasions. He stood successfully at stud in Kentucky in the 1960s and 1970s and some of his descendants have since appeared on British racecourses: his son Thatch was a multiple Group One winner in 1973 while more recently his grandson Docksider won over 12 times on British soil in the late 1990s. Argentina first became a popular destination for British stallions at the end of the nineteenth century when cattle barons were rich enough to import Derby winners such as Ormonde (1886) and Diamond Jubilee (1900). (Ormonde had a wind problem and may have been sold abroad to ensure that this was not passed on to British bloodstock; Diamond Jubilee was renowned for his vicious temper although he prospered as a sire in South America for 15 years.) Later exports included Derby winners Cameronian (1931), Pont l'Eveque (1940), Psidium (1961) and Triple-Crown-winning Bahram (1935), none of whom were a success at stud, but Craganour, famously first past the post in the 1913 Derby and later disqualified, was also sold to Argentina and proved to be an outstanding sire. Other South American countries, anxious to improve their thoroughbred bloodstock, also provided markets for British horses. Moderate animals such as Swallow Tail, third in the 1949 Derby, did well at stud in Brazil; Souepi, winner of the 1953 Ascot Gold Cup was popular in Chile while Queen Elizabeth II's first winner as reigning monarch, Choir Boy, was despatched to Uruguay. Some never made it – Hippius, third in the 1940 St Leger, died at sea in appalling weather en route to Brazil. Others, dismal failures at British studs, also ended their days in the southern hemisphere.

A few journeyed in the opposite direction. The first winner of the Grande Premio Brasil, considered to be the most important race in Brazil, was Mossero in 1933. He was sent to England where it was said that he won a race at Bath, the first South American thoroughbred to race in Britain. More recently Empery, 1976 Derby winner, was a son of Peruvian triple-crown-winning mare, Pamplona II. James Buchanan, the first Lord Woolavington, a Scottish businessman who won the Derby and St Leger in 1926 with Coronach, brought an Argentine trainer, Luis Alvarez, and jockey Santiago Gomez back with him from a trip to South America in 1898. The partnership won the Eclipse Stakes with Epsom Lad in 1901. Another raider was Panamanian jockey Braulio Baeza, flown specially to Britain to partner 1972 Derby winner Roberto in his quest to win the inaugural Benson and Hedges Gold Cup at York (now the Group One International Stakes). The race acquired historical significance as the only defeat inflicted on Brigadier Gerard in his 18-race career. The success of Roberto who won by three lengths from his British rival and in a course record time was attributed to the tactics and skill of the jockey; the horse never won convincingly again.

The greatest South American triumph in Britain, however, was probably that of Angel Penna, the Argentinian who became a trainer in Venezuela and the United States before moving to France in the 1970s. He masterminded the most successful French onslaught on the English Classics in recent times, when Flying Water, Pawneese and Crow, all ridden by Yves Saint Martin, won the One Thousand Guineas, the Oaks and the St Leger in 1976. Pawneese captured the King George in the same year, Flying Water won the Group Three Nell Gwyn Stakes at Newmarket and Crow, a half-Argentinian colt, was runner-up in the Benson and Hedges Gold Cup, enabling Penna's patron, Daniel Wildenstein, to be leading owner in Britain that year.

Racecourses in South America, with the exception of Argentina, are said to provide enthusiastic rather than quality sport. Perhaps this is why Lester Piggott, at the age of 54 and after three years absence from the saddle, chose Lima in Peru for his comeback race in 1989 – he finished third.

Further reading

Mortimer, R., Onslow, R. and Willett, P., *Biographical Encyclopaedia of British Flat Racing* (London: Macdonald and Jane's, 1978).
Scott, B. and Cranham, G., *The World of Flat Racing* (London: Peerage, 1987).

Sponsorship

Sponsorship involves a commercial decision to provide funds in cash or kind to a sports organisation or player in return for securing publicity and product awareness. Today, as in many sports, sponsorship is indispensable to the racing industry with jockeys, horses, courses and races all receiving this form of financial assistance.

In the eighteenth and nineteenth centuries race meetings often featured races sponsored by local innkeepers and tradesmen who stood to benefit from an influx of visitors to the area. In 1794, for example, the tradesmen of Newmarket provided £50 in prize money for two races to attract horse owners to the town. In those days the condition of entry to a race often required horses to be stabled for several days before the race at named inns whose proprietors had contributed money to the prize fund, so the sponsorship could pay off. The groom who accompanied the horse, and perhaps other servants and the owner, would be accommodated there, thus increasing the innkeepers' profits. Spectators also might visit the inns to examine the horses and have a drink whilst doing so. Certainly the residents of Newmarket appreciated the contribution of a meeting to the local economy as in 1875 sponsorship was still available, this time from the town council who put up £300 for the Newmarket International Free Handicap. This sponsorship with commercial intent should be distinguished from the patronage provided by wealthy aristocrats and gentry who often put up prize money as part of their paternalistic responsibility to promote local racing as an entertainment for the populace.

The first sponsorship of a major race came in 1866 when William Blenkiron, one of the earliest commercial breeders and owner of the Middle Park Stud, gave 1,000 sovereigns to establish a race for two-year-old colts at Newmarket. Nine years later Thomas Gee of the Dewhurst Stud financed the Dewhurst Stakes also run at Newmarket. Others involved in nineteenth-century sponsorship included the bloodstock auction house Tattersall's who first sponsored a race over the Rowley Mile at Newmarket in 1849. They did not venture into that area of racing again till 1880 when they put £200 into the Somerville (a Tattersall family name) Stakes at the second Newmarket spring meeting, together with £300 from the Jockey Club for two-year-olds sold by the firm. They have continued sponsorship of racing and in the mid-1980s backed the Middle Park Stakes, the race first promoted by Blenkiron. By 2002 the firm was adding money to 30 races worldwide culminating in the £100,000 Tattersalls Autumn Auction Stakes at Newmarket, open only to two-year-olds that had been sold the previous year at the Autumn Yearling Sale.

The modern period of sponsorship began in 1957. It was pioneered by Whitbread Brewers who, at the instigation of chairman Colonel Bill Whitbread, himself an amateur rider who had ridden in two Grand Nationals, put up money for the Whitbread Gold Cup at Sandown. The firm gained publicity, the course obtained funds, and National Hunt racing had a finale for its season. The longest established sponsored flat race, the John Smith's Magnet Cup began three years later. Others followed, particularly in jump racing where the lower level of prize money made less financial demands, but also on the flat as television coverage expanded and brought the sponsor's name to a wider audience. In 1984 the Classics became sponsored events and by 1989 almost all the 105 pattern races in Britain were sponsored, only Royal Ascot at that time remaining reluctant to dip its bucket into the new revenue stream. Sponsorship of races rose from £1.3 million (11.5 per cent of total prize money) in 1979 to £11.4 million in 1997 (18.9 per cent).

Not all sponsorship is at a major level. Smaller firms, who do not need national television coverage, can spend a few thousand pounds to gain local market exposure and to entertain clients. Nor need it be confined to a particular race or a particular course. A recent innovation has been the sponsoring of a series of races at several courses such as the Capel Cure Sharp Supreme Novices' Series at Cheltenham, Ascot, Sandown, Wetherby and Kempton. Most sponsorship has been by commercial firms but there have been instances coming from political groups, most notably the trade union NALGO, who, in 1989, sponsored the card at Market Rasen with race titles such as 'Help Your National Heath Service Hurdle'.

A substantial volume of sponsorship comes from within the industry itself. The Federation of Bloodstock Agents began a race sponsorship programme in 2001 and in 1997 Elite Racing, the country's largest racehorse owners' club, added £45,000 to the prize money for the Triumph Hurdle. The Tote also keeps its name to the fore. In 2002 it sponsored 29 races to the tune of over £15,000 each, including £162,000 to the Cheltenham Gold Cup, as well as adding money to the prize fund for many more minor events. Bookmakers too appreciate that racing is their golden goose and are prepared to feed it. In January 1999 Victor Chandler, the enterprising bookmaker, sponsored the whole card at an Ascot National Hunt meeting.

One area of sponsorship that proved controversial was that relating to jockeys. In 1998 the British Horseracing Board (BHB) agreed that riders could wear sponsorship logos on their breeches, but made this conditional on owners of the relevant horse also giving their permission. The Jockeys Association felt that this was an infringement of their earning rights as sponsors would be unlikely to come forward if there was no guarantee that the logo could be seen. On the other hand some owners were outraged at the suggestion that the jockey on their horse might be sponsored by a company with whom they would not wish to be associated. Gerald Leigh, a leading breeder, threatened to remove his horses from Britain if the BHB overruled an owner's right to veto his jockey's sponsorship deals. Although Victor Chandler's offer to sponsor a meeting at Ascot had been gratefully received, there was much less enthusiasm for his proposal in May 2000 to sponsor champion jockey, Kieren Fallon. Some owners simply objected to having a bookmaker's name emblazoned on the breeches of a jockey wearing their colours, but most of the media-led criticism focused on the danger to the image of racing if Fallon lost a race on which Chandler had laid special odds. Eventually Chandler withdrew the offer. No such objection was made against the Tote sponsorship of jockeys in general.

The danger with sponsorship is that it can be withdrawn. Business problems, new marketing directions or simply irritation with the recipients can end a relationship. No race or meeting has a divine right to be supported. In 1998 recruitment firm Pertemps dropped its sponsorship of the St Leger. Although the conventional platitudes were exchanged, many in racing felt that it was a show of pique by the managing director of the firm after the Doncaster stewards disqualified a horse running in the company's colours on which he stood to win £100,000. In 2000, to the surprise of many in racing Whitbread, the pioneers of racing sponsorship in the modern era, opted to pull out of the sport because they were now targeting drinkers aged 18–24, a demographic group not conspicuous at National Hunt races.

Sponsors are paying for publicity and expect the media to utilise their names. If this does not happen they might opt out. One area of conflict occurs when the sponsors have attached their names to longstanding events and the media have to choose between downgrading the traditional race names which are part of the sport's history and giving the commercial backer sufficient promotion. In many cases compromise with the print media has been reached via the use of different type faces and font sizes which emphasise the sponsor while the official racing publications retain the full title and maintain historical continuity. All this was in danger of being thrown away by a recent ill-advised attempt of the BHB to drastically increase the fee paid by newspapers for the right to print racecard data. It backfired when the press reacted by threatening to remove all sponsors' names from the titles of races. Martell, who had just increased its sponsorship of the Grand National meeting by 17 per cent, estimated that it could lose up to £2 million worth of publicity in press exposure and intimated that it would review the renewal of its contract. Racing could not afford to lose sponsorship, which in the early twenty-first century contributed over one-fifth of the sport's prize money.

Further reading

The Business of Racing: The Guide to Corporate Sponsorship (London: Sporting Life, 1990).

Stable staff

The lowest paid workers in the racing industry are the stable staff, yet without them there would be no sport. In 2000 the official weekly minimum wage of stable staff was just over £180, a low reward by any standards. One reason is that the industry as a whole is ill-financed and many smaller trainers would argue that they cannot afford to pay more. Some stable hands accept low wages because they like to work with horses; others because they have no skills transferable to other industries; and some because they have no skills at all. Wages have actually risen above the rate of inflation in the past decade, but the rise has mainly been self-financed via increased productivity; staff now look after three or four horses rather than two and sometimes work seven days a week. In 2000, aware that the restructuring of the fixture list would put new pressures on trainers and their staff, British Horseracing Board chairman Peter Savill set up a Stable Staff Resources Group to analyse the existing human resources and working practices in training yards. The report showed that low pay was ranked only third on the list of stable staff complaints, well behind 'too much racing' and 'too long hours'.

Most stable staff learn their trade on the job but formal practical training is available at the British Racing School at Newmarket. Established in 1983, the school is the only purpose-built training facility for horseracing staff in Britain. It offers a 9-week foundation course after which there is a guaranteed job in a trainer's yard: such is the shortage of labour in the industry. Any teenager weighing less than 9 st is eligible whether or not they have ever ridden a horse. For those with the aptitude further qualifications are available, though nearby Cambridge University might be surprised to know that the acronym for the Advanced Modern Apprenticeships is an MA! The facilities available at the School include a 2-furlong round all-weather gallop, a 7-furlong, straight all-weather and grass gallop, an indoor schooling area, equicisors and horse simulators. The youngsters wear radio headsets to receive instructions whilst riding and their performances are videoed for analysis. Stable staff courses are also available at the Northern Racing College near Doncaster.

Today more than half the workforce in the stables is female. Trainers appreciate (and exploit) their female workers because they love horses and are prepared to work long hours at menial tasks for little money simply to be with them. It is generally acknowledged that in many respects girls make better grooms than boys as they are considered quieter, more reliable and less likely to abuse a horse. Trainers also find them less militant. Susan Gallier, who worked as a stablehand in the 1980s in both France and Britain, felt that the girls received preferential treatment as they were paid the same rate as the boys but were rarely asked to deal with a rampant colt or unblock a stinking drain. That said, boys were also more likely to be called on to ride trial gallops, an aspect of the job that provides valuable experience for the budding jockey. This is because many trainers adhere to the view that the very qualities that make women such good exercise riders – lightness and gentleness of touch – work against them as jockeys where full control of mounts is vital. With the growing proportion of female labour in training yards, the genderless 'stable staff' has superseded 'stable lads'. But even in the old days it was an inappropriate title, covering as it did all manner of employees from striplings to grandfathers. Within the trade many women object to what they believe is the patronising use of the words 'lass' or 'girl'.

There are a few, but limited, opportunities for promotion up the stable hierarchy. The key figure among the staff is the head lad – the trainer's sergeant major – who has generally worked his way up and has become master of all equine trades, able to shoe a horse in the absence of a farrier, break in the yearlings, and organise the work of the stables. He takes charge during the trainer's absence. Larger establishments also have a travelling head lad who takes responsibility for the horses and staff away from the stables and can deputise for the trainer at the racecourse.

With so many small employers, collective action to improve conditions and wages has been difficult to organise. The Transport and General Workers Union first recruited stable staff in the 1930s when they had a drive for members from that other ill-paid set of rural workers, those who laboured in agriculture. Their aim was a minimum wage and one Sunday off in three. Newmarket trainers were willing to recognise the union but not their Lambourn counterparts who resisted negotiations. In 1969 about 10 per cent of lads were union members, a figure that had risen to 54 per cent by 1975 and encouraged the union to hold a strike. Unionism has assisted many stable staff to improve their living and working conditions, but these workers still remain bottom of the heap in the racing industry and financially are worse off than most other employees in the country.

Yet many persevere. Mucking out at 5.30 in the morning is not much fun, but shortly afterwards on the gallops the lad riding work can assume sole control of a horse worth a six figure sum. Moreover, every year brings fresh hope that this might be the season that they get to look after a horse that goes on to win a big race with the consequent financial reward and social kudos.

Further reading

Barnes, S., *Horsesweat and Tears* (London: Heinemann Kingswood, 1988).
Cassidy, R., *The Sport of Kings* (Cambridge: Cambridge University Press, 2002).
Gallier, S., *One of the Lads* (London: Stanley Paul, 1988).
www.northernracingcollege.co.uk
www.brs.org.uk

See also Apprentices, Strikes.

Starting

One of the hardest worked officials at the 1857 Derby was the recall man stationed down the track to signal a false start. Twelve times that year he had to stand and wave his flag as the jockeys, impatient to be off in the Epsom Classic, drove their mounts forward ahead of the starter's call. Starting was not an easy task in the days before stalls and tapes when the starter had to rely on shouting 'go', waving a flag and keeping the jockeys in order by force of personality and the imposition of fines and suspensions. For most of the nineteenth century there was no draw for position at the start and jockeys tried to grab any place they could. In traditional long-distance races this scarcely mattered – there is still no draw in National Hunt racing – but in shorter events starting positions could be crucial. At Croydon on 2 June 1871, one race was delayed by 45 minutes and another was abandoned after over an hour of aggravation. Two jockeys were suspended for almost a year for their behaviour.

Even when a starting gate – a cable that stretched across the track and was operated by a lever – was introduced in 1897 the starter still faced problems. He had to keep the horses in line to prevent one being left or allowing a jockey to steal a flying start. Experienced jockeys, however, learned to anticipate the rise of the tapes by observing the mannerisms and arm movements of the starters. Nevertheless the Jockey Club, appreciative of its advantages, made it compulsory for all races in 1902. Starting stalls, which further equalised chances at the beginning of a race, arrived in 1965. They were first used at Newmarket in a race won by Lester Piggott, a jockey later to be seriously injured in a stalls accident when his horse squeezed under the barriers.

Starting stalls are used for all flat races except when adverse conditions such as high winds or heavy going might make them impractical or unsafe. Standard stalls come in ten-bay units that are manoeuvred around the racecourse by a fleet of specially modified Land Rovers. This and the transportation of the stalls to the next meeting is organised by Racetech Services, the company that is also responsible for the photo-finish and other on-course technical equipment. After being formally displayed in the parade ring, horses are cantered to the stalls where they come under the authority of the starter. They are checked against the list of runners and riders with the starter calling a roll that in flat racing also serves to remind each jockey of his place in the draw. The horses are loaded into the stalls; odd numbers first then even ones. Once the starter is satisfied a white flag is raised to signal to spectators that the horses are 'under orders' and from that time all bets stand. Even those on Fetchinni, a horse that collapsed and died in the stalls at York in 1992 prior to the off in the Micklegate Selling Stakes: a dead cert only to the bookmakers! Before the runners enter the stalls, all the front gates are locked by spring loaded latches linked to an electrical system. Once all the runners are installed and the rear gates closed, the starter presses the electrical release mechanism that unfastens the latches on each gate simultaneously. Or it should. On rare occasions one set of stalls has lagged behind the other in opening, leading to demands from some irate owners and punters that the race should be declared void. That was the result at Worcester on 9 October 1979 when the starter despatched the horses before the appointed time. The 2.00 o'clock race started 30 seconds after the hour according to his watch, which he had set by the clock in the weighing room. Unfortunately that clock was fast and the race began 43 seconds early, only marginal but sufficient to have the race nullified.

Most problems at the start are equine rather than technical. At each meeting the stalls are supported by a team of at least eight professional horse handlers whose function is to lead the horses into the stalls as rapidly and efficiently as possible. Sometimes this takes a deal of pushing from behind. If a horse completely refuses to enter the stalls or if it misbehaves when in them, it has to take a stalls test before being allowed to race again. This involves being loaded by no more than one handler in front and two behind and then having to stand in the stalls for a minute without becoming unruly.

Former nineteenth-century jockey Henry Custance must feature in any honour roll of starters as he remains the only man to have ridden in the Derby (he won it on three occasions in 1860, 1866 and 1874) and also to have started it (in 1885). So too should recently retired Jockey Club starter, Gerry Scott who is the National Hunt equivalent of Custance, having won a Grand National (on Merryman II in 1960) and later started several. Pride of place, however, belongs to Alec Marsh. He was a leading amateur rider for three consecutive seasons from 1934/35 but gave up riding in 1940 after a fall too many. He had ridden in over 1,000 races, winning 163 of them, including 21 on the flat. At one stage the National Hunt Committee, anxious to protect the livelihood of paid riders, counselled him to turn professional himself but he ignored their advice. Under the existing Jockey Club regulations this would have prevented him pursuing a career as a racing official. On demobilisation from the RAF after the Second World War, he acted as a starter for the Royal Calcutta Turf Club before returning to Britain to be appointed an official starter by the Jockey Club in 1947. He officiated at his first Classic in 1952 and in that year also became the senior starter for the Club. A further 100 Classic starts were to come before his retirement in 1972 after a career in which he presided over 25,000 races.

Further reading

www.racetech.co.uk

Starting price

Most off-course punters rely on the starting price for the odds at which their winning bets will be paid out. Until 2000 two reporters, working independently, noted opening prices offered by on-course bookmakers and later market movements. They then met to decide at what odds the horses actually started. At major meetings four men worked in different sections of the betting ring. This continues but a Quality Control Inspector now manages the operation.

The concept of a starting price originated in the late nineteenth century when Valentine and Wright, a Farringdon Street, London bookmaking firm who were members of Tattersall's and the Newmarket Settling Rooms, circulated their clientele stating that their bets would be governed by the returns shown in the *Sporting Life*. The idea caught on as a form of guarantee to bettor and bookmaker alike. It was formalised in 1926 when the *Sporting Life* (now having taken over *Bell's Life in London* and *The Sportsman)* agreed to work with its remaining competitor, the *Sporting Chronicle*, to examine the odds offered at the course and, when they disagreed, accepting that an average of their views would be struck. When the *Sporting Chronicle* closed the *Press Association* took over and was joined by the Mirror Group (publishers of the *Racing Post*) on the demise of the *Sporting Life*. This composite return was to everyone's advantage in the industry.

Until the 1980s the agreed figures were given to the Exchange Telegraph Service (generally called Extel) for transmission around the country but from 1987 the contract went to Satellite Information Services. The underlying assumption is that the course bookmakers are operating in a competitive market so that their odds genuinely reflect the betting patterns on the day. Hence the observers look for the broad picture of betting rather than any special prices being offered by individual bookmakers. The big bookmakers have suggested that the starting price ought to reflect the actual betting taking place not just that on the course. In fact they often transfer money laid in their betting shops to the course for this purpose. With the possibilities of instant nationwide computerised communication, that day may not be far away.

Odds declared such as 11–10, 5–4, 13–8 are hangovers from the pre-decimal currency days when 8 half-crowns, 10 florins (2-shilling pieces) or 20 shillings made up a pound and represent the odds to certain proportions of the old currency. Yet within these bookmaking odds lurks the apparently anomalous 100–30. However, this too is explicable in terms of £.s.d. as it represents a bookmaker offering £5 (100 shillings) to someone staking £1.50 (30 shillings). Not all the old odds survived decimalisation: the betting market has rid itself of 100–6, 100–7 and 100–8 which have been rounded respectively to 16–1, 14–1 and 12–1.

See also Betting shops.

Steeplechasing and steeplechasers

It cannot be very heartening for a jump jockey approaching Becher's Brook to realise that at the moment of take-off, his mount is jumping blind. The horse can see the obstacle clearly with both eyes as it approaches but its own head eventually obscures the jump and it leaps from memory, like a plane becoming airborne on instruments only. If eighteenth-century horsemen knew that their animals lacked vision at such crucial times, they should be considered either exceedingly brave or extremely foolhardy to have devised the sport of steeplechasing. If they were not aware of the eye failings of their horses, it is perhaps just as well or the jumps branch of racing may never have developed.

Said to have originated in Ireland in the 1750s, the notion of racing horses across country, jumping obstacles along the way, derived from the hunting field. The first recorded race was held over 8 miles in 1792 between three gentlemen in Leicestershire, and 1810 saw another for bona fide hunters staged over a specially designed 3-mile course at Bedford. Although matches and similar races were sometimes arranged, especially between army officers, the first serious attempt to organise a commercial jump race had to wait until 1830. Thomas Coleman of the Turf Hotel, St Albans, is credited with establishing the St Albans or Hertfordshire Steeplechase over 4 miles with 12 st weights.

During the next few years the race, over ploughed fields and several brooks, attracted numerous runners, large crowds and 'professional' riders such as Captain Martin Becher and Jem Mason, later of Grand National fame. By 1836, however, the idea of steeplechases had spread to many other parts and the St Albans race fell into decline; in the early 1840s, over 60 other meetings were recorded from Chatham to Cheltenham.

Although its popularity waxed and waned over the following decades, certain important features developed. Races increasingly took place on and around established racecourses instead of across open country. Liverpool, venue for the original Grand National in the 1830s, came to be seen as the major steeplechase meeting and its famous race attracted countrywide interest. Perhaps most significantly the first National Hunt Committee was formed in 1866, with the approval of the Jockey Club, to govern the affairs of the sport. During its first 50 years it set about the task of bringing order to an area of racing in which disreputable practices had grown as fast as the size of fences had fallen. Even the Aintree course in Liverpool had been criticised for allowing its obstacles to be scaled down. The committee therefore brought in rules, some of which still exist, stipulating that there should be at least twelve fences in the first 2 miles of a steeplechase with a further 6 for each additional mile, and setting out measurements for ditches and water jumps. Two years later it appointed an Inspector of National Hunt courses to try to ensure that fences throughout the country were fairly uniform.

Regulations today state that plain steeplechase fences must not be less than 4 ft 6 in high. They are wooden-framed, packed with birch and fronted with a painted wooden strip which acts as a guideline for take-off. Open ditches have a low rail on the near side to aid jumping. The third type of obstacle, a water jump, used to be a mandatory feature but many courses no longer contain this particular hazard. The jumps on the Grand National course at Aintree are different, constructed from hawthorn, dressed with spruce or gorse – this forms the debris scattered around after the field has crashed through the barrier.

Towards the end of the nineteenth century there were nearly three times as many jump courses as there had been 50 years earlier – 176 in 1886. Most, whether organised by a local hunt, cavalry officers or the commercial sponsors of the new enclosed courses such as Sandown and Kempton Parks, were annual events. Prize money remained poor in comparison with flat racing and the amateur ethos was perpetuated by gentlemen riders for longer and more widely than in the older branch of the sport. Another major difference was the lack of prestigious races comparable with the Classics or what would now be called Pattern races. The first half of the annual steeplechase programme was a mundane affair. The climax of the season then as now arrived in March with the Liverpool Spring Meeting, featuring the Grand National, and the Grand Military Meeting at Sandown at which the main contest was the Grand Military Gold Cup. Racing also took place at Cheltenham where the most prestigious race from 1911 onwards was the National Hunt Chase, worth £1,285 in 1924, the inaugural year of the Gold Cup (worth only £685). In the beginning, the Gold Cup was viewed as little more than a trial for Aintree.

There were fewer outstanding horses in the first half of the twentieth century to capture the attention of the general public simply because there were insufficient competitive top-class races, and some of the great chasers sought additional prizes abroad. Jerry M, a big Irish horse, was twice sent to France for the Grand Steeplechase de Paris; second in 1909, he won the race in 1910, the year in which he was second in the Grand National. He finally captured the Aintree marathon in 1912. Another Irish champion, Troytown, won the Grand Prix in 1919 as a six-year-old, the Grand National at seven and tragically died in a fall a few months later at Auteuil. Reynoldstown became the first horse to win the Grand National in two consecutive years (1935 and 1936) since The Colonel 66 years earlier while Easter Hero was the first to win the relatively new Cheltenham Gold Cup twice in 1929 and 1930. Allotted 12 st 7 lb in the 1930 Grand National, he finished a gallant second to Gregalach. The horse who fired the public imagination most, however, was Golden Miller (see separate entry), successful five times at Cheltenham but only once at Aintree in spite of several attempts.

The 3-mile King George VI Chase first took place at Kempton Park in 1937 but it was run only twice before the war intervened. It resumed in 1947 and was won the following year by Cottage Rake, the year in which he took the first of his three Cheltenham Gold Cups. Fifteen years later, opportunities for steeplechasers to compete in quality races had multiplied with the arrival of televised racing and sponsorship. The Whitbread Gold Cup at Sandown over 3 miles 5 furlongs was the first commercially sponsored race, in 1957, and it was followed by the Mackeson Gold Cup over $2\frac{1}{2}$ miles at Cheltenham in 1960, where a 2-mile Champion Chase (now the Queen Mother Champion Chase) was first held in 1959. With the Hennessy Cognac Gold Cup of 3 miles 2 furlongs run for the first time in 1960 at Newbury and the 2-mile Tote Gold Trophy staged from 1963, the jumping year began to take on a shape which was eventually formed into a pattern in imitation of the flat-race season.

The expansion of National Hunt racing produced heroes beyond the Grand National. Mandarin was one of the first, a winner of the Hennessy and King George VI Chase in 1957 (and the latter again in 1959) as well as the Cheltenham Gold Cup and the Grand Steeple-Chase de Paris in 1962. Mill House was the Gold Cup and King George winner in 1963, but then came Arkle (see separate entry), a horse that carried everything before him for three years to 1966. Mill House, gallant loser to his Irish rival on many occasions, finally outstayed him on the racecourse, winning the Whitbread as his swansong in 1967. Flyingbolt was another jumper unfortunate enough to be racing in the Arkle era. He was the champion novice chaser of 1964/65, won what is now the Queen Mother Champion Chase in 1966 and was third in the Champion Hurdle the following day! He then took the Irish Grand National under 12 stones 7 pounds but his achievements were always overshadowed by those of Arkle. He was struck down by brucellosis at the end of that year and never recovered his former brilliance.

In the past 35 years, the National Hunt Festival at Cheltenham has come to dominate the jumps season, and the Cheltenham Gold Cup has become the coveted prize. Consequently the winners of this race, rightly or wrongly, have been identified as champions. Those who have additionally captured a race such as the King George VI Chase may deserve the title, horses such as Captain Christy from the 1970s, Burrough Hill Lad from the 1980s, The Fellow from the 1990s and most recently Best Mate. Desert Orchid (see separate entry) and See More Business are two more who have done this double but it is now uncommon for Gold Cup winners to have a crack at the Grand National, as Golden Miller did, in 1934 and very rare to be successful. The only other horse to have won both was L'Escargot, twice Gold Cup winner in 1970 and 1971 and the 'villain' that prevented Red Rum from winning three Nationals in succession in 1975. Garrison Savannah came close to achieving both victories in one year (1991) but was beaten on the run-in to the winning post at Aintree, like so many tired horses before him.

Further reading

Harman, B., *The Ultimate Dream. 75 Years of the Tote Cheltenham Gold Cup* (Edinburgh: Mainstream, 2000).
Seth-Smith, M. *et al.*, *The History of Steeplechasing* (London: Joseph, 1966).

Stoute, Sir Michael (1945–)

Michael Stoute has been one of the most successful and consistent trainers in Britain over the past 30 years. He won his first trainers' championship in 1981, his most recent in 2003; he trained his first Classic winner, Fair Salinia, in the 1978 Oaks, his latest North Light in the 2004 Derby. In between he has been leading trainer on five further occasions and has developed a reputation for bringing out the best in older horses.

He arrived in Britain from Barbados in 1965 to work in the Yorkshire stables of Pat Rohan before spells as assistant to Doug Smith and Tom Jones at Newmarket, where he acquired his own yard in 1972. Over the next few years, he won a variety of top races from the six-furlong Stewards' Cup with Alphadamus in 1973 to the $2\frac{1}{2}$ mile Ascot Gold Cup with Shangamuzo in 1978. His first winner, Sandal, had been owned by his father but by 1981 he was training for the Aga Khan, whose great horse, Shergar, won the Derby, Irish Derby and King George that year, helping Stoute to achieve his first trainers' title. His second, in 1986, came partly as a result of the same owner's Shahrastani, winner of both the Epsom and Irish Derbys, and partly thanks to Sheikh Mohammed's Sonic Lady, winner of the Irish One Thousand Guineas, Coronation Stakes, Sussex Stakes and Prix du Moulin. He has maintained a successful relationship with the Maktoum family over many years, sending out such Classic winners as Unite in the Epsom and Irish Oaks of 1987 and Musical Bliss, One Thousand Guineas winner in 1989, the year in which he was champion trainer for the third time. He even trained Sheikh Mohammed's Kribensis to win the Champion Hurdle in 1990 and he has recently handled the Queen's best horses; Blueprint won the Group Two Jockey Club Stakes in 2000.

Although he has been responsible for twelve English Classic victories, including consecutive Two Thousand Guineas winners King's Best (2000) and Golan (2001), and is the only twentieth-century trainer to win a Classic in five successive seasons (1985–89), it is his record with older horses which has enhanced his reputation in recent years. He kept Sheikh Mohammed's Opera House in training as a five-year-old and won the Coronation Cup, the Eclipse Stakes and the King George in 1993, taking the leading trainers' title for the fourth time. In 1996 and 1997 the earnings of Singspiel and Pilsudski justified their training costs as four and five-year-olds – between them they won the Japan Cup twice, the Breeders' Cup Turf, the Dubai World Cup and six European Group One races, enabling Stoute to claim the trainers' championship yet again in 1997. (Pilsudski was also runner-up twice in the Arc and once in the King George.)

Renowned for his meticulous attention to detail and extraordinary memory – he can apparently identify all of his 200-odd charges at sight – Michael Stoute has the knack of keeping horses in form for several seasons. This, together with adventurous programming for his stable strings, mark him out as a trainer of great talent. Recent successes from his Freemason Lodge base have included a second Breeders' Cup Turf in 2000 with Kalanisi, the year of his fifth trainers' championship, and the 2002 King George with Golan. His triumphant 2003 season saw not only two Classic winners in Kris Kin (Derby) and Russian Rhythm (One Thousand Guineas) but the first British success in the Breeders' Cup Filly and Mare with Islington. He ended the year as top trainer yet again. His knighthood, however, bestowed in 1998, is not an acknowledgement of his success in horseracing, but for services to tourism in his native Barbados.

Further reading

Magee, S., *Channel Four Racing Complete A–Z of Horse Racing* (London: Channel 4 Books, 2001).

Strikes

In June 1975 several hundred thousand pounds worth of races were almost disrupted over a matter of a mere £1.47. Both Newmarket Classic days were the focus of industrial action by local stable lads. They had been refused a pay rise of £1.47 a week by the Newmarket Trainers' Federation, which argued that many owners would not stand for the resultant rise in training fees. The response of the lads was, first, to come out on strike – though sufficient stayed at work to allow the training centre to continue to function – and, second, to picket the approaches and entrances to the course and, more significantly, to interfere with the racing itself. In the race preceding the One Thousand Guineas they blocked the Rowley Mile and, when jockey Willie Carson approached, he was dragged from his mount. Nearby racegoers and trainers went to his aid and there was an ugly but brief incident labelled by the press, both tabloid and broadsheet, as 'The Battle of Newmarket'. Two days later, the morning of the Two Thousand Guineas revealed that 15 holes had been made in the track with a bulldozer 'borrowed' from construction work on the Newmarket Bypass. These were repaired but as the horses were being loaded into the stalls, a group of strikers sat down across the course. Mounted policemen and dog handlers quickly cleared them away. The strike continued but there were no further attempts to disrupt the meetings, though televised racing ceased because cameramen sympathised with the lads. On their return to work 71 strikers were handed their cards. A pay rise was awarded at arbitration but wages remained below those of agricultural workers.

This was not the first time that stable staff had gone on strike. Those at Lambourn had participated in a strike for improved wages in 1936 and in 1960 they came out in support of apprentices who protested about the deplorable living conditions in Heath House, a hostel owned by the Jockey Club and leased to the Newmarket Trainers' Federation to house 75 apprentices.

Only three times have jockeys held premeditated strikes and in two of these actual racing was not involved. In May 2002 while negotiations were taking place between the Racecourse Association (RCA) and broadcasting companies over media rights Britain's riders, on the advice of the Jockeys Association, refused to be interviewed on racing's new television service, the Attheraces channel. Their grumble was not with the television group, who had actually sponsored the Association's Lester awards night only ten days before, but with the RCA over what share the Jockeys Association should receive from the rights contract. A collective refusal to talk in front of the cameras had also occurred in March 1988 when, once more on the advice of their association, no member agreed to be interviewed about the new whipping regulations. The Association wanted to ensure that no conflicting opinions were aired whilst they protested to the Jockey Club. The only dispute to affect racing came in 2003 when the Jockey Club banned jockeys from using mobile phones at the racetrack on the grounds of security. In response, till more moderate proposals were mooted, jockeys refused to ride and two meetings were cancelled.

Most confrontations involving jockeys have been flashpoint combinations of riders on safety issues, as when they refused to race at Brighton in 1981, Beverley in 1989 and at Haydock in 1996 because of what they judged to be dangerous conditions. Following a serious accident at Brighton from which apprentice Joe Blanks died, jockeys refused to ride there unless the size of fields was reduced to a number they thought safe. The stewards agreed to limit runners to 16 instead of the 21 declared. At Beverley the riders had actually gone down to the start but 5 of the 11 then refused to race. They were subsequently fined between £250 and £750. At Haydock the clerk of the course had warned that a bend could only be negotiated safely by racing on a strip of ground barely the width of two horses. After the first race in which several horses slipped, senior jockeys asked for the course to be inspected. Although it was passed fit, not one of the 21 riders ventured out of the weighing room for the second race and the meeting was abandoned. This time the jockeys escaped any penalty because the course officials had failed to follow correct procedures.

Surprisingly, in view of the low level of prize money at some courses, owners have rarely gone on strike, but, in 1992, in protest at the 'despicable' offering at Fontwell, Ken Higson and Barney Curley withdrew their horses, both of them favourites, at the off. The public protest cost them – and their jockeys – Jockey Club fines of £1,500. In 2003 the Racehorse Owners' Association called for strike action against racecourses which regularly failed to come up with adequate prizemoney, but it was rapped over the knuckles by the Office of Fair Trading who said that an organised boycott would be unlawful. Owners do have the easier option of not entering races and letting the lack of runners act as a signal to the course executives. Bookmakers went on strike in 1926 in protest at the imposition of a betting duty, but not for long; there was too much money to be made even with tax!

Industrial action outside racing has occasionally impacted on the sport. In 1921 railway and transport workers came out in sympathy with striking coal miners, and the government banned racing as a temporary measure to ease travel problems. The General Strike of 1926 led to the abandonment of meetings at Bath, Catterick, Doncaster, Haydock, Kempton Park, Newmarket, Ripon and Salisbury. In 1955 the Royal Ascot meeting was transferred from June to July because of a national rail strike (and the consequent state of emergency declared by the government). A lesser delay – just 55 minutes – occurred at Haydock in 1989 because one of the ambulance crews refused to work during a national dispute and this compromised the safety of the riders.

Further reading

Hill, C.R., *Horse Power: The Politics of the Turf* (Manchester: Manchester University Press, 1988).

Sunday racing

Sunday is traditionally the big race day across Europe and British racing professionals have journeyed to compete in France, Belgium and Germany for many years. When Sunday racing began in Ireland in 1985, leaving Britain as the only major European state outside the Sunday racing circuit, it seemed that change was only a matter of time. But although a Jockey Club working party reported in its favour in 1987 and an attempt was made in 1988 to introduce a Private Member's Bill in the House of Commons, advocating races on a limited number of Sundays each year, it was 26 July 1992 before Doncaster racecourse opened its gates to the first British Sunday race crowd. At 23,000, it was said to be larger than the number of paying spectators at that summer's Derby.

Opposition to Sunday racing had arisen not only from religious quarters but from sections of the general public and the racing industry itself, unhappy at the extension to working hours. The campaign to liberalise Sunday trading laws paved the way for change in racing but the flat meeting at Doncaster and the first Sunday jump meeting at Cheltenham in November 1992 both took place without on-course betting facilities. It was 1995 before changes to the law allowed the opening of betting shops and racecourse betting outlets at Sunday race meetings, 12 of which were scheduled that year. Since then the quality of racing has ranged from the One Thousand Guineas at Newmarket, the first English Classic to be run on a Sunday in May 1995, and the Ascot Festival in September to mundane programmes at lesser courses, where the emphasis has been on family entertainment. There are now over 130 Sunday fixtures scheduled for 2004, nearly double the figure for 2003.

The response to Sunday racing has been mixed. Generally large crowds, often of first-time racegoers with children, have pleased racecourse managers with an eye on the spectators of the future, but low betting turnover has upset bookmakers.

Trainers have been faced with staffing problems and the higher costs of Sunday racing while the attitude of the British Horseracing Board (BHB) to Sunday racing has been one of active promotion and wholehearted approval. In the face of opposition from within the industry, it sanctioned 14 consecutive Sunday race days during the summers of 2000 and 2001, resulting in an unbroken sequence of 104 days racing. This pattern was not repeated in 2002 when three blank Sundays were introduced during the summer. However, while recognising the burden placed on stable workforces, the BHB has now extended the Sunday programme to 47 days in the year.

It is not difficult to see why. Every year has seen increases in attendance, off-course betting and racecourse profitability. The BHB is particularly keen to attract women and children to the racecourse, and sees enormous benefit to the industry from providing racing as part of a package of family entertainment. The promotion of Sunday racing therefore tends to feature opportunities for picnicking, the provision of free child entry and creche facilities, and a carnival atmosphere, with music, bouncing castles and bungee jumping, summed up in the race title, The 'Family Sunday is Funday' Selling Handicap Hurdle Race at Market Rasen in August 1999. Sometimes it would appear that the wheel has turned full circle, with the racing of horses as a sideshow, much as it would have been on eighteenth-century fair days and local holidays. If racing authorities view their product as part of the burgeoning leisure industry, competing with many alternative weekend entertainments, the present fixture list and the packaging of Sunday racing is undoubtedly here to stay.

Superstition

Although generally the best horse on the day wins the race, luck can play a part in determining the result: a rein can snap, a rival can be brought down, or a gap can miraculously appear in the equine traffic. This has led some participants to adopt superstitions to secure good luck or prevent bad luck affecting their performance. Some like jockey Peter Scudamore had a 'lucky' parking spot at Ascot; others like trainer David Nicolson always wore red socks after similar garb brought him success in the 1963 Triumph Hurdle; yet others will wear charms and talismans, eat the same meal, or have a certain routine that must be followed. In taking such rituals on board racing is no different from other sports. Although there is no evidence that any of these superstitions influence luck, they may assist athletes psychologically to be in the right frame of mind to perform. Following the same pattern of behaviour before an event is a common form of ritual in many sports and makes sense if they are connected with past success, as it is a means of thinking positively. Athletes who employ pre-match rituals are providing themselves with behaviours that can convince them that they are confident, motivated and ready to perform. Superstitious behaviours are also a way of controlling pre-contest anxiety and giving the athlete something specific to focus on over which they have some control. In some cases, the superstition is used as a means of focusing and enhancing mental arousal, while in others it is viewed as a means of dissipating anxiety and helping to relax the athlete. However, in racing this can relate only to jockeys as trainers and owners cannot influence what is happening on the track and horses, so far as is known, are not aware of the concept of luck.

Nevertheless owners continue to believe that their behaviour can affect events. Ian Bryant, breeder of 1999 Cheltenham Gold Cup winner, See More Business, never backed the horse believing that it would bring bad luck. He was so superstitious that he would go behind the grandstand with his fingers in his ears so as to avoid knowing how the horse was progressing during a race. Others have believed in celestial influence. Lord Wavertree, the man who presented Britain with its National Stud, was a firm believer in the use of astrology in horseracing. He required his stud employers to note the exact minute that a foal was born and then had an elaborate horoscope prepared so that the propitious times for racing the animal could be determined. The stars sometimes lied as they led him to sell Prince Palatine who went on to win the St Leger and two Ascot Gold Cups.

Many gamblers believe in luck and those involved in racing are no different. Some hope that luck can be transferred between individuals and the lad who looked after Red Rum, winner of three Grand Nationals, often enjoyed hospitality from those who looked forward to his luck rubbing off on them. There is no evidence of such a transfer! Another superstition without foundation is that it is unlucky to change the name of a horse; hence Grey of Fallodon remained Grey of Falloden when it was misspelled in the horse's initial registration.

Further reading

Wann, D., *Sport Psychology* (Upper Saddle, NJ: Prentice-Hall,1997).

Moneybox

Santa Claus won both the English and Irish Derbys in 1964. Favourite for both races (15–8 and 4–7), he picked up a cool £125,000 (£1.5 million now) within four weeks.

Scoop 6 is a weekly Tote bet that requires punters to predict the winners of six nominated Saturday races.

Shergar and **Sir Ivor** are the only two odds-on favourites to win the Derby since 1946; at 10–11 Shergar was the shortest priced winner of the race in the twentieth century. Sir Ivor was sent off at 4–5.

Spotters are used at bloodstock sales to assist the auctioneers by pointing out bidders that they might not see immediately. They also present the 'acknowledgement of purchase' form to the buyer.

The connections of **Storming Home** paid £24,000 to supplement him for the Champion Stakes at Newmarket in 2002. It was worth the money as he won the race and £245,920.

Syndication is the term for dividing ownership of a stallion at stud into shares between numbers of breeders.

A day at the races 2000

Off to the races today. Got enough money? Entry to Tatts £10; might upgrade to the Members for another fiver but better change out of these jeans or I won't get in. Parking? Could be free; probably covered in the admission charge. Take a couple of quid just in case. Copy of *Racing Post*. That's another pound but can't do without it. No good trying to search the web for betting tips on the laptop at the track. Not sure about buying a racecard. Matter of principle. Not paying £2 for all that advertising. They should be free. But they are useful; masses of info about the course and what's going on. Okay, then I'll have one. A man of flexible principles that's me! Cash for betting? Bookies are okay for the big bets, especially if you can shade the odds down the line. But no strong fancy, so might stick with the Tote. Chat up the lady in red at the same time. Two quid's a woman's bet but I'll need about a tenner a race. Should get some of that back. I'm no mug punter choosing the pretty colours and horses that remind you of holidays and better times. Rely on the advice of the experts is my motto. Wonder why they write for the papers if they can pick winners. Eating and drinking? Lot better than it used to be. When I think of the stuff I've eaten in my time! Burgers made out of beaten favourites and burned as much as the punters that backed them. Might have a good lunch and miss the first. Probably only an apprentice race. Pity there aren't more like Wolverhampton. Okay, it's a glorified dog track but on a Saturday night you can eat and watch the races at the same time. Can't do that at Sandown. Not even a telly in view at some of the tables.

* * *

Going to the races today. Never been before. It's pretty confusing. Saw the advert offering a free bet if I came by train. But then there were no buses from the station so that was a taxi fare. Then I had no idea where to go in. I can cope with 'stalls', 'dress circle' or 'balcony' at the theatre but what is Tattersalls? Clearly I'm not a member so I opted for the Silver Ring as it sounded pretty. Big mistake. A run-down concrete enclosure with more weeds than people. And, I was so far from the winning post that if it hadn't been for the commentary I would have had no idea what had won. At least at the theatre – even in the Gods – you get a good view of the stage. I wanted to see the jockeys getting on board but the man said where was my badge. Only a couple of bookmakers there but lots next door. Asked one for my free bet but he just laughed.

Horsebox

Theatreworld was second in the Champion Hurdle on three consecutive occasions, first to Make a Stand in 1997, and twice to Istabraq (1998 and 1999).

The Dikler made seven appearances in the Cheltenham Gold Cup between 1970 and 1976, finishing third in 1971 and 1972, second in 1974, and first in 1973.

Tied Cottage was first past the post in the Cheltenham Gold Cup in 1980 but was disqualified after testing positive for a banned substance, thought to have been picked up from contaminated feed.

Time Charter won the 1982 Oaks, the last English Classic winner to be partnered by an apprentice jockey, Billy Newnes; she also has the distinction of winning a Group One race in three consecutive seasons, taking the King George in 1983 and the Coronation Cup in 1984.

The **Tote Gold Trophy**, run at Newbury in February, was abandoned nine times in 23 years because of bad weather (1969–91).

Touching Wood (1982) is the last horse to have won the English and Irish St Legers in the same year – it is possible to win them in consecutive years because the Irish race is also open to four-year-olds.

Tattersall family

The Tattersall family created the greatest bloodstock auction house in the world. Still in existence after over 200 years, it remained in family control for more than a century and three-quarters. They also gave their name to a betting area at British racecourses and to the rules under which racetrack betting takes place. Richard (1724–95), founder of the firm, became head ostler at Beevor's Repository in St. Martin's Lane, London. From there he moved to become stud-groom, and later possibly Master of Horse, for the Duke of Kingston.

By 1766 he had accumulated sufficient funds to purchase a 99-year lease from Lord Grosvenor of a property at Hyde Park Corner, where he set up as a horse and hound auctioneer. The business boomed, partly because of his reputation for integrity but also through his cultivation of potential clients with dinners and other hospitality. In 1780 he added subscription rooms which became the site for the making and settling of bets by the higher echelons of the racing fraternity. He also ventured into thoroughbred horse ownership, most spectacularly with the purchase for £2,500 from Lord Bolingbroke of the unbeaten Highflyer, who became champion sire 12 times. Richard proved to be an astute businessman and took Tattersalls to a commanding position among British bloodstock auctioneers.

By 1784 the firm was advertising itself as 'Tattersall and Son' and two years before his death Richard had begun the process of transferring the control of the firm to his only son Edmund. Far more cultured than his father, thanks to extensive continental tours, Edmund (1758–1810), a man of good looks and charming manner, was more interested in hunting than auctioneering, though he had a solid grounding in, and understanding of, the family business. Perhaps his wisest decision was to bring his eldest son Richard (1785–1859) into partnership in 1806. Of his two other sons, George (1792–1853) managed the firm's stud and Edmund junior (1789–1851) became a partner in the firm but never played a prominent role.

Richard took command on his father's death and within a decade the firm became paramount in the world of bloodstock auctioneering, with sales to the continent increasing and the development of annual yearling sales for some of the major studs. 'Old Dick', as he was known to distinguish himself from his son (also called Richard) was responsible for the expansion of the firm's activities to include sales at Doncaster and Hampton Court. Although he disapproved of heavy gambling – as a deeply religious man he never bet himself – he opened new subscription rooms in 1815 at The Corner where gambling debts could be settled.

The business was taken over by 'Old Dick's' elder son, Richard (1812–70), who had been a partner since 1840. Under his stewardship the firm moved to Albert Gate at Knightsbridge, following the expiry of the Hyde Park Corner lease. At the end of the 1860s he was instrumental in bringing in the first non-family partner, Thomas Pain, who developed a market for hunters and hounds in the Midland Shires. 'Old Dick's' other son, George (1817–49), did not enter the family business, instead achieving moderate fame as an artist, publishing engravings of racehorses and illustrating Nimrod's *Hunting Reminiscences*, and as an architect specialising in stables, kennels and other sporting buildings. For a brief period in the mid-1840s he also edited the *Sporting Magazine*. Richard's marriage was childless and control of Tattersalls fell to his cousin Edmund (1816–98). He set himself up as an independent horse auctioneer at Newmarket before being offered a partnership in the family firm in 1851. When he died in 1898 Tattersalls were responsible for 72 per cent of all bloodstock sold at auction in England.

Edmund's eldest son, Edmund Somerville (1863–1942), then became the last Tattersall to direct the firm. He became a partner in Tattersalls in 1885 and was later assisted by his younger brothers Harry George (partner 1891) and Rupert Reeve (partner 1901), though the former, fond of drink and careless with money, resigned from the firm in 1905 after a quarrel with Edmund, a man with a strict sense of decorum. Rupert lost a leg in the First World War and retired from the firm in 1919. A third brother, Richard Brooke, was not taken into partnership but sent to America to establish a branch of the business there, but he proved ineffective and died in comparative poverty in New Orleans. By the outbreak of the Second World War much of the auctioneering and direction of the farm has passed to non-family members and when the unmarried Edmund died on 26 October 1942, after a series of small strokes, dynastic control of the great auction house ended.

Further reading

Orchard, V., *Tattersalls: Two Hundred Years of Sporting History* (London: Hutchinson, 1953).
Willett, P., *The Story of Tattersalls* (London: Stanley Paul, 1987).

See also Sales.

Taylor, Alec (1862–1943)

Labelled by the racing scribes as 'The Wizard of Manton', Alec Taylor trained the winners of 21 Classics and headed the list of winning trainers 12 times, a record for the twentieth century, including 7 consecutive seasons from 1917. He came from a family of trainers. His grandfather, Thomas Taylor, had been private trainer to Lord Chesterfield and his father, also Alec, won 12 Classics, beginning with the Derby (Teddington) and the One Thousand Guineas (Aphrodite) in 1851 and ending with Rêve d'Or's double of the One Thousand Guineas and Oaks in 1887. On his father's death in 1894 Alec and his older half-brother took over the running of the Manton stables near Marlborough in Wiltshire, Alec taking full control in 1902. In that year he saddled the winners of 12 races worth £2,305. Five years later he was champion trainer with 31 winners worth £24,708 and in 1910, he gained his third title with 47 victories bringing in prize money of £52,364. By 1909 he had a reputation as a master in the art of developing stayers. This was the year he won the St Leger with Bayardo, a horse that he prepared for 25 races, 22 of which he won.

His first Classic success was with Challacombe in the 1905 St Leger, a race that he won on a further four occasions, a record he shared with Frank Butters until Cecil Boyd-Rochfort sent out Alcide to win his sixth St Leger in 1958. His speciality, however, was the fillies' blue riband and his owners celebrated eight triumphs in the Oaks. He also won four Two Thousand Guineas, three Derbys, but only one One Thousand Guineas, somewhat surprising in view of his Oaks victories. He won two war-time Triple Crowns with Gay Crusader in 1917 and Gainsborough the following year, but perhaps his best Classic training feat was to win the Derby and Oaks in the same season with Lemberg and Rosedrop in 1910.

He devoted his life to training, rarely leaving Manton for reasons other than race meetings and bloodstock sales. He was renowned for his patience with his charges, at least the equine ones. Few juvenile victories figure in the stable's roll of honour as Taylor treated his two-year-olds as little more than infants and generally preferred them to mature before being raced or even trained hard. This was in sharp contrast to his father who reputedly would gallop his yearlings. The training line of the Taylor family ended with Alec who remained a bachelor. On his retirement at the end of the 1927 season – in which he won the St Leger with Book Law – he handed on the Manton stables to his former assistant Joseph Lawson who went on to win 12 Classics himself.

Further reading

Mortimer, R., Onslow, R. and Willett, P., *Biographical Encyclopaedia of British Flat Racing* (London: Macdonald and Jane's, 1978).

Television

See Broadcast media.

Tote

On 29 November 2002 the Tote sponsored a hurdle race at Newbury to celebrate the 25th anniversary of what the organisation claims is 'racing's favourite bet', the Placepot. In it punters have to nominate a horse in the first six races of a meeting that will win or be placed; those that succeed share in the distribution of the total money bet on that option. Introduced at Newbury in 1977 over £1 billion has been speculated on the Placepot and annual turnover on the bet now exceeds £100 million. None of this could have been envisaged in 1929 when the Tote made its debut under Jockey Club Rules at Newmarket and Carlisle on 2 July. (It was first used on a British racecourse at Portsmouth on 4 May 1929 at a meeting under Pony Club Turf Rules.)

The standard totalisator system works by pooling all stakes on a race, making deductions to cover costs and the Tote's contribution to racing, and then dividing the remainder by the number of winning units to give a dividend to winning punters. In effect Tote customers bet against each other not against the bookmaker. Odds for win bets and place bets will fluctuate according to the money bet on each horse but the dividend declared is determined by the volume of betting at the 'off' unlike betting with the bookmakers who will offer odds at the time of striking the bet.

The introduction of the Tote to British racing was primarily due to Lord Hamilton of Dalzell who, when senior steward of the Jockey Club, instituted and chaired a committee that recommended that gambling be made to contribute to the maintenance of the sport. However, the Tote was never the saviour that he had hoped it might be. He had wanted the Jockey Club to be in charge of the new operation but the private member's bill of Sir Ralph Glyn was changed drastically at the committee stage in Parliament and control was instead vested in a statutory body, the Racecourse Betting Control Board, responsible to the Home Office. It was so underfunded that there was little capital available for development; not till 1934 was every racecourse supplied with the necessary equipment.

From 1931 to 1949 all bets had been for win and place with the pool divided equally between the two. Separate place-only betting was then introduced. Over the years other types of bet were brought in such as the dual forecast in which the first two horses could be nominated in any order, the Tote Trio which required the same for the first three past the post, and, of course, the Placepot itself. Recently the Tote has launched new bets intended to give greater payouts. The dual forecast has been replaced by a straight forecast where the horses have to be in designated positions. Similarly the Tote Trio has changed into the Trifecta, in which the first three horses in order have to be selected in one nominated race a day; it is hoped that this pool will rise from the 3 per cent of turnover of the Trio bet to approach 20–25 per cent as in Australia and New Zealand. More spectacular has been the Scoop6 in which punters attempt to name the winners of six televised races. A quarter of the stakes go to a place pool and another quarter to a win pool. If there is no win-ner the money accumulates. A further 20 per cent is put in a bonus pool that can be collected by those scoop winners who also name the first horse in a nominated race a week later.

At the course the Tote appeals to those punters who prefer the orderly queue to the push and shove of the betting ring, to those wishing to bet in small amounts, and to those seeking to bet each-way or even place only. Its use of red-suited 'Tote ladies' who offer help to the inexperienced bettor has helped create an image different to that of the bookmakers: it is seen as benign, safe, and even comforting.

In 1989 the Tote received permission to accept off-course telephone bets at starting prices. Ten years later it was Britain's fourth largest bookmaker owning 347 betting shops. It has also moved to accept bets on most major sporting events though racing is still its dominant income stream. It has also made arrangements with several off-course bookmakers to accept some of the special bets like Scoop6 and pay them a percentage for taking and passing on the transactions.

The Tote now has four major divisions: a credit betting facility which func-tions both on-course and via the phone; a racecourse section which takes tote bets on all race meetings; a bookmaking branch that has offices throughout the country (and on most racecourses) providing a cash betting service at either starting price or Tote declared odds; and Tote Direct which operates via on-line terminals in betting offices to enable Scoop6, Jackpot, Placepot and Trifecta bets to be transmitted to the racecourse tote pools. As a sponsor of racing its name appears on jockeys' breeches, the large television screens at most race-courses and on the racecards for big betting races such as the Ebor, Cambridgeshire and Cesarewitch.

As part of the implementation of the Labour Government's election mani-festo, there are plans for the Tote to be sold to the private sector though with only a seven-year exclusive right to run pool betting. Both the Racecourse Association and the British Horseracing Board have thrown their hats into the ring as prospective purchasers. Others have floated the idea of a Racing Trust, with representatives from across the industry, to run the privatised operation. However the Tote is proving to be a victim of its own success. Extra betting shops have been purchased and telephone betting has increased 90 per cent in a year resulting in a valuation by the Treasury of £200 million in 2002, up from £90 million three years before. Whether any sector of the racing industry – except the bookmakers! – could raise this sort of money is questionable.

Further reading

Vamplew, W., *The Turf* (London: Allen Lane, 1976).
www.tote.co.uk

Training and trainers

Trainers have to get their horses fit, keep them fit and ensure that the animals peak for selected races. Knowing their horses, being able to cajole them, and appreciating the subtleties in their behaviour changes are key aspects of training. Yet horse sense is of little use without business sense. Trainers also have to plan the racing programme for their charges. What type of race will best suit them? What is their preferred distance? Which of Britain's different courses will help rather than hinder their performance? And where will rival trainers be sending their horses? Getting horses fit is one task; getting them in the right race is another.

Man management is another vital part of the training equation. Stable staff have to be recruited, trained and retained. They are closest to the horses and with encouragement from a respected employer can yield important information. With good teaching some of these lads might develop into jockeys. 'Frenchie' Nicolson, for one, made a name for his ability to train apprentices as well as horses. Graduates of his stables included leading jockeys Paul Cook, Pat Eddery and Walter Swinburn. He taught his boys not just to ride a race but how to behave civilly and dress appropriately, traits that would stand them in good stead when seeking rides in an industry where employers tended to be conservative. Those employers too have to be dealt with. Up to the late nineteenth century most trainers served only one or two wealthy owners but, after the development of public training, a yard might contain horses from many owners, all of whom have to be kept happy. Owners are not tied to a trainer. If an owner takes umbrage because his or her horses are not winning they can take them elsewhere. Aspirations in racing rarely match up to reality but few owners are willing to admit that they have bought a duff animal. If it is not the jockey's fault then the next in line to be fired is the trainer. Lack of success is not the only reason why owners change trainers. The Aga Khan removed his horses from Luca Cumani's yard – a third of the trainer's bloodstock – because he was unhappy with stable security.

Training methods have changed significantly since the eighteenth century when, in the belief that lighter horses ran faster, trainers sweated and purged their animals. In the early Victorian years Thomas Dawson, the eldest of the four trainer brothers, pioneered the training of horses without sweating them under heavy rugs to get rid of supposed surplus flesh. His training methods produced five Classic winners and a host of imitators. At the end of the nineteenth century, American trainers came over to Britain and showed that horses could benefit from ventilated stables, previously kept sealed to prevent draughts. In the later twentieth century came another revolution in training methods when Martin Pipe (see separate entry) became a prolific winner by employing a form of interval training in which horses were ridden hard uphill for short distances with less intensive work between these efforts. He was not the first. In the 1960s, Ken Oliver, Scotland's most successful trainer who won almost 1,000 races, had developed a method of bringing his horses up to fitness by working them up the Border hills in a series of sharp canters. Many trainers now follow a regime of climbs and turns, often on specially constructed artificial gallops, the amount of work done depending on the stage of preparation that the horses are at. But not all. Racing remains a conservative industry where new ideas are treated with suspicion . . . even when they work! Pipe was also to the forefront in venturing into regular blood testing of horses. Even more science is now applied by a new generation of trainers who use electrodes to monitor the heart rate of horses during exercise and then blood test at the end to assess how much lactate is being produced, in effect measuring the effort that the horse has put in.

Historically, successful trainers have tended to come from a racing background. Cecil Boyd-Rochfort (see separate entry) was the step-father of Henry Cecil (see separate entry) who himself married Julie Murless, daughter of Noel who trained the winners of 19 English Classics and was champion trainer nine times. Luca Cumani came from Italy where his father had been champion trainer several times and he himself had won 75 races as an amateur rider. The Easterby family have been northern trainers for several generations and in 1996 Peter Easterby became the first modern-day trainer to saddle 1,000 winners under both codes of racing. Fulke Walwyn (see separate entry) and his cousin Peter became champion National Hunt and flat-race trainers respectively. Recently retired with over 1,850 winners to his credit, Peter dominated flat racing in the late 1960s and 1970s, culminating in two trainers' championships in 1974 and 1975. In the latter year he was the first trainer in the twentieth century to win more than 100 races in a season. David Nicolson, son of 'Frenchie', rode nearly 600 winners over jumps including the 1967 Whitbread Gold Cup on Mill House before turning to training where he saddled just short of 1,500 winners before his retirement in 1999. Both sons of trainers, Fred Rimell and Fred Winter (see separate entry) became champion National Hunt jockeys before turning to training themselves where they each secured trainers' titles. Rimmell is the only trainer in the twentieth century to train four winners of the Aintree Grand National. Michael Dickinson, a former jockey, took over the Harewood Yard from his father Tony and in 1983 trained the first five home in the Cheltenham Gold Cup. On Boxing Day the previous year he saddled 12 winners across the six meetings shattering Arthur Stephenson's record of seven in a day which he achieved in May 1970. Another jockey turned trainer is Aidan O'Brien. Like Vincent O'Brien (see separate entry), his unrelated predecessor at the Ballydoyle stables, the Irishman has had a major impact on British racing. He was a 20-year-old amateur jockey when he linked up as a stable rider for his future wife Anne-Marie Crowley. After winning the Irish jump trainers' title in

1992–93, she handed over the licence to O'Brien. That he won with a horse on his first day as a trainer was a sign of things to come. The next six Irish jump championships came his way before he cut back on his National Hunt commitments to concentrate on the flat where he has become a major force at the top level.

Yet belonging to a family steeped in racing is not essential to training success. Les Eyre, who averages a winner a week, was a miner's son who made millions from selling kitchens before turning to training. Six-times flat-race training champion Sir Michael Stoute (see separate entry) was the son of the Barbadian Police Commissioner and Martin Pipe (see separate entry), the most successful of recent National Hunt trainers, had a bookmaking father. Mark Johnson, a Scotsman who migrated to Middleham to become the quickest to train 1,000 winners, was a qualified vet before he took out a licence in 1987. In 2002 he trained 134 winners, more than any other flat-race trainer. Second to him in the number of winners was Mick Channon who came into training from international football where he gained 46 caps for England. Initially Channon was refused a training licence by the Jockey Club on the grounds of his inexperience. He made his reputation by buying and training two-year-olds and in 1999 he moved into the Berkshire Downs stable formerly run by Major Dick Hern, four times champion trainer.

Training is a stressful job with little security and sometimes scant reward. For many trainers the economics of the job is a delicate balance between profit and loss with the success of one horse often making the difference. As a rule of thumb most trainers aim to break even on their training fees and make their money from either the bookmaker, or more commonly, from their 10 per cent share of prize money. Not all can do this. In a survey conducted by the *Racing Post* in 2000 almost one in five trainers reported making a loss the previous year; others earned less than their own head lad; and around 40 per cent would not recommend their profession as a worthwhile career. On the other hand the majority of trainers do make a profit and some 20 per cent reported net incomes of over £50,000. The losses lead to about 50 or so trainers quitting each year but the potential profits (and excitement) tempt others to make up the numbers again. As a condition of obtaining a licence these newcomers have to attend a three-week course at the British Racing School, one week of which is devoted to business management. Where there has been a decline in trainers – from about 600 at end of the 1970s to less than 250 today – is in the number of permit holders. These are a special group of trainers who are allowed to care for horses owned by their immediate family. For many years they have been the backbone of jump racing and traditionally are the main breeders of steeplechasers. The slide has at least been slowed by the Jockey Club lowering the minimum number of horses required to obtain a licence to 6 from the previous 12 (flat and jump combined) or 9 (jump only).

As this suggests trainers' yards come in all sizes from those with over 200 horses to those with scarcely a handful. Yet the problems facing their proprietors are similar. They cannot instil talent in a horse but can inhibit its development or bring the animal to a level of fitness where the natural ability can make itself felt. Although trainers' championships are measured by prize money won it can be queried whether it takes more skill to win major races with good horses or a selling plate with a moderate one. There are many good trainers around who never get the chance to work with anything but average horses. To them a Group winner will never be anything but a dream.

Further reading

Fitzgeorge-Parker, T., *Training the Racehorse* (London: Pelham, 1973).
Nicholson, D. and Powell, J., *The Duke* (London: Hodder and Stoughton, 1995).
Walwyn, P., *Handy All the Way* (London: Metro, 2002).

Transport and travel

In mid-May 1860, John Sharp received a telegram from Scottish ironmaster and racehorse owner, James Merry, inviting him to ride Thormanby in the forthcoming Derby. The problem for Sharp was that he was training horses in Russia at the time. Additionally he would have to lose 10 lb in order to ride the weight. Nevertheless a Derby ride is a Derby ride, so he accepted the offer and on the Sunday afternoon before the race caught a train to Berlin where he arrived at five o'clock the next morning. Each time the train stopped he would disembark and exercise to reduce his weight. At 11 am on Tuesday he reached Ostend and then spent the time sweating off pounds till the cross-channel boat departed for Dover at 6 pm. London was made at 4 am on Wednesday from whence Sharp proceeded to Epsom where he continued the sweating process to good effect. At scale he was only $\frac{3}{4}$ lb above the stipulated weight. Perhaps this was too much for Mr Merry, a hard man obsessed with money. Just prior to mounting, he informed Sharp that, as 18-year-old Harry Custance knew the horse so well, he had better ride him instead. And so he did: to a $1\frac{1}{2}$ length victory. Merry is reputed to have won about £85,000 in bets, though he gave Custance only £100 as a present for winning. History has not recorded how Sharp felt about being 'jocked off' after travelling nearly 2,000 miles.

In contrast to Sharp's long and fruitless journey were the late-twentieth century flights between racecourses by plane and helicopter of jockeys Paul Cook and Gary Carter who both won three races at three different meetings. On 4 July 1981 Cook piloted home Prince's Gate in the 2.15 at Sandown, Ramannolic in the 5.00 at Bath, and finally Pavilion in the 7.50 at Nottingham. Almost ten years later, on 14 June, Gary Carter performed a similar feat with Luvly Jubly in the 1.30 at Southwell, Romany Rye in the 4.40 at York and Able Sudan in the 8.15 at Doncaster.

The vocation of jockey is significantly different from most occupations in that the main place of work changes almost daily. Few race meetings last more than three days and the vast majority are single-day affairs. In the pre-railway era riders had to travel to meetings by coach, on horseback, or even walking with their racing saddles tied to their waist. The coming of the railway eased travel problems but most top jockeys took advantage of the new mode of transport not to relax but to increase their workload and earnings. Tommy Loates, for one, travelled 2,000 miles and rode 33 times in 17 days in 1889, including successive days at Derby, Paris and Nottingham. During the late nineteenth century, following the emergence of enclosed London suburban courses, leading jockeys increasingly raced in Britain on a Saturday and in France the next day. Nat Flatman, champion jockey in 1849 when the railway network was relatively undeveloped, raced on only 75 days of the season, but by 1899 Sammy Loates, the leading rider in that season, was able to manage 179 days. Estimates of the respective distances travelled are 4,270 and 10,770 miles.

To the initial travel convenience offered by the railway can be added that of the car, plane and helicopter, all of which have enabled top riders to race more frequently than in the past, often including both afternoon and evening meetings on the same day within their itinerary. Generally a professional jockey has to cover between 50,000 and 60,000 miles annually in Britain alone. In 1995, when both Frankie Dettori and his challenger for the championship, Jason Weaver, had more than 1,000 rides in the United Kingdom, they travelled some 200,000 miles. Elite jockeys can afford to hire chauffeurs; the rest drive themselves or beg lifts from colleagues. Speeding offences are a regular occurrence for jockeys as they hasten across country to take a ride. For leading riders there is also air travel. In 1990 Ray Cochrane bought a Cesna aircraft after he calculated that he was spending a month a year in his car! As early as 1946 Tommy Weston flew 1,000 miles in a week to ride at York, Newmarket, Salisbury, Liverpool and Goodwood. Willie Carson is generally credited with pioneering the ownership of private aircraft by jockeys. Seeing how fresh he arrived at race meetings other leading riders opted to follow his lead, though, unlike Carson, few of them also studied for a pilot's licence, preferring others to take the controls. Air travel allows most top flat-race jockeys to race for lucrative prizes on the continent on Sundays (thus freeing up Sunday rides at home for lesser jockeys). Jump jockeys rarely fly to meetings: the prize money and winter weather act as deterrents, though both Richard Dunwoody and Tony McCoy have taken advantage of trainer Martin Pipe's helicopter when maximising their riding opportunities. Although jockeys raced in other countries during the close season in the days when seafaring was required, flying has eased the travel problems. It has also enabled them to venture to Europe, America or Asia for short spells or even just one meeting.

The railways revolutionised travel for horses. Prior to the coming of the locomotive there was little option but to walk animals to and from race meetings, accompanied by their grooms and sometimes their jockey. Much is made in racing literature of Lord George Bentinck vanning his horse Elis from Goodwood to Doncaster to win the 1836 St Leger. Such a journey would normally have taken 15 to 20 days walking, but Bentinck, keen to engineer a betting coup, kept Elis at his Goodwood base until only five days before the race. The odds on the horse widened and Bentinck was able to secure some good bets. However, he had arranged for a local coachbuilder to construct a van in which relays of six horses, travelling about 80 miles a day, brought Elis to the Yorkshire course. This was not the first instance of vanning. In 1788 Eclipse had been taken in a two-horse van to perform stud duties and in 1816 Sovereign travelled in a cart drawn by oxen from his Worcestershire base for an unsuccessful attempt at the Cesarewich. In both instances not tiring the horse was a more important motive than speed. Despite the victory of Elis, the era of long-distance vanning was short-lived. Within a few years the burgeoning railway network offered both faster and cheaper transportation of equine stock. By the 1850s, several hundred railway horseboxes were in use. In the late nineteenth century racehorses began to travel abroad on a regular basis to race in France and Belgium, usually taking the sea route between Folkestone and Boulogne on which the firm of Peden and Son operated with special transit boxes.

More recently the roll-on roll-off cross-Channel ferries have enabled horses to be transported in their familiar boxes, though flying has become more commonplace now that problems of quarantine, health regulations and acclimatisation have been overcome. Until recently no one was quite sure how long to allow for a horse to get used to the new environment after long haul flights. Many trainers, like Barry Hills, thought it was best to fly out the day before racing and come back the day after whereas the connections of Dancing Brave allowed ten days either side for acclimatisation on long haul flights. Research by Desmond Leaden, an Irish vet, demonstrated that four days was about right and that inflight weight loss could be countered by intravenous injections before and after journeys. Horses do not mind flying. Many are less disturbed by a long flight than a short journey in a horsebox with its braking, cornering, stopping and starting. Less than one horse in 100 needs to be tranquillised for a flight. Unlike humans, horses are not aware that planes can crash. What concerns them is the loud noise, but if it can be kept reasonably constant they will tolerate it. Hence experienced pilots will taxi to the runway and arrange to take-off without stopping first and revving the engines.

Further reading

Tolson, J. and Vamplew, W., 'Facilitation not Revolution: Railways and British Horseracing 1830–1914', *Sport in History* 23.1 (2003), pp. 89–106.

Trophies and prizes

Little attention has been paid in recent years to racing trophies. Annual presentations of cups are made for football and rugby – the well-known FA Challenge Cup, the Rugby League Challenge Cup and the Calcutta Cup. British open golf champions receive the instantly recognised Claret Jug, men's singles finalists at Wimbledon contest the Challenge Cup and women the embossed Challenge Plate. Even 'The Ashes' in cricket, though too fragile to be presented, are embodied in a small ceramic urn. The elite British horseraces, however, such as the Classics, are not associated with any similar historic trophies and the presentation of mementoes which take place almost daily at racecourses throughout the country mostly owe their existence to the generosity of commercial race sponsors.

The earliest prize in English horseracing was said to be the wooden ball decorated with flowers presented at Chester races in 1512, later made of silver and then gold. A silver bell, in imitation of those fastened to a horse's tack, was apparently donated by Elizabeth I for the races at Salisbury in 1585 but the oldest still in existence are the tiny, round Carlisle Bells (5 cm and 4.5 cm in diameter), dating from 1599. A slightly larger Lanark Bell (11.5 cm) was made in Edinburgh around 1608–10 but although the race for this prize is thought to date back to the twelfth century, no artefacts from this earlier period remain. Practical items such as saddles and other pieces of equipment were often given as prizes for winning a horserace at the numerous local fairs and festivals held throughout the seventeenth and eighteenth centuries. At more important events, bells were gradually replaced by two-handled cups or punch bowls, both intended for toasting success in alcohol! State encouragement of horseracing and breeding led to the awarding of Royal Plates and Cups by the post-Restoration Stuart monarchy. The early eighteenth century also saw more functional trophies in the form of silver or gold tea and coffee pots but, practical or decorative, the support and participation of the gentry and aristocracy resulted in items of considerable value and craftsmanship.

Improvements in metal working techniques and changes in taste produced increasingly elaborate designs with leaves, scrolls, cherubs and laurel wreaths adorning vase and urn-shaped trophies. The Doncaster Cup, inaugurated in 1766, was first presented by the stewards of the racecourse but the annual gift became so ornate and expensive that the cost was taken over by the Town Corporation. Usually in silver-gilt and some 50 cm tall, it was made, like most pieces, by London goldsmiths for whom racing commissions were a lucrative business. Many race cups featured a horse, though not always a racehorse. The grandest trophies of the Victorian era progressed from engravings of the horse based on classical antiquity to designs in the shape of St George on horseback slaying the Dragon or Good Queen Bess on a charger. Others did away with horses completely and were based on romantic images of the past, with embossed knights, kings in armour – real or fabled such as King Arthur – and heraldric features. Those presented at Ascot and Goodwood for the Cup races were amongst the most elaborate and on some occasions represented around 70 per cent of the winnings, the money from the sweepstakes making up only 30 per cent. Such valuable trophies were nearly all awarded to the winners of the top traditional stayers' races, still known as 'Cup Races'.

From the Great Exhibition of 1851 to the end of the century, high Victoriana ruled in design and the profusion of intricate detail attested to the superiority of the master craftsmen. Large sculptured pieces, candelabra, ewers and tankards were all presented as prizes. Thereafter, the enormous costs of manufacture heralded a return to the relatively simple, less highly decorated styles of earlier times and to the decline in importance of the racing trophy. Royalty continued to take an interest. King George V asked for an improvement in the design of the three prizes still donated by the monarchy, the Royal Ascot Gold Cup, the King's Gold Vase and the Royal Hunt Cup, and Ascot Cup competitions open to any craftsman or designer were held on several occasions between 1927 and 1939. For the most part, however, the prize money was of far greater significance than the memento of a winning horse.

Since the Second World War it has been the newly founded races that have tended to revive the tradition of trophies. The first commercially sponsored steeplechase, the Whitbread Gold Cup of 1957, was followed by the donation of further gold plate and silverware by drinks firms. A more original piece was commissioned by Seagrams in 1986 to commemorate their sponsorship of the Grand National; the handsome bronze, designed by ex-jump jockey Philip Blacker, shows three steeplechasers who have just cleared Becher's Brook. De Beers, the diamond company, have sponsored the King George VI and Queen Elizabeth Stakes for 30 years, with the word 'Diamond' inserted in the race name since 1975. A new and often imaginative trophy in the shape of a bowl, plate, vase or other object is commissioned every year, always decorated with diamonds. Winning jockeys and trainers also receive prizes, often diamond jewellery, and the successful owner receives a traditional cup from the Queen in addition to the sponsors' prize (and a vast sum of money!) Other more recent awards include bronzes given since 1982 by the Racehorse Owners Association for their Champion Horse of the Year. Simple cups of traditional style have also been presented for races such as the Derby and the Cheltenham Gold Cup while the Irish Derby has sometimes featured a design of Waterford crystal.

As country houses have been sold and trophy rooms emptied, old racing cups have re-appeared on the market. Some have returned to their original use, others have found new homes. The Admiral's Cup, presented since 1957 to the winning yachtsmen in a series of races at Cowes, was once a nineteenth-century horseracing trophy. The Eclipse Foot, originally mounted in gold during the 1830s and briefly competed for at Ascot, is the property of the Jockey Club as are many other traditional racing prizes. Further trophies have been purchased, loaned and donated to the National Horseracing Museum at Newmarket, the Victoria and Albert Museum and municipal galleries around the country, the custodians of a valuable heritage.

Further reading

Victoria and Albert Museum Exhibition Catalogue, *Sporting Glory, the Courage Exhibition of National Trophies* (London: Sporting Trophies Exhibitions Ltd, 1992).

Twentieth-century flat horses

The twentieth century began and ended with royal Classic victories. When Diamond Jubilee won the Two Thousand Guineas in 1900 for the future Edward VII, then Prince of Wales, it was the fourth Classic win for the British royal family in five years. None could have imagined the extent of royal success one hundred years later. When Mutafaweq captured the St Leger in 1999, it was the thirty-second Classic victory in 17 years for the ruling dynasty – of Dubai, not Britain. His owner, Sheikh Mohammed al Maktoum was a royal prince of a small member state within the United Arab Emirates, and he and his brothers dominated elite thoroughbred racing in Britain at the end of the twentieth century in the same way that the Victorian aristocracy held sway at the end of the nineteenth. The intervening years saw the pre-eminence of the English gentry as owners and breeders disappear to be replaced by a mixture of wealthy businessmen, Middle Eastern aristocrats, Muslim spiritualist leaders and powerful international breeding syndicates. It is their horses that have largely shaped late twentieth-century British racing.

The first 50 years had much in common with the Victorian era of racing. The goal of the top horses was to win a Classic (or preferably three, thus claiming the Triple Crown) or the Ascot Gold Cup, the most prestigious longer distance race. As in the nineteenth century, some continued to do both. Diamond Jubilee, a wilful and at times dangerous horse and full brother to Derby-winning Persimmon (1896), took the first Triple Crown of the century, a tribute to the hard work of his trainer Richard Marsh and jockey Herbert Jones. Gay Crusader (1917) and Gainsborough (1918) went further, winning the Triple Crown and the Gold Cup as three-year-olds but these were wartime substitutes and all the races took place at Newmarket. Nevertheless, champion jockey Steve Donoghue rated Gay Crusader the best he had ever ridden. He may not have said this had he ridden the sire of these two colts, Bayardo, one of the greatest horses of the century. The winner of 22 of his 25 starts, he was unbeaten as a two-year-old in 1908, won 11 races at three including the St Leger, the Eclipse Stakes and the Champion Stakes, and romped away with the Ascot Gold Cup the following year.

There were some exceptionally talented fillies at this time. Sceptre and Pretty Polly (see separate entries) each won fillies' Triple Crowns in 1902 and 1904, in Sceptre's case consigning the exploits of the highly rated colt Ard Patrick to obscurity although he had beaten her in both the Derby and the Eclipse Stakes. Signorinetta (1908), Tagalie (1912) and Fifinella (1916) all won the Derby, the last three fillies to do so, but they were able to claim a 5 lb allowance over the colts. Signorinetta and Fifinella also won the Oaks, Tagalie the One Thousand Guineas. Cap and Bells triumphed by six lengths in the 1901 Oaks, the first American-bred winner of the race; Cherry Lass captured the One Thousand Guineas and the Oaks in 1905 as well as the Nassau Stakes and the St James's Palace Stakes; and Keysoe emulated Sceptre and Pretty Polly by winning the St Leger in 1919, one of only seven female winners in 50 years.

Keysoe was bred by the seventeenth Earl of Derby and the next three decades were dominated by his thoroughbreds and those belonging to the other outstanding owner/breeder of the period, the third Aga Khan, spiritual leader of a Shia Muslim sect. By the time of his death in 1948, Derby had won 20 Classics, his rival 13 but the Aga Khan had 4 further winners before he died in 1958. Lord Derby only won the Ascot Gold Cup once with Bosworth in 1930 although his colt Alycidon won in 1949, the year in which this horse became the first since Isonomy in 1879 to win the stayers' Triple Crown (Ascot, Goodwood and Doncaster Cups). The Aga Khan won the Gold Cup twice with Felicitation (1934) and Umiddad (1944), and consecutive Derbys in 1935 and 1936 with Triple Crown-winning Bahram and the grey Mahmoud whose record-breaking time of 2 minutes 33.8 seconds was unbeaten for 59 years.

Another grey belonging to the Aga Khan, Mumtaz Mahal, was one of the fastest two-year-olds ever seen on an English racecourse. Strictly a sprinter, she won five top races as a juvenile and struggled into second place in the 1924 One Thousand Guineas, before reverting to shorter distances and winning the

Nunthorpe Stakes by six lengths. She was as popular in 1923 as her sire, The Tetrarch, had been ten years earlier. While she was dubbed 'the Flying Filly', he became known as 'The Spotted Wonder' because of his unusual grey and white coat. Unbeaten in seven starts as a two-year-old, he was juvenile champion of 1913 but was injured in the autumn and retired to stud. At the opposite end of the racing scale but even more popular was Brown Jack, one of the few twentieth-century horses to achieve fame outside the tight-knit racing community. His major achievement was to win the longest race in the calendar, the Queen Alexandra Stakes at Royal Ascot on six consecutive occasions, 1929–34.

The breeding careers of Bahram and Hyperion, the two greatest horses owned by the Aga Khan and the Earl of Derby, were markedly different. Bahram won all his nine races. As well as the Triple Crown, he won the Gimcrack Stakes, four other two-year-old starts and the St James's Palace Stakes. He was immediately and controversially retired to stud after the St Leger at a time when three-year-olds were usually kept in training for a further year, the only unbeaten Triple Crown winner of the century. In another unpopular decision, he was exported to America in 1940 along with Mahmoud but he failed there as a stallion and ended his days in Argentina. Hyperion, however, stuck it out in wartime Britain. The smallest horse to win the Derby in the twentieth century (he was only 15.15 hands high), he won twice as a two-year-old and three more times in his three-year-old season, including the 1933 St Leger. He was retired to stud after coming a poor third in the 1934 Ascot Gold Cup but went on to be champion sire on six occasions. By the time of his death in 1960, his offspring had won around 750 races in England and Ireland, including 11 English Classics. By a strange twist of fate, the most successful colt and filly sired by Bahram and Hyperion, Big Game and Sun Chariot, were both leased by the National Stud to King George VI and sent to trainer Fred Darling. Big Game won the 1942 Two Thousand Guineas and Sun Chariot the fillies' Triple Crown in the same year, ensuring that the king and Darling were leading owner and trainer, and giving jockey Gordon Richards 4 of his 14 Classic victories. He rated Sun Chariot the best filly he ever rode.

An honourable mention should also be given to Windsor Lad, winner of the 1934 Derby but, like Shahrastani 52 years later, overlooked because of the unexpected and controversial demise of the favourite, in this instance, the Two Thousand Guineas winner, Colombo. Windsor Lad went on to win the St Leger in a record time which still stands and followed this success with the Eclipse and Coronation Cup in 1935. (Shahrastani, on the other hand, won the Irish Derby but was trounced in all his subsequent meetings with the unlucky Epsom loser, Dancing Brave – see separate entry.)

Two of the outstanding horses of the immediate post war years were Abernant and Tudor Minstrel. Abernant was a grey grandson of Mumtaz Mahal and inherited her astonishing speed, winning 14 of his 17 races. Like her, he failed to stay a mile and was narrowly beaten into second place in the 1949 Two Thousand Guineas, the first English Classic to be decided by the photo-finish. But he then won 4 top sprints that year and repeated 3 of his successes, the July Cup, the King George Stakes and the Nunthorpe Stakes, in

1950. Tudor Minstrel was another horse who might have remained unbeaten if he had been raced at his optimum distance of 1 mile. He won 8 of his 10 starts including the St James's Palace Stakes and the 1947 Two Thousand Guineas by the widest margin of the century (officially eight lengths) but failed to stay the distance in the Derby and the Eclipse Stakes in which he finished fourth and second respectively.

The post war era saw many changes to racing in Britain, possibly the most important of which was the heightened prominence given to middle-distance races and the parallel demise of the stayer. The Ascot Gold Cup and even the St Leger began to decline in the face of competition from new 12-furlong races such as the King George VI and Queen Elizabeth Stakes, inaugurated in 1951, lucrative shorter events like the International Stakes (first run in 1972) and end-of-season overseas trophies such as the Prix de l'Arc de Triomphe and Irish Champion Stakes. The Triple Crown, once the ultimate prize, ceased to be challenged for – there has only been one winner since Bahram in 1935. The fact that the outstanding colt, Nijinsky (see separate entry) failed to win Europe's richest race, the 1970 Arc, only three weeks after completing his Triple Crown-winning St Leger has helped to ensure that other champion horses are steered away from the final English Classic by increasingly business-minded owners. The down-grading of the Gold Cup has been even more spectacular. From a prestigious place in the racing calendar at mid-century, its fortunes have fallen as the fashion for breeding speed rather than stamina has risen. When Classic Cliché won the Cup in 1996, he was the first Classic winner (of the 1995 St Leger) to do so in 50 years.

None of this was obvious in the 1950s, the final decade in which British owner/breeders dominated the Turf. Meld, a descendant of Bahram, took the fillies' Triple Crown in 1955, the last for 30 years. Petite Etoile, a grey from the Mumtaz Mahal line was first or second in all 19 of her races over three seasons, winning the 1959 One Thousand Guineas and Oaks, as well as the Sussex Stakes, Champion Stakes, Yorkshire Oaks and Coronation Cup twice. It was a good era for females in racing. Lady Zia Wernher was leading owner in 1955 as a result of Meld's triumphs and Queen Elizabeth II received this accolade in 1954 (and again in 1957) when her colt Aureole, a son of Hyperion, won the King George and the Coronation Cup.

However, there were signs of what was to come. First there were successful European raids on the top British races. Ribot, the champion of Italy, took the King George in 1956 (and two consecutive Arcs in 1955 and 1956). Five French-bred and trained colts won the Epsom Derby between 1947 and 1956, and Frenchman Marcel Boussac was leading owner in Britain on two occasions (1950, 1951). Another French horse, Sea Bird II, won the Derby in 1965 in what is widely recognised as the best performance of the twentieth century but there was another component in his breeding which many future champions were to share – American bloodstock. American owners were also becoming involved in European racing and many formed fruitful partnerships with Irish trainer Vincent O'Brien (see separate entry), the man who turned Ballymoss into champion racehorse of Europe in 1958. Following the type of international pattern which was to become increasingly familiar in subsequent decades,

Ballymoss won the Irish Derby and the English St Leger in 1957 and the King George, Eclipse Stakes and the Arc in 1958. Ten years later O'Brien and American owner Raymond Guest won the Grand Criterium for two-year-olds at Longchamp, the English Two Thousand Guineas and Derby, and the Washington DC International with the American-bred Sir Ivor. Then came Nijinsky, a son of champion Canadian stallion Northern Dancer, and Mill Reef, trained in Britain but American owned and bred, two of the outstanding middle-distance horses of the century (see separate entries). A triumvirate of world-class champions foaled in the late 1960s was completed by the unfashionably home-bred Brigadier Gerard, probably the top European miler of the century (see separate entry). These three colts between them pulverised European opposition, winning consecutive King Georges (1970–72), five English Classics, an Arc, Irish Derby and two Eclipse Stakes. In a combined total of 45 races, they won 40 and were second on the other 5 occasions, almost exclusively in top-flight contests.

Thereafter North American bloodlines dominated English racing and Northern Dancer, the 1964 Kentucky Derby winner, managed to be champion sire in Britain without ever entering the country. As his offspring filtered across the Atlantic, speed won the battle with stamina as the most prized attribute of the thoroughbred. The fastest times for four of the English Classics were all recorded in the last 20 years of the century with Intrepidity (1993 Oaks) and Lammtarra (1995 Derby) both foaled by sons of Northern Dancer. Only in the St Leger did the pre-war records continue to stand – Mutafaweq (1999) is the sole horse since Bahram in 1935 to figure in the top six fastest times for the race. The lowered status of the Ascot Gold Cup and similar long distance European races was exemplified by the case of Sagaro, the only horse in 170 years to capture the trophy three times. In spite of his achievement, the National Stud, as solitary bidder purchased him for a paltry £175,000. (Compare this with his contemporary Alleged, dual Arc winner in 1977 and 1978, whose stud valuation was $16 million.) He was predictably sent only moderate mares and died without siring a Group One winner.

The last quarter of the twentieth century finally saw the old guard give way to the new. There were three further Classic successes for the Queen (1974 One Thousand Guineas – Highclere, 1977 Oaks and St Leger – Dunfermline) before overseas dynasties and businessmen took over the English turf. The fourth Aga Khan, grandson of the 1930s leader, has continued his winning touch with five Classic wins, including the unfortunate Shergar, runaway winner of the English and Irish Derbys and the King George in 1981 but later kidnapped and presumably killed by the IRA. Leading owner in 1981, the Aga Khan repeated this success in 2000 when Sinndar again won both Derbys together with the Arc.

Multi-millionaire Robert Sangster, partnered by trainer Vincent O'Brien, was the dominant force in British racing from 1976 to 1984 and four times leading owner. Having founded the Coolmore Stud with John Magnier, son-in-law of O'Brien, he set about importing the best American yearlings as a foundation for his racing operation. His most successful horses included The Minstrel, winner of the English and Irish Derbys and the King George in 1977, and El Gran Senor, the unlucky runner-up in the Epsom Derby of 1984 but victorious in the Two Thousand Guineas and the Irish Derby. His greatest champion, however, is Sadler's Wells, winner of several Group One races in 1984 but more famously the son of Northern Dancer who perpetuated his line in Europe. Standing at Coolmore, he has been champion sire in every year since 1992 and his offspring had won a world-record 45 Group and Grade One races by June 2001.

With increased international competition, a tendency to breed milers who are not stepped up to longer distances and an even stronger trend on the part of some owners to retire successful three-year-olds to stud before they blemish their careers (and potential stud fees), it has become harder to identify the truly great horses of the late twentieth and early twenty-first centuries. The Irish-bred and trained Giant's Causeway (2000) and Rock of Gibraltar (2002) are prime examples, horses that carried all before them, winning five and seven Group Ones respectively but, unlike comparable champions Brigadier Gerard and Mill Reef, unable to consolidate their reputations as four-year-olds. Although there were several dual Classic-winning horses in the 1980s (Reference Point won the 1987 Derby and St Leger, Nashwan the 1989 Two Thousand Guineas and Derby, and Oh So Sharp the first fillies' Triple Crown for 30 years in 1985 – and the last), only one horse has won two English Classics in the past decade. (Kazzia won the One Thousand Guineas and the Oaks in 2002.) This pattern has been replicated throughout the racing world. There have been no multiple French Classic winners in the last ten years, only one Irish and no winners of the American Triple Crown since Affirmed in 1978.

Instead there has been a pick-and-mix approach to European Classics. Salsabil (1990) won the English One Thousand Guineas, Oaks and the Irish Derby; Dream Well (1998) won the French and Irish Derbys as did Montjeu (1999) and Galileo (2001). Montjeu was undoubtedly an outstanding colt, taking the Arc as a three-year-old and the King George the following year. Generous, Racehorse of the Year in 1991, won the Epsom and Irish Derbys and the King George but failed in an attempt on the Arc. Lammtarra, the first English Derby winner to be bred from a Derby/Oaks mating – sire Nijinsky (1970), dam Snow Bride (1989) – completed the Derby/King George/Arc treble in one season, 1995, but gained limited recognition, perhaps, it was suggested because he was a product of the recently formed Godolphin racing operation. The brainchild of Sheikh Mohammed al Maktoum, Godolphin buys where and when it pleases and spares no amount of money in pursuit of its goals. After taking over from the Sangster/O'Brien partnership in 1985, the Maktoum brothers (see separate entry) and their horses have completely dominated the English turf with 11 consecutive leading owner titles; since 1995, they have added 3 more while Godolphin has claimed 4. With so many horses in training and so much competition for the top prizes, it is infinitely harder to establish reputations and select the great champions of the present day.

Further reading

Barrett, N. (ed.), *The Daily Telegraph Chronicle of Horse Racing* (London: Guinness, 1995).
Randall, J. and Morris, T., *A Century of Champions* (Halifax: Portway, 1999).

Twentieth-century jockeys

Although the age of the amateur in National Hunt racing was not over, the twentieth century was dominated by paid riders. Two professional jump jockeys each won three Grand Nationals in the first quarter of the twentieth century. One of them, Jack Anthony, had two brothers who also trained National winners. The other, Ernie Piggott, divided his early career between England and Belgium. Percy Woodland also spent much time riding abroad. He rode his first winner in a steeplechase at Lingfield in 1897 when he was only 13. He went on to win both the Grand National and the Grand Steeplechase at Auteuil twice, but he was also useful on the flat and triumphed in the French Derby on two occasions as well. George Duller, one of the first jump jockeys to adopt a crouching seat, rode almost entirely over hurdles and his specialisation paid off in that he won five Imperial Cups, the Sandown event that was the most important hurdle race of the season until the inception of the Champion Hurdle at Cheltenham.

Several interwar champion National Hunt riders began their careers as jockeys on the flat. Before increasing weight pushed him into changing codes Fred Rimell had 34 winners on the flat, the first when he was only 12. He became champion over jumps in the last full season before the Second World War, attempted to join the forces but was rejected on medical grounds and came back to racing to become champion once more with just 24 winners in an abbreviated season. He tied for the championship in a second shortened season when the war ended – this time with only 15 victories – and then headed the table with 54 winners in the first full season after the war. He twice rode five winners on a card, at Windsor and at Cheltenham. His riding career ended when he broke his neck – for the second time – in a fall in the Gold Cup at the latter course. Together he and his wife Mercy then developed a successful training partnership and won four championships. He and Fred Winter (see separate entry) are the only two men to have done the double of winning both the jockeys and trainers titles. Rimmell's brother-in-law, Gerry Wilson, was champion jockey six times in the 1930s and added a further title in 1940–41. He won two Cheltenham Gold Cups and a Grand National on Golden Miller.

Another National Hunt champion who rode his first winner on the flat at the age of 12 was Bryan Marshall. This was in 1926. It took another 11 years for him to register a victory over fences which was the result of obtaining a spare ride at Carlisle. His mount, Gliding Orb, was the outsider in a three-horse race but the other two fell! He became champion in 1947–48 after finishing runner-up the year before. He retired in 1957 with over 500 winners to his credit, including two Grand Nationals and a reputation as the most successful jockey at Aintree in the post war decade.

Pat Taaffe was one of the many Irishmen who have made their mark in jump racing, aided in his case by his long association with Arkle. So successful was he as an amateur rider that he lost his claiming allowance within a year. He became stable jockey for Tom Dreaper in 1950, a position that he retained till his retirement 21 years later, fittingly at Fairyhouse where he had landed a record six Irish Grand Nationals. His career victories totalled over 500 including two Grand Nationals and four Cheltenham Gold Cups. With 25 wins he remains the most successful jockey in modern times at the Cheltenham National Hunt Festival.

Josh Gifford, a contemporary of Stan Mellor and Terry Biddlecombe (see separate entries) was another who began on the flat and in 1957 he won 28 races. Increasing weight persuaded him to change first to hurdles and then also fences. In 1962–63, not yet 21, he finished fourth in the National Hunt riders championship and then won it for the next two seasons. He was then put out of the saddle for 15 months by first a riding accident and then a car crash. On his return he won the title again in 1966–67 with a then record 122 winners.

The modern era of celebrated National Hunt jockeys includes champions John Francome, Peter Scudamore, Jonjo O'Neill and Tony McCoy (see separate entries). Four other riders, Mick Fitzgerald, Richard Johnson, Adrian Maguire and Peter Niven, have joined the select few that have ridden over 1,000 winners, though none of them has ever been champion.

Irishman Fitzgerald was set to emigrate to New Zealand in 1990 after a luck-less start to his British racing career with only three wins in two years. Then a victory at Hereford landed him a position as stable jockey with trainer Ray Callow. Elevation to the big time came three years later when he joined Nicky Henderson's stable. Generally recognised for his tactical awareness, his most memorable triumphs have been on Rough Quest in the 1996 Grand National and on See More Business in the 1999 Cheltenham Gold Cup. He has twice been leading jockey at the Cheltenham Festival. His career has been blighted by injury including broken arms, legs and the removal of a collarbone.

Injury actually forced Adrian Maguire to retire from racing after he broke his neck in a fall at Warwick in 2002. He made his debut in British racing as an unknown Irish amateur, piloting home 11-1 shot Omerta in the Fulke Walwyn Kim Muir Chase at the Cheltenham Festival. Later that season he won the Irish Grand National on the same horse. As an apprentice for Tony Balding in 1991–92 he won the conditional riders championship, en route picking up the Cheltenham Gold Cup on 25-1 outsider Cool Ground. After losing his claim his first major stable was that of Ferdy Murphy, for whom he won the Hennessy on Sibton Abbey, but he later teamed up with David Nicholson, only to return to Murphy after an acrimonious split with the 'Duke' in 1998. In 1992–93 he lost the National Hunt jockeys' championship to Richard Dunwoody on the last day of the season, his aggregate of 194 remains the highest losing total.

Cotswold jockey Richard Johnson is the perennial runner-up in the championship to Tony McCoy. Despite riding over a century of winners for seven successive seasons, he has finished behind 'A P' on each occasion. Unlike many top jockeys, Johnson still rides out most mornings, seeing schooling horses as part of the job but also becoming acquainted with the foibles of the animals he is to ride in races. He is the second most successful (runner-up yet again!) English rider after Peter Scudamore.

Unlike Maguire and Johnson, Scottish rider, Peter Niven never even challenged closely for the title. His best was third place in 1991–92 with 105 winners. Brought up around horses, he graduated through gymkhanas, show jumping and cross-country riding to have his first win on Loch Brandy in a hunter chase at Sedgefield in 1984. His mother trained the horse. After unproductive spells with both David Nicholson and Jimmy Fitzgerald, he moved to Mary Reveley's Saltburn stables as an amateur rider cum pupil assistant. However, there was no stable jockey at the time and Niven took over that role. When he arrived at Saltburn he had only two winners, one under Rules and the other in a point-to-point, hardly a precursor to the successful partnership that would develop on the northern courses. The stable did not pursue the big events, concentrating on quantity rather than quality. Hence he rode only one winner at the Cheltenham Festival, Monsieur Le Cure in the 1994 Sun Alliance Novices' Chase. His great achievement was to ride five winners on a card three times in the same season – at Kelso, Doncaster and Sedgefield in 1991–92 – still a unique performance. He was a powerful but unstylish rider. His forte was his tactical ability to be in the right place at the right time. He was also brave. In December 1999 he fractured a bone in his neck, but, despite the risk of paralysis, he came back to riding. At the time he needed 26 more victories to reach the 1,000 milestone. He achieved this on Colourful Life at Wetherby in 2001. Two wins later he retired to become a trainer at Malton.

On the flat Steve Donoghue was the dominant rider until the era of Gordon Richards (see separate entries). There were rivals to Richards. Tommy Weston won 11 Classics, including two Derbys, thanks mainly to securing the position of jockey for Lord Derby from 1923 to 1934. He was champion jockey in 1926, the year that Gordon Richards was sidelined with tuberculosis. Charlie Elliott was the same age as Richards but had collected four Classics before Richards notched his first. He also had two jockeys' championships, the first while still an apprentice. Later his taste for the high life led him into gambling and, fearful that the Jockey Club might take away his licence, he opted to ride in France. Four times Derby winner Charlie Smirke might have won even more had he not actually lost his licence for five years after being found guilty of making no attempt to start on the favourite in a two-year-old race. No such fate ever befell Harry Wragg who became known as the 'Head Waiter' because of his riding tactic of slipstreaming and then coming from behind. He argued that in the days before photo-finish cameras judges tended to favour the horse gaining ground at the post. His style brought him three Derbys.

Joe Mercer, famous as the partner of Brigadier Gerard, rode from 1950 to 1985 and is ranked sixth on the all-time list of successful British jockeys – behind Gordon Richards, Pat Eddery, Lester Piggott, Willie Carson and Doug Smith (see separate entries) – with 2,810 winners. His best season was 1979 when he gained his sole championship with 164 victories. Eddie Hide spent most of his 35-year career based in the North and rode 2,591 winners, the greatest aggregate for any non championship-winning jockey. He secured six Classics but his speciality lay in the big handicaps. Geoff Lewis, formerly a Waldorf pageboy, rode winners for both his sovereign and a prime minister, piloted Mill Reef to a Derby win, but was never able to wrest the championship from Lester Piggott.

At the beginning of the twenty-first century Kieren Fallon is the champion and Frankie Dettori the celebrity (see separate entries). Walter Swinburn, alas is not there to compete with them. He followed his father into racing and won three Derbys through his ability to settle a horse. However, in 1996 he finished in intensive care after a horrific fall in Hong Kong when his mount galloped through the running rail rather than taking a bend. He came back to win the Breeders' Cup Turf on Pilsudski but, like many jockeys before him, could not overcome the associated twin demons of weight and alcohol.

Further reading

Fitzgeorge-Parker, T., *Steeplechase Jockeys: The Great Ones* (London: Pelham, 1971).
Seth-Smith, M. *et al.*, *The History of Steeplechasing* (London: Michael Joseph, 1971).
Tanner, M., *Great Jockeys of the Flat* (London: Guinness, 1992).

See also American invasion, International.

Two Thousand Guineas

See Classics.

Moneybox

Terimon, at 500–1, is the longest priced runner-up ever in a Derby (1989).

The Minstrel became the first horse to win more than £200,000 in a British racing season in 1977, having won both the Epsom and Irish Derbys and the King George, as well as finishing third in the Two Thousand Guineas – he would have netted £750,000 in current values.

A **Trifecta** is a Tote bet in which punters have to select the first three home in the correct order – a similar non-Tote bet is a **Tricast**.

Troy went through the £300,000 prize money barrier in 1979 with victories in the Epsom and Irish Derbys and the King George, as well as third place in the Arc (that would be £900,000 now).

Tulyar finally broke the career winnings record of Isinglass (1895) in 1952, amassing £76,577 from nine wins, a second and a third.

The **Two Thousand Guineas** was worth £5,505 (almost £380,000 now) to the winner, Sceptre, in 1902 but only £174,000 to the winner, Rock of Gibraltar, in 2002.

U

Horsebox

Ubedizzy finished second in the 6-furlong Abernant Stakes at Newmarket in 1978 but was subsequently banned from British racecourses for trying to savage his lad in the unsaddling enclosure.

Udaipur won the Oaks and Coronation Stakes in 1932 for the Aga Khan and bred Umiddad, Ascot Gold Cup winner in 1944.

Unfuwain was second in the King George in 1988, and won the Chester Vase in the same year.

Unite won the Oaks and the Irish Oaks for Sheikh Mohammed in 1987, one of only six fillies (to 1990) to do the double.

User Friendly was the last filly to win the St Leger, in 1992, as well as the Oaks, the Irish Oaks and the Yorkshire Oaks, making her flat-race horse of the year.

Ushers Island won the 1994 Whitbread Gold Cup.

Moneybox

In 1940 Major A.E. Allnatt purchased 12 yearlings from the Aga Khan for £4,800. He later sold one of them **Ujiji** for £30,000 after it won the wartime Gold Cup.

Once horses are **under** starter's orders all bets stand.

The winning horse in the **United Services Steeplechase** at Newbury in 1940 was disqualified because his rider was not a commissioned officer.

A horse that finishes third may be regarded as **unplaced** for betting purposes if there are less than six runners in the race.

The **Usher-Vaux** Brewery Gold Tankard at Ayr was one of many races sponsored in the 1960s by the alcohol industry.

Uttoxeter, owned by Sir Stanley Clarke, was a favourite track for Lord Gyllene, also owned by Sir Stanley Clarke. He ran half his races there and won three as well the 1997 Grand National.

V

> **Horsebox**
>
> **Vaguely Noble** winner of the Prix de l'Arc de Triomphe in 1968, and sire of Dahlia, twice winner of the King George, and Empery, Derby winner of 1976, was trained in England as a two-year-old before moving to France.
>
> **Valoris**, ridden by Lester Piggott, won the Irish One Thousand Guineas and the Oaks in 1966.
>
> **Viking Flagship** won the Queen Mother Champion Chase twice in 1994 and 1995, as did Barnbrook Again (1989, 1990), Pearlyman (1987, 1988), Hilly Way (1978, 1979), Skymas (1976, 1977), Royal Relief (1972, 1974), Drinny's Double (1967, 1968) and Fortria (1960, 1961); Badsworth Boy won it three times (1983–85).
>
> **Vimy** was the first French-bred and trained horse to win the King George in 1955, by a head.
>
> **Volodyovski** won the 1901 Derby, the first winner to bred by a woman, Lady Meux, and the only Classic success for American jockey Lester Reiff before he was warned off.
>
> **Vulgan** was leading National Hunt sire nine times from 1959 to 1974; his offspring included three Grand National winners – Team Spirit (1964), Foinavon (1967) and Gay Trip (1970).

Veterinary practice

Vets in racing have a host of tasks to perform from treating mares with hormones to assist the reproductive cycle to putting down injured animals with a lethal injection. Some veterinary treatments can seem alarming. Injured tendons are often treated by 'firing' in which a red hot iron or sulphuric acid is applied to the skin of the affected leg – under local anaesthetic these days – in the belief that blistering will promote healing by increasing the flow of blood to the area and the consequent scar tissue will strengthen the weakened area. In 1991 this treatment was banned by the Royal College of Veterinary Surgeons, but so many vets objected that firing is now common practice again. As with human ailments medical knowledge has changed and will continue to change. For most injuries rest is usually advised – not always that easy with equine patients – but remedial exercises with a heavier shoe on one foot enabled Carvill's Hill to overcome a chronic back problem, caused by a bad fall, and go on to win the Welsh National in 1991. Other developments include the implantation of carbon fibres to strengthen tendons and the use of anti-inflammatory drugs to combat muscular spasm, though caution has to be exercised in the latter case as if the drugs are in a horse's system when it races the trainer's licence could be at stake. Vets have also turned to athletics to borrow both the idea of nasal strips to increase the flow of air to the lungs by opening up the nostrils as well as looking at how shoes could be varied according to leg length and joint angles.

One area where there has been little development in veterinary practice is that of fractured legs. Generally little attempt is made to deal with serious fractures, for although it would be possible to treat the break itself, there are significant convalescent problems, as horses cannot easily have the weight taken off the injured limb. Additionally the risks of infection following a fall on turf are very high and sometimes no amount of antibiotics can prevent infection spreading and causing irreparable damage. Basically in the event of a bad fracture the vet has the option of trying to treat an injury which will, at best, result in a protracted and painful recovery period with no guarantee of a return to racing or killing the horse with a lethal injection. Usually it is the latter procedure that is adopted apart from the most valuable stallions retained for stud purposes.

Those vets who work for the Jockey Club have four key responsibilities. First they act to safeguard the integrity of racing by verifying the identity of horses running and taking post-race samples of urine and blood for dope testing. Second they are concerned with racehorse welfare and examine them for signs of excessive whipping, monitor the return to racing of horses that have been injured, and investigate complaints about the mistreatment of animals in training. Associated with this welfare function is their role in checking racecourse veterinary facilities and personnel and the standards of their response to – and management of – injuries. Additionally they provide clinical back up at the courses. The officers are assigned to specific regions to allow them to cultivate working relationships within the area and, in particular, with the veterinary practices employed by the individual racecourses.

Until the late 1990s the Jockey Club veterinary team was used principally in a regulatory capacity, but under the leadership of Chief Veterinary Adviser Peter Webbon, their role has expanded increasingly into pro-active welfare activities. One of these has resulted in a new specification for horse ambulances which insists on them being equipped with gently inclined ramps, telescopic partitions, the ability to load and unload horses in a straight line, a winch and sling, and a driver experienced in handling and transporting horses. They have also become involved in several research projects looking at retrospective studies of risk factors for racecourse injuries and the influence of training surfaces on injury.

Further reading

www.thejockeyclub.co.uk

Virtual racing

The classic example of virtual racing was the small Cornish meeting held by the Trodmore Hunt on August Bank Holiday 1898. The card appeared in *The Sportsman* prior to the race and the results the next day with two 5–1 winners and the rest at shorter odds. But the meeting never actually took place. It was a phantom fixture organised by a betting syndicate to take advantage of a busy day in the racing schedule by pretending that Trodmore was, like several hunts, putting on an annual event. The perpetrators were certainly imaginative; not only did they invent a meeting but also the names of 41 runners, only two of which had previously appeared in the *Racing Calendar*. In contrast to the creation of a meeting, there have also been attempts to announce that racing has been abandoned as in late 1978 when false information was given to radio stations that meetings at Haydock Park, Southwell and Newton Abbot were not to take place. Fleet Street journalists were the prime suspects but no one was ever apprehended.

Charity organisations often feature 'race nights' in which pool betting takes place on filmed and videoed races. Such material is drawn from racing all over the world, as each race must contain exactly eight runners so that the betting system can operate prior to the film or video being played. The horses remain anonymous and a commentary is dubbed on to the film or video using numbers rather than names. In effect it is a glorified lottery; but so, some people would say, is horseracing itself.

Any exhibition of Victorian children's toys might feature a horseracing board game using a dice or top to determine the distance moved by each animal. More sophisticated versions have developed in the twentieth century though the basic aim remains the same: to be the first past the post. Totopoly – with the names of the horses originally based on the winners of the Lincolnshire Handicap from 1926 to 1937 – allowed for pre-race play that gave some horses advantages when it came to the races themselves. More recently the 'Really Nasty' Horse Racing Game has brought in the concept of false starts, photo-finishes, remounting, objections and stewards enquiries as well as betting odds dependent upon the actual chances of the horses determined by their draw at the start and advantages that can be gained during play. However, this can be offset by the owner opting to throw the race or by opponents deliberately blocking the progress of the horse: not that this really mirrors what might happen in real racing! Computerised racing games are now available but, as yet, they cater interactively only for bettors and owners and do not allow players to get into the saddle. This is not the case of those who participated in the Grand National Experience at Aintree where a virtual reality ride was available courtesy of jockey-cam recordings during real races.

Computers were used in March 2000 to run the Grand National in advance in Covent Garden rather than Aintree. A software programme that incorporated 18 form and performance statistics determined the outcome. The result placed Choisty, a 50–1 outsider, just ahead of Dark Stranger with Irish challenger, Micko's Dream, third and Star Traveller fourth. The stunt was sponsored by bookmaker Victor Chandler who later offered 8–1 against these four horses actually competing the course in the real race at Aintree. His money was safe. Both Choisty and Micko's Dream fell, Dark Stranger unseated his rider, and Star Traveller was pulled up! A 50–1 outsider Master Marcus also won a simulated King George VI Chase staged by the BBC in 1967 during the Foot and Mouth outbreak. Some websites now organise total computerised racing in which participants buy virtual horses, design their own silks, train the animals and race them against others on-screen in real time for prize money. Form books are kept and betting facilities also offered. In effect this fantasy racing mirrors the real thing with most 'owners' treating it as an entertaining hobby though with lower prize money and also lesser costs.

See also Internet.

Virus and other ailments

The 'virus', racing parlance for any respiratory viral infection but particularly equine flu, is bad news for a trainer. It may put a horse out of racing for several weeks if not months, but worse still it can spread like wild fire to other horses sharing the stables. Although it is mandatory for a racehorse to have a course of flu injections before he is permitted to race, nothing seems to stop the spread of the disease. Indeed once an outbreak has been detected some trainers simply opt out of racing until the affliction has run its course. Other respiratory disorders such as 'whistling' or 'roaring' are attributable to an obstruction or paralysis in the larynx that affects the horse's ability to breathe.

Many other ailments, particularly those affecting the legs, tend to stem from the fact that thoroughbreds are racehorses running at high speed on variable surfaces. 'Breaking down' occurs when tendons are excessively strained: some horses' legs can stand a lot of work but others break down relatively easily. Young horses in particular are liable to fracture their knees, especially towards the end of the race when muscles are tired, rendering the knee joint – with its seven bones – and its tendons less stable. Sore shins and other stress fractures come from the repeated concussion of immature limbs on hard ground. 'Splints', which can cause lameness, occur when one of the small bones between the knee and fetlock becomes enlarged because of a kick or by stress on the bones and ligaments. 'Overreaching' is when the front of the hind plate strikes and cuts the front foot just above the heel. It tends to occur on heavy surfaces that delay the lifting of the front feet and when a horse is being driven hard towards the end of a race.

Breaking a blood vessel is a common occurrence in horses, though in Britain there is no stigma attached to it, except for the animal being labelled a 'bleeder'. In contrast in both Australia and Hong Kong they face a mandatory three-month ban if they bleed once and a lifetime ban if it occurs again. Colic, basically an obstruction in the digestive system, can be a major killer of horses as they cannot vomit and hence are reliant on bowel lubricants. If these fail to do the trick, surgery has to be resorted to. In poorly managed stables colic can be caused by overfeeding tired horses, using poor quality forage, suddenly changing a horse's diet, and allowing tooth irregularities that prevent the animal chewing properly. Colic is much rarer in well-run yards and is generally self-inflicted by greedy feeders that bolt their food.

Injury and disease cost money in veterinary bills and in lost opportunities to race. Injury is perhaps inevitable in the nature of racing but disease, the constant fear of every trainer, is to some extent avoidable. To lessen the chances of it developing and spreading within his stables Aidan O'Brien, the star Irish trainer, insists that every one of his horses has its own equipment and any of them having a night away from the Ballydoyle yard must return to an isolation box. Owning their own horse transport can also allow trainers some degree of control over a possible outbreak of infection. Unfortunately there is little that any individual trainer can do about racecourse stables, a perennial source of contagion.

Further reading

Magee, S., *The Channel Four Racing Guide to Racehorses* (London: Channel 4 Books, 1999).

Moneybox

Vacarne at 8–1 on was beaten in the Combe Stakes at Sandown in 1959 by Bali Ha'i, a horse given to the Queen Mother on a tour of New Zealand.

The **Victoria Sporting Club** was a betting house opened in London in 1860 which became an important centre for making and settling sets.

Lorna Vincent was the first professional female rider to win under National Hunt Rules when she brought home 25–1 shot Pretty Cute at Devon on 18 August 1978, beating six male jockeys in the process.

Dr Carlo Vittadina was leading owner in 1975 (£209,493), the year his colt Grundy won the Derby and King George.

M. Leon Volterra bred both the first and second horses in the 1948 Derby. All the placed horses in the 1961 Derby were owned by women: winner Psidium by Mrs Arpad Plesch, the second Dicta Drake by **Mme Suzy Volterra** and the third Pardao by Mrs C.O. Iselin.

W, X

Wales

Wales has been virtually a racing-free zone for much of the twentieth century, with only two racecourses, Bangor-on-Dee and Chepstow, and a small number of training centres concentrated in the south and along the border. But it was not always so. The period from 1775 to 1875 saw flat racing at no fewer than 30 venues, from Conwy in the north to Cardiff in the south, from Wrexham near the English border to Carmarthen in the west. Recent plans to develop a new course in South Wales have so far failed.

Although Bangor-on-Dee, a small jumps track near Wrexham, is probably best known as the racecourse without a grandstand, the more prestigious Chepstow, operating on the flat and over jumps, is the home of the Welsh Champion Hurdle and the Welsh National. The Hurdle, held in April, has been won by stars such as Bula (1971), Night Nurse (1976 and 1977), Monksfield (1979), Sea Pigeon (1980) and the Welsh-trained Persian War (1969), who had a novice hurdle and a bar at the racecourse named after him. The Welsh National, first run in 1895, takes place over 3 miles 6 furlongs at the course in late December and has produced Rag Trade (1976), Corbière (1982) and Earth Summit (1997), all of whom went on to victory at Aintree. On the flat, history was made at Chepstow in October 1933 when Gordon Richards rode the winners of all six races on the card, following this achievement with five victories on the second day of the meeting, a feat which went some way towards ensuring both the jockey championship and a record number of wins in one season.

Welsh prestige, however, has tended to come under National Hunt rules. Grand National winner Kirkland (1905), Cheltenham Gold Cup winners Patron Saint (1928) and Norton's Coin (1990), and most famously, the three-time Champion Hurdle ace, Persian War (1968–70) were all trained in Wales, the latter by Colin Davies at Chepstow. Emblem (1863), Poethlyn (1919) and Maori Venture (1987), all Grand National winners, were Welsh-bred, as were Dick Rees, Dudley Williams and Neale Doughty who partnered Aintree heroes Shaun Spadah (1921), Kellsboro' Jack (trained by Welshman Ivor Anthony in 1933) and Hallo Dandy (1984) to victory.

Rees, the greatest inter-war jump jockey, was the first to win 100 races in a National Hunt season (1924) and was champion jockey five times between 1920 and 1927. He also rode one of the pre-1939 steeplechase stars, Easter Hero, to victory in the 1929 Cheltenham Gold Cup, having won the inaugural race on Red Splash in 1924, while fellow Welshman Evan Williams landed the race in 1936, the fifth consecutive victory for the other equine champion of the period, Golden Miller. Geoff Lewis, runner-up to Lester Piggott in the jockeys' championship of 1969 and 1970, provides a rare story of Welsh achievement on the flat but the most successful Welshmen in racing have probably been Fulke Walwyn (see separate entry), five times champion trainer and winning Grand National jockey in 1936 on Reynoldstown, and the Anthony brothers.

Sons of a Carmarthenshire farmer, Jack, Ivor and Owen Anthony were all jump jockeys at one time. Jack, who was both amateur and professional champion, won the Grand National three times in 1911, 1915 and 1920 (on Glenside, Ally Sloper and Troytown) before moving on to a career in training. He won the Cheltenham Gold Cup twice as trainer of Easter Hero, as did brother Ivor with Morse Code (1938) and Poet Prince (1941). Ivor also sent out two Grand National winners, Kellboro' Jack in 1933 and Royal Mail in 1937 but is probably best remembered as the trainer of Brown Jack, six times winner of the Queen Alexandra Stakes at Royal Ascot. Although Owen became known as the last handler of Golden Miller, he also lifted the Cheltenham Gold Cup on two other occasions with Thrown In (1927) and Roman Hackle (1940), and won the Grand National with Music Hall in 1922.

Like the Scots, the Welsh have had to move away from their native land in order to pursue careers in racing, although neither the Anthony brothers nor Fulke Walwyn, based in Lambourn, had to settle a great distance from the border. Certainly none will have travelled as far as Sheila Laxon in pursuit of glory. Born in Pontypridd, she is the successful trainer of Ethereal, winner of the Melbourne Cup in 2002, and a resident of New Zealand!

Further reading

Pitt, C., *A Long Time Gone* (Halifax: Portway, 1996).
Smyly, P., *Encyclopedia of Steeplechasing* (London: Hale, 1979).

Walwyn, Fulke (1910–91)

Fulke Thomas Tyndall Walwyn had a remarkable career as a National Hunt trainer. In addition to five training titles his horses brought him the prestigious Hennessy, Whitbread and the Grand Military Gold Cups seven times each, the King George VI five times, the Cheltenham Gold Cups four times, the Champion Hurdle and the Scottish Grand National twice and one Aintree Grand National. Ironically for a man brought up near Chepstow racecourse he never won the Welsh National. Overall, prior to his retirement in 1990, he trained the winners of 2,188 races over jumps and hurdles.

His father had been Master of the Monmouthshire Hounds and Fulke learned to ride and hunt at an early age. His first racing win was on Ciren in a point-to-point in April 1930 and his first under National Hunt rules on Alpine Hut at Cardiff the same month. He became a successful gentleman rider, winning the amateur championship three times and piloting Reynoldstown to victory in the 1936 Grand National despite losing both his whip and an iron. After resigning from the army he turned professional and won several races before a near-fatal fall at Ludlow in 1939 fractured his skull and rendered him unconscious for a month.

He then began training, operating a small establishment at Delamere House in Lambourn and winning 18 races before the outbreak of war. In 1944 he purchased Saxon House Stables in Upper Lambourn and became champion trainer in three successive seasons beginning in 1946–47. For a number of years he was also a successful flat-race trainer. Much of his early success over jumps and hurdles was due to Dorothy Paget's horses. Although she had a reputation for dismissing her trainers at whim, Walwyn lasted nearly ten years and even curbed her habit of late night phone calls and nocturnal visits to the stables. On one memorable occasion Walwyn and jockey Bryan Marshall almost took her horses through the card at Folkestone on 29 September 1948, winning five and coming second in the last race. Ultimately he broke with Miss Paget after having 'had enough' of her difficult behaviour.

When Paget's horses departed in 1954 his boxes did not remain empty for long. He attracted some outstanding animals, including Mill House, who in 1963 won the Cheltenham Gold Cup, the Hennessy and the King George, and Diamond Edge, twice a Whitbread winner in 1979 and 1981. Team Spirit was another of his champions which when it won at Aintree in 1964 meant that Walwyn had become the first man to both ride and train a Grand National winner. His favourite, however, was the diminutive Mandarin who arrived in 1954 with a reputation as a poor jumper but, under Walwyn's tuition, went on to win both the Hennessy and King George twice and also the Cheltenham Gold Cup. In 1973, following the death of Peter Cazalet, the Queen Mother transferred her horses to Saxon House and Walwyn went on to win 150 races for her.

Walwyn lived for his horses. He understood them and treated each one of his string as an individual animal. He was a genius with doubtful legs and never hurried an injured horse back into serious training. He had infinite patience with horses, less so with people: jockeys who failed to ride to orders or who were too hard on his horses could expect a loud reprimand even before they dismounted.

He was appointed CVO in 1983 but probably would have felt more honoured by the posthumous renaming of the Kim Muir Memorial Chase, the 3-mile race for amateur riders on the opening day of the Cheltenham National Hunt Festival, as the Fulke Walwyn Challenge Cup Chase.

Further reading

Fuller, B., *Fulke Walwyn: A Pictorial Tribute* (London: Lambourn, 1990).

Weather

Horseracing is particularly susceptible to the vagaries of weather. Frost, snow, rain and fog can cause abandonment because of treacherous surfaces, water-logging or poor visibility but dry or hot weather can present problems associated with firm ground, including potential damage to fragile limbs. All-weather racing was introduced to Britain in 1989 in an attempt to combat the worst of the British winter but even it has occasionally fallen victim to combinations of snow, frost and fog.

Newspaper reports for nearly 200 years are peppered with references to inclement weather. The 1839 Derby was run in a snow flurry. The frozen conditions at Aintree in 1845 resulted in a vote by owners to determine whether the Grand National should take place and in 1901 it was the turn of jockeys to protest at the raging blizzard in which they were required to compete. The bad weather which caused the abandonment of the National Hunt Festival at Cheltenham in 1937 also deprived Golden Miller of the opportunity to win a sixth consecutive Gold Cup. The opening meeting of the flat season at Lincoln in 1947 had to be abandoned because the course was flooded, a misfortune that affects Worcester racecourse on the frequent occasions when the adjacent River Severn bursts its banks. There is an apocryphal story that a local rowing eight was once seen racing down the submerged course, screaming 'photograph' as they passed the winning post. The severe winter of 1962–63 necessitated an 11-week layoff for the entire racing industry with only one meeting, at Ayr, between 22 December 1962 and 8 March 1963, the longest weather-induced break in racing history. In the winter of 1967, a shorter spell of bad weather led a London evening newspaper to organise computerised racing using information about well-known steeplechasers. A commentary for the 'races' was provided and bookmakers offered betting facilities.

Hot, dry weather can also cause problems. The drought of summer 1976 led to abandoned fixtures because of the restrictions on watering courses. It was said that some high-class two-year-olds never appeared at a racecourse that year and trainers sometimes refused to run their charges either because they feared injuries or because they were unable to prepare the horses properly on bone-dry gallops at home. In recent years, however, waterlogging became a particular problem with wet springs and autumns in 2000 and 2001.

The financial consequences of bad weather can be disastrous. When the Boxing Day race programmes were wiped out in 1995, the estimated loss in betting turnover was £50 million, and ten racecourses, only partially protected by insurance, missed out on lucrative holiday fixtures. The abandonment of its Boxing Day meeting to frost and waterlogging in five consecutive years to 1999 led Newton Abbot racecourse in Devon to exchange the fixture for a summer jumps day instead, overturning a 150-year tradition in the process. The loss of betting levy resulting from the absence of turf racing for two weeks over Christmas and New Year 1996–97 was estimated at over £1million, despite a programme of replacement meetings on the all-weather tracks. For self-employed jockeys, a racing shutdown can mean no income.

Although it is sometimes the prevailing weather conditions which result in abandoned meetings, it is the impact of weather on racing surfaces that can cause long-term difficulties for racecourse officials and trainers. Many horses have a preference for a particular state of the ground and prolonged periods of wet or dry weather can interfere with campaigns mapped out for individual horses, result in reduced or greatly enhanced fields, and influence the outcome of races. Trainers are unable to prepare their animals if the gallops are waterlogged or frozen although this is less of a problem in the age of all-weather training areas. While stables have to combat the problem of keeping horses fit, owners are faced with training bills that cannot be recouped on the racecourse. Further frustration can be caused by raceable courses whose car parks and access roads are impassable.

The difficulties of racing in the unpredictable British climate have been partly ameliorated by all-weather racetracks and gallops but with only three such racecourses – operating solely on the flat – their impact in providing punters with a betting market has probably been greater than the opportunities they afford trainers to keep horses employed. All-weather racing is geared towards inexperienced or modest horses and is no substitute for abandoned National Hunt meetings. The best that can usually be achieved for jump racing is the provision of replacement fixtures and the rescheduling of significant races. When the Grade One Tolworth Hurdle at Sandown Park was lost to waterlogging on Saturday 4 January 2003, it was transferred to Warwick the following weekend, only for that fixture to succumb to frost. After bad weather caused the abandonment of all turf meetings for the first fortnight of the new year, the race finally took place on 18 January at Wincanton.

British racing, however, is not alone in having to contend with the elements. The Dubai World Cup, held at the desert racecourse of Nad al Sheba, was washed out by storms and torrential downpours in March 1997 and had to be rescheduled for five days later, once the track had dried out.

Further reading

Kay, J. and Vamplew, W., *Weatherbeaten. Sport in the British Climate* (Edinburgh: Mainstream, 2002).

See also Abandonment, All-weather racing.

Weatherbys

Weatherbys is often referred to as the civil service of racing but it actually takes a wider role than that might imply, including running a bank and an insurance firm. One-third of its profits are ploughed back into racing, mainly via sponsorship of races. The firm has been entrepreneurial for many years and is famously associated with the *Racing Calendar* and the *General Stud Book*, though the former publication was not begun by the family who, seeing a profit to be made from providing a service to racing and breeding, took over the idea from the originators.

The firm has three main departments: racing administration, racing operations and editorial services. The first of these registers the names of horses and the colours of their owners, allocates weights to horses (working closely with the official handicappers), and processes the race results. The operations group handles each transaction connected with every race in Britain – up to 3,000 a day at busy times – from the initial entries through to the final list of runners and riders, including the details of the draw, whether blinkers will be worn, and the weights to be carried on the day. This information is then transmitted by computer to newspapers, broadcasters and the racecourses. The editorial department has the responsibility for the compilation of a wide range of publications including the *Programme Book* that provides all the details of conditions pertaining to individual races (a vital tool to trainers in selecting the events for their charges), the *Racing Calendar*, the *General Stud Book* and the flat and jump racing *Pattern Race Annuals*. They also supply the majority of British racecourses with their racecards.

Weatherbys is also a registered bank (keeping accounts for owners, trainers and jockeys), a leading bloodstock insurance agent, and a specialist in providing asset finance for such items as horseboxes, horse walkers and veterinary equipment. In 2001 the work of the National Jockeys Booking Agency became part of Weatherbys' internet operations. Based at the offices of the Jockeys Association, for nine years the Agency had acted as link between jockeys seeking rides and those seeking jockeys especially when declaration time was looming. It is also Weatherbys' technology that is behind the Racecourse Association's PASS (Privileged Access Swipe System) operation under which owners, jockeys, trainers and others with regular business on the racecourses are issued with a swipe card.

Until 1970 the firm was based in London, but this location was not ideal for access to the major British training centres. The headquarters were therefore moved to Wellingborough in Northamptonshire which is only a couple of hours drive from Newmarket, Malton, Middleham, Lambourn and Epsom, as well as being close enough to London to facilitate liaison with the Jockey Club and British Horseracing Board.

The relationship with racing's authorities dates back to 1771 when James Weatherby was appointed Keeper of the Match Book, Stakeholder and Secretary to the Jockey Club. From then till the death of Simon Weatherby in the 1980s a family member always held that important secretarial position.

Further reading

www.weatherbys-group.com

See also General Stud Book, *Racing Calendar*.

Weight

Almost by definition there is no such person as a fat jockey: if riders cannot make the weight then they do not have a job. There is also a fine line between losing enough weight to get a ride and maintaining sufficient strength to control the horse. The nineteenth-century jockey relied on eating little and combating even that with a regimen of long walks in heavy clothes, Turkish baths and purgatives. Little changed for many years. Records kept by northern jockey Eddie Hide in the 1960s and 1970s show that he sweated off an average of 18 st a season. Modern jockeys use a combination of diuretics, laxatives, rubber suits, saran wraps, and pre-race saunas. Nevertheless, like their earlier counterparts, the primary method of weight control is still diet. Ex-champions Lester Piggott and Pat Eddery chose to eat very little, especially after they had conquered the hunger of the first few months and got used to having to go without, the former using cigars, the latter cigarettes to help suppress the appetite. Self-discipline is vital. Current National Hunt champion, Tony McCoy, who rides $1\frac{1}{2}$ st below the normal weight for a man of his build, often survives on a cup of tea and a bar of chocolate on a day when he is racing. Fortunately for today's jockeys they no longer have to rely simply on doing what their forefathers did. When Michael Turner became Chief Medical Adviser to the Jockey Club in the early 1990s one of his early decisions was to treat jockeys as professional athletes and offer them scientific advice on nutrition and weight control. Jockeys have also resorted more to the gym over the past five years to help them lose weight and keep fit.

Jockeys accept wasting as a normal part of their routine in the same way as other elite athletes who adopt disciplined training regimes. Successfully making the weight demonstrates their personal competence and self-determination. Other sports also have weight categories, but unlike boxing and amateur wrestling, jockeys do not have the luxury of rehydrating or eating after they have weighed out for competition. They have to weigh in again with only a 1 lb margin permissible. The demands of the sport lead to undesirable eating patterns and practices that can involve sessions of rapid weight loss of up to 5 per cent of bodyweight. However the racing environment may not only precipitate eating disorders, it can also legitimise them. As the great majority of riders use the sauna and waste regularly, any young jockey attempting to control his weight is likely to be influenced to engage in the same practices. Those jockeys who have a constant battle with their weight are glamorised within the industry and congratulated for their efforts by owners, trainers and the media.

There are health implications to wasting, particularly when it involves the use of laxatives, diuretics, appetite suppressants and vomiting. Stress fractures are more likely after falls, dehydration can affect the kidneys, and there can be a psychological effect via depression, confusion and tension. Associated with wasting is a high incidence of smoking and relatively high alcohol consumption, both of which can bring their own health problems. Continued efforts by jockeys to keep their weight artificially low are dangerous to their health. Although Eddie Hide, who used to go running wrapped in sweaters and a mackintosh, found life was more relaxing and easier once saunas became available, sauna-induced dehydration and long periods of inadequate nutrition reduce the ability to concentrate, affect the body's thermostatic qualities and blood flows, and deplete liver glycogen – all of which can lead to accidents and serious illness. Leading flat rider John Reid was hospitalised by kidney stones caused by chronic dehydration. Nineteenth-century rider, George Barrett, was known to eat well then stick his fingers down his throat. Such practices have not ceased. Steve Cauthen, who rode a stone under his natural weight, exhibited bulimic behaviour and Walter Swinburn was eventually forced out of racing by this eating disorder. Others, such as champion National Hunt jockey Richard Dunwoody, have suffered from anorexia. Ultimately wasting can have fatal consequences. Constantly trying to lose weight contributed to the early deaths of Victorian riders Tom French, John Charlton and Tom Chalenor, all of them Classic winners, John Wells, twice champion jockey, and the great Fred Archer; and in the early twentieth century to those of three times champion, Danny Maher, and Australian Brownie Carslake.

Why jockeys have to be so small is not clear. In the mid-eighteenth century 9 st seems to have been a minimum in racing for normal thoroughbreds. The emergence of lighter weights probably owes something to gambling owners – and most of them were – realising that they gave an advantage in a race as well as lessening the risk that a valuable thoroughbred would break down. Such weights contradict the oft-used nineteenth-century rationale for horseracing as a racecourse test that produced horses from which quality army remounts could be bred. Put simply, army officers rarely weigh less than 8 st! There is more logic to the argument if it is applied to National Hunt racing where, perhaps because of its origins in the hunting field, average weights carried are normally 2–3 st higher than on the flat.

Over time the Jockey Club has raised the minimum weight to be carried by a horse to its present level of 7 st 10 lb in contrast to the 4 st of 1850, the 5 st 7 lb of 1875 and even the 7 st introduced after the First World War. The recent legislation has recognised that, even for jockeys, average body weights have risen, but in the nineteenth century this was done to protect horses and owners rather than jockeys. Too little weight implied insufficient strength to control a fractious mount which might have led to accidents or to erratic running in a tight finish, both of which could have serious financial consequences for those who owned valuable horseflesh. The raising of the minimum weight backfired in one respect in that it reduced opportunities for lightweight apprentices who would have had to carry too much deadweight for the liking of most trainers. In the early twentieth century the Jockey Club brought in the apprentice weight allowance to help rectify the situation. A recent study by Michael Caulfield has shown that only 9 per cent of flat race jockeys can ride at the minimum weight of 108 lb and only 16 per cent of trainee jockeys can make the 101 lb minimum.

Jockeys' weights are illogical, artificially imposed and dangerous to health, but they are unlikely to change as there are too many vested interests, including most existing jockeys who fear even more competition in the labour market if weight levels are raised significantly.

Further reading

Caulfield, M., *Weight Loss and Psychological State Among Jockeys*, M.Sc. thesis Brunel University 2002.
Vamplew, W., 'Still Crazy After All Those Years: Continuity in a Changing Labour Market for Professional Jockeys', *Journal of Contemporary British History* (2000), 115–45.

See also Jockeys.

Whipping

A whip is the only artificial aid that a jockey is allowed to use to balance a horse, to steer it, to keep it concentrated, and, some would argue, to give it a necessary adrenalin rush of terror. Beating animals is cruel and the Royal Society for the Prevention of Cruelty to Animals (RSPCA) is under increasing pressure to take jockeys to court under the 1911 Protection of Animals Act. Indeed they have been compiling evidence using thermal cameras that will show whip marks more clearly than conventional ones. The Jockey Club is caught between wanting to protect horses whilst allowing riders some use of the whip for control and safety purposes, and responding to a public, many of whom do not understand racing and believe all whipping to be brutal.

The response of the Jockey Club was initially to outlaw some target areas on the horse's body, and then to change the rules to allow stewards some discretion in determining how the whip had been used rather than merely counting the number of strokes. Vets were authorised to examine all placed horses and a selection of the also rans for indications of excessive whipping. Next in 1996 came additional suspensions for those riders who had already been given 15 days within a year. Such legislation has led to further bans of 15 or more days for, among others, champion National Hunt jockey, Tony McCoy. He was even sent to the British Racing School to learn a new whipping technique. Currently new technology is being tried to produce gentler, air-cushioned whips or some made of carbon fibre with foam coverings that can be used for balancing, straightening or reminding without causing real pain.

The next generation of riders are being educated. Following an agreement between the National Trainers Federation, the Jockeys Association, the Jockey Club and the RSPCA, races are being run for apprentices in which whips can be carried but not used. Nevertheless most jockeys regard use of the whip as both a necessary skill acquisition and a way of ensuring victory in a tight finish. This perhaps explains why stewards still detect almost two 200 whipping offences each year. Big races are especially tempting. In 1996 Frankie Dettori won the Two Thousand Guineas and the St Leger and was suspended after both for whip offences. In 1998 French jockey Olivier Peslier drove High-Rise home in the Derby but incurred a two-day ban for overuse of the whip. Clearly jockeys, especially in key races, regard a suspension from riding as a reasonable price to pay for victory. Even though longer bans have now been introduced for whip offences in major races, they do not seem to have acted as a deterrent. Until the authorities bring in disqualification as a punishment, or possibly the loss of the jockey's percentage of the prize money, they are open to the charge of tacitly approving the actions of the riders.

Winter, Fred (1926–2004)

One of the few men in National Hunt racing to make the transition from great jockey to great trainer – indeed only the second champion jockey also to become champion trainer – Fred Winter came from a racing family. Fred Winter senior had been champion flat apprentice in 1911. He rode till 1929 and then took up training at Epsom. Fred junior had his first public ride, also on the flat, aged 13, weighing 5 st 7 lb, but he had been riding out for his father before his fifth birthday! His eighth official ride in May 1940 brought his first win. When old enough he joined the army, became an officer, and served until 1948. By then his weight ruled him out of a flat-race career and he turned to hurdles and jumps. His first winner under National Hunt Rules was on Carton at Kempton Park 27 December 1947. After two more successes, however, he broke his back on only his eleventh ride over jumps when his mount, the eleven-year-old Tugboat Minnie, a mare that had never been placed, fell at the first hurdle at Wye. Taking that spare ride – as aspirant jockeys have to do – cost him the rest of the season.

Five years later he was champion National Hunt rider with 121 winners, a record total at the time. He was unable to defend the title as in his first race of the next season he fell in a novice hurdle at Newton Abbot, broke his left leg in several places and was out for the rest of the year. He returned to win the championship a further three times. In all he rode 923 steeplechase and hurdle winners including three Champion Hurdles, two Grand Nationals and two Cheltenham Gold Cups. He also had over 300 falls, most of which he accepted as part of the job, but, after failing to finish on 11 of the 12 rides he had at Plumpton, he refused to ride over jumps there again.

He was a strong man and could drive a horse home in a tight finish, almost lifting the animal across the line! Such was his upper body strength that his party trick was to walk around a room on his hands. His ride on Mandarin in the Grand Steeplechase de Paris at Auteuil in 1962 has entered racing folklore as an example of horsemanship and courage. Sick from breaking a 48-hour fast too indulgently, then hampered by a broken bridle which made steering the horse next to impossible for most of the race, his skill and strength kept Mandarin going even when the brave animal broke down about half a mile from home. Exhausted jockey and horse triumphed in a photo-finish.

One day, in his last season as a jockey, he rode four winners at Newbury, not all of them on fancied horses. As he walked into the changing room every rider stood up and applauded him, a demonstration of their respect and admiration.

When he quit riding he had hoped to become a starter, but was turned down by the Jockey Club who believed that he would be unable to control the jockeys. This was a blessing in disguise for National Hunt racing as he turned to training and in 1965, only three years after riding Kilmore to victory in the Grand National, he saddled Jay Trump who repeated the feat. A year later another of his horses, Anglo, also triumphed in the Aintree event. In 1975–76 he trained 99 winners, thus only just missing out on being the first Briton to both ride and train a century of winners.

In September 1987 he had his most serious fall, down the stairs at his home following a stroke. He fractured his skull and was in a coma for three weeks. He was left partially paralysed, confined to a wheelchair and unable to express himself with his usual clarity and humour. He handed over his training licence to his assistant Charlie Brooks who later purchased the Uplands stables.

Four times champion National Hunt rider, eight times champion National Hunt trainer, he is the only man in racing to have both ridden and trained winners of the Grand National, the Cheltenham Gold Cup and the Champion Hurdle. In 1993 he was inducted as a founder member of the National Hunt Hall of Fame at Cheltenham, the course where he had 189 winners, 67 as a jockey and 122 as a trainer.

Further reading

Lee, A., *Fred: The Authorised Biography of Fred Winter* (Pelham: London, 1991).

Women

Women have never played a significant part in the history of the turf. Although Queen Anne is said to have been a keen follower of racing in the eighteenth century, introducing additional prizes during her reign, and both the present Queen and the late Queen Mother have been enthusiastic and successful owners and supporters throughout the twentieth, there is little evidence that women contributed greatly to core activities in the sport. Even today, they are still most numerous in the least prestigious areas – as grooms and work riders, secretaries and 'Tote ladies' – and most visible in the traditional female roles of looking decorative and sexy, whether parading at Royal Ascot or marketing the sponsors' products. A few high profile trainers and even fewer jockeys at the top level cannot conceal the absence of women at the sharp end of the sport.

The story of women in racing is a succession of 'firsts'. At the end of the nineteenth and beginning of the twentieth centuries, women were undoubtedly involved in horse breeding. There are 22 named in the *Racing Calendar* for 1888 and 39 in 1910 but it is the female members of the aristocracy whose success is best documented. Lady Meux became the first woman to breed a Derby winner when Volodyovski won in 1901 while Lady James Douglas, having bought a stud in 1910, became the first woman to own and breed a Derby winner. Her colt Gainsborough not only won this race but also the Triple Crown in 1918, making her the first woman to be leading prize money winner of the year. She bred and owned Bayuda who won the Oaks in 1919 and bred Rose of England, the winner in 1930. Gainsborough went on to a highly successful stud career: he was champion sire in 1932 and 1933, his most famous son being Hyperion.

It has always been alleged that women were forbidden by the Jockey Club from racing horses in their own names but there is no evidence for this. Although some may have followed the nineteenth-century owners' practice of using a pseudonym, the *Racing Calendar* again demonstrates that a small number of women had registered their own colours and were racing horses before 1900. There are 24 female owners listed in *Ruff's Guide to the Turf* in 1904, divided equally between flat and jump racing. The commonly held view that women had to race incognito may stem from the high profile activities of some who did. The actress Lillie Langtry who owned Merman, the 1897 Cesarewitch winner, assumed the name of Mr Jersey but by 1900 when the horse won the Ascot Gold Cup, she had married Hugo de Bathe and was perfectly happy to be known in racing circles as Lady de Bathe.

There have been few female owners to challenge men at the elite end of the sport. Dorothy Paget was leading flat owner in 1943 when her colt Straight Deal won a wartime Derby; Lady Zia Wernher topped the list in 1955 thanks to her Triple Crown-winning filly Meld (and also bred notable sires Precipitation and Persian Gulf); and the Queen was champion owner in 1954 and 1957. Lady Beaverbrook was consistently among the top owners over a period of 30 years with horses such as Bustino and Minster Son, winners of the 1974 and 1988 St Leger, King George winner Petoski in 1985 and Mystiko, the Two Thousand Guineas champion of 1991. In recent years the name of Mrs John Magnier has cropped up regularly in the leading owner statistics, either in her own right or in partnership with others involved in the Coolmore Stud operation.

A greater number of women have been successful in jump racing where costs – and financial rewards – are much lower although many have also been wealthy, titled or both. Miss Paget was the leading prize winner on three occasions (1933–34, 1940–41 and 1951–52) and was the first and so far the only woman to have achieved the Derby–Grand National double. (Her Cheltenham Gold Cup winner Golden Miller – see separate entry – won the National in 1934.) Anne, Duchess of Westminster, is best known as the owner of Arkle (see separate entry) but she has since featured amongst the top British jump owners with Cheltenham Gold Cup winner Ten Up (1975) and Grand National winner Last Suspect (1985). Others have become leading owner on the strength of National victories – Mrs Lurline Brotherton (Freebooter 1950), Mrs Mary Stephenson (Jay Trump 1965) and Miss Juliet Reed (Rhyme 'n' Reason 1988) – but there is more scope for women to succeed at all levels of jump racing than on the flat.

Women have been accepted when they pay the bills but they have struggled for recognition as active participants in horseracing. Florence Nagle trained her first winner in 1920 but the Jockey Club refused to acknowledge women trainers and demanded that the licence be held in the name of a man, normally the head lad. This nonsense was finally overturned in 1966 when Mrs Nagle took them to court. She was granted a judicial review, the Court of Appeal noting that racing's ruling body was 'entirely out of touch with the present state of society in Great Britain'. The Jockey Club backed down before the action could be heard. This was too late for Helen Johnston Houghton who trained Gilles de Retz to win the 1956 Two Thousand Guineas but was not officially recognised. (She became one of the first women to be elected to the Jockey Club in 1977.) The record books show that Norah Wilmot was the first woman to train a winner under Jockey Club rules, in August 1966, and that Criquette Head, of the famous French racing dynasty, was the first woman to saddle an English Classic winner (Ma Biche, One Thousand Guineas, 1983). A glance at recent training statistics confirms, however, that it is a formidable challenge for a woman to train successfully on the flat in Britain. Amanda Perrett is alone in the list of top 50 trainers by prize money; cynics and misogynists will point out that she inherited a going concern from her father, trainer Guy Harwood.

It is a different picture in jump racing where there are currently three women in the top ten. Henrietta Knight took out a licence in 1989 and handles both Edredon Bleu, winner of the King George VI Chase in 2003 and the most popular steeplechaser of the day, three time Cheltenham Gold Cup winner, Best Mate. Venetia Williams won the King George in 1998 with Teeton Mill, only three years after she began training on her own, and the Welsh National in 2000 with Jocks Cross. She also won the Group Three Ormonde Stakes at Chester in 1998 with her first runner on the flat, Stretarez. Mary Reveley trains under both codes and has probably been most successful in the big flat handicaps such as the Cesarewitch and the Cambridgeshire. She started as a permit holder, sending out her first winner in 1970, was the first woman to train 100 winners in a calendar year (1991), and in 1992 became only the third trainer to achieve 50 winners in consecutive flat and jump seasons. Sue Smith is another northern trainer who has been increasingly successful in recent years. The best known female trainer to date has been Jenny Pitman (see separate entry), the only woman so far to train both a Cheltenham Gold Cup and a Grand National winner (or in this case, two National winners: Corbiere in 1983 and Royal Athlete in 1995).

Although women jockeys have been permitted since the 1970s (first in women-only amateur flat races in 1972, then against male riders in 1974, as professionals from 1975 and under National Hunt rules since 1976), this is an area in which progress has been limited. There have been many firsts – in 1972 Meriel Tufnell was the first woman to ride a winner under Jockey Club rules, at Kempton; in 1974 Linda Goodwill won the first race between men and women at Nottingham; a year later Jane McDonald rode as the first professional female jockey, at Doncaster, and in 1976 Diana Thorne was the first woman to win over jumps, at Stratford. Charlotte Brew was the first to compete in and Geraldine Rees the first to complete the Grand National. Gay Kelleway was the first to ride a winner a Royal Ascot in 1987. Alex Greaves won the Lincoln Handicap in 1991, dead-heated in the Group One Nunthorpe Stakes in 1997 and was the first women to ride in the Derby in 1998.

Isolated examples of success, however, cannot conceal that fact that women jockeys are still overlooked by top trainers (the same individuals who often rate female stable staff and work riders more highly than their male counterparts) and often viewed with suspicion by the public at large. Recent statistics suggest that punters will underestimate a horse's chance if it is ridden by a woman, which can provide trainers with good opportunities for landing a gamble. The advent of all-weather racing in 1989 increased the chances of more moderate or inexperienced jockeys picking up rides: Greaves made her name riding on the all-weather and other women have followed, including Kim Tinkler and Joanna Badger. But once they have ridden out their apprentice claim, women, like most aspiring male jockeys, find it increasingly difficult to obtain rides. Although there were 40 professional female riders licensed by the Jockey Club in 2000, the majority were apprentices, with only four fully-fledged jockeys on the flat. The excuses which are trotted out for not employing women – not strong enough in a finish, wrong sort of shape, not mentally hard enough – somehow fail to apply in other parts of the world such as North America where female riders appear to be more readily accepted. American jockey Julie Krone, who rode three winners from five horses in a meeting at Redcar in 1992, retired from the saddle in 2000 with a total of 3,545 wins including the Belmont Stakes (part of the American Triple Crown) in 1993.

The increase in women managers and media personnel has been reflected to some extent in racing, where there have been several high profile female executive appointments and prominent television presenters who discuss the races, not the fashion. There is a higher percentage of female racegoers than ever and the old guard, and with them old attitudes, are dying out. Nevertheless, the future for most women in racing does not seem appreciably brighter at the beginning of the twenty-first century than it did 20 years earlier.

Further reading

Vamplew, W. and Kay, J., 'Horseracing' in Christensen, K. *et al.* (eds), *International Encyclopedia of Women and Sports* (New York: Macmillan, 2001), 537–44.

See also Royalty.

Moneybox

The **Walton** property group purchased Aintree racecourse in 1973 and gave a five-year guarantee on the future of the Grand National.

Peter Walwyn was leading trainer in two consecutive years, 1974 (£206,784 from 96 races) and 1975 (£382,527 – a British record – from 121 races, including the Derby and King George with Grundy).

Wayward Lad held the record in 1985 for career earnings for a National Hunt horse trained in Britain – £278,064 from 28 wins, 12 seconds and 7 thirds, the equivalent of £500,000 now.

Bookmakers are not obliged to pay out on winning bets until it has been announced that jockeys have **'weighed in'** that is the riders have proved that they carried the correct weight throughout the race.

Lady Zia Wernher is the only woman apart from the Queen to have topped the table of leading flat-race owners twice, thanks to the success of Triple-Crown winning Meld (a filly she bred herself) in 1955, and her Derby-winning colt, Charlottown, a son of Meld, in 1966.

Whitbread brewers became the first commercial sponsors of racing in Britain when the inaugural Whitbread Gold Cup was run in April 1957 – they ceased sponsorship in 2002.

Y

Horsebox

Yaazir was the original name of Sheikh Mohammed's great horse, Dubai Millenium.

Yahoo was the 25–1 outsider who nearly beat Desert Orchid in the 1989 Cheltenham Gold Cup, having led him over the last fence.

Ya Malak, ridden by Alex Greaves, was involved in a dead heat for the Nunthorpe Stakes in 1997, with Coastal Bluff, ridden by Kevin Darley.

Yavana's Pace, trained by Mark Johnston, recorded his first Group One victory in 2002 – as a ten-year-old. His 16 wins have been gained in 7 different countries.

Yellow God, second to Nijinsky in the 1970 Two Thousand Guineas and a winner of five races in England and France, sired Nebbiolo, the race winner in 1977.

Your Majesty, owned by J.B. Joel, won the St Leger in 1908, was leading money winner of that year and finished up as a sire in Argentina.

Year (racing)

The shape of the racing year, once determined largely by physical factors such as weather, ground conditions and transport, has undergone significant change since the late twentieth century with the advent of all-weather courses, flood-lit racing, summer jumps fixtures, Sunday meetings and easier long-distance travel. The pattern of flat racing's major events, however, has altered surprisingly little in 150 years, with many taking place in roughly the same weeks as they did in the reign of Queen Victoria. All this may soon change if radical plans for the future of British racing are implemented.

Racing under both sets of rules now takes place all year, but although moderate flatracers can earn their keep between November and March on the artificial tracks of Lingfield Park, Southwell and Wolverhampton, the winter months are still dominated by National Hunt racing. In the first quarter, all roads lead to Cheltenham and Aintree. The season for many good hurdlers and steeplechasers is mapped around an appearance at one or both of these fixtures, held in mid-March and early April, and while the Grand National meeting attracts great public interest, the National Hunt Festival at Cheltenham remains the outstanding event of the jumping calendar.

The end of March sees the start of flat racing at Doncaster with the first big handicap of the year, the Lincoln, but the major spring meetings, the Craven at Newmarket and the Newbury meeting in April provide early trials for the three-year-olds that will contest the year's Classics. The first two of these, the One Thousand and Two Thousand Guineas, are held at Newmarket at the beginning of May. Meanwhile, the last week of April sees the elite National Hunt season draw to a close with the final major gold cup at Sandown Park. Jumping continues at many smaller tracks throughout May and, since 1995, a programme of summer jump meetings has operated at a handful of courses from June to September.

The flat season gathers pace with the long-established May fixtures at Chester and York, but for some, the racing year peaks in early June with the Epsom Derby meeting. Thereafter the focus swings away slightly from the three-year-old cohort to encompass both older horses and the first outings of the two-year-old crop. Summer sees the fashionable meetings, Royal Ascot, 'Glorious' Goodwood and the July meeting at Newmarket, all providing opportunities for top middle-distance horses of different ages to compete against each other. But for most racehorses and their trainers, summer racing means travelling between the less prestigious courses, to seaside meetings at Folkestone, Yarmouth or Redcar, to evening meetings or Sunday 'fun' days countrywide, to Saturday and Monday meetings which originated as local fair days and holidays. The volume of racing increases from May to September, with over 130 meetings staged each month and sometimes over 100 consecutive days of racing.

Many classier British horses are now campaigned abroad, turning out for the Irish Derby and Oaks at The Curragh, or their French equivalents at Chantilly, but forays into Europe are not confined to the cream of the three-year-olds. Group races in Italy and Germany attract British entries throughout the season, and the major French meetings at Saint-Cloud in June, Deauville in August and Longchamp in September are popular with British trainers.

Early autumn sees the final Classic of the year, the St Leger at Doncaster, and the two traditional October fixtures at Newmarket, featuring the top two-year-old races of the season, pointers, perhaps, for the following year's Classics. National Hunt racing begins again in earnest but as the domestic flat season winds down, thoughts turn to the big international contests which now dominate the final quarter of the year. The Arc at Longchamp on the first Sunday in October is the greatest race in Europe, but it is soon followed by a trio of overseas events, the Melbourne Cup for stayers, the Japan Cup for middle-distance specialists and the American Breeders' Cup series, all of which regularly attract British entries. For the majority, however, early November heralds the last flat-race meeting on turf at Doncaster. For the next four months, the all-weather tracks provide the only opportunities for flatracers and the field is left to the jump specialists, whose season gathers pace towards the Christmas holiday meetings, notably at Kempton Park.

There are other cycles in the racing year, involving yearling sales and breeding but these have also been affected by long-distance air travel. Stallions whose season used to last from February to July now find themselves shipped off to the southern hemisphere to fulfil stud duties there. The racing year, once curtailed by considerations of weather and distance, and split sharply into summer flat and winter jumps, now operates on all fronts for a full 12 months.

Further reading

Magee, S., *The Channel Four Book of Racing* (London: Hamlyn, 1995).

York

York is the premier racecourse of the north. It hosts 15 flat race days a year, stages three Group One races at its prestigious August meeting and recently won the accolade of best British course in a nationwide survey. It is renowned for its history – it has the longest unbroken sequence of racing records anywhere in the world, starting in 1709 – and for the tantalising smell of chocolate which wafts over the course from the nearby Terry's chocolate factory!

Although meetings were initially held at Clifton Ings, and were considered sufficiently important to warrant the donation of a gold cup by Queen Anne, York races shifted to the newly designed Knavesmire course in 1731. Racing was timed to coincide with the county assizes when the great and good of Yorkshire together with the circuit judges were assembled in the city; they were responsible for the public hangings which frequently took place before the races, swelling the crowd of onlookers. The most famous race ever staged at the Knavesmire, the rematch between Derby winners Voltigeur and The Flying Dutchman in 1851, was said to have attracted 100,000 spectators. The same number had allegedly watched the notorious 1804 battle of the sexes when Alicia Thornton and Captain Flint engaged in a public horserace.

The course on which they raced is very similar today. An elongated C shape, flat, wide and 2 miles long, it is regarded as a very fair test of the racehorse. The main meeting still takes place in August as it would have done 250 years ago although another important fixture is held in May, featuring two major Classic trials, the Dante Stakes for colts (named after the local Derby-winning hero of 1945) and the Musidora Stakes for fillies (commemorating the Malton-trained Oaks winner of 1949). It is the three-day summer meeting, however, which brings the cream of the racing world north to contest several top-flight races. The first of three Group Ones, the International Stakes is one of the three major 10-furlong races in Britain alongside the Eclipse and the Champion Stakes. Dating back to 1972, when Roberto infamously inflicted the sole career defeat on Brigadier Gerard in what was then the Benson and Hedges Gold Cup, it has been won by numerous class horses from double winner Dahlia (1974, 1975) and Derby-winning Troy (1979) to Singspiel (1997) and Giant's Causeway (2000). The Yorkshire Oaks, first run in 1849, is one of only three Group One races for three-year-old fillies, the others being the filly Classics. Recent victories have gone to Epsom and Irish Oaks winner Ramruna (1999) and

Petrushka, Irish Oaks winner of 2000. The Nunthorpe Stakes is the only Group One race over 5 furlongs and one of the major sprints of the year. First run in 1922 and raised from Group Two status in 1984, it was won by Dayjur (1990) and Sheikh Albadou (1991) on their way to Breeders' Cup Sprint runner up and victory, and by Lochsong (1993) before her Prix de l'Abbaye triumph. Open to two-year-olds and upwards, it has only been won four times by juveniles, three 1950s' colts and, in 1992, the diminutive filly Lyric Fantasy.

As if these were not enough, the August meeting also stages the Ebor Handicap, first run in 1843, the John Smith's Cup, the oldest sponsored flat race in the calendar since its inception as the Magnet Cup in 1960, and the Group Two Gimcrack Stakes, named after one of the most successful eighteenth-century racehorses and run since 1846. The Gimcrack Club still hosts an annual dinner in December at which the principal speaker is the winning owner of the race. Traditionally a speech on racing politics, it has been used in recent years by Sheikh Mohammed as a vehicle for criticising the levels of prize money in British racing, and was given in 2001 by Sir Alex Ferguson, long-serving manager of Manchester United FC after the success of his colt, Rock of Gibraltar. A relative newcomer to racehorse ownership, Sir Alex used this opportunity to urge the various factions within racing to pull together for the greater good of the sport.

York manages to combine a respect for history – it retains several Georgian buildings – with ultramodern facilities. It was the first course to install close circuit colour television and now boasts several new stands, a raceday radio station and a reputation second to none. On the strength of this, it has been awarded the royal meeting in 2005 when Ascot is closed for the refurbishment.

Further reading

Lee, A., *The Course Inspector* (London: CollinsWillow, 2001).
Magee, S., *The Channel Four Book of the Racing Year* (London: Sidgwick and Jackson, 1990).
Tyrrel, J., *Racecourses on the Flat* (Marlborough: Crowood Press, 1989).
www.yorkracecourse.co.uk

Yorkshire

Yorkshire has always been the heartland of northern racing. It was well established by the early eighteenth century, with 25 race meetings recorded in 1730, and at the beginning of the twenty-first century it still boasts nine racecourses, more than any other region. It is the home of two of the largest British racehorse training centres outside Newmarket, at Middleham and Malton, and hosts the oldest Classic race, the St Leger, first run in 1776 at Doncaster, a course which continues to shape the flat-racing year by staging the opening and closing meetings of the season.

The importance of Yorkshire in racing was recognised as early as the reign of Queen Anne (1702–14) when the monarch sponsored several gold cups and plates throughout the county, and entered her own horses for races at York.

The county town, a centre for fashionable society throughout the eighteenth century, and either Hambleton or Richmond, continued to receive two Royal Plates, the most prestigious races of the day worth 100 guineas each, for over 150 years, the only venues outside Newmarket to be granted more than one. Both York and Doncaster regularly held two race meetings a year at a time when most racecourses staged one annual event, and for much of the nineteenth century, Yorkshire was the only county in which meetings reached double figures. Doncaster, with around 30 flat and jumps race days each year, is surpassed only by Newmarket and Haydock in the number of fixtures staged in the twenty-first century.

Racehorse breeding was always important to the area. The Darley Arabian, his son Bartlet's Childers and Regulus, a son of the Godolphin Arabian and eight times champion sire, were all at stud in Yorkshire, while Squirt, the sire of Marske and grandsire of Eclipse, was also bred there. At one time up to 80 per cent of thoroughbreds came from studs around the Vale of York and the area was still sufficiently important as a breeding centre for Tattersalls to hold their premier yearling sales at the Doncaster St Leger meeting for 120 years, from 1838 to 1958. Regular bloodstock sales continue to be held at Doncaster.

Middleham, near Richmond, and Malton, near York, were also significant nineteenth-century training centres, with Thomas Dawson, brother of the famous Mathew based in the former and John Scott, the first great public trainer at the latter. Dawson trained five Classic winners at his stable but Scott sent out 41 from 1827 to 1863. Nothing comparable has been seen since. William I'Anson, like the Dawsons, moved south from Scotland to Malton and in 1857 his filly Blink Bonny won both the Derby and the Oaks. When her son Blair Athol won the Derby and St Leger in 1864, she was the first mare to have become and bred a Derby winner. Members of the Peacock dynasty trained in Middleham over an 80-year period – Matthew Peacock trained most winners in a season on five occasions as well as the last Yorkshire Derby winner, Dante, in 1945 (and the first since 1868!) – while Noel Murless, champion trainer nine times from 1948 to 1973, spent the first 12 years of his career near Thirsk.

However, there has been limited Classic success in the post-war era. Captain Charles Elsey of Malton trained four fillies, Musidora (One Thousand Guineas, Oaks), Honeylight (One Thousand Guineas), Frieze (Oaks) and Cantelo (St Leger) to Classic victories between 1949 and 1959, and one colt, Nearula, Two Thousand Guineas winner of 1953. He was champion trainer in 1956 and headed the numerical list eight times. His son Bill Elsey achieved an Oaks victory with Pia in 1967 and a St Leger with Peleid in 1973. Bill Watts sent out Waterloo, the 1972 One Thousand Guineas winner from his Richmond stable while Mick Easterby training at Sheriff Hutton near York was responsible for Mrs McArdy, 1977 winner of the same race. His nephew, Tim, saddled the most recent Yorkshire Classic success when Bollin Eric won the 2002 St Leger. Other Yorkshire flat trainers included Sam Hall, also from Middleham, a big handicap specialist who carried off the Ebor in 1949 and 1957, the Cesarewitch in 1958 and the Manchester November Handicap four times.

In National Hunt racing, the first three home in the 1950 Grand National, won by Freebooter, were all trained in Yorkshire. Neville Crump, training at

Middleham, won the Grand National three times with Sheila's Cottage (1948), Teal (1952) and Merryman II (1960) who had also won the Scottish Grand National in 1959. Crump won the Whitbread Gold Cup on three occasions and was twice leading National Hunt trainer. Peter Easterby, brother of Mick, operating from Malton, won five Champion Hurdles, two each with the brilliant Night Nurse (1976 and 1977) and the much-loved Sea Pigeon (1980 and 1981), once with Saucy Kit (1967). He won two Cheltenham Gold Cups with Alverton (1979) and Little Owl (1981), was champion jumps trainer in three consecutive seasons from 1978–79 and also turned out a number of useful flat-race handicappers, winning the Lincoln in 1965 and 1973. His son Tim took over the yard on his retirement in 1995. Michael Dickinson, training at Harewood, made a meteoric rise to fame as a jumps trainer with consecutive Cheltenham Gold Cup winners in 1982 (Silver Buck) and 1983 (Bregawn), the year in which he was responsible for the first five placed horses in the race, a feat unlikely to be repeated. He was champion trainer in three seasons out of four before quitting to train on the flat; he emigrated to the United States in 1987. Malton trainer Jimmy Fitzgerald also went through a purple patch in the 1980s, capturing the Gold Cup with Forgive'n Forget in 1985 and the Scottish Grand National twice with Ardroma in 1984 and 1985.

With a concentration of money, stables and top-class flat racing in the south of England, Yorkshire has struggled in recent years to recapture the glories of the past. However, a revival seems to be under way at Middleham, largely thanks to the Mark Johnston stable. Johnston trained Mister Baileys, the Two Thousand Guineas winner of 1994, the first Yorkshire Classic success for 17 years and has twice trained the most winners in a season. In 2001 he captured the Ascot Gold Cup with Royal Rebel and 2002 saw him finish third in the trainers' championship with prize money of over £$2\frac{1}{4}$ million. Although stalwarts such as Fruits of Love and Yavana's Pace have been favourites with the racing public, his most popular horse has possibly been Double Trigger who notched up seven wins in the three major Cup races for stayers between 1995 and 1998. Three victories at Goodwood, three at Doncaster and one at Ascot made him the most prolific winner in the history of these races, and probably the only racehorse to have a high-speed train named after him.

The nine regional racecourses, Beverley, Catterick Bridge, Doncaster, Pontefract, Redcar, Ripon, Thirsk, Wetherby and York operate a joint marketing initiative and between them offer over 125 flat-race days a year and around 30 National Hunt fixtures. Malton is still a racing town (even if the stables are actually located in the adjacent village of Norton) and a Malton Stables Open Day is held annually in August while Middleham puts on a similar event in April. Yorkshire remains an important racing county.

Further reading

Mortimer, R., Onslow, R. and Willett, P., *Biographical Encyclopaedia of British Flat Racing* (London: Macdonald and Jane's, 1978).

Randall, J. and Morris, T., *A Century of Champions* (Halifax: Portway, 1999).

Moneybox

A **Yankee** is a bet which involves four horses, backed in six doubles, four trebles and one four-horse accumulator.

Trainer Arthur **Yates** was severely criticised for withdrawing Cloister, one of the hottest pre-race favourites, from the 1894 Grand National on the grounds that the horse had aggravated an old strain.

At the Houghton Sale of 1998 the average price of **yearlings**, horses still too young to be raced, was 171,357 guineas.

York was granted a prestigious Royal Plate worth 100 guineas in 1711.

Mr Zenya Yoshida paid £23,000 for Lassalle as a yearling. The horse went on to win the Ascot Gold Cup in 1973.

Mr T.C. Yuill, a Scottish dairy farmer, had only three horses in training but all three won races including Rockavon in the Two Thousand Guineas at 66–1.

Z

Horsebox

Zabara won the One Thousand Guineas and Oaks in 1952.

Zafonic won the 1993 Two Thousand Guineas in a course record time.

Zarathustra won the Irish Derby and St Leger in 1954, the Ascot Gold Cup in 1957 and a total of 13 races from 5 furlongs to 2 miles 5 furlongs.

Zeta's Lad won the Racing Post Chase in 1993, not to be confused with Zeta's Son who won the Anthony Mildmay/Peter Cazalet Memorial Chase in 1977 and the Hennessy Cognac Gold Cup in 1976.

Zilzal was rated 135 in 1989 as a three-year-old, winning the Sussex Stakes and the Queen Elizabeth II Stakes at Ascot.

Zino won the 1982 Two Thousand Guineas, one of eleven French-trained winners, but never won another race.

Moneybox

Zahia, a 100–1 outsider in the 1948 Grand National, was among the front runners after jumping the penultimate fence; unfortunately her jockey took the wrong course and failed to jump the last.

Zambo (second in the St Leger) and **Zionist** (second in the Derby) were not good enough to maintain the Aga Khan as leading owner in 1925, after he had achieved that accolade for the first time in 1924 with record twentieth-century winnings of over £44,000 in one season (a massive £1.5 million in today's values).

Mr H.R.K. Zeisel was the principal shareholder in the six-man syndicate that owned Rheingold, winner of the Grand Prix de Saint-Cloud and beaten by only a short head in the Derby of 1972. He was owner of a club in London which he named unsurprisingly The Rheingold.

Zev, trained in the United States, became the top money earner in world racing in 1923, surpassing the 28-year-old record of Isinglass. He also beat Papyrus in a match race between the English and Kentucky Derby winners for $110,000 at Belmont Park.

In 1976 French trainer **Maurice Zilber** won both the English and French Derbys with Empery and Youth respectively.

Zucchero was bought for £60,000 by Baron Guy de Rothschild in 1953 to stand at stud but he failed a fertility test and the sale was automatically cancelled.

Chronology of British Horseracing

1540	Racing recorded at The Roodee, Chester, the oldest surviving racecourse in Britain
1622	First recorded match race at Newmarket
1640	Racing recorded at Epsom
1671	Charles II the first (and only) British reigning monarch to ride the winner of the Newmarket Town Plate, a race he founded six years previously
1687	The Byerley Turk imported
1704	The Darley Arabian brought to Britain
1711	First race meeting at Ascot
1727	John Cheny published first *Racing Calendar*
1729	The Godolphin Arabian imported
1740	Parliament bans races with less than £50 prize money
c.1750	Jockey Club founded (?)
1750	Parliament rescinds the £50 prize money regulation
1752	Allegedly first recorded steeplechase in Co. Cork
1758	All jockeys to weigh in after races at Newmarket
1762	Racing colours first registered at Newmarket
1766	Richard Tattersall began Bloodstock sales at Hyde Park Corner
1773	James Weatherby took over publication of the *Racing Calendar*
1776	First St Leger at Doncaster
1779	The Oaks established at Epsom
1780	Diomed won first Derby at Epsom
1791	First volume of the *General Stud Book* published
	Prince of Wales withdrew from racing at Newmarket after Jockey Club inquiry into running of his horse Escape
1792	Earliest recorded steeplechases in England in Leicestershire
1798	Sir Harry won the Derby, the first winner to be sired by a previous winner (Sir Peter Teazle in 1787)
1802	First recognised meeting at Goodwood
1807	Ascot Gold Cup run for the first time
1809	Wizard won first Two Thousand Guineas at Newmarket
1812	Goodwood Cup inaugurated
1814	Charlotte won first One Thousand Guineas at Newmarket
1821	Jockey Club issued first warning-off at Newmarket

1825	Tontine won One Thousand Guineas by a walk over, the only such instance in the history of any of the Classics
1828	Cadland won the Derby after re-run following a dead-heat
1829	First meeting at Aintree
1830	First St Albans Steeplechase
1831	Jockey Club refused to arbitrate in disputes unless races held under its Rules
1834	Racehorses at Newmarket began to celebrate their official birthday on 1 January instead of 1 May
1836	Liverpool Grand Steeple-Chase at Aintree
1839	The first Liverpool Great Steeplechase won by Jem Mason on Lottery
1844	Derby was awarded to Orlando after the initial winner Running Rein was disqualified for being over age
1847	The Grand National was officially adopted as the name of the major Aintree steeplechasing event
1850	Admiral Rous published *The Laws and Practice of Horse Racing*
1851	Abd-el-Kadar became the first horse to win the Grand National twice
1853	West Australian became the first horse to win the Triple Crown (Two Thousand Guineas, Derby and St Leger)
	Betting offices closed down after the passing of the Betting Houses Act
1855	Admiral Rous produced first weight-for-age scale
1857	William I'Anson bred, trained and owned Derby winner Blink Bonny
1858	All horses had their official birthday on 1 January
1859	Yearling races banned by Jockey Club
1864	The French filly, Fille de l'Air won the Oaks, first overseas-trained winner of an English Classic
	William I'Anson again bred, trained and owned the Derby winner, this time Blair Athol
1865	The French colt, Gladiateur won the Triple Crown, the first foreign horse to do so
1866	Grand National Steeplechase Committee formed, later to become National Hunt Committee
	Lord Lyon won Triple Crown
1867	John Day trained 146 winners in a season, a record that was to stand for 120 years
	On 18 June George Fordham rode six winners and a dead-heat at Stockbridge, losing the re-run in the latter race
1868	The filly Formosa won the St Leger to add to the One Thousand Guineas, the Oaks and a dead-heat in the Two Thousand Guineas
1870	Jockey Club restricted the length of the flat season
1871	Hannah won fillies' Triple Crown
1872	The Derby first run over its present course
1874	Apology won fillies' Triple Crown
1875	Sandown Park opened as the first enclosed racecourse in Britain
1877	Draw for starting positions introduced
	Fred Archer rode all six winners at Newmarket on 19 April

1879	All jockeys in Britain had to be licensed
1881	Iroquois first American-bred colt to win the Derby
1882	Fred Archer rode all six winners at Lewes on 5 August
	All Classics won by fillies for the first and only time
	Minimum requirements laid down for number and size of hurdles and fences in a race
1886	Inaugural running of the Eclipse Stakes at Sandown Park, the first £10,000 race in Britain
	Tattersalls' rules on betting introduced
	Ormonde won Triple Crown
	Fred Archer committed suicide
1889	Racing colours became compulsory
	Grand National Steeplechase Committee changed its name to National Hunt Committee
1891	Common won Triple Crown
1892	La Flèche won fillies' Triple Crown
1893	Isinglass won Triple Crown
1894	Lord Rosebery the first serving Prime Minister to own a Derby winner, Ladas
1895	The Derby first race to be recorded on film
1897	Starting tapes used for the first time, at Newmarket
	Galtee More won Triple Crown
1899	Flying Fox won Triple Crown
1900	American Lester Reiff the first overseas Champion Jockey
	The Prince of Wales won Triple Crown with Diamond Jubilee and the Grand National with Ambush II
	Flying Fox brought 37,500 guineas at auction, a British record for a horse in training that stood until 1967
1901	Champion jockey Lester Reiff warned off for not trying to win a race at Manchester
1902	Sceptre won all Classics except the Derby
1903	Jockey Club banned doping
	Rock Sand won Triple Crown
1904	Pretty Polly won fillies' Triple Crown
	George Thursby rode John O'Gaunt to second place in the Derby, first amateur rider to be placed in the Classic
1905	Jockey Club introduced licenses for trainers
1906	Newbury racecourse founded
1907	Orby the first Irish-bred and -trained Derby winner
1908	Signorinetta, bred, trained and owned by Italian Chevalier Ginistrelli, only the third filly to win both the Oaks and the Derby
1909	Lutteur III won the Grand National, the first to be French bred and owned and the only five-year-old ever to win the race
	Edward VII became first reigning monarch to own a Derby winner, Minoru
1910	National Hunt trainers had to be licensed
	Racing suspended for two weeks after death of Edward VII

The National Hunt Committee banned doping and made number cloths compulsory

Frank Wootton won third consecutive jockeys' title

1911   Only one horse, the winner Glenside, of the 26 starters in the Grand National went round Aintree unscathed

1913   The 'Jersey Act' passed by the Jockey Club, virtually prohibiting the import of American thoroughbreds

Minimum race distance fixed at 5 furlongs and horses over two-years-old no longer allowed to run unnamed

Suffragette Emily Davison killed by a horse at Tattenham Corner during the Derby

Of 22 starters in the Grand National 20 fall

1914   Durbar II became the first French horse to win the Derby since 1865

1915   Flat racing outside Newmarket banned for the duration of the war

First ever Derby away from Epsom

Pommern won substitute Triple Crown

1916   National Stud founded at Tully, Co. Kildare in Ireland

Grand National run at Gatwick

1917   Gay Crusader won wartime Triple Crown

1918   Gainsborough won wartime Triple Crown

1919   Two-year-old Tetratema the leading stakes winner and headed Free Handicap by 12 lb

1920   Owners no longer allowed to use assumed names

Amateur riders banned from competing against professionals in flat racing

First Prix de l'Arc de Triomphe won by Comrade

1921   All but one of 35 starters fall in Grand National

Racing cancelled because of miners' strike

1922   Number cloths carried for first time in British flat racing

1923   Steve Donoghue won third consecutive Derby and tied with Charlie Elliott for the jockeys' championship

1924   First running of Cheltenham Gold Cup

Protective skull caps made compulsory in National Hunt racing

Fontwell opened

1925   21-year-old Gordon Richards became champion jockey for the first time

1926   Betting tax introduced

Racing press agreed to make a combined return for starting price

Chepstow opened

1927   First running of Champion Hurdle at Cheltenham

Taunton opened, the last new course in the twentieth century

First BBC radio broadcast of the Grand National and the Derby

Jockey Club required all horses to be run on their merits; previously one could be stopped in favour of another with same owner

1928   Racecourse Betting Control Board established

	Tipperary Tim won a Grand National in which 42 runners started and only two finished, one of whom had to be remounted after the last fence
1929	Betting tax abandoned
	Record 66 runners took part in the Grand National
	Bookmaker killed by lightning at Ascot
	Tote introduced at Newmarket and Carlisle on 2 July
	Jockey Club abolished 'void nominations' rule by which an owner's death rendered void all race entries for their horses
1930	Patrol camera used for the first time in Britain, at Newmarket
1931	Dead-heats no longer allowed to be run off
1932	The Derby first race in Britain to be televised
	Solario, a ten-year-old stallion, brought a record 47,000 guineas at auction
1933	Gordon Richards rode 12 consecutive winners, 11 of them at Chepstow
	Gordon Richards broke Fred Archer's record of 246 winners in a season with a total of 259
1934	Golden Miller won the Cheltenham Gold Cup together with the Grand National, a feat still unequalled, setting a record time for the National in the process
	Brown Jack ridden by Steve Donoghue won his sixth consecutive Queen Alexandra Stakes at Ascot
1935	Bahram won Triple Crown for the Aga Khan
	Racing suspended for funeral of George V
	Blandford champion sire in both Britain and France
1936	Golden Miller won fifth successive Cheltenham Gold Cup
	Mahmoud set a record Derby-winning time, unbeaten till 1995
1937	Golden Miller prevented from attempting sixth win in Cheltenham Gold Cup as meeting abandoned because of bad weather
	First King George VI Chase at Kempton Park
1938	Bruce Hobbs aged 17, riding Battleship, became youngest ever winner of the Grand National
1941	Fred Darling equalled the record of John Porter by training his seventh Derby winner
1942	National Hunt racing abandoned until January 1945
	Sun Chariot, racing in the colours of King George VI, won fillies' wartime Triple Crown
1943	National Stud transferred to England from Ireland
1946	No unnamed horse allowed to race
1947	Photo-finish introduced at Epsom Downs on 22 April
	First evening race meeting at Hamilton Park on 18 July
	Grand National held on a Saturday rather than Friday in interests of British industry
1948	BBC introduced first televised racing from Sandown Park on 24 January
	A record 58 runners for a flat race went to post for the Lincolnshire Handicap
	Newport racecourse closed

1949   Two Classics decided by a photo-finish, the Two Thousand Guineas and the Derby, both won by Nimbus

1950   Gordon Richards the first British jockey to ride 4,000 winners
French horses won four Classics

1951   The King George VI and Queen Elizabeth Stakes inaugurated at Ascot
Record field of 44 for Cambridgeshire (43 in 1862)

1952   Electrical timing introduced at Newmarket
Racing suspended for funeral of George VI
Loudspeaker commentaries used at Goodwood
Aga Khan won his fifth Derby and equalled 126-year-old record of Lord Egremont

1953   Gordon Richards won his first Derby in 28 attempts and became first professional jockey to be knighted

1954   At 18 Lester Piggott the youngest jockey to win the Derby but later in the season has licence withdrawn for six months for dangerous and erratic riding

1955   Two people killed by lightning at Ascot
Captain Cecil Boyd-Rochfort the first trainer to have career winnings of over £1 million
Meld won fillies' Triple Crown
First evening meeting in London at Alexandra Palace

1956   The Queen Mother's horse Devon Loch slipped over only 50 yards from the winning post in the Grand National. E.S.B. won

1957   Alec Russell rode all six winners at Bogside on 19 July

1959   Jockey Manny Mercer killed in accident at Ascot

1960   Grand National televised for first time
Patrol camera introduced at Newmarket on 30 June

1961   Betting shops became legal on 1 May
BBC gave starting prices with racing results
Racecourse Betting Control Board reconstituted as Horserace Betting Levy Board

1962   Seven horses fell in the Derby coming down Tattenham Hill
First Saturday evening meeting at Wolverhampton
Hurst Park racecourse closed

1963   On 5 January Ayr held the solitary meeting in Britain between 21 December 1962 and 7 March because of severe winter

1964   Last Lincolnshire Handicap at Lincoln as race transferred to Doncaster
Lewes and Lincoln racecourses closed

1965   Starting stalls introduced at Newmarket on 8 July
Duke of Norfolk Committee published report on future of racing
Birmingham, Bogside and Rothbury racecourses closed

1966   Jockey Club forced to grant trainers' licenses to women
Betting Tax re-introduced
Doug Smith won record sixth Cesarewitch
Arkle wins third consecutive Cheltenham Gold Cup

1967   Starting stalls used for the Classics

Foinavon, a 100–1 outsider, won the Grand National when the rest of the field was caught in a pile up at the 23rd, now known as the Foinavon Fence

Vaguely Noble sold for 136,000 guineas to shatter the record auction price for a horse in training

Racing abandoned because of foot and mouth

1968 The Jockey Club and the National Hunt Committee amalgamated
Betting duty doubled

1969 Arthur Budget bred, trained and (half)owned the Derby winner Blakeney

1970 Nijinsky won Triple Crown for Charles Engelhard
Alexandra Park racecourse closed

1971 Pattern race classifications introduced in Europe

1972 Races for women riders permitted
Mill Reef broke a leg but was saved for stud duties

1973 Centralised computer-assisted handicapping started

1974 Graded handicaps introduced to flat racing
Women allowed to ride as amateurs against men
Wye racecourse closed

1975 Women allowed to apply for professional licences as jockeys
Stable lads struck for higher wages and attempted to disrupt both the Guineas Classics at Newmarket
Grundy beat Bustino in the King George VI and Queen Elizabeth Stakes, the 'race of the century' according to many
Graded handicaps introduced to British flat racing
L'Escargot first horse since Golden Miller to win Cheltenham Gold Cup and Grand National

1976 Eclipse winner, French horse Trepan disqualified following a positive dope test

1977 Red Rum the first horse to win three Grand Nationals
Jockey Club lifted ban on women members
Last races at Lanark racecourse

1979 Troy ridden by Willie Carson won Derby by seven lengths, largest margin for 54 years

1980 Nureyev disqualified for barging after winning the Two Thousand Guineas

1981 Bob Champion rode Aldaniti to an emotional victory in the Grand National. Champion was recovering from cancer and Aldaniti had suffered from severe leg injuries
Shergar won the Derby by a record 10 lengths
Stockton racecourse closed
First Japan Cup

1982 John Francome shared National Hunt riders' title with injured Peter Scudamore after refusing any more mounts once he equalled Scudamore's total
Trainer Michael Dickinson saddled 12 winners on Boxing Day

1983   Derby-winner Shergar abducted and presumably killed by terrorists
        The mounts of jockeys guilty of careless riding now placed behind
            their victim not automatically last
        Michael Dickinson trained first five in Cheltenham Gold Cup
        Jenny Pitman first woman to train a Grand National winner
1984   All the Classics sponsored
        European Breeders' Fund inaugurated
        Inaugural Breeders' Cup programme
        Dawn Run the first horse to win the English, Irish and French
            Champion Hurdle in one season
1985   Oh So Sharp won fillies' Triple Crown
1986   Dawn Run won the Cheltenham Gold Cup to become the first horse
            to complete the Cheltenham double of Gold Cup and Champion
            Hurdle
        Betting shops allowed to show televised races
1987   Satellite Information Services telecasts began
        Henry Cecil beat John Day's record by training 180 winners in a season
        Sheikh Mohammed the leading owner for the third consecutive year
        Steve Cauthen beat Pat Eddery for the jockeys' championship
            197–195, the closest margin for 24 years
1989   Lingfield Park held Britain's first meeting on an all-weather surface
        Peter Scudamore broke Jonjo O'Neill's record for the highest number
            of jump winners in a season with 221, the first double century by
            a National Hunt rider
1990   Aga Khan withdrew all his horses from Britain in protest at 'flawed'
            drug-testing procedures
        Desert Orchid won his fourth King George VI Chase
1991   Martin Pipe first National Hunt trainer to win £1 million in first-
            place prize money in a season
        Scottish National Hunt rider Peter Niven rode a five-timer at
            Sedgefield, a record third in a season
1992   Doncaster held Britain's first Sunday fixture but without betting
1993   British Horseracing Board was founded
        Vintage Crop the first European-trained winner of the Melbourne Cup
        Grand National declared void after false start
        Betting shops allowed to stay open till 10 pm to cater for evening
            racing
1994   All-weather hurdle racing discontinued because of the number of
            equine fatalities
        Three-year, £3.5 million Derby meeting sponsorship by Vodaphone
        Trainer Alex Scott shot dead by former employee
1995   Sunday racing with betting facilities at Newmarket and Salisbury
        Summer jump racing introduced
        One Thousand Guineas first Classic run on a Sunday
        Lammtarra first Derby winner to be bred from a Derby/Oaks mating
1996   First listed race on all-weather track
1997   Racing suspended for funeral of Princess Diana

1998   First public auction of bookmakers' pitches
2000   Istabraq won third consecutive Champion Hurdle
       The Aga Khan first non-Maktoum to be leading owner on the flat
          since 1984
2001   Racing abandoned because of foot and mouth
       New generation all-weather Polytrack at Lingfield Park
2002   Racing suspended for funeral of Queen Mother
       Betting tax and betting levy abandoned
       Announcement that Tote to be privatised
       Rock of Gibraltar first horse to win seven consecutive Group One
          races
       Tony McCoy smashed Sir Gordon Richards' record by riding 289
          winners in a season
2003   Jockeys strike in protest at ban on use of mobile phones Jockey Club
       announces it is to cede powers to a new independent regulatory body
2004   Best Mate emulates Arkle by winning three consecutive
       Cheltenham Gold Cups

Index